£30

POWER AND GLORY

THE HISTORY OF GRAND PRIX
MOTOR RACING

POWER AND GLORY

THE HISTORY OF GRAND PRIX MOTOR RACING

VOLUME 1: 1906 — 1951

William Court

Patrick Stephens

First published in 1966 by Macdonald & Co (Publishers) Ltd
This facsimile edition first published 1988

British Library Cataloguing in Publication Data

Court, William
    Power and glory: the history of Grand
    Prix motor racing.
    Vol. 1: 1906-1951
    1. Racing cars. Racing. Races. Grand
    Prix, to 1965
    I. Title
    796.7'2

    ISBN 1-85260-184-1

Both Author and Publisher are mindful that in some cases fault may be found with the quality and detail of some of the illustrations. They have been at pains to find illustrations which illustrate points made in the text and particularly with some of the older ones beggars cannot be choosers. Thus some slightly imperfect illustrations are presented without apology in the belief that readers would prefer the text to be properly illustrated in this way, particularly as in many cases these have proved to be the only discoverable photographs of the subject concerned.

This book was designed by Gwyn Lewis, with drawings by Peter Helck, and maps by Dr. L. J. Stretton.

Patrick Stephens Limited is part of the Thorsons Publishing Group, Wellingborough, Northamptonshire NN8 2RQ, England.

Printed in Great Britain by Butler & Tanner Limited, Frome, Somerset

10   9   8   7   6   5   4   3   2   1

Contents

Circuit Maps

Foreword

by Laurence Pomeroy, F.R.S.A., M.S.A.E.

Motor racing has now passed its 70th anniversary, a span considerably beyond that which can be compassed in terms of direct experience by any living person. Additionally history written by participants in the events themselves can be biased, and those who look back over long periods of time as observers all too frequently mis-remember that which they have seen, or that which has been told to them.

From this historical point of view it is a matter of regret that there was no substantial body of books about motor racing until 20 years ago, and that those which were written earlier are all too frequently merely personal impressions, the value of which in some cases diminishes when it is well known that ghost writers were all too often employed by those famous figures who had apparently put pen to paper.

It is a further misfortune that a number of the few able authors who have surveyed motor racing have been most enthusiastic, and most accurate, when writing of the years in which they were personally associated with the sport, and with the great figures participating, but have paid less regard to what had gone before their time, and in some cases have plainly been bemused, if not repelled, by more recent races.

It is thus clear that there should be merit in a work written by one who would not be biased by personal connection at any given time, who would have the patience, energy, and imagination to trace the long story from its beginning up to the present, and to relate the various kinds of racing and the differing types of car as a continuous story, with each phase articulated with what had happened before and with what has subsequently emerged.

Measured in terms of labour involved, and any possible reward other than fame and gratitude, the task looks so onerous as to discourage anyone other than a fanatic; and yet a sane appreciation of events to be recorded is vital to the success of such a work.

Having myself had some experience of what is involved, even when the task is simplified by eliminating everything which has no engineering significance, I would not have supposed that there was a man alive who would volunteer to tackle a history in which every major motor race would be described in some detail, and with an accuracy transcending the immediate reports of the time which have, to say the least, varied degrees of truthfulness arising from the fact that they have had to be set up in type and widely distributed within a few hours of the fall of the winning flag.

In view of all these adverse circumstances I was therefore amazed to hear that W. E. Court had set his hand to this truly monumental task; honoured when he asked me to write a Foreword to it, and amazed at his aptitude when I came to read his manuscripts. That he has been able to marry facts and statistics with literary skill and poetic allusion came as a further and welcome surprise. It is even more remarkable that he has been able to couple the plain narrative of what happened with so many perspective judgments on the course of events, at the same time forswearing technical analysis which might confuse the general reader to whom this work is plainly addressed.

As a record of what has gone on in the higher echelons of motor racing it stands alone. It will be particularly valuable to those who are now actively engaged in motor sport in their late twenties and early thirties, who may well never have seen a supercharged car in action, or a wheel change and refuelling with sixty gallons of alcohol blend in less than half a minute, and to whom the 500 h.p. cars built in the thirties are just as remote in time and perspective as the 50 h.p. cars racing from one European capital and another at the beginning of the century.

The reader of this book will have the unique experience of seeing the whole map of motor racing, over these many decades, spread out before him. He will find that it is in reality a relief map with the peaks standing up, and, to pursue the analogy, beacons lit upon them so that signals can be exchanged between one generation and another.

In his enormous task the Author has in fact succeeded well and deserves grateful thanks from all those many people who to-day are interested in one of the greatest pursuits of our time.

Author's Introduction
to this new edition

April, Mr Eliot assures us, is the cruellest month of the year, but for the life of me I never know why. More cruel by far are those dark days, that are scarcely days at all, between Twelfth Night and St Valentine's Day. How uplifting, then, to have a voice from the past illumine the murk with a tentative enquiry about a re-issue of *Power and Glory* after all these years: and was I interested? Was I indeed?!

By early March the preliminaries were accomplished fact and two decades had telescoped themselves as if their Nineteen Long Winters had never been.

There are few things more galling than to stand idly by watching a Great Project crumble to dust without being able to do a blind thing about it. Thus *Power and Glory* suffered the frustrating, rock-bottom indignity of premature remaindering, described by a colleague as 'an incredible case of commercial impatience', leaving the real spoils to the antiquarian book trade!

It is always good to know where your friends are and in the aftermath of 1968 I surely needed them, with *Power and Glory* a goner and *Speedworld International*, to which *Power and Glory* had led me, as dead as its own guiding light, dear departed Gregor Grant.

For a time I found a home with the BRSCC doing a regular stint for their in-house monthly, *British Racing News*. Of course there was no money in it, but that was not the point: the good offices of this Club and its manager, Dennis Southwood, enabled me to keep in touch with the Grand Prix and sports car scene as an active Sort of Journalist till 1973 when other necessities and disciplines intervened. Thereafter I became a simple observer of the glittering scene with no more facilities than an ordinary spectator beyond what I could occasionally finagle for myself.

In the meantime—in between time—ain't we got—well, not exactly Fun so much as the odd contact about another book that never seemed quite to materialize and the possibility of a sequel to *Power and Glory*—'Vol 2' as it came to be known— to take the story on from the end of 1951 to the Lord knew where. Ironically, before they would countenance *Power and Glory*, the original publishers required me to sign up for what ultimately became the first version of 'Vol 2'—covering up to the end of 1965. They received this in mid-1966 and then sat

on it for eighteen months before deciding they were not interested in racing cars any more and returned my dusty manuscript just in time for at least half of it to be serialized in *Speedworld* through 1968 before the Long Nothing.

However humbly, *Power and Glory* claimed a kinship with and even succession to Gerald Rose's classic *Record of Motor Racing*. Although Rose came to live in my part of Kent I never had the pleasure of meeting with him, which was a regrettably lost opportunity. He had himself given up chronicling motor racing after 1908 and was not re-published until 1948. In retrospect, therefore, I should be grateful that my own rehabilitation has taken little more than half that time!

Apart from the pleasurable renewal of an old contact with PSL and their Patrick Stephens and Darryl Reach, I must particularly mention a friend of many years in Eoin Young and thank him for his never-failing support of *Power and Glory* which has extended to enlisting the public and moral support of Cyril Posthumus and, another friend of long standing, the well-known collector of motoring curios, Peter Blair-Richley. Nor should I forget my friend and professional colleague, Mr Official Solicitor David Venables, author and co-publisher of the distinguished *Racing Fifteen Hundred*. All these good people—and, for all I know, many more, have long advocated the need to re-publish *Power and Glory*, no less its proposed successor: and, God Bless Them All and PSL, they have now brought off the Double for me, with the possibility of 'Vol 3' on the Turbo Age, now drawing to its close, thrown in: and what a Trilogy of Power that would be!

When the dice are heavily stacked on the side of non-alignment, it is hard to speak too highly of friends like these, especially as they have had so little to gain from their support. Perhaps it would all have been very different if *Speedworld* had survived into the 'seventies and beyond, but that, again, is not in point. It failed for all the wrong reasons and, not for the first time nor the last, I found I had backed the wrong horse and thanked my lucky stars for a humdrum back-up profession, while putting away my glittering eagles and trumpets for the duration. And now the fly-wheel is poised again at top dead centre for a new power stroke, albeit with The Mixture very much as before, warts and all!

William Court, Rhodes Minnis, 1988

Whosoever in writing a modern history shall follow truth too near the heels it may haply strike out his teeth.

Sir Walter Ralegh: Preface to History of the World

Ancient myths very rarely tell a straightforward and consistent story. The reader therefore must not be too surprised if some of the details of my story cannot be reconciled with those recorded by every story-teller and historian.

Diodorus Siculus: Book IV, 44: 5, 6

'Nothing is new,' says the writer,
'It's all from the books on the shelf.'
'Nothing is new,' says the reader,
'If I'd thought, I'd have said it myself.'

Owen John in the Autocar, 24th December 1910

PART ONE
1894 to 1911 · Setting the Stage

Let's start at the very beginning,
A very good place to start.
Oscar Hammerstein II: The Sound of Music.

1 Above MISPLACED IDEALISM: The Gordon Bennett Trophy

2 Left ROAD TO HISTORY: The Paris–Bordeaux route used in 1895, 1898 and 1901 was the first and only part of the fatal Paris-Madrid in 1903

3 Below . . . 'the important and historically significant Circuit des Ardennes inaugurated in 1902 over a 53½-mile closed circuit . . .'

PARIS
(VERSAILLES)

CHARTRES

CHÂTEAUDUN

VENDÔME

TOURS

CHÂTELLERAULT

POITIERS

RUFFEC

ANGOULÊME

BARBEZIEUX

BORDEAUX

BAYONNE

VITORIA

BURGOS

VALLADOLID

MADRID

PARIS-MADRID

ARDENNES
LAP DISTANCE 53½ Miles

BASTOGNE
START

VAUX LES
ROZIÈRES

LONGLIER

MARTELANGE

LÉGLISE

ANLIER

HEINSTERT

HABAY-LA-NEUVE

Chapter One
1894 to 1906 · The Earliest Days

The history of motor racing from its first splutterings in the Paris-Rouen reliability run of 1894 to the Edwardian splendours of the 1908 Grand Prix has been imperishably set down by Gerald Rose in his Record of Motor Racing. The origin of this book lay in an attempt to compile accurate tables of every competitor's time at every stage of every race of consequence which had then been run. Rose obtained access to many official records and as a result he was able to attain a level of statistical accuracy that would be hard to repeat in a book of similar compass and which has only been rivalled for a short time by the then quarterly magazine Autocourse in its halcyon days following its first appearance in 1951. The original scheme had been to use Rose's tables in conjunction with Charles Jarrott's equally classic Ten Years of Motors and Motor Racing, but when it became apparent that their bulk precluded this course, Rose added a narrative text of exceptional brilliance and the whole was published in 1909 by the Royal Automobile Club. I have not attempted to include in this book tables of the kind and on the scale furnished by Rose: with the multiplicity of the racing calendar since the late twenties this would be tantamount to a publishing impossibility even supposing complete records of all the events still to exist. In this sense, therefore, this book cannot claim to be a continuation of Rose's work, of which, in spite of the addition of his narrative, the tables remained not only the skeleton but the very soul.

It can still claim some degree of kinship, however humble, in the sense that it continues the story of Grand Prix racing from the point where Rose left it at the end of 1908. Thus I originally planned to start the story with the revival of the French Grand Prix 1912, but it has been urged upon me that this can be likened to starting a History of England with the Wars of the Roses instead of with either the Norman Conquest or the accession of the Tudors. Therefore, in order to enable the reader to understand the significance of the events that followed 1908 it is necessary first to go back in history for some ten years even if this means a brief recapitulation of ground already covered quite incomparably by Rose himself.

No matter how feebly, the Paris-Rouen amble set a pattern for the great series of inter-town races that were motor racing until 1903. In these events, which generally started from Paris at prodigiously early hours of the morning, competitors were sent off one by one and competed on a basis of elapsed time less that taken in towns and other neutralised sections that was similar in general principle to the Mille Miglia of 1927-57. A century before, the great roads of France had echoed to the marching feet and rumbl-

ing guns of the Grande Armée as they bore the Imperial Eagles all over Europe. Now these same roads were bringing a new message of thundering steel from Paris that was soon to spread to the uttermost parts of the globe and it is an interesting coincidence that the Ave de la Grande Armée passed through the old Porte Maillot which was the spiritual centre of French motor sport in the early days.[1]

Between 1894 and 1903 thirty-five of these events were held, the greatest being Paris-Bordeaux-Paris (1895), Paris-Marseilles-Paris (1896), Paris-Bordeaux and Paris-Amsterdam-Paris (1898), Paris-Bordeaux and Tour de France (1899), Paris-Lyons and Paris-Toulouse-Paris (1900), Paris-Bordeaux and Paris-Berlin (1901), Paris-Vienna (1902) and Paris-Madrid (1903). Now while these races undoubtedly provided almost the entirety of motor sport during these nine years, the important and historically significant Circuit des Ardennes series had been inaugurated in 1902 over a 53½ mile *closed* circuit with no neutralised sections as the first large scale event of its kind. Charles Jarrott, who won the race for Panhard, regarded it as a distinct experiment in which he took very little interest until he 'arrived at Bastogne the day before the race and realised from the nature of the roads and the number of the competitors that the race would offer a great amount of sport'.

Interwoven with these two basic themes was the Coupe Internationale or Gordon Bennett Cup, neglected brainchild of the American newspaper magnate. Very briefly, the Coupe was for competition between teams of three cars from each country nominated by its premier motor club; the entirety of each car had to be made in its country of origin and it was the duty of the winning club to organise the following year's event. Gordon Bennett was better known for sending out H. M. Stanley on his quest for Livingstone, and his venture into motor racing was less felicitously attended in that, although the French were pleased enough to win the first event over the road from Paris to Lyons in 1900, they found the international opposition so poor that they combined the event with their own Paris-Bordeaux and Paris-Vienna races in 1901/2, regarding it as a rather poor relation to be tolerated but kept well in the background.

While in theory with its emphasis on international competition, the Gordon Bennett should have been the major international event after 1900, it was in fact always overshadowed by the inter-town events and it is doubtful if its survival would have been tolerated by the French had it not been for the fortuitous win of S. F. Edge's Napier in 1902. The following year, 1903, was a very decisive one in motor racing history. First, the tragic Paris-Madrid race brought

---

[1] *For an elaboration of this see Chapter 11, W. F. Bradley's* Motor Racing Memories, *pub. 1960 by* Motor Racing Publications Ltd.

1

6 NIGGER IN THE WOODPILE: Jenatzy who won as 'France failed to regain the Trophy . . .'

the series of inter-town classics to an end. Secondly, the Gordon Bennett attracted full teams from France, Germany, Great Britain and the U.S.A. Thirdly, France failed to regain the Trophy. Thereafter, following the example of the British organised Gordon Bennett and the Circuit des Ardennes, racing took place on closed circuits, albeit of appreciable length, and for the time being manufacturers concerned themselves mainly with the Gordon Bennett.

This sudden fierce concentration of the entire resources of the French industry on the Gordon Bennett was rather more than that unhappy competition could bear, for, even in the space of four years, its regulations had become sadly out-moded and none more so than the Fourth, which restricted each country's entry to three cars irrespective of the size of its motor industry.[2] France therefore spared neither expense nor trouble to regain the Trophy in 1904 even to the extent of holding an eliminating trial earlier in the year, which was a race of major stature in itself. The 1904 event was held in Germany and enjoyed an unprecedented standing being graced by the presence of the Kaiser and his Court, who were much disappointed not to see Mercedes triumph a second time. The race was won by a Richard-Brasier driven by Théry who had also won the French eliminator and, al-though the A.C.F. finally agreed to organise the event in 1905, they made it quite clear that the advent of their own brainchild, the Grand Prix, was only to be postponed for one year. In taking this course the A.C.F. were representing the interests of the French industry, but, combined with the industry's subsequent abandonment of racing after the German victory in the 1908 Grand Prix, their action in sup-pressing the Gordon Bennett has attached to the French a stigma they have not altogether deserved. No doubt but they had played fast and loose with the Gordon Bennett when it suited them, yet it is hard to fault their logic on that score and in any case nobody ever took up the Third Condition to challenge France to a renewal of the contest in 1906 and to this day nobody ever has. Moreover their approach to the problem posed by the Fourth Condition was a good deal more honest than the German ruse in 1904/5 which enabled them to bring two teams of Mercedes to the line by having one team assembled in compliant Vienna and racing under 'Austrian' colours, a rather charming revival of the old diplomatic hexameter

'Bella gerant alii, tu felix Austria, nube!'

In 1903 the principal races had been the Gordon Bennett, organised on a closed circuit of public roads in Ireland by Great Britain as winning nation, the Paris-Madrid, or-ganised by the A.C.F. and stopped after the first day at Bordeaux as a result of many accidents en route, and the Belgian Circuit des Ardennes. The following year the mes-sage had spread in three very significant directions—across the Rhine to Germany in the wake of the Gordon Bennett Trophy, across the Alps where that great and lifelong bene-

[2] *The whole of these conditions can be found in Appendix A to* A Record of Motor Racing.

2

factor of the sport, Vincenzo Florio, organised his first race at Brescia and across the Atlantic Ocean itself where William K. Vanderbilt, in many ways the American counterpart to Florio as gentleman, race promoter and driver, founded the Vanderbilt Cup series. Following Paris-Madrid all these races took place on closed road circuits and the Florio Cup brought a new nation on to the honours' board which had hitherto been almost entirely dominated by French names.

The new winner was the Fiat of Vincenzo Lancia, who had driven one of two Fiats in their first big race—the Light Car section of Paris-Madrid, and if the Fiat was slightly looked down upon at the time as a 'Mercedes assembled in Turin', there could be no such criticism of the 1905 cars which started in the Gordon Bennett on the mountainous Auvergne circuit. This race lay between the French Richard-Brasiers of Théry and Caillois, the de Dietrich of Duray and the three Fiats of Cagno, sometime chauffeur to the King of Italy, Lancia himself and another new name, Felice Nazzaro son of a Torinese coal merchant, who had been singled out by Florio as his own chauffeur. Slight of build, gentlemanly of mien and immaculate in dress, Nazzaro was then starting on a career that involved nineteen years of successful motor racing in two continents. Lancia opened at his usual furious pace and led for the first two of the four laps from Théry, Cagno and Nazzaro on the first lap, and Théry, Duray, Cagno and Nazzaro on the second. At this point Lancia had an advantage of almost 13 minutes and one doubts if even the famed clock-pattern methods of Théry would have made this up had Lancia not suffered a punctured radiator and a seized piston during his third circuit, when he had actually passed Théry on the circuit, although starting a quarter of an hour behind: Peter Helck[3] tells of Théry's remark to his mechanic—'He is going faster than I but I think we shall see him again before the end!' They did—a few kilometres from the end of the third circuit, motionless by the roadside as dejected as the rain showers falling over the gloomy scene. Théry thus kept his winning sequence, but the new star Nazzaro was not far behind and Cagno followed him home ahead of Caillois, Werner's Mercedes and Duray.

The Circuit des Ardennes was also run in 1905 as well as the Florio and Vanderbilt Cups: Hemery, another great

8 . . . 'the Gordon Bennett of 1903 run on a closed circuit of public roads in Ireland . . .'

TOTAL LAP DISTANCE —103 Miles

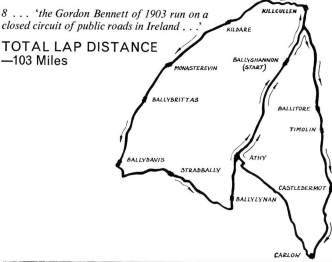

9 IMPERIAL PATRONAGE: 'the 1904 event graced by the Kaiser and his Court . . .'

7 William K. Vanderbilt (in many ways the American counterpart to Vincenzo Florio) chats with friends at Long Island in 1908

[3] From The Checkered Flag, by Peter Helck. Used by permission of Charles Scribner's Sons, New York.

10 ROCK OF AGES: the steadiness of Théry was the rock upon which the industry of Jenatzy and the brilliance of Lancia both foundered

11 MOUNTAIN PROSPECTOR: Vincenzo Florio setting out to survey the circuit on his 24 hp Itala

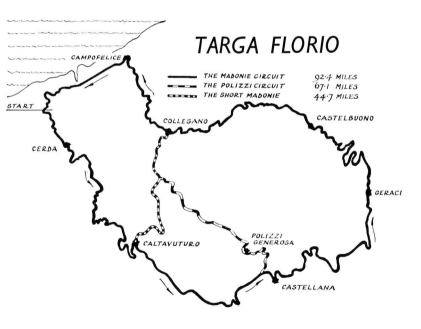

TARGA FLORIO

THE MADONIE CIRCUIT	92·4 MILES	
THE POLIZZI CIRCUIT	67·1 MILES	
THE SHORT MADONIE	44·7 MILES	

CAMPOFELICE

START

CERDA

COLLESANO

CASTELBUONO

GERACI

CALTAVUTURO

POLIZZI GENEROSA

CASTELLANA

veteran driver who survived long into the twenties, won both the Belgian and American races with a Darracq and the Florio Cup went to Raggio driving another famed Italian car of those times—Itala.

During these two years an enduring pattern of internationally founded races on long closed circuits had been established and by the end of 1905 much of the driving force in motor racing had passed from the A.C.F. Thereafter the A.C.F. sought to restore the situation by organising their first Grand Prix, but not before Vincenzo Florio had successfully run his first Targa Florio in Sicily on the famous Madonie Circuit, the 90-mile marathon that has dwarfed every other closed circuit and almost every other motor race before or since. Thus by a matter of 50 days the Targa Florio enjoys the fame of being the oldest race series still extant.

Technically the Grand Prix broke no new ground in that it perpetuated the old Gordon Bennett formula based on a maximum weight of 1000 kg. (2204 lbs.) with an additional 7 kg. for an engine driven magneto or dynamo used for ignition, although it was newly and harshly provided that only the driver and riding mechanic could work on a car. Prior to 1902 the inter-town races had catered for a series of classes based on weight, with the biggest cars enjoying no limit at all. Thus in 1901 the outstanding car was the 60 h.p. Mors with four cylinders measuring 130 × 190 mm. (10,087 c.c.) and weighing 1300 kg. Driven by Henri Fournier this car won both the Paris-Berlin and Paris-Bordeaux races, the latter at an average of 53 m.p.h. The vastly improved performance of the lighter cars in these races, particularly Paris-Berlin, had not escaped the attention of enlightened observers and it was argued that if the 12 h.p. 640 kg. Panhard of Giraud and the 8 h.p. Renault weighing only 395 kg. could average 35.5 and 36.9 m.p.h. respectively in Paris-Berlin (as against the winner's 44.5 m.p.h.) then it was high times these 'sortes de locomotives' were restrained. The seventh of the Gordon Bennett conditions prescribed a weight limit of 1000 kg. and this was adopted in and after 1902 for most of the great races including the 1906 Grand Prix. In fact however engine capacity steadily rose during the years of the weight limit, starting with the '70' Panhard of 1902 (160 × 170 mm. = 13,672 c.c.) and culminating with their '130' model in 1906 which had grown to the staggering proportions of 185 × 170 mm. = 18,279 c.c., making them the largest cars ever to have raced in a Grand Prix with the possible exception of the American Christie of 1907[4]. The Gordon Bennett cars were, in some cases, larger still, notoriously the 1905 Dufaux of 26,400 c.c. (4 × 225 × 166 mm.) and Hotchkiss of 18,816 c.c. (4 × 185 × 175 mm.).

The natural answer of a primitive[5] era to a series of maximum weight formulae was to insinuate the largest possible engine into the most exiguous chassis that human ingenuity could devise and then piously hope the driver was

[4] *See Chapter Two, p. 18.*

[5] *The answer of the German constructors in 1934/7 was much more sophisticated and placed much emphasis on chassis design as well.*

equal to his task. The climax of this process was probably reached in some of the Paris-Madrid cars and it contributed in no small measure to the disasters on the way to Bordeaux. The old couplet could well be applied to the attitude of some manufacturers to their drivers:

'Thou mayst not kill but needst not strive
Officiously to keep alive',

and safety factors were often seriously strained throughout the Age of Monsters although serious efforts were made in 1907 and 1908 to re-orientate designers' thinking with a fuel consumption limit (1907) and a formula based on maximum bore and minimum weight (1908). In this context it is instructive to recall what Jarrott wrote immediately after Paris-Madrid in the Automotor Journal of 13th June 1903:

'Restricted cylinder capacity with a minimum weight will put before the constructors problems in regard to efficiency and strength which cannot but have a marvellous effect on the evolution of motor carriages sold for ordinary use commercially. . . .'

but his views were five years in being recognised by the A.C.F.

There has never been quite the same distinction in motor racing as in cricket and other sports between professional and amateur, although in these early times the social distinction could be very sharply drawn. In the same way as Lord Chesterfield would always have kept at least one door between himself and that dusty Dr. Johnson, the aristocratic German Automobile Club sought to exclude the Mercedes works testers, Hieronymus and Werner from its membership and thus from the 1903 Gordon Bennett team. In the end the team was made up of Jenatzy, Baron de Caters and the American amateur Foxhall Keene who were completely acceptable socially, whether or not they all had the same skill as the works drivers. In 1904, when there were in effect two Mercedes teams in the race, the 'German' team still bore the tang of the Almanac de Gotha with Fritz von Opel joining Jenatzy and de Caters, while the works testers Braun and Werner raced under 'Austrian' colours. What that ultimate in aristocrats the Emperor Franz Joseph, who would not even recognise a Countess as wife of his heir apparent, would have said of such a distinction beggars description, and it was perhaps as well that he did not attend the Gordon Bennett race with his Imperial neighbour.

The manufacturer often took the view that his drivers or testers were simply paid to keep their cars on the road and win races, and if they objected or failed, why there were plenty more fish in the sea: labour in Edwardian times was cheap, abundant and thus eminently expendable. The team manager's reply to the driver who left the road in favour of a water hazard was to remind him that he was paid to win

13 LIGHT CAVALRY: the 12 hp Panhard of Giraud

14 QUART INTO PINT POT: . . . 'the largest possible engine into the most exiguous chassis' actually a 120 hp Clément-Bayard of 1905

15 MULTUM IN PARVO: the seating accommodation on the Darracq with which Wagner won the 1906 Vanderbilt

16 MAN OF SPIRIT: Louis Wagner shewing his paces in the 1906 Circuit des Ardennes on Darracq

17 INTREPID LADY: Madame le Blon (Hotchkiss) sets off into the mountains in the first Targa Florio

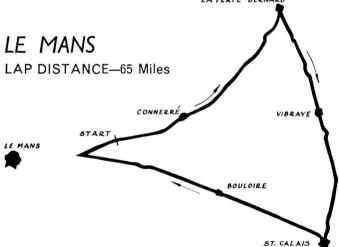

LE MANS
LAP DISTANCE—65 Miles

18 Six laps of a 65 mile circuit based on Le Mans had to be covered each day

races not to go bathing. For his time, therefore, Louis Wagner must have been a man of rare spirit as well as skill, and when Alexandre Darracq, a famed martinet, sought to explain away his defeat in the 1907 Targa Florio by blaming his leading driver, Wagner gave him the reply he deserved:

'Well, if you put the blame on me, you will regret it.'

It may be coincidence that Fiat were first and second in that race but Wagner promptly crossed the Alps and stayed with Fiat until he felt his honour had again been impugned by his employer—after the Brescia races of 1921.

The famous epigram—'We build cars to go not to stop; let us hear no more of this foolish talk about brakes!'—has been attributed both to Darracq and another autocrat, Ettore Bugatti, although he was cast in a different mould, and typified the attitude of many constructors. Some, however, were more go-ahead, though none perhaps so much as Peugeot who went so far as to allow their works drivers Georges Boillot, Jules Goux and Paul Zuccarelli to form a development unit of their own. Thus this great trinity of drivers left their mark on the social evolution of the racing driver no less than on the development of the modern high speed engine in the years immediately before 1914 and can truly be regarded as the archtypes of the modern class of professional driver.

Apart from the Cuban affair, there were four principal races in 1906: the Targa Florio in May, the Grand Prix on two days in June, the Circuit des Ardennes in August and the Vanderbilt Cup in October. According to W. F. Bradley[6] the suggestion to hold a race in Sicily was made in 1905 to Florio by the Editor of L'Auto to which Florio's initial response was that there were no roads! At all events, 90-miles worth of route had been found in that mountainous island by May 6th 1906 as well as ten competitors including several of the leading drivers of France and Italy, notably Lancia (Fiat), Henri Fournier, and his lesser known brother Maurice on Clément-Bayards, Paul Bablot on Berliet, de Caters, Cagno, Victor Rigal, who had succeeded Nazzaro as Florio's chauffeur, H. R. Pope and one Graziani on Itala and le Blon, accompanied by his wife as riding mechanic, on a Hotchkiss. For the record it was Cagno who won, covering the three laps (277 miles) in nine hours thirty two minutes and twenty two seconds at an average of 29.07 m.p.h. which compared interestingly with the fastest average over this long circuit in 1931 by Nuvolari on the new 2.3 straight eight Alfa Romeo of 40.28 m.p.h. over four laps. It was really an Itala benefit, as Graziani was 2nd, Rigal 4th and de Caters 5th out of six finishers.

Not to be outdone by any upstart Sicilian event, the A.C.F. ordained two days of racing for their Grand Prix over a 65 mile circuit based on Le Mans. Six laps had to be covered each day, making a total racing distance of 780 miles and the circuit followed the example set by the Italians at Brescia in

---

[6] *See his* Targa Florio (*pub. G. T. Foulis & Co. Ltd.: 1955*), *p. 25.*

that it aimed at very high speeds whilst conforming to the triangular pattern set by the Belgians in the Ardennes. In order to avoid traversing any towns a special wooden road was constructed to connect the two main Routes Nationales along which the majority of the circuit lay. The French had aimed a shrewd blow at Teutonic cunning by restricting the entry of each team to three cars, but there were still three Mercedes, three Fiats and three Italas to give the race a good solid international flavour. Mercedes were led by the great Jenatzy, whose win in the 1903 Gordon Bennett had really sparked off the whole chain reaction that resulted in the Grand Prix, but his team mates, Mariaux and Vincenzo Florio were, as racing drivers, little known. After their Sicilian Triumph Itala retained the victor Cagno and de Caters, deserting his almost traditional Mercedes, and Fabry on the third car. Fiat, deprived of Cagno, brought in an unknown amateur, Dr. Weillschott, to join the redoubtable Lancia and Nazzaro. Such then was the foreign challenge—nine cars with five drivers of the first rank—drawn up to meet the cohorts of French cars ranging from the 18-litre Panhards to the diminutive 7½-litre Gregoires.[7]

The American amateur Heath, who had won the Ardennes and Vanderbilt races for them in 1904, was still driving for Panhard in 1906 and led the team with Tart and Teste, survivors of early motor cycle and light car racing, in support. Next in order of size were the de Dietrichs, also of 18-litres, with what was possibly the strongest team of drivers—Gabriel, winner of Paris-Madrid, Rougier and Duray. Le Blon, back from the Sicilian mountains, led the Hotchkiss team with the better known Salleron, who had previously driven for Mors, and an American amateur Shepard. Then there was Rigolly with the vertically opposed Gobron-Brillié, the first car known to have exceeded 100 m.p.h., a mere stripling of 13½-litres. After the death of Marcel Renault in the Paris-Madrid, the firm had retired from racing temporarily, but had made the beginnings of a successful comeback in the 1905 French eliminating trials with a 13-litre model which François Szisz, erstwhile mechanic to Louis Renault, had driven into 5th place. The same combination of car and driver were back again in 1906 with former Darracq driver Edmond who had also driven in the 1905 race and another unknown, Richez. The name of Clément was well known in early motor racing, but for 1906 'patron' Adolphe Clément himself had retired in favour of his son Albert, who teamed up with Villemain and de la Touloubre, both drivers of considerable experience, if limited success.

As we have seen, Alexandre Darracq had attained considerable success in 1905 with a relatively small car of some 10-litres and he enlarged this to over 12½-litres for 1906 retaining his successful 1905 drivers Wagner and Hemery, whilst bringing in Hanriot to replace de la Touloubre who

19 LE MANS LEVIATHAN: The Panhard-Levassor of Teste was the largest car in the 1906 Grand Prix

20 STRONGEST TEAM: 'Next in order of size were the de Dietrichs . . .' Gabriel, Rougier, Duray (left to right)

21 ODD MAN OUT: . . . 'then there was Rigolly with the vertically opposed Gobron-Brillie . . . a mere stripling of 13½-litres . . .'

[7] The dimensions of the principal cars will be found in the table at page 18 infra.

14 Circuit de la Sarthe 1906

Virage à la sortie de Lamnay ... *de la Touloubre (Equipe Bayard-Clément)*

L'Hirondelle - Paris

22 DARRACQ TURNCOAT: ... 'de la Touloubre who had gone over to Clément-Bayard ...'

23 ... 'with their non-detachable wire wheels Hotchkiss (Shepard up) were at as much of a disadvantage as the other entrants with non-detachable rims'

24 FIRST STARTER: Gabriel, here shewn studying the map before setting off among the peat bogs in 1903

had gone over to Clément. In 1905 the most famous racing name in France, if not in the whole of Europe, was that of Richard-Brasier, but perhaps ill fatedly Monsieur Brasier had now lost the Richard and also, perforce, his great instrument of victory—Théry. His three drivers were Baras, Barillier and Pierry; the first two were old hands and Baras had at one time held the world kilometre record while Pierry was almost completely unknown. Finally there were the Gregoires of de Bosch and Tavenaux and Barriaux' Vulpes, the last two of which non-started.

Allowing for the fact that there were 23 French starters and six from Italy, it might almost as well have been the Gordon Bennett all over again but for the significant technical innovation by Brasier, Fiat, Itala and Renault of detachable rims. Perhaps foolishly Panhard decided they were not worth the extra weight involved (in the region of 36 kg.) and put their trust in brute force instead. By contrast the Hotchkiss had wire wheels of a non detachable pattern, while the Renault team had done much of their practising on similar wheels, but had reverted to the more normal pattern artillery wheels with detachable rims for the race. Detachable wheels were of course not permitted under Grand Prix regulations until 1912, and therefore Hotchkiss were at as much of a disadvantage as the other entrants who continued to rely on the artillery type of wheel with non-detachable rims.

The Chevalier René de Knyff had given up motor racing after losing the 1903 Gordon Bennett to Jenatzy, not in any spirit of pique, but simply because he felt the time had come to give place to younger men. He continued, however, to be present for many years in the counsels of the A.C.F. and the years had in no way dimmed his appetite for early morning rising by 1906, for prompt at 6 a.m. there he was to start the field, beginning, appropriately enough, with his old rival and Gordon Bennett colleague—Fernand Gabriel. One by one the 32 starters were sent on their way at 1½-minute intervals and after all the times were in for the first lap, it was Baras who led for Brasier, from Duray, Szisz, already well up with the leaders, Weillschott, Lancia and Pierry—two unknowns both very well placed. For all his inexperience Pierry improved the fortune of Brasier mightily on the 2nd lap when he went up to 2nd behind Baras with Weillschott now 3rd for Italy, and then Szisz, Hemery (Darracq) and Teste (Panhard). This, however, was Pierry's finest hour for his 3rd lap took him more than 2 hours, but now it was the turn of Barillier on the third Brasier to work his way into 2nd, after being 12th on the first lap. Baras was still 3rd, behind Szisz who had assumed the lead he was to hold for the rest of the two days' racing. Barillier had trouble on the next lap and the sun of Brasier was now only shining fitfully through the efforts of Baras and even he was gradually dropping back.

At this stage in the race the foreign challenge seemed to

25 EASY WINNER: François Szisz (Renault)—note the detachable rims

have been effectively settled for behind Szisz came Teste on the Panhard, with Shepard 3rd, then the falling Brasier of Baras, then Nazzaro, and Tart on another Panhard 6th, so that France's traditional champions old and new were dominating the race thus far. Another lap passed and as the leaders went through on to their last of the day Szisz still led, but now it was Clément appearing with the leaders for the first time in 2nd, then Weillschott back again in 3rd, then Shepard in spite of his slower tyre changes. Nazzaro still lurked ominously well up in 5th and then came the third Panhard of Heath. Weillschott's magnificent drive was abruptly terminated on the 6th lap when through sheer fatigue he ran off the road on the wooden section, which let Nazzaro into 3rd behind Szisz and Clément at the end of the first day's racing, when the main order was:—

1. Szisz   5–45–30 65·8 m.p.h.   4. Shepard 6–30–45
2. Clément 6–11–40   5. Barillier 6–31–48
3. Nazzaro 6–26–53   6. Richez   6–35–47

then Heath, Teste, Lancia, Hemery, Rigolly, Mariaux, Baras, Duray, Pierry, Jenatzy and Rougier—17 survivors out of 32. After the race Shepard reckoned he had had three tyre changes on the first day and that each one had taken him at least ten minutes longer than those with detachable rims ahead of him so that his was, on any account, a fine performance especially as he had had to stop and transfer some spokes to le Blon who had buckled a wheel. Perhaps even more remarkable was the 2nd place of the Clément-Bayard which also had fixed rims.

Szisz started first the following morning and drove straight to his pit where he spent 12 minutes compared to

26 Lancia watches the camera while a tyre is filled from a compressed air bottle

Clément's five and Nazzaro's immediate getaway, but even so his advantage was more than sufficient. Shepard made a poor start spending over half an hour at the pits and then melted away, ultimately leaving the road on the 8th lap at the same point as le Blon, when he damaged a wheel, this time too badly to continue. It had been arranged that cars were to be sent off on the second day in the order and at the intervals in time that they had finished the previous day so that the first car to complete its six laps would automatically be the winner. This was the nearest the Grand Prix got to running a race on this basis until 1922, when there was a

9

27 NEATEST RACER: Hanriot's Darracq at Longlier in the Ardennes

28 INSTRUMENT OF VICTORY: By the Ardennes race all the entrants had opted for the detachable rim as on Baras' Brasier (above)

29 NOT SO WEAK: 'Baras . . . "of the brilliant past . . . weak-looking until one forgot all about that in admiration of his handling of the car" '

mass start for the first time. By the second day the road was breaking up badly and the surface preparation was also causing considerable suffering to some of the drivers. Mr. J. T. Burton-Alexander,[8] who took over from Jenatzy on the second day at an hour's notice without having driven on the circuit, described it as full of loose stones and holes except, one hopes, on the wooden section. In spite of this handicap and his relative inexperience in racing Burton finished and averaged only 4 minutes less than Jenatzy for his 6 laps.

The second day's racing was relatively uneventful: Szisz ran out an easy winner from Nazzaro who had displaced Clément during the 10th lap, although the winner had a few bad moments after breaking a rear spring on the 11th lap. Lancia too had completed the Fiat revival by climbing from 9th to 5th, but Mercedes, shorn of their six car entry, had put up a very poor showing even allowing for Jenatzy's eye troubles. Burton claimed that 'the car was quite capable of winning but for tyres' and told how 'Baras caught and passed me once and I picked him up and left him again like anything,' (and Baras it was who put in the fastest lap in 52 mins. 25 secs. (73.3 m.p.h.) but it was all to no avail for Mercedes.

In all probability it was tyre changing that was the decisive factor in the race: decisive firstly because those without detachable rims lost heavily on each tyre change, both in terms of time and sheer driver fatigue, and secondly because the rough road surface wrought havoc with primitively designed tyres on two really blazing hot days of racing. Herbert Austin (later Lord Austin) who watched the race formed the impression that the Renaults were the most carefully and scientifically designed cars in general and that the arrangements for the mechanic's comfort on the Renault were better than on any other car which aided him the better to play his part in wheel changing and other tasks.

Although they were probably the fastest cars on the course, the Brasiers had been inexplicably unlucky, or perhaps it was that their lack of litres proved a fatal handicap on a circuit where maximum speed counted for more than anything else. At all events they were the only firm to finish a team of cars intact, although, on this score, the Fiat team must be counted unlucky to have lost Weillschott due only to fatigue at the very end of the first day. Neither the Italas nor the Mercedes had played any serious part in the racing although Fabry had been going fast until his accident on the first lap. The road surface, as in 1921, was appalling causing injuries to drivers' bodies and, worse, to their eyes and even the iron Szisz was shown receiving medical treatment from Dr. Pascal (Baron Henri de Rothschild).

It was generally felt that two days racing on such a circuit coupled with the somewhat inhuman restriction on the number of people allowed to work on the cars had been too much of a good thing and these requirements were materially relaxed for the Circuit des Ardennes two months later on

[8] *also known as J. T. Burton.*

30 BEST RECORD: Albert Clément's Clément-Bayard which was 3rd at Le Mans, 4th in the Vanderbilt and 6th in the Ardennes

31 LITTLE SHORT OF CRIMINAL: Lancia's Fiat thunders through the ill-controlled crowd in the Vanderbilt Cup

August 14th. The circuit was that used for the first race when Jarrott had won and in addition tyre depots were set up at several points around the course by Michelin and Dunlop manned by their own fitters. As a final Sybaritic touch the start was delayed until seven in the morning. The race lay between teams of Darracq, de Dietrich, Brasier and Clément driven by Hemery, Wagner and Hanriot (Darracq), Duray, Rougier, Gabriel and Sorel[9] (de Dietrich), Barillier, Baras, Pierry and Bablot on Brasier and Clément, Villemain and a well known French rugby footballer Pierre Garcet in place of de la Touloubre, on Cléments. The rest of the field comprised Demogeot on a light Darracq, Count d'Hespel on a Corre and the three Mercedes of Jenatzy, Salzer and Burton-Alexander, now promoted to a regular driver.

H. Massac Buist who attended the race provided the Autocar with a most vivid eye-witness account of 'such well known motorists as de Knyff, Heath, de Caters and de Crawhez wandering about the square of this little village for hour after hour as though in search of a job, while Théry, the invincible, passes among the crowd utterly unheeded, and has to peer between the railings among the crowd to get glimpses of those who have come into prominence since his retirement from racing.' Significantly all the entrants opted for detachable rims apart from Hemery who evidently preferred to be conservative even though he was observed unkindly to have 'grown more stalwart during the last twelvemonth.' The new Darracqs of Wagner and Hanriot won much praise as 'the neatest little racers yet made' in contrast to poor Baras 'of the brilliant past ... sunken-chested and weak looking (until) as the car got going one forgot all about that in admiration of his handling of it.' Then there was Albert Clément with 'his head encased in the wood enforced casquet worn by all the Clément-Bayard drivers' and the inevitable Gabriel, this time sporting 'a tasselled smoking cap of many colours.'

Like Baras' in the Grand Prix, the fastest lap in the race was the first—this time by Wagner. Following this early proof of his brilliance, his inevitable ill luck was not long delayed when he lost many places on the next lap. After lying 2nd on lap one, Salzer too fell away and the race was

fought between Duray and Clément in the first half and Duray and Hanriot in the second, with victory finally going to Duray by the narrow margin of 1 min. 42 secs. and even this could well have been closer had Hanriot not slowed in the final kilometre. Ten minutes behind Hanriot there had been a mighty tussle for 3rd place with a bare two minutes covering Rougier, Barillier and Gabriel—making the race a real triumph for de Dietrich which was celebrated by the erection of a triumphal floral arch by their workmen to greet the victors' return to the factory. Clément who eventually finished 6th had had misfortune on his 6th lap which took $64\frac{1}{2}$ mins. otherwise he would undoubtedly have finished in the first three and there must have been many who shared Massac Buist's view that 'the driving in general was perhaps finer than any that has been witnessed in long distance racing,' even though there had been no Fiats or Renaults in the field.

No Renaults crossed the Atlantic to Long Island for the third Vanderbilt Cup in October, but three Fiats and their Le Mans drivers did, along with three outstanding French entries—Duray (de Dietrich), Wagner (Darracq) and Clément (Clément-Bayard). The last named had been rumoured to be building a 6-cylinder car for the race with the same square dimensions as their 4-cylinder model (160 × 160 mm.). Heath on Panhard and Shepard on Hotchkiss brought French entries up to five, with de la Touloubre a sixth on an American Thomas. The ubiquitous Jenatzy appeared with Mercedes as did Cagno and Fabry on Itala, the American challengers being Lawyell (Frayer Miller) Tracy (Locomobile) Harding, and Christie on a car of his own make.

As at the Ardennes the racing was close in the extreme, but unhappily the Belgian Club's notices warning spectators of the dangers of motor racing had failed to accompany the European invasion and the organisation of the race was little short of criminal. As a spectator put it

'*Where the crowd was greatest a fence of wire netting had been erected ... but no sooner had the first car started than this was entirely swept away and the course swamped by the crowd.*'

[9] *The same Colonel Sorel so well known to Bugatti enthusiasts in England before the war.*

11

32 WORTH CROSSING THE ATLANTIC: Duray (de Dietrich) shews talent as a slip fielder when a detachable rim and his mechanic both break loose

33 'To hear the tale of peril': a meditative Louis Wagner at the finish (centre) with Jenatzy (left)

This was all the more regrettable as the race itself was thrillingly contested by Wagner, Lancia, Duray, Clément and Jenatzy, now driving his last really outstanding race. Wagner led on time throughout but the intervals and starting places were such that on the road Jenatzy, Lancia and Wagner were 'neck and neck ... throughout the day, lap by lap, these giants were pitted against each other for a Titanic struggle ... (with) rarely more than a minute's interval on any part of the course. Hour after hour they were in sight of each other, passing and repassing. I was fortunate enough' wrote an eye witness 'to see perhaps the most thrilling moment of the whole race ... (when) Jenatzy, Wagner, Lancia and Tracy arrived at this corner at practically the same moment. The excitement was terrific ... and it was worth going across the Atlantic to see.'

Surprisingly perhaps Tracy on his Locomobile made the fastest lap although he was never higher than 9th and it may well be that the European drivers were so troubled by the poor spectator control that they were unwilling to risk everything: indeed Wagner was quoted as saying that he could have gone quicker had he not been unnerved by the crowds who swarmed all over the course. Behind Wagner the other four finishers—Duray, Lancia, Jenatzy and Clément—were constantly changing places and at the end of the day's racing Lancia was 2nd, a mere 16 secs. ahead of Duray; there was a gap of $8\frac{1}{4}$ mins. between Duray and the 4th man Clément, but he in turn was less than 3 mins. ahead of Jenatzy and on its American showing the Mercedes could at least begin to lay claim to the extravagant praise bestowed

upon it by Burton-Alexander at Le Mans.

Although in terms of prestige and numbers of entrants the Grand Prix had dominated the year's racing it was far from producing the best racing or racing conditions and the Circuit des Ardennes had undoubtedly been the best event of the year, judged all round, while the Vanderbilt would certainly have been but for the unpleasant taste left by its disgraceful organisation. Thus although other countries were palpably encroaching on French leadership in organisation and racing generally, the obstinate fact remained that France still enjoyed, if not a monopoly, at least an appreciable advantage in the matter of cars and drivers. With 2nd place in two of the main events of the year Fiat could look happily towards a brightening future, even though the fortunes of Mercedes were still sadly in decline. However their decline in no way affected the prestige of motor sport in Germany, and for 1907 the All Highest himself had decided that the time had come to excel mere mortals like Vanderbilt and Florio by inaugurating his own race—the Kaiserpreis.

After the disasters of 1906, the Vanderbilt Cup went into cold storage, but the Targa Florio was back again in the lists, and so was the Grand Prix after a great deal of characteristic prima donna behaviour from the A.C.F. and the French motor industry. In addition the Brescia races were revived and the Circuit des Ardennes was run for the last time, although sadly declined in its status as an event for Grand Prix cars.

Chapter Two
1907 · The Grand Prix Becomes Established

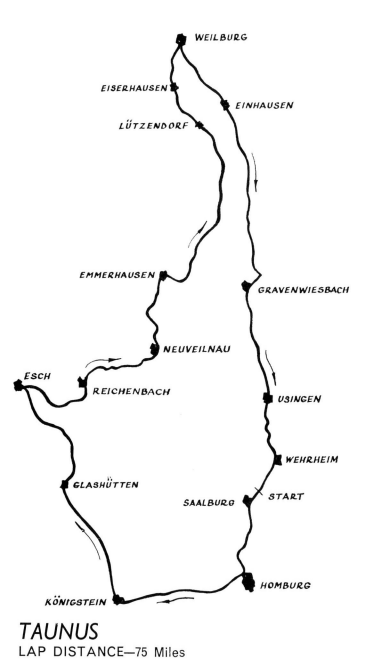

TAUNUS
LAP DISTANCE—75 Miles

34 . . . 'the Kaiserpreis circuit used much of the old Taunus Gordon Bennett course of 1904 . . . '

During 1906 the bad relations between the French motor trade and the A.C.F. had been coming to a head. Some years before, feeling that the Club cared little for the Trade, some manufacturers had formed the Motor Union, but this had not prospered and gave way presently to a stronger body altogether, under the august presidency of the Marquis de Dion, one of the three founders of the A.C.F.—the Chambre Syndicale de l'Automobile, to which most of the leading French manufacturers belonged. The Club invited members of the Chambre to help in organising the annual Paris Salon and also promised to consult it on all other matters involving the Trade including, of course, motor races. However, even this did not satisfy some extremists in the Trade, notably the bellicose Alexandre Darracq, who set about founding what he hoped would become an even wider and more powerful body—the Fédération des Chambres du Cycle et de l'Automobile, which de Dion, with a characteristic flourish, described as 'born of self-interest and jealousy.' Darracq of course put it rather differently (while carefully avoiding calling out the Marquis, a famous duellist, for satisfaction)—claiming it was his intention 'to make manufacturers masters of the situation as regards the organisation of all sporting manifestations, such as races, trials, exhibitions and the like.'

35 FAMOUS DUELLIST: The Marquis de Dion

13

36 *LIQUID DIVERSION: Gabriel's Lorraine-Dietrich is given its ration under the watchful eye of the Chevalier René de Knyff*

37 *SUCCESSFUL REPEAT: 'the second Targa attracted 46 starters . . .'*

In fact the French motor trade was at a very touchy stage in its history largely because the traditional supporters of racing were finding it very tough at the top in the face of competition from foreign entrants and 'parvenu' home competitors. What they really wanted was the freedom to have given up racing altogether, but this could only be done if everybody else did and the infamous self-denying ordinance was then several years away. The trade were also displeased with the Club because it only organised its Grand Prix so that French constructors were obliged to travel to Italy, Sicily, Belgium and even America to keep in the competitive swim. This, they claimed, was undesirable on two counts—first it added immensely to costs and secondly it ensured the growth of interest in racing in these other countries, most notably in Italy, where the rising fortunes of Fiat, Itala and Isotta-Fraschini were obviously not going to be denied victory for very much longer. In this connection the proposed re-entry of Germany into the field of race organisation in 1907, backed by the stimulus of full Imperial patronage, must have awakened many uneasy memories of the Mercedes triumph in the 1903 Gordon Bennett and the tremendous battle the following year on that same Taunus circuit where the Kaiserpreis was to be centred.

The calamitous organisation of the 1906 Vanderbilt Cup did not help matters either, pointing as it did to the necessity of choosing shorter circuits which were easier to police and maintain and even then there was talk in informed circles of a move towards setting up some form of permanent circuit, although not necessarily on private ground like the new Brooklands Track then fast approaching completion in England. To resolve its difficulties or possibly to quieten its critics the Club put a referendum to the Chambre on the following points:

1. Should they hold a Grand Prix in 1907?
          and if so
2. How was it to be organised?
3. Were engines to be limited in capacity? and
4. Should detachable rims be allowed?

The Chambre did not take long to say "Yes" to the first question and recommended the selection of a small circuit which could be used for one race each year. Having lost £3000 on the 1906 Grand Prix, the Club welcomed the suggestion that the race organisation should be farmed out to a contractor and the debate then passed to the third question, where opinion favoured a formula based on maximum fuel consumption. In terms of a circuit, de Dion was busily urging the claims of the Auvergne as a permanent venue, but in the end the Club opted for a 48 mile circuit based on Dieppe where it was thought the higher performance cars would have a better test. The town also offered a financial guarantee of some £4000, and after a winter of alarum and excursion the Grand Prix was in business again backed by 34 entries at single fees.

The fuel consumption limit was finally set at 30 litres per 100 kilometres which worked out at about 9.41 miles per gallon and plainly failed in its avowed object of diverting constructors' thoughts from maximum engine size on to chassis design. It was averred that even the most thirsty of the 1906 cars consumed only 28 or 29 litres per 100 kilometres, which made the 30-litre limit seem positively extravagant. Faroux virulently denounced the Club's prodigality and openly preferred the approach of the German Kaiserpreis, which postulated an engine limit of 8-litres coupled with a minimum weight of 1175 kg. Notwithstanding this small engine Faroux forecast a winning average of 100 k.p.h. (c. 62 m.p.h.) which would compare very favourably with Szisz' speed at Le Mans of 63 m.p.h. on a circuit where little gear changing was needed. Faroux also rubbed home the lack of progress in design by citing Gabriel's winning speed of 65.3 m.p.h. in Paris-Madrid. As it turned out, Faroux was rather wide of the mark for Nazzaro only averaged 52.5 m.p.h., albeit in poor weather, but it is worth mentioning that the Grand Prix class in the Circuit des Ardennes was won at a slightly slower speed than the class for the Kaiserpreis cars, while on the very fast Brescia circuit the Grand Prix class winning speed was only fractionally faster than that in the Kaiserpreis class. In neither of these latter events, however, was there anything like the entry for the Grand Prix—or for that matter for the Kaiserpreis.

Not to be outdone, Florio produced some rather more ingenious rules for his 2nd Targa which were ultimately adopted in principle by the A.C.F. in 1908. Here weight was to some extent in proportion to engine bore, which was limited to between 120 and 130 mm. for 4-cylinders and 85-90 mm. for sixes. Minimum weight was set at 1000 kg. with an allowance of 20 additional kg. per millimetre of bore in the case of a four cylinder and 40 kg. per millimetre in the case of sixes. Although the regulations were more complex than any others and the race was as early as April 21st, the second Targa attracted 46 starters including Darracq (Wagner and Hanriot), and Lorraine-Dietrich (Duray and Gabriel) from France, Benz of Erle and others plus Opel's Opel from Germany and a strong contingent from Italy led by the Fiats of Nazzaro, Lancia and Weillschott, the Isotta-Fraschinis of Trucco, Minoia, Tamagni and Sorel and the Italas of Cagno and Fabry. There were also some Clément-Bayards but not of the first order. Course and distance were as before but this time a magnificent race was produced between Lancia, Nazzaro, Wagner, Duray, Gabriel, Fabry and Cagno. From the start it was Lancia who took the lead, but by a bare 14 secs after lap 1 from Cagno, Trucco, Nazzaro, Minoia and Wagner. During the second lap the Isottas faded, but in their place Wagner moved right up to 2nd place harrying Nazzaro on the leading Fiat until he

38 *Primitive pit area with mountainous backcloth for the 1907 Targa Florio*

39 *where the entries included Erle's Benz*

40 *. . . and the Itala of Cagno the 1906 winner*

41 BELGIAN SENSATION: . . 'the Pipe of Hautvast whose performance was the sensation of the meeting'

42 IMPERIAL PREFERENCE: The Opel (Michel's) which ran so excellently, with Wagner's Fiat behind

43 Fournier's Itala which finished 8th

finally ran out of transmission half way through the third and last lap. By this time Lancia had fallen to 3rd place with Duray and Gabriel 4th and 7th sandwiching the Italas of Cagno and Fabry.

When the Darracq's transmission gave out, Lancia crept back to 2nd and on the last lap Fabry managed to catch Duray to give the home cars a 1-2-3 finish, the times being:

1. Nazzaro	8–17–36	5. Cagno	8–39–16
2. Lancia	8–29–29	6. Gabriel	8–39–46
3. Fabry	8–32–40	7. Tamagni	8–41–45
4. Duray	8–39– 7	8. Weillschott	8–42–52

The Targa Florio set a pattern for the very close racing that was seen throughout 1907, even though full teams from the available constructors never entered for all the events. With three basic formulae applying to the five principal meetings, this was perhaps not surprising, but it was none the less disappointing. The most varied international entry was obtained for the next race—the German Kaiserpreis—where battle was joined between home teams of Mercedes, Opel and Benz, French Lorraine-Dietrich and Darracq, Metallurgique, Pipe and Minerva from Belgium, Fiat, Itala and Isotta from Italy and even a Daimler from England. Amongst a host of lesser known and easily forgotten makes was an Italian Bianchi driven by one Maserati. The circuit used much of the old Taunus Gordon Bennett course of 1904 and once again the Kaiser was mightily in evidence in his usual variety of resplendent uniforms. Originally there had been an entry of 92, but this tailed away and although the entry was divided into two eliminating heats, only 25 started in the first and 29 in the second so that the entry could probably have all been run off in the same race. As it was, there was considerable dissatisfaction at the principle of choosing the first 20 in each heat for the final, irrespective of racing time; as a result, the 19th finisher in the first heat was slower than those finishing 21st, 22nd and 23rd in the second, and the 20th in heat I was slower than 24th, 25th and 26th in Heat II.

However, none of this affected the principal actors—the Fiats of Nazzaro, Lancia and Wagner, newly brought over after his fracas with Darracq, the Belgian Pipes of Hautvast and Deplus, whose performance was the real sensation of the meeting, and the Opel of Opel himself. Others who qualified well were Wilhelm on Metallurgique, who unfortunately crashed early in the final, Geller's Adler and Cagno's Itala. With Cagno in the Itala team was the renowned Henri Fournier pursuing the minor comeback which he had made with Clément-Bayard in the 1906 Targa Florio.

The closeness of the racing in the final was well in keeping with the quality of the entry: thus on lap 1 Nazarro led Wagner by a mere 7 secs; the next lap it was Hautvast's turn to lead his team-mate Deplus by the slightly greater margin of 23 secs. while Nazzaro held a very narrow advantage of 63 secs. over Hautvast as they entered the fourth and last circuit. On the first lap the Pipes had occupied 3rd and 4th behind the leading Fiats, but in the middle part of the race they really challenged the all-conquering Italians and even led them; nor were the Opels of Jörns and Opel himself much behind throughout the race and when Deplus and Wagner fell back, they quickly seized their opportunity.

By contrast Lancia was more than usually unlucky, making a very slow first circuit when he lay 28th. During the rest of the race he improved prodigiously, being 17th after 2 laps, 11th after 3 and actually finishing 6th within 68 secs. of Wagner who had led him by more than quarter of an hour two laps before. Lancia, needless to say, put in fastest lap at 53.5 mph. on his last circuit, but even this tremendous tour-de-force was overshadowed by Nazzaro's second victory and the wonderful display of the Pipe and Opel cars. Deplus sadly had a steering failure on his last lap, but Hautvast held 2nd place only 4 mins. 24 secs. behind Nazzaro and a mere 29 secs. ahead of Jörns on the first Opel. The Kaiser, it was noted, received the winning drivers, mechanics and constructors with great warmth and none more 'than his own subjects the makers and drivers of the Opel car which ran so excellent a third'. Contemporary accounts spoke glowingly of the bearing of the All Highest and the applause which greeted him everywhere and, as the *Autocar* summed up: 'It is when engaged in such acts as these at the close of a great international contest which His Imperial Majesty had encouraged to the utmost that we admire him most'. If only he could have been content with motor racing!

Behind Nazzaro, Hautvast and Opel came the Opel of Michel, the Fiats of Wagner and Lancia, then Minoia (Isotta), Fournier (Itala), Salzer (Mercedes), Cagno (Itala), Schmidt (Eisenach) and only then in 12th, the French de Dietrich of Rougier. Coming on top of their disappointing showing in the Targa Florio, this cannot have given much satisfaction or encouragement to the French constructors, who must have approached their own Grand Prix with sore misgivings at the late entry of three Fiats at double fees, whilst perhaps breathing a sigh of relief that foreign participation did not include any of the Belgian and German upstarts who had so thoroughly thrashed them in the Kaiserpreis.

Both the races thus far run had been astonishingly successful in terms of organisation, entry and racing and it was feared that the Grand Prix itself might prove somewhat of an anticlimax. It had been hoped that the proximity to England, which was at that time obsessed with the Edwardian ideal of l'entente cordiale, would bring over King Edward VII as a counter to the Kaiser's encouragement of the German race, but in the end English participation was limited to a brace of bizarre eight-cylinder Weigels. The great Dieppe circuit, then being used for the first of its three

44 FALLEN ANGEL: . . . 'by contrast Clément-Bayard who had done so well in 1906 were having a poor year' (above is Shepard)

45 AMERICAN GOLIATH: the most notable curio was the V-4 front wheel drive Christie of 19,618 c.c. driven by its designer

46 BELGIAN DAVID: The Germain which was the smallest car in the race

17

47 BLOOD AND THUNDER: 'Behind Lancia, Duray was making tremendous speed in his Lorraine-Dietrich . . .'

48 LUCKY JIM: Triple winner Felice Nazzaro

49 VERSATILE SPORTSMAN: Ex-Rugby footballer Garcet who finished 8th on Porthos

50 RETURN TO GLORY: 'the sun of Brasier had been brighter at Dieppe with Baras finishing 3rd'

Grands Prix, measured just under 48 miles and began at the almost obligatory fourche, in this instance situated just outside the town at the junction of N 25 and N 320. In 1907/8 the circuit was run anti-clockwise and the start was on the slight downhill slope on N 320, which ran for about 25 kilometres east to Londinières, where it branched left and ran north west for another 25 kilometres along N 314 to a hairpin just south of Eu where it doubled back sharply on to N 25 for the 30 kilometres run back to Dieppe and the start.

The circuit was basically triangular like the one laid out at Le Mans, but where Le Mans had been flat, the Dieppe circuit contained an interesting variety of mild uphill and downhill sections. The total of 10 laps gave a racing distance of $477\frac{1}{2}$ miles, which was appreciably less than Le Mans, and the field contained a mere 37 starters making it the smallest of the year, although for racing quality it was probably better than anything else in 1907. Lorraine-Dietrich and Fiat had supported both previous races and were the principal contestants at Dieppe, but the Darracqs, which had also raced in Sicily and Germany, could not be ignored any more than the entries of Brasier and Renault.

By contrast Clément-Bayard, who had done so well in 1906, were having a poor year and it must have required all the famed fixity of purpose of Adolphe Clément to have continued with his entry after the fatal accident to his son Albert while practising. The fuel consumption restriction had not really had much effect on engine size and it is interesting to compare the engines of the cars that ran in 1906 and 1907 at this stage:

	1906	1907
Panhard	$185 \times 170 = 18,279$ cc.	$170 \times 170 = 15,435$ cc.
de Dietrich	$190 \times 160 = 18,146$ cc.	$180 \times 170 = 17,304$ cc.
Fiat	$180 \times 160 = 16,286$ cc.	$180 \times 160 = 16,286$ cc.
Mercedes	$175 \times 150 = 14,432$ cc.	$175 \times 150 = 14,432$ cc.
Gobron-Brillie	$140 \times 220 = 13,547$ cc.	$140 \times 220 = 13,547$ cc.
Renault	$166 \times 150 = 12,970$ cc.	$166 \times 150 = 12,970$ cc.
Clément	$160 \times 160 = 12,868$ cc.	$160 \times 160 = 12,868$ cc.
Darracq	$170 \times 140 = 12,711$ cc.	$170 \times 140 = 12,711$ cc.
Brasier	$165 \times 140 = 11,982$ cc.	$165 \times 140 = 11,982$ cc.

Thus, only Panhard and de Dietrich made any reduction and neither of these was particularly significant, while everyone else maintained the status quo.

There were, however, several distinct curios in design at the 1907 Grand Prix. The most notable of these was the American Christie, which was an immense V-4 front wheel drive affair allegedly measuring 184 x 184 mm. (19,618 c.c.) which, if true, made it the largest car ever to have taken part in a Grand Prix. The designer, who actually drove his car, claimed 135 developed horse power for it, coupled with a speed of 120 m.p.h. and a weight, incredibly, of 16 cwt. none of which is likely to have been true. The two English Weigels, in their way, were equally bizarre with their straight eight engines measuring some $7\frac{1}{2}$ feet in length. A contemporary photograph shewed the maker standing by one of the four-throw crankshafts, looking for all the world like a Scots music hall comedian with traditional Harry Lauder stick. Two other straight eights were on show: first, the Swiss Dufaux which had previously appeared in Gordon Bennett days—this had a bore and stroke of 125 x 130 mm. (12,763 c.c.) and employed chain drive and a three-speed gearbox in contrast to the Weigel, which only used two speeds. The other was the Porthos, which had already appeared in a sense in the Kaiserpreis. Due to the 8-litre limit the cars had then had six-cylinder engines of 119 x 120 mm., but now for the Grand Prix they were brought up to fully 'square' dimensions and given an extra two cylinders for good measure to give a total capacity of 10,857 c.c.

The 37 starters were to be let off at intervals of one minute and prompt at 6 a.m. a cannon was discharged to commence the proceedings and then at 6.1 Lancia was despatched on his long journey. It was notable that very little of the precious fuel allowance was wasted on warming up, but apart from two of the Panhards most of the cars found little difficulty in starting, and Lancia's Fiat, now painted traditional Italian red, was back again in 41 mins. 33 secs. Behind him, however, Duray was making tremendous speed in his Lorraine-Dietrich and had in fact lapped in 1 min. 33 secs. less than Lancia. Duray had started three minutes behind the Fiat and, after a second lap in 39 mins. 54 secs., he had closed to just over a minute behind Lancia on the road. Notwithstanding this electrifying duel between two of the fastest drivers of the time, it was the new Fiat driver Wagner who actually led the race on time and after three laps he was no less than 1 min. 20 secs. faster than Duray. By this time Duray had actually passed Lancia on the road and led the procession of cars, if not the race itself; however, this was the last the stands saw of the dashing Wagner, who met with an accident on the fourth lap, and from then until the 8th lap the race was mightily fought out between Lancia and Duray. The fact that they were generally in sight of each other added pepper and mustard to the excitement of spectators all the way round the long circuit.

The visible battle between Duray and Lancia had tended to obscure the fact that it was Wagner who led for the first three laps and that Lancia, during the early part of the race, was not 3rd but 5th, behind Gabriel and Szisz, so that the anticipated engagement between the leading French cars and the Fiats was being well fulfilled. After Wagner's retirement Duray led from Lancia and, ominously, the patient, methodical but ever formidable Nazzaro who had been biding his time after his wont. Now, all Duray had to do was to keep up a good pace and keep Lancia in sight and, accidents excepted, he might expect to win. On the 7th lap things improved still more for him when Lancia began to slow on to three cylinders while Nazzaro came up into 2nd and as they went on to the 9th lap Duray had a relatively

comfortable 4-minute lead over Nazzaro. The hapless Lancia might be almost crippled with misfiring, yet his work for Fiat had been faithfully done for Duray was soon back at the stands, but from the wrong direction and on foot with 'a bearing seized in his gear'.

This left the race to Nazzaro with the steady Szisz in 2nd place behind him, for Lancia suffered a deranged clutch when only a few miles from the finish, leaving the places behind the Italian winner to be well packed by the French defenders:—

1. Nazzaro 6–46–33 = 70·5 m.p.h. 3. Baras 7– 5–5.3/5
2. Szisz 6–53–10.3/5 4. Gabriel 7–11–39

then, 5. Rigal; 6. Caillois; 7. Barillier; 8. Garcet; 9. Shepard; 10. Hemery; 11. Courtade; 12. Bablot.

The sun of Brasier which had shone with fitful brilliance at Le Mans had been brighter at Dieppe with Baras and Barillier finishing solidly in 3rd and 7th, even if they eschewed their fireworks of the previous year; Bablot had been unlucky in being involved with Richez's Renault when its driver lost control on the first lap, which cost Bablot upwards of half an hour; otherwise he would certainly have finished very much higher as he had gained 4 mins. over the 16 miles he had covered before the accident to catch up with Richez. Darracq, with 5th and 6th, had the satisfaction of beating the renegade Wagner and the Lorraines had undoubtedly been the fastest cars racing and Duray most unlucky not to have won. Finally, if France had not actually carried off the first prize, her entries and drivers had dominated the event and, apart from Nazzaro, the only foreign car to finish with any credit was the Mercedes of Hemery, down in 10th. The foreign menace was certainly not strong enough to warrant any talk of abandoning Grand Prix racing—and as for Nazzaro, he had just been lucky right to the point of finishing with only 11½ litres of petrol—enough to take him a mere 20 miles!

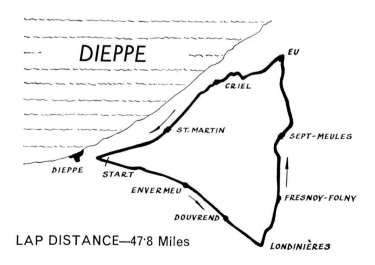

LAP DISTANCE—47·8 Miles

52 BELGIAN VICTOR: the successful Kaiserpreis Minerva here with Albert Guyot at the wheel in the German event

53 POPULAR WINNER: Baron de Caters (on his 1906 Targa Florio Itala) who won the G.P. class in the Ardennes races

Needless to say the French Trade was by no means as satisfied with the event as the A.C.F., who had reputedly made a profit of 70,000 francs and after the race an international conference was convened at Ostend to determine a formula for future racing car events. Whilst the presence of three different sets of rules in 1907 had undoubtedly added variety and, in the context of the times, provided a valuable period of experiment for organisers and designers alike, it was obviously too costly an arrangement to endure for very long. Not unnaturally the Germans favoured a capacity limit, while France and England backed the yardstick of a maximum bore and, perhaps surprisingly, Italy favoured formule libre. In the end the Anglo-French view prevailed and a maximum bore of 155 mm. with a minimum weight of 1100 kg. was laid down—in fact, a modified Targa Florio formula. At long last a truly concrete step had been taken to encourage the beginnings of sophistication in engine design and possibly some improvement in general features, such as handling and chassis design.

No sooner had all this been decided than it was time for the Ardennes meeting which included separate races for Kaiserpreis and formule libre cars. Benz, Adler, Mercedes, Gaggenau (Germany), Aries (France), Minerva, Imperia, Pipe and Metallurgique (Belgium) all entered for the former and after their brilliance in Germany one would have thought the race a foregone conclusion for the Pipe team of Hautvast, Deplus and now the great Jenatzy. Hautvast led for the first two laps, arousing much interest by completing his first with a dog neatly skewered on his starting handle, while the other two cars held 2nd and 4th on lap 1, and 3rd and 4th on lap 2. This, however, was high noon for the Pipes, as Jenatzy and Hautvast crashed on the 4th lap and Deplus on the 5th. In the meantime the Minervas of Guinness and Brabazon had been hotly challenging Hautvast, and Guinness

took the lead on the 3rd lap and held it almost to the end. Unhappily his 7th and last lap took him over an hour compared to his 3rd (47 mins. 59 secs.) and 2nd (48 mins. 18 secs.) which were the two fastest laps by any competitor in the race. His team-mate Brabazon more than upheld British honour by picking up three places on his last lap to win by 27 secs. from Koolhoven, with the unlucky Guinness 3rd another 52 secs. behind. All three had driven Minervas and Warwick Wright on the fourth finished 7th, with Hanriot's Benz 4th and Hieronymus now on Gaggenau in 5th.

British hopes stood high for the Grand Prix class thanks partly to the poor entry of only six cars—Harrison and Laxen on Grand Prix Weigels, Guinness' Darracq, the Laminne-Duchesne of Laminne and those two grand old timers of Mercedes—Baron de Caters and Camille Jenatzy, both driving what was to be their last race on the cars they had driven with such distinction for so long. The Weigels never rose higher than 4th and the race, such as it was, lay entirely between de Caters, Jenatzy and Guinness. Thus Jenatzy led for the first lap, de Caters for the next two and then Guinness came through again and seemed to have the race completely in hand when he held a lead of 5½ mins. over de Caters with one lap to go. Like Lancia at Dieppe, however, he had only three good cylinders at this vital stage and once more his last lap occupied more than an hour, which gave de Caters a narrow win by 1 min. 24 secs. Jarrott[1] had written of de Caters:

'. . . *he has never been fortunate in winning a big event. I am certain that were he successful he would be congratulated as no other man would be congratulated, because all automobilists know him for what he is.*'

and, greatly as Guinness must have been disappointed at losing both events in identical circumstances, neither he nor

[1] *In* Ten Years of Motors and Motor Racing.

20

54 NEW ITALIANS: (left to right) The Isottas of Tamagni, Minoia, Trucco and Sorel

any one else present grudged the gallant Baron the victory that he had so long and selflessly sought. Jenatzy, too, had shewn glimpses of his old form and made the two fastest laps of the race, his fastest lap of 47 mins. 48 secs. being slightly faster than Guinness' in the Kaiserpreis class. However, on a combined basis, six of the seven finishers in the Kaiserpreis class would have beaten de Caters.

This pattern was closely followed in the Brescia races in September which wound up the 1907 calendar. The preponderance of the entry for the Florio Cup, which was run to Kaiserpreis rules, was Italian, with the Isottas of Minoia, Trucco and Sorel and the Italas of Cagno, Fabry and Fournier the leading entrants; Hemery, Hanriot and Erle were back with their Benzes and there were also two Darracqs for Demogeot and Airoldi. As a matter of interest Maserati was again in the lists on Bianchi and there was even a team of three Wolsits (made by Wolseley) from England in the 34 starters. The circuit had been shortened to

37¾ miles and was to be covered eight times to give a distance of just over 300 miles, which seems hardly to have warranted a start at 5.31 a.m. However, promptly at this horrifying hour Ceirano on his Spa set out followed by the rest of the field at intervals of half a minute. Minoia was away like a rocket and led throughout the race, followed at various times by Trucco, Cagno and Fabry during the early stages; the French drivers on Benz and Darracq seemed to have been taken by surprise by the fast pace of the Italians and preferred to bide their time prudently after the manner of Nazzaro. However, they were either not so good at piling on the pace when it was needed or not such good judges of a race as Nazzaro and, although Minoia was delayed by tyre troubles on the last two laps, he still had enough in hand to lead Hemery home by nearly ten minutes.

Notwithstanding the example of Nazzaro and Cagno the *Autocar's* correspondent commented that 'the Italians drove with their accustomed impetuosity, which would savour of

55 CROSSING THE BAR: Kaiserpreis class regulations were relatively complicated involving height—here is Fabry's Itala being checked before the Florio Cup

56 CHAMPION OF THE FUTURE: 'Maserati was again in the lists on Bianchi in the Florio Cup . . . '

57 BRESCIA ROCKET: Minoia who led throughout winning the Florio Cup at 64.7 mph

recklessness if it were not for the remarkable skill with which they handled the cars. . . . As drivers the Italians show extraordinary aptitude and their driving is of the type which brings them through if they do not wreck their cars. At the same time they run greater risks of such troubles, inasmuch as they take even more out of their cars than the Frenchmen.'

I was sceptical of this view even from such a generally well informed source, and W. F. Bradley's comments in a recent letter are interesting:

'It is incorrect to suggest that in the 1907 period Italian drivers were more reckless and took greater risks than their French counterparts. The important firms frowned on recklessness. When Louis Wagner left Darracq to join Fiat, Signor Agnelli was not afraid to say to him—"We want no car wreckers on our team". . . . In the 1908 Brescia, one of the crack Clément-Bayard drivers walked back to the pits and announced that his car was in a river. He expected sympathy. Instead he got a broadside he was not likely to forget for a long time. My impression is that even serious newspapers of that period played up accidents and sympathised with the drivers. There was no such sympathy on the part of the manufacturers.'

Whilst the bulk of the entries in the Florio Cup might be German or Italian, this was not the case in the Coppa Velocita for Grand Prix cars which concluded the meeting and was subject only to the Dieppe fuel limit. Only 14 cars started—Duray, Gabriel and Rougier (Lorraine-Dietrich), Garcet, Alézy and Shepard (Bayard-Clément), Buzio (Diatto-Clément), Darracq (Demogeot), Itala (Cagno, Fabry, Fournier) and Spa (Ceirano, M., Ceirano E. and Raggio). Once again 5.30 was the starting time but in this race the cars departed at one minute intervals.

Shepard shewed the promise of the Bayard by leading on the first lap from his team-mate Garcet, then Fabry followed by Gabriel and Duray—first blood definitely to France. Cagno, however, had made a slow start losing eight minutes while he cleaned fouled plugs and now began carving his way through the field with two tremendous laps in 31 mins. 56 secs. and 31 mins. 31 secs.; his first lap, allowing for his 8 minutes loss at the start, would also have been accomplished in much the same time. In the meantime, however, Fabry improved his speed to take the lead on the 2nd lap, followed by Shepard still and then Duray. On the 3rd lap Duray caught Shepard and then he went to the head of affairs, still followed by Shepard but with the Italas of Fabry and, at last, Cagno challenged strongly.

About this time rain started falling and the Italians took time out to change to non-skid tyres, while the French preferred to save time by continuing on their smooth tyres. This possibly accounted for Shepard's crash on the 5th lap when he was lying 2nd to Duray. At the same time Fabry had engine troubles and this all let the persevering Cagno

58 UNIQUELY ON HIS METTLE: Cagno carves his way through the rough to win the Coppa della Velocita

59 . . . 'the unspectacular Rougier' who was 3rd, here taking his Lorraine-Dietrich round Longlier in the Ardennes

into second place about five minutes behind Duray. Poor Duray! luck just simply was not going to play it his way all through 1907 and on his sixth lap he lost over a quarter of an hour due to a skid when he damaged his steering. This brought Cagno to the lead after six laps with an advantage of almost five minutes over Demogeot's Darracq and, as if his steering troubles were not enough, Duray's car caught fire during its seventh lap. Although Demogeot was fastest on the 5th and 8th laps and Gabriel on the 7th, their efforts came too late and Cagno romped home 3 mins. 17 secs. ahead of Demogeot with the unspectacular Rougier 3rd, Gabriel 4th and the Bayards of Alézy and Garcet 5th and 6th. On a combined basis the result would have been (with Kaiserpreis cars in capitals):—

1. Cagno	4–37–36 = 65·25 m.p.h.	6. Gabriel	4–50–35
2. MINOIA	4–39–55 = 64·7 m.p.h.	7. Alézy	4–53–58
3. Demogeot	4–40–53	8. HANRIOT	4–57–47
4. Rougier	4–45–31	9. Garcet	4–59–22
5. HEMERY	4–49–49	10. TRUCCO	5– 5–56

Both races had been closely fought, but the Grand Prix cars had to some extent vindicated themselves by their slightly superior speed. It should be remembered first that there had been rain in the Coppa Velocita and secondly that many of the Grand Prix cars had lapped appreciably faster than Minoia's best Kaiserpreis lap of 33 mins. 16 secs.

Afterwards it emerged that Demogeot's car had never been driven before the actual race and also that it went through the race on the same set of Dunlops—slotted on the front and steel-studded on the back. One of the Wolsit drivers, M. Wild, in an interview after the race underlined what the *Autocar* said about the recklessness of the Italians . . . 'they take too much out of their cars. If everything goes well this spells victory but the comparative reserve[2] of the Frenchmen brings about a higher percentage of finishers than the brilliantly or perhaps madly reckless style of the majority of the Italians.' Cagno actually had driven what was noted as a very fast and consistent race, eschewing fireworks as befitted a former chauffeur to Royalty.

[2] *Reserved or not it is notable that the Italians had the deliberation to change tyres during the race to suit the change in weather.*

On their Brescia showing it was much to be regretted that the Italas did not attend the Grand Prix as they were clearly every bit as fast as the Lorraine-Dietrichs in the hands of their Grand Prix drivers and over a course similar in nature to the Dieppe circuit. Had they done so, and with Cagno in anything approaching his Brescia form, 1907 might perhaps have seen an Itala victory, though W. F. Bradley doubts this. Cagno, in fact, never drove such a race again, being normally renowned for the steadiness of his driving, but the long delay for new plugs at the start had served to put him supremely and uniquely on his mettle.

During 1907 Grand Prix racing had erupted into Germany and Italy besides Belgium, all this more than making up for the temporary disgrace of American racing. For 1908 the Americans were returning with not only the Vanderbilt Cup but also a new event—the Grand Prize. In addition the stature of the Grand Prix itself had been increased by the universal accord reached at Ostend, the financial success achieved by the A.C.F., to say nothing of the report that there would be no big racing in Germany, and the fact that the Targa Florio was to be open only to 4-cylinder cars of between 120 and 130 mm. bore. Having pioneered the principle of the new Ostend Rules, it seemed both odd and ironical that Florio should now effectively cut the throat of his fledgling Targa as a great racing event, but this was the effect of his new set of regulations and it was not until its great days in the twenties that the Targa Florio returned to the status it had fleetingly enjoyed in 1907. Whilst one said a long 'au revoir' to the Targa in 1907, it was final farewell to the Circuit des Ardennes which, almost more than any other event, had shaped the destiny of motor racing after the tragic end of the old inter-town races. However, if Florio lost out with his Targa, he certainly produced a wonderful race with his 1908 Coppa Florio, run as an event for Grand Prix type cars. The Grand Prix itself too enjoyed an Indian Summer before its four-year disappearance, and at the end of 1907, motor racing stood poised on the edge of one of its greatest seasons.

Chapter Three
1908 · Vanishing Edwardian Splendours

60 WINNING LINE-UP:The Mercedes Grand Prix team (left to right) Lautenschlager who won, Salzer who made fastest lap and Poege who was 5th

If there was comparative peace in French circles it was not to endure very long for that automotive firebrand S. F. Edge was abroad again—this time on the warpath of the detachable wire wheel. Now there was nothing especially new about wire wheels, in 1906 Hotchkiss had used them in the Grand Prix and Renault had certainly practised extensively on them, while several of the Peugeots in the Paris-Rouen had used them. Equally there was nothing vitally novel about a detachable wheel or, for that matter, about the time honoured rule in all the A.C.F.'s great races that the wheel, like the engine and gearbox, was an integral part of the car, so much so that in the days when seals used to be affixed, one was invariably put on the hub to prevent an illicit wheel change.

As we have seen, Hotchkiss were at an appreciable disadvantage in not having detachable rims in 1906, and nobody repeated their fixed wire wheel experiment in 1907 or 1908, although Weigel used wire wheels with a detachable rim in 1908. However after their trials at Le Mans all the doubters swiftly went over to the detachable rim, that had been pioneered in France by Michelin, and Dunlop in particular were not slow in applying this to racing uses in conjunction with their racing tyres. But it happened that in England a further development had been pioneered in the shape of a detachable wire wheel and there is little doubt but that this had its first serious test in long distance speedwork when Edge opened Brooklands with his historic 24-hour run on 29th/30th June, 1907. The efforts of Mr. John Pugh and

Rudge Whitworth Ltd. had put England well in the lead in this field and it was only natural that Edge should decide to use them on the Napiers he was preparing for the 1908 Grand Prix.

On the 24th January, 1908 Edge read a paper to the Coventry Engineering Society, under Mr. Pugh's chairmanship, on The Results of Racing on Design. One of the twelve items discussed was the detachable wire wheel and Edge very rightly claimed that its use had been well proved by Napiers both in their record breaking at Daytona Beach in 1906 and over longer distances by himself at Brooklands. In addition whenever a Napier raced at Brooklands it used similar wheels. To some extent this was a characteristic Edge 'Aunt Sally', because, in fairness, the A.C.F. had not taken any point on safety: indeed they would have been singularly ill advised to do so, as the detachable rim was far from satisfactory on this count and there were several instances of it coming adrift in the Grand Prix and other races.

The A.C.F.'s arguments centred on two points : —

(1) that the detachable wire wheel was not established as practical for touring cars,

(2) that it was too late to modify the existing rules.

The first point was really just as much of a French 'Tête de Turque' as anything Edge ever dreamed up: it was an extraordinary criterion for the French of all people to adopt in the first place and secondly it was arrant nonsense. Looking through the correspondence of the times it is quite clear that many motorists shared the view of Mr. Hubert Egerton that the R.W. wheel

'has been the greatest comfort and convenience and seeing that it is so infinitely more secure and much more quickly fitted than the best of detachable rims, I cannot help regarding it as one of the greatest improvements that has been devised of late.'

Viewed with the always questionable eye of hindsight the arguments for the R.W. wheel are so devastatingly right that it is satisfying to find such a body of contemporary proof of this view, and none more telling than the fact that they were allowed for the Prince Henry Trials later in 1908. Had the A.C.F. listened to Mr. Egerton or Prince Henry it is doubtful if they could have held their position for very long, although, in fairness, it should be stated that there was an equal body which viewed the wheel as unsafe, excessively costly and likely to add too much bulk to the equipment of a touring car. All these, in the context of the times, were very legitimate objections.

The A.C.F. were, however, on surer ground with their second point. D. M. Weigel had written to the Club on Edge's behalf suggesting the wisdom of allowing detachable wheels to which the Chevalier René de Knyff replied

61 *THE CONTENDERS: Firebrand Edge (right) and the 'reactionary" de Knyff centre) who were the main actors in the detachable wheel drama with Charles Jarrott (left) whose return on Mors was eagerly awaited*

62 *THE BONE: The 1908 G.P. Napier which wouldn't play in the A.C.F.'s yard*

63 *THE PROOF: Earp on a Napier fitted with detachable wire wheels stirs the sand on Ormonde Beach in 1906*

64 *DYING GAUL:* . . . 'even Mors made an entry at the eleventh hour including . . . the lesser known Landon'

65 . . . 'Bayard-Clément were back again with a new team (left to right) Hautvast, Gabriel and Rigal . . .'

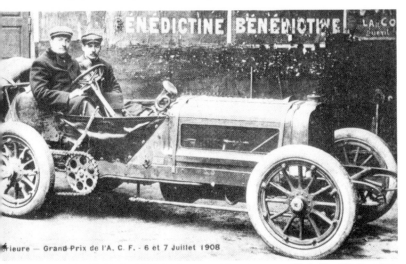

66 *SEMPER FIDELIS:* . . . 'Brasier . . . filled Barillier's place with the greatest of his drivers—Théry'

I have the honour to inform you that the rules . . . having been adopted and published, it is absolutely impossible to modify them on the demand of one competittor.

I am of the opinion that the plea you are putting forward in favour of one of your compatriots is not of a nature to prevent English manufacturers from participating in the event as you yourself state that you see no hardship in Article 17 . . . that prevents the changing of wheels.'

Weigel made the following reply:

'. . . might I point out that it was impossible for any would-be competitor to place before your committee for their consideration any suggestions as to what the rules might be, inasmuch as the rules were not published and no draft was at any time submitted. It only therefore became possible for Mr. Edge to question Rule 17 after he had seen it.'

He then went on to agree that there was no advantage in altering Rule 17 and suggested that, if all competitors agreed to Edge running on his detachable wheels, he should be allowed to do so as a preferable alternative to seeing 'would-be competitors refrain from entering through so trivial a matter.' How well Weigel knew Edge! In fact de Dietrich agreed to this idea, but the A.C.F. did not take it up, and before many weeks were out the whole atmosphere had become clouded by accusations of ill manners and bad sportsmanship flying to and fro across the Channel and hope of any reasoned compromise had completely evaporated.

I incline to the view that it simply did not cross Edge's mind before the rules were published that his wheels would not be permitted, although, as a motoring competitor of very long standing, he certainly ought to have contemplated the probability that the old rule would be perpetuated. However, once the rules were published his conduct becomes very hard to understand. Had he gone quietly to Paris to argue his case, as was suggested at the time, it would have been more tactful and comparable as an exercise in good manners to the visit of several dignitaries of the A.C.F. to the works of Austin and Weigel to measure their cylinder bores well in advance. De Knyff's strict adherence to rules was well known where his watchword was always *Fiat Justitia ruant coelae* and Weigel himself was happy to accept the French ruling:

'Personally I look upon it in the way of a sporting event more than a business one, and should like to see the best car win, even if the driver changed the engine on the road.'

Poor Duray, had he read this, must have longed for a spare gearbox in 1907! Unfortunately Edge was every bit as much of an extremist as de Knyff and the French were forced by his bellicose approach to take up positions they would have preferred to avoid and it is possible that had Edge approached the problem by the diplomatic backstairs with a measure of tact, and even of champagne, then the undoubted common sense view might have prevailed, instead of the A.C.F. taking the stand of Pontius Pilate on the written word. Most competititors would undoubtedly have shared the views of Baron de Türckheim of Lorraine-Dietrich:

'I should not have hesitated to compete with Mr. Edge even under conditions which he considers more favourable to himself seeing that he is sheltering himself behind the clause of the regulations in order to avoid taking part in the Grand Prix.'

Of course Edge's answer ought to have been to have taken his Napiers across to Dieppe, detachable rims and all, and to have trounced the others fair and square. However, for reasons of pique or principle, he refused to do this—rather, one fears, in the spirit of Miss Peggy Lee

*'I don't want to play in your yard
If you can't be good to me.'*

At all events, if Napiers were going to ignore the Grand Prix, practically nobody else was and even Mors made an entry at the eleventh hour, including in their team two mighty veterans—Jenatzy and Charles Jarrott with the lesser known Landon. Sadly a works driver crashed Jarrott's car before the race and he therefore did not start. Panhard had also delved into history by resurrecting one of their veteran drivers, Henry Farman, along with Heath and the ex-racing and world record motor cyclist Cissac. Bayard-Clément were back again with a new team of Victor Rigal, Gabriel, brought over from Lorraine, and Hautvast, after his great driving in 'Kaiserpreis' events in 1907. In place of Gabriel, Lorraine-Dietrich engaged Minoia and kept their great stalwarts Duray and Rougier. No Darracqs were racing and Caillois had now gone over to join Szisz at Renault, the third place going to another unknown—Dimitri. Barillier had retired, but Brasier still had Bablot and Baras and filled Barillier's place with the greatest of his drivers—Léon Théry. Teams of Motobloc (Pierron, Courtade and Garcet) and Porthos (Stricker, Gaubert and Simon) completed the 24-strong French entry that reached Dieppe.

Germany stood next in weight of numbers. Mercedes were making a descent in force on the Grand Prix, after their succession of failures, with Poege, well known in sporting Germany, Salzer and a new works tester Christian Lautenschlager. Benz were French almost to a man with Hemery and Hanriot joining designer Erle, who, like Poege, was a well known competitor in Prince Henry and Herkomer events. Finally, spurred on by their Kaiserpreis success, Opel had built a team of cars which they entrusted to their very successful 1907 drivers—Jörns, Opel and Michel.

Had Napiers not played sulky, England would have matched this entry in number if not in quality: as it was her

NEXT IN WEIGHT OF NUMBERS

67/8/9 Traditional fare was provided by Mercedes—here is Salzer about to start on his record lap (top), (centre) and by Benz—here is Hanriot who finished 3rd Rising Teuton—'spurred on by their Kaiserpreis success Opel had built a team of cars' (Michel's above)

70 UNLUCKY FOR SOME: *Harrison's Weigel passes the trouble stricken Thomas a few minutes before his own accident*

71 LONE AMERICAN: *Strang who had been mechanic to Christie in 1907 now boasts his own Thomas*

72 ADVANCED ANGLICAN: *The single O.H.C. Weigel engine with inclined valves and hemispherical combustion chamber*

hopes rested on the slim shoulders of Weigel (Laxen, Harrison and Shannon) and the unspectacular ones of Austin-Brabazon and Warwick Wright after their good work in the Ardennes and a newcomer to the continent, Dario Resta, destined to win great fame as a Sunbeam driver in a few years.

No Isottas came to Dieppe for the Grand Prix, although they had a putative 'Bugatti' in the voiturette event, which explains Minoia's translation to his erstwhile rival, but Itala and Fiat were back again. Cagno, Fournier and Piacenza were a good team, but, as usual in these years, it was Fiat who stole the driving thunder with Nazzaro, Wagner and Lancia—surely one of the all-time strongest teams of drivers, for all the world as if Ferrari or Auto-Union had succeeded in uniting Nuvolari, Varzi and Fagioli in one team in the thirties.

Germain had entered some more of their attractive 'little' cars in the yellow of Belgium for Degrais, Roch-Briault and Perpère and finally there was one American entry, the Thomas of Strang, who had been mechanic in 1907 to Christie.

With any formula based on limited bore a designer's problem centres around breathing and constructors approached this in several interesting directions. Everyone, apart from Austin and Porthos, built right up to the maximum bore permitted although that of the Thomas was sometimes expressed as 154 mm., but then the Americans always measured in inches and perhaps the Atlantic was a little far even for the politely minded officials of the A.C.F. to travel to verify bores in advance. The approach of the largest and smallest of the 155 mm. bore constructors was the most advanced. Both Weigel and Bayard-Clément produced monobloc four cylinder engines with hemi-spherical combustion chambers and overhead valves inclined at 45 degrees operated, if not by two, at least by a single overhead camshaft. In each engine the camshaft was driven by an external vertical shaft at the front of the engine. Benz, Lorraine-Dietrich, Fiat and Mors also adopted the inclined valve but in each instance they were driven by one or two side camshafts and pushrods and rockers.

Renault and Brasier, although eschewing chain drive, were conservative in retaining the ancient side-valve layout, while Itala and Mercedes retained the inlet-over-exhaust pattern. Panhard, Thomas, Austin, Germain, and Porthos on the other hand preferred T-head. Alone of the 17 marques Mors and Brasier retained the gilled tube radiator. On transmission opinion was well divided—eleven used four, and six 3-speed gearboxes, while ten employed chain and seven shaft drive.

Bayard-Clément and Opel produced the largest cars at 155 × 185 mm. (= 13,963 c.c.) and thus far at least the formula was having some effect as these cars would have been well down the size list both in 1906 and 1907. Mercedes had two different strokes: the larger was of 155 × 180 (as on the Lorraine-Dietrich) = 13,586 c.c. and the smaller 155 × 170 = 12,831 c.c., like the Panhard, Mors and Motobloc. Benz and Germain had strokes of 165 mm. each (12,454 c.c.) then Renault, Brasier, Fiat and Itala on 160 mm. (12,076 c.c.) then Weigel and Thomas at 150 mm. (11,321 c.c.). Finally came the bore-dissenting 'sesquipedalian'[1] brigade —Austin with 127 × 127 (9677 c.c.) and Porthos 127 × 120 (9244 c.c.), the smallest cars in the race.

Early in 1908 the A.C.F. had made the decision to use the Dieppe circuit again. Everything points to an anti-clockwise or left handed race again, with the start at the same point. Gerald Rose who had a practice run with Strang on a 40 hp. Thomas touring car with W. F. Bradley gave this impression of the circuit, which he surveyed from what Kipling picturesquely called 'the hinder parts of a carbonadoed stink'

'... the general impression one carries away is that of its immense speed possibilities. Endless straights seem to rise before one's eyes, broad and open, and always of a blackish asphalt colour from the tarred surface. Sometimes flat, more often undulating, one feels that there are few places on the circuit where cars cannot go all out. There are half a dozen bad corners ... but outside these and on two others, the course seems practically a succession of "lignes droites" strung together by slight curves.'

This should have produced a classic race with an entry of such varied quality and size, but unhappily the A.C.F. allowed a voiturette race to be run off on the day before the Grand Prix which visibly affected the road surface and the Grand Prix very largely degenerated into a mere matter of tyre survival. In addition the tarred surface became pulverised and the cloud of heavy brown dust thus disseminated caused drivers to cover their entire faces 'and as each had a headgear of the same colour as his car the effect was distinctly curious.' Starting No. 1 that year was Dario Resta on Austin, but there ended the comparison with Guyot who had won the voiturette event for Delage from this position, for Resta, although he might astonish the spectators by the silence of his getaway, certainly produced nothing surprising in the way of speed, and six cars passed him on his first lap.

In fact it was the short stroke Mercedes of Salzer which led with a record lap of 36 mins. 31 secs. after one lap, but then came a solid French bloc of Bablot, Théry and Szisz, followed by Wagner's Fiat and Baras on the third Brasier, all within 73 secs. of one another. Lancia made a sad farewell to the Grand Prix with a poor first lap by his standards at 38 mins. 58 secs. and then retired with engine troubles of an undisclosed nature. As so often in the past this now left things to Nazzaro and, as usual, he did not disappoint, as the 2nd lap found him moving up into the lead

73 *VARIED QUALITY: A group of cars waiting to leave the paddock —Lautenschlager (No. 35), Courtade (Motobloc –36), Dimitri (Renault –37), Minoia (Lorraine-Dietrich –38)*

TYRE SURVIVAL

74 *'Spirit of Health': A splendidly silhouetted Jenatzy replenishes his Mors*

75 *'... or Goblin Damned?': Hemery and his mechanic take on four new rims for the 48-mile lap*

---

[1] *I am indebted to Kent Karslake for the application of this word to the 6-cylinder engine.—See* From Veteran to Vintage *at page 203, pub.; Temple Press Ltd. 1956.*

76/7 'Tyres might have swayed the race against Lautenschlager had he had any trouble during his last two laps when there was not a single new tyre left in his pit . . . '

78 NORSE GODS: 'Lautenschlager (behind car) had won . . . '

while Salzer plummetted down to 35th. Nazzaro led by a whole minute after 2 laps from the new man Lautenschlager, now replacing Salzer as the Mercedes pacemaker, with Théry, regular as ever, 3rd, 12 secs. slower, then Wagner, then Duray and Minoia now challenging for Lorraine-Dietrich. Nazzaro fell back on the 3rd lap, but the day was still bright for Fiat, as Wagner assumed Nazzaro's lead by nearly two clear minutes, while the home defenders on the leader board were now reduced to the eternal Théry and even he was as far away as 6th, almost 8 minutes behind Wagner. In between came the Benzes of Hemery (2nd) and Hanriot (5th), the Mercedes of Lautenschlager in 3rd and Nazzaro (4th). The 3rd and 4th laps were the graveyard of the previous winners, Szisz falling out on the 3rd and Nazzaro on the 4th, and to complete the Italian tale of woe Wagner was also put out on that decisive 4th lap.

With all the Fiats out of the running, Lautenschlager took the lead, followed by Hemery and Hanriot and then four French cars, Théry, Heath, Bablot and Cissac. The pattern of the race was now beginning to settle down into one where the pace was being made by the German cars for whom victory was beginning to look tolerably certain. To underline this Lautenschlager, Hemery and Hanriot stayed in their positions for the rest of the race. Behind came Théry, driving with all his famed precision, which kept him in 4th from the 4th to the 9th lap. This, however, took him no less than 55 mins. 48 secs. and he never finished his tenth and last lap. As if the German landslide of Mercedes and Benz was not enough Jörns now took turns with Cissac and Heath to hold 5th place behind Théry until Cissac on his 9th lap lost a tyre and crashed fatally.

The 9th lap ended the hopes of the once proud House of Panhard for Heath took 1 hr. 7 mins. 31 secs. over his and these tragedies allowed the Germans to pack two more places in the first six. Hautvast had been 8th on lap four, but his effort had then fallen away with a fifth lap in very nearly two hours, culminating in his retirement on the 6th. Gabriel had been well up on the first lap but his second occupied him over 70 mins. and put paid to any chances he might have had. Rigal, however, kept going in between no less than nineteen tyre changes, in spite of which he managed to average about 45 minutes for each lap which compares interestingly with Salzer's record of 36 mins. 31 secs. The only lap which was probably free of trouble was his 8th when he took 37 mins. 28 secs. This, coupled with Rigal's fourth place and Hautvast's speed of 105.1 m.p.h. over a measured kilometre, has suggested to posterity that the Cléments were the fastest cars at Dieppe. Possibly they were, but this was not borne out by their performance on the comparable circuits at Bologna and Savannah later in the year. Tyres exercised a considerable influence on the race and might even have swayed it against Lautenschlager had

79 . . . 'With all the Fiats out Lautenschlager took the lead . . .' —here he is on the tricky Ancourt section

he had any trouble during his last two laps when there was not a single new tyre left in his pit. His 9th lap was accomplished in the rapid time of 38 mins. 42 secs. which was perhaps pushing his luck, but it held and after a more cautious last lap he finished 1st with a lead of nearly 9 minutes from Hemery's Benz.

Hemery was very unlucky when he had his goggles broken early on by a flying stone which caused portions of glass to be driven into his eye. Stoically he finished the lap and then had medical treatment at the pits before continuing. But for this he would most likely have won the race though, as it was, Benz did wonderfully well in their first Grand Prix, finishing the only complete team in 2nd, 3rd and 7th. Mercedes, with 1st and 5th and Opel with 6th (and 21st) completed the German triumph and, indeed, it was only Rigal's 4th place that saved the French from an even more terrible thrashing by the German cars. As it was their defeat on such an unprecedented scale was enough to shock the crowds into abject silence until, 35 minutes after Lautenschlager had won, the Marseillaise rang out for Rigal's Clément-Bayard.

At the time this beating aroused in the French a very noble lust to sweep to their revenge with all speed and for this reason the forthcoming Circuit des Ardennes seemed likely to regain much of its old prestige after its poor year in 1907. However it was to be 18 years before Belgium staged another classic motor race, and, as in 1914, so in 1908 the French lost their opportunity to avenge a German defeat in a race on Belgian soil. In 1908 the trouble lay in a clash of dates with the races at Bologna, which was eventually resolved by the Belgians giving way to the Italians for 1908 on the understanding that their event would have priority in 1909. The French sought to explain their defeat away by

complaining of their tyres—again as they were to do in 1914, and they also inveighed against their detachable rims, which had given trouble to Szisz, Gabriel, Hautvast, Bablot and Baras. By contrast the English Dunlop rims fitted to the Austins and Weigels gave no trouble at all but it may be that their lack of performance did not subject them to the same stresses as those set up on the faster cars. Michelin had devised a new type of rim which could be removed and refitted by about two dozen quick turns of a brace and this proved unreliable, although the Germans apparently used a similar rim without trouble. The other fault was that the French had reduced their tyre pressures in view of the poor state of the circuit, whereas the Germans had blown their tyres up as hard as they could. It is, however, unlikely that, Rigal's Clément-Bayard apart, the final result was as seriously affected by tyres as all that, and in reality the French were fairly beaten by superior cars, underlined by the fact that the Brasiers who had put up the strongest challenge in the race were among the most antiquated in design.

Charles Faroux conducted two timed tests, one over the first 300 metres from the start to test acceleration and the other over a flying kilometre on the straight part of N 25 back from Eu to the start, which makes it clear that the race was once again run anti-clockwise. Of course the cars were not timed on each and every lap and the times of certain competitors were not taken—notably Hemery, Lancia, Théry, Opel, Rigal and Cagno—but those taken showed that Hautvast's Clément-Bayard was fastest at 105.1 m.p.h., with the Mercedes of Salzer and Gabriel's Clément next fastest, then the Mercedes of Lautenschlager and Poege, all over the 100 m.p.h. mark, as were the Brasier, Benz, de Dietrich and Fiat teams. It was noted that the Mercedes accelerated best even though the Cléments were possibly

Circuit de Dieppe. — Piacenza et Fournier

80 LAST OF THE VINTAGE: Fournier dwarfs Piacenza with the 1908 racing Itala in the background

81 . . . 'the way was clear for Nazzaro to win (the Florio Cup) with his usual ease . . .'

82 HAPPY VICTORY: the 1908 Vanderbilt Cup gave George Robertson 'a welcome and much appreciated victory'

faster on sheer maximum speed. Perhaps it would have been best if the French had allowed Mr. Pugh's 'bicycle' wheels after all!

It was very noticeable in 1906 how quickly detachable rims became universally adopted between the Grand Prix and the Circuit des Ardennes. In 1908, however, there was no corresponding rush to get the detachable wheel sanctioned for the Florio Cup at Bologna early in September.

Even if the German victors of Dieppe were absent, the presence of Fiat, Lorraine-Dietrich and Bayard-Clément, supported by Mors, Itala and Motobloc was enough to guarantee a worthy race. Rougier had retired from Lorraines since Dieppe and his place was taken by Trucco who thus joined his compatriot Minoia and Duray; Rigal too was in retirement and Shepard took his place beside Hautvast and Gabriel. Itala and Fiat fielded their Grand Prix team and cars, while Mors kept Landon but replaced Jenatzy and Jarrott with Garcet and Demogeot. Finally Motobloc had one Gauderman, and Charles Faroux making his one and only appearance in a race of Grand Prix stature. Michelin had modified their new rim after all the trouble at Dieppe and apparently the result was entirely successful.

The first lap brought disaster to both Motoblocs: Faroux broke a universal joint in the transmission and Gauderman, running on fixed rims, burst a tyre and damaged the rim too badly before he was able to stop. Finally Hautvast missed a turn and could not stop in time and ran off the road into a ditch to become the victim of the team manager's broadside.[2]

After these early excitements it was Lancia's turn to electrify all the spectators with a lap at 82.3 m.p.h. and he led the race with increasing ease for the first four of the ten laps. Then came his wonted débâcle, this time the breakage of a valve and a rocker arm, although he was able to limp home 5th. Both Gabriel and Duray of Bayard-Clément broke valves, while Wagner broke his front axle clean in two. He made a temporary repair by the homely expedient of a log of wood and a liberal amount of rope and in this way saved himself and his mechanic, together with Duray and his mechanic, a long trail home. Henri Fournier was driving his last great race in Europe and put up a performance worthy of the occasion on his Itala. After one lap he lay 9th; a lap later and he was 3rd, ahead of Nazzaro and behind Wagner and the flying Lancia, and then on the 3rd lap he was past Wagner and gaining on Lancia himself. He had in fact caught Lancia too before he was blinded by Cagno's dust and narrowly failed to negotiate a sharp bend which materialised awkwardly (the one that had already caused Hautvast's undoing), and thus Lancia held his lead for one more lap. With Fournier, Lancia, and Wagner gone the way was clear for Nazzaro and he led with his usual ease for the rest of the race to win by a substantial margin from Trucco,

[2] *See Letter of W. F. Bradley p.22 supra.*

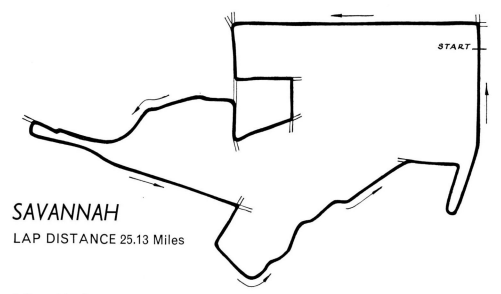

SAVANNAH

LAP DISTANCE 25.13 Miles

83 . . . 'the circuit was relatively short and wound its way along roads between 30 and 60 feet wide lined with palm trees or avenues of oak . .'

followed by Cagno, Demogeot, Lancia and Garcet.

Although some European cars competed in the Vanderbilt Cup, it was, driver-wise, an entirely American affair and need not concern us here, except to record the fact that it gave Robertson on 'Old 16', the big Locomobile that had achieved fastest lap in 1906, a welcome and much appreciated victory, the first by an American car and driver in a major event.

In sharp contrast came the first Grand Prize of the Automobile Club of America which was held at Savannah, Georgia, on Thanksgiving Day (November 26th) 1908. No motor race had ever then been held so late in the year and the entry was of a character to match the uniqueness of the occasion. The circuit was relatively short (25.13 miles), and wound its way along roads between 30 and 60 feet wide lined with palm trees or avenues of oaks, heavily festooned with moss. It was also most rigorously policed by armed soldiers who did not hesitate to use real Frontier methods on transgressors whether it was the rash local who tried to drive a horse and buggy across the circuit during the race or Hanriot himself. All this was very warmly appreciated by the drivers—years after Louis Wagner wrote thus of his memories:

'The climate, the nature of the country, everything was new to me. . . . The course was marvellously policed. It also had a particular charm . . . . we were all captivated by the kindness of the organisers as well as by the forethought of all towards the race drivers from beyond the Atlantic. . . . . It was a wonderful life. We hated to leave.'[3]

Wagner was not alone in his pleasure: Hanriot actually presented his gloves and goggles to a Police Captain after the incident when he was fired upon for an infringement of the regulations. Good old Henri Fournier, now ending his

[3] *From* The Checkered Flag, *by Peter Helck. Used by permission of Charles Scribner's Sons, New York.*

great career, had an oyster supper given in his honour by a prominent local family where Madame Fournier created some stir by wearing long white kid gloves! Fournier returned the compliment in true Italian fashion with a spaghetti supper in the Itala camp. In between these delectable junketings there were ten whole days set aside for practising immediately before the race, in spite of which the circuit seems to have remained in excellent condition. In every way the New World had really shown how is could organise a motor race in the grand manner once it gave its mind to the task.

American starting customs were more civilized than European and the drivers can hardly have credited their good fortune in starting as late as 9 a.m. and, as if this was not enough, it was then postponed for 45 minutes because of fog. The starting order was : —

1.	Rigal	Clément	11.	Harding	National
2.	Mulford	Lozier	12.	Cagno	Itala
3.	Seymour	Simplex	13.	Hautvast	Clément
4.	Haupt	Chadwick	14.	Wagner	Fiat
5.	Burman	Buick	15.	Hanriot	Benz
6.	Nazzaro	Fiat	16.	Strang	Renault
7.	Zengle	Acme	17.	Fournier	Itala
8.	Hemery	Benz	18.	de Palma	Fiat
9.	Duray	de Dietrich	19.	Erle	Benz
10.	Szisz	Renault	20.	Piacenza	Itala

The home products were little known although Burman and Mulford were drivers of considerable ability and the Chadwick has a place of its own in history as the first car to race with a forced induction device. The most distinguished American driver was, however, Ralph de Palma, taking Lancia's place as third member of the great Fiat team. This was the first big race since Fiat's entry into racing in which Lancia had not driven and de Palma carried a big responsibility as well as Lancia's personal riding mechanic, Pietro Bordino, who was to become the greatest Italian driver of

84 Cagno about to start on his Itala

"HOME PRODUCTS":

85 Burman on the modified underslung Buick

86 Haupt's Chadwick 'has a place of its own in history as the first car to race with a forced induction device . . .'

the early twenties. Nazzaro's own mechanic, Fagnano, was soon to have a Grand Prix Fiat to drive, as was Heim, who rode with Hanriot, to have a Lorraine in 1912 while with Rigal rode Jean Chassagne, future Sunbeam driver before and after 1914. Duray's mechanic is given as 'Mathys' but one feels almost certain that it was the Alsatian Mathis who was actually there, and one also wonders if the 'Marindo' programmed as accompanying Cagno was not in fact the same Moriondo who drove the rotary valve Itala in the 1913 Grand Prix.

After their ill luck at Dieppe Fiat had struck back with their great win at Bologna, although Fournier had perhaps been unlucky not to have challenged Nazzaro. At Savannah, however, the race lay almost entirely between the Fiat and Benz teams and, to the surprise of many, it was not Hemery, Hanriot, Wagner or Nazzaro who made the pace from the start, but the unknown de Palma; he was followed by Wagner, Hanriot, Szisz and Erle, with Nazzaro as usual biding his time in 6th. De Palma inherited the ill luck of Lancia almost throughout his career and this, his first big race, was no exception, when on his 3rd lap he had tyre and oiling troubles which sent him down to last position. Hanriot now forged ahead, with Szisz 2nd, then Erle, Cagno and Nazzaro with Wagner fallen to 6th, and he retained this lead until he fell to 5th on the 8th lap. At this point Benz were well placed having Hemery 2nd and Erle 5th, with the Fiats of Nazzaro and Wagner 3rd and 4th. Erle now moved up to 4th, but the three leading positions changed constantly between Hemery, Nazzaro and Wagner—two Fiats to one Benz now that Hanriot had fallen behind. On the 11th lap Erle was knocked unconscious by a bursting tyre and the car travelled another quarter of a mile before it left the course and overturned: miraculously the mechanic was uninjured and Erle only received minor injuries, but the contest between marques was now even.

Among the leaders, Wagner had led for Fiat after eight laps, then Hemery held it for two laps, then Wagner again for one and then the patient Nazzaro thrust forward and led first Wagner and then Hemery for four laps. In this way Nazzaro went on to the last lap with a lead of nearly two minutes over Hemery, who in turn led Wagner by only two seconds, while 4th man Hanriot was another 12 minutes to the bad. It really did seem all over bar the shouting, but, incredibly, Nazzaro's luck for once was out and he lost a tyre within 15 miles of the finish, which in racing of that closeness brought him down to 3rd. Now all depended on the Wagner-Hemery duel. Hemery had started six minutes ahead of Wagner and put in a relatively quick last lap of 22 mins. 50 secs., compared with de Palma's record of 21 min. 36 secs. Wagner, however, made victory sure with a lap of 21 mins. 52 secs. (second only to his 8th in 21 mins. 50 secs.) to win by the unheard of hair's breadth of 56 secs. To have won against that speed Hemery needed to break 22 minutes for

87 *MOST DISTINGUISHED: de Palma on his Fiat with mechanic Bordino*

88 *LONG FAREWELL: Szisz who held 2nd in the early stages and retired when 4th makes Renault's final Grand Prix appearance*

89 *ALSO RAN: Len Zengle's Acme rounds Solomons Corner*

90 *SHORT HEAD: Wagner (Fiat) the winner 'by the unheard of margin of 56 secs . . .*

91 *LONG ISLAND PERILS: A scene from the 1905 event shews why European drivers dread the New York crowds*

his last lap and this, in fact, he had never succeeded in doing throughout the race where his fastest speed had been 22 mins. 3 secs., while Hanriot had put in the best Benz time of 21 mins. 52 secs.

At long last the Americans had shown themselves capable of running a motor race properly, and the organisers were more than rewarded by the magnificently close contest provided by the three leading drivers, while the drivers' pleasure was reflected in their remarks when the 1910 Grand Prize was switched at the last moment from the dreaded Long Island course to Savannah. Hemery is reported as greeting the news with 'It will be grand. Not even Europe has ever furnished a more perfectly patrolled course. I shall be happy on the day I get back to Savannah. I wonder if they will give us any more of those fish dinners?' Wagner, whose dislike of Long Island was well known, was even more delighted—'I am ready to go South tonight.... Neither of us (he and Nazzaro) ever stopped telling our countrymen how good the people were to us. I dreaded the race on Long Island but now I am anxious to begin training.' Nazzaro was equally enthusiastic and averred that there would have been many more leading European drivers over had it been known that the race would be held at Savannah.

However, while the Bologna and Savannah races had been occupying drivers a struggle of a very different nature had been going on in the boardrooms of racing constructors. For the first time since the dawn of the automobile age supply was beginning to exceed demand and as a further consideration the racing car had developed into a complete freak, being 'big, heavy, over-engined (and) quite out of touch with the touring-car except in the broadest details.' In short, by 1908, the Grand Prix car had become, for the engineering purist, a highly expensive and singularly unedifying luxury, which constructors were beginning to have difficulty in affording. Yet they had no wish to abandon racing—least of all the French ones; their aim was that perennial Philosopher's Stone—cheaper motor racing, coupled with more direct advantage to their production models. Moreover in the case of French constructors, one has the darker suspicion that they were once more on the hunt for a formula which would ensure their habitual monopoly of success. At the same time they had to make sure that they did not lose face by retiring from racing or, for that matter, get stabbed in the back by some upstart constructor. They therefore hit on the idea of entering into a Bond in the form of a Self Denying Ordnance, under which all the signatories should undertake to give up Grand Prix racing for a period of years on pain of a fine of £4000. The French, having now protected themselves all round, were free to concentrate on the voiturette class of racing where for the time being they enjoyed undisputed leadership.

At this point one must say that the A.C.F. had a clear conscience: for 1909 they published regulations, chose a new circuit in Anjou and opened an entry list, and continued to offer their services to organise similar races for 1910 and 1911. One cannot, however, thus easily whitewash the French constructors. Although immediately after Dieppe some were concerned with revenge, they took some hard knocks at Bologna and Savannah, where the races were overrun by Italian and German cars and all their pique aroused by their loss at Dieppe in 1907 and their utter humiliation in 1908 was reborn. Never before had the French been so spineless and it should also be said that only 12 of the 17 signatories to the Bond were French. Moreover although Fiat, Mors and Itala were the principal abstainers from the Bond, only Mors backed words with deeds and entered a team for the 1909 Grand Prix, and, although Great Britain expressed lively disapproval of the continental system, it did little except preach the virtues of stock (i.e. production) car racing. As usual, everyone was only too

happy to say far too much and do far too little and so it came about that on the 31st December 1908, with only nine entries before them, the A.C.F. acknowledged defeat and abandoned the Grand Prix.

During 1909/11 the initiative in motor sport passed across the Atlantic and the English Channel, but, on the whole, both England and America signally failed to take advantage of the lull in French interest in racing design. During this period Brooklands Track was in the first flush of its Edwardian heyday and in February 1909 began the construction of the Indianapolis Speedway, built with the avowed intention of licking Brooklands to a frazzle, as the Americans put it. In terms of speed it was to be over twenty years after the last racing exhaust died away at Weybridge before Indianapolis speeds matched those of Brooklands! The speedway was no more successful in another of its objects— that of giving American constructors a road where they could tune their racing cars to such a pitch that they could get on terms with their European rivals. As the *Autocar* pithily observed of this 'Eheu fugaces! There *are* no more races.' In England constructors were getting to grips with their problems much more realistically as we shall see when we consider their improved showings in the Coupe de l'Auto races in the next chapter.

At the time, however, the loss of the Grand Prix seemed like the end of motor racing; as the *Autocar* remarked after the race itself:

'*The races of 1907/8 carefully plotted and planned as they were to preponderate enormously in favour of France have ended so disastrously for the French industry and have so sorely wounded the French* amour propre *that the Grand Prix of 1908 is more than likely to be the last of such contests.*'

The acrimony and misery of the whole situation was a long way from the beautiful sporting idyll Rose had penned for the *Autocar* on the eve of the 1908 Grand Prix

'*Let non competing firms carp as they like about useless expense and wasted time. The very fact of having competed in the Grand Prix adds a lustre to the name of a car which no amount of reliability trials and local hill-climbs can ever hope to give. It is proof that the designer does not hesitate to submit his production to the severest trial possible and that under the very eyes of the world. It shows that the firm is not ashamed to learn the lessons which only racing can teach, and through such dearly-bought experience has the whole fabric of the modern automobile been built up.*'

Chapter Four
1900-1913 · Voiturette Interlude The First

92 FIRST GLORY: '. . . a tremendous triumph for the smaller cars . . .'—Louis Renault in Paris–Vienna, 1902

93 . . . 'Louis Renault (with mechanic Szisz) arrived at Bordeaux at 12.15 p.m.'

'*In a sense, of course, the racing voiturette is as old as motor racing. The Panhard et Levassor with which Emile Levassor won the first real motor race of all from Paris to Bordeaux and back in 1895, had a 1200 c.c. engine, which would hardly have looked full-size against its 70 h.p. 14-litre successor of 1902. . . .*'
Kent Karslake: Racing Voiturettes.[1]

By the turn of the century the racing car had grown to the 10-litres of the Brasier-designed Mors while the largest voiturette in Paris-Toulouse-Paris was a Cottereau of 1400 c.c. The Heavy Car class there was won by Levegh's Mors at 40.2 m.p.h. against Louis Renault's voiturette winning speed of 18.8 m.p.h. on his single-cylinder of 499 c.c. In that year Renault was slower than any of the finishers in the Heavy Class, but this pattern was now soon to change. For 1901 new rules were introducing four classes based on weight:

A. Over 650 kg. C. 250–400 kg.—'Voiturettes'
B. 400–650 kg.—"Light" Cars D. Under 250 kg.

At this point the voiturette really grew up into a light car,

and a racer at that, and, as Kent Karslake says, 'to consider the one without the other is a practical impossibility, and besides if the Voiture Légère was never a voiturette, then certainly the so-called voiturette of say 1903 was nothing other than a Voiture Légère,' or as the poet has it :

'*But who Pretender is, or who is King—*
God Bless us all—that's quite another thing.'

At all events we shall not go very far wrong if we accept voiturettes for racing purposes between 1901 and 1905 as cars weighing between 250 and 650 kg.

The new cars were not long in showing their quality as the following table of the results in Paris-Bordeaux, Paris-Berlin (1901) and Paris-Vienna (1902) demonstrates. (The placings refer to overall classification) :—

	PARIS–BORDEAUX	PARIS–BERLIN	PARIS–VIENNA
Heavy	10-litre Mors 1st 53 m.p.h.	10-litre Mors 1st 44·1 m.p.h.	13·6-litre Panhard 2nd 38·4 m.p.h.
Light	3·3-litre Panhard 6th 40·2 m.p.h.	3·3-litre Panhard 14th 35·5 m.p.h.	3·7-litre Renault 1st 38·9 m.p.h.
Voiturette	1-litre Renault 12th 34·3 m.p.h.	1-litre Renault 8th 36·9 m.p.h.	1·8-litre Darracq 19th 30·6 m.p.h.

[1] *Published in 1950 by Motor Racing Publications Ltd., this book deals in great detail with the voiturette movement down to 1925 and is highly recommended for anyone seeking further information on this subject.*

Paris-Vienna, in particular, was a tremendous triumph for the smaller cars, although some wiseacres might have tried to shrug it off with talk of the harsh roads being the grave-yard of the heavy cars which, paradoxically, had been hampered by their ultra-light construction which had made tyre, chassis and mechanical failure inevitable. Rose gives another table based on the three stages of Paris-Vienna: 'Paris-Belfort for speed, Bregenz-Salzburg for hill-climbing and brake efficiency and Salzburg-Vienna for endurance.'

Panhard 13·6-litres	54·4 m.p.h.	34·3 m.p.h.	39 m.p.h.
Mercedes 6¾-litres	46·1 m.p.h.	36·5 m.p.h.*	39·4 m.p.h.
Darracq 5·8-litres	48·5 m.p.h.	33·1 m.p.h.	39·6 m.p.h.
Renault 3·7-litres	46·1 m.p.h.	35·2 m.p.h.	44·8 m.p.h.

Unofficial speed.

The great race of 1903 was to be Paris-Madrid with a first day's racing to Bordeaux that would place a higher premium on sheer speed than even Paris-Belfort: the next two days, however, were to be on the rough and mountainous roads of Spain from Bayonne through Vittoria to Madrid after a final burst of speed through the lonely woods of Les Landes to the Franco-Spanish border. With the fast stretches of France in mind, Renaults increased their cars to 6276 c.c., but still kept within the 650 kg. limit to meet the assembled might of Mercedes (12½-litres), Mors (12-litres), Panhard (13½-litres) and de Dietrich with results that were a classical Greek combination of Triumph and Tragedy.

Louis Renault had the inestimable advantage of drawing starting number 3, while brother Marcel started 39th. Ahead of Louis, de Knyff on No. 2 was soon out and Jarrott with No. 1 de Dietrich was delayed slightly in the early stages. Thus Louis had a clear road from Rambouillet to Bordeaux while the others struggled their way through the inevitable growing dust cloud, the heat and the mounting tide of disaster by the roadside. Louis Renault arrived at Bordeaux at 12.15 p.m. after about 8½ hours on the road, having averaged 62.3 m.p.h. after allowing for neutralizations. Only 16 mins. later Jarrott drove up on his new and untried de Dietrich and then, after another 40 mins. came No. 168! —Gabriel's Mors which had actually started 82nd, completing 'one of the most wonderful feats of skill and courage on the part of the driver that has ever been reported in the annals of motor racing.' So much for the Triumph.

Behind Louis Renault stark Tragedy had been enacted time and again, and never more so than when Marcel Renault crashed fatally trying to pass Théry's Decauville in a cloud of dust. Had he continued through to Bordeaux it is likely that Marcel's time would have been very similar to his brother's and, even allowing for Les Landes and the genius of Gabriel, the Renaults must have been prime favourites to win the race. But Fate and the French Government decreed otherwise and the inter-town races ended on that hot, dusty,

94 . . . 'only 16 minutes later Jarrott drove up . . .'—here he draws up at Rambouillet with mechanic Bianchi and Edge in cap on car's left

95 IMMORTAL HOUR: Gabriel at Bordeaux after performing 'one of the most wonderful feats of skill and courage in the annals of motor racing . . .'

96 FATAL COURSE: Marcel Renault before the race at scrutineering

97/8 The Sizaire-Naudin which won the 1907 Sicilian Cup. Giuppone's Lion-Peugeot which won at Turin in 1908

99 FIRST WIN: . . . 'the G.P. des voiturettes of 1908 gave Louis Delage his first win through the medium of Guyot'

100 VOITURETTE UBIQUITOUS: Goux drives his Lion-Peugeot into the winner's enclosure after the 1909 Catalan Cup

fatal 24th day of May, 1903, with the final result for all time—

1. Gabriel	5–14–31.1/5	65·3 m.p.h.
2. Renault	5–29–39.1/5	62·3 m.p.h.
3. Salleron (Mors)	5–47–1.4/5	59·1 m.p.h.
4. Jarrott	5–52–55	58·2 m.p.h.

Both the principal actors in this drama ultimately died more wretchedly than Marcel Renault, Gabriel in an allied air raid under the ruins of his house in 1943 and Louis Renault in the jealousies and suspicions that so viciously ripped apart post-1944 France. 'If this was the alternative', wrote Kent Karslake, 'what racing driver would not have chosen Marcel's end at Couhé-Verac?' As we have seen motor racing managed to survive at what we may call 'Grand Prix level', but Paris-Madrid was very nearly the end of the racing voiturette. In 1904/5 only the Circuit des Ardennes catered for these cars and by 1906 as Kent Karslake picturesquely puts it—'the old order had creaked to an inglorious close.'

In fact, of course, this had been bound to happen anyway as a result of the evolution of the racing voiturette into a full-blooded racing car every whit the equal of the big cars. Perceiving the need for an entirely new set of regulations for voiturette racing the proprietors of l'Auto offered a new trophy for competition in 1905—the Coupe des Voiturettes, or Coupe de l'Auto as it was always known. The organisers aimed at producing a competition for everyday cars and not freak racers and to emphasise this they stipulated a six days' trial before the actual 'race', imposed a limit on weight and restricted engine capacity to 1-litre only. The 1905 event was run off in the snows of November and was such a fiasco that the results were annulled and the Coupe was not awarded.

Nothing deterred, l'Auto elaborated the rules for 1906 by imposing a bore limit of 120 mm. for single-cylinders and 90 mm. for twins and a *minimum* weight of 700 kg. in contrast to the *maximum* figure for Grand Prix cars of 1000 kg. Although the event followed the basic pattern of 1905, it was a tremendous success, sparking off a revival of voiturette racing that now was to be spread far beyond the frontiers of France. Thus in 1907 there were two voiturette events. The first was the Sicilian Cup on Florio's Madonie Circuit, where the little cars were set the formidable task of covering two laps of the Long Madonie! This occupied no less than 7 hrs. 47 mins. and 9 secs. of Monsieur Naudin's time on Sizaire-Naudin and just over 8 hours of that of Florio himself, who was driving a de Dion-Bouton.

For their 1907 race l'Auto altered the rules slightly again: first they reduced bores from 120 to 100 mm. for singles and from 90 to 80 mm. for twins and then brought back maximum weights—670 kg. for singles and 850 kg. for twins. While the weather was slightly better than in 1906, speeds were considerably improved: this time Naudin increased his partner's winning speed to 40.7 m.p.h. and Sizaire finished

2nd, with a familiar name for the future in 3rd—Goux on Lion-Peugeot. One of the oldest names in French motoring and racing, Peugeots were continuing their return to competition motoring with their new voiturettes, which they had begun in 1906 when Giuppone had finished 3rd in the Coupe de l'Auto behind Menard-Lucas' Delage and Sizaire. The oddity about the name is explained by the fact that there were two Peugeot factories—one in Paris, where the big cars were built and one in South East France where bicycles, motor cycles and small cars were built under the name Lion-Peugeot.

The following year (1908) saw not two but four voiturette events. The first two were Italian and fittingly enough provided victories for Giuppone on Lion-Peugeot. As a matter of interest he improved Naudin's Targa speed by 4.8 m.p.h. (or 1 hr. 15 min. 39 secs.). The third event I have already mentioned in passing as being responsible in part for breaking up the Dieppe circuit before the Grand Prix and giving the drivers and their tyres such a rough time. This race, the Grand Prix des Voiturettes, gave Louis Delage his first win through the medium of Guyot, who drove Grand Prix Delages during 1913/14 with both distinction and ill luck. The ubiquitous Sizaire and Goux were 2nd and 3rd respectively.

Last in the season, almost by tradition now, came the Coupe de l'Auto and for the first time the rules admitted 4-cylinder engines as follows:—

CYLINDERS	MAX. BORE	MAX. WEIGHT
1	100 mm.	500 kg.
2	80 mm.	600 kg.
4	65 mm.	650 kg.

There were also some body restrictions aimed at reducing the sporting aspect of the cars. 47 cars started in the Dieppe Grand Prix des Voiturettes including, for the first time, the young Georges Boillot, now taking his place beside the 'old-timers', Giuppone and Goux.

Delage did not attend the Coupe itself at Compiègne but Peugeot and Sizaire did and this time it was Naudin's turn to win from Sizaire and Goux.

Gerald Rose enthused over the 'dignity and . . . sense of unharnessed power about the old racing cars . . .' and in his writings he obviously took the same view of the upstart voiturettes as many of us in more recent times took of the early English 500 c.c. Formula Three 'pipsqueaks'. Yet it was from the voiturette theme that the modern age of racing emerged in 1914, just as the new Grand Prix cars of the 1959-65 era are the lineal descendants of those very 500s. By 1909 however, the Coupe de l'Auto was so firmly established that the organisers were offered no less than fifty-six circuits and in the next three years the event went from strength to strength. The measure of its place in the public esteem was that, in 1912 when the Grand Prix was finally revived, the cautious A.C.F. combined their race with the Coupe de

101/2 'Dignity and Unharnessed Power' are exercised to the full as Duray's de Dietrich passes the stands (top) and takes a fast bend (bottom) in the Ardennes Circuit of 1906

103 'in some cases the driver had to peer round . . . ' Goux's Lion-Peugeot starts in the 1910 Coupe (top). 104 . . . 'and in others the exhaust pipe passed over their heads . . . ' (bottom)

105 Cesare Giuppone . . . 'a very successful and spirited driver . . . '

l'Auto to ensure the success of the so-called premier event! The influence and value of the voiturette movement during this anxious period was fourfold: first, it kept public interest in the sport alive; secondly, it ensured that the long series of annual classic road races going back to Paris-Bordeaux-Paris in 1895 was kept alive; thirdly, it provided a new generation of drivers to take their places beside the old veterans of the Inter-Town and Gordon Bennett days; and fourthly, once a 3-litre capacity limit had superseded the limited bore rules in 1911, it proved that a vast multi-litre engine was not a universal pre-requisite for the design of a successful Grand Prix car. In so doing the movement unknowingly set the standard for the new age of motor racing that had its birth pangs at Dieppe in 1912 and was finally delivered at Lyons in 1914. Thus it was that the débâcle which overtook Grand Prix racing in 1909 was put to good use after all.

For 1909 another variant of the formula was devised to assist development of 4-cylinder engines:—

CYLINDERS	BORE AND STROKE (mm.)
1	100×250 to 120×124
2	80×192 to 95×98
4	65×150 to 75×75

and a minimum weight for all cars of 600 kg.

Although these regulations were supposed to favour the 4-cylinder engines, this would have involved their designers being able to produce crankshaft speeds of 8000 r.p.m. if they were to rival proportionately the revolutions produced by the single and twin cylinder brigade. As a result constructors pressed on with abnormal Stroke : Bore ratios. There were three races in 1909 all of which were won by Lion-Peugeot, Goux winning the Sicilian Cup and the new Catalan Cup at Sitges and Giuppone the Coupe de l'Auto itself. It was significant that in none of these races did a 4-cylinder car finish in the first three. The fastest car in the Coupe had been Boillot's single-cylinder Lion-Peugeot, built right up to the engine limit and employing the fantastic number of six valves—three inlet and three exhaust. This freak was comparable to the de Dion engine of the same stroke which enjoyed an overall height of more than three feet and of which Kent Karslake drily remarks:—

'further progress in this direction, if carried to its logical conclusion, would eventually prevent voiturette racers from passing under such bridges as there might be on the course;'

in some cases drivers actually had to peer round the side of the bonnet containing these fantastickal engines and in others the exhaust pipe passed like some ancient locomotive horizontally above the heads of the driver and mechanic.

The same three events continued in 1910, with Boillot, Giuppone and Goux scoring a great Lion-Peugeot win in Sicily, while Goux went on to repeat the dose at Sitges, with

106–6a SPANISH RATIONALE: Chassagne (Hispano) leads Goux in the 1910 Coupe

Boillot 2nd, and, now significantly, a 4-cylinder Hispano-Suiza 3rd, driven by Paul Zuccarelli. The Hispano had first raced at Boulogne in 1909, with a 4-cylinder engine of 65 × 140 mm. and one of the Catalan cars in 1910 still had this engine measurement, but the other three had longer strokes of 180 mm. For the 1910 Coupe de l'Auto however, the multi-cylinder cause had obtained an even more remarkable recruit in Lion-Peugeot, even though they were still lurking round the shallow end in using what was in effect a pair of V-twin engines with the characteristic measurements of 65 × 260 mm. compared with the Hispano's stroke of a mere 200 mm. These new cars were to be driven by Giuppone and Boillot, but in an unofficial practice run Giuppone was obliged to brake sharply to avoid some cyclists and the unstable car overturned with fatal results. At the time this deprived Lion-Peugeot of a very successful and spirited driver, but in retrospect it may be that it had an immeasurable effect on the subsequent history of the high speed engine, for Giuppone's loss led to the engagement of Zuccarelli as a Peugeot driver in association with Boillot and Goux in the ensuing years.

While the Lion-Peugeots were still faster than the Hispanos in the race, the Spanish cars were undoubtedly more soundly designed in every department and happily for the future of the voiturette movement Zuccarelli defeated the twin cylinder Lion-Peugeot of Goux with Chassagne finishing 3rd on another Hispano. Boillot brought the surviving 4-cylinder Lion-Peugeot into 4th, although his was certainly the fastest car on the course, and it may be that the Spanish use of detachable wire wheels swayed the issue as much as anything else, for these had been permissible in the Coupe since the previous year when the English Calthorpes had used them.

107 SPANISH RATIONALE: Zuccarelli winning the 1910 Coupe de l'Auto

43

108/9 Richards on the first Coupe de l'Auto Sunbeam in the 1911 race (top)–Resta at Eu in 1912 when the English cars swept the board (bottom)

110 PEUGEOT DOLDRUM . . . 'the one entry (1912) suffered from the greater attention paid to the team for the Grand Prix . . .'

Realising that the limited bore and stroke rules were now producing cars every bit as freakish as some of the old Grand Prix and Gordon Bennett racers, the organisers drastically revised the rules for the remaining pre-war years, although with the return of Grand Prix racing in 1912, less notice tended to be paid to the voiturettes and in 1911/13 the Coupe de l'Auto was the only event run for them other than two poorly supported races at Le Mans in 1912/13. During these years a capacity limit of 3-litres was imposed, but designers were still restricted by a stroke/bore ratio that had to be between 2:1 and 1:1; additionally, in 1912, there was a minimum weight of 800 kg. and the next year a maximum of 900 kg; coupled with an embargo on superchargers, following the experiments for the 1912 race carried out by Hispano-Suiza. In 1911, the Coupe was the only Voiturette race and the principal contestants were Lion-Peugeot as usual and Delage, making a comeback, but with some very different cars from his last racers of 1908. Delage was successful with what was a more balanced car than the Lion-Peugeot, which still clung to its mechanical ancestry with a V-4 engine, now of 78 × 156 mm. compared to the Delage's 80 × 149 mm. It was left to the English school (Vauxhall) to produce a more enlightened dimension of 90 × 118 mm., but Pomeroy's employment of side valves in an L-head represented retrograde thought or practice.

Retrograde or not, side valves dominated the 1912 event which was run off at Dieppe in conjunction with the Grand Prix, when the English Sunbeams and Vauxhalls were the fastest cars in their own class and faster than almost all the Grand Prix cars into the bargain. The one Lion-Peugeot entry suffered from the greater attention paid to the team of three Peugeots entered for the Grand Prix itself and, notwithstanding its employment of the 'New Model' engine lay-out of twin camshafts, four valves per cylinder etc. the car could do no better than retire well down during the first day's racing.

With the Coupe put back to September again following the re-establishment of the Grand Prix in 1913, Peugeot were able to concentrate their attention on both sets of cars and their 1913 Voiturette represented a great improvement on its 1912 predecessors. In fact, as we shall see, it was really the outstanding car of the year and was able to outpace the English Sunbeams and Vauxhalls most convincingly and take round vengeance for the defeat of 1912.

Both in 1912 and 1913 the Le Mans programme included a voiturette event. In 1912 it was called the Grand Prix de France and was won by Zuccarelli although his team mate Thomas was still pursued by his Dieppe luck and retired. The 1913 event was not attended by the Peugeots at all and was relegated to the inferior status of Coupe de la Sarthe, giving the deserving house of Gregoire a rare taste of victory.

By 1913, therefore, the voiturettes, having enjoyed their

111 PEUGEOT TRIUMPH ... 'their 1913 voiturette represents great improvement on its 1912 predecessor'

112 PROPHETIC ... 'the promise that a new epoch had begun ...' as the 500s line up for their first long race in October 1948 at Silverstone

years of glory, were being forced to take a back seat by the revived Grand Prix. But their work had been well and faithfully done and was in a sense consummated in 1920/21 when the Grand Prix events were all for 3-litre cars although without restraint on stroke/bore ratio. This was the first instance of an erstwhile Voiturette growing up into a Grand Prix car.

History has a tendency to defy orderly classification because the development of its subject matter is generally too gradual to enable any single date to be pin-pointed as a dividing line in any particular process of historical evolution. But if a date has to be set for the emergence of the modern era of motor racing, it must be 1912. What is often described as the Heroic Age of Motor Racing ended with the 1908 season, although the Monsters that typified it still appeared in the Savannah races of 1910/11, at Le Mans in 1911 and, of course, at Dieppe in 1912. Their day, however, was done with the advent of the 1912 Peugeot. These cars were inspired by a unique combination of drivers and practical engineers in Boillot, Goux and Zuccarelli, whose ideas were put on paper by a Swiss draughtsman, Ernest Henry who has in the past tended to receive the greatest credit for their developments. However, whoever was responsible for it, the Peugeot of 1912 set a basic trend in design that was to win ten out of the seventeen principal events between then and 1922 when new lines of development superseded what is often wrongly referred to as the 'Henry theme'.

The twenties produced two great technical advances—the perfection of the straight-eight engine and the adoption of the supercharger, coupled with a gradual diminution in engine size from 3 to 1½-litres. This culminated with the 1927 Delage, one of the high water marks of racing car design. After 1927 a slump set in for various reasons and what was in practice a formule libre prevailed until 1934 when a return was made to a formula based on maximum weight and the new German cars swept through the vintage type racers of France and Italy in much the same way as had the Peugeots and Sunbeams at Dieppe in 1912.

The German ideas tended towards increasing complexity,

the Mercedes-Benz in particular graduating from a relatively simple straight eight in 1934 to a highly complex two-stage blown V-12 in 1939. The ultimate development of this trend of design is to be found in the 1½-litre Cisitalia and B.R.M. V-16 cars of post-1945 and it continued as the dominant trend right through to the end of 1951 when the 1½-litre blown/4½-litres unblown formula finished its days.

It is a recurring theme in motor racing history to find an erstwhile voiturette category becoming the Grand Prix formula, thus

	VOITURETTE	GRAND PRIX
3-litres	1911/13	1920/1
1½-litres	1921	1926/7
	1935/9	1946/51
	1957/60	1961/5
2-litres	1948/51	1952/3

and this had happened most especially in the post 1945 period.

The developments since 1951 are too recent for really meaningful consideration, and 1951 may conveniently be regarded as the end of the period that began in 1934 with the years 1952/8 forming a bridging period between the post-vintage 'modern' and newer 'modern' themes. The dawn of what I call the newer modern theme came in 1958 when Rob Walker's Cooper won the Argentine and Monaco Grands Prix. By 1959 the Cooper was the mount of World Champion Jack Brabham and yet another racing voiturette had made the grade. More than any other driver Stirling Moss has epitomised the emergence of this particular type of car as a Grand Prix contender, a process foreseen by Kent Karslake in the concluding sentence of Racing Voiturettes, published, let it be remembered, in 1950:

'No one with the history of what has gone before in mind who watched these new racing voiturettes in their first long distance race at Silverstone in 1948 could fail to see the promise that a new epoch had begun.'

Just how promising perhaps not even the prophetic Karslake could see.

45

Chapter Five
1909-11 · Le Grand Prix des Vieux Tacots[1]

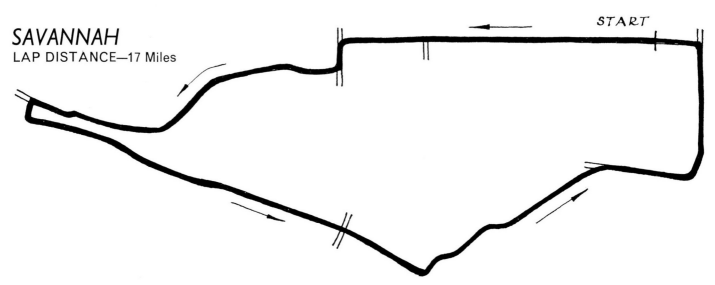

SAVANNAH
LAP DISTANCE—17 Miles

START

113 *The new circuit at Savannah that was laid out in a month for the Grand Prizes of 1910/11*

'Restraint and Obstruction constitute the principle of Movement': Renan

No races of Grand Prix status took place in 1909, but the situation brightened a little in 1910/11 starting with the United States Grand Prize which was revived at Savannah 12th November 1910. The venue was decided upon in a hurry following yet another lethal Vanderbilt Cup event on Long Island in October. The organisation of this race had prompted a sarcastic French observer to comment

'Comme toute course Amèricaine qui se respecte elle a été marquée par des nombreux accidents.'

The news of the transfer of the Grand Prize to Savannah was received with great joy by the European drivers in America for reasons that one suspects were not entirely connected with the improved safety factors down South if Hemery's delighted gastronomic anticipation of more fish dinners is to be credited. A course of 17.3 miles was laid out in the space of a month with a plentiful supply of convict labour, which was happily rewarded by a special enclosure for the prisoners on race day. The circuit was to be covered 24 times to give a distance of 415.2 miles. The European starters were de Palma, Nazzaro and Wagner on S.61 Fiats, designed the previous year and of the type which won the 1911 Grand Prix de France, and Hemery, Haupt and Bruce-Brown on Benz. The last two drivers were American: Haupt had driven a Chadwick in 1908, while Bruce-Brown was hardly known apart from having scored two small successes at Florida in the annual Ormonde-Daytona Beach races in 1909. More, however, was to be heard of this most brilliant driver before his untimely death in 1912.

Their American competitors were on less out-and-out racing cars, the highest placed being Chevrolet's Marquette-Buick which was a modified production car; a similar car was driven by Bob Burman, two Pope-Hartfords were driven by Basel and Disbrow, an Alco by Harry Grant and two Marmons by Ray Harroun, winner of the first Indiana-polis '500', and Joe Dawson. Grant and Dawson had finished 1st and 2nd in the recent ill fated Vanderbilt Cup. Finally there were two Loziers for Ralph Mulford and Joe Horan.

The race itself started at the late hour of 9 a.m. and from the start it was Hemery who made the pace by leading for the first eight laps, initially from Chevrolet's Buick and Wagner's Fiat. The Buicks, however, were in trouble with their tyres and did not last and the main race was again contested between the Benz and Fiat teams: when Hemery lost the lead on the 9th lap it was Wagner who stepped into the breach till he in turn had to give best to Haupt on the

[1] *'Old Crocks'*

114 CHAIN GANG: Convict labour creates the Savannah circuit

11th lap. Haupt put in three electrifying laps in 13 mins. 43 secs. (10th and 11th) and 13 mins. 23 secs. on the 12th to lead Nazzaro by nearly four minutes at half distance, with Wagner a further minute astern, followed by de Palma, Hemery and Bruce-Brown. In all 6 mins. 52 secs. separated these six leaders after close on three hours racing—a veritable pocket handkerchief for those times—leaving the race still absolutely wide open.

Haupt's 13th lap was his last—sadly, after his wonderful showing, he took a right-angle corner too fast and landed in a mass of bushes. The car was hopelessly damaged and the Fiats of Nazzaro and de Palma went ahead followed by Bruce-Brown and Wagner. Hemery had been delayed by a stop on his 9th lap, but was now beginning to get back into the hunt and moved up to 4th when Wagner fell back until he too had an accident on his 17th lap.

The Fiat position still seemed tolerably secure in spite of the loss of Wagner, with Nazzaro and de Palma still 1st and 2nd, but still only 5 mins. 5 secs. separated the four leaders at 16 laps. The 17th was a bad lap for Fiat with first Wagner's accident and then a delay at the pits for Nazzaro, which tumbled him to 2nd on the 17th and 4th on the 18th. He finally retired with a broken chain a lap later. This left de Palma still in front with Bruce-Brown, driving very steadily, less than a minute behind and Hemery about $2\frac{1}{2}$ mins. further behind in 3rd. By the 22nd lap stage de Palma had increased his lead but on the 23rd his ill luck reasserted itself and he was out with a punctured radiator.

Nothing now seemed likely to check the two Benz cars and on the 23rd lap Bruce-Brown took the lead for the first time and went into his last lap 79 secs. ahead. He took over quarter of an hour for this lap, while Hemery pulled out a real flier in 13 mins. 54 secs., reducing the winner's margin to the incredible figure of 1.42 secs. after close on six hours' racing. This put even the close finish of 1908—again with Hemery on the losing end—into the shade.

115 Haupt who joined Hemery and Bruce-Brown in the 1910 Benz team

116 MOST HAPPY FELLA: A delighted Victor Hemery anticipates Savannah's fish dinners

INDIANAPOLIS
LAP DISTANCE—2½ Miles

117 AMERICAN FOLLOW-UP: Built with the intention of licking Brooklands to a frazzle it was over 20 years after Brooklands finished before speeds at Indianopolis matched those of the English track

118 CREATORS ALL: Henry Ford (1) with the four founders of Indianapolis—A. C. Newby, Harry Wheeler, Carl Fisher and James Allison

119 VIEU TACOT: Anthony's Porthos starts at Le Mans

The Buicks had been hampered by tyre troubles but by steady driving Burman brought his into 3rd, just over 18 mins. behind Hemery, followed by the Loziers of Mulford and Horan and Harroun's Marmon the last of the finishers. When the Buicks were going they had done well—Chevrolet had been 2nd on lap one and 3rd on the next and on his 12th lap Burman had achieved the excellent time of 13 mins. 40 secs. in comparison with the other fastest laps by the European cars

Haupt	13m. 23s.	Wagner	13m. 53s.
Nazzaro	13m. 42s.	Brown	14m. 3s.
Hemery	13m. 50s.	de Palma	14m. 4s.

The performance of the Buicks was much the best that American cars had achieved against their European competitors to date and in addition, their drivers, de Palma, Haupt, Bruce-Brown, Chevrolet and Burman had shown themselves worthy rivals of Hemery, Nazzaro and Wagner, then three of the best drivers in Europe. Could they but have taken advantage of Indianapolis in the same way as England did of Brooklands it might not have taken America another eleven years to achieve success in the Grand Prix.

There is no evidence that the inaugural meeting at Indianapolis in 1910 was one of Tex Rickard's promotions, but the proceedings were certainly worthy of his best, being conducted by the great American heavyweight boxers, Jack Johnson and James Jefferies. The Black Demon was no mean driver, having at one time owned a 1908 Grand Prix Austin and, as a contemporary put it, 'il réussit avec succés à faire son Nazzaro,' in contrast with James J. who struck terror into even hardened American souls.

The fantastic could be propagated at Brooklands too, as witness the journalist who naïvely suggested levelling speeds by means of fitting the cars with wind-resistance devices to the 'enormous benefit' of the sport. The raconteur's icy comment is worth repeating

...'certainly the spectacle of a host of big Fiats and Mercedes trying to get round the Byfleet Banking or across the Fork on a gusty day, each burdened with a superstructure like an advertisement hoarding would have been terrific.'

During 1910 the A.C.F. was split by a feud which culminated with the resignation of the Marquis de Dion and at this low ebb in the Club's annals the spirit of Puck seems to have entered the French Establishment who chose such a moment to bestow upon the Club's President the Legion d'Honneur—a truly Gilbertian paradox to provide a final and perhaps fitting piece of stage dressing for the stumbling revival of a Grand Prix race in Europe in 1911, derisively described in the French press as the Grand Prix des vieux tacots. Initially a brilliant entry was promised for the Sarthe Club's Le Mans race, including four Lorraine-Dietrichs, three Rolland-Pilains, three Lion-Peugeots and three Hispano-Suizas with three Nationals and a Buick from America. From the first nothing went right for the Sarthe Revivalists; for a start the date had to be changed several times, then the European constructors remembered the Ordnance and the American entries just melted away, leaving the organisers no choice but to admit defeat and the monsters if there was to be any race at all.

The new circuit was just under 34 miles in length and lay to the south of Le Mans covering some of the ground later used for the Twenty-four Hour Races. Starting from the suburb of Pontlieue it ran down the Mulsanne straight and further to Ecommoy where it turned left through St. Mars and then left at the junction with the road back to Pontlieue by way of Parigne L'Evêque. In 1912/13 the circuit was run clockwise, but the impression gained from contemporary accounts is that in 1911 it was run anti-clockwise, although this is contrary to Mr. Bradley's recollection. Twelve laps had to be covered to give the distance of 405 miles.

By race day on the 23rd July the competitors had been whittled down to:

Maurice Fournier (Corre-la-Licorne)
Barriaux   (Alcyon light car)
Duray   (1906 G.P. Lorraine-Dietrich)
De Vere   (Côte 2-stroke)
Rivière   (Excelsior light car)
Anthony   (1908 G.P. Porthos)
Rigal   (Rolland-Pilain)
Deydier   (Cottin-Desgouttes)
Hemery   (Savannah Fiat)
Friederich   (Type 13 Bugatti)
Fauquet   (Rolland-Pilain)
Ollier   (Côte)
Gabriel   (Rolland-Pilain)
Leduc   (Côte)

The Rollands should have started firm favourites—Rigal and Gabriel were fast and experienced drivers and the cars had been specially built for the race. They were reputed to develop 110 b.h.p. at 1800 r.p.m. out of their engines of 4 × 110 × 160, though it is odd that they were so well within the capacity limit of 110 × 200. The Alcyon, Excelsior and Côtes had all taken part in the Coupe de l'Auto at Boulogne a few weeks previously; the Porthos, Lorraine and Cottin were survivors from the real age of monsters. Fournier's Corre was a 1907 car which he had rebuilt in his own garage at Le Mans, as La Vie Automobile put it 'de bric et de brac sans toutes précautions d'usage'—with tragic consequences as it turned out.

Finally there was Friederich's little Bugatti. The brilliant display of this tiny car, so charmingly described by Faroux as 'cette boîte de vitesse liliputienne' transformed the whole character of the race and gave it some small degree of justification. Opinions vary as to the derivation of this car. At one time it was suggested that the engine was a derivative of the putatively Bugatti-designed 1908 Isotta-Fraschini

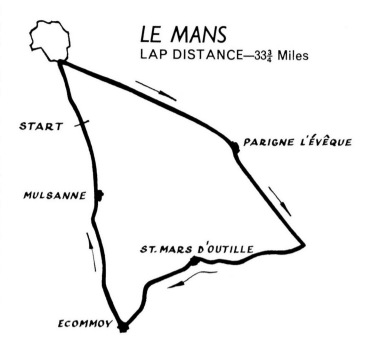

LE MANS
LAP DISTANCE—33¾ Miles

START

PARIGNE L'ÉVÊQUE

MULSANNE

ST. MARS D'OUTILLE

ECOMMOY

120 The new Le Mans circuit that was used in 1911-13

voiturette. Bore and stroke of this car were 62 × 100 and of the Bugatti 65 × 100 and there is definite similarity in the engine layout, but there the matter ends. The latest and probably wisest judgment is H. G. Conway's:—[2]

'It is difficult to be exact in this matter. It is possible that Bugatti had a finger in the Isotta pie, but as he was the last person not to seek credit where credit was due, the fact that he never mentioned Isotta-Fraschini .... is significant. To the engineer only the layout .... is similar—the detail is quite different. The conclusion is inescapable. Bugatti must have seen the Isotta .... cars and as a result was stimulated to abandon the monster cars he had been designing and try something smaller—and what a success his attempt was to be. It is unreasonable on the evidence to credit him with a design he certainly did not claim himself.'

This brings me to another Bugatti conjecture connected with this race. With his characteristic ingenuity[3] Pomeroy has suggested that Bugatti was also responsible for the 1909/11 S 61 Fiat which raced at Savannah in 1910 and won the Le Mans race. Pomeroy puts his case like this:—

'It is ... known that Bugatti designed a small 4-cylinder engine for Isotta-Fraschini having basically the same camshaft design as on the Deutz (which he unquestionably did design—WEC). The relation between Bugatti and Fiat in the design of their overhead camshaft S 61 model is less certain, but there is at least the probability that it existed and there is no doubt at all that the Fiat engine and

---

[2] Bugatti, *published by G. T. Foulis & Co. Ltd. 1963.*
[3] *Whilst this is an entertaining exercise in deduction the fact remains that this car was the work of a technical team headed by Avv. Fornaca.*

the Black Bess type are highly similar and that both bear a close resemblance to the Type 13 which was derived from the Isotta-Fraschini. The logical likelihood is . . . . that Bugatti's engine design came in the following order: In 1905 the s.v. Hermes; in 1906 the o.h.c. with sliding quadrant tappets Deutz; in 1907 the little Isotta with o.h.c. In 1908 (probably) the basis of the S. 61; in 1909 the Type 13 derived from Isotta and around 1910 "Black Bess" derived from the Fiat.'

In his biography of Bugatti[4] Bradley mentions nothing of any connection with Fiat (or Isotta for that matter on which he has told me he has no definite information) and also the obstinate fact remains that Bugatti himself claimed credit for neither the Isotta nor the Fiat designs. The former is possibly understandable as the Isotta did not do particularly well in the Dieppe race and never reappeared, but, a Bugatti victory at Le Mans in 1911 would have been an irresistible publicity boost to any young designer, particularly when it was coupled with his little car's second place. Psychologically Conway's verdict is almost conclusive and the various similarities can equally be explained by the fact that Bugatti had a sight of the Isotta and possibly of the S 61 Fiat as well! Is it not a coincidence that 'Black Bess' is the only Bugatti with chain drive, which Fiat did not abandon till their 1914 models? Can it be also that a Fiat designer had a look under the Isotta bonnet at Dieppe in 1908?

It is a delightful paradox that a dull race should have given rise to such an interesting historical guessing game, which has happily not generated anything like the heat endured by the competitors on the 23rd July 1911. The day was torrid and the roads were in a terrible state so that the drivers were sorely troubled by dust and the pit area gradu-

121 VIEU TACOT: Hemery's Fiat which won

ally turned into an inland sea as the grilling day wore on. The cars started in the order in which they were listed earlier at one minute intervals and the race soon developed into a three-cornered struggle between Fournier, Duray and Hemery. To everyone's surprise Fournier did not lose his leading position on the road although Deydier's Cottin was fastest on lap one. He lost his position with a steering failure, leaving Fauquet's Rolland-Pilain in the lead, till its axle broke on lap three. De Vere's Côte did not complete one lap, the Porthos cracked a cylinder on the 2nd and Ollier's Côte also, and the race became more like Ten Little Niggers than ever, when Rivière's Excelsior lost its timing gears and Then There Were Nine, with Fournier, Duray, Barriaux, Hemery and Rigal in the first five places.

Water and tyres now became the besetting troubles on the cars in the blazing heat, the only car seemingly unafflicted being the little Bugatti which only weighed 6 cwt. The race had started at 8 a.m. and shortly before noon rumours of an accident to Fournier began to circulate; in fact he had been having a duel down the Le Mans to Ecommoy stretch with Hemery's Fiat when his front axle broke, both he and his mechanic being fatally injured.

By half distance the race had resolved itself into a duel between Duray's Lorraine and Hemery's Fiat—old style racer against modern tourer, with the old just having the upper hand by slightly under eight minutes, Hemery's car being fitted with a big dashboard, high chassis and very upright driving position. It was seen to handle badly, but still put in the fastest lap at 67.75 m.p.h. on its fourth circuit. Eventually the Lorraine's differential gave way, leaving the race to Hemery as he battled his way through troubles with tyres, springs and gears—being obliged to cover the last half of the race on top gear.

The roads were to be re-opened at 4 p.m. and by this time Hemery had been proclaimed winner in 7 hrs. 6 mins. 30 secs. (52½ m.p.h.) The Bugatti had covered ten laps in 7 hrs. 16 mins. 50 secs., Gabriel's Rolland-Pilain nine in 8 hrs. 4 mins. 38 ³⁄₅th secs. and Leduc's Côte voiturette eight in 6 hrs. 19 mins. 33 secs. Hemery's was a popular victory as he was a local man; also he had not won a race since the Vanderbilt Cup of 1905, although he had been 2nd in two American Grand Prizes (by incredibly close margins) in the 1907 Florio Cup and the 1908 Grand Prix.

The reputation of Grand Prix racing was to some extent redeemed by the highly successful American Grand Prize at Savannah on the 30th November. On this occasion the event was preceded by the Vanderbilt Cup, in which some of the same cars were taking part, although the interval of three days meant cutting things rather fine. The principal European entries were once again Fiat and Benz; Wagner again led the Italian team but this time he was supported by Bruce-Brown and Caleb Bragg, an American amateur who had

[4] *Ettore Bugatti, by W. F. Bradley, pub.* Motor Racing Publications Ltd. *1948.*

managed the Fiat team the previous year. Hemery led the Benz team against his great friend and rival Wagner for their third and final meeting and he, too, was supported by two Americans, Hearne and Bergdoll. There were also two Mercedes—1908 Grand Prix type cars—entered privately by de Palma and Spencer Wishart. The remainder were American cars—Ralph Mulford's Lozier, the Vanderbilt Cup winner, two Marmons (Burman and Patchke), two Buicks (Basel and Cobe), two Abbot-Detroits (Limberg and Mitchell) and Disbrow's Pope-Hummer.

Dr. Quattlebaum tells us that November 30, 1911 was one of the coldest days ever witnessed and that 'a number of negro waiters, each carrying a tray suspended from his neck, and containing a number of glasses and bottles of liquor in each corner ... did a land office business selling straight whisky without a chaser for 50 cents a drink ... This was a time when prohibition was a burning political issue, but there were few supporters of the idea among those thoroughly chilled spectators.'

The Fiats were new cars, specially built for the event, with their bonnet tops almost shoulder high to a standing man and very similar outwardly to the 1912 Dieppe Grand Prix cars. From the start these great Monsters—the last of the vanishing race—dominated the proceedings, Bragg leading for the first three laps. On the second he was followed by Bruce-Brown and Wagner with Hemery and de Palma close by.

The next lap Hemery fell back with valve troubles and his race was nearly (but not quite) run—letting de Palma into 3rd with his old Mercedes, which had already finished 2nd in the Vanderbilt Cup. The other two Benz were 4th and 5th and the Americans did not look like repeating their Vanderbilt win: the big European cars were just too quick. However, if it could not be an American car, an American driver was the next best thing and there was great rejoicing, no doubt well celebrated at 50 cents a time, when de Palma went up into the lead after four laps. This was largely because all three Fiats were stopping for tyres and de Palma was down to 5th on the next lap, but a further boost was given to the home supporters when Burman brought his Marmon up into 4th place. This triumph, too, was short-lived, for the car went out on the next lap with magneto failure only to have its challenge taken up by Mulford in his Lozier who stayed well up with the leaders till almost the end of the race.

The 5th lap was Hemery's farewell to Savannah, which he accomplished at the record average of 81.6 m.p.h. finally retiring two laps later too far behind to exert any influence on the race. Hemery's retirement was by no means the end of the Benz effort; although Bergdoll also fell out on lap 8, Hearne took over de Palma's lead on lap six and held it for much of the rest of the race. He was displaced first by Patchke's Marmon on laps seven and eight, but, two laps of

122 SAVANNAH FAVOURITE: Ever popular at Savannah here is Wagner in 1911: he never forgot his three races and the hospitality of that 'wonderfully beautiful old Southern city ...'

123 SAVANNAH FLIER: ... 'from the start it was Hemery who made the pace ...'

124 *AMERICAN FACE-SAVER: Limberg (Abbott-Detroit) passes the stands and the abandoned cars of Hemery (56) and Wishart (54)*

125 *LARGEST MARGIN: "Bruce-Brown made assurance doubly sure with a barn-storming last lap to win by 2 m. 4 secs. . . ."*

126 *Ralph Mulford (Lozier) who won the 1911 Vanderbilt and made a powerful challenge in the Grand Prize*

this pace finished this home challenger and Hearne then stayed in the lead from the 9th till the 20th lap. Behind him the Fiats were going tremendously fast between tyre changes and in addition Bragg had to replace an oil line but the overall pattern was of the remaining Benz being stalked by the three great Fiats with de Palma's grey Mercedes sometimes breaking up the red and white pattern.

Wagner had to retire with deranged steering after 14 laps when he was almost within striking distance of Hearne. About this time Mulford began to reassert the American challenge, moving up into 3rd when Wagner retired behind Hearne and de Palma; by the 19th lap he was in 2nd, a mere 16 secs. behind Hearne, but only 28 secs. in front of Bruce-Brown, who was once again playing a waiting game. On the 20th lap the Fiat and the Benz changed places, with Mulford still 2nd and 31 secs. between the three of them, which after 4½ hours was racing with a vengeance. These laps were Mulford's Indian Summer for he fell back to 3rd for the next two, and then when only 32 secs. behind Bruce-Brown (in 2nd) he had to retire when his driveshaft broke. This was mortal ill luck as the car might easily have won, although the strain of two races in four days cannot be discounted.

Mulford's Lozier was not the only contestant to feel the strain; on the 22nd lap Hearne lost his lead when he stopped to change tyres and finished the 23rd lap 1½ mins. behind Bruce-Brown who made assurance doubly sure with a barn-storming last lap to win by two mins. 4 secs.—the largest margin by which a Savannah Grand Prize had been won.

This in itself is a sufficient epitaph for the three Grand Prix races run at Savannah in 1908, 1910 and 1911. At a time when European racing was at its lowest ebb, the Savannah series had produced three of the fastest and closest races ever run, besides throwing up one American driver of real world class in David Bruce-Brown. Dr. Quattlebaum, in his most delightful work on these races,[5] concludes his account of the 1911 Grand Prize with these words:

'Once again Savannah had staged a perfect motor car race. There was nothing but praise for everyone who had helped make Savannah the greatest racing centre in the world. Everyone seemed to feel, even before the Grand Prize was finished, that Savannah would not again hold a big race. Wagner and Hemery, the two great foreign drivers who had participated in each of the Grand Prize events, remained in the city a few days. . . . Many friends were at the station to see them off, and . . . no doubt they expressed the feeling of the thousands of visitors who had seen the races, as well as themselves, when they declared that neither of them would ever forget the kindness and warm hospitality of this wonderfully beautiful old Southern city.'

[5] The Great Savannah Races of 1908-10-11, *published privately by the author in 1957, is at present undergoing revision with a view to a 2nd edition. Dr. Quattlebaum tells me he 'compiled (the) book solely for the purpose of preserving a very unique episode in the history of our unique city . . .' and it is certainly a beautiful and worthwhile possession containing details of all the races and full lap time-tables.*

PART TWO
1912 to 1921 · From Veteran to Vintage

Beneath the acting of a dreadful thing
And its first motion. . . .
The Genius and the mortal instruments
Are then in Council.
William Shakespeare : Julius Caesar

Chapter Six
1912 · The Struggle for Revival

'. . . facilis descensus Averno
Sed revocare gradum superasque evadere ad auras
Hoc opus hic labor est . . .' Virgil: Aeneid VI

By the time the Grand Prize had taken place it was settled that a 2000 km. Grand Prix was to be held on the Dieppe circuit at the end of June 1912. To cap this it was announced that the Paris Salon would be revived in 1912 if only to recover the prestige lost by the tremendous success of the London Show in 1911. 'Mon Dieu', wrote Charles Faroux 'nous ferons en 1912 un Salon épatant à Paris et nous reprendrons la première place.' Still, to run a Grand Prix there had to be an entry and when only four Lorraine-Dietrichs had been entered it looked as if all the fine talk in the world could not beguile the shy constructors from their long chastity; nor were the French the only offenders, for there was a complete German and partial Italian boycott on the event so that by December 31st not even Fiat had entered!

In order to avoid another Le Mans fiasco, the A.C.F. decided to combine their Grand Prix with the Coupe de l'Auto in the teeth of fierce opposition from manufacturers and press alike. They had also taken the wise course of abandoning fancy formulae and leaving the Grand Prix to all intents and purposes formule libre. This was plain common sense to the organisers but not to those journalistic idealists who were opposed to the Cult of the Monster—a criticism that had derived fresh impetus from the field in the recent Grand Prize. The apotheosis of these monsters was undoubtedly the great 300 h.p. Fiat record breaking car, which appeared several times in this country, with four cylinders of 240 × 320 mm. which, as a contemporary naïvely remarked made it 'a bit high for corners.' All this added fresh fuel to the fire of Faroux in denouncing formule libre as a 'Formula of idlers.'

Against this background events proceeded towards the 25th June, which was to be the opening day of the 1912 Grand Prix and the veteran Gobron, of 1904 and even earlier, was entered! As if to give the public a real money's worth, the circuit was to be covered 10 times each day making a total distance of 956 miles, which made it by far the longest race in the century and the 3rd longest up to 1912. Unhappily the quality and quantity of the entry did not measure up and the final tally numbered one Excelsior, three Fiats, four Lorraines, one Mathis, two Rolland-Pilains and three Peugeots. This was a sorry collection compared to the large fields of 1906-8 and underlined the wisdom of the A.C.F. in combining the race with the Coupe de l'Auto, for which there were thirty-three starters—making forty-seven in all, one fewer than had started in the 1908 Grand Prix.

The Rolland-Pilains were the 1911 Le Mans cars—with long pointed tails and attractive modern lines, but, like the Excelsior, they were appreciably slower than many of the Coupe de l'Auto cars. The Fiats of 150 × 200 mm. were very similar to the 1911 Savannah cars, and the Lorraines even bigger with 155 × 200 mm. bore and stroke; the Mathis was only in the Grand Prix because it was too small for the Coupe de l'Auto, like the Bugatti in 1911, though there the comparison ended! Finally there were the new Peugeots. Compared to most of the voiturettes, and indeed the Grand Prix Rolland-Pilains, the Peugeots were very traditional in aspect with a high bonnet line, large drain-pipe exhaust, two exposed seats and a bolster tank. Under the bonnet, however, there was much novelty and, if in the end, Boillot's victory perhaps owed more to his detachable Rudge-Whitworth wheels, the Peugeot engine design set an enduring basic pattern.

It is trite to say that there is nothing new under the sun and to this end it matters not who first designed an engine with (1) one or more overhead camshafts or (2) inclined overhead valves or (3) monobloc casting or (4) central plug location. The fact remains that the 1912 Peugeot was the first to unite all these features, using, in fact, two such camshafts and four such valves per cylinder. The cars, designed and built almost independently of the factory by the energy and enterprise of the 'driver' team of Boillot, Goux and Zuccarelli supported by their Swiss draughtsman, Ernest Henry, represented a remarkable advance in technical design with their 7½-litre engines running up to 2880 ft. per minute of piston speed. About the same time Bugatti had entered into an agreement with Peugeot to design two cars—the Bébé Peugeot and a larger one. Bradley[1] has said that there was a plan to sell the 5-litre design (100 × 160 mm.—'Black Bess' type) to Peugeot and one can only speculate on the possibility that this was the design contemplated

---

[1] *Biography of Bugatti.*

by the Peugeot-Bugatti agreement. Conway[2] infers that it was not, but the possibility is intriguing, particularly when one considers the performance of the special version of the 5-litre Bugatti at Indianapolis in 1914. With shaft drive and a longer stroke of 180 mm., Friederich drove it until it went out with rear axle failure, at one time, according to one source, holding 2nd place in competition with the faster Peugeot and Delage Grand Prix cars of 1913. Pomeroy concludes that the 1913 cars were on average four per cent. faster than the 1912 ones, all of which makes the presence of a 5-litre Bugatti at Dieppe a tantalizing might-have-been.[3]

Whilst the engine, with its single overhead camshaft operating three valves (two inlet, one exhaust), may not be as exciting as the Peugeot, Bugatti was on a sounder track in eschewing the very long stroke that always haunted the Peugeot design school—an uneasy relic from their early Coupe de l'Auto days. Bugatti was also experimenting with an 8-cylinder car in 1913 consisting of two 68 × 100 engines in tandem (2.6 litres) but using three valves per cylinder. The car was reputed to be 'fast but not very successful in racing' but a Peugeot-supported team of these cars would have caused a furore at Boulogne in 1913 to say nothing of a 4½-litre straight eight at Lyons in 1914! It is curious how often the name of Bugatti crops up in considering these byways of motoring history—all part of the legendary character of this unique man; Boillot is thus described by Scott-Moncrieff in Three Pointed Star—

'Boillot at the wheel of a Peugeot had acquired almost legendary fame. An overpowering swollen headed man who played to the gallery he might in his general attitude have stepped right out from the pages of a Dumas novel. He was a virtuoso of the road and he knew it; his long string of triumphs had brought sporting France to his feet. He was the idol of his countrymen as were Lenglen and Carpentier when they were at their zenith'

and the clash of personalities between him and Bugatti might well have strangled the idea at birth, so to return to the realities at Dieppe....

128 ... 'the Rolland-Pilains were the 1911 Le Mans cars with their attractive modern lines ...'

129 ONCE AND FOR ALL TIME: Bruce-Brown's driving in 1912 deeply impressed observers: here he sets off on the first morning

127 LIVING LEGEND: 'Boillot at the wheel of a Peugeot (here a 1913 G.P. car) had acquired almost legendary fame ...'

130 NOT SO GAY: a rather subdued Hemery in his Lorraine-Dietrich at Dieppe

[2] Op. cit.
[3] Against this must be set the fact that after the driver team had been formed, Bugatti offered to build a racing car for Peugeot, which was presented and tested but as the results were inferior to the cars built by the driver team, Bugatti's design was not accepted.

131 FIRST BLOOD TO THE MONSTERS: One of the Lorraines approaching the Ancourt bridge

132 ... 'if Boillot were to share the lot of Goux and Zuccarelli (above)...'

As in design so in choice of drivers Lorraine had stuck to tradition in retaining Hemery, Hanriot and Bablot; Hemery and Hanriot had finished 2nd and 3rd on Benz in 1908 while Bablot had been team-mate to the great Théry on Brasier. Their fourth driver, Heim, completed one circuit and then vanished into the relative oblivion from which he had sprung. Like some latter-day Ferrari teams, Fiat did not have a single Italian driver and retained a strong American influence with Bruce-Brown and de Palma, with their stalwart Wagner. The remaining drivers were Esser (Mathis), and Anford and Guyot on the Rollands. Guyot, although competing in his first Grand Prix, had won the 1908 voiturette event on the Dieppe circuit and finished 3rd in the 1911 Coupe de l'Auto for Delage.

The residue of the old Grand Prix drivers were turning their talents to the voiturettes—Barriaux, Duray and Page (Alcyon), Garcet (Calthorpe), Gabriel (Côte), Caillois, Rigal and Resta (Sunbeam). The remaining drivers came from the new generation which had sprung up in the intervening voiturette years—in the Grand Prix Boillot, Goux and Zuccarelli and in the Coupe, Champoiseau (Th.-Schneider Hancock, Watson (Vauxhall) Thomas (Peugeot) and another, Chassagne, who was only riding mechanic to Rigal despite his 3rd place for Hispano in the 1910 Coupe de l'Auto.

Practice wiseacres thought the race would be between Fiat and Lorraine, though this was probably because the Peugeots were little in evidence. In accordance with the spartan European traditions the first competitor, Rigal's Sunbeam, was sent off on his long haul at 5.30 a.m. and the rest followed at thirty second intervals. At 5.33 the Grand Prix proper was under weigh again when Hemery, fittingly enough, let in the clutch of his 17-litre Lorraine and he it was who re-appeared first at 6.12 a.m. precisely. A mere ten seconds behind on the road came Rigal, then Goux around 6.14 a.m. and Boillot a couple of minutes later. It was not until 6.22 a.m. that the race leader, Bruce-Brown, appeared with his great Fiat, having taken 37 mins. 18 secs. to lead from

2. Boillot	38m. 40s.	4. Goux	40m. 16·4s.
3. Hemery	39m.	5. Heim	40m. 26·3s.

with Christiaens, Wagner and de Palma next up—first blood to the Monsters. The 2nd lap was a sad setback for the old timers; Hemery and Heim both had engine failures, Boillot was round in 37 mins. 52.2 secs. to be within 13 secs. of Brown and Goux moved up to 3rd ahead of Wagner, Christiaens (Excelsior), de Palma and Resta, on the leading voiturette in 7th!

Boillot fell back on the 3rd lap, being physically overtaken by Brown on the Dieppe straight while Goux toppled from 3rd to 40th and Wagner moved up to 3rd less than a minute behind Boillot; by the next lap Wagner had climbed to 2nd, Boillot to 4th with de Palma 5th, Hanriot 7th and Anford (Rolland) 10th. This was the Indian Summer of the Monsters and as the day wore on it became increasingly apparent that the small cars were the real heroes. At quarter distance the order was (voiturettes in italics)

1. Brown	3–14–54·1		*6. Resta*	3–37–22
2. Boillot	3–21–24·1		7. Hanriot	3–37–28
3. Wagner	3–22–1·4		8. Anford	3–39–10·2
4. Hancock	3–33–58·3		*9. Rigal*	3–39–26·2
5. de Palma	3–35–38·2		*10. Medinger*	3–39–28

Behind the first three a race, close even by American standards, was taking place and Hancock's performance, in particular, was quite staggering.

During the ensuing five laps the voiturettes and Boillot gradually improved their positions, although Caillois (Sunbeam) fell out on the 7th. At the end, Brown still held the lead, but Boillot put in two fire-cracking laps, both well under 38 mins., to round off the day which brought him to a mere 2 mins. 1 sec. of the leader. The final order was:

1. Brown	6–36–37·6		*6. Hancock*	7–16–42·6
2. Boillot	6–38–38·6		7. Anford	7–21–9
3. Wagner	7–3–12		8. de Palma	7–24–24·2
4. Resta	7–10–54·6		*9. Medinger*	7–33–19
5. Rigal	7–14–21		10. Hanriot	7–47–43·6

with nine other survivors.

Incredible though the performance of the light cars might be, it was Bruce-Brown who had earned the greatest praise. The Fiats, with their great height and short wheelbase ought to have been devils to drive but clearly were not. The S-bend under the railway bridge at Ancourt was a favourite vantage-point and during practice Bruce-Brown had a tremendous moment there; to the surprise of observers the car went 'across the road without any swing whatsoever' and the cars were described as 'running with gyroscopic steadiness as solidly as the proverbial rock'. With his flair for graphic description of these great veterans, Gerald Rose thus described them at full speed:

'The Fiats with their great high bonnets and rattling chains seemed to tear through the air with a painful effort, as if fighting against a great resistance. . . .'

and thus in writing of Bruce-Brown:

'. . . I confess I had expected he would be abnormally rash being accustomed to the highly banked corners of the American circuits. . . .'

although it was on the road circuits at Savannah that his two great victories had been won. Rose of course added that 'he drove magnificently' never taking Ancourt in anything ap-

133 . . . *'Boillot put in two firecracking laps to round off the day . . .'*

134 . . . *'the Fiats (Wagner's above) seemed to tear through the air with a painful effort . . .'*

proaching a dangerous fashion. It is clear, however, from a contemporary Gordon Crosby impression of him 'side-stepping' round one of the dangerous hairpin bends that the progress of the faster cars on the loose surfaces was a highly exhilarating affair. Corners were negotiated

'... by momentarily locking the rear wheels with a touch of the brakes the lateral momentum of the car swinging the rear wheels across the road to the position required for the new direction of the car which is maintained by sudden but accurately formed movements of the steering wheel.'

On a very different plane it was driving of this spirit that was shewn by one J. F. Gonzalez at Silverstone in 1951 when he broke the long Alfa-Romeo supremacy in Grand Prix racing with his unblown Ferrari.

The scales were interestingly balanced between Monster, Peugeot and Voiturette at the day's end and if Boillot were to share the lot of Goux and Zuccarelli on the morrow the outlook for France (and also possibly the future of the Grand Prix!) was a sorry one indeed. Illicit refuelling brought disqualification to Goux, de Palma and, ultimately, to Bruce-Brown, it being laid down that fuel could only be taken on at the pits, while Hanriot's car never re-started, so the first ten were rapidly thinned out. To start with, both Wagner and Brown gained appreciably on Boillot and it still looked as if Fiat would pull off the impossible until Bruce-Brown's tenuous lead vanished utterly when he suffered a leaking fuel system on his 14th lap which took him over 65 mins.

From that point Boillot moved into a lead which he never lost although he was delayed on the 18th lap for long enough to let Wagner's Fiat come up to within 6½ minutes of him. The big car was losing too much time wheel changing to be a really pressing rival; it was unfortunate that the Fiats were hard on their tyres, but their persisting with detachable rims could well have been monumental folly for the Rudge Whitworth wheel was well proved in competition by 1912. Thus, in Kent Karslake's words, 'the race which for so long had looked a certainty for Fiat was slipping through the Italian's fingers. If only they had used wire wheels...'[4] In addition the big car was handicapped by the wet condition of the course during the second day after a night's rain; thus Boillot was able to gain 5 mins. 22 secs. on Bruce-Brown during the 12th and 13th laps before the Fiat ran into fuel troubles.

On this occasion Boillot had carried Peugeot and France to victory in spite of having had to fight the Fiats and voiturettes alone for almost all the 946 miles: two years later at Lyons he was to know the despair of defeat after a long uphill struggle against another new order. At Dieppe, however, it was Boillot who represented the new order and we can leave him for the time being secure on the verge of a

fame equal to that of any of the great pioneers who had gone before him. In those times races were few and far between and reputations could be made overnight; if it had taken four patient years in voiturette events to qualify Boillot for his position, his legendary reputation was made on that wet Wednesday at Dieppe. Jules Goux, far the more successful till then, was henceforth the second string, the Fidus Achates ready to step into the Master's shoes should occasion arise. Dieppe did not make Boillot's name alone; as at Lyons in 1914, so at Dieppe the non-finisher was in a sense the true hero and many plaudits were reserved for David Bruce-Brown. With his characteristic woollen windsock hat trailing in the wake of the great red Fiat he had kept going to the end, though technically disqualified as of the 14th lap. To its incalculable loss and sorrow, Europe was to see no more of this young and talented driver who ranks with de Palma, Milton and Murphy as the only great road racing drivers (by European standards) to come out of America until very recent times.

135 ... 'hardly less meritorious was the achievement of the Sunbeams ...'. Rigal who finished third overall passes the stands

Hardly less meritorious was the achievement of the Sunbeams in finishing 3rd, 4th and 5th in the overall category. True they had lost Caillois en route but their victory in the Coupe de l'Auto was the most crushing achieved up to then in any major race: 'One-Two-Three' was without precedent in the inter-town classics, the Gordon Bennett, the Coupe de l'Auto or the Grand Prix, until Sunbeam pulled it off with contemptuous ease almost at their first attempt. Hancock's wonderful run on the first day was another highlight and it is a sobering thought to relate the first day's racing to the 1907 and 1908 races which had been over 10 laps of the circuit:—

1.	Bruce-Brown	(1912 Fiat)	6–36–37
2.	Boillot	(1912 Peugeot)	6–38–38
3.	Nazzaro	(1907 Fiat)	6–46–33
4.	Szisz	(1907 Renault)	6–53–10
5.	Lautenschlager	(1908 Mercedes)	6–55–43
6.	Wagner	(1912 Fiat)	7–3–12
7.	Hemery	(1908 Benz)	7–4–24
8.	Baras	(1907 Brasier)	7–5–5
9.	Hanriot	(1908 Benz)	7–5–13
10.	*Resta*	*(1912 Sunbeam)*	*7–10–54*

[4] *In fact the Fiats are said to have come to Dieppe with R.W. wheels only for Bruce-Brown and Wagner to find handling unsatisfactory so that the cars went back to the Paris Depot of Fiat to have wood wheels fitted.*

This last is the really instructive placing and it is for the speeds of the voiturettes as much as the triumph of Peugeot over Fiat that Dieppe—1912 marks the end of that age which had been ushered in by the great Mors and Panhard of 1901/2: the Decade of the Monsters.

Technically, perhaps, there was little to be said in favour of these huge cars but they had enriched the motoring scene for ten great pioneering years and at the end they had left it on a sustained note of magnificent defiance. The 1912 Grand Prix rang down the curtain irrevocably and poignantly on the Heroic Age of Motor Racing and never again has a car of over 10 litres come so close to winning a classic road race. Peugeot had won through but like the Battle of Waterloo it had been 'the nearest run thing you ever saw in your life' and, like Wellington, Boillot might well have remarked (and probably did) 'By God! I don't think it would have been done if I had not been there.'

136 EVER VICTORIOUS: 'By God! I don't think it would have been done if I had not been there . . .'

Reviewing the racing for the Autocar Gerald Rose praised the influence of Brooklands as a proving ground for the English voiturettes and finished with a stirring call to 'show a clean pair of heels to the fastest product of La Belle France. . . . We have scooped the motor cycle honours throughout . . . France; cannot we do likewise with the racing car? . . . Now is our chance . . . it may not come again—we must take it while we may. So here's to the Grand Prix of 1913. . . .' Faroux summed it all up in two succint sentences:

'Il nous faut au plus vite un autodrome'—and—*'Sans Peugeot quelle terrible défaite pour nous.'*

England was unhappily not quick enough on the draw and neither in 1913 or 1914 did her cars come so close to winning

the Grand Prix in spite of Brooklands, which then had no counterpart in the Old World.

The 1912 season was not yet completed and in the two further events of significance the Peugeot cars consolidated their supremacy. First at Le Mans Boillot and Goux completely eclipsed the 1911 speeds, Goux winning at 74.56 m.p.h. and Boillot putting the lap record up to 80 m.p.h. in 25 mins. 9 secs. As if to rub in the salt the second car home behind Goux was an 18 h.p. Spa tourer driven by Leduc in 6 hrs. 35 mins. 18 secs. in contrast to Hemery's winning time in 1911 of 7 hrs. 6 mins. 30 secs. Sceptical after their unhappy experience in 1911, the A.C. de la Sarthe had copied the A.C.F. in combining their 'Grand Prix' for the Coupe de la Sarthe with a voiturette event which they had made the principal event and called the Grand Prix de France. As the only Grand Prix cars were the two Peugeots they were clearly right.

The season was effectively continued at Indianapolis in 1913 when a substantial European challenge appeared for the first time. In 1911 and 1912 the race had been run to a 600 cu. in. capacity limit (about 9850 c.c.) reduced to 450 cu. in. (about 7400 c.c.) for 1913. In 1911 the European cars were a 90 h.p. Mercedes with which Wishart led the race for a while, two Fiats and a Benz of 1910 Savannah Grand Prize type. With one of these Fiats Bruce-Brown finished 3rd at 72.70 m.p.h. in front of Wishart's Mercedes. Harroun won with a 7.3 litre Marmon at 74.59 m.p.h. followed by Ralph Mulford's 9-litre Lozier at 74.28 m.p.h. Speeds increased substantially in 1912, de Palma leading for 197 of the 200 laps on the 1908 Grand Prix type Mercedes which he had driven at Savannah the year before. Then, with a 10-mile lead he was overtaken by mechanical troubles and his valiant attempt to push his car home from half way through the 199th lap was too much for him. This enabled Joe Dawson to win on his National at 78.72 m.p.h. from Tetzlaff's Fiat (76.75 m.p.h.) and a small 4.9 litre Mercer at the very creditable speed of 76.13 m.p.h.

137 Bruce-Brown in the 1910 Savannah Fiat with which he finished third in the 1911 '500' at 72.70 m.p.h.

138 ... 'the season was continued at Indianapolis in 1913 ...

139 SLEEPERS AWAKE! – *'Jules Goux had caught America well and truly napping ...'*

In 1913 America was warned very picturesquely of the seriousness of the European attack

'America will be called upon to defend its speed laurels on Friday, ominous Friday, but America is ready, as America ever is.' (Motor Age).

Two Peugeots, linered down to 7.4 litres were to be driven by Goux and Zuccarelli plus Guyot on a Sunbeam, Pilette on a sleeve-valve Mercedes and three Isotta-Fraschinis for Trucco and the Americans Grant and Tetzlaff. In addition Mulford was to drive the 1908 Mercedes, also suitably linered down; eight foreign cars and five foreign drivers all without previous Indianapolis experience—'swarthy skinned aliens' as the American press called them.

From the start the race lay between the two Peugeots, Guyot's Sunbeam and Burman's 7.2 litre side-valve Keeton. Apart from Goux the Europeans had little experience of track work but Goux had spent a considerable time at Brooklands with a Peugeot in March and April 1913 to such good purpose that he put in a lap at 109.22 m.p.h. in a record attempt. Curiously enough he did not run the Peugeot in streamlined form in America, although it was fitted with a cowling and a long tail at Brooklands. The Sunbeam was a private entry of Guyot's being a 1911 car (Toodles iv) driven at Brooklands by R. F. L. Crossman. In two handicaps in March Goux had successfully given the Sunbeam 10 secs. over $5\frac{3}{4}$ miles and 15 secs. over $8\frac{1}{2}$ miles. Crossman accompanied Guyot as riding mechanic and some observers thought this entry would have done better had their positions been reversed. Whilst giving him high praise for finishing 4th, H. Massac Buist strictured his poor race control organisation and pit work and remarked that although the car had run like a watch throughout it had never been really extended and had made a relatively *poor* showing in finishing 4th! Compared to some cars the Sunbeam was very fortunate in tyre selection, changing only one Dunlop in 500 miles.

Goux apparently decided to use a tyre of half an inch less diameter on the left (inside) front wheel though this did not do him much good as his bursts of leadership in the early stages were interspersed with stops for tyres after which 'he was out in pursuit of the field at a terrible speed'. Goux's principal challenger, Burman, fell out of the running during the second 100 miles and although a Stutz led on two occasions, the Peugeot was never seriously challenged again. Zuccarelli did not have much luck; after holding 2nd place in the early stages and putting in a record lap at 93.5 m.p.h. he fell out with carburettor troubles. In the end Goux won by a margin, which I have seen reported as variously as 23 mins., 14 mins. or 3 mins. 22.55 secs. from Wishart's 4.9 litre Mercer and Merz's Stutz. Both Wishart and Merz are reported in different accounts as having finished in flames, so it may well be that some of the six bottles of champagne Goux reputedly consumed en route found their way into the pagoda-like press-box. The most reliable records give the following result:

1. Goux	75·92 m.p.h.	4. Guyot	70·92 m.p.h.
2. Wishart	73·49 m.p.h.	5. Pilette	68·14 m.p.h.
3. Merz	73·38 m.p.h.		

6th Wilcox, 7th Mulford

No other European cars finished, two Isottas having split fuel tanks and one being disqualified. Jules Goux had caught America well and truly napping and passes into history as the first European to win at Indianapolis and probably the last to do so on a liberal champagne diet.[1] His efforts netted him £8,750 in the days of golden sovereigns so his golden training fluid was both fitting and merited.

We much revere our sires
Who were a mighty race of men
For every glass of port we drink
They nothing thought of ten.

is as good a note as any upon which to leave the triumphant House of Peugeot whose first Grand Prix car had proved in every sense of the word a true World Beater, and if the 1912 cars have been little heard of since then may it not be that they have had no more worlds to conquer?

Not to be outdone by his colleague, Boillot met the visitors at Le Havre and then leaving after the Paris express drove W. F. Bradley back to Paris in his racing car 'in such time that we were able to wash, change, purchase bouquets of flowers for the visitors and drive in a taxicab to the Gare St. Lazare to await the arrival of . . . the express train. It was an epic run and one which probably would have been impossible for any other than a Georges Boillot, who not only knew how to get the best out of a car but had a highly developed road sense such as is given to few men.'

140 . . . 'Goux had spent a considerable time at Brooklands . . .'

141 The Sunbeam with (left to right) Bob Burman, Guyot, Ralph de Palma and Crossman

---

[1] *There seems a certain amount of doubt about the amount and the actual champagne. Al Bloemker insists this is factual and gives a detailed account in '500 Miles to Go'. W. F. Bradley denies the story, which he claims started with Hearst correspondent Burton's report of the race and the news photo of Goux's pit-stop showing champagne bottles being lofted and consumed. Bradley says the contents were water and that he had never seen champagne consumed during a race. This does not quite accord with the inference from the* Autocar's *comment on Resta refreshing himself with hot water during the 1913 Grand Prix (see infra page 69) and Peter Helck, puzzled by the contradictions, has written to me—'So . . . . I checked with Jules himself. It* WAS *champagne and he even remembered the brand! I personally doubt any such quantity as 5/6/7 bottles tho'.' And so do I. In a letter to Helck dated 2nd November, 1963, Goux wrote: 'Mais je peux vous affirmer que, pour la bouteille de Champagne ce n'etait pas de l'eau mais du vrai et bon Champagne brut que m'avait procuré avec des grandes difficultés Mr. Kaufman de New York le représentant de Peugeot pour l'Amérique.'*

142 SKY THE LIMIT? . . . 'no more worlds to conquer' for Boillot as he nears the summit of Mont Ventoux in 1912

63

Chapter Seven
1913 · Old Giveth Place to New[1]

The final nail was driven into the coffin of the Monsters when the A.C.F. announced their regulations for the 1913 Grand Prix which to the progressive Faroux atoned for 'les déplorables errements de l'année dernière.' Weight was to be between 800 and 1100 kgs. and cars were to be allowed 20 litres of fuel per 100 km. (about 14 m.p.g.). The race was to be moved from Dieppe to Amiens and early in the New Year great preparations were reported in train and enthusiastic sightseers were advised against visiting the circuit. Apart from anything else they might have interrupted the assiduous Boillot as he practised and practised over the circuit. Peter Helck tells of another innovation used by Boillot in practice—'a tape recording device for checking his precise speeds over every inch of the circuit. The subsequent analysis of these readings enabled that great master to exactly edit the Peugeot's power and braking potential and was reflected in the saving here and there of a second, at significant points on the course.'[2]

Peugeots were back in the lists with Boillot and Goux and a third car for one Delpierre who had driven in two Coupes de l'Auto without distinction save that in 1911 he had finished too late to be timed. In outward appearance the cars were narrower than the 1912 cars and the engine was reduced to 100 × 180 mm. (5654 c.c.) though retaining its characteristic mechanical features. Also in French colours were two newcomers to the Grand Prix—Delage and Th. Schneider. Two Delages of 105 × 180 mm. (6234 c.c.) were entered for Bablot and Guyot both veteran Delage voiturette drivers; the cars were bull-nosed and slightly higher than the Peugeots having horizontal overhead valves to give a simply shaped combustion chamber free from pockets. Like the 1911 Coupe de l'Auto winner, the new Delage had a five-speed gearbox. In their outward aspect the Schneiders were different from any of the other cars; their radiators were behind the engine, like the Renault, and the V-shaped sloping bonnet had a semi-human aspect, the open-fronted touch being reminiscent of the visored casque of a mediaeval knight. The engines were of 96 × 190 mm. (5½ litres) and four cars were to be driven by Croquet, Gabriel, Champoiseau and René Thomas. From Belgium came two Excelsiors of 90 × 160 mm. (6106 c.c.) to be 'steered', in the idiom of the times, by Christiaens and L. G. Hornsted; Germany sent Jörns on an Opel of 5021 c.c. (100 × 160) and Esser's outclassed Mathis, (70 × 140 = 2154 c.c.). After their defeat at Dieppe no Fiats came to the Grand Prix in 1913 nor Lorraine-Dietrichs though both firms had supported racing almost throughout the century.

Italy was however represented by three rotary valve Italas of 125 × 160 mm. (7853 c.c.), appreciably the largest cars in the race. Strike troubles at Turin had nearly necessitated their completion at the company's Weybridge Works and exhaustive tests had been carried out at Brooklands. The great Nazzaro was returning to Grand Prix racing to lead the team with Moriondo and H. R. Pope in support. Finally Sunbeam had taken the plunge into the Big League with an entry of four cars originally intended for Caillois, Resta, Rigal and A. Lee Guinness. An accident in practice for the Spanish Grand Prix eliminated Rigal and made way for his mechanic Chassagne. Rigal accepted this with both philosophy and sportsmanship remarking, 'I can only rejoice that my bad luck has given Chassagne his chance. You will find he will make marvellously good use of it.' Chassagne did indeed, but he did not have particularly promising material.

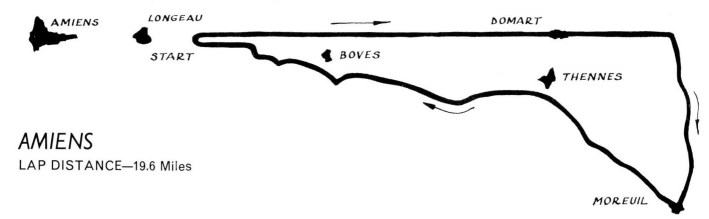

AMIENS
LAP DISTANCE—19.6 Miles

143 The Amiens circuit was different from any used in Europe and embraced several unpleasantly tight corners

[1] *The substance of this chapter has already appeared under the title—* The Forgotten Years *in the Bulletins of the English V.S.C.C. and appears by kind permission of the Editor.*
[2] *From* The Checkered Flag, *by Peter Helck. Used by permission of Charles Scribner's Sons, New York.*

The Sunbeams, although loudly acclaimed in the British press before and after the race, were rather pedestrian cars, being in effect, a 6 cylinder version, side-valves and all, of the 1912 cars, measuring 80 × 150 (4523 c.c.). They employed a solid rear axle and were reputed to develop 110 b.h.p. like the Italas, and to be capable of 103 m.p.h.

If Peugeot were still alone in their cylinder head lay-out all of the 20 cars were new and 8 different marques were represented, only one of them very slightly exceeding the size of the 1912 Peugeot and none employing chain drive. It was feared that the fuel limit would reduce speeds and,

TWO FRENCH NEWCOMERS

presupposing lap speeds of 80 m.p.h. for Delage and Peugeot, this would have meant their running out of fuel six laps before the end. Both cars were claimed to be capable of such a speed and it is not surprising to find the fastest race lap to be as low as 76.6 m.p.h. and the timed kilometre speeds appreciably less than the cars' known potential. This limit certainly made the competitors think; Sunbeam experimented with radiator blinds, and Itala conducted elaborate tests to see whether more fuel was used by keeping the engine running rather than switching off during stops.

The course, too, was different from any used previously for big racing in Europe, being of only 31.6 kms. (19.6 miles)

144 *The cockpit of Guyot's Delage*

146 . . . *'the great Nazzaro was returning to Grand Prix racing to lead the Italas'*

145 *Champoiseau's Th. Schneider with visored casque slides at Moreuil*

147 *THOUGHT PROVOKING FORMULA: Chassagne's Sunbeam receives its fuel allowance*

and had to be covered 29 times to give a racing distance of 916.8 kms. (560 miles). What Théry would have thought of such a circuit I dread to think in view of his reported remark on the 28 mile circuit chosen for a 1905 race—'as it appears that the circuit selected has only a length of about twenty miles he says that he is not disposed to risk his neck by turning like a squirrel in a cage.' The general nature of the circuit can be seen from the map; it embraced several unpleasantly tight corners, particularly two in the region of Boves, and the roads were also narrower and in poorer condition than those at Dieppe. All this is reflected in the relatively low fastest lap speed, for which fuel limits alone were not responsible. Amenities, too, were nowhere near Dieppe standards as many visitors found and none more than the wretched Itala team whose accommodation was so inadequate that they had to do most of their work at the roadside like so many gipsies. Sunbeams, with a French 'patron', had things much better organised in the Château de Moreuil.

The wind of change had not permeated as far as the hour of starting which was scheduled for 5 a.m. but a co-operative thick mist delayed matters for half an hour. With visibility about 300 yards Caillois was sent off on No. 1 Sunbeam at precisely 5.31 a.m. and the rest of the field followed as promptly as their evil-tempered engines would allow. Even wood and steel were beginning to rebel against the A.C.F.'s iron regimen.

Apart from the injured Rigal, Hanriot, Hemery, Duray and Wagner were notable absentees who had not previously missed a Grand Prix; in tragic circumstances there were no American drivers, de Palma having been seriously injured in the 1912 American Grand Prize at Milwaukee and Brown killed in practice. Like Goux, Bruce-Brown had proved himself a remarkably fine all round driver in road and track racing on both sides of the Atlantic, even contriving to win a Handicap Race at Brooklands at the 1912 Whitsun meeting on Gordon Watney's revamped 1903 '60' Mercedes reputedly the car with which Jenatzy had won the Gordon Bennett cup and at one time supposedly entered by Watney for the 1913 Grand Prix! I use the word 'reputedly' because of the belief that Jenatzy's car, although a stock '60' chassis did have an 85 h.p. engine in it. This originates in an interview given by Jenatzy to le Monde Sportif in July 1903. It is only right to say that all official records, including Gerald Rose's, give the engine as the normal '60'. In addition Scott-Moncrieff's exhaustive schedule of Mercedes cars[3] refers to several ratings for racing and touring cars in 1903 but no '85'. How wise Kent Karslake is to sound a warning against accepting the post-race evidence of competitors as 'gospel'. In two seasons Bruce-Brown had won 2 Grand Prizes, finished 3rd at Indianapolis and dominated the 1912 Grand Prix and his loss, following a burst tyre at the very beginning

148 IDEAL RACING MAN: Bruce-Brown after his last great win, at Savannah in 1911

of such a career was truly tragic. Peter Helck has written of him:

'Big in stature, strong in heart and hands with the requisite competitive spirit and a passion for thundering speed he was the ideal racing man in any period. For many close followers of the sport he was supreme.'[4]

Peugeot, too, had suffered a grievous blow some three weeks before the race in another tragic and needless accident. Zuccarelli had been testing on a long straight in Normandy frequently used by the team when the inevitable deaf and blind rustic had driven a hay cart out of a barely discernible side-turning leaving the driver with no escape. Thus it was that Delpierre found his way into the team and Peugeot lost a talented driver and an even more talented engineer. Strangely enough, nothing went wholly right for any 'Henry' design originated after Zuccarelli's death be the car Peugeot, Ballot, Sunbeam or Schmid.

At first sight one might have been pardoned for forecasting the result as Peugeot first, the rest nowhere, but the race turned out very differently. In the end the familiar pair of Boillot and Goux finished first and second but there must have been times when they might gladly have settled for the certainty of a place. The two Delages, in particular, proved formidable opponents while the Sunbeams ran so steadily as to be a constant danger should the least trouble befall their swifter opponents.

The mist was still thick when the cars started and Boillot and Goux did much to consolidate their success in those early mist ridden laps. In spite of the presence of the so-called Godfather of Carburation, Monsieur Claudel, many of the cars were very sulky in the damp morning and the Sunbeam driver Caillois assured an observer that he

[3] In Three Pointed Star.

[4] Op. cit.

noticed the difference 'the moment the sun peeped through the mist even for a few seconds.' Both the Peugeot stars knew the circuit intimately, but in a way it merely heightens their skill that they had so thoroughly memorized its every detail. By contrast Delpierre was slow off the mark and relatively swift to find trouble at the tricky Boves corners. According to the race numbers he started ten minutes after Boillot yet according to a report he is supposed to have crashed in an effort to *overtake* Boillot at a point about three quarters round the first lap, which occupied a mere 16 mins. 39 secs. of Boillot's time! It makes a delightful legend anyway.

The Delages crept very unwillingly to their work and could well be said to have lost the race by their indifferent performance in the early stages. With the exception of Caillois on No. 1 the Sunbeams ran like trains, although their solid rear axles gave them a skittishness on corners belied by their sober broadcloth appearance, for all the world as if Oliver Cromwell or Praise-God Barebones had designed a Grand Prix car. The detachable wire wheel having been pioneered in England, it is odd to find Sunbeams throughout 1911/13 sticking to the ponderous artillery wheel. Albeit Chassagne, Guinness and Resta kept a stranglehold on the places behind the leaders as they went up and down the ladder. If Peugeot had made the least serious slip it would have been Dieppe-1912 all over again and Mr. Massac Buist's dearest wish would have been realized.

Boillot led from Goux for the first two laps and even at this stage Chassagne on the leading Sunbeam was in 3rd was 38 secs. behind Boillot. The flying Georges dropped to 4th during the third lap and did not regain the lead for another fifteen laps. At first Goux stepped into the breach but as the mists dispersed the fortunes of Delages began to follow the sun and by the 9th lap Guyot had assumed the lead with Bablot in 5th place, just over 5 minutes behind the leader and Goux, Boillot and Chassagne sandwiched in 2nd, 3rd and 4th. Either Goux or his car could not have been in their best form for neither were a match for Guyot who made a tremendous effort between the 6th and 16th laps, all of which he covered in under sixteen minutes. By contrast Goux's fastest lap was 16 mins. 8 secs. one second slower than Chassagne's. Bablot was the fastest with 15 min. 22 secs. and his last nine laps were all under 16 minutes. Boillot, however, put in no less than thirteen successive laps in this manner in the middle of the race and was in fact steadily gaining on Guyot all the time, although his fastest time was 2 secs. slower than Bablot's record.

When Guyot first passed Boillot on elapsed time he established a lead of 2 mins. 41 secs. at the end of lap 7; nine circuits later Boillot had reduced this by 1 min. 25 secs. to 1 min. 16 secs. and as Guyot never bettered 15 mins. 43 secs. it was clear that Boillot would regain his lead by

. . . 'Chassagne, Guinness and Resta kept a stranglehold on the places behind the leaders . . .'

149 *Chassagne passes the pits*

150 *Resta on the circuit*

151 *Guinness passing Moriondo's Itala which has just been righted after overturning*

152 HAPPY WINNER: ... 'the mantle of Théry had fallen on a worthy successor ...'

153 UNLUCKY LOSER: Albert Guyot with Delage chief tester Achille Seuss

the end of 25 laps unless Fate took a hand. This it most decidedly did during the 17th lap when Guyot had to stop on the course for a wheel change. In his haste his mechanic Semos sadly contrived to be run over by the rear wheel and by the time Guyot himself had changed the wheel and brought Semos back to the pits the lap had taken over half an hour. The pit stop to take on a spare wheel and mechanic ensured that the next lap took 23 mins. 12 secs. and for one reason or another Guyot never broke 16 minutes for the rest of the race. During all this time Boillot had been driving a superb race pulling out everything he knew and his persistent effort was rewarded when he regained the lead on the 17th lap. Boillot found himself with a lead of 2 mins. 12 secs. over Goux at this stage, which he had almost doubled by the 25th lap, when he was obliged to stop for water. This nearly proved his undoing for the mechanic lost minutes finding the radiator cap, there being no snap-on filler, and Goux found himself within 6 secs. of the leader the next lap. Like all truly great drivers, Boillot could always produce that something extra when it was most needed and his last three laps were all accomplished in under 16 minutes; the 27th was his fastest in 15 mins. 24 secs. only slightly slower than Bablot's record.

But for Guyot's calamity Boillot in the ordinary course of events would have regained the lead during the 26th lap, on which he lost over 4 minutes, all of which he would have had to regain during the 3 final laps after his delaying stop. Even for him this would have been almost impossible and whilst Boillot's stop on the 26th lap was unlucky, Guyot's débâcle was nothing short of tragic and robbed the race of a Savannah-type finish. The final order was:

1.	Boillot	7h. 53m. 56·8secs.	72·2 m.p.h.
2.	Goux	7h. 56m. 22·2secs.	71·8 m.p.h.
3.	Chassagne	8h. 6m. 20·2secs.	70·3 m.p.h.
4.	Bablot	8h. 16m. 13·6secs.	68·9 m.p.h.
5.	Guyot	8h. 17m. 58·8secs.	68·6 m.p.h.
6.	Resta	8h. 21m. 38·4secs.	68·1 m.p.h.
7.	Champoiseau	8h. 44m. 37·2secs.	65·1 m.p.h.

Boillot thus became the first man to win the Grand Prix twice, and in successive years for good measure. The mantle of the then recently deceased Théry had fallen on a worthy successor. After his two slow laps Guyot never recovered his speed and could do no better than finish a relatively indifferent 5th, being caught in the final laps by his team-mate Bablot who finished the race with a sequence of very quick laps, the last five being of astounding speed and regularity:

15m. 29s.
15m. 27s.
15m. 27s.
15m. 25s.
15m. 26s.

That Bablot could put in speeds like this at the very end of the race underlines the claim of the Delage to have been the fastest car at Amiens even though it was beaten by both Sunbeam and Peugeot. The Sunbeams, too, were not without their disappointments; Chassagne had a trouble-free run never falling below 4th, thoroughly justifying Rigal's faith in him; Guinness ran between 5th and 7th until his accident on the 16th lap at Boves when he was lying 5th. Fortunately neither he nor his mechanic were seriously hurt though the car made a spectacular departure from the road. Resta was persistently delayed by a burst reserve oil tank, it being noted that the driver refuelled himself with plain hot water 'for the typical British method of motor racing does not call for the use of champagne nowadays.' Perhaps this was what Goux lacked!

Of the other cars the Schneiders ran steadily behind the Sunbeams; Jörns' Opel completed one slow lap, Pope and Delpierre did not manage even that. The other two Italas did no particular good and whilst Nazzaro had by no means concluded his Grand Prix career, Amiens was the swansong of the House of Itala. Finally the two Excelsiors were plagued with plug troubles and both Hornsted and Christiaens and their mechanics became so black as to be styled the Christie Minstrels!

Although the contest between Delage and Peugeot had at times been as close as anything seen in the Grand Prix, the 1913 event is not generally considered one of the classics in the series. The contest was unhappily not resumed in the Grand Prix de France at Le Mans in August, the Peugeots being non-starters 'au cas de force majeure' having reputedly in the meantime found American buyers. They met again in three American events in 1914 with results that left the balance of power rather on the Peugeot side. The Le Mans race was still of great interest by reason of Pilette's team of Mercedes cars which had been refused at Amiens ostensibly because they were not factory entries. Three Delages came to the line for Bablot and Guyot with Duray on the reserve Amiens car; the Mercedes were driven by Pilette himself (4 × 130 × 170 = 8.7 litres), Lautenschlager and Salzer (6 × 105 × 140 = 12.5 litres) and Elskamp on a private entry of a 1908 Grand Prix type car with Knight sleeve valve engine; two Excelsiors and four Th. Schneiders were back with their Amiens drivers and two relics of the Age of Monsters, Moraes' 1908 Benz and one Soldatenkoff reputedly on Théry's 1905 Gordon Bennett Richard-Brasier.

The six-cylinder Mercedes had the 75/80 aero engine with one overhead camshaft which had been developed during the previous year and the cars were all much larger than any of those at Amiens. According to A. E. Ullman the new engines were put into the old 1908 Grand Prix type chassis and it would be instructive to know their weight and fuel consumption as either of these factors could have accounted for their non-attendance at Amiens. In the race itself the cars ran steadily enough but never looked like repeating their 1908 triumph although both Salzer and Pilette pressed the winning Delages. Bablot in fact led the race throughout,

154 . . . 'Bablot (at Moreuil) who finished the race with a sequence of very quick laps . . .'

155 CHRISTIE MINSTRELS: Christiaens Excelsior at Boves

156 . . . 'the contest between Delage and Peugeot had been as close as anything seen in the Grand Prix . . .' – here Boillot leads Guyot past the stands

69

157 *Elskamp's Mercedes-Knight weighing in*

158 *and leading a Delage*

159 *Salzer weighing in*

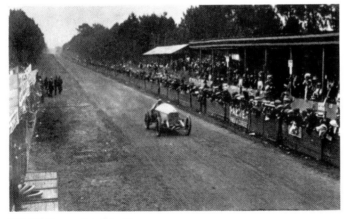

160 *Pilette passing the pits*

... '*No inkling of the* Furor Teutonicus *that was to come ...*'

although he actually shared it with Guyot and Christiaens on the 2nd lap; the Excelsiors had evidently found some speed since the Grand Prix but Christiaens' fine form availed him nothing for he stripped a timing gear and Gabriel displaced him. Gabriel's skill had declined little with the passing years; even though he did not finish, he, Bablot and Guyot were the only drivers to break 25 minutes for a lap.

Bablot stopped to change rear wheels after 4 of the 10 laps when the order was:

1. Bablot	1. 39. 4.	5. Lautenschlager	1. 48. 15.
2. Duray	1. 42. 38.	6. Salzer	1. 51. 16.
3. Guyot	1. 43. 54.	7. Thomas	1. 56. 7.
4. Pilette	1. 45. 57.	8. Elskamp	2. 0. 21.

All the remaining cars had retired by this time, including the veteran Brasier which burnt itself out on the 4th lap. Four laps later Bablot had a lead of 11 minutes over Pilette and stopped to change front wheels, and switched off his engine. Even in those times 11 minutes should have been a winning lead but the Delage then obstinately refused to start and for an agonising time it seemed that the unpretentious Mercedes come-back would succeed and Delage again be foiled. This time Fate intervened in a friendly manner—in the herculean shape of Léon Molon—Bablot's face lost its 'crispation' and the recalcitrant engine roared into life with its substitute mechanic clinging to the car for dear life as Bablot strove to consolidate his narrowing lead. Even for one 'd'ailleurs accoutumé à ces actes d'abnégation', the goggleless Molon must have endured dire discomfort on those two furious closing laps. Happily it was all in a good cause and Bablot crossed the line with nearly 5 minutes to spare. Ironically enough Pilette was attacked by tyre troubles on the last lap which let Guyot into 2nd place and made the final order:

1. Bablot	4. 21. 50·8 = 76·5 m.p.h.
2. Guyot	4. 26. 50
3. Pilette	4. 27. 53·6
4. Salzer	4. 34. 55
5. Duray	4. 35. 3·6
6. Lautenschlager	5. 13. 15·6
7. Elskamp	5. 18. 15
8. Thomas	5. 25. 55·6

Thus, after three years of patient endeavour the deserving Sarthe Club was rewarded with a race filled with interest and drama; less than 15 minutes had separated the first five finishers and speeds were such that Goux's 1912 Peugeot would have finished no higher than 6th, though in fairness it should be said that he was never pressed. Finally, Bablot had increased the lap record from Boillot's 80 m.p.h. to 82.5 m.p.h. The most interesting feature was the shy return of Mercedes; it had not been especially stirring and certainly gave no inkling of the Furor Teutonicus that was to come in eleven months at Lyons. It is unlikely that the real reason for their abstention at Amiens will now ever be known; several have been advanced:—

161 A COMPLETE TRIUMPH:
'Thomas' Delage was the winner . . .'

(1) *The cars were specially built for Le Mans in view of the formule libre (La Vie Automobile)*

(2) *The A.C.F. refused Pilette's entry as not being a direct factory entry (Pomeroy & King-Farlow)*

(3) *Mercedes deliberately refrained from making too public a comeback (Kent Karslake)*

The second accounts for their absence but the factory could easily have remedied the position had they wished. Kent Karslake's is probably the reason nearest the truth and is all of a historical piece with the carefully graduated return by the firm in 1952/3 before their Grand Prix cars reappeared at Rheims in 1954. The 1922/4 come-back cannot really be compared because the A.C.F. refused entries then from non-Allied countries.

Enigmatic abstentions seem to have been a feature of 1913 and it was not until 1915 that the three principal European contestants appeared in the same race—in the Vanderbilt Cup and American Grand Prize races at San Francisco. The Peugeots had reputedly already been sold to America, although the *Autocar* reported that they had been scratched at Le Mans because Boillot had a strained arm and the firm could not allow Goux to start alone! It is unlikely that they had in fact been sold at this time as the 1913 cars appeared at Indianapolis in 1914 as factory entries and the *Autocar's* report is probably nearer the truth, coupled with the fact that having won the Grand Prix

Peugeots had commercially nothing to gain and everything to lose by racing at Le Mans against strong opposition.

Emboldened by Goux's victory the Old World amassed a veritable Armada for the 1914 Indianapolis '500' led by the incomparable Georges Boillot in person driving a 1913 Grand Prix car with the faithful Goux in support. In addition there was a team of independents managed by W. F. Bradley consisting of René Thomas and Guyot on 1913 Delages and Duray on a 3-litre 1913 Coupe de l'Auto Peugeot. There were four other European cars, Christiaens (Excelsior) Chassagne and Harry Grant (Sunbeam) and Friederich (Bugatti); the first three were Amiens cars, while the Bugatti was a shaft-driven and enlarged version of the Garros 'Black Bess' type with a bore and stroke of 100 × 180 mm. = 5657 c.c. The Sunbeams were supposed to have been specially rebuilt for the race with 80 × 150 mm. 6-cylinder engines and only two speeds, the higher being 3 : 1. The three Peugeots are reported as having their left hand frame members fitted with lead to counteract centrifugal force on the high speed banked turns.

The race was a complete triumph for the European cars; Thomas' Delage was the actual winner, like Goux in 1912 bearing the number '16', Duray's little 3-litre Peugeot the hero in finishing second and Boillot the fastest on the course raising the lap record to 99.5 m.p.h. after qualifying at 99.95 m.p.h. In the early stages the Peugeots of Boillot and Goux made the running, but they soon ran into terrible tyre

162 EUROPEAN ARMADA: ... 'led by the incomparable Boillot (in car) in person with the faithful Goux (right of Boillot) in support ...'

A COMPLETE TRIUMPH

163/4 'Duray's little 3-litre Peugeot the hero in finishing 2nd (above) and Boillot the fastest on the course (below)'

troubles for which several reasons have been given and ceased to play any decisive part in the race. Goux must have gone very fast to finish only 14 minutes behind the winner in spite of many burst tyres and a stop at half distance to replace his front spring shackles. Boillot had a bad moment around the 400-mile mark when a rear tyre burst and wrapped itself round a brake lever administering the chassis such a shock that the frame cracked and he left the track. Chassagne had an accident when one of the welded steel wheels Sunbeams persisted in fitting gave way, and was at first rumoured dead (though these rumours proved happily to be greatly exaggerated).

René Thomas succeeded in winning most of the distance prizes apart from the 200-mile which went to Duray on the unbelievable 'little' Peugeot. The third member of Bradley's team, Guyot's Delage, completed the Independents' Grand Slam. Thomas did not lead throughout the race, having to give best from time to time to Guyot and Boillot besides Duray and also to the Mercers of Caleb Bragg and Spencer Wishart. He also had one anxious moment when his exhaust pipe broke loose during the race and another one after it when he found his winnings amounting to $37,000 delivered to him in the form of a cheque.

The race was an utter walk-over for European cars; six of the eight starters occupied six of the first seven places. As La Vie Automobile remarked, their clear-cut victory provided the complete answer to those who were all too keen to belittle the home products abroad. France had verily conquered, even though the official Peugeots had fared comparatively badly. Bradley provides the most convincing and authoritative reason for their tyre troubles. Originally, Boillot required the use of another tyre which cost nothing and gave a substantial premium, in spite of Goux's insistence on Palmers. Practice troubles convinced Boillot of Goux's wisdom and orders were sent to Victor Rigal to send over a consignment from England. Rigal disliked sea journeys and sent French Palmers from Cherbourg; while Delage with English Palmers had no troubles, the French version on the Peugeots was quite disastrous. Kent Karslake suggests the reason lay deeper—'it must be supposed that some feature of the Indianapolis track disagreed violently with the car's suspension.' This could be so, but the cars did go fast between their tyre troubles and, on balance, Bradley's seems a more likely explanation.

At all events Delage had his revenge for Amiens in a convincing manner, the final order being:

1. Thomas	6.	3.	46	= 82·47
2. Duray	6.	10.	20	= 80·99
3. Guyot	6.	14.	1	= 80·27
4. Goux	6.	17.	24	= 79·49
5. Oldfield (Stutz)	6.	23.	51	= 78·14
6. Christiaens	6.	25.	30	= 77·42
7. Grant	6.	36.	22	= 75·68

The Bugatti has been variously reported as leading, holding 2nd place and retiring in 3rd place after 425 miles, while the lap chart shews it retired after 335 miles when 13th!

The final rounds between the 1913 cars were contested in the Grand Prize and Vanderbilt Cup races in March 1915 at San Francisco. In both events Resta had a Peugeot, Newhouse a Delage, Marquis a Bugatti and de Palma one of the six cylinder Mercedes. Resta won both races, the Delage finished 6th in the Vanderbilt and was flagged off in the Grand Prize; de Palma finished 4th in the Vanderbilt and retired in the Grand Prize and the Bugatti retired insignificantly twice.

It is always difficult to judge works cars once they leave the care of their racing departments; when evenly matched, Peugeot and Delage each won one victory over the other, even though each race might easily have gone the other way with a little change in luck. When they lost works or semi-works status, however, the Delage did little good whereas the Peugeot won two races in very quick succession before retiring into obscurity. In all other respects, however, the 3-litre Coupe de l'Auto Peugeot was the outstanding car of 1913, both for the ease of its triumph at Boulogne and the manner in which it so successfully challenged the heavier metal at Indianapolis. On a circuit where maximum speed mattered less it might well have succeeded in winning outright and its appearance at Amiens would have been even more of an eye-opener than that of the Sunbeams in 1912 at Dieppe. In road-racing trim this car achieved a mean speed over a kilometre of 93.82 m.p.h. and 95.07 m.p.h. in one direction; in the 1913 Grand Prix the *Autocar* had the cars timed over a kilometre on perhaps not the most favourable section of the straightway, the fastest being Boillot at 97.62 m.p.h. and the best Delage 92.1 m.p.h. Amiens figures are a little misleading because of the fuel consumption limit and the Grand Prix car would certainly have the edge on maximum speed but in the 565 mile race over the twisting Amiens circuit anything might have happened. In fact the 3-litre car had been designed for the 1912 race, but the works had concentrated on the three Grand Prix cars and René Thomas on the single 3-litre had done no good at all. The design underwent detailed alteration before 1913 although the engine dimensions of 78 × 156 remained unchanged. Albeit the possibility is near enough to be tantalising that a thoroughly prepared and designed 3-litre Peugeot might have walked through them all at Dieppe or Amiens.

165 GREATLY EXAGGERATED: Chassagne's accident with the Amiens Sunbeam was not so serious as first rumoured

BEST AMERICANS

166/7 Caleb Bragg whose Mercer led on occasions (above) and Barney Oldfield whose Stutz was the highest home finisher in 5th (below)

73

Chapter Eight
1914 · Le Plus Grand des Grands Prix

On the idle hill of summer,
Sleepy with the sound of streams,
Far I hear the steady drummer,
Drumming like a noise in dreams.
                    A. E. Housman[1]: *A Shropshire Lad*

The success of the capacity formula in the Coupe de l'Auto between 1911 and 1913 had not escaped the notice of the A.C.F. and for 1914 they decided to break new ground by choosing a capacity limit for the first time—4½ litres being selected with a weight limit of 1100 kgs. A few cranks still hankered after another fuel limit but their complaints were fast swallowed up in the general approval which greeted this final blow to the reign of the large engine. It was successful too, for it was not until 1936 that a car as large as 6-litres re-appeared as a successful Grand Prix contestant, if one excepts the SSKL Mercedes as an overgrown sports car. Technical opinion forecast outputs of 140 b.h.p. and a

variety of dimensions for four and six cylinder engines though nobody seemed to fancy an eight: oh for a Bugatti-Peugeot! In fact 140 h.p. was not realised until the advent of the 5-litre Ballot in 1919, Peugeot and Mercedes, the principal contestants, being estimated to develop 112 and 115 b.h.p. respectively.

In the face of fierce competition from more traditional sites the A.C.F. finally chose the great industrial centre of Lyons. The hilly and tortuous circuit measured 23.3 miles and was the most arduous since the Auvergne circuit devised for the 1905 Gordon Bennett; it would clearly call for fast flexible engines, quick gear changes and superb road-holding and thus test the skill of engineer and driver to the utmost. The race was to be over 20 laps—468 miles—and was the shortest yet held and the cars were the smallest Grand Prix cars to date. The course, which is shewn on the map, began at the fork roads at Les Sept Chemins, 9 miles out of Lyons on the main road to St. Etienne; thence the cars ran first for five miles along the valley of the Garon, skirted

168 ROBIN GOODFELLOW: 'Sailer soon warmed to his task . . .'

[1] *Permission to reproduce these lines has been granted by the Society of Authors as the literary representatives of the estate of the late A. E. Housman and Jonathan Cape Ltd., publishers of A. E. Housman's* Collected Poems.

Givors and for the next eight miles followed the winding corniche road along the valley of the Gier, turning sharp right where this joined the main road again near La Madeleine. From here it climbed steadily up to what was called 'La Montagne Russe', a 6 mile straight of gentle undulations where the maximum speeds would be reached; this ended in a wicked descent by way of a couple of right angle bends and a hairpin picturesquely described as 'le piège de la mort' leading back to Les Sept Chemins.

Having chosen such a circuit the A.C.F. spared no expense to endow it with corresponding spectator facilities, the crowning glory of which was a superb grandstand costing reputedly £12,000. This palatial edifice provided a fortunate 4,000 with a view of the cars for about $2\frac{1}{2}$ miles as they swept up La Montagne Russe through the Jaws of Death on to the finishing straight. 'Thus', wrote St. John Nixon, 'each car could be seen in the distance approaching the first corner at high speed, slowing down, accelerating again, slowing once more for the final corner and then with a mighty burst of acceleration tearing past the grandstand.' Can it be that it is time the Grand Prix returned to the old Lyons circuit?

By contrast their conduct of the pre-race arrangements left much to be desired. First they gave competitors a bare 48 hours notice of the 2 days' official practice sessions; this, of course, made little difference to most of the continental participants who had long since carried out their preliminary tests on the circuit. The Opels had been fully prepared for at least six months and the Mercedes team were obviously not concerned to do anything but effect minor detailed adjustments during official practice. The English, however, were gravely discomfited; Chassagne put in three days' practice, Resta two laps and Guinness three quarters of a lap. Great confidence was expressed in the Vauxhall, it being reported that the weaknesses shewn up in the T.T. had been eliminated from the new cars and Mr. Pomeroy himself 'more confident than we have ever seen him on the eve of a great race.' In the event, the first of these cars was only ready a fortnight before the race so that the most novel cars in the field were also the most untried. Needless to say, Boillot had photographed every detail of the circuit in his mind by diligent practice, but even so he still thought it necessary to refresh both his memory and his stomach by driving his Peugeot to a luncheon engagement at Givors two days before the race when practice was normally forbidden. Need one add that at the conclusion of his luncheon he went home round the remainder of the lap!

The second shortcoming of the A.C.F. lay in their apparent inability to prevent the circuit from being victimised by scores of enthusiasts settling their private rivalries right up to the start of the race.[2]

Appropriately enough the first entry came from Alda—a car produced by the great pioneer Charron which had

LYONS
LAP DISTANCE—$23\frac{1}{2}$ Miles

169 SUPREME TEST: the hilly and tortuous circuit was the most arduous since the Auvergne and would test the skill of engineer and driver to the utmost

170 Wagner's Mercedes on the back leg

[2] *The ruination of the road surface before the Grand Prix itself was a practice that was seemingly endemic to the A.C.F. in the 'open road' period of the Grand Prix; in 1908 it was done in the G.P. des Voiturettes and in 1923 and 1924 by a Touring Car Grand Prix.*

171 THE FORK AT SEPT CHEMINS: Lautenschlager the winner – note the condition of the surface

172 . . . 'the winding corniche road along the valley of the Gier . . .' – Boillot about to engulf an Alda

173 Jörns who led the Opel team

appeared with very little success in the 1913 Coupe de l'Auto. To lead his team Charron had engaged none other than Szisz, who had won the first Grand Prix and followed it up with a second place in 1907. All France's Amiens representatives were in action again with teams of three. Peugeot had dropped the tardy Delpierre and retained their Coupe de l'Auto team of Boillot, Goux and Rigal. Delage, too, put their trust in familiar faces—Bablot and Guyot and, another great veteran, Duray. Th-Schneider re-engaged Gabriel and Champoiseau and brought in a newcomer Juvanon for René Thomas.

Italy came next in quantity with eleven entries from Fiat, Aquala-Italiana, Caesar and Nazzaro. The Caesars melted away as did two of the three Aquilas, the one starter being driven while it lasted by the then unknown Bartolomeo Costantini. Fiat had by this time mislaid their old drivers and uncorked one of their veterans in Cagno along with Fagnano and their English works tester, Jack Scales. Nazzaro himself led his own team of himself, Porporato and de Moraes. Germany's representatives were formidable: the Mercedes team was the maximum permitted, in which the Dieppe stalwarts, Lautenschlager and Salzer were joined by Pilette, their Belgian agent and Louis Wagner who had missed the 1913 event. Lastly there was a relatively unknown driver, one Max Sailer. Opels were making a third attempt again with Jörns, this time supported by Erdtmann and Bruckheimer. Since 1911 English participation in European road racing had been growing more and more serious, with very creditable results. On this occasion both Sunbeam and Vauxhall had designed new cars and entered teams of three; both factories relied on their 1913 Coupe de l'Auto drivers, Vauxhall adding the outstanding American Ralph de Palma. The lesser countries were represented by Belgium with a brace of Nagants, driven by Esser and Elskamp and Switzerland by the two Piccard-Pictets of Tournier and Clarke.

Thirty-seven starters there certainly were but at least a quarter of them were mere scaffolding. All four previous Grand Prix winners were driving, although only Boillot and Lautenschlager had any serious chance of winning. Gabriel, Bablot, Cagno, Duray, Jörns, Lautenschlager, Nazzaro, Rigal, Szisz, Salzer and Wagner represented the older generation of drivers; Boillot, Champoiseau, Chassagne, Goux, Guinness, Guyot, Esser, Hancock, de Palma, Pilette, Porporato, Resta and Watson the new. The rest were newcomers whose reputations were not fated to endure, apart from Sailer and Costantini.

The outstanding technical development was the adoption by Delage, Fiat, Piccard and Peugeot of front wheel brakes; on Fiat they operated simultaneously whereas on the other three front and rear wheels worked independently as on the old Austin Sevens. All the cars, even Mercedes, had shaft drive and all save Mercedes had cylinders cast in one block.

174 INTO THE JAWS OF DEATH – rode – Resta's Sunbeam, showing clearly the stands and their view of the road to and from Sept Chemins

Aquila had the only 6-cylinder engine; Fiat and Vauxhall were the nearest to being 'square' while the rest varied from 92 × 169 to 97 × 150 in bore and 97 × 150 to 93 × 164 in stroke, the favourite being 94 × 160 (Alda, Delage, Nazzaro, Opel, Schneider and Sunbeam). Peugeot and Fiat had the prettiest and most aerodynamic bodies, the Piccards and Nazarros also having pointed tails. With their marine-type steering wheels and ship's ventilators the Vauxhalls had a distinctly nautical aspect, but it was the Mercedes which made the greatest impression at the weighing-in

'Most striking in appearance were the white painted Mercedes, whose acute V-fronted radiators, straight line bonnet and dash, and curved pocket tail—gave them that complete-from-every-point-of-view appearance which gives such an individuality to war vessels of the British Navy and to many of the great railway express engines. . . . They have lines which a camera cannot portray; a white marble of one would be a priceless possession.'

Oddly enough the Mercedes were rather more traditional in aspect and design but this seems to have paid dividends as the four most individual cars—Fiat, Vauxhall, Piccard-Pictet and Aquila—did very little good. Tyre sizes varied little save that Mercedes and Delage chose a 135 mm. section for their rear tyres while the others favoured a mere 120 mm. Mercedes at 900 kg. were the lightest[3] Peugeot, Sunbeam and Delage weighed 10 kg. more with the Schneiders carrying top weight at 1050 kgs. so everyone was well within the

175 ANCIENT MARINER: the Vauxhall cockpit

176 . . . 'a white marble of one would be a priceless possession . . .' —Lautenschlager on the descent to Sept Chemins

[3] *This does not agree with the* Autocar, *Vol. XXXIII, p. 66, although this source adds that the weights quoted do not show dead weight as many cars carried an unknown quantity of fuel, etc.*

177 RECORD CLAN GATHERING: The Peugeots of Goux and Rigal weigh in—note the humps containing the fatal spare wheels

178 LYONS DISAPPOINTMENTS: Delage (Bablot–9) and Sunbeam (Chassagne–10) at the start

prescribed limit and there were no scenes like the frantic slimming of the Italas at Amiens.

Even in 1914 practice times had not acquired their present significance and although the Delage had the reputation of being very fast there must have been something decidedly odd about the timing as the cars never lived up to this either in the Grand Prix or anywhere else[4]. The English entry was regrettably very ill prepared which was a thousand pities as the Sunbeams showed outstanding form in the race and the Vauxhalls proved they had great potential in post-war Brooklands racing. Now that a Grand Prix has become such an every-day and well disciplined affair it is almost impossible to imagine the fervour aroused by one annual Grand Prix. Nobody near the circuit seems to have slept for nights and the whole area round the circuit was given up to fiesta; the only modern equivalent is perhaps the Le Mans 24-hour race. The scene is beautifully set by the *Autocar's* description of the Night before the Race from which there is space only for a few extracts : —

'Few who have not witnessed the scene on the eve of a great motor race in France can conceive of the noise which prevailed all day and all night before the race.... Just why so many hundreds of cars tore about screaming and blasting all night no one seemed to know but... (this) ... is a characteristic premonitory symptom of a great race in France and we should be seriously concerned for the virility of the nation did ... the people near a race circuit patronise their beds or make less than a perfectly gigantic pandemonium of noise all night long before the event ... on the course itself hundreds of cars of all sizes and ages were driven many circuits at wild speeds ... indeed some of the visitors may have had more practice on the circuit than many of the racers themselves. By the side of the road little camp fires burned and Chinese lamps swung in the wind disclosing merry noisy groups.... The roadside cafés were surrounded, almost besieged and the whole countryside seemed to pulsate with noise and to teem with restless people.... France had indeed organised a record gathering of the clan automobile which knows no country.'

Edwardian Europe was gathering for its last and greatest Motor Race, little knowing how long it would be before another Grand Prix was to be held. Perhaps the circuit was much the worse for wear by 8 a.m., perhaps there was no sleep for the spectators and perhaps it was all a little disorganised but, with all its faults, there was a wonderful air of uninhibited abandon about the old Edwardian motor racing which the present-day streamlined slick circus can never remotely recapture. This was what Rose put so movingly in the Preface to the 1949 Edition of his Record of Motor Racing:

[4] *Bablot was timed by an* Autocar *observer at 74 m.p.h. which he acknowledged might be an error but 'certainly not large if there was an error.' Vol. XXXII, p. 1252.*

'the man who never saw—and heard—the tremendous rush and roar of the Clément Bayard coming down the straight towards Dieppe at 100 m.p.h. . . . has missed something which modern racing cars and conditions can never again give him in the years to come.'

A full mass start at Lyons would have been the final touch and crowning glory.

As it was the A.C.F. had so far broken with tradition as to start the cars in pairs at half-minute intervals, beginning at the unusually civilized hour of 8 a.m. This was to avoid the overlapping that had occurred on the 'squirrel cage' of a circuit used at Amiens. Appropriately No. 1 off the mark was Szisz's Alda, not that he had any chance in a race which lay entirely between Mercedes, Peugeot, Sunbeam and Delage. The race proper began at 8.1 a.m. when No. 5, Boillot's Peugeot, left to the rousing cheers of all France; ninety seconds later Sailer made a fierce and brutal start on No. 14 Mercedes and soon warmed to his task[5] of harrying the very daylights out of the great Boillot. This he did to such fantastic purpose that by quarter distance he led Boillot by 2 mins. 44 secs. gaining furiously on every lap as the following times show:

	1	2	3	4	5
0801 Boillot	21'29"	21'19"	20'59"	20'49"	21'24"
0802·5 Sailer	21'11"	20'51"	20'28"	20' 6"	20'40"
Lap Gain of Mercedes	18"	28"	31"	43"	44"
Lead of Mercedes	+ 18"	+ 46"	+1'17"	+2' 0"	+2'44"
Gap on the road	−1'12"	− 44"	− 23"	+ 30"	+1'14"

Thus during the 4th lap Sailer had passed Boillot on the road and established a road lead of half a minute and an overall race lead of 2 minutes, which must have brought home to Boillot the enormity of his task. Even at this early stage it was clear that failing a miracle Boillot could not possibly make it three-in-a-row for Peugeot and that *for sheer speed on the Lyons circuit* the Peugeot was beaten all ends up.

These sorry reflections were to some extent driven underground by the retirements of Pilette after 3 laps, and of Sailer himself along the Gier valley stretch on the 6th lap with a broken connecting rod. His work, however, had been accomplished with devilish efficiency and even though no Mercedes came into his sight again he had ensured that Boillot would know no peace of mind for the rest of the race and that at the very thought of his unseen pursuers the great Georges would drive as only he could, straining every nerve to extract the maximum performance from an inferior car and the maximum advantage from his superior braking. The inevitable result was that his stops for tyres exceeded those of his strongest competitors and that his car finally broke under the strain, while those of the more temperate Goux and Rigal lasted the distance but way behind.

All this was perhaps not so readily apparent when Boillot assumed the lead on the 6th lap, with two Mercedes out

[5] *It is improbable that Sailer had specific instructions to do this; he just drove as fast as he could and his racing sense did the rest.*

179 INEVITABLE RESULT: . . . 'Boillot's stops for tyres exceeded those of his strongest competitors . . .'

BELGIAN EFFORTS

180 Elskamp refuels his Nagant (top); 181 André Pilette, Mercedes' Belgian agent, on the fifth team car is the last to start—note the dust masks

182 FORWARD LIKE ROBOTS: Salzer at the top of the descent

183 BRILLIANT FAILURE: ... 'Alas Boillot was fated never to finish his greatest race ...'—here he crouches in pursuit of Guyot's Delage

184 ... 'Coatalen had shewn himself their equals'—here Chassagne leads Goux

already; the nearness of Lautenschlager caused Boillot to make his 7th lap his fastest in 20 mins. 20 secs. increasing his lead to over a minute. This precipitated a tyre change as did his 9th lap of 20 mins. 23 secs. so that at half distance his lead over Lautenschlager was a mere 1 min. 9 secs. Goux lay in 3rd, three and a half minutes behind the Mercedes, Wagner was 51 secs. behind Goux and in 5th was Salzer with the remaining Mercedes another 64 secs. further astern. Now the gloves were really off and the Mercedes were at the throats of Boillot and Goux with no further interference from Delage, Sunbeam and Fiat.

At half distance came the routine Mercedes pit stops which compared sadly with their general race organisation and some of the French pit work. As a result Boillot found himself with an advantage of 4 mins. 7 secs. as he entered his 12th lap. At this stage Wagner showed his hand after a sluggish start when he had been delayed by an official. His stop had been accomplished rather more expeditiously than Lautenschlager's and this, coupled with three fast laps, brought him into 2nd place after 14 laps, 1 min. 36 secs. behind Boillot and 61 secs. ahead of Lautenschlager. Goux had now fallen to 4th over 2 minutes behind and with Salzer gaining on him. It was on this 14th lap that the famous 'duel' between Goux and Lautenschlager took place through the downhill bends to Les Sept Chemins when Goux tried the old trick of late braking to tempt the Mercedes driver into error. Wisely Lautenschlager let the Peugeot through and took Goux again on the straight and the merciless struggle continued. The 15th lap saw Wagner in the pits for a wheel change and Lautenschlager gained 11 seconds on Boillot; he was yet 2 mins. 28 secs. behind and there was still every possibility of Boillot holding out for the remaining quarter of the race. After all, it had taken Sailer five laps of unparalleled speed to establish a lead of 2 mins. 44 secs. when car and driver were fresh and was not this very situation as much meat and drink to Georges Boillot as had been the challenge of the Hundred Days to Napoleon Bonaparte a century before?

In fact, however, Boillot was beginning to feel the pace and did not succeed in breaking 21 minutes after his 13th lap, while Lautenschlager, Wagner and Salzer went forward like robots, the lap times telling the story painfully clearly:

	16	17	18	19	20
Boillot	21'39"	22'44"	21'20"	21'32"	—
Lautenschlager	21'16"	20'53"	20'33"	20'58"	20'54"
Wagner	21'13"	21'15"	20'58"	21'40"	21' 7"
Salzer	21'11"	21'14"	21'17"	21'22"	20'50"
Goux	21' 2"	22'57"	24'19"	22' 8"	22'

In the early stages Sailer, leading the field to destruction like Robin Goodfellow, had set the trap; ever since his retirement Boillot had been in the most fatiguing of all racing predicaments—the leader with dwindling resources and no hope of relief. Now in the closing stages the time was ripe for the trap to be sprung and in the end Mercedes won almost as they liked speeding up all the way, rowing down the more brittle Peugeot as one has so often seen the might of Cambridge cut through Oxford between Hammersmith Bridge and Mortlake.

Boillot had set out on his 17th lap with a lead of 2 mins. 5 secs. which dwindled to a mere 14 secs. by the following lap; on the 18th lap Lautenschlager regained the lead for Mercedes for the first time in 5 hours, and as the cars went on to their final laps there was no hope for Boillot who was then 67 secs. behind the leader and only 16 ahead of Wagner. Alas Boillot was fated never to finish what I regard as much his greatest race; his stricken car came to a full stop during the first half of the circuit with a malady variously reported as a seized engine, a broken propeller shaft, back axle or valve— it matters not which. For France Lyons was a tragic defeat but it had taken the strongest and best equipped racing team yet seen to defeat their great champion. The true measure of Boillot's performance lies in the comparative failure of his compatriots on Peugeot and Delage who could muster between them but 3 of the 30 fastest laps, a very different story from 1913. Delage are supposed to have made a last-minute adjustment to their valve-gear to their detriment, but this does not explain Goux or Rigal whose best laps, in any event, did not touch that of Duray.

The French failure was underlined by the fact that Louis Coatalen had shown himself at least their equal at producing the Peugeot type of racing car. The Sunbeams of 1914 were blueprints of the 1913 Coupe de l'Auto Peugeot, an example of which Coatalen had bought and copied slavishly after the race. Contemporary accounts speak of the excellence of the Sunbeam cars and drivers, particularly bearing in mind their lack of four-wheel brakes and proper preparation. Maybe H. Massac Buist was overstating the case in these extracts from his Gossip About The Grand Prix, but the promise of the 1914 Sunbeams is not as generally known as it ought to be

'So the Mercedes and the Sunbeams showing themselves the fastest cars on the course found themselves at a disadvantage on every bend by reason of the braking, though the brilliance of the British drivers enabled them to take those turns faster than their rivals and so reduced this handicap to a minimum.'

Buist reckoned the Peugeot brakes were worth anything up to a minute a lap to them and then suggests that a f.w.b. Sunbeam would have beaten them by a wide margin and even pressed the Mercedes. But all the while Mercedes could have fitted f.w.b., and then what would have happened? Sad as it may be that Sunbeam eschewed development along 6-cylinder lines, the fact remains that, Boillot's apart, their cars were as fast as any Delage or Peugeot and faster than all the others, Mercedes apart. In the race Resta held 4th place for the first four laps and was 5th, only one second behind

185 *CAT WITH CREAM*: Patron *at the wheel of Guinness' car*

186 *Resta who held 4th for the first four laps and finished 5th at 62.46 m.p.h.*

187 *SECOND ONLY IN INTEREST*: Cagno and Fiat make their comeback

81

Lautenschlager, at quarter distance. Between laps 7/9 Resta put in times of 20 mins. 45 secs., 20 mins. 41 secs. and 20 mins. 38 secs. and only Sailer (laps 3/5) and Boillot (laps 7/9) put in faster sets of three consecutive laps. Guinness had been 6th on the 6th lap and Chassagne, after a slow start, had risen to 7th by half distance. All this must have been a heartening as well as a tantalizing experience for the young Sunbeam Company, though nothing to their disappointment at Lyons ten years later.

Also well to the fore, if not in the running for the lead itself, were two other great rivals of the twenties—Delage and Fiat. Duray's best lap was his 16th in 20 mins. 57 secs., slightly faster than Goux's, and he had also held 3rd place for the first 6 laps and 4th for the next three before plummetting down to 11th and 12th place. Neither Bablot nor Guyot with best laps of 22 mins. 38 secs. and 22 mins. 9 secs. respectively came within hailing distance of repeating their Amiens performances. Ever since Nazarro's Year of Victory in 1907, Fiat fortunes had been on the decline, in spite of their American successes in the face of diminished opposition, so that their emergence in modern guise in 1914 was second only in interest to that of their great early rival Mercedes. By comparison it was not especially spectacular and certainly did not herald their supremacy in the early twenties. Solid worth rather than brilliance was the theme of Fiat at Lyons although the neat futuristic lines of the car with its simultaneously operated front wheel brakes and square-type engine gave it an air of originality. Kent Karslake attributes the square engine to the fact that Fiat had never favoured the voiturette movement, but then neither had Mercedes, who had the longest stroke, and the tallest car on record was not a Lion-Peugeot but the giant 300 h.p. Fiat record-breaker. Fagnano was the best Fiat driver rarely being out of the first ten till the last lap of all and holding 6th for much of the last part of the race, which must in some measure have redeemed the short-stroke school after the Vauxhall disasters.

But all this, and other fine performances such as Porporato's lap in 21 minutes with the Nazarro and the steady drive of Esser (Nagant) from 17th on the 1st lap to 6th at the finish, passed virtually unnoticed beside the great battle between Boillot and the Mercedes. The curtain on this motor drama fell finally when Lautenschlager crossed the line shortly before 3.15 p.m. thus making it at last plain that the incredible had really happened; the legendary and invincible Boillot had fallen and the hated Boches had gained as great a victory as Mercedes and Benz in 1908, only this time one team had finished—1-2-3 for the first time in the Grand Prix.

To forestall the inevitable witch hunt Faroux claimed that France had been defeated by minor pettifogging details and wound up with a characteristic flourish

'Mais pour Dieu ne recommençons pas le gesté enfantin et boudeur de 1909'.

Actually French reaction on this occasion was a burning desire for vengeance in the forthcoming Belgian Grand Prix, originally scheduled to take place later in July. It was, however, put off till August and by that time a struggle of a very different nature was being fought on Belgian soil between France and Germany and for the time being the Lyons Grand Prix was forgotten except in allied departments concerned with the development of aircraft engines. With commendable Gallic logic the French had decided that if the Germans were going to use their Grand Prix to perfect the means of their destruction they might as well derive some benefit from the proceedings so that the belief has developed that one of the cars was detained in France till the outbreak of war and an engine found its way to Rolls-Royce. In fact a maze of legend has grown up about the destiny of those five Mercedes cars, at least three of which are known to survive today, along with two of the Opels, at least one Peugeot and a modified Fiat. They began, when the Grand Prix had hardly finished, with Gordon Watney's alleged purchase of the winning car for the August Brooklands meeting at a price of £1200 and a whole chapter could easily be filled with them, all of which does nothing but bear out Mark Twain's old aphorism about the fragments of the True Cross.

A. E. Ullman has written that in a sense this German victory has remained unavenged to this day. It has also tended not to receive its full due from writers who have tried to explain it away rather than accept it at face value, largely because of the erstwhile obsession of technical writers with the progressive Peugeot theme in engine design. The myth of Peugeot invincibility during this period has indeed died a hard death, at the expense of the clean-cut razor edged racers from Stuttgart and their less inspiring but no less successful drivers. Notwithstanding their superior speed and overwhelming victory the idea has been fostered down the years that the Peugeots were the fastest cars on the course. This is plain nonsense as it pre-supposes that every Peugeot stopped at least once on every lap which is both unlikely and uncorroborated by any contemporary source other than one Major Galliot quoted by Pomeroy. As the Major was speaking at an interval of many years from memory and even misplaced the position of the timing posts in relation to Boillot's pits, we need not attach too much importance to this report. In any event this is now conceded by Pomeroy in later editions of The Grand Prix Car.

La Vie Automobile details Boillot as making 6 stops, and Pomeroy 8 and on the evidence of the lap times I incline to the view that Boillot covered all his 5 laps in under 21 minutes non-stop as well as his standing one of 21 mins. 29 secs. A possibility I have not seen canvassed is that the cars

may have made stops out on the circuit to change wheels for there is clear evidence that spare wheels were carried and replaced at the pits. According to La Vie Automobile, Boillot and Goux each took on one 'roue de rechange' during the race, so this line of enquiry does not take us much further. Faroux at the time preferred another view, blaming the narrow section of tyre and the choice of non-skid as opposed to smooth tyres. Yet, notwithstanding a 135 mm. section, Duray had to make four stops, as many as Goux and one less than Rigal. In the light of this Kent Karslake is undoubtedly right when he writes that if Boillot had been in constant tyre trouble it would have been most remarkable to observers.

Admittedly Boillot changed more wheels than Lautenschlager, but the likelihood is that Boillot's 'high-speed cornering and last-minute braking imposed such strains that failures were inevitable.' Boillot himself claimed to have been 6 m.p.h. faster on the straights and that his f.w.b. had enabled him to 'ridicule' the Mercedes on the corners, though apparently he was unable to do much about Sailer during the early stages or the other Mercedes later on. Boillot was driving all he knew that day but on a car that was not in the same street as the Mercedes and probably no better than the Sunbeams or Delages, on the Lyons circuit at least. Facts are unpleasant things but to anyone who had read the signs aright the Peugeot eclipse in 1914 should not have been too surprising but for the legend of Boillot, for the

victories in 1912 and 1913 had been close indeed apart from the Coupe de l'Auto. No doubt the 3-litre car would have been a winner in any year but by 1913 interest in voiturettes was waning and Boillot and Goux did not really have any pressing opposition. Goux himself has put forward another explanation that the streamlined tail, containing two spare wheels mounted lengthways behind the rear axle, caused road-holding difficulties at high speeds and stops to change types of cover and adjust pressures as often as worn tyres. This could well explain the poor showing of Goux and Rigal who decided that discretion was the better part. It is also likely that several of Boillot's closing laps were covered with a broken valve although his eventual retirement was attributed to several causes, all of which were possibly true. The theory of the broken valve certainly lends colour to the stresses imposed by Boillot's almost superhuman efforts to overcome the inherent weakness in his car.

Boillot had been superb and drove without question the greatest race of his life; as a motor racing tour de force it must take its place alongside such famed achievements as the victories of Nuvolari, Fangio and Moss in the German Grands Prix of 1935, 1957 and 1961, and the unforgettable occasion when Raymond Sommer passed the entire Alfa-Romeo team whilst refuelling to lead the 1950 Belgian Grand Prix on an antiquated Talbot. Much was expected of Boillot on that day and the measure of the German success is that not even his transcendent best was enough to bring victory to France. To have seen him at Lyons must be one of motor racing's most prized recollections and to have defeated him an equally prized achievement. Let us finish with this picture of Boillot driving his last race, which I recently re-read whilst listening to the slow movement of Beethoven's Violin Concerto and found somehow deeply moving

'The figure of Boillot will remain in the writer's eye for many a day; the lithe and shapely blue car, with its air of speed enhanced by the very attitude of the man himself, his hair streaked on his head by the wind, his tense yet easy figure, with a strong brown right arm always peculiarly visible over the side of the car . . . the man himself looks the spirit of racing. Boillot does not somehow suggest excitement in his driving but daring and dash.'

Whether the 1914 Grand Prix merits the title of the Greatest of All Time does not matter overmuch; it provided a magnificent and moving finale to the Edwardian era of motor racing. The entry in 1908 had been larger, better and no less representative and the racing in general closer, yet it is to Lyons that the eye of posterity has turned—partly for the glory of Boillot and perhaps also because the eye of hindsight sees the struggle that day on the circuit as symbolic of the age-old rivalry between Teuton and Gaul which was so soon to be revived and with such tragic consequences for France's leading competitor. Therein lies the true appeal of the 1914 Grand Prix and for this reason it has remained and will continue unique in its fame. Let Sammy Davis, himself a survivor of two great World Wars, who saw the race have the last word—written twenty years later

'There was something more than motor racing in the atmosphere as the crowds made their way dustily from the course. Never before had there been that curious indefinable feeling and everyone was extraordinarily quiet. Had the gift of foresight been ours, what, I wonder, would one have thought; as it was there was quite distinctly the feeling that a menacing though invisible presence had been manifest. The thing disappeared in an hour or two, normality returned; but though we knew nothing of it, there had come faintly on the wind the echoing thud of guns. The brooding shadow was death, the end had come to a generation. Never again would the Grand Prix seem the same. Castles in the air had vanished beyond return. The roads we had known were to see not racing cars but millions upon millions of men, to bear armoured fighting machines and countless numbers of guns. When next we saw the Mercedes Grand Prix engine it was in a fighting aeroplane—had in fact been the beginning of one before the race. Team headquarters, which were so pleasant a memory, vanished in a hell of shellfire, their shattered debris to hide the still more deadly machine gun. Men had reached their journey's end. Perhaps it was as well as we did not know.'

189 SPIRIT OF RACING: . . . 'the figure of Boillot will remain . . .'

Chapter Nine
1915/19 · Redressing the Balance

Although Europe was at war within a month of Lyons by no means the last had been heard of many of the cars or drivers in the Grand Prix. The great Mercedes—Peugeot rivalry was continued in various races in America in 1915/16 with Delage and Sunbeam in walking-on rôles; the Fiats, Nazarros and an Aquila re-appeared in the 1919 Targa Florio, as did a 1914 Coupe de l'Auto Peugeot. Some of the 1914 cars were considerably modified and even supercharged by Mercedes for races in the early and mid-twenties and a variety of these cars appeared at Brooklands during this period, though none seem actively to survive in England today apart from one Mercedes and two Opels.

The central figure in 1915/16 was Dario Resta with his Peugeot and the American results show that the 1914 Peugeot had the edge over de Palma's Mercedes and that Sunbeam were superior to Delage. For the most part these races were track events on board or brick and not particularly favourable to the Mercedes which had been designed for a slower type of racing. At Indianapolis the cars were very evenly matched and in the 300-mile Chicago event in 1916 de Palma and Resta raced neck and neck for 296 miles until the Mercedes had plug troubles. In a special series of sprints at Chicago the Peugeot was .6 m.p.h. faster. These and other results will be considered in more detail later but

190 CENTRAL FIGURE: Dario Resta at the start of the 1916 '500'

191 LONE STAR: de Palma's Mercedes which won the 1915 '500'

192 Porporato on the 1914 G.P. Sunbeam with van Raalte in the mechanic's seat

193 . . . 'a funny little old chain driven car . . . '—Marquis on a similar Bugatti at Santa Monica in 1916

in bare outline they hardly support Pomeroy's original contention, admittedly based on Major Galliot's inaccurate observations, that the Peugeot was inherently capable of lapping the Lyons circuit in 19½ minutes against Boillot's best of 20 mins. 20 secs. and Sailer's 20 mins. 6 secs. Whatever its potentialities on a fast circuit the Peugeot with its characteristically narrow power band had an inferior low-speed-circuit performance. It was a thousand pities the Belgian Grand Prix was never run in 1914 as the rules particularly forbade tails to project more than eight inches beyond the rear dumb-irons and 'Manx' Peugeots would have put Goux's theory to a practical test on a similar type of circuit. As it is the cars have yet to meet again under true road racing conditions and whilst such a contest is theoretically possible as at least three Mercedes and one Peugeot are known to survive, chance would be a fine thing.

Their first meeting at Indianapolis in 1915 produced a struggle every bit as epic as Lyons when Resta's Peugeot, supported by Bob Burman on a linered down 1913 car and Babcock on a 1913 3-litre, opposed de Palma's lone Mercedes. John de Palma had the 1913 Delage which had won in 1914, Porporato and van Raalte two 1914 Lyons Sunbeams, Harry Grant the artillery-wheeled 1913 car and one G. Hill, a 'Black Bess' type Bugatti, described in The Autocar as 'a funny little old chain-driven car' which cannot have amused Bugatti overmuch. The main American opposition came from three Stutzes, three Duesenbergs and three Maxwells, all built up to the limit of approximately 4.9 litres. Several of these cars had taken part in the Vanderbilt and Grand Prize races at San Francisco earlier in the year, when Dario Resta had been so conspicuously successful in winning both events with his 1913 Peugeot. As the races were of substantial duration and usually run off within three or four days of one another this was no mean test of endurance for car and driver and was, incidentally, the only time this car-and-driver double was ever achieved.

de Palma was fastest qualifier at 98.6 m.p.h. slightly slower than Boillot's larger 1913 Peugeot the year before at 99.9 m.p.h.; Resta was fractionally slower with 98.5 m.p.h. and then Porporato's Sunbeam with 95.1 m.p.h. Both cars made two pit stops, the Peugeot changing seven wheels to the Mercedes five and the Mercedes pit work was reported as the smarter, which probably sufficed to keep it in front. By contrast with Lyons the Peugeot was faster on the straight but the Mercedes was still better through the corners as might have been expected. Both cars were assailed by serious troubles in the closing stages; Resta's steering gear grew less and less effective and two laps from the end the Mercedes broke a valve. By this time de Palma had a safe lead and, unlike Boillot at Lyons, he managed to limp home without losing his place.

In the early stages the Stutzes, proudly labelled, with the

Maxwells, as America's first 16-valve cars, had hotly challenged de Palma and Resta, first Wilcox and then Anderson holding the lead but neither the Stutzes nor the Sunbeams had quite the speed to cope with the winner. Porporato managed to stay well up, being only nine seconds behind de Palma after 400 miles but the car was put out with mechanical troubles. Van Raalte was even more unlucky missing an almost certain 6th place due to losing bonnet straps and his magneto working loose. In finishing 10th, however, he was the only Englishman to be 'in the money' at Indy until Jim Clark's memorable drive in 1963. The American cars packed the places behind the European winners to give the home products much their best year since the early years of the event. Rather optimistically, as it turned out, the Autocar's reporter remarked

'The Mercedes and Peugeot ought to be good for racing in America during the present year but it is to be anticipated that the newer American cars will be too hot for these old warriors next year.'

In fact one or other of the 'old warriors' managed to win the race until 1920 and de Palma's winning speed in 1915 stood unbeaten until 1922. The final touch to the achievements of these magnificent cars was provided in 1949 when Lindley Bothwell entered a 1914 Peugeot and practised at over 103 m.p.h. though, needless to say, failed to qualify.

During June of the same year the 2-mile wooden banked track at Chicago was opened and battle was again joined over 500 miles between most of the Indy field with the significant absence of de Palma's Mercedes which could not be made ready in time. Average speeds were substantially higher than at Indianapolis and Resta won a close race by 3 mins. 23 secs. from Porporato's Sunbeam. The first four cars broke the then existing record for 500 miles of 94.74 m.p.h. made at Brooklands on October 1st 1913 by a 1913 Sunbeam, similar to that raced by Harry Grant in both 1915 track events. The winners in the two events were as follows:

INDIANAPOLIS		CHICAGO	
1. de Palma (1914 Mercedes)	89·8	Resta (1914 Peugeot)	97·60
2. Resta (1914 Peugeot)	88·9	Porporato (1914 Sunbeam)	96·50
3. Anderson (Stutz)	87·6	Rickenbacker (Maxwell)	95·80
4. Cooper (Stutz)	87·1	Grant (1913 Sunbeam)	95·06
5. O'Donnell (Duesenberg)	81·5	Cooper (Stutz)	94·09
6. Burman (1913 Peugeot)	80·3	Anderson (Stutz)	94·04
7. Wilcox (Stutz)	80·1	Alley (Duesenberg)	91·70
8. Alley (Duesenberg)	79·3	Chevrolet (1913 Delage)	91·60
9. Carlson (Maxwell)	78·9	Burman (1913 Peugeot)	91·20
10. Van Raalte (1914 Sunbeam)	75·8	Cooper (Sebriey)	90·30
11. Haupt (Emden)	70·7	Van Raalte (1914 Sunbeam)	

By the 9th October more Peugeots than ever before were in circulation and in the Astor Cup on this day no less than five took the field led by Resta, Aitken and Wilcox on 1914 Grand Prix cars, Burman on the 1913 Amiens car he had driven in the previous races and Ralph Mulford on the 1913

NEWER AMERICANS

194 and 195 The White Squadron Stutz of Earl Cooper at Indy in 1915 (top) and O'Donnell's Duesenberg in 1916 (bottom)

196 OLD WARRIOR: Lindley Bothwell's 1914 Peugeot when it lapped at over 103 m.p.h. in 1949

3-litre[1] which had been competing in the States since its defeat at Indianapolis the previous year. This race and several others of a shorter nature were run off on a 2-mile oval at Sheepshead Bay, Long Island, consisting of two ½-mile straights and two banked turns also of half a mile each, the banking being 25 feet high. The track was formally opened on September 10th when Resta covered 10 miles in 5 mins. 32⅘ (108 m.p.h.)—a new American record. In the eliminating trials for the Astor Cup the fastest qualifiers were:

Resta (Peugeot)	106 m.p.h.	1m. 8·2s.
Aitken (Peugeot)	105 m.p.h.	1m. 8·65s.
Oldfield (Delage)	104 m.p.h.	1m. 9·25s.
Burman (Peugeot)	103 m.p.h.	1m. 9·78s.
Anderson (Stutz)	102 m.p.h.	1m. 10·84s.
Romey (Stutz)	102 m.p.h.	1m. 10·93s.
Wilcox (Peugeot)	101 m.p.h.	1m. 11s.

The trials were marred by the fatal injuries sustained by Harry Grant, who had won the Vanderbilt Cup twice and had driven the old Amiens Sunbeam in 1914/15. On this occasion he had switched to Maxwell.

The Mercedes was seemingly still licking its Indy wounds and, although the 350 mile race was largely dominated by the Peugeots of first Resta and then Aitken, it was the American cars that eventually took the first five places. Throughout the season the home products, in particular the Stutzes, had been showing greatly improved form and Anderson it was who wound the year's racing up with a firm win, the first American car to win a major event in the States since 1911, except for Pullen's win with the Mercer in the 1914 Grand Prize where the opposition was very unworthy. As Anderson defeated no less than five Peugeots and two Delages, at least one being a 1914 car, the Americans were fast on the way to producing a racing car with a real hope of winning a European road race. The American formula catered for cars of 300 cu. ins. or 4916 c.c. which was slightly larger than the 1914 European limit so that the Europeans were at a slight disadvantage in races where maximum speed was a decisive factor. Besides the Stutzes, the 16 valve Maxwells and the Duesenbergs had also done well. The final result was:—

1. Anderson (Stutz)	3–24–32	= 102·6 m.p.h.
2. Rooney (Stutz)	3–25–29	= 102·19 m.p.h.
3. O'Donnell	3–39–55	= 95·45 m.p.h.
4. Alley	3–47– 3	= 92·52 m.p.h.
5. Henderson	3–47–26	= 92·31 m.p.h.
6. Limberg (Delage)	4– 9–23	= 84·22 m.p.h.

Fastest Lap: Resta @ 109·75 m.p.h.

Mortality was high and 14 retired including all five Peugeots and one Delage.

Later in the month Resta won a 100-mile race at the same track in 56 mins. 55.7 secs. (= 105.39 m.p.h.) fast, but just slower than Chassagne's 1913 record at Brooklands of 55 mins. 35.5 secs. (= 107.93 m.p.h.). Burman in a Peugeot

197/198 UNWORTHY OPPOSITION: The Oldfield-de Palma duel in the 1914 Grand Prix (top) and Carl Limberg's 1914 Delage (bottom)—note the tail and cowling added since Lyons. This car was 6th at Sheepshead Bay in 1915

[1] *This is not universally agreed. In the* Autocar *it is stated that as only five cars of one make were allowed, 'the arrival of Mulford's larger Peugeot from France forced out the 3-litre racer which was to have been driven by Hughes'.*

took 58 mins. 38.95 secs. (= 102.43 m.p.h.). In a 3-cornered match de Palma, with the record-breaking 12 cylinder Sunbeam, covered four miles in 2 mins. 8.6 secs. and six miles in 3 mins. 9.8 secs. defeating Burman's Peugeot and the Blitzen Benz. Finally, J. G. Vincent took a specially modified V-12 Packard round at 102.25 m.p.h. for a lap, the car being of 6916 c.c. (= 76 × 127 mm.). This car affords a pleasing illustration of the Biter Bit, for at the end of 1916 Louis Coatalen told the Sunbeam Company's A.G.M. that his own 12-cylinder car would have been marketed but for the war. 'As it was they sent it to America where it was bought by a firm of perhaps the highest reputation in that continent. In consequence that firm copied the engine and standardised the 12-cylinder car.'

The Stutz engine was made by the Wisconsin Motor Co. and was an interesting amalgam of Mercedes and Peugeot practice. It measured 97 × 165 (= 4916 c.c.) and reputedly developed over 130 b.h.p. (26.5 h.p. per litre) peaking at around 3,300 r.p.m. In comparison the Mercedes developed 115 b.h.p. at 2800 r.p.m. giving about 25.5 h.p. per litre. The valve operating gear, rockers and camshaft design followed Mercedes, and the camshaft drive Peugeot. Four valves per cylinder and 1 o.h.c. were adopted together with a crankshaft divided at the centre and run in three ball bearings. Wet sump lubrication and a one-piece block were employed. At its best the car was slightly slower than the fastest Peugeots but quite capable of winning if any ill overtook them.

Following the Peugeot disaster in the Astor Cup, Resta came back to Europe to replenish his spares with a reputed £7,550 in winnings, compared with those of Anderson (Stutz): £7,400, Cooper (Stutz): £6,150, Rickenbacker: £4,800 and O'Donnell £3,800. In the round the Peugeot was much more successful than any other car including de Palma's Mercedes and, in addition to these wins, Resta had already dominated the 1915 Grand Prize and Vanderbilt Cup events with the 1913 Amiens car. With less need for low speed torque the Peugeot was just the better car and de Palma's car very rarely came out at all. In 1915 the Sunbeams gave a fair account of themselves, but again were never really up to the Peugeots and the only cars to beat them convincingly were the Stutzes.

For the following year there was little new on the American scene apart from a team of special Sunbeams. If the *Autocar*[2] is to be believed the 6-cylinder engines were originally intended for the 1914 Grand Prix and three cars were scheduled for completion. The engines were presumably enlarged to the American 300 cu. in. limit and measured 80 × 156 = 4915 c.c.[3]; the last 6-cylinder car had been the

[2] Page 538, Vol. 36. '*Two years ago . . . the Sunbeam Motor Co. built a set of special engines which were to have been fitted to their racing chassis. Unfortunately the time between T.T. and Grand Prix was too little to allow of any change in the engine . . . . Now and then the tension (of war) . . . has relaxed allowing half forgotten engines to be brought out and tuned up.*'

[3] *Other sources give 81·5 × 157 mm. (British Competition Car, p. 46).*

199 Hughie Hughes (No. 11) with the 12-cylinder Sunbeam at the start of the Corona Road Race

200 Bob Burman with Blitzen Benz

201 SPECIAL SUNBEAM: Former Excelsior driver Christiaens with mechanic Frank Hill in the 4.9-litre Indy car

202/203 (top) the start of the 300-mile race with de Palma (No. 10–Mercedes), Christiaens (No. 6–Sunbeam) and Resta (No. 2–Peugeot) (bottom) Christiaens just makes the flag after 100-mile race with Jimmy Murphy

204 A Sheepshead Bay line-up with (left to right) Christiaens, Aitken, Rickenbacker and de Palma

4½-litre side-valve measuring 80 × 153 mm. for the 1913 Grand Prix. The new cars employed twin overhead camshafts, ball bearings for the mains and four valves per cylinder. Two wheel brakes and a transmission brake were fitted as well as a pointed-tail, staggered 2-seater body. In fact the car did not live up to its promise and failed 'to show the American manufacturers that there is much difference between the machines of the Grand Prix which last year they competed against and the same design improved.'

One of these cars started at Indianapolis on May 30th driven by Christiaens and was opposed by no less than four 4½-litre Peugeots in the hands of Resta, Mulford, Aitken and Merz and the two Lyons Delages of Oldfield and le Cain. The race was cut to 300 miles and resulted in a fairly easy win for Resta, showing that there was still little wrong with the Old Warriors. Speeds were slow, particularly in view of the shorter distance and I am inclined to accept the reason given by Pomeroy that the event was stopped through rain making the track dangerous, although other accounts claim the weather to have been hot and dry on race day. Shades of Diodorus Siculus! For the first time since 1913 an American car achieved 2nd place, the first five being:

1. Resta	2. d'Alene (Duesenberg)	3. Mulford
4. Christiaens	5. Oldfield	

Significant absentees were the White Squadron Stutzes and the white Mercedes of de Palma. It is said that de Palma tried to raise excessive starting money by withholding his entry and in the end found his bluff called and his entry refused. Be this as it may he brought the Mercedes out of its seclusion for the Chicago '300' a few weeks later where Resta won again (but only after a desperate battle with de Palma) at the record speed of 98.61 m.p.h. by 1 min. 54 secs. from the Mercedes. With only four miles to go and a short lead the Mercedes had a plug failure and Resta just scraped home. Third, apparently with plenty in hand and closing on the Mercedes, was Christiaens in the Sunbeam at 95.78 and Cabria on the other Sunbeam was fifth at 94.54 m.p.h.

Thereafter the two great adversaries steadfastly avoided each other in long distance events, although the Peugeot won three short match races against the Mercedes. On the 15th July Resta won the 150 mile event at Omaha at 99.02 m.p.h. and de Palma the 50 mile at 103.45 m.p.h. and later in the year Aitken scored a double for Peugeot at Sheepshead Bay.

The last of the 'pre-war' racing took place over the 8.4 mile road circuit at Santa Monica on 16th and 18th November for the Eleventh Vanderbilt Cup and Seventh Grand Prize races. These were both for 300 cu. in. cars over the same circuit as had been used for the events in February 1914 when they were still dominated by the great chain driven racers. Resta was all out to repeat his great double of February 1915. On the 16th November he won his third successive road classic at 86.98 m.p.h. by 7 mins. 56 secs. from Cooper's Stutz. Aitken on the other 1914 Peugeot retired on the 20th of 35 laps with a broken valve and a hard day's work ahead of him to be on the starting line for the Grand Prize.

This was over 48 laps and it was not Resta's lucky day for once. Howard Wilcox added his Peugeot to those of Aitken and Resta. Tragedy brought Aitken down during the very first lap this time with a broken piston and the American championship at stake. Resta, however, forged ahead until he had ignition failure on lap 19 and Wilcox took over the lead. A rather undignified series of manoevres then ensued between Resta and Aitken, his nearest challenger for the richly endowed A.A.A. championship. First Aitken took over from Wilcox and then Resta tried to buy Cooper's Stutz (lying 2nd) after having protested unsuccessfully against Aitken's take over! Aitken ran out winner at 85.59 m.p.h. by 6 mins. 12 secs. from Cooper's Stutz but Resta remained champion as the A.A.A. declared Wilcox winner of the Grand Prize. At all events the two seasons had been very largely a triumph for the Peugeot cars, a triumph that was to be renewed when the Victory Sweepstakes were run off in 1919, the last great Peugeot win in motor racing.

The 1917 '500' would have been an interesting event as a team of re-vamped Lyons Fiats were entered and their meeting with Mercedes, Peugeot, Delage and Sunbeam promised well. As it was the '500' went into cold storage till May 30th 1919. Within a fortnight of the Armistice, French circles were prophesying the return of the Grand Prix if the manufacturers approached the Commission Sportive—W. F. Bradley's idea being to hold the event in Alsace-Lorraine to celebrate its restoration to la belle France. There was even talk of a British Victory Road Race 'on Gordon Bennett lines' in that golden summer of 1919, whilst the press were expatiating on the scandal of the rotting military surplus cars in Cumberland Market and Kempton Park Racecourse. Evidently the post-1918 vacuum did not throw up too many scrap dealers in war surplus.

Whilst Brooklands and most of Europe languished in inactivity, de Palma was busy breaking records at Daytona in February with a V-12 Packard and in March 1919 a stout trinity of French drivers, Bablot, Guyot and Thomas made their way across the Atlantic to join in the American fray. All this time intense activity was going on in the Ballot works to produce Monsieur Henry's answer to the post-war challenge—the Hundred-and-One-Day miracle of a straight-eight 5-litre Ballot. Ernest Ballot was a dour French marine engineer who is supposed to have decided to build his car on Christmas Eve 1918. At all events a team of four cars took ship from le Havre on 26th April, 1919 to be driven by Bablot, Guyot, Thomas and Wagner. Both Packard and Duesenberg had also produced cars for the event; the latter

205 Cooper's Stutz passes Aitken's disabled Peugeot in the 1916 Vanderbilt Cup, the last for 20 years

206 A revamped Lyons Fiat of the type entered for the 1917 '500'

207 101 DAY MIRACLE: Louis Wagner with the 5-litre Ballot which set a new lap record at Indy of 104.7 mph

208 *'Willcox was not seriously challenged . . .'*

was a straight-eight, but the Packard was something new in 'formula' motor racing—a V-12. Both Henry and Duesenberg had come into contact with Bugatti's straight-eight aero engine during the war and the lesson had not been lost on either of them. Their main 4-cylinder rivals were the Chevrolet-designed Frontenacs, the old Stutzes, one of which was masquerading as a Durant Special, and the five Peugeots of Wilcox, Klein and Goux (1914 Lyons), Howard (1913 3-litre) and André Boillot on a 1914 2½-litre designed for the Coupe de l'Auto that never was. On 21st May 1916, the great Georges had flown to his death over Verdun and another brother having been killed in the infantry, it was left to André Boillot, the youngest brother, to carry on the great traditions of his family. Although he was lying 4th (or 3rd on some accounts) a mere 22 miles from the end with a car half the size of most of its competitors, the new Boillot's greatest hour was yet to come with this same car which had been used throughout the war by Georges Boillot and Charles Faroux, having thus covered 200,000 kilometres by the time it came to be raced! The Frontenacs, designed and driven by the Chevrolet brothers, were notable for their solid rear axles and extensive use of aluminium. Like the Stutz Wisconsin, their engines were an amalgam of 1914 Mercedes and Peugeot practice in principle—dry-sump lubrication, ball-bearing crankshaft with a single overhead camshaft operating four valves per cylinder driven by bevel gearing and a vertical shaft. The engine was cast in one block, measuring 98.5 × 162 (4915 c.c.) and supposedly developed 135 to 140 b.h.p. The result of the use of aluminium was reflected in a weight of 14¼ cwt. compared to the 20 cwt. of Wilcox's Peugeot.

The Duesenberg was a new straight-eight, using a single overhead camshaft and three valves per cylinder, even in 1919 a well-defined Bugatti practice, although, following his experience with the eight and 16 cylinder Bugatti aero-engines, Duesenberg had discarded Bugatti's hit-or-miss lubrication methods.

Like the Bourbon monarchs Henry learnt and forgot nothing, or as Pomeroy puts it—'Henry sowed but did not reap so far as the eight-cylinder in-line engine was concerned.' Personally I beg leave to doubt if he even sowed this engine design to any great extent for his Ballot was basically a rehash of the old Peugeot cars, with its transverse bolster fuel tank behind the driver somehow underlining its fundamental lack of basic originality. In the race the cars were unlucky as they were found to be overgeared, so smaller American wheels and tyres were fitted as they had no spare ratios with them—a surprising omission in a team of cars reputedly costing £30,000 to build. The smaller wheels gave constant trouble and possibly cost them the race.

The early part of the race was dominated by a struggle between de Palma and Gaston Chevrolet with Wilcox's Peugeot and Cooper's Stutz next up. de Palma led at 150 miles at the record speed of 92 m.p.h. and it looked as if his 1915 record with the Lyons Mercedes would at last fall. When a pit stop delayed him, Chevrolet went ahead, still at over 90 m.p.h. but he too fell back at the 200 mile mark. At half distance Louis Chevrolet led from Wilcox by 1 min. 50 secs. followed by de Palma, Hearne (Durant/Stutz) and Gaston Chevrolet. 1919, however, was not the Chevrolets' year and soon after half distance Wilcox went into a lead he was not to lose again. At one stage Earl Cooper on another Stutz was close to Wilcox but valve troubles delayed him and Wilcox was not seriously challenged for the rest of the race. He finished after 5-40-42.87 at an average of 87.95 m.p.h. adding yet more lustre to the car formerly driven by the late Johnnie Aitken; his speed, however, was still nearly 2 m.p.h. slower than the Lyons Mercedes in 1915. This car was again a regrettable absentee, one of its team-mates, reputedly the Lyons winner,[4] having been sold shortly before the race to Baron Petiet for £2,500.

The Final result was:—

1. Peugeot 1914 4½ litres (Wilcox)	5–40–42·87	
2. Durant/Stutz 1915 4·9 litres (Hearne)	5–44–29·04	
3. Peugeot 1914 4½ litres (Goux)	5–49– 6·18	
4. Ballot 1919 4·9 litres (Guyot)	5–55–16·27	
5. Bender (Alley)	6– 5– 3·92	
6. Frontenac 1916 4·9 litres (L. Chevrolet)	6–10–10·64	
7. Packard 1917/19 4·9 litres (R. de Palma)	6–10–10·92	

Goux's car had been fitted with a Premier engine during practice which was an exact copy of the Peugeot; although many miles behind, the Frontenac/Packard fight, which had so dominated the first half of the race, still held the crowd to the very end, Chevrolet winning by the finical margin of

[4] *As to this Gordon Watney was also under the impression in July, 1914, that he had bought the winner. W. F. Bradley, in* Motor Racing Memories, *claims the Baron's car was actually the one driven by Sailer and that in 1930 the Baron gave it back to Mercedes-Benz for their Stuttgart Museum (pp. 134/5).*

209 Louis Chevrolet's Frontenac

.28 secs. The Ballots fared ill, Wagner and Chassagne/Bablot both coming to grief and Thomas finishing 11th, although Thomas achieved a new record lap at 104.7 m.p.h. making the cars clearly the fastest on the course. This must have been some consolation to Marshal Foch who watched the race as one of the highlights of a victory tour of the United States, and one hopes enjoyed it as much as the Huitres Foch created for him in New Orleans.

A minor mystery of the Sweepstakes concerns the British Sunbeams entered for Resta and Chassagne. They were very similar to the 1916 cars but were reported as having a slightly larger bore of 81.5 mm. with the same stroke of 156 but the apparently lesser capacity of 4883 c.c.[5] According to one view the cars were found to be four cubic inches oversize on measurement, according to another, cited by Pomeroy, they were withdrawn 'because Resta's report on the torsional oscillations in the crank at 2500 r.p.m. was decisive.' When one remembers that the cars had allegedly been thought up for the 1914 Grand Prix and raced in America in

1916, it all adds up to a very odd tale! At least one chassis was made into a very desirable four-seater tourer; two engines found their way into the chassis of the 1921/2 3-litre cars and took part in the 1922 Coppa Florio, and one was later used for motor boat racing. The various discrepancies in engine size favour a theory that the Sunbeam engineers were caught napping, or at any rate did not show Augie Duesenberg's presence of mind, when confronted with a similar situation, when an official measured one cylinder and multiplied it by the number of cylinders to arrive at the conclusion—'Oversize'. Duesenberg bade him measure each cylinder explaining—'if we score a cylinder we do not rebore the entire block, but merely work on the defective cylinder and adjust the weights. In that way we keep within the limits.' With six cylinders and an engine possibly enlarged from its original state such a situation could well have arisen. I am disinclined to accept the suggestion of mechanical trouble in a design already tested in a season's racing in America in 1916.

[5] *See p. 89 supra.*

Chapter Ten
1919/20 · A New Boillot

210 ONE SPEECH HAMILTON: André Boillot with his remarkable 2½-litre Peugeot

211 SURPLUS POWER: Thomas had little chance to use the full power of the Ballot in the Targa although he set up a new lap record at Indianapolis with the car

Europe had endured over four years of total war on a scale of unprecedented ferocity and, when it came to organising races, lacked the resilience of the new world. There was much enthusiasm but, with factories undergoing conversion, there were few practical prospects of new racing cars in 1919. Indeed the French Chambre Syndicale and similar trade bodies went so far as to advise members that no competitions would be sanctioned for 1919 to give the industry a chance to recover its breath. Similarly, a petition in England to hold a stock car race in the Isle of Man met with little favour from manufacturers. The prevailing form of motoring sport seems to have been 'tractor management'—a poor substitute for Lyons 1914, though this pleasing rustic diversion might be seen to contain the embryo of the modern trial.

In 1919, as now, the Targa Florio had the distinction of being the oldest extant motor race in the world and Count Florio determined that, Come Hell or High Water, his race would be revived in 1919 even if it were held on mid-Winter's day. In the event, all these elements had their place in the 1919 Targa which was run off on November 23rd over the traditional circuit, though shorn of 26 of its 93 miles, which had to be covered four times for a total distance of 268 miles. The race shares with the 1933 Pau Grand Prix the distinction of being run in snow, for the night before the race a violent storm had drenched the low-lying coastal areas and laid a two-inch carpet of snow in the Madonie mountains.

When Florio first organised the Targa in May 1906 it was said that his remarkable circuit 'out-Auvergned the Auvergne in the matter of twisting hills and hairpin bends', but since 1908 its importance had been sadly on the decline. Now it was about to enter upon its Golden Age and European road racing could have had no more dramatic curtain-raiser than the 1919 Targa Florio. Even already the event seems so lost in the mists of time in that no two sources agree on the number or identity, let alone spelling, of the competitors.

The only new car of any note was René Thomas' Indianapolis Ballot, specially fitted with four-wheel brakes and fresh from winning the Gaillon Hill Climb. The entry was made so late that Thomas had to drive it all the way from Paris to Naples,—a sobering thought in these times when even trials cars are so special that they are frequently transported to events. It must have been pretty sobering at the time for poor Thomas too, as the roads in Italy were so bad that at one point he had to wait while scaffolding was put up to replace a road which had been washed away. Thomas' principal opponents were a pair of the revised Lyons Fiats in the hands of Antonio Ascari and Count Masetti and André Boillot's 1914 Coupe de l'Auto Peugeot, all fitted with four-wheel brakes. Other pre-war survivals were a pair of rotary valve Italas from the Amiens race driven by Moriondo and Landri, the 1914 Aquila of the younger Masetti, Baldoni and Negro on 1914 Nazzaros, Lopez on a similar Fiat, and one

Reville on a second 2½-litre Peugeot. The rest of the field comprised Alfas, Diattos, C.M.N., Eric Campbells, Lancia and Gallanzi, the only drivers of note being Campari (Alfa), Ferrari (C.M.N.) and Scales (Eric Campbell). At that time, in spite of Lancia, Cagno, Minoia and Nazzaro, the great Italian motor racing tradition was still in its infancy; the renowned name of Ascari was just beginning to be known in Italy as a successful and amateur hill climb driver; Enzo Ferrari was driving his first big race, and although that of Campari had been bracketed with Alfa in the 1914 Targa, both were still obscure.

Promptly at 7 a.m. the pitiless starter sent Enzo Ferrari on his cheerless way, followed at 3-minute intervals by the other competitors. Although he started 7th, René Thomas was round first in 1 hr. 58 mins. 25 secs. a remarkable time considering the car had been designed for Indianapolis and, like most 'Henry' cars, had a characteristically narrow power band—to say nothing of the atrocious conditions. However, when all the times were posted it was seen that Boillot's remarkable Peugeot was in the lead with a time of 1 hr. 54 mins. 36 secs. with Gamboni (Diatto) third in 2 hrs. 8 mins. 11 secs. and Count Masetti (Fiat) fourth 14 secs. later. This lap of Boillot's turned out to be the fastest of the day and, even allowing for the fact that Thomas had little or no chance to use the full power of his car, Boillot's drive has taken its place as one of the epic drives in racing history. Not even the Great Georges had ever done anything finer as W. F. Bradley was quick to state in his report of the event:

'Georges Boillot had the reputation of being the most skilful and the most daring driver in the world. His brother André has shown that he has the same qualities with a recklessness which even his brother did not possess ... his only hope of victory lay in taking chances which no other man would take; this display was so thrilling that it is to be hoped for his own sake ... he will not repeat it.'

Like the proverbial 18th century Member of Parliament who won the nickname 'One Speech Hamilton', André Boillot never again put up a similar performance, seemingly having burnt up his entire quota of fire and luck in eight dramatic hours over the Sicilian mountains.

The fiery Ascari had left the line at great speed and gave a striking foretaste of his ability by covering the 31 kilometres between Cerda and Caltavuturo in three minutes less than Thomas. Unhappily he had not then learnt to temper fire with discretion and, shortly after, overdid things to end his race thirty yards down a ravine. There, but for the thousandfold Grace of God, would also have gone André Boillot who made at least six dramatic departures from the circuit during his drive, one of which is depicted in a Gordon Crosby drawing when at the end of the first lap he skidded, struck a bank, leapt three feet in the air, dropped on to two wheels, tottered for a second and was only prevented from falling

212 *Great veteran Henri Fournier, who died in December 1919, here shewn on the Mors with which he dominated racing in 1901*

200 feet by a pile of stones! His final departure was equally dramatic in character. Thomas, still behind on time, had broken his differential on the last lap and, although he must have overtaken his principal adversary, Boillot pressed on with undiminished verve towards the finish only to find his victorious passage barred by a solid wall of spectators opposite the Tribunes. Almost miraculously he had sufficient brakes to pull up, but not before the car had spun three times and crashed into the grandstand. For the sixth time (at least) the exhausted crew leapt out, restored the errant car and crossed the line—but in reverse, thereby entailing disqualification. Ernest Ballot himself is reported as putting the crew back in their car and despatching them back to their point of departure where they turned round and crossed the line once more—this time the right way! Then, as if to add a final coup de théâtre, he collapsed over the steering wheel with a cry of 'C'est pour la France!'—another touch never rivalled by his brother.

Despite all this scurrying to and fro at the finish, the Peugeot had a half hour's margin over Moriondo's Itala, who had eschewed his Amiens acrobatics on this occasion. The final list:—

1. Boillot (1914 2½ litre Peugeot)   7–51– 1   34·2 m.p.h.
2. Moriondo (1913 Itala)   8–21–46
3. Gamboni (Diatto)   8–33–28
4. Masetti (1914/7 4·7 litre Fiat)   8–41–19
5. Negro (1914 G. P. Nazzaro)   8–42– 5
6. Masetti (1914 G. P. Aquila)   9–13– 5
7. Sivocci (C.M.N.)   9–26–35
8. Baldoni (Nazarro)   9–59–47

Ferrari (C.M.N.) and Lopez (Fiat) were still running at the end, Ferrari having fallen somewhat from his proud starting position and ruefully remarking that Count Florio had better get his Targa run off in May another year!

The year closed on a note of sadness with the death of the great veteran Henri Fournier in Paris on 18th December. He had taken little part in racing since the Heroic Age, but, in the days of one or two great events in a year, he had won the

two races of 1901, Paris-Bordeaux and Paris-Berlin with the Mors on which he was undisputed champion in that year. His last appearance was at Savannah in 1908 and his career stretched back to the days of cycle racing from which came so many of the early sporting motorists.

There was the usual plethora of idle speculation during what remained of the winter on the prospects for 1920; at one minute there was to be a Grand Prix at Le Mans for 3-litre cars weighing not less than 750 kg. with a prize of 100,000 frs. for which entries were expected from Ballot, Delage, Peugeot, Gnome-Rhone, Rolland-Pilain, Renault, Panhard, Sunbeam, Bentley, Fiat, Packard, Chevrolet and Frontenac; yet at the next, the manufacturers were ready to sign the Pledge again. Still, hope springs eternal and as the Sunbeam Company had paid a 10 per cent. dividend in the middle of 1919 the optimism of *The Motor* was understandable:

'*It is with more than ordinary expectancy that we look forward to the many and varied sporting events which are to be held during the coming year and there are welcome indications that the industry is not forgetting the value and importance of races and trials.*'

All this was in vain, however, for by the beginning of 1920 the triumph of the Pledgers was plain for all to see, although some diehards were still holding out for a voiturette race at Le Mans for 2-litre cars and further races were mooted at Aix and Marseilles. But it was to be good-bye to the Grand Prix for another year and, soon after, the Isle of Man racing programme was shelved for yet another season. In March 1920 a stirring contribution appeared in *The Motor* aptly enough signed by one 'Jehu':

'*The whole situation now rests with the manufacturer. Is he willing to put his cards on the table and openly pit his wares in friendly rivalry ... or has he lost his sporting instinct?*

'*Claims have been made regarding quality. Ought they not to be proved in public?*

'*The beneficial effects of racing may not perhaps be felt by manufacturers during the coming year (because) the demand for cars exceeds supply in too great a proportion. But the wise virgin trimmed her lamp.*'

The ancient house of Peugeot were far from virginal in motor racing but showed some lack of wisdom in their new design for 1920. In all, six races were run to the 3-litre or 183 cu. ins. formula between 1920 and 1922—three at Indianapolis, the Grand Prix and Brescia events in 1921 and the R.A.C. T.T. in 1922. For the first of these no less than three new French cars were designed, of which the Peugeot was the most revolutionary and the least effective. A prize fund of £15,000 was worth competing for, but Monsieur Gremillon of the Peugeot racing department really went one too far in endowing his cars with three overhead camshafts, and five valves and two plugs per cylinder: quite where cooling water was supposed to fit can only be left to the imagination. The cars were reputedly driven under their own power from Paris to Le Havre and certainly looked very good with narrow racy lines, and beautifully proportioned tails. On paper they had good power to weight ratio figures, with 105 b.h.p. at close on 4000 r.p.m. and a weight slightly in excess of the minimum of 14 cwt. 82 lb. Between 1913 and 1920 the 3-litre engine had been slightly 'squared' from 78 × 156 to 80 × 149 mm. bore and stroke, but the essential pre-war Peugeot characteristics and appearance had been retained, along with Goux and Boillot (André) as drivers. The third was the 1919 winner, Howard Wilcox, receiving the official accolade for the last great race of Peugeot.

Gregoire, another old French racing name, was also singing its swansong in this race; the cars had four separate cylinders of 78 × 156 mm. and four horizontal valves per cylinder, operated by exposed push rods impelled by two low camshafts mounted externally on either side of the upper part of the crankcase. These conservative cars were held up by a shipping strike and late preparation, so Porporato and Scales had little chance even of surviving the eliminating trials.

213 DISAPPOINTING SWANSONG: The French Gregoire at Indianapolis in 1919

The cream of the European entries were the three Ballots of Thomas, Chassagne and de Palma and, like the other French entries, the Ballot, too, had a touch of finality for it was the last flowering of the classic 'Henry' school of design. The story is told of Clive Gallop, despatched by Count Zborowski to buy an Henry design for Aston-Martin, being ushered into the Great Presence who solemnly drew his T-square and bisected the line drawing of the straight-eight Ballot and gave this to Gallop in exchange for a bag of gold. Whether true or not, this story makes a good parable illustrating, if cruelly, the sterility of Henry. As we have seen, when he wanted an 'eight' he doubled up the last pre-war design[1] and now the wheel had come full circle. No expense or trouble had been spared in the preparation of these cars, short of hiring a Fiat engineer to design them, and Ernest Ballot was keenly anticipating the victory that had eluded him the year before.

Finally from Europe there was the promise of a team of three entirely new Fiats to be driven by the great veterans Wagner and Minoia and, the successor to Lancia and Nazarro, Pietro Bordino. As it turned out a combination of labour and experimental troubles prevented the appearance of these cars not only in 1920 but also in the Grand Prix the next year, their one and only appearance being at Brescia in 1921 where Wagner ran 3rd behind the Ballots of Goux and Chassagne.

Of seven 500's so far, five had fallen to European cars and an American car had not won since 1912, although they had been breathing down the Europeans' necks in the last two races. 1920 was to see the American breakthrough and was the last year a European car even came near to winning until Wilbur Shaw's 8-cylinder Maserati in 1939/40, while René Thomas' 2nd place in 1920 was to be the highest achieved by a European car and driver in the 47 years between Resta's win in 1916 and Jim Clark's 2nd place in 1963. The main American challenge would come from the Monroes and Frontenacs, both Chevrolet designs based on the pre-war Peugeots, and the 8-cylinder Duesenbergs which had done so well the year before. In the ten mile elimination trials de Palma was much the fastest, but behind him there was a

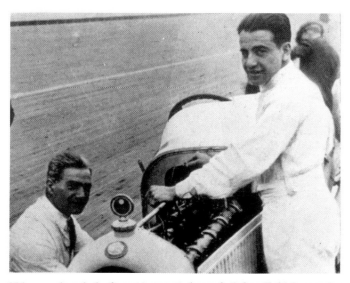

214 . . . . 'much the fastest in practice' was de Palma (left) here tuning his Ballot with his nephew and mechanic Peter de Paolo

[1] *The cylinders of the 2½-litre car of 1914 measured 75 × 140 mm. and those of the 1919 straight-eight 74 × 140 mm.*

215/16 Gaston Chevrolet's winning car in 1920 (left) and Tommy Milton's eight-in-line which was 3rd

solid phalanx of Americans mixed with the other two Ballots:

1. de Palma	Ballot	6– 3·08	:11. Milton	Duesenberg	6–39	
2. Boyer	Frontenac	6–11·49	:12. Wilcox	Peugeot	6–45·41	
3. Chevrolet	Monroe	6–13·91	:13. Murphy	Duesenberg	6–45·99	
4. Chassagne	Ballot	6–17·14	:14. O'Donnell	Duesenberg	6–48·23	
5. Thomas R.	Ballot	6–23·27	:15. Hearne	Duesenberg	6–49·06	
6. Thomas J.	Monroe	6–27·89	:16. Haupt	Meteor	7– 1·04	
7. Klein	Frontenac	6–28·31	:17. Boillot	Peugeot	7– 1·48	
8. Chevrolet G.	Monroe	6–33·30	:18. Howard	1913 Peug't.	7– 5·55	
9. Sarles	Monroe	6–36·74	:19. Goux	Peugeot	7– 7	
10. Hill	Frontenac	6–37·57	:20. Boling	Richards	7–19·89	

Slowest of the 23 competitors was Porporato's Gregoire in 7m. 30 secs.

According to these times de Palma should have run all the opposition into the ground and pulverised his own 1915 record, but he made a bad start and it was Joe Boyer with the Frontenac who dominated the first half of the race. When he made a routine pit stop, Thomas took over the lead and it was not until the 300 mile mark that de Palma asserted himself by leading at the record average of 90.78 m.p.h. from Boyer, Gaston, Chevrolet, René Thomas and Chassagne: Ballot v. Monroe/Frontenac with the rest merest also-rans. Five out of the seven 'Chevrolet' cars had steering fractures, none with fatal results although Chassagne nearly met with an unpleasant accident when one of these breakages occurred in front of him at speed on a main straight.

During the latter half of the race, with Boyer in trouble, it was Gaston Chevrolet against the full might of the Ballots, with de Palma going away lap after lap and the other two Ballots closing the gap from behind. Then everything seemed to happen at once to poor Ernest Ballot; first some slovenly pit work delayed Thomas after 400 miles; then, with the race all but won, de Palma's car stopped at the top

of the home straight with 50 miles to run. The trouble was eventually traced to a fault in one of the two magnetos, so that de Palma was able to finish the closing laps having lost four cylinders and places. The wanton Gods had not even then finished their sport with poor Ballot, for disaster now struck down Chassagne. When de Palma first stopped, Chassagne was signalled to challenge Chevrolet for the lead and, at least in the opinion of W. F. Bradley, would have succeeded but for an error of judgment due to reaction from his previous incident; having been delayed after hitting a retaining wall he finally finished 7th, leaving Thomas to lead the Ballots home 6 mins. 20 secs. behind Chevrolet. The final results, including half distance places, was:

1. Chevrolet G.	Monroe	5–38–32	=88·16 m.p.h.:	2–46–15	(3)
2. Thomas R.	Ballot	5–42–51·6	=87·47 m.p.h.:	2–46– 8	(2)
3. Milton	Duesenberg	5–45–2·43		2–52–26	( )
4. Murphy	Duesenberg	5–52–31 35		2–54–10	( )
5. de Palma	Ballot	6– 5–19·15		2–46–47	(4)
6. Hearne	Duesenberg	6–10–21·55		3– 6–26	( )
7. Chassagne	Ballot	6–15–16·65		2–47– 2	(5)
8. Thomas J.	Monroe	6–21–41·55		2–58–36	( )
9. Mulford R.	Mulford	7–17–14·25		3–55–13	( )
10. Henderson	Revere	7–23–53·95		3– 1–33	( )
Boyer	Frontenac			2–44–26	(1)

From a European viewpoint these results were full of foreboding; while the Chevrolet cars were probably track specials and not especially reliable, the Duesenbergs were true racers in the best European traditions and only O'Donnell's had given any trouble. The very convincing performance of the American cars in this race gave special menace to the suggestion made at the public banquet that followed that the City of Indianapolis should finance a national team at the next Grand Prix.

Chapter Eleven
1921/22 · The Sorrows of Ernest Ballot

217 HISTORIC OCCASION: *Jubilation at Le Mans as Murphy wins the Grand Prix for Duesenberg and America*

Undaunted by their previous failures and inspired, and perhaps even shamed by the success of the Voiturette Grand Prix the previous August, the A.C.F. made a further effort to revive the Grand Prix in 1921. Originally it was to have been held over a 10½-mile circuit near Strasbourg to celebrate the return of Alsace-Lorraine, but this project failed to materialize due to the indeterminate attitude of the local authorities. So in the end it was left to that good old standby, the A.C. de l'Ouest, to fill the gap over their new circuit first used for the 1920 voiturette race and subsequently for the early 24 hour races. This measured 17 km. 420 m. (c. 11 miles) and formed a small part of the old 34-mile circuit used in 1911-13; whilst it had no connection with the original 1906 circuit, it was still historically fitting that Le Mans had been chosen to usher in a new age of racing. The roads were subjected to intensive preparation, including complete relaying and treatment with calcium chloride, costly measures which proved of little avail, the race being run off in a cloud of flying dust and larger missiles, many of which wrought considerable havoc among the cars and drivers and prompted the famous American wisecrack about stone throwing contests.

Early on Fiat and Ballot were described as firm starters and there were promises from Bugatti, Darracq, Mathis, Peugeot and Sunbeam, besides a titillating rumour of a bid by Renault to regain their laurels of 1906. Both Ballot and Peugeot had cars ready from the year before while the Fiats were certainly then in existence. The newly formed Sunbeam-Talbot-Darracq combine published plans for the new season on a scale worthy only of Stuttgart, for the building of no less than ten cars, seven for Le Mans and three for Indianapolis. In the States the cars were to be 'Sunbeams' and driven by Boillot, Resta and Thomas, while for Le Mans, Resta was to switch to another S.T.D. marque to make room for one H. O. D. Segrave, then a complete newcomer to Grand Prix work. Boillot the fearless and Thomas were two of Europe's outstanding drivers; little had been heard of Resta since 1916 but his European and American successes between 1912 and 1916 were formidable indeed.

Fiat had enlisted their great veteran Louis Wagner to lead Minoia and the then unknown ex-mechanic, Pietro Bordino, for their new 3-litre cars. They did not in fact come to the start for reasons that have never been entirely clear—some

218 UNSUCCESSFUL EUROPEANS: The 1921 Sunbeams at Indianapolis (left to right) André Boillot (retired), Ora Haibe (5th) and Thomas (retired)

219 INSPIRERS OF VICTORY: (left to right) Louis Chevrolet, Harry Miller, Fred and Augie Duesenberg

said they did not consider the opposition worthwhile but it is more likely that they were just not ready, as they did appear later in the year at Brescia opposed by only three Ballots. Bordino and Minoia got no second offers but Wagner was promptly snapped up by Ballot to join Chassagne and de Palma on 3-litre cars, with Goux driving a smaller 2-litre four cylinder version, which was later the first production twin overhead camshaft design to be marketed on any scale.

Oddly enough the field did not include any previous winner of the Grand Prix, Szisz and Nazzaro being in retirement, Georges Boillot deceased and Lautenschlager an enemy alien. Quite why entry fees should have been so astronomical at a manifestly difficult economic period is hard to understand, but at 15,000 francs per car (or about £1,200) they must have been somewhat discouraging. The 1921 Grand Prix was a very chancy affair with only the four Ballots to be counted remotely certain starters; screaming international chaos reigned in the S.T.D. works and the Fiats were known to be in difficulty. Then, at the last minute, W. F. Bradley, like Canning, called in the New World to redress the balance of the Old with the entry of no less than four Duesenbergs at double fees to the tune of 86,500 francs. This entry, coupled with the almost miraculous arrival of four S.T.D. cars on the starting line gave the race at least an appearance of respectability even if the 1921 Indianapolis line-up undoubtedly overshadowed it.

This was the last year of an appreciable European challenge there until the Ford-Lotus, with the possible exception of the American entered straight-eight Maseratis in 1939/41. As in 1920 de Palma's Ballot made all the running, leading for 112 laps until a familiar Henry trouble struck the car—lubrication failure causing a broken connecting rod. de Palma had led at ever increasing and record speeds but in the end his old 1915 record with the Lyons Mercedes remained intact. Tommy Milton with his Frontenac could only average 89.62 m.p.h. but, for the first time in '500' history, no European car finished in the first three, the highest being Ora Haibe's S.T.D. 'Sunbeam' in 5th at 83.86 m.p.h., which would barely have won in the race even seven years previously. Thus unless Fiat could pull something fairly remarkable out of the bag the European larder looked unpromisingly bare for the Grand Prix.

Duesenberg, Miller and Chevrolet in particular had all learned extensively from the Peugeot and Mercedes cars that had dominated the American scene in the 1913/16 era and from the Bugatti aero-engines which had been exhaustively developed during 1917/18 in America. The straight-eight was the basic Grand Prix design between 1919 and 1951 and had been seen in racing as early as the first Dieppe Grand Prix in 1907 when the Dufaux, Porthos and Weigel cars had all had such engines. Indeed Weigel had a positive penchant for being unsuccessfully ahead of his time, for, having failed with an eight-in-line in 1907, he resorted, with equal lack of success, to single o.h.c. in 1908. Thereafter the Coupe de l'Auto was the chief inspiration for designers until the war and this event did not cater for development along straight-eight lines so that the next designer to take up the torch was, almost inevitably, Bugatti.

If not the actual progenitor of the straight-eight, Bugatti became at least its god-father when he put two Type 13 engines in tandem to give an eight-in-line of 68 × 100 mm. (2905 c.c.) which first appeared in 1913, at least two cars being produced. With the outbreak of war Bugatti was swept into the aircraft industry and by 1915 he had produced yet another straight-eight, this time of 12½-litres, by coupling up two of his 6.25-litre engines. Thus by some homely adaptation of ready-to-hand materials Bugatti had paved the way for designers of the next four decades and better than ever he knew, for by a series of war-time coincidences his aircraft engines came under the scrutiny of three men well qualified to benefit from them—Ernest Henry and the Brothers Duesenberg. The original aero-engine was licensed to Delaunay-Belleville and, according to Bradley, to Diatto also, this too being significant in spreading the new learning to the factory whence the first Maserati designs were soon to spring. Nothing loath, Bugatti went one better and produced a 'twin-eight', which was bought up by the Bolling mission and put into production in U.S.A. chiefly chez Duesenberg. It was also produced at the Bara factory at Levallois where Ernest Henry must undoubtedly have seen it. Whilst it is now thought very doubtful if any of Bugatti's engines ever actually left the ground[1] the lesson his designs spread was to have lasting effect and it is small surprise to find the straight-eight taking over where the Peugeot-based cars had left off in 1914. Of course the new cars were not true copies of the Bugatti and in any case further development followed swift-ly. Inevitably Henry added a fourth valve to each cylinder and a second camshaft and in 1923 Fiat added a super-charger, both embellishments which Bugatti resisted like the plague, the blower till 1926 and twin o.h.c. till 1931. As Conway says,[1] 'for all his brilliance' Bugatti was truly 'unusually conservative'. For all their known maritime skill the ancient Greeks would always sail round rather than across the Mediterranean, and so it was with Bugatti so that one must occasionally regret his lack of a formal engineering training.

Although he had repeated his 1911 triumph in the Voiturette Grand Prix at Le Mans in 1920, Bugatti's great Grand Prix days were then still to come and at Le Mans in 1921 he has to be left still dreaming in the wings of what might have been if Peugeot had not preferred their own development team in 1911/12.

Eventually by miracles of midnight oil burning, four S.T.D. cars reached the line for Thomas and André Boillot ('Talbot-Darracq') and K. Lee Guinness and the young Henry

Segrave ('Talbots'), with Zborowski, J. M. Cooper and Resta unhorsed. Joe Boyer and Jimmy Murphy headed the Due-senberg team with veteran Albert Guyot and wealthy amateur André Dubonnet in support. Originally one Inghi-bert was to have driven the fourth Duesenberg but he turned his car over in practice when seeking instruction from Murphy and nearly spelt FINIS to the American's chances as well. The four Ballots and the last of Mathis' minuscule Alsatian bêtises made up the field. Apart from Segrave and Dubonnet the drivers were all professionals, mostly of the old school, in particular the evergreen Wagner who had driven not only in the first Grand Prix but in the legendary Paris-Madrid itself. Segrave was in his very first great race and was to become so swiftly one of the greatest drivers of his age. By contrast Dubonnet was an amateur cast in the tradition of Baron de Caters, having reputedly paid hand-somely for the right to drive his car and came to the line impeccably accoutred with his head and mouth swathed in blue silk. With all the dust let loose on the circuit this was an eminently practical touch and his driving in the race was equally polished and competent.

The five marques disclosed no very great variety of tech-nical interest; the Henry school were represented by Ballot and S.T.D.; the Duesenbergs had three valves per cylinder, one o.h.c., a detachable head and a very slightly longer stroke. Four-wheel brakes were universal, even the Duesen-bergs had applied after Indianapolis a system that was 'hydraulic ... in the fullest sense of the word as they were operated by water—an arrangement which must have strained the confidence of the drivers to the utmost.' What-ever that strain, the brakes stood up very well and the Americans were not only the fastest goers but also the best stoppers on the course.

As at Lyons the cars were sent off in pairs at half-minute intervals, the order being:

de Palma (Ballot) and Mathis (Mathis)
Guinness (S.T.D.) and Thomas (S.T.D.)
Guyot (Duesenberg) and Chassagne (Ballot)
Segrave (S.T.D.) and Murphy (Duesenberg)
Boillot (S.T.D.) and Wagner (Ballot)
Boyer (Duesenberg) and Goux (Ballot)
Dubonnet (Duesenberg)

De Palma of course left Mathis standing, and the S.T.D. cars were very level; Guyot was a bad starter, letting Chassagne go right away. Murphy had the edge over Segrave but, surprisingly, Goux and Boyer were evenly matched over the first 100 yards. Finally Dubonnet departed in solitary immaculacy and the Grand Prix was a reality again after a seven year gap, in the teeth of such criticisms as that of Malcolm Campbell that the race would be 'more or less of a fiasco'. For Europe perhaps it was so, but no American could be expected to agree as a Duesenberg led for 23 of the 30 laps and the Ballot effort failed sadly.

When the first lap times were posted Boyer and de Palma

[1] See H. G. Conway, Op. cit.

220 Goux at weighing-in with the 2-litre Ballot

221 REALITY AGAIN: After seven years the Grand Prix was under way again—de Palma (1), Mathis (3), Guinness (4) and Chassagne (8).

222 FAMILY LIKENESS: The S.T.D. cars of Guinness (No. 4, Talbot) and Thomas (No. 5, Talbot-Darracq) were very level

were equal 1st with 8 mins. 16 secs. followed by Murphy and Chassagne on 8 mins. 21 secs. Wagner on 8 mins. 38 secs. and Boillot and Guinness one second slower. First blood slightly in favour of Ballot, but by the 2nd lap the two American drivers were equal 1st, 6 seconds ahead of Chassagne. On this lap the S.T.D. effort began its sad decline into a wearisome succession of tyre troubles brought on by totally inadequate tyres, the makers of which, wrote Segrave, 'had evidently during the war had no opportunity to gain experience in constructing covers for racing work'. This was sad, not merely for the drivers and mechanics, but because the cars had evidently found some speed since Indianapolis, Guinness putting in second fastest lap in the race between nine wheel changes. On the lap times Murphy was far the fastest and most consistently fast driver—between the 2nd and 12th laps he built up an 87 second lead over Chassagne who had worked into 2nd ahead of Boyer. These three fought out the early stages of the race as de Palma was unable or unwilling to sustain his fast first lap, being appreciably slower than Chassagne and giving way to Guyot on the 9th lap. At 10 laps the order was

1. Murphy	1–18–51	2. Chassagne	1–20–18
3. Boyer	1–20–43	4. Guyot	1–21–47
5. de Palma	1–22– 5	6. Dubonnet	1–24–59

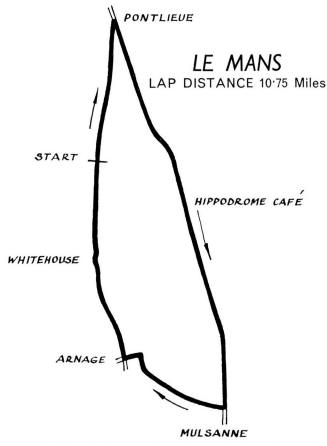

223 1921 THROWBACK: . . . 'it was historically fitting that Le Mans had been chosen to usher in a new age of racing . . .'

with Duesenberg well on top, Ballot going down grimly fighting and the rest firmly nowhere. What was especially striking was that the Ballots, which had run away with Indianapolis for the last 2 years while they lasted, were being convincingly out-run on their own ground.

Further back Boillot was leading the struggling S.T.D. contingent and exhibiting his special brand of brio in his unhappy task. Thomas had had trouble early on, taking over 1½ hours for his first 3 laps. Wagner had made too vigorous a start and was delayed after 2 laps with clutch, and later with carburetter troubles. Goux was driving with characteristic regularity and Segrave with the determination of Jarrott in Paris-Vienna, for on his showing depended his whole future with S.T.D.

After 12 laps Murphy lost the lead when he stopped for fuel and new wheels. This left Chassagne 27 secs. ahead of Boyer and 70 secs. ahead of Murphy. During the ensuing five laps Murphy regained 37 secs. on Chassagne and Boyer fell back at about the same rate. On the 18th lap both Chassagne and Boyer retired, the former with a petrol tank adrift and the latter with a run big-end brought about by overheating due to a flying stone having punctured the radiator. The circuit was visibly disintegrating, especially round Arnage, and de Palma also had a stone hit his fuel tank. These incidents left Murphy still more securely in the lead after 18 laps:

1. Murphy	2–25–5	4. Boillot	2–37–41
2. Guyot	2–26–9	5. Goux	2–37–45
3. de Palma	2–33–9	6. Dubonnet	2–39–12

Boillot's was the best place reached by any of the S.T.D. team and is a remarkable tribute to his resolution. Murphy went on lapping regularly under 8 minutes till at least 20 laps were past and drew steadily away from Goyot. With 7 laps left Guyot began to slow with a slipping clutch and on the 28th lap he stopped at his pit. On re-starting he had another dose of mechanic trouble, which make his remarks on the mechanic controversy in 1924 significant and heart-felt—'Of late years the mechanic has never helped to win a race and he has often been a handicap'; this time he was unable to crank the car and, as for Bablot in 1913, another spectating driver came to the rescue. This time it was not the Herculean Molon but Guyot's former Delage team mate Arthur Duray who hopped in beside Guyot, hatless but otherwise faultlessly clad in dark suiting and white cuffs replacing the great cross of Lorraine he had worn at Le Mans fifteen years before and in this manner the two veterans finished the race.

Jimmy Murphy drove serenely on in spite of a punctured radiator and the physical pain of his broken ribs; Guyot's misfortune had made way for de Palma whose closing laps were faster than anyone else's. The only driver to better even one of de Palma's laps at this stage was Goux, of all people,

224 Joe Boyer with Georges Carpentier

INTO THE ROUGH!

225/226 . . . 'further back Boillot was leading the S.T.D. contingent and exhibiting his own special brio (top) and fast finisher de Palma put in closing laps quicker than anybody else's (bottom)

227 *WEARISOME SUCCESSION: The labours of Segrave*

228 *EVERYTHING'S BUSTLE, FLURRY AND FUSS—What would the R.A.C. say nowadays—Segrave leaves (10) the pits, Murphy (12) seems to have forgotten his mechanic while Dubonnet stops to change a wheel*

229 *ONLY ONE WINNER: The Man Who Got Home First— Murphy, bruised and grimy, relaxes after his great victory*

whose 29th in 8 mins. 13 secs. was his fastest. By driving steadily throughout and profiting from the misfortunes of others, he finished a creditable 3rd in spite of giving away a whole litre to the other finishers. Great steadiness had also been displayed by the S.T.D. drivers Boillot, Guinness and Segrave. Guinness was the individual fastest and Boillot the best finisher, while Segrave had done all the sardonic Coatalen could have expected of him, and probably rather more, in finishing just over an hour behind the winner. By sticking to their work the S.T.D. drivers had kept faith with the great traditions of their group. Boillot had changed 7 wheels, Guinness 9 and Segrave 14 and Segrave summed up this experience with a true piece of British understatement— 'I am never likely to forget it!' In addition to all these wheel changes, he and his mechanic, Moriceau, had had to stop to re-time the engine and later to caulk a hole in the oil tank caused by a stone. Then to add injury to insult another flying stone had rendered the wretched Moriceau unconscious. Thomas, laps behind, had driven grimly on taking just over 5 hours to cover 23 laps while Guinness had at one stage to resort to wayside carpentry to plug a leaking oil tank. Segrave's own words admirably describe the S.T.D. effort:

'But still in spite of it all I am inclined to think that if during this first road race of mine the engine had fallen into pieces or one of the axles had cracked in the middle, I would somehow have succeeded in finishing the full distance. To get there meant more than anything else in the world to me at that time.'

The main havoc had been wrought by the break-up of the road surface in spite of the vaunted preparations made by the organisers. Practically all the retirements and delays had been caused by this, directly or indirectly, in that there had been hardly any mechanical troubles which had not sprung from mischiefs brought about by dust, road surface or tyres. Murphy, Goux and Dubonnet had enjoyed comparatively trouble-free runs; de Palma had had his delays but he had not been fast enough to make any real impression on Murphy; the tragedy had been Chassagne's retirement as he might well have been able to press Murphy to destruction in the closing stages of the race when the Duesenberg was in trouble with overheating. All this was in Ernest Ballot's mind when he vociferated on the injustice Fate meted out to him after the race, but as Albert Guyot acidly told him from the depths of his own experience at Amiens eight years before, 'there's only one winner in any race . . . the man who gets home first.'

The absence of the Fiats was regrettable especially when one reads contemporary reports such as the *Autocar's* which appeared before the Brescia races in September

'So fast are these cars that it is reported that one of the technical staff of the Fiat works expressed the opinion that

no human driver could avail himself in the race of the speed possible with these machines.'

However fine words polish no trophies, and I doubt if even the Fiats could have done much better than the Ballots at Le Mans. The lap times show that there was nothing fortuitous about the Duesenberg victory—they were appreciably the fastest cars in the race and both Murphy and Boyer were well up to the best European driving standards. At least if they were not, the cars must have been potentially even faster than would appear. Moreover the attitude of the Americans was an example to the cocksure and blasé continental attitude to race preparation and their victory was, in a sense, as complete as that of Mercedes in 1914. It is pleasant to record that their team manager had been none other than George Robertson who had won the first great American victory in road racing in the 1908 Vanderbilt Cup on 'Old 16', the great Locomobile.

Unfortunately the Duesenbergs could not remain in Europe for the Brescia Grand Prix in September as the Fiats appeared on this one occasion, opposed by the Ballots with three Italas and two SCAT non-starters. de Palma, Chassagne and Goux were on Ballots, Wagner, Bordino and Sivocci on Fiat. The Fiats had the same engine dimensions as their rivals and shared the twin o.h.c. lay-out but were very different in other respects. In many ways they were based on the war-time amendments to the 1914 cars and even took after them in outward appearance having the same wedge-shaped tail in contrast to the torpedo or cigar effect characterized by the French and American cars of the period. The engine had two large valves per cylinder, with cylinders in blocks of four which were steel forgings with sheet steel water jackets welded on in accordance with time honoured Mercedes practice. In contrast to the prevailing designs the crankshaft was in one piece with roller bearings for mains and big ends, split cages and races being employed for the first time. Engine and gearbox were in unit and the car was supposed to develop 115 b.h.p. at 4,600 r.p.m. in contrast to the figures for Ballot—107 b.h.p. at 3,800 r.p.m. and Duesenberg—115/120 at 4,250. The course was the classic triangle, measuring 17 km. 400 m. (just under 11 miles) and had to be covered thirty times and an exceedingly fast race was promised.

At 8 a.m. the six cars were sent out at one minute intervals —Wagner, de Palma, Bordino, Chassagne, Sivocci, Goux. Making his first appearance in an international event Bordino streaked away from the field for the first 13 laps by which time he had a lead of 1½ mins. over Chassagne at an average of 93 m.p.h., having set a record lap of 96.3 m.p.h. Initially Wagner had held 2nd place ahead of Chassagne, Goux and de Palma, Sivocci having crashed on his 1st lap. Tyre troubles, from which the Ballots almost always seemed immune, crowded in on the Fiat drivers; Wagner had to

change five wheels and Bordino's great run was slowed on the 13th and 14th laps by temporary tyre troubles and finished on the 15th by a broken oil connection. These sudden reverses to the fortunes of their favourites had a nettlesome effect on the Italian crowd and their passions were freely vented on the hapless Wagner. Suspecting that his repeated stops were occasioned by excessive caution rather than strict necessity, some malevolent person displayed to the crowd three apparently unburst and unpunctured tyres from Wagner's car. This prompted one of nature's self appointed orators to mount an oil-drum and demonstrate by voice and gesture the fate that should overtake any foreigner who dared by such cowardice to throw away a race. Sadly, W. F. Bradley, who has perpetuated this incident, was not able to film it so that the gestures employed by this fiery gentleman must for ever challenge the imagination. By chance this puppet show was interrupted by Wagner's arrival at the pits with a tyre in ribbons thus deflating the orator as well, and causing the fickle crowd to cheer the foreigner whose agility, for a man past 40, in changing wheels elicited especial comment from Bradley. All in all, it seemed as if tyres rather than drivers were the limiting factors on the Fiat's performance and the best Wagner could do was to finish well down in 3rd place behind Goux and Chassagne both of whom ran through the race non-stop:

1. Goux (Ballot)   3–35– 9 = 89·9 m.p.h.
2. Chassagne (Ballot) 3–40–51 = 88·9 m.p.h.
3. Wagner (Fiat)   3–45–53 = 86·9 m.p.h.

Thus after three seasons of disappointment it was Ernest Ballot's turn to find that the race was not always to the swiftest and profit by another's misfortune, for the Fiat had shown itself clearly the faster car. The effect of American participation sadly remains an idle if tempting speculation. Pomeroy has indexed the three leading cars as—Fiat 117, Duesenberg 116, Ballot 115, which may be sound theory; albeit, on the Le Mans evidence it would be a bold man who would gainsay the Duesenbergs a repeat of their Le Mans triumph. Personally I believe the Duesenbergs, with their ability to achieve 5,000 r.p.m. with comparative safety, would have carried the day at Brescia although Murphy and Boyer might well have found it hard to hold Bordino in the early stages. Bordino's fastest lap had been 3.31 m.p.h. faster than the Ballot's, while on the slower Le Mans circuit Murphy's best had been faster than that of the fastest Ballot. Really it is anyone's guess and it might well have turned out that the rivals would have blown each other up and let the Ballots through anyway. If I had had to make a book, though, I should have backed the Duesenberg to win *and* make fastest lap—in fact to be the fastest car on the circuit.

Two more 3-litre races took place in 1922, although in the end the Grand Prix was for 2-litre cars. In the Indianapolis '500' Murphy won with the same Duesenberg chassis, now fitted with a Miller engine; at long last the old Lyons Mercedes' record was broken although the 1919 lap record still stood. A 3-litre Ballot driven by Eddie Hearne was the only European car of consequence finishing 3rd. From this time begins the long domination of the event by American track cars. The R.A.C. T.T., the last to be run in the Isle of Man, was a domestic affair with three 3-litre Grand Prix Sunbeams, three Bentleys and three 4-cylinder Ricardo-designed Vauxhalls. I always feel that Pomeroy has allowed family tradition to influence his judgment in his assessment of these and the Lyons Vauxhalls:

'It is a real irony of motor racing that Vauxhall . . . should have produced one of the three fastest 4½-litre cars and one of the two fastest cars of the 3-litre formula and failed to secure international honours with either. . .'

When the first modern racing car saw the light of day before the 1912 Grand Prix there had been a 3-litre formula governing the voiturette class and it is one of the recurring themes of motor racing history that the voiturette of today turns into the Grand Prix car of to-morrow. The first example of this is to be found in the 3-litre Grand Prix cars of 1920-1922 and the Edwardian age of motor racing which ushered itself in with the twin-cam Peugeots and 3-litre Sunbeams of 1912, bowed itself out in the relative obscurity of the 1922 Tourist Trophy and Indianapolis events. Ever since 1912 the so-called 'Henry School' had been regarded as the acme of engine design and practice. Its basic layout had been copied by old and new world alike but by 1921 it was only too clear that there were others in the field with very decided ideas of their own—notably Miller and Duesenberg in America and Bugatti and the Fiat engineers in Europe. The Peugeot racing department produced two of the three outstanding designs of the Edwardian period in the 1912 Grand Prix and 1913 Coupe de l'Auto cars. The Grand Prix cars of 1913 and 1914, the 1914 Coupe de l'Auto cars and especially the 1920 Indianapolis cars were by no means remarkable and neither the 1913 nor 1914 cars were the fastest in the Grand Prix. The 1912 car was a true milestone in the evolution of the Grand Prix car and the 1913 3-litre carried this development to its logical conclusion so that, in a sense, all that followed it was idle repetition. Alas for Peugeot and Henry no fame is eternal and no design proof against time and human ingenuity and after breaking new ground in 1912/13, these sources made no further contribution to Grand Prix design apart from adopting the 4-wheel brake in 1914 and the straight-eight in 1919—neither of which were in any sense original or even originated by Peugeot/Henry. Moreover this school of engine design which relied on a long stroke with its limited range of performance and perfidious lubrication system had really been on the wane since 1914 and even the engrafting of the straight-eight by Henry in 1919 failed to shore up the tottering structure. Henry had passed from originality through

repetition into sterility and, like the old monsters he had banished at Dieppe in 1912, he, too, was doomed in spite of the Ballot win at Brescia. Henry had sowed and now it was for others to reap.

It might have been so different if the driving force of Boillot had survived the war and the so-called roaring twenties certainly failed to throw up another driver who so utterly epitomised the spirit of his age, as Nuvolari did for the early and Caracciola for the late thirties and Fangio and Moss for the forties and fifties. The deaths, first of Zuccarelli in 1913 and then of Boillot, were blows from which the Peugeot Racing Department never recovered; one suspects too, that Zuccarelli was a key figure if only on the empirical basis that nothing really shone as brightly for Peugeot or Henry after 1913.[2]

Apart from the decline of Henry and the advent of the straight-eight engine, the other important theme of the period is the increasing influence of America in racing throughout the ten years under consideration. First Bruce-Brown and de Palma had shown themselves drivers to be reckoned with Europe's best and then the American engineers, under the impetus of European example and competition on their home circuits, had gradually improved their cars and drivers to the point of their resounding victory in the 1921 Grand Prix. Both from an engineering and a driving angle this was something towards which the Americans had been working steadily since the Savannah days of 1910/11 and it is greatly to their credit that they were eventually able to make up the immense start gained by European engineers and drivers over the period from 1900 to 1912. If anyone has any doubt of the skill and ability of, for example, the Duesenberg engineers then the story of their amendments and improvements to the Bugatti war-time aero engines told by H. G. Conway[3] will prove instructive reading. If Bugatti could have overcome his conceit in his own handiwork, the Duesenberg triumph should have been no surprise to him. Like Mercedes in 1914 they had shown that honesty of purpose, coupled with a certain measure of simplicity, paid rich dividends.

230 HUMBLE BEGINNING: a flashback to the 1903 Gordon Bennett when the American entry was slow and trouble-ridden

[2] *This has also been confirmed by Goux in his lifetime.*
[3] *Op. cit.*

106

PART THREE
1922 to 1933 · The Vintage Years

Great Works are performed not by strength but by perseverance.

Samuel Johnson

Chapter Twelve
Vintage Prelude

'It is not necessary that the Traditions and Ceremonies be in all places one, and utterly alike; for at all times they have been divers, and may be changed according to the diversities of countries, times, and men's manners. . . . '

Articles of Religion No. xxxiv

All the ingredients of vintage motor racing had appeared at one time or another during the preceding nine years. The 1912/13 racing cars had been fitted with bodies that were, almost universally, refinements of the racers of the Heroic Age involving some slight degree of cockpit protection for driver and mechanic and ending in the transversely mounted bolster fuel tank with its array of spare wheels strapped on behind. Decreasing engine size contrived to scale the 1914 cars down to more modern proportions and some even had pointed tails to conceal their fuel tanks and spare wheels. Track racing at Brooklands and Indianapolis had inspired a certain amount of streamlining with a tendency towards conical or cigar-shaped tails of which the prettiest examples were the 1921 Duesenbergs. It was left to Fiat, however, to produce the first characteristically vintage racing car in that immense leap forward they made from the monsters of 1912 to the highly sophisticated 1914 racers. These cars, with their narrow razor-edged windcheating bodies and wedge-shaped tails set the pattern for racing car bodywork for the next twenty years.

It was Fiat who also set the standard for vintage engine design by bursting out of the bonds that fettered the 'Henry' type of engine with its severe limitations on engine revolutions. The Fiat attack had two prongs—the first was developed in the cars of 1921 and 1922 whose engines were made to turn over at the high speeds of 4400 and 5200 r.p.m. respectively. This was achieved by employing two large and widely angled valves per cylinder at the top and a one-piece crank-shaft at the bottom of the engine with its system of split-cage roller bearings and big ends. In this way they were able to make their engines breathe and revolve freely without lubrication failure. In 1923 the Fiat engineers launched the second prong by applying the supercharger which, at least in those happy times was anything but that means of wasting power to make a pretty noise which it was said to have become in latter years. Indeed even to its most rabid addict there must be now something sadly dated about Pomeroy's

words written in 1949 when an unblown Grand Prix car had hardly won a major event since 1923:

'None of these changes (twin O.H.C., front brakes and the straight-eight engine) had such potentially far reaching consequences as supercharging which added ... an extra dimension in engine design. . . . '

We have considered the first blown racing car in the 1908 Savannah races and followed W. F. Bradley as he industriously ferreted out the Hispano secrets of blower development in 1911, while Pomeroy has stated that Arnold Zoller certainly designed vane and centrifugally blown engines before 1914.

At this stage the irrepressible Mercedes engineers took over and to them must go the credit of placing the first blown racing car on a European starting grid. This was Max Sailer's 6-cylinder 28/95 car which won the 1921 Targa Florio. Their next blown racers, a pair of $1\frac{1}{2}$ litre cars, were very unsuccessful in the 1922 Targa Florio; one of these cars was beautifully restored by Peter Hampton in this country before the war and has been extensively written up both in Motor Sport and by Pomeroy. In 1923 Fiat brought a blown car to the start of the Grand Prix. Like the Mercedes, the Fiat blower blew air into the carburetter and was also not permanently engaged. The Grand Prix Fiats were unlucky at Tours with their vane-type blowers which were replaced with permanently engaged Roots-type instruments for the Italian Grand Prix later in the year. By 1924—and with all respect to Ettore Bugatti—all the fastest and most successful Grand Prix cars were supercharged and Sunbeam in that year introduced to Europe the more satisfactory principle of the blower deriving fuel-and-air from the carburetter and delivering the compressed mixture to the cylinders.

A matter of days before the Fiats raced at Tours in 1923, Mercedes had made their one and only official entry at Indianapolis with a team of three blown 2-litre four cylinder cars, this being the first German appearance in an international 'formula' race since 1914. The cars were not particularly successful though Max Sailer and his nephew brought their car home 8th and Werner 11th. The wail of the Stuttgart sirens had not fallen on deaf airs and the following year three centrifugally blown Duesenbergs started, one winning at the record speed of 98.24 m.p.h. an improvement of nearly four m.p.h. on the old record. These Duesenbergs, like their

Sunbeam contemporaries, were among the first to have the blower deriving mixture from the carburetter.

It was the blower, as much as anything else, which was responsible for the cleavage between European and American racing in the years that followed. It is a characteristic of the centrifugal blower than it produces little boost at low engine speeds but a most considerable effect in the upper reaches of engine performance. This made it an admirable instrument for events such as Indianapolis, but quite hopeless for any European road event—even on the combined road and track Monza circuit. The Roots-type blower produced much the same b.m.e.p. characteristics as an unsupercharged engine except on a higher plane and tended to lose efficiency at pressures in excess of 10 to 12 p.s.i., making it an equally unsuitable proposition for the Indianapolis type of event. Thus, the more the different types of engine were developed, the more widely divergent did their characteristics and interchangeability become, although occasionally the gap was bridged notably in the years 1939/41 by the 3-litre Maserati.

The success of the capacity formula ensured its retention for the first part of the vintage period down to 1927 for a series of races that swelled in number as year succeeded to year. There had been 'splinter-group' Grand Prix before the Italian Grand Prix in 1922, notably the series of American events which had attracted many of the great European cars and drivers principally in the Long Island and Savannah races. There had also been a Belgian Grand Prix for 'formula' cars scheduled for August 1914, but the Italian event in 1922 was the first time that any European country outside France had presumed to hold its own national Grand Prix for Grand Prix or 'formula' cars, although it has become fashionable in recent years to style the Brescia event of 1921 as the first Italian Grand Prix. Fittingly, too, that country was Italy, whose fortunes had not been of the best since the great days of Fiat and Nazzaro in 1907 and even more fittingly it was the great Felice himself who led the Fiats to consummate the Italian risorgimento in 1922 which had begun with those futuristic oversize cars at Lyons in 1914. Strictly the race was called the European Grand Prix but the principle of a non-French national event was established and the habit spread to Spain and Belgium in 1924, England and Germany in 1926, Monaco in 1929 and Czechoslovakia in 1931. During this period of Grand Prix expansion the nucleus of the modern fixture list was established and in the ten years that followed 1927 a pattern of races almost every week-end during the months from April to September came into being, with each country having a multiplicity of minor events as well as its own Grand Prix. Whilst the status of the French Grand Prix remained on the whole undimmed, it became no more than primus inter pares during the years after 1924.

Racing remained the preserve of the officially entered teams of the constructors until depressed economic conditions took charge of the situation in the dark years that followed the great Delage domination of 1927. These conditions paved the way for a new figure in the racing fields—the independent entrant, who was usually a wealthy and often gifted amateur, but for whom there had previously been no car apart from a works entry. The cars were provided by constructors like Alfa-Romeo, Maserati and principally Bugatti who was entering on his golden age in the late twenties. For a while the initiative had been taken away from the great factories which had contested the Grands Prix of 1922-7 and had come to rest with either independents or small manufacturers who built racing cars on a very limited production schedule such as Bugatti and Maserati. A third category was the independent racing organisation—Stable, Ecurie or Scuderia according to your accent. The most famous and lasting of these was founded in 1929 by Enzo Ferrari, the Alfa-Romeo driver, who, since the war, has stepped into the niche vacated by Ettore Bugatti, in so far as this is possible for any one man.

The cars of the 1928-31 period were for the most part developed survivors of the previous Grands Prix or quasi-sports cars such as the 1750 and 2.3 Alfa-Romeos and 2.3 litre Bugattis. Maserati was the significant exception and the only constructor who built out-and-out racing cars until the P3 or monoposto Alfa-Romeo, appeared in 1932. It was also a time of freak cars, such as the twin-six Alfa-Romeo and V-16 Maserati and to a lesser extent the Type 54 4.9 litre Bugatti, none of which were particularly successful. Earlier in this paragraph I used the expression 'sports-car', which begins to appear around this period. The twenties saw the establishment of three great classic events for this type of car—Le Mans in 1923, the Mille Miglia in 1927 and the R.A.C. T.T. revived in 1928. These events were frequently contested by thinly disguised racing cars or, if you prefer it, many of the so-called Grand Prix cars of the period were in reality stripped sports cars. The most outstanding example of this type of car was the big Mercedes usually outstandingly driven by Caracciola which appeared in such divers events as the Grands Prix of France, Germany and Monaco on the one hand and the three sports car classics on the other, besides winning at Avus in 1931 and 1932.

During the first half of the period the drivers were very largely drawn from the old professional school which was still recruited from the ranks of works testers and riding mechanics, but even before 1927 a new type of driver was making himself felt. A social revolution was slowly taking place which was changing the status of the racing motorist —drivers like de Palma, the Guinness brothers and Segrave were the successors of the wealthy amateurs of the heroic days, de Caters, Vanderbilt, Foxhall-Keene, Bruce-Brown and Jenatzy, but with the difference that like Georges Boillot and Goux before the war, most of them were in the racing game on a much more commercial basis and motor racing was on its way to becoming a profession rather than a trade. After 1927 the old artisan class of driver, who graduated from the testers' bench or machine-shop became a very exceptional bird except in that most conservative of institutions, the Daimler-Benz A.G. who made Hermann Lang a champion as late as 1939.

The 'gentleman' professionals came into prominence during the twenties with such names as Masetti, Antonio Ascari, Benoist, Chiron, Nuvolari, Caracciola, Fagioli, Campari, Boillot, Birkin, Brilli-Peri, Etancelin, Varzi and Segrave. The old school was represented by such ex-riding mechanics and testers as Divo, Moriceau, Bordino, Salamano, Costantini and Christian Werner and the pre-war drivers, Goux, Resta, K. Lee Guinness, Guyot, Hemery, Wagner, Friederich, Chassagne, Thomas and Minoia. The old distinctions of class, so notable in the Gordon Bennett days had worn very thin by the end of the vintage period, though they still persisted in the Mercedes camp at least

down to 1939 in the ill feeling between Brauchitsch and Caracciola on the one side and the arriviste Lang on the other.

Back in 1922, however, these developments were all in the future though clearly foreshadowed by history. There was some initial uncertainty during 1921 about the formula for the Grand Prix, when it was given out that the Grands Prix of France, Belgium and Italy and the Indianapolis and T.T. races would be governed by a 3-litre capacity limit and a fuel consumption of about 18 m.p.g. in the case of the French race. Gradually, however, the change to a 2-litre formula was made and by the autumn, it was clear that the French and Italian events would be for 2-litre cars and that Indianapolis would make the change in 1923. Unhappily Vauxhalls managed to be caught between the two fires and, in the result, the 3-litre cars they had been to so much trouble to prepare ran in one race only against purely British opposition. As it turned out, they did not do tremendously well in the T.T. sadly failing to realise their potential, and I feel it unlikely that they would have been a match for the Ballots, Fiats and Duesenbergs in an international field.

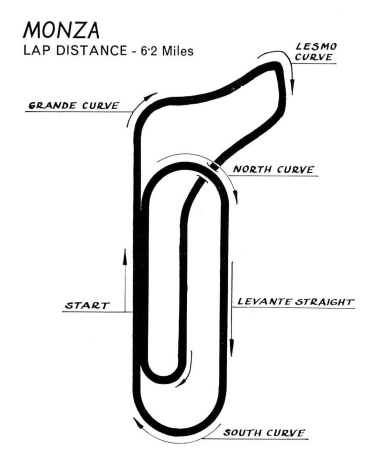

MONZA
LAP DISTANCE - 6·2 Miles

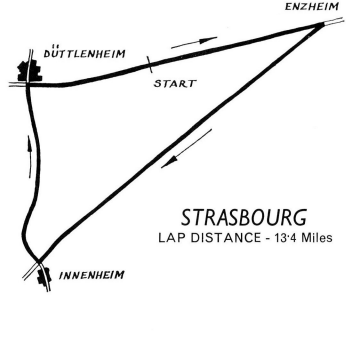

STRASBOURG
LAP DISTANCE - 13·4 Miles

231 EXPRESS EARTHWORK: . . . 'the track itself was built in 110 days and within six months of the first earth being turned the first race had been held . . .'

232 . . . 'the 1922 Grand Prix was again of triangular shape . .

Chapter Thirteen
1922 · Italian Risorgimento

With the withdrawal of Ballot from official competition after 1921 Louis Coatalen was at last able to secure the services of his idol—Ernest Henry—which proved an expensive way of shutting the stable door after the horse had bolted. As well as maximum capacity there was a minimum weight of 1433 lbs. and Henry produced a typical pre-war design for Sunbeam and was also represented by the sports model 2-litre Ballot of the type Goux had driven at Le Mans. There was initial uncertainty about the venue and even some idea of holding the Grand Prix in the Bois de Boulogne. Almost before choosing a site the A.C.F. made the much needed cut in entry fees from 15,000 to 5000 francs per car and then in December an 8.3 mile circuit near Strasbourg was officially chosen. The local authorities were to guarantee an expenditure of 150,000 francs on the preparation of the circuit and a further 200,000 francs towards general expenses. Preliminary reports indicated that there would be entries from Sunbeam, Rolland-Pilain, Delage, Bugatti, Mathis, Ballot, Fiat and possibly Peugeot, but nothing, strangely enough, from the new world, while non-Allied Countries were still excluded.

Although it had dominated European and American minds since the war none of the established constructors—Ballot, Delage, Fiat and Sunbeam—prepared straight-eights for the new formula and it was left to the relative newcomers, Rolland-Pilain and Bugatti to build the smallest eight-in-lines then raced. Pomeroy is quite right when he describes the 1922 cars as representing one of the lowest ebbs in Grand Prix history and 'the slowest ... models to be built, for it is doubtful if they could hold their own with, say, the 1908 cars in respect of maximum speed and acceleration.' In the same way some thirty years later the unblown 2-litre cars of 1952 were a fearful and comparable anticlimax after the surge and thunder of the small and highly super-charged 159 Alfa-Romeos and the big unblown 4.5 litre Ferraris of 1951. Aston-Martin, Ballot and Sunbeam were typical Henry creations, all three being either directly or indirectly designed by him, each having four cylinders, twin o.h.c. and four valves per cylinder of 65 × 112 (Aston-Martin) 69.9 × 130 (Ballot) and 68 × 136 (Sunbeam). The engine dimensions of the Aston-Martins lend credence to the

233 CLASSIC PATTERN: 'Two of the sides were absolutely straight ...'—here Segrave leads a Fiat

234 POOR REWARD: . . . 'The Astons were unlucky or inadequate'. Lionel Martin directs operations while the mechanic refuels Gallop's car

235 FLYING CIGARS: Goux's Ballot (left) and P. de Vizcaya's Bugatti (right) race neck-and-neck past the stands

236 TROUBLED ENTRY: The attractive and advanced Rolland-Pilains of Guyot (6) and Wagner (19) weigh in

tale told earlier on of Gallop's visit to M. Henry and they were the same as the superb little 1½-litre Talbot-Darracqs of 1921. There, however, any comparison must end, for the Astons were unlucky or inadequate and gave Zborowski a poor reward in terms of results for his enthusiasm, enterprise and expenditure in organising their entry. One feels that the little Talbot-Darracq voiturettes would have made a better showing at Strasbourg than the Astons and possibly even their new 2-litre cousins the Sunbeams. These vicarious Henry designs would probably have done him more credit in 1922 than any of his actual creations.

The Astons were to be driven by Zborowski and Clive Gallop; Goux remained faithful to Ballot where he was joined by Foresti and Count Masetti. Bugatti had the biggest entry with Friederich, de Viscaya, Marco and Mones Maury, while Sunbeam renewed their trust in K. L. Guinness and Segrave, and brought back Chassagne. The new Rolland-Pilains bristled with technical interest with their straight-eight engines and hydraulic brakes, but for drivers they went back to Gordon Bennett days with Guyot, Hemery and Wagner, Hemery making a return to the Grand Prix after ten years' absence and Wagner having left Fiat following the Brescia incident. Originally the engines were to have employed desmodromic valves like the Th-Schneider in 1913 and Delage in 1914, but these were abandoned before the race. Like their 1912 predecessors the 1922 Rolland-Pilains were very pleasing to the eye with low rakish lines giving a beauty that turned out, unhappily, to be only skin deep. At one time it was hoped to have two cars ready for Indianapolis on the 30th May but in the end it was as much as the works could do to have the cars ready for the Grand Prix nearly two months later.

The Fiats were scaled down versions of the 1921 3-litre cars having six instead of eight cylinders measuring 65 × 100 mm. and most of the detailed mechanical features of the earlier cars, as well as much the same appearance. Once again Bordino was in the team but this time he was supported by the great Felice Nazzaro and his nephew Biagio. Bugatti, like Aston Martin, was making his Grand Prix debut and his straight-eight engine followed closely on the 3-litre one he had shown at the 1921 Paris Salon, with a one-piece block and detachable cylinder head measuring 60 × 80 mm. and three valves per cylinder. Ball bearings were used for the crankshaft bearings and plain bearings for the big ends. The twin magnetos were driven off the rear end of the camshaft which allowed 'them to project through the dashboard and permits of verification even while running', as The Autocar somewhat naïvely remarked.

In 1922 Bugatti's Grand Prix cars had not acquired their classic lines and shared with the Ballots the dubious distinction of some pretensions to streamlining, both cars employing rounded cigar-like front cowlings with a cooling hole in the centre and, in the case of Bugattis, a similar hole in the centre of the tip of their conical tails. The tail-view of the Ballot was reminiscent of Jenatzy's 19th century record-breaker *La Jamais Contente*. The Ballots were streamlined versions of the car which Goux had driven at Le Mans the previous year and with considerable success in the 1922 Targa Florio.

These then were the 18 cars and drivers who were to contest the Strasbourg Grand Prix over 60 laps of the 8.3 mile circuit, which again was of the classic triangular shape. Two of the sides were absolutely straight and the third wound uphill; the main bends were the two right angles and one hairpin at the bases of the triangle. The surface was reported to be 'perfect so far as the absence from dust and loose stones is concerned but slightly wavy for cars running at speeds approaching a hundred miles an hour.' Following two-by-two starts in 1914 and 1921 the A.C.F. decided to go the whole hog and allow a mass flying start for 1922 in accordance with long established Indianapolis practice. Most of the teams had been dogged by last-minute troubles—and none more than the unhappy Rolland-Pilains; first they had to abandon their desmodromic valves, then Guyot's car took fire, and Wagner's was lost in transit, but by some miracle they were all on the grid. The Fiats and Sunbeams were the best prepared, the Sunbeams in particular coming to the line with gauze and Triplex aero-screens and an offside front mud deflector. It rained hard all the night before the race and then two hours before the start rain fell again in torrents, conditions which were almost unprecedented for the Grand Prix, although it had rained before the second day of the 1912 event.

At about 8.15 a.m. the cars streaked past the stands behind the pilot motor cycle and already the veteran Nazzaro had snatched an early lead from his front row position which he held for the first lap by a bare length from Friederich, Guyot and Goux, with Bordino and Segrave 5th and 6th. Wagner was last with his Rolland-Pilain and Guyot's effort cost him a broken crankshaft on the 3rd lap, when Wagner also retired with a broken connecting-rod. Hemery completed a three-fold disaster for his team when he disappeared shortly after. During that eventful 3rd lap Friederich put his Bugatti ahead of Nazzaro, but Bordino was now finding his speed and, on a signal, darted in front and then went right ahead, even of Nazzaro. Before very long the Sunbeams of Chassagne and Guinness were in trouble with their valve-stems and out of the race. While his Sunbeam lasted, however, Segrave kept ahead of Biagio Nazzaro's Fiat in 3rd, but slowed and eventually retired with valve stem troubles around half distance when lying 5th. This and the loss of Friederich's Bugatti left the race an utter walk-over for the Fiats.

They stopped around half distance for fuel for which they had devised special filler tanks which were mounted on the tails and which then allowed the fuel to pour in unattended

237 FIRST MASSED START: Nazzaro leads from Friederich (5), Guyot (6) and Goux (7)

238 . . . 'While his Sunbeam lasted Segrave kept ahead of Biagio Nazzaro in 3rd . . .'

239 Bordino changing plugs and refuelling with the special filler tank which could be left unattended. On the counter is the signal board shewing No. 2 Fiat as leader (Bordino), then No. 1 (Nazzaro)

while the mechanics busied themselves on other tasks. Nazzaro's stop took 1 min. 52 secs. but young Biagio was less lucky, finally having to change his fuel tank, which was accomplished in the remarkable time of $14\frac{1}{2}$ mins. This enterprise had a sad sequel when two or three laps later the car lost a wheel due to a rear axle fracture and crashed, killing the driver. Bordino, in the meanwhile, had lost his lead thanks first to running his main fuel tank dry and later to a plug change. With five laps to go he was over 12 mins· behind Nazzaro and not even Bordino could hope to recover that much time. However, Fate had another shock in store for the Fiats, for on the 59th lap Bordino had the same axle fracture as young Nazzaro though with less serious results. Thus 1-2-3 had been dashed tragically from them in the last stages, although true to form 'Lucky' Nazzaro ran out the winner and by the all-time record margin of 57 mins. 52 secs. This enormous lead, coupled with the fatal accident, made the 1922 finish a very lame affair and robbed Fiat of the thorough-going triumph their beautifully engineered little cars deserved. Nazzaro had covered the 500 miles in 6 hrs. 17 mins. 17 secs. at an average speed of 79.2 m.p.h. ahead of

2. P. de Viscaya (Bugatti) 7h. 15m. 9s. = 69·2 m.p.h.
3. P. Marco   „   7h. 48m. 4s. = 63·8 m.p.h.

Mones Maury had covered 57 laps when the race was halted and so did not rank as a finisher and all the others had retired. In spite of Bordino's great speed it was Nazzaro who put in the fastest lap at $87\frac{3}{4}$ m.p.h. Interviewed after the race Nazzaro said that his car had given him no trouble and that he changed tyres only as a precaution, disdaining the use of a spare. . . . 'I never found it necessary to run at full speed. For most of the time I kept . . . down to 4100 r.p.m. and only increased to 4500 r.p.m. towards the end of the race. The instructions given to Bordino were to drive faster and but for his mishap he would have won.'

During the latter part of 1921, when people still thought in terms of a 3-litre formula for 1922, Grand Prix events had been envisaged for Belgium and Italy plus the Indianapolis and T.T. events. In the end, however, only the Italian event was run off under the 2-litre formula. The Belgian race did not materialize and the T.T. was a purely domestic affair contested by Sunbeam, Vauxhall and Bentley. In actual fact the Italian Grand Prix for 1922 was for $1\frac{1}{2}$-litre cars, the 2-litre event being designated the European Grand Prix; this was originally schedule for the Brescia circuit and was to have seen the first German Grand Prix cars since the war. Soon after, however, the venue was moved to the new Monza autodrome, where work began in March, being started by Lancia and Nazzaro with the female interest maintained by Baroness Avanzo who had won the Ladies' Cup at Brescia in 1921. The track itself was built in 110 days and within six months of the first earth being turned, the first race had been held.

As a result of being able to charge for admission, the organisers were able to make a Grand Prix something of a commercial proposition for the first time in European racing history, and for the European Grand Prix a prize fund of American proportions was set up. These ranged from 100,000 lire for the winner to 5,000 for the tenth finisher and 10,000 for the leader at 40 laps, and two prizes of 20,000 each for the leader at 50 and 60 laps. The total fund was half a million lire or nearly £6,000. The track itself was 6.2 miles long and followed the lines of the present autodrome in general outline, but without the super elevated banking, the north and south curves on the 'track' part being in reality four moderately banked turns as at Indianapolis. The 'road' section contained several sharp corners and the organisers had very successfully contrived to reproduce and combine the best features of European and American racing, without falling into the dwarfing absurdity of Brooklands that had been manifest to Mr. Massac Buist as long ago as 1914. The Brooklands authorities had dreamed up a 500 mile race for September 30th 1922 and Mr. Massac Buist renewed his plea for 'grafting road racing features on to a transformed Brooklands track' by introducing chicanes to simulate corners. In fact it took the Brooklands pundits sixteen years to learn the lesson of Monza and the tremendous asset and advantage that this country had enjoyed and used to build up its racing cars up to 1914 was criminally frittered away in the twenties. A Campbell circuit in 1921/3 might have saved Brooklands from its 1945 ignominy but the sad truth is that even in 1922 it was dated and dead as an element in Grand Prix history with its valuable years already behind it. That most un-motoring of papers the New Statesman had seen this long before Sir Henry Birkin and the holding company's shareholders:

'Brooklands is not too well managed. It cost a fortune and has never earned substantial profits. The owners refuse to sell except at a figure which is of no real commercial interest. The track is too large for thrills. Speed on it is barely spectacular for its size dwarfs 100 m.p.h. until it is no more impressive than 30 m.p.h. in a Devon lane . . . the exits are few and awkward and the owners are unwilling or unable to spend money in improving their splendid property.' (May 1927)

On the 10th September 1922 some 150,000 people gathered together in Monza Park for the first European Grand Prix which like the French and Italian Grands Prix was rendered one of the dullest races on record by the utter superiority of the Fiats. A brilliant entry finally resolved itself into eight starters—Bordino, Nazzaro and Giaccone on Fiat, de Viscaya (Bugatti), Heim and Stahl (Heim) and Meregalli and Maserati (Diatto). Originally Friederich, Marco and Mones Maury should have supported de Viscaya but they were withdrawn at the last minute for the surprising

240 *During that eventful third lap Friederich (above) put his Bugatti ahead of Nazzaro*

reason that the gear ratios were wrong and Bugatti had not been able to get the correct wheels. Eventually Fiats loaned him a set of wheels which enabled de Viscaya's car to start although this had to be delayed half an hour for the car to be prepared. The race was run off in drizzle and as if to emphasize the farce Giaccone's Fiat suffered a broken clutch at the mass start and de Viscaya was almost immediately back at the pits with plug troubles, although he managed to lead Nazzaro behind Bordino for a short time. The Heims were not fit to be on the same circuit, the Diattos were not really racing cars anyway and the Bugatti was manifestly outclassed so the less said about the actual race the better. The finishers were:

1. Bordino 5–43–13 = 86·90 m.p.h.
2. Nazzaro 5–51–45 =
3. de Viscaya still running when flagged off 7 laps behind 2nd and 9 behind 1st.

The others had all retired apart from Maserati who was reported as 'showing considerable recklessness in the bends' and met with an accident which wrecked his car, but left him unscathed. Bordino stopped twice, once for fuel in 56 secs. and once to change rear wheels as a precaution in 1 min. 14 secs., when he stayed in the car himself leaving the riding mechanic to do the menial work. He also put in the fastest lap on a drying track at 91.3 m.p.h. A week earlier in similar conditions Bordino had won a 373-mile race at 83.25 m.p.h. so that his expressed preference for a left hand track like

Indianapolis was not, perhaps, something to be taken too seriously.

Outside formula racing only one event of interest took place in 1922—the Targa Florio. The significance and standard of these races varied enormously, but the 1922 event had both, largely because it saw the first German re-entry into international racing, two of their cars being fitted with forced induction devices. In addition the racing was exceedingly close, Masetti winning by less than two mins. after nearly seven hours' racing. The variety of cars entered more than compensated for the fact that most were somewhat dated and the entry for this event during the twenties is reminiscent of nothing so much as a good contemporary English vintage race meeting. Mercedes had six official entries, two of the blown 1½-litre cars (Minoia and Scheef), two 6-cylinder 28/95 models of 105 × 140 mm. (Sailer and Werner) and two enlarged and improved 1914 cars of 4900 c.c. (Lautenschlager and Salzer). As if this armada was not enough it was supplemented by the great Targa driver, Count Masetti on a privately entered 4900 c.c. car, this being the last appearance of these classic cars in international racing, although their '1914' element then savoured somewhat of the proverbial axe of my grandfather. Their r.p.m. had been increased from 3600 to 5000 and the valves and pistons modified and four-wheel brakes fitted, besides the enlargement of the engines, which possibly pointed towards the cars' having been intended for Indiana-

241 The Mercedes of Masetti which won

242 Goux's 2-litre Ballot (complete with Champagne at the ready) which was less than two mins. behind

polis in the old 4.9-litre days. The principal opposition came from a team of 2-litre twin o.h.c. Ballots driven by Goux and Foresti and four Fiats, two being the 1½-litre twin o.h.c. engines in the standard 10/15 chassis for Giaccone and Berghese and a third standard 10/15 for works tester Lampiano. The fourth was Wagner's Brescia 3-litre now driven by the ill-fated Biagio Nazzaro. In addition there were several 4½-litre Alfa-Romeos, principally those of Ascari, Ferrari, Sivocci and Campari and, as an afterthought, a 1½-litre Austro-Daimler driven by one Alfred Neubauer, with Baroness Avanzo intrepidly driving a similar Alfa in traditional red with matching costume, cap and flowing veil, which for sheer colour must have outdressed even an American golfing professional.

Jules Goux drove one of the finest races of his life, which he also personally considered one of the hardest he had ever driven, to finish second to Masetti, these two occupying the first two places throughout the race, thus:—

	1ST LAP	SECOND	THIRD	FOURTH
1. Masetti	+2m 7s.	—	—	+1m. 47.1/5s.
2. Goux	—	+1m. 11s.	+2m. 7s.	—

On the first lap Nazzaro had been 3rd, but, like Thomas in 1919, he found his big powerful racer too much of a handful and ran out of road and the race on the next lap, sparking off a rumour that not he but his renowned uncle, Felice, had been fatally injured. Giaccone on the small Fiat then assumed 3rd place for two laps but both he and Goux met with misfortune on the 4th lap. Giaccone had a flat tyre which he had continually to inflate by hand; Goux ran out of brakes and bent his chassis and then found his tyres worn to the breaker strip, all of which made his last lap his slowest and cost him the race by the excessively narrow margin of 1 min. 47 secs. Whilst M. Henry and Jules Goux had not beaten all the Mercedes, they had well and truly humbled the Stuttgart entry with a much smaller car and Goux and, for that matter, Masetti, had plainly utterly outdriven the German drivers as W. F. Bradley puts it:

'*it was interesting to watch (the German) men and cars in comparison with those of Italy and France. The four big white cars ... gave the impression of immense power, dominated by men of almost superhuman strength.*'

a far cry from the 1914 view of the same men and cars, but to return to Bradley:

'*The most striking example was Sailer ... who drove as if he were at war with his car but meant to bring it to its senses. It was strikingly sensational but it was a method which nevertheless failed to bring real speed out of the machines. Goux, on the other hand, gave the impression of a rider in sympathy with his mount who was coaxing it to its utmost and not driving it by whip and spur. In comparison the Ballot never seemed fast ... (nor) hair-raising, but the stop-*

watch showed that it was a very much faster method than that adopted by the German drivers. . . .

'While Masetti obtained excellent results out of his car . . . the two similar machines in the hands of Lautenschlager and Sailer were far from being as fast. The difference lay with the drivers rather than with the cars.'

'The successful racing driver of today is a much more highly developed organism than his prototype of twenty years ago.'

The true skill of the professional lies in the readiness with which he adapts himself to changing conditions and it is notable that men like Nazzaro, Wagner, Goux, Resta, Guinness, Chassagne, and René Thomas were every bit as formidable in the twenties as they were before the old war.

Unlike the Grand Prix events, the Targa Florio produced a large number of both starters and finishers, and the first 20 of the 26 finishers is worth recording for sheer antiquarian interest, if only because of its wonderful variety, and to show that some of the less credible Italian names are not just a feat of the imagination:

1. Masetti	4·9 1914 G.P. Mercedes	6–50–50.2/5
		=39·2 m.p.h.
2. Goux	2-litre Ballot	6–52–37.3/5
3. Foresti	2-litre Ballot	7–4–58
4. Ascari	Alfa-Romeo (4×102×130)	7–6–48.2/5
5. Giaccone	Fiat (4×65×112)	7–11–23.1/5
6. Sailer	Mercedes (6×105×140) (S)	7–12– 8
7. Hieronymus	Steyr	7–15–41.2/5
8. Werner	Mercedes (as Sailer) (S)	7–16–12
9. Sivocci	Alfa-Romeo (as Ascari)	7–16–25
10. Lautenschlager	Mercedes (4·9, 1914)	7–17–50
11. Campari	4·5-litre Alfa-Romeo	7–19–32
12. Moriondo	Itala (4×83×130)	7–20–17.2/5
13. Salzer	4·9 Mercedes	7–24– 0
14. Lampiano	1½-litre Fiat	7–32–36.2/5
15. Ritzler	Steyr	7–40–14
16. Ferrari	Alfa-Romeo (as Ascari)	7–40–58
17. Saccomani	Ceirano (4×85×130)	7–43–14
18. Ceirano	Ceirano (4×85×130)	7–46– 6
19. Neubauer	1½-litre Austro-Daimler	7–49–54
20. Scheef	1½-litre Mercedes (S)	7–52–46

It is sad to record that within a month of his racing return on the Steyr, Otto Hieronymus was killed testing a racing car after a career including the Paris-Madrid and the last Gordon Bennett in the Auvergne. Later in the year, when everyone was celebrating the revival of Fiat's Edwardian glories, another of the real pioneers, Leonce Girardot, the original 'Eternal Second' died at the early age of 58.

For Fiat it had been a true Annus Mirabilis to rank with Nazzaro's Kaiserpreis—Targa Florio—Grand Prix slam of 1907, with the ever youthful Nazzaro himself again playing a leading part, at the same time willingly yielding pride of place to Bordino, who was at last putting into practice what he must have learnt riding with Lancia and de Palma. The triumph of the Italians had been more absolute than any-

thing known in motor racing and they seemed to have such an advantage that it must have been difficult to see who could hope to challenge them for years to come, particularly when they had plans for 8-cylinder cars for 1923. The irrepressible Coatalen had a firm answer—in his cheque book—and promptly sent M. Henry packing off to Citroen and brought over the new prophets Bertarione and Becchia to bring lustre to the last years of the S.T.D. dream. Not only had the Fiats been much the fastest cars, but their organisation had been of the highest order; their pit-work had been speedy, and organised with remarkable foresight—as witness their refuelling methods and the replacement of Biagio Nazzaro's fuel tank—and also the elaborate code of signalling they had devised for the Grand Prix. If you have the fastest cars and drivers, plus the best organisation you are bound to grind the rest in the dust, and this the Fiats did in 1922 in a manner which has barely ever been equalled, let alone surpassed. As a tailpiece, this short letter written to the *Autocar* by one L. P. Openshaw on October, 20th, 1922, seems not inappropriate:

'It would be very interesting if some of the famous designers who last year proved the absolute unsuitability of the six-cylinder engines for racing purposes were to explain to us the success of the 2-litre Fiat in this year's racing.'

TOURS
LAP DISTANCE - 14·18 Miles

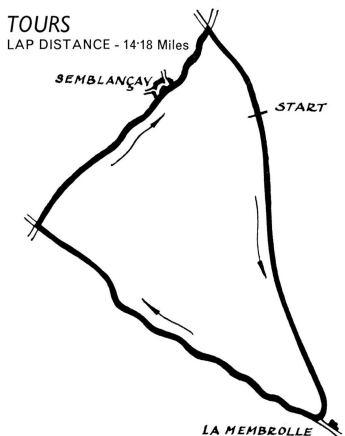

243 The Touraine Grand Prix circuit for 1923 where in the opinion of Pietro Bordino 'practically all the bends can be taken at full speed!'

Chapter Fourteen
1923 · A Famous Victory

'*Ridiculous even to imagine such a thing! He's (Sala-mano) miles in front.*'

Sir Henry Segrave : The Lure of Speed.

The 2-litre regulations governed the principal racing events in both worlds for 1923, these being Indianapolis on 30th May, the Grand Prix on July 2nd, the European Grand Prix at Monza in September and several Spanish races scheduled for the Autumn. The circuit of Touraine, which had to be covered 35 times (496½ miles) was 14.18 miles round, and followed the basic triangular pattern, although to everyone but the formidable Bordino it was expected to be slower than the simpler and straighter Strasbourg course. After trials early in the year with the 1922 cars, Bordino decided the race could be won at between 80 and 84 m.p.h. and expressed the view that although at first sight the course seemed more difficult than Strasbourg, 'after a little practice I find that practically all the bends can be taken at full speed, and that only the right angle and hairpin turns have to be taken slowly as was the case at Strasbourg.' Bordino was, however, discreetly silent as to the potentialities of the new Fiats—as well he might be. Reading the contemporary accounts it is quite evident that Fiat's use of superchargers caught everyone by surprise—even the perspicacious W. F. Bradley has described them as a complete surprise. In principle the Fiats were similar to the 1922 cars apart from having 8 cylinders in line of 60 × 87.5 mm.; like Mercedes their superchargers were not in constant engagement and blew into the carburetter. Like the Sunbeams, the Fiats employed straight sided tyres and in addition the Italians had applied hydraulic operation to their four wheel brakes. The cars presented their usual clean, simple and highly attractive lines, matched by the 'very harsh healthy crackle' of their engines which merged with the terrific whine of the supercharger. Marvellously the cars were driven ON THE ROAD over the Alps from Turin to Tours, Bordino, need-less to say, getting ahead of the party until he found himself at ten o'clock at night with neither lights nor spare tyres. His early training as a mechanic stood him in good stead when he rose at daybreak the next day to patch the tyre and arrive at Tours in time for a lap's practice.

The palatial quarters of the Fiats at the Château de Pouillé contrasted with the more rustic simplicity of their principal rivals and copyists, the Sunbeams, at the Hotel du Boeuf Couronné, where Wolverhampton was spread against a back cloth of 'chickens, an indolent pig, a passive mule . . . (and) . . . a mechanical piano. Now and again a mechanic winds up the organ and a wheezy foxtrot fills the air until its sound is drowned by the braying of the mule or a sudden rapid-fire from the exhaust of one of the cars.' The so-called English cars were in most respects copies, albeit improved, of the Strasbourg Fiats, right down to the streamlining of the exhaust pipes in the body side. For drivers they had Guin-ness and Segrave and the erstwhile riding mechanic Albert Divo. At one time there had been a possibility of Nazzaro leading the Fiats, but in the end he stood down and Bordino was supported by two works testers, Giaccone and Carlo Salamano, both voiturette drivers.

The other notable entry was René Thomas' Delage; al-though this car had been rumoured for 1922, the new 12-cylinder design did not leave the drawing board until Febru-ary 1923 when the chassis was already under test with another engine. It must rank as a very fine technical tour de force to have constructed such an engine in the space of 120 days, to say nothing of getting it to the starting line. In original form the car had the oval radiator and general aspect of the special hill-climbing Delages I and II built by the factory in the early post-war years, rather than the low square squat appearance it had acquired by 1924/5. Bore and stroke were 51.4 × 80 and the cylinders, with solid head, were cast in two blocks of six at an angle of 30°. Four carburetters were used on the outsides of the vee with the exhausts in the centre emerging high above the engine in traditional Delage style. Since his win at Indianapolis in 1914 René Thomas, now head of the Delage competition department, had met with indifferent luck or cars and, whilst it was too much to hope that such a design would win the Grand Prix in an utterly untried state, it was clearly capable of immense development, particularly with the advent of supercharging.

These seven cars were the leading examples of 6, 8 and 12 cylinder design. In the second class there was an equally interesting variety of thought shown by Rolland-Pilain, Bugatti and Voisin. The first-named eschewed their desmo-dromic valve gear yet again and had two of the Strasbourg type cars for the veterans Hemery and Guyot and a third car with a new kind of cuff valve engine for Jules Goux. This engine was the work of M. Henry who was supposed to have run it at 6000 r.p.m. under load. All these cars were traditional in aspect compared to the Voisin and Bugatti entries. Having produced a mobile cigar in 1922, Bugatti went one worse in 1923 with a racing 'tank', with the incredibly small dimensions of 6 ft. 6 in. wheelbase, 2 ft. 7 in. height and 3 ft. 4in. track front and rear. The engines were the same as 1922, indeed two of the three cars' engines had been prepared for the 1922 Monza race where they had not started. The Voisins were the most unorthodox looking Grand Prix cars ever built. Gabriel Voisin was an individualist at least on a par with Bugatti and an aviation expert into the bargain who had protested vigorously against the conservative type of body ordained by the regulations for the Touring Grand Prix. He took the view that designers would be better advised to spend six months studying wind resistance than six years on engine design and the resulting car was obviously the work of an aircraft designer in all respects apart from the speed derived from its 6-cylinder 62 × 110 mm. sleeve-valve engine. Streamlining was carried to the point of shaping the steering wheel in such a way that its highest part did not project above the scuttle line and a propeller mascot was mounted on the front of the radiator grille. The drivers were the veterans Rougier and Duray, co-designer Lefebvre and Morel. Oddly enough the Fiat bodies, though designed by their aviation department, differed at every turn from the Voisins, the Fiat experiments having shown that it was detrimental to bring the under surface too near the road and that this clearance should increase as the tail was reduced to release air imprisoned under the car. Practice, however, indicated what everyone believed, that the race would be another Fiat benefit if the cars held up; Bordino was fastest Fiat at 85.6 m.p.h. (9 mins. 56 secs.) and Segrave for Sunbeam at 81 m.p.h. (10 mins. 3 secs.). Even then the full potential of the Fiats had not been realised as Bordino showed in his electrifying opening laps in the race.

With such a variety of cars representing all the racing nations apart from America, whose cars were growing unsuitable for road racing, and Germany, whose cars were non grata to the A.C.F., the 1923 Grand Prix was on the way to recovering its pre-war standards. Hotels were packed, and overcharging rife and the usual 'army of open exhaust enthusiasts ... were most successful in defeating the end of those few sober minded individuals who had sought their beds; outside the places where 'on-y-danse' confetti and streamer festooned cars were stationed all night. Touraine was enthusiastically en fête!' In the end only 17 cars came to the start, the exception being Jules Goux whose cuff-valve engine had collapsed during practice, thereby keeping him from his first Grand Prix since 1912. The cars started 200 yards from the start line to which they were paced by a motor cyclist, their places being determined by lot.

244 *TOURS PIT AREA: Even with canvas covers in 1923 the effect is still that of a Tartar caravanserai as Guyot's Rolland-Pilain leads Divo's Sunbeam*

245 *TOUR DE FORCE: 'the other notable entry was Thomas' Delage' with the original oval radiator looking 'very early vintage' compared to (below)*

246 *the low square squat appearance it had acquired by 1925*

121

247 LAST FLING: the six-cylinder cuff valve engine of Goux's Rolland-Pilain was Ernest Henry's last contribution to Grand Prix design

248 RACING TANK: Friederich's Bugatti at the pits

249 MOST UNORTHODOX: . . . 'the resulting car was obviously the work of an aircraft designer'—the Voisin at Membrolle

René Thomas took advantage of his No. 1 position and an initial lead, but before they were out of sight of the grandstands it was Bordino who had swept to the front and, hardly had the spectators in their magnificent grandstands recovered from the thrilling, dust-kicking start than it seemed the harsh crackle and scream of the Fiat was heard again blasting its way on to its second lap. Bordino had eclipsed all his practice times with a first lap in 9 mins. 45 secs. (87.18 m.p.h.) and led by 41 seconds from Guinness followed by Thomas, Giaccone, Salamano, Segrave and Divo. At Strasbourg the Fiats had had an elaborate signalling code and had there been any need for them they would doubtless have produced some carefully evolved race tactics as well. For 1923 their tactics seemed only too clear with Bordino setting a matchless pace and Guinness neatly sandwiched between the Fiat team. It was not to be expected that Thomas' untried Delage would last very long and so it turned out; the Sunbeams, however, were not going to give in without a fight and in fact Guinness substantially increased his lead over Giaccone and Salamano during the first 10 laps; and, when Guinness fell back, Divo was ready to pile on the pressure. Bordino's tremendous run came to an end on the 8th lap when he led Guinness by nearly 4 minutes at an average of 87 m.p.h. having left the lap record at 87.75 m.p.h. The trouble was first given out as a stone having broken the crankcase but really turned out to be stones and dust causing supercharger troubles.

Guinness thus assumed the leadership which he held for four laps till his routine fuel stop let the Fiats ahead; he then ran into clutch troubles which dropped him down to 6th after 15 laps. Thomas had retired early on after a very creditable run and further back Guyot had been keeping the only surviving Rolland-Pilain going very steadily so that he held 4th for the middle part of the race behind the changing fortunes of Fiat and Sunbeam. As Guinness faded, Divo and Segrave moved up into the attack; Segrave had started the race with a slipping clutch which would not fully engage because of a maladjustment in the clutch stop. This ceased when the stop broke off and Segrave found himself with a virtually unstressed car after 400 miles of the race when he was lying 3rd, behind Divo and Salamano. This, however, is to anticipate, for at 15 laps, with Guinness in difficulty and the remaining Fiats firmly in 1st and 2nd the Italians seemed set for a brilliant repetition of Strasbourg. The following table of the 15, 10 and 5 lap positions shows clearly how the leadership swung from red to green and back to red again with a thin strand of blue running through:

	15 LAPS		10 LAPS		5 LAPS	
1.	Giaccone	2–40–47	Guinness	1–43– 6	Bordino	48–41
2.	Salamano	2–42–24	Giaccone	1–47– 4	Guinness	51– 1
3.	Divo	2–42–41	Salamano	1–47–14	Giaccone	53–22
4.	Guyot	2–44–34	Guyot	1–49–59	Salamano	53–40
5.	Segrave	2–48–15	Divo	1–50–11	Divo	53–52
6.	Guinness	2–52–52	Segrave	1–52–24	Thomas	55–21
7.	Friederich	2–54–48	Friederich	1–57–57	Guyot	55–44
8.	Rougier	2–59– 4	Rougier	1–58–25	Segrave	56–13
					Friederich	59–32
					Rougier	59–57

Everything changed after 16 laps when both Fiats came to the pits; Giaccone pulled in slowly, refuelling and changing plugs and rear wheels, and drove off unhappily, stopping again a lap later to retire with the same troubles as Bordino. On the same lap Rougier's steady drive with the best placed Voisin came to an end and Divo found himself leading after 20 laps by the narrow margin of 51 seconds from Salamano; Sunbeams still had their team intact making up in regularity what they lacked in speed. Victory must still have seemed a far away thought to Divo and Segrave after Salamano had showed his hand to catch Divo and pull out a lead of 2 mins. 20 secs. on lap 25 which he had increased to 4 minutes by the end of 30 laps to make another Fiat victory almost certain, the order then being:

1. Salamano 5–28–48
2. Divo 5–32–59
3. Segrave 5–38– 2
4. Guinness 5–57–25
5. Friederich 6– 0– 6
6. Lefebvre 6–41–16

Guyot had only just dropped out and at this vital point Divo suffered one of those soul destroying delays that make or mar a race; when he stopped for fuel he was unable to remove the filler cap. After wasting a quarter of an hour they decided to work on the reserve tank which would involve a stop on every lap till the finish. While all this was going on Salamano was fighting adversity out on the circuit having, as he thought, run out of petrol. In reality he had been struck down by the same supercharge of Touraine grit and dust. The Fiats had done all their development on the smooth dust-and-grit-free surface of Monza and were not prepared for the appalling loose surface at Tours, which had been considerably aggravated by the Touring Car Grand Prix. His mechanic ran nearly 2 miles for more fuel and then, setting off back on a bicycle, he was ordered to his feet to the great displeasure of the crowd. Sad to relate all this fine effort was wasted as the car never restarted. Thus it was that on the 33rd lap an Englishman found himself at the head of the premier road race in the world for the first time since S. F. Edge's fortuitous win in the Gordon Bennett 21 years before. Like Edge, Segrave by patient endeavour had outrun his swifter and more fragile opposition, besides enjoying a generous measure of good fortune in the shape of Divo's jammed filler cap. The impossible possible began when Dutoit

'letting go everything and making a funnel of his hands close to my ear shouted; C'est le quatorze qui est en panne! Nous sommes en tête!'

How different, yet equally nerve-racking, must those last miles have been from Segrave's painful closing laps to the finish at Le Mans two years before when his Sunbeam career was in the balance. Now as he puts it

'I could scarcely believe my ears—for the first time in history an English car was leading in the Grand Prix with only one lap to go.

250 DIFFERENT APPROACH: 'the Fiat bodies though designed by their aviation department differed at every turn from the Voisins . . .' —here is Giaccone's car

251 . . . 'Guinness then assumed the leadership . . .'—note this fine driver's calm and relaxed style

252 . . . 'and further back Guyot had been keeping the only surviving Rolland-Pilain going very steadily'

253 . . . 'Everything changed after 16 laps when Giaccone changed plugs and drove off unhappily'

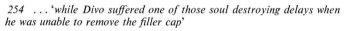

254 . . . 'while Divo suffered one of those soul destroying delays when he was unable to remove the filler cap'

255 Pride Goeth . . . 'Victory must have seemed a far away thought to Divo and Segrave after Salamano (above) has showed his hand . . .'

256 . . . Before a Fall . . . 'Salamano fighting adversity out on the circuit . . .'

257 FINEST HOUR: Segrave, winner in 1923, at speed in the 1924 Grand Prix

258 Two Fiats and the revolutionary white Benz at Monza

'How can I ever forget these last few miles—every noise in the engine seemed magnified a hundredfold, every corner seemed impossible, my brain refused to wok in complete co-ordination with my hands and feet.

'But luck was with us....'

and Segrave crossed the line with a margin over Divo of 19 mins. 6.1/5 secs. The Sunbeams' attempt to equal Mercedes' Grand Slam of 1914 was sadly and narrowly worsted by Guinness' sick car stalling momentarily on its last lap and losing 2 minutes in the process which was enough to let Friederich into 3rd place on the surviving Bugatti:

1. Segrave   6–35–19.3/5 = 75·31 m.p.h.
2. Divo   6–54–25.4/5
3. Friederich 7– 0–22.4/5
4. Guinness   7– 2– 3
5. Lefebvre   7–50–29.3/5

Thus ended what the *Autocar* described as 'the most thrilling Grand Prix ever seen.' Whilst an English account of Segrave's triumph may be pardoned for such a judgment and admitting the immense improvement in the race over the two previous events, the Grand Prix had still some way to go before it regained the classic stature of the 1914 event. In fact it had precisely 12 months until that great moment when with the race to be run over part of the 1914 circuit, Segrave on No. 1 Sunbeam swept to the head of a field that included Bordino (Fiat), Ascari (Alfa-Romeo), Campari (Alfa-

Romeo), Thomas, Divo and Benoist (Delage) and the classically beautiful Type 35 Bugattis. At that moment Segrave and the great S.T.D. empire enjoyed their proudest hour, when on sheer merit of car and driver The Green went to the front of the Grand Prix from its very start and held off the greatest Italian and French cars and drivers of the day till trivial engine troubles set in, leaving Segrave with the poor consolation of the fastest lap. On that day Segrave, Guinness and Sunbeam were at the pinnacle of their racing lives.

Whether it was fear of defeat or too nice an observance of the supposed tradition that the winner of the Grand Prix should not race elsewhere, the absence of the Sunbeams from the European Grand Prix at Monza was deeply regrettable. Having won the Grand Prix for the first time it seemed a pity indeed that England should pass up a chance to win the European Grand Prix. By contrast the beaten Fiats could not wait for a chance to be back at their rivals' throats; these rivals included three American Millers which arrived in Europe for practice early in August led by the great Jimmy Murphy. These cars had dominated the Indianapolis race setting a new lap record of 108.17 m.p.h. in the hands of Tommy Milton, the winner, and they had 4-carburetter unblown straight-eight engines. Bugatti and Sunbeam stood aside on their Touraine laurels but Rolland-Pilain and Voisin were to be there as well as two newcomers to the post-war field—the one, Benz, was one of the most illustrious

259 OLD NAME REVIVED: Benz was one of the most illustrious names in history besides being the first German entry in a European Grand Prix event since the war

260 SCION OF A NEW LINE: The original P 1 Alfa-Romeo in practice with Sivocci and mechanic Marinoni

names in motor racing history besides being the first German cars to race in a European formula event since the war and, the other, Alfa-Romeo was to found a victorious dynasty that held sway until the firm's retirement from Grand Prix racing in 1951. The history of the Alfa-Romeo is almost synonymous with that of motor racing between 1924 and 1951 and it is historically disappointing that the cars were withdrawn at the last minute following a fatal accident to Sivocci in practice. Fiat also had their share of tragedy during practice, when a stub axle broke on Bordino's car costing passenger Giaccone's life and injuring Bordino to the extent that he had to have the gears changed by his mechanic during the race. Since the Grand Prix the Fiats had replaced their Wittig vane blowers with conventional Roots instruments running in constant engagement while the Alfas employed Wittig blowers on their 6-cylinder P.1 cars. The other entries were all unsupercharged, only the Benz calling for any detailed comment. These cars were the work of one Dr. Rumpler and had 6-cylinder 65×100 mm. twin o.h.c. engines mounted behind the driver in a well streamlined cigar shaped body with a torpedo shaped oil tank mounted above the engine on a level with the driver's head. The chassis was equally unconventional employing independent rear springing through swing axles and inboard rear brakes. The cars were credited with a speed of 114 m.p.h. which, if true, comes close to the 122 m.p.h. officially recorded by Bordino's Fiat at Tours. Their drivers were the Italian veteran, Minoia and two little known Germans, Walb and Horner. The Millers were twin o.h.c. straight eights of 58.7×88.9 mm. with four valves per cylinder and eight carburetters. For Monza they had been fitted with four wheel brakes and developed about 120 b.h.p. at 5000 r.p.m. which compared very favourably with the published figures of 118 b.h.p. at 5600 r.p.m. for the Fiats and 102 b.h.p. at 5000 r.p.m. for Sunbeam. Besides Murphy the drivers were Zborowski and a wealthy Argentine named Alzaga, elsewhere described as the first husband of the fifth Mrs. Clark Gable.

Guyot and the erstwhile mechanic Delalandre drove the two Rolland-Pilains on which they had won a minor event at San Sebastian in August. Evidently the years since Savannah and its fish dinners had weakened the former sailor's stomach, so that Delalandre had taken the place of Hemery who had been seriously affected by Spanish fare and even Guyot had had to rest during the race. It is pleasing to find even this small victory for these enterprisingly constructed and attractive looking cars. The field was completed by the three Voisins of Silvani, Rougier and Lefebvre and the revised Fiats of Bordino, Salamano and Felice Nazzaro standing in for Giaccone, as their veteran reserve driver Cagno had apparently and improbably departed for Russia the day before the race. Surprisingly there was no entry from Mercedes; perhaps there was some truth in the suggestions that they were boycotting the race because of Italian support for the French occupation of the Rhineland but, equally, they had good reason for being dissatisfied with their cars' showing at Indianapolis in May. Bordino was driving in spite of injuries to his left arm and wrist and had to receive medical treatment before the start but, once away, he was out in front immediately, followed by Salamano, Nazzaro and Murphy who spent most of the race in that order. The Fiats were back to the dog days of 1922, although Murphy's Miller was not as completely outclassed by them as any other car was or would have been. The main interest lay in the astonishing performance of Bordino whose mechanic had to do all the gear changing and the keen struggle between Nazzaro and Salamano for 2nd place behind him. At half distance the order was:

1. Bordino	2–38– 2 = 94·3 m.p.h.	5. Minoia	2–54–57
2. Nazzaro	2–38–43	6. Horner	2–59–20
3. Salamano	2–38–47	7. Guyot	
4. Murphy	2–42–45	8. Alzaga	

The Voisins, Delalandre's Rolland, Walb's Benz and Zborowski's Miller had all disappeared with various engine troubles long since and shortly after half distance the lead changed with the Fiat routine stops. Bordino's work was done entirely by his mechanic while he received medical treatment and took 5 mins. 54 secs. as against 3 mins. 42 secs. for Nazzaro and 3 mins. 25 secs. for Salamano. Two laps later Bordino lost a rear tread and was so overcome by holding the resulting slide with only one arm that he felt unable to go on; in the absence of reserve driver Cagno, en route for Muscovy, the car had to be withdrawn after a truly heroic drive. By contrast Murphy's pit work was swift in the extreme, his stop only taking 1 min. 41 secs., not that it seemed to do him much good as he was still as far away as ever by the 60 lap stage.

Salamano's lead was short lived and, like Bordino's, was cut short by tyre trouble obliging him to run nearly a lap on the rim and leaving Nazzaro in a seemingly impregnable position. Salamano made a spirited recovery and was only 22 secs. behind with 10 laps to go, but still too far behind until, with 2 laps left, Nazzaro found himself with a broken oil pipe which necessitated a hurried refill. For once Nazzaro's luck was out and Salamano caught and passed him, drenched with oil, during the last lap to win the European Grand Prix at a record speed of 91.08 m.p.h.—nearly as fast as Bordino's record lap in 1922. Bordino himself put in fastest lap just outside the magic century at 99.8 m.p.h. the final order being:

1. Salamano 5–27–38	4. Minoia 76 laps
2. Nazzaro 5–28– 2	5. Horner 71 laps
3. Murphy 5–32–57	6. Alzaga 70 laps

The other retirement had been the Rolland-Pilain of Guyot, who had been burnt by the exhaust pipe and was disqualified for having handed over to Delalandre. The European Grand Prix had now made a very successful beginning and, so far from being regarded as an upstart, the A.C.F. had elected to hold it for their own Grand Prix in 1924 with the possibility of England having it the next year.

261 SUNBEAM IN SPAIN: Resta (centre) seems very bored with his return to European racing while an official holds forth to Coatalen (left) and Divo (right)

Having declined to give battle at Monza the S.T.D. combine were equally careful to avoid meeting the 1½ litre Fiats in the 200 mile race at Brooklands, preferring instead the sunny shores of Spain where they cleaned up two voiturette and one formula event at Barcelona and Sitges on the newly opened track. These races deserve mention for two reasons—first because they marked the return of Dario Resta to European competition and secondly because of the first appearance in a non-national event of one Nuvolari. The 2-litre race at Sitges was a very poor affair with the Grand Prix Sunbeams of Divo and Resta and Zborowski's Miller the only cars of any note. Resta had troubles but Divo and Zborowski had a great battle throughout the 248 mile race which resolved itself in Divo's favour when Zborowski had to change a tyre in the closing stages. Divo's speed was just under 97 m.p.h. Nuvolari drove a Chiribiri into 3rd place at Sitges and 5th in the road race at Penya-Rhin, both events being dominated by the S.T.D. Talbot-Darracqs, but in 1923 the hour of neither Nuvolari nor Alfa Romeo had struck as they stood impatiently biding their time in the wings of history.

After the relatively uninteresting Fiat dominated events of 1922, the 1923 season had been one of absorbing technical interest with the two principal races contested by 10 different marques from five different nations if one includes the German Steigers and Italian Alfa-Romeos which non-started at Monza. In addition the Indianapolis '500' had seen Mercedes on the line again with 'formula' cars for the first

127

time since 1914. This was the last '500' to have any meaningful European cars in it till 1939 and the first to permit single-seater cars; in the race Mercedes were the only cars to have riding mechanics and the first to race a supercharged car in a genuine 'formula' event. Bugatti went in for the race in tremendous style entering five cars for de Vizcaya, de Cystria, Alzaga, Riganti and Zborowski; the engines were the normal 2-litre straight-eights and the bodies beautiful single-seaters built by the S.P.A.D. aircraft concern and mounted on the off-sides of the chassis. Brakes were hydraulic and the cars had certain points of minor difference in mechanical detail. The race marked the first return of Dario Resta, who with de Palma and Joe Boyer was driving a new 6-cylinder Packard of 63.5 × 101.6 mm. bore and stroke. The other important American cars were fitted with 8-cylinder twin camshaft Miller engines under various aliases with the significant exception of a Barber-Warnock driven into 5th place by L. L. Corum. This consisted of a souped up Model T Ford engine in the conventional chassis complete with 2-speed epicyclic gearbox. The engine had a type of Frontenac head with two push-rod operated valves per cylinder in place of the 1922 sixteen valve twin o.h.c. heads. The Miller-engined cars comprised two H.C.S. (Stutz) Specials (Milton and Wilcox), one Miller properly so called and eight Durant Specials (Harry Hartz, Jimmy Murphy,

Eddie Hearne, Elliott, Durant, Earl Cooper and others). In practice Count Zborowski likened the superiority of the American cars to that of the Strasbourg Fiats and it was no surprise to find him racing one in Europe later in the year. Milton on the soi-disant H.C.S. made the fastest practice laps, averaging 108 m.p.h. and dominated the race winning all but three of the distance prizes as well as the race itself.

The German drivers impressed the Americans on the track no more than they had W. F. Bradley in the 1922 Targa Florio and Lautenschlager and Max Sailer had unhappy experiences not in keeping with their distinguished records. Sailer had bruises and a sprained wrist from an accident in practice, and Lautenschlager hit a wall on the 14th lap and retired. Christian Werner redeemed Stuttgart honour by holding 3rd place for much of the first half of the race until he had to be relieved by Max Sailer, whose own car was being driven by his nephew Carl. Later Werner relieved Carl Sailer on uncle Max's car and finally finished the race on his own car—Teutonic musical chairs (or more probably bumps!) with a vengeance with the whine of the blowers supplying the music. The four and eight cylinder Mercedes of the twenties were clearly most difficult cars for almost anyone to drive, certainly none of the German drivers bar Caracciola and Werner seemed able to cope with them and even the gifted Count Masetti had his work cut out.

Four of the Bugattis retired at various stages in the race—Alzaga, Riganti and Zborowski fairly early on and de Vizcaya after 450 miles when lying 5th. De Cystria on the surviving car finished 9th. The final order was:

1. Milton	90·95 m.p.h.	7. Durant	82·17 m.p.h.
2. Hartz	90·05 m.p.h.	8. Sailer	80·68 m.p.h.
3. Murphy	88·08 m.p.h.	9. de Cystria	77·64 m.p.h.
4. Hearne	86·65 m.p.h.	10. Morton (Duesenberg)	74·98 m.p.h.
5. Corum	82·58 m.p.h.	11. Werner	74·65 m.p.h.
6. Elliott	82·22 m.p.h.		

Technical variety had not exactly abounded at Indianapolis but in Europe there had been 4, 6, 8 and 12 cylinder engines employing single or multiple carburetters, in two cases superchargers, and in one, rear engine mounting with independent rear suspension. Valves were operated mainly by twin overhead camshafts, but both sleeve and cuff valve designs had been raced and desmodromic operation tried out. Four wheel braking was universal and in some cases hydraulically operated and a real attempt was being made to streamline and tidy up bodywork. Experiment of all kinds had been rife throughout 1923 all of which paved the way for the immense advances in speeds and engine design seen in the next two years. Motor racing was now ready for its next great stride forward and, fittingly enough, it was led by an absolute new-comer to Grand Prix racing—Alfa-Romeo. The season closed on a tremendous conflict of opinion on the admissibility of the supercharger, many designers, notably Bugatti and Coatalen, expressing strong views against its use. Bugatti continued in obstinate opposition for some years, but Coatalen was quick to turn it to his own ends and turned out the fastest cars of 1924 with the most progressive system of forced induction.

263 Reactionary Mercedes still kept to riding mechanics however

265 Bugatti went in for the race in tremendous style with a beautiful single-seater

264 Dario Resta made a comeback with the new six-cylinder Packard

266 Tommy Milton, the winner, on his Miller-engined H.C.S., which dominated the race winning all but three of the distance prizes

129

Chapter Fifteen
1924 · The Trèfle à Quatre Feuilles Crosses the Alps

Motor racing had been improving steadily since the war and 1924 was a Vintage Year. A new record was set up at Indianapolis, the Grand Prix was contested by much the best field since the war, there was a rattling good Targa Florio, Mercedes re-entered Grand Prix racing and the Spanish Grand Prix attracted its best entry to date. To many, however, the year was most noted for the tremendous success of the new Alfa-Romeo team racing under the badge of the Four Leafed Clover previously borne by the conquering Richard-Brasiers in 1904/5. Starting as a humble offshoot of the great Darracq concern the Alfa had been seen in racing before the war and in Italian local events and the Targa Florio in the post-war years. A team of vane-supercharged 6-cylinder cars had been entered for the 1923 European Grand Prix but withdrawn due to Sivocci's fatal accident in practice. These P1 cars were replaced for 1924 by the P2 Alfa-Romeo, which became one of the most long lived and successful racing cars, its design strongly reflecting Fiat practice. As if the Gods were jealous of all this progress, tragedy was never far off; Count Zborowski, Dario Resta, Joe Boyer and Jimmy Murphy were four great drivers who held their last wheel during the year, and K. Lee Guinness retired after the accident in which his mechanic was killed in the Spanish Grand Prix.

New tracks were opened at Miramas and Montlhéry; the Swiss Grand Prix made its debut, if only as a voiturette event, and the riding mechanic was finally dropped in the regulations for the 1925 season. Sadly enough Fiat made their last appearance in the Grand Prix just as Alfa-Romeo had arrived to take on the torch that Fiat had carried for Italy with such distinction since 1904. Four events were run to the 2-litre formula—Indianapolis, the European Grand Prix at Lyons, the Italian and Spanish Grands Prix. The first can be dismissed in a few words. Only one European car started—one of the 1923 Mercedes cars now called a Schmidt Special and driven by Ora Haibe who had driven a Sunbeam there in 1921. The only European driver was A. E.

Moss, Stirling Moss's father, driving a 1923-type Barber-Warnock which was flagged off after 440 miles. The principal feature of the race was the return of the brothers Duesenberg to the limelight with a team of three centrifugally supercharged cars, and a fourth fitted with eight Miller carburetters. These blowers operated at eight times engine speed and were the first raced to derive mixture from the carburetter. The cars themselves had duralumin frames, two having two valves and two four valves per cylinder. The blower cars were entered for Joe Boyer, L. L. Corum and Ernie Ansterberg and the fourth unblown for Peter de Paolo, Ralph de Palma's nephew and sometime riding mechanic, thus neatly preserving a form of Apostolic succession which went back to Vincenzo Lancia and Paris-Madrid. Fourteen Millers, three Barber-Warnocks and the 'Schmidt' Special completed the field with such well known Indy drivers as Tommy Milton, Jimmy Murphy, Earl Cooper and Harry Hartz driving the leading cars.

Murphy, Milton and Hartz were in the front row, but it was Boyer on the blown Duesenberg who stormed through from the second to lead on to the 2nd lap. Soon after disaster struck the Duesies a double blow when Ansterberg hit a wall following a steering fracture and Boyer's car sheared a key off its supercharger gears. The race then settled down to a duel between Murphy and Cooper followed by Hill, Hartz and Corum, and it looked as if the American blown cars were to share the fate of the Fiats at Tours. This, however, was to reckon without Fred Duesenberg and Joe Boyer; when Corum came in after 109 laps he was replaced by Boyer whose instructions from Fred are variously reported as 'I want you to finish the race in his car'[1] and 'Put that ship out in front or burn it up!'[2] Whichever be true, there can be no doubt of Boyer's electric reaction. Hill and Hartz were relatively easy game but at 350 miles Cooper still led him by 1 min. 25 secs. and Murphy by 33 secs. After this stage the leaders found themselves in tyre troubles through having to drive harder through the turns than they had bargained and

[1] *Bloemker*—500 Miles To Go, *p. 157.*
[2] V.S.C.C. Bulletin No. 69, *p. 66.*

Boyer narrowly won after a most thrilling duel in the closing laps with the veteran Cooper. Speeds were well up on the 1922 record of Jimmy Murphy (94.48 m.p.h.)

1. Corum-Boyer   Duesenberg (S) 98·24 m.p.h.
2. Cooper   Studebaker   97·99 m.p.h.
3. Murphy   Miller   97·27 m.p.h.
4. Hartz   Durrant   96·55 m.p.h.
5. Bennett Hill   Miller   96·46 m.p.h.
6. De Paolo   Duesenberg   94·30 m.p.h.

These results had little bearing on the European scene although Zborowski raced a Miller at Lyons and American cars appeared at Monza in 1925. The Americans can, however, claim to have beaten the Sunbeams to a racing car on which the mixture was supplied to the engine via the blower, an arrangement which ultimately led to the wider use and development of alcohol fuels.[3]

The European season had started a month earlier with the Targa Florio on 27th April for which an intriguing variety of cars had been entered. Three were supercharged, the two 1923 Indianapolis Mercedes of Werner and Lautenschlager and the 1½-litre Fiat of Bordino. At the other end of the scale was Dubonnet's Hispano Suiza with its tulip wood boat body built by the Nieuport Aviation Company. Other leading entrants were Ascari, Campari, Masetti and Louis Wagner (Alfa-Romeo), Boillot, Foresti and Dauvergne (Peugeot) and Goux (3-litre Ballot). After the 1st lap of 67 miles, only half a minute separated the first five cars on time, Dubonnet being in 2nd place on one of the most unsuitable cars ever to race in Sicily, behind Masetti and ahead of Werner, Boillot and Ascari. The field became more spread out on the 2nd lap when Werner went to the front with a total elapsed time of 3 hrs. 11 mins. 47 secs. followed by:

2. Ascari   2 m. 3 secs.   5. Campari   6 m. 44 secs.
3. Boillot   3 m. 24 secs.   6. Bordino   6 m. 58 secs.
4. Masetti   5 m. 52 secs.

Bordino, finding that his light racing car was singularly unsuited to the Madonie circuit, was taking a terrible hammering and even the reliable Jules Goux had left the road on his 3-litre Ballot. Needless to say the dashing Boillot had a rare moment when he was faced with the choice between skidding round and ruining his tyres or dropping six feet into a bean field. He chose the beans and was observed driving across this extension of Count Florio's circuit pursued by his mechanic and the starting handle! This escapade only dropped him one place, changing places with Masetti; Bordino also overtook Campari after three laps when Werner came in for a wheel change. The Targa has never been as other races and the manner of Werner's pit stop was truly in keeping, for no sooner was the car at rest than two stalwart Germans lifted each road wheel (and thus the car and its driver) whilst others slipped jacks under the axles—no fancy restrictions on numbers of mechanics prevailed in Sicily!

For a detailed treatment of this subject see chapter headed The Beginnings of Blowing, in The Grand Prix Car by Laurence Pomeroy.

267 Jimmy Murphy, who died in 1924, at the wheel of the Miller on which he finished 3rd in the '500'

268 Veteran Earl Cooper who had a thrilling duel with the winning Duesenberg in the closing stages of the '500'

269 GERMAN COMEBACK: 1924 saw the first German win in post-war racing by Werner's Mercedes in the combined Targa and Coppa Florio

The final lap produced a finish equal only in drama to André Boillot's in 1919. Werner with starting number 10 finished in 6 hrs. 32 mins. 27 secs.; before he went away on his last lap he had had a lead of 2 min. 53 secs. over Ascari which had been lost by his pit stop in spite of his crew of Teutonic weight lifters. Thus Ascari, with starting number 24, had twenty-eight minutes in which to finish which, on all accounts, he should have been able to manage. At last the warning gun boomed and the red Alfa shot into view with a very narrow advantage. Poor Ascari! 1924 was not his lucky year and the car came to a stop with a seized engine a matter of yards from the finishing line, being finally pushed over in 2nd place. As if all this excitement was not enough, Bordino completed his four laps and collapsed in a faint from which neither water, ice nor 'restoratives' could rouse him until after Nazzaro had driven the car off to complete the 5th lap for the Florio Cup. The final order for the four lap Targa was:

1. Werner (Mercedes (S)) 6–32–27 = 41·1 m.p.h.
2. Ascari (Alfa-Romeo) 6–41– 4 5. Campari (Alfa-Romeo) 6–46–51
3. Masetti (Alfa-Romeo) 6–42–30 6. Boillot (Peugeot) 6–47– 1
4. Bordino (Fiat) (S) 6–46–34 7. Dubonnet
                                        (Hispano-Suiza) 6–50–24
(all within the existing record of 6–50–50).

The season continued on the 9th June at Cremona, where the new Alfa-Romeos made their first appearance. Ascari had the consolation of winning at 98.3 m.p.h. also achieving the fastest lap at 100.8 m.p.h. and a timed speed over 10 kilometres of 123 m.p.h. This compared very favourably with the speed of the 1923 Fiats over a very short stretch at Tours and established the new cars as strong contenders for the forthcoming European Grand Prix. The previous season had concluded with a tremendous dispute about the ethics of the supercharger particularly amongst French designers and it was at first not certain if its use would be sanctioned for the European Grand Prix. These doubts were favourably resolved, and Sunbeam, Fiat and Alfa-Romeo were all busily experimenting with blowers as well as Delage and, so it was rumoured, was Bugatti. Early in the year Resta had been down to Lyons renewing his acquaintance with the circuit where he had driven in his last Grand Prix. The 'new' Lyons circuit covered only part of the great 1914 course; start and finish were at the same point and, once again, the grandstand spectators were to have the same view of the cars sweeping down off the straight switchback of 'les montagnes russes' through the Esses and the piège de la mort to the hairpin at Sept Chemins. The old circuit was cut short at Givors where the cars now turned sharp right along a tricky winding back leg on to the 'montagnes russes' section.

Early in the year the commercially minded René Thomas was proposing lap prizes for the Grand Prix as at Indianapolis where he had won ten years previously and soon after a prize of quite another character was devised. In addition to

270/1 MADONIE MISFITS: Not even Bordino (top) could make a success of the blown 1½-litre Fiat which finished 4th, 14 mins behind the winner and (bottom) Dubonnet's big Hispano-Suiza, which finished 7th

its silks, Lyons was very proud of its sausages and the Hartford Shock Absorber Company gave a dinner at Lyons to leading drivers at which it presented a monster sausage, 12 ft. in length and 10 stones in weight to be awarded to the winner. Potential winners of this wondrous comestible were Alfa-Romeo (Ascari, Campari, Ferrari and Wagner); Bugatti (Chassagne, Costantini, Friederich, Garnier and Vizcaya); Delage (Benoist, Divo and Thomas); Fiat (Bordino, Marchesio, Nazzaro and Pastore); Miller (Zborowski) Schmid (Goux) and Sunbeam (Guinness, Resta and Segrave).

Little appeared in the press about the Alfas but their speed at Cremona made them more formidable than the views of the *Autocar* might indicate :

'*Personally*', wrote W. F. Bradley, '*I should bracket Sunbeam, Fiat and Bugatti together, with Delage, Alfa-Romeo, Schmid and the privately owned Miller in the second grouping.*'

The cars had engines of 61 × 85 mm. with their eight cylinders cast in blocks of two, closely following Fiat practice in such details as welded-up cylinder construction, roller bearing big ends and mains and permanently engaged Roots blower. Body shape was squatter than the Fiats, an impression which was enhanced by their 'bull-nose' radiators and

balloon tyres. Vittorio Jano was the designer and as he had been connected with Fiat for 13 years the resemblance was not hard to understand. Their drivers were all well known in Italian national events, but were all making their first appearance outside their own country. Ascari and Campari are famous names and Ferrari was the self-same Enzo Ferrari. These new drivers had the leavening experience of Louis Wagner to back them up.

Supercharging helped Sunbeams overcome the basic difficulty in ensuring even distribution of mixture over their 6-cylinder engines and the new blown cars produced 138 b.h.p. at 5500 r.p.m. in comparison to the figure of 135 b.h.p. given for the Alfas. Even as early as 1924 Fiat were rumoured to be experimenting with a blown two stroke, although such a car only appeared experimentally in 1926 as a 1½ litre. For 1924 they raced improved versions of the 1923 cars; two were new and two were rebuilt. Modifications had brought the power output up to 146 b.h.p. at 5500 r.p.m. Delage, too, was sticking to established practice in running the same type of unblown V-12 car, but Monsieur Lory had altered the body and chassis considerably and had also experimented with twin Roots blowers. The Schmid was merely a repeat of the Schmid-Henry engined cuff-valve Rolland-Pilain that had run at Tours and the Miller was

LYONS
LAP DISTANCE - 14·3 Miles

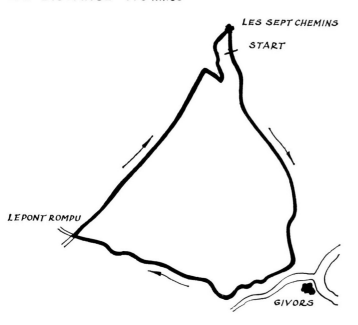

272 LAST OF THE LINE: the 'new' Lyons circuit covered only part of the 1914 course but was just as severe a test of man and machine and was the last of the great open road circuits.

273 'To many the year was most noted for the tremendous success of the Alfa-Romeo team . . .'—Ascari's car (3) carries a spare wheel behind Campari's (10), which won

274 . . . 'once again the grandstand spectators had the same view of the cars sweeping down . . .'

275 The Miller was Zborowski's 1923 car, here with driver and mechanic S. C. H. Davis on the weighbridge

276 GRAND MANNER: the Bugatti team at Lyons (left to right) Chassagne, Friederich, P. de Vizcaya, Garnier and Costantini

277 CAUSE AND EFFECT: . . . 'it was expected that conditions after two hours' racing would be worse than on the stoniest parts of the Tours circuit . . .'

Zborowski's 1923 car. It was left to Bugatti to spring the best surprise of the year with his new Type 35 Grand Prix cars.

For the European Grand Prix Bugatti went motor racing in the grandest manner. As a start he cast out all primitive attempts at streamlining and re-designed the body and chassis of his cars and also did a certain amount of rethinking on their engines. Then he proceeded to build no less than ten cars, five for practice and experiment and five for the race itself. As a final individualist's touch he brought his own accommodation with him and, knowing Bugatti's reputation as a lover of the good things of life, his équipe must have been the envy of all the other competitors. In the engine department Bugatti increased the main roller bearings for the crankshaft from three to five and converted the big ends from plain splash lubricated to roller bearings with a meticulously engineered built up crankshaft. Improvements were also carried out to the chassis, steering and brakes. Lastly, in discarding his misguided attempts at streamlining, he produced one of the most aesthetically satisfying cars of all time with its low sloping pointed tail, and polished axle well ahead of its narrow horseshoe radiator. Small wonder that the car has caught and held the imagination of successive motoring generations—

'It was so well finished, with its nickelled axles and controls, its almost show-polished engine and its shapely radiator, that it was the kind of toy which an enthusiast had only to see to desire.'

At the time Bugatti would not have been himself had he not given out that he had abandoned his beetle-back body, not because he found it inefficient, but because such odd looking cars would not be easy to re-sell! The final touch of *le patron's* genius was reserved for his caravanserai which enabled all the cars, spares and drivers to be under canvas with 'specially devised cooking facilities and all the comforts usually found in an hotel. For the use of himself and his family he had a specially designed (Bugatti?) four-wheel caravan which was a marvel of comfort and ingenuity. . . . Bugatti had brought Jean aged 15, and Roland, a curly headed youngster of two. The atmosphere was one of gaiety, high spirits and optimism. Le Patron was justly proud of his work, he was surrounded by a devoted team, every member of which regarded himself as belonging to the family . . . even if defeated . . . they had accomplished something worthwhile, something of which they could be justly proud.'[5] According to Bugatti himself 'the racing cars went to Lyons under their own power and the supporting supply vehicles carried a total load of 30 tons.'[6]

Practising was relatively uneventful save for an accident to Bordino whose car had to be returned to the works. The course was clearly both rough and testing; after three hours

[5] *W. F. Bradley: Ettore Bugatti, p. 50.*

[6] *Circular letter issued by Bugatti c. 1924.*

practice Guinness said he felt like 'a pea on a hot plate' while Segrave had a steel box fitted to the steering column with motor cycle grips attached to either side for the driver to grip with his legs, and the old campaigner Nazzaro fitted the seats of his Fiat with rounded upholstery to avoid all sharp or hard edges. The main danger lay in the twisty section from Givors to Le Pont Rompu, where it was expected that conditions after two hours' racing would be worse than on the stoniest section of the Tours circuit. As W. F. Bradley concluded, it would be a wonderful car and a master driver who won the Lyons Grand Prix. Just such a car and driver combination was that of Sunbeam and Segrave. It is a charming tale that the Alfa-Romeo drivers suggested a deal with the Sunbeams before the race to ensure them 2nd and 3rd behind the winning Sunbeam and there must have seemed much wisdom in the idea when Segrave shot to the front from the start on No. 1 Sunbeam.

Matched against the greatest assembly of Europe's cars and drivers since 1914 the domination of the green Sunbeams driven by the holder of the Grand Prix title was a sight and sound to swell the hearts of every Englishman. At long last an English car and driver were leading the Grand Prix not by right of survival but by sheer right of speed even though it might be designed by Italians. By the time he had reached *les montagnes russes* Segrave had cleared the opposition and when the cars reached the hill down to the Death Trap Ascari was 2nd, followed by Guinness, Campari, Bordino, Wagner, Chassagne, Divo, Friederich and Resta—Sunbeam and Alfa-Romeo hard at each other's throats with Bordino and Bugatti thrown in for good measure. During the 2nd lap Bordino began his great effort which took him first past Campari, and then on the next lap, past Guinness and Ascari in pursuit of Segrave. To the intense disappointment of spectators (and drivers) there was to be no duel between the two most successful drivers of the day, for after three laps Segrave let Bordino through and halted to change all his plugs. After five laps (one-seventh distance) there was the familiar spectacle of Bordino in the lead, challenged fiercely by the rising star Ascari a mere six seconds behind, followed by Guinness (−53 secs.), Campari (−1 min.), Wagner (−1 min. 15 secs.), Divo (−1 min. 28 secs.), Resta (−1 min. 32 secs.) and Benoist (−1 min. 45 secs.). Segrave had fallen to 14th, 3 mins. 49 secs. behind Bordino. The three Alfa-Romeos in 2nd, 4th and 5th. had taken as firm a grip on the race as the Mercedes ten years before and consolidated it during the ensuing laps. Ascari took the lead on the 10th lap at the end of which he led Bordino by three seconds at 73.6 m.p.h. with Guinness still holding grimly on 62 secs. behind, followed by Campari (−1 min. 20 secs.), Divo (−2 mins. 7 secs.), Wagner (−2 mins. 12 secs.), Chassagne (−2 mins. 14 secs.) and Resta (−2 mins. 24 secs.). At this stage the race was unbelievably open with less than 2½ minutes between the first eight cars which were all good enough to win.

278 SUNBEAM PINNACLE: . . . 'a sight and sound to swell the hearts of every Englishman' as Segrave leads off the grid

279 Bordino's great effort (No. 12) took him past Campari, Guinness and Ascari in pursuit of Segrave (No. 1)

280 FALL FROM GRACE: . . . 'after three laps Segrave let Bordino through and halted . . .'

281 . . . 'sadly enough it was the dashing Bordino with brake trouble after he had regained the lead . . .'

282 . . . 'all efforts to restart were unavailing and Ascari's gallant run ended at the foot of the hill . . .'

283 TOO MUCH IN RESERVE: Benoist tries to make up for lost time leaving Sept Chemins

Something was bound to crack under this pace and sadly enought it was the dashing Bordino with brake troubles, after he had regained the lead on the 12th lap. This was a sadder occasion than anyone then knew, marking as it did the last significant appearance in Grand Prix racing of both Fiat and Bordino, who was considered almost universally the greatest driver of the 'twenties and the lineal successor to Boillot and forerunner of Nuvolari in the transition from Ancient to Modern. During the first third of the race Ascari had fought the great Bordino and held him—the hardest possible baptism in the Grand Prix; now he could reap his reward though he had precious little chance to relax with Guinness driving another inspired race, having gained half a minute between the 10th and 15th laps, followed by Campari (−56 secs.), Divo (−1 min. 55 secs.), Benoist (−6 mins. 21 secs.), Thomas, Wagner and Segrave. Bugatti and Fiat were dropping back and Delage were now packing the places behind the leaders as they gathered for the kill. The first four were still closely bunched and Alfa-Romeo's grip on the race stronger than ever. In spite of this Guinness raised British hopes by taking the lead on the 16th lap when Ascari had his pit stop; however nothing could halt the lucky Four Leafed Clovers who were on their way to founding a motor racing legend that hot, dusty, August day forty and more years ago. By 20 laps the four leaders were still less than three minutes apart but with the Alfa-Romeos in the lead :

1. Ascari   4–1–15 = 71·5 m.p.h.   5. Benoist 4– 8–45
2. Campari 4–3–5   6. Wagner   4–11–25
3. Guinness 4–3–36   7. Segrave 4–16–13
4. Divo   4–3–57   8. Thomas 4–16–39

The only change in the ensuing five laps came when Guinness retired on the 21st lap and from this lap till the 31st the first four stayed as they were. After the excitement of the first 20 laps the race seemed to be settling to a peaceful old age, but Ascari had been slowing visibly and on the 33rd lap he was passed by Campari who then had a lead of two seconds with Divo only 73 seconds astern. At the 25 lap stage the order had been

1. Ascari   5–0–28 = 71·8 m.p.h.
2. Campari 5–3–50
3. Divo   5–5–15

so, for the first time since 1913 there seemed a possibility of a French victory and Divo was urged on by the crowd all the way round the circuit, even as Boillot had been ten years before, only this time it was a Frenchman who was doing the pursuing. In the end the effort was just too much for the gallant Divo who slowed during the final lap when it became clear he could not close the gap; otherwise he would have finished within a minute of Campari. In the meantime Ascari pulled in on his last lap to change plugs; his engine was red hot and water was pouring out of the exhaust pipe. All efforts to restart were unavailing and Ascari's gallant run ended at the foot of the hill past the pits—thus again had the leader for so many of its laps lost a Lyons Grand Prix in the last minutes. In the end it was a case of 1st Campari, 2nd Divo, and the rest really nowhere:

1. Campari	7– 5–34.3/5	= 71·0 m.p.h.	6.	Thomas
2. Divo	7– 6–40	= 70·7 m.p.h.	7.	Chassagne
3. Benoist	7–17– 0.4/5	= 69·0 m.p.h.	8.	Friederich
4. Wagner			9.	Garnier
5. Segrave			10.	Resta

For the first time the winner received a cash prize—of 100,000 francs.—to say nothing of the Lyons Sausage—a singularly appropriate award for the renowned gourmand Campari. The revolutionary Delages had lasted better than their six and eight cylinder rivals—almost too well and one has the feeling that they had held themselves too much in reserve in the early stages, of which Divo must have been very mindful as he fought to close with the flying Alfas in the last ten laps. They had also fitted higher gears following irregular running in practice which must have affected their speed over the slower sections if not their long distance reliability.

The Sunbeams supported their claim to have been the fastest cars on the course with Segrave putting in fastest lap (his 29th) at 76.7 m.p.h. and his perseverance in adversity brought him from 14th to 5th at the finish. It is one of the tragedies of history that Sunbeams heeded the blandishments of the Bosch firm to fit new magnetos on the very eve of the race which kept Segrave in trouble throughout the race. Tragic but, in retrospect, almost incredible. Bugatti, as he was at pains to assure his customers, suffered with unsuitable tyres and it was widely held that he might well have had a car in the first three otherwise, in spite of his aversion to the supercharger and his protestations that 'this car must not be considered as a racing car ... since I do not propose ever to race with a machine that is not strictly that that the customer can buy.'[7] The Schmid of Foresti non-started and Goux's might as well have done, while Zborowski's Miller after a plucky run had to give up with chassis and steering troubles. Apart from Bordino's the Fiats exerted no influence on the race. Bordino lost his right front brake and the other cars found their brakes inadequate. It was a sad end to the firm's racing career of 19 years in two continents and those of Nazzaro and Bordino. Pastore and Marchesio were below par as drivers and Salamano, recovering from an accident in the Targa Florio, was sorely missed. The suddenness of Fiat's disappearance from the racing scene after this race has been explained to me by W. F. Bradley, who says that the defeat of their cars in successive Grands Prix by cars designed by old Fiat men (Bertarione, Becchia and Jano) made the Directors weary of their racing department being used as a training ground for other firms.

Alfa Romeo had been slightly lucky to win; the Delages had finished a whole team in better shape and both Segrave

284 SPOILS OF WAR: A triumphant Campari with the Great Lyons Sausage

285 LYONS VETERANS: Wagner (2nd in 1914) finishes 4th and leads Resta (5th in 1914) who was 10th

286 Dario Resta drives his last Grand Prix before his tragic death at Brooklands in September

E.B. Circular, Op. cit.

HERNANI

URNIETA

ALDEAMURO

START ORIA

LASARTE

RIVER ORIA

287 The Lasarte circuit was narrow, twisty and poorly surfaced

and Bordino, with faster cars, had fallen out of the running with faults of detail. Perhaps it was a coincidence that an article on 'Luck in Racing' appeared earlier that year in the *Autocar* which ended with these words:

'there still remains a certain proportion of incidents so utterly beyond human control that, despite all our logic and all our reasoning, we have to call on Luck—malicious or otherwise—to furnish the necessary explanation.'

Lucky or not, the Alfa-Romeos had dominated a superb motor race which had kept the crowd on its feet to the last minute of its seven hours. After Lyons the remaining 2-litre races seemed tame affairs even though the cars and speeds continued to improve.

Alfa-Romeo and Fiat did not attend the San Sebastian Grand Prix—latterly called the Spanish Grand Prix—but Sunbeam, Bugatti and Delage did as well as Mercedes, Schmid and Diatto. The race was run over the 11 mile Lasarte circuit, which was narrow, twisty and poorly surfaced and not improved by rain the previous night and drizzle on race day. The Diatto was the product of one Alfieri Maserati, who drove it; Goux and Foresti persevered

288 Segrave was content to let others make the pace as Divo leads the field from the start at San Sebastian

with the cuff-valve Schmids, Count Masetti and Sailer had two of the four-cylinder blown Mercedes, Morel, Benoist Divo and Thomas the formidable 12-cylinder Delages, and Vizcaya, Costantini and Chassagne had Bugattis and, sadly, only two Sunbeams for Segrave and Guinness, who was driving his last Grand Prix. Sadly, because Resta, who was to have made up the team, had been killed earlier in the month making a record attempt at Brooklands, after a Grand Prix career which had begun at Dieppe in 1908 on the Austin with starting number 1. In the same tragic month Jimmy Murphy, still the only American to win the French Grand Prix on an American car had been killed in a dirt track event at Syracuse, N.Y.

Segrave had drawn a fourth row starting position and was content to let others make the pace in the opening laps of the 386 miles (35 laps). The Sunbeams seem to have been over-geared for the course or the weather conditions as neither Guinness nor Segrave could use their fourth speed, although Benoist's Delage had been fitted with an indirect fifth speed for the race. At the outset Masetti, Benoist, Divo, Maserati, Guinness, Segrave and Sailer fought the race keenly on their various cars. By the 5th lap things had settled down and Masetti had established a useful advantage with the Mercedes; it was a great pity that this talented driver, so adept at driving the difficult Mercedes cars of the period, was not seen in more Grand Prix events and he certainly proved himself among Europe's best that day at San Sebastian. By the 10th lap he was leading Segrave, Guinness and Maserati, both Sailer and Benoist having left the road and Divo being delayed with a leaking fuel tank. Guinness had a pit stop which put him temporarily behind Maserati, but he caught him half way round the 11th lap and then came disaster when the car's wheels were diverted by the rutted surface causing it to leave the road. Driver and mechanic were thrown out, the mechanic sustaining fatal and Guinness serious injuries. Segrave stopped at the scene on the next lap losing more ground to Masetti, but the dashing Count's race was nearly run for he too skidded in the wet and damaged

289 DRIVER OF THE YEAR: By winning the long and difficult Spanish Grand Prix Segrave had some reward for his upset at Lyons

his car too much to continue. Segrave then ran out a relatively easy winner though Costantini, as formidable an opponent in Spain as he was in Sicily, thanks to a record last lap at 71.7 m.p.h., was not far behind—arousing strong speculations of what might have been at Lyons, for the Delages had been well beaten by both Bugatti and Sunbeam in the result—

1. Segrave   6–1–19   4. Divo   6–11–11
2. Costantini 6–2–44   5. Vizcaya   6–29– 9
3. Morel   6–3–47   6. Chassagne 6–46–30

In winning this long and difficult race Segrave set a great seal on his career for the conditions made it as hard a race as any since André Boillot won the 1919 Targa Florio. To add to everybody's troubles the organisers had tried to improve adhesion by spreading sand on the road—a dubious enough experiment in itself—but the order had been misunderstood by the peones and in the result clay was used instead. Everyone must have been very glad to leave the inhospitable Spanish shores for sunny Italy where the last event of the year, the Italian Grand Prix, was to be held at Monza on 19th October. Even in 1924 with at least two other well supported international Grands Prix manufacturers still had the maddening habit of not supporting all the events so that it was no surprise to find no Sunbeams, Delages, Fiats or Bugattis at Monza. Four Alfa-Romeos (Ascari, Campari, Wagner and Minoia) met four Mercedes (Neubauer, Werner, Masetti and Zborowski), two Schmid (Goux and Foresti) and two 1½-litre Chiribiris. Fiat had entered but in the end found themselves 'too busy' to start!

The Mercedes were entirely new straight-eights designed by Dr. Porsche and really not ready for racing. The engines were of 61.7 × 82.8 mm. with the traditional Mercedes cylinder construction and four valves per cylinder, the

exhaust valves being sodium cooled. A single Roots-type blower was fitted and represented a two-fold departure from Mercedes supercharging practice in that it derived mixture from the carburetter and was permanently engaged. At Monza, Masetti made a brief and not very significant challenge to the Alfas and then the cars fell further and further back until they were withdrawn after Zborowski's fatal accident. They were reputed to develop 160 b.h.p. at over 7000 r.p.m. and to have achieved 130 m.p.h. at Monza but their steering and chassis made them almost impossible to drive. The engine was very advanced even though it suffered from a poor pick-up and many of its technical features were to re-appear in the 1934 cars, for Mercedes were ever conservative. So ended the one unsuccessful Mercedes comeback; even though the cars won the Avus and Solitude events in 1926 their handling was never really improved and these victories must rank as a tribute to the skill of the young Caracciola rather than to the car.

The 500 mile Grand Prix ran out to a drear and sad conclusion with the P2 Alfas winning the sort of victory one came to associate with the Type 158 cars in the post-1945 period—

1. Ascari   5– 2– 5 = 98·76 m.p.h.   4. Minoia   5–22–43
2. Wagner   5–18– 5   5. Goux   10 laps behind
3. Campari 5–21–55   6. Foresti 13 laps behind

The accident to the popular Zborowski cast a gloom that extended far beyond the shadow of Brooklands where he was best known. In a career as brief and meteoric as his father's he had achieved his life-long ambition at Monza in handling the latest works Mercedes and, like his father, he perished at the wheel of one. Whilst perhaps not in the same class as Murphy, Resta and Boyer, Zborowski had a fine record, particularly in the 1922 and 1924 Grands Prix and the 1923 Indianapolis 500, and all this he had done, as an obituary put it, 'by sheer personal courage and intense enthusiasm ... not as a professional but for the real love of the game. ... He drove, as his father drove, with all his heart and soul, but with his head as well and the sheer intoxication of it he delighted to show. ... Racing will be different without him.' Like Joe Boyer, Zborowski was gifted with great wealth with which he financed his racing from the construction of the diminutive Strasbourg Aston Martins to the great track specials he built at Higham in Kent. Zborowski was an Englishman with catholic sporting tastes and it pleases me to think that a friend of mine still uses a shooting bag with the Count's distinctive 'Z' marked on it.

For some time the rising cost of racing had been troubling organisers, constructors and drivers alike, particularly in the straitened financial conditions of the twenties and in yet another way the New World came in to redress the balance of the Old. Immense cash prizes had been a feature of the American events for many years not least because they were generally held at tracks like Indianapolis where admission money could easily be collected. It was otherwise in Europe on circuits of closed roads often of great length where the local authorities and the organising clubs had to find the money to promote the event and hope that it could pay its way. Under such conditions there was little or no margin for a prize fund, let alone starting money, and constructors had to race for the honour and glory of winning the Grand Prix of the A.C.F. and the hope of increased sales and advertising revenue. Financially, if the prize money was to be the criterion, it was about as worthwhile for a manufacturer to enter for the Grand Prix as it was for Walter Hagen to win that British Open Golf Championship prize of £100 which he promptly gave to his caddy. W. F. Bradley has written of the mercenary instincts of René Thomas after winning the 1914 '500' and, when prizes for 1st, 2nd and 3rd were announced for the 1924 Grand Prix, it was no surprise to find him campaigning for prizes for the fastest on each lap of the race as at Indianapolis. Far from regarding this as bourgeois commercialism the Chevalier René de Knyff himself opened the fund with the first 500 franc prize. In the long run, however, this sort of approach was not going to solve a problem which could only be attacked by reducing overheads and increasing revenue. The obvious way of achieving both these ends was to lay down a series of permanent circuits for each major event and the spread of these privately promoted tracks or autodromes was one of the principal developments of the mid 'twenties.

Brooklands remained the first of such sites, but this was a track pure and simple; Indianapolis followed suit and then came Monza (1922), Sitges (1923), Miramas and Montlhéry and Avus (1926). Initially Monza and Montlhéry had combinations of road and track while Sitges, Miramas and Avus were pure speedbowl. Later came pure road circuits in private grounds such as Nürburg Ring (1927) and Donington Park (1931/3). All this added up to the death of the old system when the classic race venue varied from year to year over a pure road circuit of appreciable length. From 1925 the sites of the French and Italian Grands Prix became established and remained almost entirely at Montlhéry and Monza for a decade. Thus it came about that Lyons contrived to stage both the last great Edwardian road race and also the last great road race in the old traditional manner, both of which were fittingly perfect examples of their kind.

Drivers anyway might heave a sigh of relief at the prospect of better money and also better roads, for those at Le Mans, Strasbourg, Tours and Lyons had left much to be desired. Opinion was rather more divided, however, on two other developments that were announced at the end of 1924. The 2-litre capacity limit was to continue into 1925 with a minimum weight of 12 cwt. 89 lb. and then for 1926 the limit and minimum weight were to be reduced to 1½-litres and 10 cwt. 92 lb. respectively but with 2-seater bodies and from 1925 the riding mechanic was to be dropped as had already happened at Indianapolis. The fatalities to four prominent drivers during the year and other accidents, particularly in the Spanish event, had brought in their wake an exceptional realisation of The Price of Speed. Thus the idea of faster, lighter and better streamlined cars after 1925 was met with cries of horror from both drivers and manufacturers, while opinion on the dropping of the mechanic was reasonably divided. In 1921 Louis Coatalen had seen Segrave's Brescia Bugatti with its bolster petrol tank and very exposed cockpit and remarked rather disparagingly "She is old now".' Three years later such was his opposition to increased speed that he was writing in the *Autocar*:

'I should strongly favour also, the suppression of the tail on the body of the racing car. This also should reduce the maximum speed.'

In the same article he was half advocating, half deprecating streamlining and the single-seater body but in his published writings Coatalen was a real Mr. Facing-Both-Ways and it is often no more easy to follow his published thought processes than to navigate the Hampton Court maze.

The arguments for the mechanic were that he helped the driver watch his instruments, the condition of his car and the movements of other drivers, besides assisting in whatever work had to be done to the car away from the pits. With the wisdom of hindsight it is difficult to see any sense in most of these arguments but in 1924 drivers of the experience of Divo, Segrave and S. C. H. Davis were all firmly convinced the mechanic had a useful job to do and to dismiss their views as nonsense is to take an unjustifiable view of history. Nevertheless there existed an equally authoritative body of contrary opinion—'Do away with the mechanic all the time and every time ... if the driver is incapable of watching his revolution counter he ought to fit a governor to his engines,' said André Boillot; 'We have plenty of proof that racing cars can be so designed that one man can handle them with safety; why, therefore, risk another man's life needlessly?' was the view of Louis Wagner. In Divo's opinion the mechanic was useful for running repairs en route and because the mechanic's seat was a good apprenticeship in racing 'and if we rule out the mechanic we are likely to reduce the number of drivers ... mechanics are always volunteers and I believe there are plenty of applicants.' Signor Cavalli, assistant chief engineer of Fiats, took an opposite stand... 'We have' he said, 'almost as much difficulty in finding mechanics as in selecting drivers. Men are willing to work on the preparation of racing cars, but they do not show any enthusiasm for going out in the mechanic's seat.... There is nothing for (the mechanic) to do on the racing car and he should not be allowed to take a seat thereon.' With opposition from manufacturers, many drivers and mechanics coupled with the example of Indianapolis, the final dropping of the mechanic seems now no surprise. Probably the remarks attributed to Paul Bablot, with his memories of Molon in the 1913 Le Mans race, sum it all up as well as anything:

'I would not be a racing mechanic for millions. ... Sharing the risk, having none of the glory, useless, powerless, the mechanic is merely a bundle carried around as a concession to an old practice ... as he understands a good deal about the handling of a car and has no duties to keep him occupied his mind is constantly fixed on the dangers of the next turn. ... When there was time to change a valve and still win a race there was some need for a mechanic, but his place nowadays is at the pit.'

If there were two schools of thought on the mechanic, drivers and constructors spoke with one voice about rising speeds and the 1926 regulations:

'The cause of the unfortunate accidents is that now the cars are too fast and only by reducing the speed can one make them safer.'
Louis Coatalen

'I am certain that those responsible (for the new rules) have never ridden in a modern racing car. The present cars are too fast even for the best of us. ...'
Pietro Bordino

'I consider the new rules the utmost folly ... in two years' time (the cars) will be faster still and as they will be appreciably lighter no man will be able to hold them. It will be almost fatal to the motor movement to put these new rules into force.'
Louis Wagner

290 SEAT PERILOUS: the mechanic's perch—in a 1922 G.P. Fiat

'The new rules are stark madness. They will produce a type of car which will be a death-trap and because of the accidents which will follow the entire movement will be set back. This year at Lyons it was impossible to hold the cars on the straightway. In 1926 we shall have just as much power and considerably less weight.'
André Boillot

'The great defect of modern racing cars is that their road adhesion is so low that they are dangerous.'
J. E. Scales

'The result will be that we shall have an overpowered engine in a featherweight chassis having a low co-efficient of safety and exceedingly difficult to hold on the road at high speeds.'
René Thomas

In the midst of all this argument about the mechanic having nothing to do the inevitable Heath Robinson came forward in the shape of one E. A. Hellstrand with this suggestion for improving road adhesion

*'Would it not be practicable to fit light racing cars for track use with a couple of ailerons one projecting each side of the car about the back of the driver's seat and at the level of the chassis frame ... the adjustment could be partly by hand and interconnected with a pointer and scale in view of the driver so that settings found suitable ... could quickly be made with certainty.
Has any reader tried devices on the lines indicated?'*

Well if any of the *Autocar's* readers HAD, they certainly were not owning up to it in print and to this day no racing car has been fitted with ailerons.

Chapter Sixteen
1925 · Alfa-Romeo Triumph and Tragedy

Three major races took place in Europe in 1925, all of which were dominated by Alfa-Romeo; all three counted towards the newly ordained manufacturers' World Championship, the fourth event in the series being the Indianapolis '500'. Although at one time Great Britain had been in the running for the honour, the European Grand Prix for 1925 was awarded to Belgium and it was on the historic Spa circuit that this, the first Grand Prix of the year, was held. At the time the 15-kilometre circuit represented a very considerable break with tradition; first, it was rather shorter than most of the classic road circuits previously chosen, and secondly it lacked those long straight stretches of Routes Nationales connected by hairpins that had hitherto characterized the Grand Prix circuits. The Lyons circuit of 1924

SPA
LAP DISTANCE - 8·76 Miles

291 BREAK WITH TRADITION: the historic Spa circuit was considerably shorter than the previous road circuits and lacked their long straight stretches

had been a step in this direction and Spa continued the process of picking circuits to test acceleration and brakes no less than maximum speed. The original version embodied much of today's circuit with its fast corners that could be taken at nearly full speeds by the skilled drivers. It was less severe than Lyons, faster than San Sebastian, but clearly slower than the Strasbourg, Tours or Le Mans circuits.

Twelve starters were prospected but Sunbeam eventually scratched and then the sleeve-valve Guyots followed suit, leaving the four Delages of Thomas, Benoist, Divo and Torchy to oppose the Alfa-Romeos of Ascari, Campari and Brilli Peri. Both marques had improved their existing cars for the new season, Alfas by detail work and Delage by adding a supercharger. Divo's car was a new machine, while the other three were 1924 models fitted with superchargers. The race was an Alfa-Romeo benefit, Ascari winning by 22 minutes from Campari at an average of 74.46 m.p.h. for the 500 miles. There were no other finishers. In the early stages Benoist and later Divo, held 3rd behind Ascari and Campari; Benoist had a split fuel tank on the 2nd lap, Torchy retired soon after and Thomas caught fire in the 7th lap, burning his left hand. Divo struggled on and at one time set a lap record at over 79 m.p.h., although Ascari finally left it at 81.5 m.p.h. Divo retired shortly after half distance and Brilli Peri spoilt a complete Alfa coup when he retired about the same time with a broken spring. Ascari, still preferring a slab tank surmounted by spare wheel in 1913 style, led from start to finish without any apparent effort and the French Grand Prix a month later boded remarkably ill for Delage in spite of his having prepared four brand new cars for his highly experienced team of Thomas, Benoist, Divo and Louis Wagner, back at the wheel of a French car once again. The new cars had two superchargers, one serving each bank of cylinders, drawing mixture from the carburetter and delivering it through a straight manifold on the outside of the block. A vast revolution counter dominated the instrument board, tinted in green from 5000 to 6200 r.p.m. and in red from 6200 to 7000 r.p.m. In appearance the cars were lower and better streamlined in all directions.

The Montlhéry Autodrome had been opened in 1924 but most extensive preparations were still being made under the supervision of the A.C.F. for its first great race. In addition to the despised Delages, Bugatti had entered five unsupercharged cars for Costantini, the de Vizcaya brothers, Goux and Foresti, Alfa-Romeo had their three Spa drivers and Sunbeam completed the field with three 1924 cars for Segrave and Counts Masetti and Conelli. Not surprisingly Alfa-Romeo were firm favourites, with Sunbeam second, nobody having much faith in the wretched Louis Delage after Spa. As in 1924 Segrave had drawn No. 1 starting position but he cannot have faced his adversaries with any show of confidence. Poor Segrave! 1925 was his last Grand Prix year on a circuit he manifestly disliked, with a slower car and the recollection of the recent Le Mans '24' which, like so many other Grand Prix drivers, he had roundly detested. As a race the Grand Prix was dull and tragic, bringing the death of Ascari when securely in the lead shortly after quarter distance. Before the race Thomas' Delage was withdrawn and there was a tremendous furore when Bugatti refused to remove the cowlings with which he had covered the 'mechanic's seat' on his cars. Bugatti argued that as the rules merely required a width of 31 ins. and two seats side by side, his cars should qualify, and refused to modify them. The Commission Sportive were equally adamant but finally Bugatti gave way and cut back the offending cowlings.

De Vizcaya's Bugatti took a temporary lead, but the first car to appear on the piste de vitesse at the conclusion of the first lap was Ascari's red Alfa-Romeo with a lead of nearly quarter of a mile from Divo, Masetti, Wagner, Campari, Segrave, Brilli Peri, Benoist, Conelli and the unblown Bugattis. During the next lap Ascari pulled out almost another half mile from Divo, whilst Campari moved into 3rd and Brilli Peri into 6th; to make things worse Divo came to the pits with plug and carburetter troubles on the 3rd lap and by the 5th lap Ascari had amassed a lead of 1 min. 32 secs. in under 40 miles of racing! Campari lay 2nd, 28 secs. ahead of Wagner with Masetti only another second behind, so it was level pegging between Sunbeam and Delage but Alfa-Romeo had already established a stranglehold that had taken them half the race to achieve the year before. During the next five laps Divo gave up with supercharger troubles and Brilli Peri had a long pit stop which dropped him to 12th on the tenth lap. Ascari had only increased his lead to 2 mins. 8 secs. over Campari, who had pulled out to 1 min. 21 secs. ahead of Wagner and the race, as a contest between marques, seemed as dead as the European Grand Prix a month before. Ascari had his first routine pit stop after 15 laps when he led by 2 mins. 42 secs. but did not lose his lead to Campari. Wagner also had a brief stop and all these comings and goings let Benoist into 2nd place at quarter distance (20 laps):—

1. Ascari   2–1–54   4. Masetti   2–5–22
2. Benoist   2–4–54   5. Segrave   2–7–44
3. Campari   2–5–1   6. Conelli   2–9–51

292/3/4 NELSON TOUCH: The P 2 Alfa-Romeos had a sweeping triumph at Spa: Ascari (top) before and (centre) after his last victory, with riding mechanic Giulio Ramponi behind the bonnet in the top picture

143

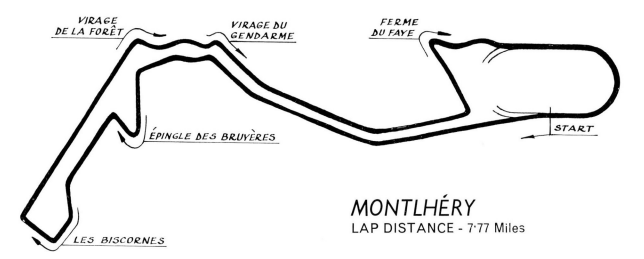

VIRAGE DE LA FORÊT   VIRAGE DU GENDARME   FERME DU FAYE

ÉPINGLE DES BRUYÈRES

START

LES BISCORNES

MONTLHÉRY
LAP DISTANCE - 7·77 Miles

296 '. . . at one moment the flying red car had seemed the very embodiment of speed . . .'

297 DOMINATING ENTRY: The P2 Alfa-Romeos being prepared before the start of the Grand Prix

The Delages were just slightly faster but seemingly less reliable than the Sunbeams at this stage, but neither would have had a vestige of hope against the fleeting Alfa-Romeos, had not stark tragedy intervened. On his 22nd lap Ascari skidded whilst negotiating an easy left hand bend and found his car out of control when its hubs became entangled with the light garden type of paled fencing put up all round the course· Had he met a retaining wall it is at least possible the accident would not have been fatal. As it was the car tore down 130 yards of fencing before it finally went out of control and overturned in a ditch. The driver died on his way to hospital and the news was immediately given out, casting a terrible gloom over the whole circuit. At one moment the flying red car with its burly bronzed driver had seemed the very embodiment of speed with utter safety, and now it lay crumpled by the wayside whilst the remaining cars roared sadly past into the increasing rain. It was this very rain suddenly dampening the circuit that probably caused the great and dashing Ascari to make this one and fatal error.

Campari soon was past Benoist's car again, now with Divo driving, and had established an easy lead by the 30-lap stage, followed by Masetti, Wagner, Segrave and Costantini at ever increasing distances. A lap later and Segrave was out with a broken valve, leaving Masetti with the sole surviving Sunbeam, Conelli already having dropped out with deficient brakes. At thirty laps Campari had led Divo by almost 5 minutes; much of the fight had gone out of Campari's driving and Divo for his part was going for all he was worth and at half distance (40 laps) he had caught up to within 2 mins. 13 secs. of the leader : —

1. Campari	4– 7–28	4. Costantini	4–23–41
2. Benoist-Divo	4– 9–41	5. Wagner	4–25–47
3. Masetti	4–16– 3	6. Goux	4–27–31

Soon after both Campari and Brilli Peri came into the pits, raced their engines 'for a few seconds, causing them to emit a note which sounded like a wail of despair' and retired

144

following the sad tidings of Ascari's death. This left two Delages, one Sunbeam and all five Bugattis still running; Divo now held an easy lead which he was increasing all the time until he handed over to Benoist after having driven 29 out of 50 laps, leaving Benoist the final thirty and a two lap lead over Masetti. Wagner passed on the tedium of his drive to Torchy for twenty laps at much the same time, while Masetti drove all the way himself.

Rain continued intermittently right through the afternoon and at 4.30 p.m. the President of the Republic arrived in the midst of yet another shower. At the 60 lap ($\frac{3}{4}$ distance) stage Benoist had a lead of over 14 minutes, but Wagner was closing on Masetti, now delayed because floor boards had worked loose and jammed the accelerator. So the race ran on to its appointed conclusion with the eight finishers separated by nearly an hour after the longest single-day's Grand Prix then held :—

1. Benoist-Divo   8–54–41.1/5 = 69·7 m.p.h.
2. Wagner-Torchy   9– 2–27.2/5 = 68·7 m.p.h.
3. Masetti   9– 6–15.1/5 = 68·2 m.p.h.
4. Costantini   9– 7–38.2/5 = 68   m.p.h.
5. Goux   9–15–11.1/5
6. F. de Vizcaya   9–20–48.2/5
7. P. de Vizcaya   9–41–1.3/5
8. Foresti   9–49–38.3/5

Benoist received a prize of 150,000 frs. (nearly £1,500), Wagner 30,000 frs. and Masetti 20,000 frs. for their long day's work; Masetti is reputed to have described the circuit as more difficult than the Madonie and one cannot resist the feeling that the race was at least 150 miles too long, in spite of the *Autocar's* comment that 'given a good field and fast cars there need never be a moment lacking in interest even over such a tremendous distance.' In fact the only result of the extended distance had been to fatigue the spectators rather than the cars, the only material change being the displacing of Count Masetti. The Alfa-Romeos which had dominated the race till their withdrawal, ran on specially doped fuel with their superchargers geared up to run at 6000 r.p.m. for 5000 r.p.m. of the engine. The Sunbeams employed a mixture of 6-4 petrol and benzole, while the Delages ran on straight petrol, with the relatively low compression ratio of $5\frac{1}{2}$: 1 and a reputed fuel consumption of 11 to 12 m.p.g.

With the demise of the prospected Brooklands '500', due to troubles over complaints of noise, the Italian Grand Prix at Monza on the 6th September was the final European event to count for the World title and interest was again heightened by the presence of an American entry. The 1925 American '500' was the first to be won at over 100 m.p.h. and was contested by cars of basically Miller or Duesenberg design, with the spice of Bordino's 1924 Grand Prix Fiat thrown in. Two new names appeared in Millers—Ralph Hepburn and Leon Duray—both of whom obtained considerable reputations in the ensuing years. Hepburn retired after 144 laps

298 Count Masetti in crash helmet gets into his Sunbeam which finished 3rd

299 Conelli who drove the third Sunbeam

300 Wagner (left—14) and Benoist (right—10) with Louis Delage between the cars wearing cap after the Grand Prix

145

301 RECORD WINNER: Peter de Paolo whose record at Indy stood from 1925 to 1932 and who drove an Alfa into 5th later in the year at Monza

302 Bordino who managed to finish 10th in the '500' with his monoposto 1924 Fiat

with a leaking petrol tank, while Duray finished 6th. Ralph de Palma drove a Miller into 7th and his nephew, Peter de Paolo, shared the wheel of the winning Miller with Norman Batten. Bordino managed to finish 10th at 94.75 m.p.h. compared with the winner's 101.13 m.p.h.—a record which was not lowered until 1932. Three of these record breaking cars were entered for Monza to be driven by de Paolo, Tommy Milton and Peter Kreis and a special dispensation allowed them to run in single seater form but with a minimum width of 31 ins. by the provision of a dummy body round the normal shell. The American cars differed at almost every point from European practice with their use of balloon tyres, plain bearings throughout their engines, centrifugal superchargers, and single seater bodies. Like most Europeans though, Tommy Milton expressed the view that the 2-litre cars were too fast for safety and that the proposed reduction to $1\frac{1}{2}$ litres was a step in the right direction.

In the end it turned out that one of the Duesenbergs was not ready and de Paolo was paid the great compliment of being given Ascari's place in the Alfa-Romeo team beside Campari and Brilli Peri. The opposition consisted of the two other Americans on Duesenbergs, Materassi on a blown straight-eight Diatto and Guyot on one of his sleeve-valve cars. The Alfas were running on balloon tyres, doped fuel and a reputed compression ratio of $7\frac{1}{2}:1$, very much higher than the Americans. In fact the Americans, making their last serious challenge in a European race, put up a tremendous fight and with a little more fortune Milton might easily have defeated the Alfa-Romeos on their own ground and annexed the title for America. As it was he stalled at the start and had to drive 450 of the 500 miles on top gear only; by the end of the first lap he had caught Materassi and a lap later was lying 5th behind de Paolo (4th), Brilli Peri, Campari and Kreis who had a length's lead. On the 3rd lap at Lesmo, Kreis met trouble and withdrew; Guyot fell out after 7 laps and Materassi after 10, leaving Milton to fight it out with the Alfas. This he did with great purpose in spite of his gearbox troubles and a broken rear shock absorber; first he overhauled his compatriot de Paolo and then he went after the two burly Italians. His method of driving provided an entertaining contrast with their fiery style, tending 'to give the impression that the struggle was not terribly severe. Frequently when running down the straight at more than 100 m.p.h. he would look right round to see if anyone was behind and on one occasion ... (addressed) Foresti on the circuit with the greeting ... How do sporty boy!' On the 33rd and 34th laps the leading Alfas had their routine stops and Milton went ahead, while Campari slowed with misfiring and handed over to his reserve driver Minozzi. Milton then led for 7 laps till he stopped on his 39th lap, taking the appallingly slow time of 4 mins. 50 secs. to refuel and change wheels. This dropped him to 5 minutes behind Brilli Peri whom he had previously led by about 1½ minutes and two laps later he was in trouble again with a broken oil pipe which it took 20 minutes to repair.

Thereafter Brilli Peri continued to lead unchallenged from de Paolo and Campari with Milton going great guns but hopelessly behind. A 1½-litre race run at the same time was dominated by five Bugattis and Constantini actually managed to get by Milton in the closing stages; de Paolo also had troubles with an exhaust pipe falling off during the last ten laps which cost him 2nd place, the final order being:

1. Brilli Peri 5–14–33 = 94·76 m.p.h.
2. Campari 5–35–30
3. Costantini 5–44–40
4. Milton 5–46–40
5. de Paolo 5–48–10
6. de Vizcaya F. 5–50–49
7. Foresti 5–55–18
8. de Vizcaya P. 6– 1–32

Fastest laps: 2 litres—Brilli Peri 104·03 m.p.h. (elsewhere given as Kreis at 103·21 m.p.h.)
1½ litres—Costantini 92·91 m.p.h.

Thus the Italians clinched the first championship with a clear cut victory on their own ground amid scenes of frenzied jubilation although apparently the strength of their fervour was not enough to enable them to bear the weighty victor shoulder high! With a little more luck Tommy Milton might have carried the day and, whilst Brilli Peri claimed he was being signalled down all the time, a pressing Delage with Divo at the wheel might possibly also have told its tale. Yet the odd fact remains that even with the improved 1925 cars, the 1924 race and lap records were not beaten in the 1925 event, in which, if anything, the competition was keener.

Delage raced once more in the year gaining a hollow win in the Spanish Grand Prix at San Sebastian for Divo from Benoist and Thomas. The race was marred by a fatal accident to Torchy on the fourth Delage; Costantini accomplished fastest lap at 82.75 m.p.h. but crashed, the remaining Bugattis finishing 4th, 5th, 6th and 7th in their habitual style. Masetti's Sunbeam withdrew and no Alfa-Romeos started, thus robbing the race of any real importance.

The 2-litre formula of 1922/5 set the course of motor racing for the next twenty five years and provided an interesting if almost bewildering variety of technical developments. As a result of all this experimenting with 6, 8 and 12 cylinders, supercharging centrifugal and otherwise, blowing through or from the carburetter, tyres with beaded edge straight side or balloon, front and rear engines, poppet cuff and sleeve valves, streamlining, and even independent rear suspension, the basic design of the racing car settled down to the hard-sprung, Roots-blown straight-eight with balloon tyres and front mounted engine. Significantly, all the 1½-litre cars of 1926/7 followed this basic pattern. The mechanic was finally dropped in 1924, apart from the J.C.C. '200' in 1925 held at Brooklands—where else? The tendency towards tracks increased gate money and consequently prize

303 AMERICAN INVADER: Peter Kreis with the Duesenberg he drove at Indy and Monza

304 EUROPEAN DEFENDER: Brilli Peri who won the Italian Grand Prix

305 HOLLOW WIN: Divo's Delage takes the lead as the pace car pulls off at San Sebastian, with Masetti's Sunbeam (5) challenging

306 By 1925 the successful Delage had lost much of the smooth outline of its predecessors

funds and this in turn served to create a new school of professional drivers—the well-to-do amateur, like Antonio Ascari, who started as a prosperous motor agent and became one of the greatest drivers of the period.

France went through a bad patch in spite of two Delage wins in 1925 and was lucky indeed to score her first Grand Prix win in 12 years. For the two middle years the Anglo-Italo-French Sunbeams had a fleeting hey-day, but the dominant country was undoubtedly Italy, first with Fiat and then Alfa-Romeo and equally it was their big bronzed drivers who inevitably caught the eye, Bordino and Nazzaro of the old guard, Ascari, Campari and Brilli Peri of the new. German racing cars re-appeared without any great distinction and France in her turn produced two very fine drivers in Divo and Benoist besides the pre-war veterans, Goux, Thomas and Wagner, who were all still capable of more than holding their own, though really past their prime.

Competition in the middle years of the formula had been very keen, both the 1923 and 1924 Grands Prix having been very fine races; not every constructor had been fully prepared in 1922 and interest was waning by 1925 which accounted for the pre-eminence of Fiat and Alfa-Romeo in those years. Even America was still capable of putting up something of a show in a European event—a great deal better than Europe's in America although neither Delage, Sunbeam nor Alfa-Romeo appeared at Indianapolis during the period.

Tragedy had struck repeatedly at such fine drivers as Resta, Zborowski, Boyer, Murphy, Biagio Nazzaro, Sivocci, Torchy, Giaccone and Antonio Ascari and there were frequent calls for reduced speeds and some futurists even suggested fitting the cars with a form of anti-roll bar and strapping the drivers in! In reality the idea of reducing speeds was not particularly meaningful, as a correspondent to the *Autocar* pointed out—'When a car leaves the road at over 100 m.p.h. it is immaterial by how much that figure is exceeded.' At long last, however, the driver had only his own life in his hands for the mechanic was now out in all races of consequence just as the supercharger was in on all cars of consequence, with all deference to those two institutions the J.C.C. '200' and Ettore Bugatti. At long last Bugatti secured a win in a relatively important race in the 1925 Targa Florio, although the 1925 version was by no means a great one in the series. Bugatti, however, though he might not have known it, was standing on the threshold of his greatest days. Great they undoubtedly were, but it is well to remember that much of the opposition in the years between 1926 and 1931 was second class compared to the fields in the years 1923/5, consisting as it so often did of sheep-in-wolf's-clothing sporting cars thinly disguised as racers.

Chapter Seventeen
1926/7 · The Harvest of Louis Delage
Part One—Burning the Tares (1926)

The first 1½-litre formula would have been as outstanding as the 1914 and 1923/5 formulae if all the cars built for it had raced in anything like all the races. However, like its 1945/51 counterpart it never realised the competitive distinction of which both were inherently capable. The post-war formula was distinguished by an outstanding design in the 158/9 Alfa-Romeo and the competition of the 4½-litre unblown Ferrari. In 1926/7 there was an equally outstanding design in the Delage, which like the Alfa was developed over a period of many years until its ultimate performance and form bore little resemblance to the original. With the possible exception of the P2 Alfa, no two cars have lasted so long as these two cars built to 1½-litre restrictions; oddly and fittingly enough the Alfa (or Alfetta as it was originally and rather unpleasingly known) succeeded in 1938 to the voiturette crown which the rejuvenated Delage of Richard Seaman had vacated at the end of 1936. Even more strangely the two cars raced against each other on several occasions during the post-war years, at least as late as 1950. A similar juxtaposition of the ages, outside vintage racing, would have been provided by a 1914 4½-litre unblown car in a 1938/40 formula Grand Prix. The situation after the greatly increased speeds of 1924/5 and 1935/7 was much the same in that the governing body in each case sought to limit speeds; as we have seen the formula brought cries of protest from such diverse authorities as Louis Wagner, Pietro Bordino, Louis Coatalen and René Thomas. The odd thing is that a 1½-litre limit had been *de facto* accepted for Voiturette racing ever since 1920 without any complaints about safety, but now the A.I.A.C.R. sought to impose one *de jure* you could hardly hear the exhausts for the welter of complaint. The capacity limit was accepted on both sides of the Atlantic but the more contrary Europeans added an increased weight minimum of 700 kgs. (13 cwt. 87 lbs.) and kept the minimum cockpit width at 80 cm. (31.5 ins.).

For the new formula the S.T.D. cars were designated Talbots and built at Suresnes, perhaps to keep them further from the disapproving thoughts of English shareholders at a time when the combine's finances were sadly on the wane.

Bertarione's last design was a good one but was spoilt by lack of time, interest and finance. The engine was a straight eight of characteristic Fiat construction measuring 56 × 75.5 mm., producing in the region of 145 b.h.p. at 6500 r.p.m. and running up to 7000 r.p.m. The chassis, however, was much more refreshing. First, the whole thing was much lower and, as a result of having no mechanic to cater for, it was possible to lower the engine and transmission by setting this across the centre line. With the driver actually sitting in the undertray there was a mere eight or nine inches of ground clearance which must have made the bumpy roads and tracks of those times at the very least interesting. The cars had swept pointed tails and steeply raked radiators giving them a most distinctive appearance. The second feature was the split front axle which was made up of two hollow halves joined by flanges at the centre. Thirdly, the chassis frame itself eschewed the usual channel section construction being 'made from a double length of channel with suitable vertical spacing members, each side member being pressed out as one piece . . . rather like a Lancia Lambda frame on a small scale.' This chassis was cross braced by tubes and girder type members providing an immensely stout construction in an age when chassis tended to flex like aspen trees.

307 MOST DISTINCTIVE: the 1926/27 Talbots with their swept pointed tails, steeply raked radiators and low racy lines

308 SHATTERING FORETASTE: in original form the 1926 Delage exhaust pipe passed close to the driver and caused him dire discomfort. Here Senechal works on the car while Wagner cools off during the British Grand Prix

Apart from engine and gearbox in unit and similar dimensions (57.5 × 75), the Delage differed at almost every turn. In the 1927 version of this car Grand Prix design reached one of its all time peaks and it merits detailed consideration in the form of extracts from Pomeroy's description in 'The Grand Prix Car' upon which improvement is impossible and paraphrase impertinence. In a sense Louis Delage had been preparing himself for this car since 1913 when he had so nearly won the Amiens Grand Prix; it will be remembered that these cars won the subsequent Grand Prix de France at Le Mans and the 1914 Indianapolis '500' whilst his 5-speed positively-closed-valve cars had met with rather less success in Europe and America in 1914 and later. After some unsuccessful experiments with a 4-cylinder 2-litre engine in 1922, he went to the other end of the scale with the 12-cylinder car which he developed steadily and thoroughly throughout the great years of the 2-litre formula to the point where it won two Grands Prix in 1925, though it never actually defeated the P2 Alfa-Romeo, which must be regarded as Top Dog of that formula. M. Lory had been largely responsible for the development of this most original design of M. Plancton his predecessor and it is not surprising to find many similar details of design and general appearance between the 1925 and 1926 cars; these, however, underwent considerable changes following their showing in the Spanish and British Grands Prix of 1926 where, although they were 3rd and 1st respectively, they contrived to give their drivers a shattering foretaste of the flames of hell-fire. Now for Pomeroy. . . . 'On the 1926 models the exhaust pipes were placed on the right hand side of the car and throughout the year much trouble was caused by and races

lost on account of the driver's feet becoming burnt. In 1927 the exhaust pipe was changed to the left hand side and this involved removing the twin blowers previously mounted centrally and substituting a single blower on the nose of the timing cover. Other changes were a different design of radiator, thicker camshafts and considerably stiffer steering arms. These alterations had a considerable effect upon the fortunes of the design. Whereas the 1926 edition had only one win to its credit in 1927 the cars carried all before them, winning the French, the British, the Italian and Spanish Grands Prix.'

By means similar to those employed on the Talbot overall height was drastically reduced and in consequence although the body width could not be reduced to less than 31.5 ins. the frontal area of the car came to the remarkably low figure of $9\frac{1}{2}$ sq. ft.

'Thus, supposing that the engine power was in proportion to the capacity, one would have expected this $1\frac{1}{2}$-litre model to have compared quite favourably with the 2-litre which had preceded it. In fact however the power-per-litre was increased to a remarkable extent and although the sustained maximum r.p.m. cited were 6500 the engine could be run at 8000 r.p.m. at which speed it gave 170 b.h.p. in its original form. This is within 20 h.p. of the 1925 twelve-cylinder Delage and is equivalent to an m.e.p. of 177 p.s.i., a particularly fine figure in view of the low boost pressure (7 p.s.i.) and moderate compression ratio. Whether the engine could be run continuously at 8000 r.p.m. is somewhat doubtful . . . and it is likely that 132 m.p.h. at 6500 r.p.m. was the maximum ever attained on this gear (overdrive 5th) in exceptionally favourable circumstances. However, the driver had the option of running at say 128 m.p.h. at either 6300 in overdrive or 7500 r.p.m. in direct. A multiplate clutch lay between the engine and gearbox and the latter was of extreme length which, taken in conjuction with the engine mounting, resulted in there being virtually no cross bracing between the radiator and the driver's seat. This gave the car a characteristic weaving motion that affected the steadiness on the straight and impaired handling qualities on corners. . . .

'A touchstone by which we may fix the success or otherwise of a racing car is the advance which it represents in power output, subject to its achieving reasonable standards of reliability. By this test the $1\frac{1}{2}$-litre Delage engine was TRULY A MILESTONE IN DESIGN, for whereas in 1925 the 2-litre twelve-cylinder Delage developed 190 b.h.p.—*viz.* 95 b.h.p. per litre—in 1926 the $1\frac{1}{2}$-litre model developed 170 b.h.p., equal to 113.5 b.h.p. per litre or a gain of nearly 20 per cent.' Pomeroy's calculations that with a 15 lb. boost the Delage could have equalled the post-war 158 Alfa-Romeo cannot therefore be terribly wide of the mark.

'Reliability was first class. The Delage Company ran twenty cars in seven races during the period 1926/7, out of which they won five, finished first, second and third in two, and had three retirements due to engine trouble. Ten years afterwards Richard Seaman ran for a complete season without engine trouble and, in fact, won three races in succession (within 14 days and in countries as far removed as England, Switzerland and Italy) without any adjustment being carried out, probably a record in the history of the racing automobile.' During this time Seaman was getting a reliable 195 b.h.p. by very simple modification to the existing components, which in fact was more than that of the early 158 Alfa-Romeo which in its initial tests in 1938 produced 190 b.h.p. at 6500 r.p.m. and was timed in its second race at 139.53 m.p.h. on the straight at Pescara in the Coppa Acerbo. The Alfa did not win this race but it was won by a Maserati at 82.06 m.p.h. compared with Seaman on the Delage in 1936 at 77.25 m.p.h. though it is fair to add that this was a touring average with no opposition and in fact slower than his 1935 average on a B-type E.R.A.

As on the 2-litre V-12 the engine construction was complex and costly, a characteristic feature being the 'mass of the timing and auxiliary drive gears which have secured an almost legendary fame. . . . The camshaft drive involved no less than eight gears, to which should be added seven to the magneto, two to the oil pump and two to the water pump, whilst originally there were a further four for the supercharger installation, all . . . on roller bearings.'

'The block and head were an integral single iron casting, the block having open sides covered by steel sheets, the engine representing a technical *tour de force* both in design and construction the casting of the eight-cylinder block in itself being an achievement of no mean order. On the other hand the engine was heavy and measured 55 ins. from the timing case to the rear universal joint. This in conjunction with the method of engine mounting led, to a frame which was very weak in tension and it can be argued that excellent engine design was offset to a material extent by deficiencies in chassis layout.' The car's last international appearance in anything approaching original form was in the 2nd heat of the Daily Express International Trophy at Silverstone in August 1950, when A. P. R. Rolt failed to finish due to gearbox trouble. Thereafter it appeared with an E-Type E.R.A. engine driven by Rolt and P. D. C. Walker, a 1939 engine, but still in that deficient 1927 chassis instead of the E.R.A.'s own de Dion axled affair. Another of its more interesting post-war appearances was at Gransden Lodge in 1947, which, as in 1946, was the only motor racing meeting to be held in England! On this occasion it was driven by R. Habershon and opposed by G. Radford on a Talbot carrying on where Louis Wagner left off in July 1927. 'Both drove from the second the flag fell as if they were driving in a 1927 Grand Prix and as if they had been ordered by Lory and Coatalen to break up the opposition factory's

309 OUT OF ITS TIME: The last appearance of the Delage in formula racing was in the 1950 Silverstone meeting driven by A. P. R. Rolt

team, (and) it was bad luck for Radford that history should repeat itself twenty years later when he was forced out to leave that mechanical marvel the 1927 Delage securely settled in first place.' A similar, if not the same car had also raced in 1946 in a heat before the Grand Prix des Nations at Geneva, the first post-war race of any consequence and also at Albi when Nuvolari scored his last victory, strangely enough on a car borrowed from Gigi Platè, who had frequently driven the 1927 Talbots. By one of those quirks of fate it was Nuvolari who dropped the starting flag when the Delage set out on its last Grand Prix event at Silverstone.

M. Lory, as a designer, did not survive so well into the post-war period with the ill fated C.T.A. Arsenal which was the first entirely newly designed car of its time, if one accepts its similarity to the old vintage Delages. The car practised at Lyons for the 1947 French Grand Prix, but the luckless Sommer, after constant troubles in practice, failed to leave the starting line with a clutch that started by refusing to free and finished by going in with such force that the back axle broke. Three years later when the Delage was making its final appearance at Silverstone, the same thing happened to the unhappy Sommer on another National Project, the fabulous V-16 B.R.M. the ultimate in 1½-litre engine complexity. Time may have its revolutions but it is uncanny how often the wheels of history stop at the same place.

If the Delage was 'the crowning achievement of the Vintage decade', there were several other very outstanding cars about in 1926/7, of which the Talbot was but one. Miller, Duesenberg, Maserati, Bugatti, Alvis and Parry Thomas all built straight-eights, Frank Halford a six, Itala a 60 degree V-12, Fiat a twin six, following a six-cylinder two-stroke with 12 horizontally opposed pistons and Duesenberg also experimented with a straight-eight 2-stroke. Of these various cars Bugatti and Maserati were almost entirely

310 UNLUCKY SURVIVOR: Monsieur Lory (extreme left) during trials of his post-war C.T.A.-Arsenal with Sommer at the wheel

311 DEAD STOP: three years later the same thing happened to Sommer with the B.R.M. (another national project) when the 1926/27 Delage was making its final appearance

312 ENTIRELY CONVENTIONAL: the 1½-litre straight-eight was the first Maserati and proved heavy and slow: here is Ernesto Maserati in the 1926 Targa Florio where he finished 8th

conventional; Ettore at long last succumbed to the blower and produced the Type 39 which had the Type 35 bore of 60 mm. and a reduced stroke of 66 mm., making the squarest of the eights. The Maserati was heavy and slow and long-stroke (62 × 88 mm.) and gave no hint of the great days that in 1927 were just round the corner. The Millers followed Delage and Talbot practice with engines of 55.5 × 76.2 mm. the Duesenbergs being almost the same. The Miller reputedly developed 154 b.h.p. at 7000 r.p.m. and could be taken safely up to 8000 r.p.m., with its centrifugal supercharger geared up to five times engine speed. In record breaking trim that gifted driver-engineer Frank Lockhart persuaded over 200 b.h.p. out of one of these engines and his car to average 171.02 m.p.h. over a flying mile in 1927, setting the average in both directions at 164.009 m.p.h., at a time when the world's mile record stood at 203.79 m.p.h. to the credit of an aero-engined monster of 44.8 litres. In 1928 Lockhart created Black Hawk Stutz for the world land record and actually exceeded 200 m.p.h. on Daytona Beach before he crashed fatally. This car had two of the Miller engines geared together as a twin eight and performance was such as to make it a real contender for the world record itself. Like the Alvis the car had front wheel drive and employed a de Dion type front axle.

The Alvis had engine dimensions of 55 × 78.75 mm. with two camshafts operating two horizontally opposed valves per cylinder in 1926; these were replaced by a more conventional twin o.h.c. layout the next year, but with no more success. Parry Thomas' 'Flat-Iron' Specials shared the Maserati engine dimensions and, like the Talbots were immensely low on the ground; Thomas, like Lockhart, was a skilled and courageous track driver and a highly gifted engineer, who was also killed in quest of the world land speed record, which brought development on these promising cars to an end. The final British contender was a 6-cylinder special constructed by Major Frank Halford, who was the last one-man constructor to race his own car in a Grand Prix till Jack Brabham in 1962. The 63 × 80 mm. engine, with a cast-iron detachable head with twin o.h.c. and an aluminium block with separate wet liners, was coupled up to an Aston-Martin transmission and fitted into an Aston chassis. Initially the engine was boosted by an exhaust driven turbo-supercharger and also a centrifugal blower, which later gave way to the conventional Roots type blower. The engine gave 69 b.h.p. at 5300 r.p.m. which coupled with its inadequate transmission gave it a very poor performance not materially improved when 24 extra horses and 200 extra r.p.m. were hunted up in 1927. Notwithstanding, it won a handicap race of two laps (5¾ miles) at Brooklands at the Whit Monday meeting in 1926 at 95.75 m.p.h. from a standing start and a three lap (9½ mile) event in July at 102.04 lapping at over 110 m.p.h. and held 4th for most of the 1926 British Grand Prix behind the Delages and Talbot.

313 TRACTION AVANT: Milton with a f.w.d. Miller at Indianapolis in 1927

315 ENTERPRISE OF ENGLAND: C. M. Harvey with the f.w.d. Alvis

314 ENTERPRISE OF ENGLAND: Purdy's Thomas ('Flat Iron') Special leads Eyston's Bugatti in the 1927 British Grand Prix

316 ENTERPRISE OF ENGLAND: Frank Halford's Special follows Benoist's Delage in the 1926 British Grand Prix

Remarkable as these eights and sixes were, it was left to the Italians to produce the three most breathtaking designs, two of which never raced and the third winning the only race for which it was ever started. Itala produced two 60 degree V-12 engines of 1100 c.c. (46 × 55 mm.) and 1500 c.c. (50 × 55 mm.) with two horizontal valves per cylinder operated by a single camshaft within the V. The firm were reported as being "ready or sufficiently advanced to be capable of being ready for a race" as early as February, but the car never

raced and the reason for the construction of such a complex machine must remain as mysterious as its performance. The car was written up in some detail in the Autocar on 25th June 1926, when it was disclosed that the total weight was 10 cwt. 90 lb., height $33\frac{3}{4}$ ins. and clearance seven inches, although from its illustrations the car looks infinitely higher and heavier than the Delages and Talbots. R.p.m. were given as 8000 and compression ratio as $5\frac{1}{2}$ to 1, with a Roots blower running independently of the carburettors merely

153

317/8 BREATHTAKING ITALIAN: (top) The 1926 Itala (in the background are (right to left) a 1924 Bugatti, a revamped 1914 G.P. Fiat and a 1914 G.P. Aquila and (bottom) the revolutionary Itala engine

319 ENGLISH EGG HEAD: Eldridge's 1926 Special with two seater Indianapolis body

supplying compressed air to the cylinders through ports at the bottom of the cylinder barrels which were uncovered by the pistons at the bottom of their stroke. The compressed air which thus entered at the end of the firing stroke scavenged the cylinder and at the end of the induction stroke air was admitted to dilute the mixture to the correct degree. Apart from a raked front cowling the general wedge shape followed conventional Italian bodywork with a true single-seater cockpit. The engine was very short being only 29½ ins. long, and readers of the *Autocar* must have been surprised to find that this mechanical curiosity was not only to be raced, but to be produced 'as special sporting models to meet the fairly high demand existing for speedy cars of this class.' This car still exists in the Turin Museum.

Not to be outdone, Fiat produced two designs, the 6-cylinder 451 and the 12-cylinder 406; the 451 was quite the most curious device of the decade, with its 6-cylinder 52 × 58.55 engine mounted vertically containing two geared crankshafts and 12 vertically opposed pistons with communal combustion chambers; tests first gave 152 b.h.p. at 5200 r.p.m. and later reputedly 170 at 6000. Bordino tested the first car at Monza in the early summer of 1926 obtaining 'wonderfully good results' though the condition of his ear-drums must be left to the imagination. Whether for this or mechanical reasons work was abandoned on the project and switched to the slightly less revolutionary 406.

This car was a twin six with side-by-side crankshafts geared together as on Bugatti's war-time aero engines. Three camshafts operated the 24 valves, and, while the cylinders were of the usual Fiat pattern, plain bearings replaced the classic Fiat rollers, although a built up crankshaft enabled them to retain one-piece big ends. 160 b.h.p. at 8000 r.p.m.[1] was claimed with reliability and 187 at 8500 r.p.m. was reputedly achieved in bench testing, which gives some idea of the potential of a design that was prepared with almost incredible speed, following the demise of project 451. Cyril Posthumus suggests that 'it is to be doubted whether more than the one car existed'[2] when a team of three was entered for the 1927 British Grand Prix, although W. F. Bradley writing of the design in the *Autocar* on 12th August 1927 stated 'During the past few days 1500 c.c Fiat racing cars have appeared on Monza track and *these* have twelve cylinders. . . . ' The *Autocar* reported later in the year that the Fiats had spent a considerable time on the track and that experience with the test car had shown that certain modificaion should be carried out *on the other machines*. In the same article Bradley foretold the advent of more dual engines. . . . 'History has shown that the present vogue of the straight-eight is attributable to war experience. . . . This undoubtedly led other makers to adopt the same type of engine. It would not be surprising, therefore, if the dual engine, also a war product, should eventually become a normal type.' The

[1] *This is Pomeroy's figure but Posthumus (The Racing Car at page 116) prefers 175 b.h.p. at 7500 r.p.m.*
[2] *The Racing Car, p. 116.*

perspicacious Bradley thus very accurately forecast the trend of design to be adopted in the 1929/31 by Bugatti, Maserati and Alfa-Romeo, the three principal racing constructors of the period.

With the least amount of modification to a well tried design, Bugatti, for once, was ready in plenty of time for the opening of the Grand Prix scene on the windswept Camargue desolation of the Miramas Autodrome. This automotive white elephant, the brainchild of the veteran race driver Paul Bablot, was one of the closed circuits that sprang up in the vintage decade and the decision to run the French Grand Prix there had been much criticised and had no visible merit at all, reducing the great series of annual French classics to the level of vulgar farce. It was thus no surprise that at the end of the old year the Secretary of the Racing Board of the A.C.F. was still sitting looking at an empty entry list. Talbot announced their drivers early on before entering a car, Divo returning to his first loyalty with Segrave and Count Masetti. The opening entries were three four-cylinder two-stroke Sima-Violets to which the Talbot team had been added by the time entries closed at single fees. By close of entries, Delage and Bugatti had also entered, but of the four teams only the Bugattis of Goux, de Vizcaya and Costantini came to the line. By March informed opinion was expressing concern at the future of the French Grand Prix for *and after* 1926, cost being being regarded as the villain of the piece. The Miramas track was $3\frac{1}{4}$ miles round with wide radius slightly banked turns and the 1926 Grand Prix must rank as the dullest race ever to be held in France, worse by far than the derisory Grand Prix des Vieux Tacots, and there were actually twice as many European entries for Indianapolis as there were starters at Miramas!

Albert Guyot, an old hand at Indy, had built four cars for this race, three of which he sold to M. Albert Schmidt, who prepared and ran two of them, the third not being ready; the fourth car was driven by Guyot himself. These were our old friends the Grand Prix Rolland-Pilains, now with $1\frac{1}{2}$-litre 6-cylinder McCallum sleeve-valve engines. The *soi-disant* Schmidts were ill prepared and brought little gain to L. L. Corum, co-winner in 1924, and S. Nemesh, their American drivers. Guyot's own car had to be rebuilt on the eve of the race and, not surprisingly, lasted only eight laps. Some accounts speak of a 'Grand Prix Bugatti', and Jules Goux was even mentioned as its driver, but this does not seem to have achieved any notoriety, if indeed it ever ran, and the other two European cars were specials constructed by E. A. D. Eldridge, the well known English track driver. These cars had 4-cylinder supercharged, roller bearing Anzani engines with a special twin overhead camshaft cylinder head designed by Eldridge and built for him in France· One car had an egg-shaped two seater body of 31 ins. width, while the other had a narrow American type single-seater body.

320 OLD HAND AT INDY: Albert Guyot in 1926 on one of his specials

321 GIFTED AMERICAN: Frank Lockhart who won the '500' at his first attempt in 1926

322 LONG LIVED AMERICAN: Ralph Hepburn, who first drove in 1925, in the Tucker Special in 1947

155

Like the Talbots, Delages and Itala, the Eldridges were very low slung, but in spite of the ingenuity and experience of their designer they did little good in the race. Douglas Hawkes retired after 91 laps with mechanical troubles, variously ascribed to camshaft or supercharger, while Eldridge himself retired after 45 laps with a broken steering arm and, according to some accounts, then replaced Hawkes. These were the last English cars to race at Indianapolis until Jack Brabham's Cooper in 1959.

The race itself was halted after 400 miles due to a deluge of rain when Frank Lockhart was leading at an average of 95.88 m.p.h.; Lockhart had actually come to Indianapolis to prepare another car in the hope of getting a drive, but luck was with him when the well known Kreis fell ill during the time trials and Lockhart was given the chance of qualifying. Even then he very nearly failed due to tyre and mechanical troubles, during which he set a new one-lap track record at 115.488 m.p.h., but he finally qualified at 95.78 m.p.h. and then applied his very great engineering skill to preparing Kreis' Miller for his first '500'. It is no mean achievement to break the Indy record on a first appearance. and this, coupled with his win on the day in very difficult conditions, set him at the very forefront of America's drivers. Lockhart stayed well up prior to taking the lead after 59 laps and then after 71 laps the cars were flagged in for an hour and a quarter to enable the track to dry out. When racing was resumed Lockhart retained his lead till the end apart from a short pit stop when the persevering Harry Hartz took over. Hartz was the Girardot of Indianapolis in the 'twenties, finishing 2nd in 1922/3/6 and 4th in 1924/5, a record of most remarkable consistency. It is a happy thought that he had his reward in 1930 with the car he designed while convalescing after an accident. The engine of the so-called Miller-Hartz was an enlarged 2-litre Miller and the car was noteworthy as being the first frontwheel drive car to win the '500'.

The f.w.d. Millers both failed to finish in 1926 as did the blown 2-stroke Duesenberg of the 1925 record winner, Peter de Paolo. This record in fact stood until 1932, equalling the seven-year record of his uncle Ralph de Palma, who had held it from 1915 to 1922. Considering the weather it is remarkable to find that Lockhart won the 400-mile race at a higher speed than his 10-lap qualifying average. For the record those 'in the money' were :

1. Lockhart	Miller	95·88	6. Elliott	Miller	90·91
2. Hartz	Miller	94·48	7. Batten	Miller	90·27
3. Woodbury	Boyle	94·13	8. Hepburn	Miller	89·88
4. Comer	Miller	92·32	9. Shafer	Miller	87·55
5. de Paolo	Duesenberg	91·54	10. Duff	Elcar	87·09

This was the first 'place' obtained by Ralph Hepburn, one of the most colourful and daring Indianapolis drivers, who later became associated with the controversial f.w.d. Novi cars. Twenty years later on the first of these cars in 1946 he

established a track record at 134.449 m.p.h. which lasted until 1950; four years is a long span for the Indy record and twenty an amazing span of time for a man to retain supreme ability through decades in which the record had been lifted by nearly 20 m.p.h. from Lockhart's 115.488 m.p.h.

Fourteen years had gone by in 1926 since Jules Goux had driven in his first Grand Prix and thirteen since he had triumphed at Indianapolis or, indeed, anywhere else and it is the only redeeming feature of the Miramas Grand Prix that it enabled Goux's name to be added to the long roll of winners of the great annual French classic races stretching back, as they did, to the very beginning of history. Three Bugattis started—de Vizcaya soon retired while Costantini lasted till 16 laps before the end, both being put out with supercharger troubles. Goux covered the last 50 miles in solitary splendour to win at an average of 68 m.p.h. for the 500 kilometres of the most unsatisfactory Grand Prix ever to be run.

The European Grand Prix for 1926 was held at San Sebastian for which prospects were a little brighter but of the 21 entries only six faced the flag on the 18th July—the three Bugattis of Costantini, Goux and Minoia and the new Delages of Benoist, Bourlier and Morel, with Wagner as spare driver and René Thomas team manager. It was quite apparent that not even one Talbot would be ready to honour its entry; the Eldridges and Guyots were still *hors-de-combat* after their American endeavours; the Sima-Violets and O.M.s melted away and the brace of mysterious 'Jean Graf's' likewise. Surveying these entries before the race the *Autocar*, remarked—'All the cars being new, surprises may be expected and the European Grand Prix will serve particularly as *a preliminary* to the British Grand Prix at Brooklands in August'—a marvel really that the Editor was not called out by some offended Spanish motoring dignitary!

Eight days before the European Grand Prix there occurred an event which attracted but little attention at the time when Rudolf Caracciola on the ill fated 8-cylinder 2-litre Mercedes won the first of his six German Grands Prix, at the Avus track. He accomplished this at an average of 84.5 m.p.h. and appears to have carried a riding mechanic. The Mercedes lived up to its killer reputation when Rosenberger crashed while leading in the 15th lap, killing one of the occupants of the timekeeper's box.

If any of the nine drivers who actually took part in the Spanish race had ever heard of the Duke of Plaza Toro they would, unlike him, have positively longed for the watery shores of Venice, after the events of the 18th July. As the *Autocar* put it :

'A hot sun and a scorching sirocco blowing down the course and bringing with it, from time to time, blinding clouds of white dust, were the weather conditions prevailing just before the start of the race. It would have been difficult

to imagine more strenuous conditions for the men, and events, indeed, were soon to prove the terrible nature of the ordeal through which the drivers had to pass.'

Jules Goux, the eventual winner, nearly missed the start but just made it, thanks, partly, to the pacemaking car having starter troubles itself, and led from Minoia, Benoist, Costantini, Morel and Bourlier after the first lap. Benoist, however, soon found his speed and overtook both Bugattis during the 2nd lap, holding the lead until he stopped 'for supplies' after 7 of the 45 laps. It seems surprising that after so short a distance (75 miles) he should require a routine pit stop but, at all events, he did and it dropped him down to 5th ahead only of Minoia who was in trouble with overheating. Benoist set about recovering lost ground with a record lap at 78.4 m.p.h. but then the heat struck down Morel in the lead, he being removed for treatment for sunstroke and burnt feet whilst Wagner replaced him. No sooner had this happened than Benoist too stopped for relief with 14 laps covered. The Frenchmen in the crowd then called for René Thomas, who prepared himself with understandable reluctance for 'the prospect of roasting one's lower members, being asphyxiated by the exhaust gases and of being roasted by the sun . . . not at all enticing for a man of middle age who has acquired a respectable fortune. . . .' He was spared by the intervention of René Seneschal who emerged from a nearby pit and immediately offered himself for immolation.

Needs must when the Devil drives and Seneschal was allowed to take over Benoist's car despite never having sat in a Delage racer, let alone practised—oh happy carefree bygone days! Wagner, on Morel's car, was faring little better and constantly devised reasons for stopping—after one round for gloves and after three for a liberal douche of water and to 'receive restoratives'. Wagner was one of the most seasoned and tough drivers of the old school but 30 miles had been more than enough for him especially with a strange car on a circuit of which he had covered only two practice laps. One cannot but be struck by the extraordinary lack of preparations by so experienced an équipe as Delage managed by René Thomas. For all his keenness Seneschal drove but six laps and then there were two Delages standing idle, with Morel in hospital, Wagner in a state of collapse and Benoist and Seneschal similarly unable to continue.

For some reason Bourlier had been able to drive grimly on during all this commotion behind Costantini and Goux and ahead of Minoia's ailing Bugatti. When the two Delages had been stationary for about an hour the wind veered round to come from the sea, freshened itself and summoned up the Delages drivers like Gabriel's horn, Benoist taking over Morel's original car from Wagner, who later also revived and took over the Benoist-Seneschal car. Morel himself returned from hospital to bring much needed relief to Bourlier in the latter stages of the race, which were livened up by

323 RELUCTANT DRAGON: An aldermanic figure, René Thomas, found the Spanish G.P. 'not at all enticing for a man of middle age . . .'

324 . . . . 'an event which attracted but little attention . . .' Caracciola after winning his first Grosser Preis in 1926 with the difficult eight-cylinder 2-litre Mercedes

successive raisings of the lap record, first by Benoist at 78.8 m.p.h. then by Costantini to 81 m.p.h. then by Benoist again and finally by Wagner, now really finding his form, at 81.7 m.p.h. Once again Costantini had misfortune in the closing stages, though this time he was able to complete the distance in 3rd place behind the Delage of Bourlier and Seneschal and Goux's Bugatti. The other two Delages and Minoia's Bugatti were still running when the race was stopped. So ended the Grilling Grand Prix, although when the official results were promulgated the Bugattis of Goux and Costan-

325 JACK OF ALL TRADES: Segrave with the 12-cylinder Sunbeam talking to King Alfonso XIII before the Spanish Grand Prix of 1926

326 and later getting a move on in typical Lasarte countryside

tini were given 1st and 2nd places and the Delage of Morel 3rd, the other three cars being disqualified for unauthorised driver changes. Equally Wagner's fastest lap was discounted, as if anybody was really concerned. These decisions were reversed at a meeting of the A.I.A.C.R. in Paris later in the year.

A week later, on the same circuit, the Spanish Grand Prix, run on a free-for-all basis, attracted ten entries, the three 2-litre V-12 Delages of Benoist, Morel and Wagner, three works 2.3 litre Bugattis with Costantini, Minoia and Goux, three independent Bugattis and a 4-litre V-12 Sunbeam driven by Segrave. This highly versatile car comprised two of the 2-litre blocks mounted on a special crankcase at an angle of 75 degrees and was, as Posthumus says 'a real jack-of-all-trades racing car which broke the world's land speed record, contested Continental road and track races, hill climbs and sprints, and later held the Brooklands lap record.' As these words are written it has had its crankshaft and rods converted from the original roller bearings to plain ones—another interesting instance of the revolutions of time. In recent years it has been a stirring sight in English Vintage racing in the hands of R. C. Symondson and George Burton and it is a heart warming thought that there are men with the skill to drive these historic cars and the taste and enthusiasm of Sir Ralph Millais, its owner, to keep them going.

Although Segrave considered Costantini the greatest threat, it was Benoist's Delage which led at the start—the Sunbeam's three speed gearbox was a disadvantage there—and Morel's Delage which passed Segrave to take the lead after four laps. On the 6th lap, when trailing the Delage, Segrave saw his front wheels begin to tilt inwards and by luck and very skilful driving he managed to avert disaster—luck because the tubular front axle had broken (through inaccurate boring) exactly in the centre. The Delages of Morel and Benoist then led till they ran into trouble letting Costantini through. In the later stages Benoist relieved Wagner but Segrave's prophecy was as true as Bugatti's and Costantini ran out an easy winner, setting up a new record lap at 83.8 m.p.h. on the way and to round things off Goux neatly pipped the surviving Delage for 2nd place :—

1. Costantini	5–35–47 for 374½ miles = 76·8 m.p.h.	
2. Goux	5–52–16	
3. Wagner	} 5–56–57	
Benoist		
4. Minoia	5–57–26	

Bugatti had evidently decided that his French and Spanish victories were enough for the time being when added to those of the Grands Prix of Rome and Alsace and the Targa Florio and for him the Spanish races were anything but a preparation for the first British Grand Prix on 7th August. Almost exactly 12 years since he had first suggested it, Mr. Massac Buist's dreams of a quasi road race at Brooklands had come true—sandbank chicanes and all. The R.A.C. were rewarded with the best field of the year, though it was disappointing not to have any works Bugattis and both the Alvis and Thomas Specials non-started. The three Talbots were driven by Divo and Segrave and the erstwhile mechanic Moriceau taking the place of Count Masetti who had crashed fatally in the Targa Florio. Seneschal's performance at San Sebastian had earned him a second Grand Prix drive along with Wagner and Benoist. Malcolm Campbell had a new Bugatti which he fitted with wire wheels which involved new hubs and also apparently the use of ordinary instead of racing brakes which slowed him in the race. Finally, there were the Aston-Martin of G. E. T. Eyston and Halford's Special.

From the start the three Talbots took the lead, Divo ahead of Segrave and then Moriceau, whose run was abruptly ended after one lap when his front axle gave way like Segrave's at San Sebastian. Behind the Talbots came Benoist, Campbell, Halford and Eyston, then Seneschal— 'all excitement and violent action'—and finally Wagner with a sick engine already. First Wagner and then, after only 18 miles, the leader Divo was in the pits, changing plugs, leaving Segrave in the lead, trailed by the calm figure of Benoist, 'a slightly satirical smile on his face.' Wagner had already decided to call it a day when he found his exhaust setting fire to the body of his car as well as his own feet and then after 13 laps Segrave stopped to change rear wheels, losing the lead to Benoist but still getting away in 2nd ahead of Seneschal, whose fiery methods seemed to show some results, and Halford. This order continued for some time until at 25 laps there was no less than 25 miles between Benoist's leading Delage and Divo in the Talbot in 7th and last place. It was apparent that the Talbots were the fastest cars on speed and acceleration, but the Delages scored heavily on braking for the sandbank chicanes and in general handling.

Segrave, on the surviving Talbot, was sickening with carburation as well as braking troubles and by 50 laps Seneschal had got into 2nd place behind Benoist and ahead of Segrave, Halford, Campbell, Divo and Eyston. The Talbot then hit trouble in an even bigger way making four more stops in the next seven laps and, for all practical purposes, fell out of the race, although Segrave did have the satisfaction of the Stanley Cup for his fastest lap at 85.99 m.p.h. About the same time Eyston decided to retire the Aston-Martin with gasket trouble—a distressingly frequent happening in those early days of supercharging—and then there were five. Campbell's Bugatti now began to gain on Halford and, with the leading Delage in obvious difficulty, the race began to re-open particularly when the lion-hearted Divo managed to raise his Talbot to 3rd place behind the Delages, gaining on Seneschal with every lap. For some time

327 Campbell's Bugatti and Divo show off the sandbank chicanes at Brooklands

328 ABRUPT END: Moriceau's broken front axle

329 . . . 'Segrave was sickening with carburation as well as braking troubles . . .'

BROOKLANDS
LAP DISTANCE - 2·8 Miles

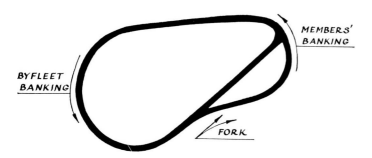

330 PIONEER TRACK: opened in 1907 Brooklands was in the first flush of its heyday in 1909/11

331 BEST FIELD OF THE YEAR: Divo gets right away at the start

Benoist had been suffering from a severely leaking exhaust, which allowed flames to play on the dash and controls, and, after a stop to alleviate this, he found great difficulty in restarting though he still led at 75 laps, by five miles from Seneschal, who had an 8-mile advantage over Divo, followed by Halford and Campbell.

After 80 laps even the fiery Seneschal had had enough and sought relief in Wagner and a foot bath of cooling water. Then within the next eight laps disaster fell first upon Halford who retired with a broken gearbox, then Divo with a multitude of ailments resulting in an engine which refused to start and finally Benoist who had led for nearly the whole race. After 80 laps Benoist made slowly for his pit and had more work done to the exhaust pipe and handed over to André Dubonnet who drove off in his ordinary clothes and, needless to say, without practice. Divo had been a constant menace to the Delages and had he been able to keep going he would surely have been able to exploit the agonies of their drivers during the closing 22 laps. As it was the Benoist-Dubonnet car had fallen to ten miles behind the Seneschal-Wagner car after 100 laps and Campbell's Bugatti was on the same lap and gaining fast. Campbell caught Dubonnet two laps later and the cars finished in the order:—

1. Seneschal-Wagner 4– 0–56   71·61 m.p.h.
2. Campbell   4–10–44   68·82 m.p.h.
3. Benoist-Dubonnet 4–18– 8   68·12 m.p.h.

Whilst Campbell's Bugatti finished the 287 miles in better fettle, nobody could grudge the Delage drivers their triumph in a race which must have been increased to twice its length by their second ordeal by fire. They seem to have borne their designer no ill will in contrast to Divo and Moriceau who spent much of the rest of the day assuring Vincente Bertarione of the poor quality of his designs, ancestry and the like.

The last formula race was the Italian Grand Prix at Monza which was another Bugatti benefit. 'Sabipa', Costan-

tini, and Goux were opposed by two Maseratis and a Chiribiri driven respectively by Ernesto Maserati, Emilio Materassi and Serboli. For the opening laps the Maseratis hounded Costantini, but once they had fallen out it was Miramas all over again. Goux retired with a broken oil pump around half distance and, with 2½ laps to go Costantini's ill luck struck again when he had a lead of 25 miles over Sabipa. His engine seized but was finally persuaded into action again, emitting what was described as 'quite a consumption cough' and the unknown 'Sabipa' (in fact an amateur named Charavel) won at 85.87 m.p.h. with Costantini 2nd at 83.77 m.p.h. with fastest lap at 98.3 m.p.h.

The following week Monza staged a 'free for all' race for the Grand Prix of Milan with supercharged 2-litre Bugattis the main contestants but leavened by Segrave's presence on the 4-litre Sunbeam. This was clearly the fastest car setting up a fastest practice lap at 110.5 m.p.h. which was in all probability a record at that time. As at San Sebastian the Bugattis were quicker away but this time Segrave decided to go to the front and stay there. This he did with ease until about half-distance when the gearbox ran dry and the race was again left to Costantini who this time finished an easy winner covering the 40 laps (240 miles) in 2 hrs. 36 mins. 18 secs. = 95.4 m.p.h., Goux was 2nd in 2 hrs. 47 mins. 19 secs., Farinotti 3rd on Bugatti in 2 hrs. 56 mins. 51 secs. and one 'Chinon' (*sic!*) 4th on a similar car in 2 hrs. 58 mins. 39 secs.

Segrave had some consolation for his three disappointments when he won the J.C.C. 200-mile race in September against indifferent opposition at 75.56 m.p.h. with Divo 2nd, .90 m.p.h. slower. Two of the Alvis cars had started but had both retired without exerting any influence on the race. The Talbots won the race much as they pleased and one cannot help feeling that a brisk outing at Monza earlier in the month ought to have been more satisfying to their competitive instincts if not perhaps to the S.T.D. shareholders.

Chapter Eighteen
The Harvest of Louis Delage:—
Part Two — Harvest Moonshine: 1927

1926 had been a poor season, promising much but fulfilling little. Bugatti had won the World Championship for what it was worth but there was quite obviously some much heavier metal lurking in Europe, to say nothing of the American cars if only somebody could be persuaded to give them a chassis and transmission to stand up to European racing conditions. Slightly amended rules were brought in for 1927 to standardise European and American racing, the chief change being to abolish the stipulation of two seats side-by-side. The four international Grands Prix were as in 1926 plus Indianapolis and there were already three teams of cars in existence from 1926 plus Maserati, Alvis, O. M. Guyot, Eldridge and Halford which had all appeared in one race or another, as well as the Fiats and Italas, to say nothing of the various Duesenberg and Miller based cars in America. If even most of this talent could be assembled for but three of the five Grandes Epreuves a most memorable series of races would be guaranteed and there were plenty of drivers to be found in England, France, Italy and America besides a rising young German motor agent called Caracciola. A certain amount of post-season shifting went on, Delage kept Benoist, Bourlier and Morel, his first strings from the flames of San Sebastian but René Thomas decided to sever his long connection with Delage. Perhaps the prospect of actually having to drive one of his fireships in a race had unnerved him, or perhaps he had other fish to fry, for, soon after, one begins to see the René Thomas sprung steering wheel advertised complete with a 'caricature of the famous French driver and facsimile of his signature on one of the spokes.' Bugatti's drivers tended to vary around this period but he was stated to have fixed on Minoia, Dubonnet and Count Conelli, and Talbot retained Divo and Segrave with the third place open.

After the 'farce provençale' of 1926 the A.C.F. returned the Grand Prix to Montlhéry for which an entry of ten cars was received from Delage, Talbot and Bugatti plus the Halford—enough to run the race but not really sufficient to produce a classic, especially with the brittle showing of Talbot and Delage in 1926. The Delages had been extensively revised during the winter and Benoist actually had a car ready for the Grand Prix de l'Ouverture at Montlhéry on March 13th. As a matter of interest no Grand Prix car had then taken part in a race so early in the season in the history of European Grand Prix racing. Divo too had been out with the Talbot but withdrew with a hand injury and the car was scratched, a circumstance which, we are told, 'the public plainly indicated that it neither appreciated nor believed', especially with Moriceau actually present at the track. Benoist set the pattern for the year by winning as he pleased on a wet track at an average of 76.3 m.p.h. for the 155 miles.

However, two weeks later at Miramas a team of Talbots opposed Benoist's lone Delage, several Bugattis and a Buc in the 1½-litre section. Torrential rain marred the meeting and, before the combined final of all three capacity classes, the Talbots were withdrawn. Benoist, out on a warming-up lap, was astonished to find the field lined up on the grid when he completed it. He did what he could but was unable to avoid striking Duray's Amilcar broadside on. Thus, with the main contestants out, the soaked crowd went berserk, running riot over the track, stopping what remained of the racing and storming the Talbot garage. This dangerous and ill mannered outburst effectively wound up racing at the dreary Miramas circuit, which must have been a sorry disappointment to its patron the distinguished veteran driver Paul Bablot. One should not forget, however, that in the 15 mile heat Moriceau's Talbot was the winner over Benoist at an average of 73 m.p.h.—a small but almost entirely forgotten reverse for the universally triumphant 1927 Delage.

No European cars or drivers raced at Indianapolis but the

332 . . . 'the winner at Indianapolis, George Souders, brought his Duesenberg to Monza later in the year . . .'

333 . . . 'the burly Divo blasted his Talbot to the front . . .' ahead of Benoist, Bourlier and Morel

334 TROUBLED TALBOTS: . . . 'shortly before half distance Divo's (No. 4) race was run with every kind of trouble . . .' with Williams (No. 10) in the foreground

winner, George Souders, brought his Duesenberg to Monza later in the year, with the veteran Earl Cooper and Peter Kreis on Cooper Specials. These were slightly modified f.w.d. Millers on which the footbrake operated on the rear wheels only—a pleasing American archaism for a European road race in 1927! Souders won at the relatively low speed of 97.45 m.p.h. after Lockhart had led for 275 miles from the start and qualified at the new record of 120.1 m.p.h. with a one lap record of 120.918 m.p.h. This was the '500' in which Norman Batten steered his blazing car for over a mile with one hand whilst sitting on the scuttle. Another car of historic interest was Tommy Milton's Detroit Special, a f.w.d. Miller fitted with a two-stage centrifugal blower the work of a Dr. Moss of G.E.C. The f.w.d. transmission of this car re-appeared in a Special in the 1947 event.

Back in Europe it was all eyes on Montlhéry for the Grand Prix on the 3rd July where the Delages of Benoist, Bourlier and Morel were to meet the Bugattis of Emilio Materassi, Conelli and Dubonnet, who had recently finished 1st, 2nd and 5th in the Targa Florio, the Talbots of Divo, W. G. Williams and Wagner and Eyston's Halford. Segrave was now more pre-occupied with record-breaking and other matters and passes from the Grand Prix scene as did so many of the other drivers after that 1927 French Grand Prix. Bugatti staged another of his last-minute tantrums, claiming to be beaten in advance and refusing therefore to hazard his drivers, and, unlike 1925, this time he stuck to it though he must have kicked himself during the race and after the Spanish Grand Prix at the end of the month. Just as he had done the year before at Brooklands the burly Divo blasted his Talbot to the front at the start, pursued by Benoist and Williams on the second Talbot and after only one lap there was already a substantial gap between these three and the supporting Delages, then, more gap and Eyston, and finally Louis Wagner obviously in trouble after a delay on the grid. Speeds rose, with first Wagner, then Benoist and Williams pushing up the lap record till Benoist left it at 81.99 m.p.h. Benoist had inexorably pursued Divo till he took the lead on the 4th lap and held it to the end of the race. While the leader drew away, Divo and Williams fell back to the other Delages; Williams had a stop after 10 laps and had fallen to 5th behind Wagner, Bourlier, Divo and Benoist at quarter distance, when Benoist had a lead of 11 minutes over Divo!

Shortly before half distance Divo's race was run with every kind of engine trouble supervening, leaving Benoist and Bourlier in utter command and Wagner still pressing on hard, perhaps too hard for his fragile car which gave up the ghost with a series of stops each more dismal than the last soon after half distance. Eventually Wagner retired in the country, while the loudspeakers, with characteristic under-statement, gave it out that he could not restart because the starting handle was at the pits and the career of the last survivor of the original Grand Prix was at an end. This gave Delage a 1-2-3 win in the order:—

1. Benoist   4–45–41.2 = 77·24 m.p.h.
2. Bourlier   4–53–55·6 = 76·1 m.p.h.
3. Morel   5–11–31·4

The Williams/Moriceau Talbot was credited with 4th place in 5-24-30, and Eyston was flagged off with 93 of the 372 miles to go! In rather better weather, over a much shorter distance and under rather less pressure from rivals Benoist had improved his 1925 average by 7.5 m.p.h.

Perhaps surprisingly Divo had run his Talbot in the free-for-all race the day before the Grand Prix against the two twelve-cylinder Sunbeams of Wagner and Williams, de Courcelles on a sleeve-valve Guyot, two blown 2.3 Bugattis (Louis Chiron and Eyston) and an 1100 c.c. Salmson, driven by Mme. Devancourt. The pouring rain deprived the big Sunbeams of their power advantage and, although Williams led on the first lap, Divo led thereafter while Wagner did not even cover one circuit. Divo's average for the ten laps was 74.75 m.p.h. and he finished with a lead of 31⁴/₅ seconds over Chiron, with Eyston 3rd and Mme. Devancourt 4th. The two Sunbeams retired with their perennial transmission troubles and de Courcelles crashed fatally on the Guyot. If Divo's Talbot could have achieved similar speeds the following day, Benoist would have had a really hard race of it for at least the opening stages, instead of walking straight through the Suresnes opposition the moment he put his foot down and 1927 Grand Prix history might well have been different. As it was this proved the swansong of the great S.T.D. combine in Grand Prix racing, for, although the cars were entered for both the Spanish Grand Prix and formule libre races later in the month they never in fact left the factory and the great potential of their design was unrealised.

1927 had seen the failure of the dullest ever closed circuit at Miramas and shortly after it also saw the opening of the most fantastic closed circuit when the first German Grand Prix was run off on the Nürburg Ring on the 17th July, making the Ring the oldest Grand Prix circuit still in current use. The race was run off in three classes, the unlimited being won by Otto Merz on a Mercedes, that same Merz past whose ears had whistled the assassin's bullets that hot 1914 June day at Sarajevo while the world speculated on an earlier Grand Prix Mercedes. These amazing old cars had not finished their careers even in 1927, when Rosenberger made f.t.d. at Freiburg hill climb with what was reputedly the Lyons winner. Madame Junek won the 1½/3-litre class in a Bugatti and a Talbot the 1½-litre class. A week later Materassi (Bugatti) won the Spanish formule libre race at 78 m.p.h. from Dubonnet and Conelli on similar cars. Bugatti seemingly had no objection to risking his drivers at high speeds when they had every chance of winning. In the

335 . . . 'Benoist had inexorably pursued Divo . . .'

336 Eyston's Halford, which was flagged off with quarter of the distance still to cover, follows Wagner pressing on perhaps too hard for his fragile car

Spanish Grand Prix over the same 430 mile distance these three Bugattis faced the Delage team and Palacio on a Maserati. Up till half distance Benoist had no trouble keeping ahead of Materassi, but Conelli and Dubonnet decidedly had the better of Bourlier, while Morel retired.

A stop to change plugs was enough for Benoist to lose his lead and, after Materassi's refuelling stop, an exciting battle developed between two men of vastly different temperament —the sphinx-like Benoist calculating every move, and the volatile Materassi driving with inspired abandon. The Bugatti appeared to handle better on the tricky San Sebastian circuit, which was slightly faster than Montlhéry and might even have made Bugatti regret his decision not to race there. After their stops Materassi was left with a lead of 27 seconds which Benoist reduced fairly quickly. During the next three laps the cars duelled fiercely until Materassi overdid things on a corner with only 8½ laps to go; Benoist was hard on his heels and did a complete spin in the dust to avoid the Bugatti. Once satisfied that all was well with Materassi, the ever chivalrous Benoist went on his victorious way for the remaining 80 odd miles to finish:—

1st Benoist 5–20–45 = 80·5 m.p.h.
2nd Conelli 5–23– 2
3rd Bourlier 5–28–12

337 RISING BUGATTISTI: Chiron leads Materassi who both made their Grand Prix debuts in 1927

During the closing stages Louis Chiron made his Grand Prix debut taking over from Dubonnet and driving so well that he would certainly have finished 2nd but for a breakdown 5 laps from the finish.

There was no racing in August but rumour was rife throughout the month with entries for the European and British Grands Prix of American cars and the double-six Fiats. The Monza meeting on September 4th was a most exciting affair, if only for the appearance of Bordino's Fiat and the Cooper Specials of Earl Cooper and Peter Kreis, and Souders' 500-winning Duesenberg. The proceedings began with a race for 1½- and 2-litre cars, principally contested by Bordino on a Fiat, Campari on a P2 Alfa-Romeo, and Materassi, Count Maggi AND Nuvolari on Bugattis.

Bordino covered the 5 laps in 20 mins. 4 secs. (92.88 m.p.h.) against Maggi's 20 mins. 35 secs. (90.4 m.p.h.), Campari's 20 mins. 37 secs and Materassi 2/5 secs slower. Bordino had won very convincingly with a fastest lap on the rain soaked track in 94.96 m.p.h. in spite of the engine having been replaced overnight. It was stated that on the Friday evening before the event Bordino had wrecked the only engine in full running trim—a significant fact having regard to the *three* cars entered for the British Grand Prix on the 1st October, and one which may explain his reluctance to embark on the 300 mile grind for the European Grand Prix.

Benoist, as usual, left the start of this event at the front and, this time, stayed there to the finish without any shadow of a challenge. It was a gesture of supreme audacity to start one car only in the premier event of the year with an unbeaten record to preserve and is really without peer in Grand Prix history. Benoist made one stop for fuel and oil and that was that until he received the chequered flag after 3-26-59⅘ (90.04 m.p.h.) of his time, with a fastest lap of 94.31 m.p.h. Kreis wrecked an already suspect engine after half a lap and later took over Cooper's car in a haphazard half-hearted way in contrast to his fastest lap in the 1925 race. Perhaps they had an off-day or just did not like the rain, but the Americans were a sad disappointment although Souders managed to stay in second place and on the same lap as Benoist for the opening twelve laps. Like Fiat, O.M. made their only Grand Prix appearance in the 1½-litre formula, sending Minoia and Morandi to the start. Both cars finished though never offering any serious challenge. Places were filled by: 2nd Morandi 3-49-32⅗: 3rd Kreis 4-2-54⅘: 4th Minoia 4-2-28⅖.

Benoist had qualified for the final race for the Grand Prix of Milan, but declined to start saying he was tired and that the fuel was not quite right for his carburetter. With only five laps to cover this all sounds as lame as Divo's hand at Montlhéry though the actual race was anything but lame, with Bordino, Campari, Maggi and Materassi renewing their rivalry with intense vigour. Bordino drove with all his legendary greatness and fire, holding skids in the wet with classic disdain and putting up one astounding lap at 96.49 m.p.h.; his winning time was 19 mins. 42⅗ secs. (94.57 m.p.h.—a faster average than Benoist's fastest Grand Prix lap) from Campari in 20 mins. 24 secs. and Maggi's 21 mins 22⅖ secs. On this evidence it is by no means unfair to claim superiority of speed for the Fiat over the Delage and a five lap duel with no quarter given between Benoist and Bordino, two of the greatest drivers of the period on two of its fastest cars, is another cherished might-have-been.

At the time it was believed to be only a postponement for a matter of weeks till the British Grand Prix, which, judged on its entry list, should have provided the greatest race of the Twenties. For it to rank with Lyons—1924, the list wanted but Segrave and Wagner with Talbots, and, as i was, it included six 8-cylinder Bugattis which were down for Eyston/Davis, Campbell, Prince Ghica, Materassi, Conelli and Chiron, now a fully fledged Grand Prix driver; three Fiats for the 1924 team of Bordino, Salamano and Nazzaro; C. M. Harvey with the original Alvis; W. B. Scott and Purdy in Thomas Specials; Benoist, Bourlier and Divo on Delage and, finally, Souders' Duesenberg. Much of the tinsel failed to shine in the cold light of day; in retrospect it seems almost impossible to take the Fiat entry at all seriously and the cars never left the factory any more than did Souders. The lone Alvis had a major mechanical disorder the day before the race, but there were still eleven starters, to make a double-figure field for the first time in the formula! Materassi and Chiron took a momentary lead at the start, but by the end of the first lap the three Delages had established a lead they retained throughout the race, the sole point of interest being to see if Benoist would complete his Grand Slam. Unlike the other races, Benoist hardly led till the closing stages, Divo and Bourlier making most of the running, the eventual order being:

1. Benoist   3–49–14.3/5 = 85·59 m.p.h.
2. Bourlier 3–49–21.3/5 = 85·58 m.p.h.
3. Divo   3–52–20   = 84·46 m.p.h.
4. Chiron

The Thomases were hopelessly slow and the Bugattis retired with an assortment of troubles apart from Chiron's, never having really been in the race after Materassi's electrifying start. Delage achieved the rare distinction of the 'Not-Victory-But-Annihilation' category and this was crowned with the award of the Legion d'Honneur to Robert Benoist in appreciation of his services to the motor industry.

Of the Grand Prix contenders only the Alvises and the Bugattis of Campbell and Eyston took part in the Junior Car Club's 200-mile race at Brooklands on October 15th; at the start the low ugly tank-like Alvises led the pack but by the end of one lap their challenge had been stilled and Oats on the O.M. fared little better, breaking a piston.

The failure of the British contenders twice within a matter of weeks on their own home ground brought a spate of demands for a British racing équipe subsidized either by a big constructor or by a fund. In the outcome nothing was done and plans for a big British road race in 1928 eventually materialized in the revival of the R.A.C. Tourist Trophy as a sports car race in Ulster, following the lead suggested in an article in the *Autocar*

'... development can be fostered just as well, and possibly more rapidly, by racing cars approximating much more nearly to the touring car than to any Grand Prix machine. Races for the former type do not lack entries and certainly do not lack excitement ... last, but not least ... British teams ... have been in the very forefront ... and have ... (upheld) ... British prestige against really strong foreign competition.'

338 DOUBLE FIGURE FIELD: (left to right) Benoist, Bourlier, Campbell, Divo, Purdy, Materassi, Conelli, Scott (behind), Chiron and Ghika

339 NOT TO THE SWIFTEST: Bugattis were never in the race after Materassi's electrifying start—here he leads Benoist the winner

By the end of 1927 the great technological and economic burst that had carried the 'modern' Grand Prix car from its muling and puking origins at Dieppe to the triumphant Delage apotheosis at Brooklands had exhausted itself. Even in 1926/7 these signs had been terribly apparent; half the designs for the formula had never appeared and of those which actually did race not even Delage had been really fully developed. The first time the constructors had run out of breath (or money) had been in 1908 when French pique as much as anything else had been to blame. The reasons in 1927 were very different and had been gradually building up for some years.

Economics were primarily responsible. In those days the idea of prize money had only just percolated through to the A.C.F., who considered the sheer honour of winning THE Grand Prix a sufficient reward. With no starting money and inadequate prize funds the manufacturer was obliged to race for publicity and little else unless he was lucky enough to win at Indianapolis. If you were as big as Fiat, Mercedes or S.T.D. it was perhaps economically viable to go motor racing year in, year out, but smaller factories such as Delage, Itala O.M., Alfa Romeo or Alvis were bound to feel the draught sooner or later and the marvel is that Louis Delage managed to survive as long as he did when making cars of such complexity as his 1923/7 racers. The economics of specialist builders like Bugatti and Maserati have never been really explained—it is one of the few frustrations of Hugh Conway's fascinating book on Bugatti that it does not explain the economics of Ettore's business—perhaps they defy it or perhaps, like the 17th and 18th century composers and writers, they were dependent upon wealthy patronage— but whatever the truth, these two constructors enabled racing to avert its complete eclipse of 1909/11. The odd paradox was that during the 1928/30 period the number of races increased enormously and during these years one can discern the beginning of the present-day Circus with a succession of races almost every week-end from May to September.

Without being too disparaging of other Clubs' and countries' efforts, much of the history of motor sport revolves around events organised by the A.C.F. and the A.C. de l'Ouest. If the A.C.F. organised the first Grand Prix, then it must be to the Sarthe Club's credit that they organised the first Grand Prix de France, or 'splinter-group' event for Grand Prix type cars. I except the pre-1915 Tourist Trophy series which catered for non-formula cars in Europe. If one excepts the American Grand Prix series which started in 1908, the Belgians were the first to propose a National Grand Prix for formula cars (in 1914), but instead of conquering German cars they found themselves overrun by conquering German troops and had to wait till 1925 for the privilege of running their first true Grand Prix. By that time the Italians had run off three (or possibly four) of their own Grands Prix and the Spaniards one, and England followed suit in 1926, unless one accepts the 1922 Tourist Trophy as a formula event, which in truth it was at least as much as the 1922 Indianapolis '500'. The next step in the process was the rise of the local Grand Prix. In the mid-Edwardian period from 1902-7 these had been relatively commonplace with the circuit des Ardennes (1902-7) in Belgium, Vanderbilt Cup (1904-8) in America, Coppa Florio/della Velocita (1904-8) in Italy, and the Kaiserpreis and R.A.C. Tourist Trophy races but, after the 1912 revival, this type of race lapsed in importance or turned into events for voiturettes or production cars. After the war there was a tentative revival of these lesser races, the first of which had once more been held in Italy— the Brescia Grand Prix of 1921 where the Ballots had defeated the Fiats. The Italians followed this up with the Circuit of Cremona in 1924, although this race would never

have become memorable if it had not been the racing debut of the P2 Alfa-Romeo.

When the former voiturette limit of $1\frac{1}{2}$ litres became the Grand Prix formula in 1926, several of the erstwhile voiturette events continued to be eligible for Grand Prix cars, such as the J.C.C. 200-mile race at Brooklands, G.P. du Salon at Montlhéry and the G.P. de Provence at Miramas. In addition several countries took to running formule libre or free-for-all races at the same meeting as their Grands Prix so that there was still some scope for pensioned off Grand Prix cars, chiefly the 2-litre Delage, Bugatti and Alfa-Romeo and the 4-litre Sunbeam. For many years it had also been the practice of the A.C.F. to precede the Grand Prix by an event for Touring or Stock Cars and from this series of races what we now know as Sports Car racing came to be born. In 1923 and 1927 came two milestones in the history of this type of racing—the first Grand Prix d'Endurance and Mille Miglia. On a rain-swept midsummer afternoon in 1923 a motley horde of 33 touring and sporting cars formed up to race for 24 hours non-stop over the circuit that had been used for the voiturette and Grand Prix events of 1920 and 1921. The idea for the race is said to have been germinated on the Rudge-Whitworth stand at the 1922 Paris Salon in the minds of Georges Durand, the Club Secretary, Charles Faroux, and Emile Coquille of Rudge-Whitworth. Accepting Faroux as a godfather of this event and of the Edwardian Coupes de l'Auto it is difficult to find any other one man who has so shaped the history of motor racing. As we have seen, the Vintage period of motor racing, that lasted in principle from 1914 to 1933, was begotten very largely out of the 1910-13 Coupe de l'Auto series and, subsequently, one of the vital influences in the survival of any form of Grand Prix racing between 1928 and 1933 was the growth of the sports car movement, which provided many of the cars and the drivers who rose to fame during those difficult years. What Roger Labric wrote in 1949 of this great man of motor racing would be as true then as in any other year since the first Coupe de l'Auto in 1906.

'... une personnalité de premier plan en matière automobile et sportive.... Ses idées toujours neuves ont declanché les formules heureuses. Sa grande expérience jointe à sa science de théoricien réputé, son bel esprit sportif, son impartialité, sa connaissance approfondie de toutes les questions qui se rapportent à l'automobile, firent de lui un directeur de course avisé et apprécié de tous.'

It was perhaps no coincidence that the Mille Miglia was also the handiwork of a Club with traditions going back to the Edwardian days. As long ago as 1899 the 18-year old Ettore Bugatti had finished 2nd in the Tricycle Class of a race from Brescia to Verona and back and the following year, as part of a motor week, a road race of 223 kms. was

340 *MAN OF INFLUENCE: Charles Faroux (right) with Alfred Neubauer*

341 *REMARKABLE THROWBACK: a view from a competing car in the Mille Miglia*

342 *HALF PAGE RATING: Minoia and Morandi at the start of the first Mille Miglia*

343 *UNMISTAKABLY SPORTS: Caracciola on the Raticosa Pass during his winning drive in the 1931 Mille Miglia*

run from Brescia to Cremona, Mantua and back. Karslake describes this as for the first Florio Cup, when Vincenzo was but 17; this ties up with the Record of Motor Racing where Rose refers to the 1904 event as 'the second Florio Cup contest over the Brescia-Cremona-Mantua-Brescia circuit.' On the other hand the *Autocar's* account of the 1900 event makes no mention of the Florio Cup simply chronicling the affair as 'a road race of 223 kilometres' and Bradley in his history of the Targa Florio makes no reference to this purported first Florio event, writing that 'in 1904 Mercanti organised the first of a series of races at Brescia' and later tells how Florio, inspired by the examples of Gordon Bennett and Vanderbilt, 'decided, in 1904, to offer a permanent challenge, the Coppa Florio, which was first competed for at Brescia, in 1905.' The Mille Miglia, run in traditional form on 23 occasions between 1927 and 1957, was a truly remarkable throw back to the old days that had ended with Paris-Madrid. However, as well as making trains run to time, Mussolini permitted such speed contests from town to town. The first classic rated only half a page in the *Autocar* and was won by Minoia and Morandi in 21 hrs. 4 mins. 48⅕ secs. (47.9 m.p.h.) on an O.M., followed by two similar cars. This lineal successor of the early races always remained a very strictly Italian preserve, being won only twice by foreign car or driver—Mercedes on both occasions, the drivers being two of the absolutely outstanding men of their ages, Caracciola in 1931 and Stirling Moss in 1955.

344/5 HALCYON DAYS: the years 1919/32 were the great ones for the Targa Florio where Bugatti (left) exerted a great ascendancy (de Vizcaya in 1925) while Borzacchini's Salmson (right) in 1927 passes through some very typical Targa surroundings in Collezano

Sports car racing kept the constructors interested in racing during the Dark Days and Bugatti and Maserati with their semi-production racing cars, plus some rejuvenated old timers, made up the Grand Prix fields until Alfa Romeo and Maserati produced some newer single-seater racers in 1932/33. Sometimes it became rather difficult to distinguish between sports and racing cars, Bugattis being particularly chameleon-like in this respect; Bentley and Mercedes were unmistakeably 'Sports' in their origins, but inevitably the Bugatti, by preserving its traditional biposto appearance right down to his first single-seater in 1935, remained more of a Racer and the same applied to Maserati and Alfa-Romeo. As time went by in the thirties the 'Sports Cars' contesting the Mille Miglia became more and more racerish culminating in the winning Alfas of the 1935/7 period.

The years from 1919 to 1932 were the great ones for another curious survival—the Targa Florio, which then as now had the distinction of being the oldest surviving motor race. The Targa Florio always remained a tremendous test of man and machine but, judged by the standards of actual Grand Prix cars taking part, some races were more memorable than others. Thus I have so far considered in detail the events of 1919, 1921, 1922 and 1924. From 1925 to 1929 Bugatti reigned supreme as King of the Madonie Mountains, winning each time and placing his cars in the first five places sixteen out of a possible twenty-five times. Out-and-out Grand Prix cars rarely dominated the Targa, as witness the failures of René Thomas' Ballot in 1919, the 2-litre Delages in 1926 and Bordino's Fiat in 1924, and it was because Bugatti's cars in some mysterious way contrived to be neither mere sports cars nor out-and-out racers that they proved such a signal success on the Madonie circuit. Can this mystic half way house in racing design be the true definition of that elusive expression 'Throughbred' or 'Pur Sang'?

During the early twenties the outstanding driver in the Targa had been Count Masetti, who won in 1921/2 and finished 2nd in 1924 and 4th in 1919 and 1923, non-starting in 1920 and 1925. After driving for the S.T.D. works in 1925, he was chosen for their team again in 1926 and would have raced the new 1½-litre cars with Segrave and Divo but for his tragic death on a 2-litre Delage in the early stages of the 1926 Targa. Bradley's explanation of his accident ('just as if some malicious giant had taken the car and placed it face downwards in the road without even scratching the paint') is that the car had run up a steep bank by the roadside—failing to stop because of the time lag in the operation of the brakes, a defect of which other drivers had complained—and had then rolled over and slipped back on to the road upside down. After this tragedy the works Delage drivers, Benoist, Divo and Thomas, all retired having little inclination to continue. The race marked Thomas' final appearance at the wheel of a racing Delage, with whom he had been primarily associated since the Grand Prix des Voiturettes in 1908; on both these occasions he was opposed successfully by Jules Goux who finished 3rd on Lion-Peugeot in 1908 and in the Targa on Bugatti in 1926, Thomas finishing 5th in 1908. Goux and Thomas could thus claim to have raced on the great Dieppe circuit in the Age of Monsters, but the ever-green Louis Wagner had actually been leading in the Grand Prix itself there in 1907 on a Fiat when he retired on the 4th lap. These three survivors of the Heroic Age ceased to take any decisive part in racing after 1927.

Even in 1927 W. F. Bradley was a doughty champion of the old time drivers to whose defence he promptly came in November 1927 following an article in a Sunday paper written by Segrave maintaining that these drivers were incapable of driving the modern cars successfully. Segrave took as his text the choice of Wagner, Hemery and Guyot to drive the 1922 Rolland-Pilains. Bradley pointed out that the cars had retired with two broken crankshafts and one broken connecting rod and then debunked Segrave's indictment of Victor Hemery, whom we last remember putting up an electrifying lap record on his Benz in the 1911 Savannah Grand Prix. As a final touch he added that the choice of the 1922 Grand Prix was a trifle unfortunate for Segrave's thesis as it had been won by one of the greatest of all the pre-war drivers, Felice Nazzaro, and dominated by Bordino who had some twenty years' experience in racing as driver or mechanic.

After his win in the 1922 Grand Prix at the age of 42 it had been remarked how fresh Nazzaro had seemed, but like his English contemporary S. F. Edge he was tireless. A few days after Strasbourg, Edge, aged 54, drove two 12-hour spells on successive days at Brooklands averaging 74.27 m.p.h. and 'coming on top of the successes of the veteran drivers in the Grand Prix and Touring Grand Prix his achievement forms an additional proof that the younger generation of racing drivers has yet something to learn from those who served their apprenticeship at the very commencement of motoring history.' The Touring event had actually been won by Rougier with Duray second—both drivers who were also prominent in the Heroic Age.

A correspondent later remarked that in all probability the world land speed record holder 'was in such a hurry that he did not allow himself time to think'; at any rate he must have been too busy to consider these criticisms as he went on to cite the incident of Hemery wrenching out the gear lever at the start and the steering wheel at his first corner *in extenso* without actually naming the driver in 'The Lure of Speed' published in March 1928. He concludes:

'This little illustration serves to indicate my point that a successful racing driver of today is a much more highly developed organism than his prototype of twenty years ago.'

In fact there was a very substantial 'carry forward' of veteran drivers into the twenties, when many of them continued to race with great success beside the new generation; some, like Goux, enjoyed a veritable Indian Summer at the relative end of their careers, others, like Wagner, Thomas and de Palma drove resolutely and professionally for whatever firm retained them. Before the war Wagner had driven for Darracq, Fiat and Mercedes and after it, his tastes were every bit as catholic, taking him to Ballot, Fiat, Guyot, Alfa-Romeo, Delage and, finally, Talbot in Grand Prix events, to say nothing of Peugeot in the Targa Florio—every équipe of note except Bugatti; did the Alsatian in each prove mutually exclusive or were Ettore's views on brakes too like those of Alexandre Darracq?

In more recent times one can only point to another Frenchman as having had so long and varied a record—

346 it was remarked how fresh Nazzaro seemed at the age of 42 after his win at Strasbourg

347 Rougier who won the Touring Grand Prix at Strasbourg

348 Hemery, still with cap reversed, drives No. 13 Rolland-Pilain at Tours

349 INDIAN SUMMER: 'Some like Goux (above at Lyons in 1924) enjoyed a veritable Indian Summer at the relative end of their careers'

350/1 RESOLUTE PROFESSIONALS: Others like Wagner (bottom) and de Palma (top) drove resolutely and professionally for whatever firm retained them

Louis Chiron, who, fittingly enough, was beginning his great career just as Wagner was ending his and even raced against him on a few occasions. In 1952 the late Lord Charnwood had the great joy of being driven round Montlhéry in his 1911 Coupe de l'Auto Delage by Wagner and found that in spite of the loss of a leg the veteran's touch had still not left him:

'After lunch Wagner took his place behind (the) wheel . . . and took me round the famous road circuit. He went fast and I am a bad passenger but I can truthfully say that I have never enjoyed being driven so much; a master's hand had lost nothing of its cunning. Two days later when Mons. Petiet showed me his wonderful collection of photographs of races and told me to notice that Wagner's mechanics always looked comfortable and relaxed, I knew why.'

There must have been many who wished that Georges Boillot had remained as a driver to French generals and survived to electrify the twenties on both sides of the Atlantic with his own especial panache. As it was the great men of the twenties tended to be less flamboyant than those who preceded or succeeded them: or perhaps it is because they make less appeal to the imagination for the lack of dramatic power in their cars and the racing. Apart from one or two outstanding examples, the Formula events of the twenties were not notable for any great struggle between drivers or marques and whilst the technical variety of the cars has made it a period of absorbing interest, it is one slightly lacking in the true dramatics of motor racing, which require intense competition between drivers and cars.

Chapter Nineteen
1928/9 · Decline and Fall

The pattern of the years from 1928 to 1933 is, season by season, very close in essence to that of 1909 to 1914. Like 1909/10, 1928/9 were seasons of almost unrelieved gloom, during which even the classic French Grand Prix fell into decay. As in 1911, so in 1930 there was an attempt at reviving the French classic; in 1911 the A.C. de l'Ouest's Grand Prix de France was contested by a touring Fiat, converted for the day into a racing car, and the minuscule Bugatti of Friederich. In 1930 Goliath made his re-appearance in the shape of Birkin's 4½-litre Blower Bentley, with Bugatti reliving his 1911 role many times over, but principally through one of motor racing's greatest characters, Philippe Etancelin the exuberant Rouennais, then in the sunrise of his racing days, driving a Type 35C. History was not exactly repeated, for on this occasion while sentiment lay with Goliath, victory went to David by a narrow margin. During these dark times the great past of Grand Prix racing was sustained, amongst organisers, almost single-handed by Vincenzo Florio. In addition to keeping his Sicilian Targa as one of the great races of the period, he also took over the annual Monza Grand Prix meeting which produced the best racing and the most technically interesting cars. Count Florio in fact fulfilled the role of the Coupe de l'Auto during the previous abeyance of the Grand Prix.

1931 was like unto 1912 with the revival of the French Grand Prix on more acceptable principles and fittingly it also saw the real rise of an individualist as great as the immortal Boillot—Tazio Nuvolari. During the ensuing years 1931/33 Nuvolari reigned as *Primus inter Pares* against his principal adversaries—Varzi, the man of ice in the school of Nazzaro as Nuvolari was the man of fire in the school of Lancia and Ascari; Luigi Fagioli, Louis Chiron, then in his greatest days, Rudolf Caracciola, the rising star of the New Germany and, last of the veterans, Cavaliere Giuseppe Campari. The youthful Giovanni Lurani tells many delightful tales of 'the good old Campari' singing 'the Barnaba' air from Gioconda on the way to the start of a race or being 'absolutely unbeatable in disposing of dozen after dozen of snails' at the Escargot prior to his second win in the French Grand Prix in 1933. Later Lurani sadly writes 'a few moments before his last fatal run Campari had stopped and talked with me, his jovial face lit up with a smile as he recalled the gargantuan snail luncheons we had shared at Montlhéry.' Behind these great men came a whole host of drivers who rose to fame as independents between 1930 and 1933—Borzacchini, Birkin, Czaikowsky, René Dreyfus, Raymond Sommer, Guy Moll, Jean-Pierre Wimille, Goffredo Zehender, Marcel Lehoux, Etancelin, Whitney

352 GREAT CHARACTER: Philippe ('Phi-Phi') Etancelin, the exuberant Rouennais with a mid-thirties Maserati

353 NEW BOILLOT: Nuvolari in the mid thirties, wearing the d'Annunzio tortoise charm

354 VERSATILE ARTIST: Taruffi near the end of his career in the W196 Mercedes-Benz in 1955

Straight, Antonio Brivio, Count Trossi and Piero Taruffi—every one of them capable of pursuing the Great Six to the utmost and even beating them on occasions. Racing has rarely been blessed with so much young and rising talent, some of whom survived well into the post-1945 period. In 1955 the Italian Grand Prix was held on the full road and track Monza circuit for the first time since 1933 and Taruffi finished 2nd in an event which he had nearly won twenty-two years previously. In 1957 he finally won the Mille Migilia, the last to be run in the Grand manner. Besides his longevity, Taruffi is to be admired for his extreme versatility—class performer on two and four wheels, record-holder on both, designer, author of the standard work on racing technique, Gilera works team manager, team driver for Alfa-Romeo, Maserati, Ferrari, Lancia and Mercedes to say nothing of Olympic bob-sledder: truly a career to be marvelled at in an age of specialization.

In the free and uninhibited atmosphere of independence, competition thrived and everyone joined in the cut and thrust of the early thirties with the abandon of the Town-to-Town races; neck-and-neck finishes were almost two-a-penny, with nothing staged (except for one famous exception at Tripoli) Nuvolari and Varzi nose to tail for hour upon hour, hurtling burning rubber and blistering Latin imprecations in one another's wake. Even Le Mans caught the fever and staged a grandstand finish in 1933 with the lead changing several times on the last lap of all. If the true drama of motor racing lies in competition on a cut-and-thrust winner-takes-all basis then 1932/33 was a Golden Age indeed. Even if the technical standards, attained by the cars were not particularly high, the standard of competitive driving was something the like of which has rarely been equalled. Whatever may be said in denigration of the process which reduces motor racing to a 'mere struggle between drivers', it is the human element that weighs most in a visual sport—the mastery of man over machine and his fellow men—and even the coolest technician will be carried away by a closely fought race to the extent when he forgets the designers and even the marques involved. At all events it was this very 'degeneracy' that made the years following the Great Depression so truly memorable and turned it to good effect. If the Depression had temporarily killed the tradition of Grand Prix racing for Works Entries only, it also ultimately broadened the whole basis of Grand Prix competition by enabling a body of independents to take their places as seasoned Grand Prix drivers on terms of equality with the old factory men. Credit must also be given for this notable development to constructors like Bugatti and Maserati who sold cars to selected drivers at the same time as fielding works entries and thus brought about the spread of real racing experience.

The process was now to all intents and purposes complete whereby the traditional 'works-tester-driver' was replaced by the new style of professional who paid his own expenses and relied on his skill to win him prize and starting money and bonuses. The only 'testers' to drive works Grand Prix cars for any length of time during the following 30 years were Lang of Mercedes and Sanesi of Alfa-Romeo. I cannot but regard Ferrari's designation in recent years of his works 'drivers' as 'testers' as other than part of the Ferrari legend or, if you prefer it, humbug. Undoubtedly there are many modern drivers with very great engineering skill in the manner of Paul Zuccarelli—Richie Ginther, Graham Hill, John Surtees and Jack Brabham spring particularly to mind —but this is not quite the same thing. Many people agreed with S. C. H. Davis that the bonus system was bad, demoralizing and unnecessary but, as Davis added 'the inevitable and devastating answer is that racing cars could not

355 EARLY THIRTIES VARIETY: the emphasis was on two seater racing cars in 1928/31

356 MID THIRTIES CONSOLIDATION: Monoposto Alfa (12 and 18), Monza Alfa (4) and Type 51 Bugatti (2)

be run without it unless—and this is the important point—prize money in sufficient quantities could be won. What really ought to be stopped with great violence is the habit some people have of claiming a bonus for something which has not been used. . . . Anyhow the real solution of the whole difficulty is prize money on Indianapolis lines.' One could not but look wistfully back to the early Brooklands days when the prize fund for the first three in the first race totalled 2,600 Edwardian English sovereigns. Davis summed the whole thing up a few years later with characteristic wit and charm after hearing a friend complain of 'the awful expense of the modern team. I wonder what he would have thought . . . of a fifteenth century jousting "team" . . . of three knights, thirteen horses, nine squires with twenty-three horses, a chaplain with two horses . . . (etc., etc.) . . . two cooks, a forager, a smith, an armourer all on single horses, eight sumpter horses with the "pit" gear (and, one is tempted to add, a partridge in a pear tree). . . . After that, the fact that that particular team drew 7000 crowns in "bonus" before it started seems only necessary'.

The 1928 formula placed no limit on engine capacity but imposed a sliding weight limit that varied between 550 and 750 kgs. empty with a minimum race distance of 600 kms. The European Grand Prix had consistently eluded the British R.A.C., who now handed the honour over to the Italian Club for 1928 and it alone was run off to the prescribed formula at Monza on the 9th September. The following year the Grands Prix of France and Spain were run off to an even more muddled formula, based on fuel consumption, minimum weight and certain regulations on body shape including Louis Coatalen's long sought requirement of 'an uncovered fuel tank of non-streamlined shape.' Needless to say neither of these so called Grands Prix were memorable, yet the same formula continued into 1930 with a slight

hotting up of the permitted fuel. That year only the European Grand Prix at Spa complied. Having had three bites at the cherry the A.I.A.C.R. embarked on an even more foolish formula for 1931/3 which manufacturers and organisers alike rejected. For the record the proposals restricted engines to 5 litres, covered body and wheel track dimensions, laid down a sliding scale of minimum weights at 20.8 kgs. per 100 c.c. with a minimum of 794 kgs. and finally barred superchargers except on two-strokes. Having dreamed up this nonsense the A.I.A.C.R. had the wit not to enforce it to the bitter end and finally ordained two-seater bodies and minimum distances of 10 hours as the only regulations for the national Grands Prix. For 1932 they reduced distance to 5 hours and did away with the body restriction and finally in 1933 distance was reduced still further to 500 kms.

Initially races were contested by the surviving time-expired formula cars, notably the P2 Alfa-Romeos and 1½-litre Talbots, substantially developed and improved, and the 1½- and 2-litre Bugattis, Delages and Maseratis. In addition Bugatti had available from previous formule libre events his blown 35B (2.3-litre) and 35C (2-litre) types. The first new car was the twin-eight Maserati driven by Alfieri in the 1929 Monza Grand Prix. In 1926 W. F. Bradley had forecast the use of dual engines, initiated by Bugatti in his wartime aircraft engines, followed by Duesenberg, and first used in a racing car by Fiat. Now in 1929/32 first Maserati, then Alfa-Romeo and then Bugatti experimented with this device with varying success. Maserati built two of these cars, the first being powered by a pair of their 2-litre engines and the second by their 1930 2½-litre engines. These 2½-litres were the first really new cars to be designed since 1927 and followed the pattern of the 1921 Duesenberg, more than any other car, in employing plain bearings (apart from a central roller main bearing for the crankshaft which was carried in five bearings in all) and a detachable cylinder head which thus appeared for the first time on a European Grand Prix car. Two valves per cylinder and the mandatory twin o.h.c. were used with cylinder dimensions of 65 × 94 mm. Another novel feature was the extensive use of electron in engine and transmission components. Running on a compression ratio of about 8 : 1 the engine developed a conservative 175 b.h.p. at 6000 r.p.m. which was sufficient to show a very clean pair of wheels indeed to its competitors at the time.

This inspired both Alfa-Romeo and Bugatti to better things. Bugatti struck first with a cylinder head conversion on the 35B which made the car into the twin o.h.c. Type 51, with only two instead of three valves per cylinder. This simple expedient increased the b.h.p. from 135 to 160,[1] and the car in this form lasted Bugatti virtually till the end of 1933. Bugatti also developed the 4.9-litre twin o.h.c. Type 54 racing car from the Type 50 sports car which he had brought out in 1930 and inserted this engine into a 9ft. chassis originally brought out in 1928 for his two 'twin-eight' machines, the Type 45 and 47 models. These cars, reputedly built for the abandoned 1928 French Grand Prix, employed either a 3.8-litre engine in a racing body (Type 45) or a 3-litre engine in a sports body (Type 47). They appeared in a few sprints and hill climbs in 1930 and are all three still in existence. The Type 54 racer was put together in 13 days for the 1931 Monza Grand Prix as the Type 51 could not cope with the new Maseratis and Alfas on sheer speed. The car won a few victories between 1931 and 1933, notably in the 1933 Avus event, but it was not generally successful on either road or track; it was not as amenable to control as most Bugattis and its weight was also against it so that the potential of its 300 b.h.p. was never realised. Bugatti also conceived a four-wheel drive car (the Type 53) during this period, which was based on the Type 54 engine. Two of these cars were built, one being still in existence; like the Type 45 and 47 this car competed in a few sprints and hill climbs in 1932/4. Jean Bugatti, after a reputedly sensational climb up Shelsley Walsh in practice in 1932, crashed his Type 53 on his first run in the event and it was left to Ferguson in 1961 to show that such a design was a practical proposition in racing. As with the straight eight and dual type of engine, however, it had taken the original mind of Bugatti to point the way. It has often been said that Bugatti derived his twin o.h.c. lay-out from the Millers Leon Duray left behind at Molsheim after his disastrous visit to Monza in 1929. Conway writes:

'. . . it is more than probable that he realised that the time had come to follow the clearly established practices of others also successful in the racing car business. After all Duesenberg had copied his 8-cylinder engine ten years previously!'

to say nothing of his twin-eight on their 1921 record car.

In Milan Signor Jano tackled the problem in two sharply differing ways, both in a sense derived from the very successful blown six-cylinder 1750 c.c. sports model, which had won (inter alia) the 1930 Tourist Trophy and Mille Miglia, besides finishing 4th in the Targa Florio. The first machine was the 8C (or 'Monza' model as it came to be known) which was a plain bearing, blown, straight eight of 60 × 88 (the same dimensions as the 1750 c.c.). Power was much the same as the Type 51 Bugatti, 160 b.h.p. at 5400 r.p.m. being cited usually; this was a substantial improvement on the 1750 c.c. but still below the P2 model, which had been producing 170 b.h.p. at 6000 r.p.m. even in 1925 and had been revamped in the ensuing years until it ceased to be able to stay on terms with the new Maseratis and Bugattis. It was in its improved chassis that the very versatile 8C scored over the 1924 car and it succeeded in winning the first Grand Prix for which it was entered at Monza in May 1931, a fortnight after winning the Targa Florio. Its average for ten hours racing was below Chiron's record average of 99.4 m.p.h. in the 1928 European Grand Prix on the Type 35B Bugatti, but Ascari's 7-year old lap record of 104.24 m.p.h. had at long last been fractionally bettered by Nuvolari at 105 m.p.h. The other Alfa-Romeo at Monza that day was the Type A monoposto, a double-six powered machine using two 1750 c.c. engines, each with its own clutch and gearbox; this William-and-Mary theme was carried right through to the transmission, which was by two propeller shafts to a back axle containing two differentials. Although they developed well over 200 b.h.p. these cars were not successful and appeared only twice, both times at Monza in 1931. However, this car which few remember was the precursor of the P3 or Type B Monoposto of glorious memory, and like John of Gaunt and Katherine Swynford who ultimately sired the Tudor monarchs, the Type A fulfilled the ancient prophecy:

'Thou shalt get kings though thou be none.'

All three constructors said their final words in 1932/3. First Alfa-Romeo produced the 2.6-litre monoposto, the Type B or P3 as it has come to be called. Like the Monza, power was developed on a very conservative scale, but the car weighed just over 15 cwt. and handled well and these features were sufficient to ensure that its original 190 b.h.p. at 5400 r.p.m. kept it a step ahead of its competitors until the end of 1933. Like the Monza it was a straight eight twin o.h.c. engine with plain bearings, but bore and stroke were changed to 65 × 100 mm. and two blowers were fitted blowing up to 10 p.s.i., each serving a group of four cylinders, as on the 1927 Delage. If the engine was based on the Monza the body and transmission were inspired by the Type A; these were the first European team of cars to be raced with a pure single seater body, following the indi-

---

[1] This is the generally accepted figure given by Pomeroy, though Conway (Op. cit. p. 221) cites 187 b.h.p. at 5200 r.p.m. on test.

357 FIRST ICE-BREAKER: the 2½-litre Maserati of 1930/31 was the first new car to be designed after 1927. Here is Dreyfus in the 1931 French Grand Prix

360 LAST WORD: 'first Alfa-Romeo produced the 2.6-litre monoposto' —Nuvolari at the 1932 French Grand Prix

358 DUAL PURPOSE RACER: The 2.3 Monza Alfa in racing guise

361 LAST WORD: . . . 'Maserati simply improved their eight-cylinder cars throughout the period'. Here is Nuvolari in the 1933 single-seater at Nice

359 THINLY DISGUISED: the 2.3 Alfa in sporting trim in the 1931 Tourist Trophy with Campari in full sail

362 LAST WORD: the 2.8-litre Bugatti (Type 59) grew up into a 3.3-litre car in 1934

vidual lead of Bordino's 1927 Fiat, and the drive from the gearbox was taken from a differential via two propeller shafts set at approximately 30 degrees and geared to twin final bevel drives. The bore of this engine was increased in size from its original 65 mm. to 69 mm. (= 2.9 litres) in 1934 to 72 mm. (= 3.2 litres) and finally to 77 mm. (= 3.8 litres) in 1935, the respective increases in horse power at the same 5400 r.p.m. being 210, 265 and 305. As in 1924, Signor Jano had lain down a far-sighted design capable of substantial development but, unlike 1924, he had this time ultimately to contend with some new designs from Germany infinitely more far-reaching than the Mercedes and Benz cars of the twenties.

Maserati simply improved their eight-cylinder cars throughout the period. The 2½-litre grew up in 1932 into a 2.8-litre by increasing the bore from 65 to 67 mm. and this car was improved still further in 1933 when the 2.9-litre single-seater was developed with a 69 × 100 straight eight engine and hydraulic brakes. In many ways this was a better car than the original monoposto Alfa and, with a little more luck in 1933, it might well have overshadowed its more renowned rival. Unlike Alfa-Romeo, who either raced as a factory or through the Scuderia Ferrari, Maserati spent a lot of their time and energy making racing cars for sale to the racing public and seldom therefore produced a proper works entry and, when they did, as often as not, it did not receive the full attention it deserved. With everybody an independent, Maserati could rule the roost as they did in 1929/30, but with the full might of Alfa-Romeo weighted against them they never quite succeeded in the ensuing years.

Finally Bugatti, after many characteristic alarums and excursions, produced a new straight-eight, the 2.8-litre Type 59 for the 1933 Spanish Grand Prix at the very end of the season. This had a bore and stroke of 68 × 100 and was additionally conventional in employing twin o.h.c., two valves per cylinder and plain bearings. Later in its history the bore was increased to 72 mm. (= 3.3 litres) and a 3.8 litre engine was also fitted. In its 3.3-litre form in 1934 it developed 240 b.h.p. at 5400 r.p.m. and in original form it probably gave out over 200 b.h.p. which should have given it the edge on power over the Alfa and on handling over the Maseratis in the 1933 season if it could have been ready earlier. As it was they finished 4th and 6th in the last race of the year without seriously challenging either rival.

One has only to read the impressions of present-day observers on driving such cars as the W125 Mercedes of 1937 to realise that even such clearly defined terms as 'Vintage' in relation to cars are purely relative in many senses. Nevertheless these three 1933 cars—the Type B Alfa, the Monoposto Maserati and Type 59 Bugatti were between them the final statement of the Vintage Era of motor racing, the era that had its lineal beginnings at Lyons on 5th July 1914 and breathed its last with the Spanish Grand Prix of 1933 if one is to be tidy, but with the Monaco Grand Prix on 2nd April 1934 to be strictly accurate. Twenty years less three months had seen an incredible variety of progress, accelerated by the impetus of the war years on technical knowledge. The 'Pomeroy' relative lap speed had risen from the '112' of the 1914 Mercedes to the '140' of the Type B Alfa-Romeo of 1932/3 in an age of tremendous experiment during which every variety of engine was tried. Even the lean years produced an intriguing crop of new cars and a whole troop of new drivers, which was more than could be said for the next 'falling off' period in 1952/3/4 after the demise of the 1½/4½-litre formula and before the W196 Mercedes-Benz had truly established itself. It is a point for endless debate and depthless dispute as to which of the three Vintage Archtypes is the most characteristic. Alfa-Romeo because it was the most successful is a popular choice; Bugatti, because of the mystique of Molsheim and because it was the most aesthetically satisfying, almost equally so. Being a perverse soul, I am tempted to pick Maserati, if a choice has to be made, as the car which most exemplifies the ruggedness of the age and which, more than any other marque, set the standard for the others to aim at with their 2½-litre car in 1929, the car which Faroux held up as a rude lesson by which he hoped French constructors would profit. To my mind there is no sight that more epitomizes these years than the classic photograph of the burly Campari, sitting almost literally astride his monoposto Maserati, as he speeds to his last great win in the 1933 French Grand Prix, the wind blowing out his overalls till he seemed like Mr. Bibendum himself—as well he might with all those Escargots. Nothing quite like this Gargantua was to be seen again in Europe till the equally imposing figure of Jose Froilan Gonzalez first electrified English spectators by defeating the assembled might of the Alfa-Romeo team at Silverstone in July 1951.

363 CLASSIC YARDSTICK: the Maseratis of 1929/33 set a standard for others to aim at. Here is Campari offering a substantial sitting target at Nice in 1933

364 EQUALLY IMPOSING: nothing quite like Campari was to be seen until the electrifying Jose Froilan Gonzalez in 1951

In many ways the American pattern followed the European during these years except that it took two years longer for the 91 inch (or $1\frac{1}{2}$-litre) formula to be killed off at Indianapolis. No European cars started at Indianapolis in 1928, although a Bugatti failed to qualify. Early in 1929 Louis Chiron was reported to have paid a visit to the track when four feet of snow were removed to enable him to try out a variety of American cars but in the end he started on a $1\frac{1}{2}$-litre 1927 Delage. At a time when the fastest Americans were qualifying around the 120 m.p.h. mark the best Chiron could manage was 107 m.p.h. finally finishing 7th at 88.73 m.p.h. compared to the winner's 97.58 m.p.h. Comotti's Talbot never started and Moriceau, on a bored out voiturette Amilcar, retired after 30 laps having contrived to hit the wall four times. All in all the Americans had taken round vengeance for their Monza defeat by Benoist in 1927. Indianapolis now virtually passes out of the Grand Prix picture till 1938; in 1930, to widen the scope of entries, the organizers adopted the so-called 'Junk Formula', which was as remarkable a piece of retrogressive thinking in its way as some of the nonsensical regulations dreamed up by the A.I.A.C.R. at the same time. All cars had to carry riding mechanics in what was renownedly the most hazardous race in the calendar; engines of 366 cu. ins. ($=$ 6-litres) were allowed but only two valves per cylinder, a minimum weight of 1750 lbs., or $7\frac{1}{2}$ lbs. per cu. in. of piston displacement (whichever was larger) and finally no superchargers except on two-stroke engines. Shorn of its superchargers the 4-litre V-16 Maserati, driven by Borzacchini, with Ernesto Maserati as riding mechanic, could only qualify at a meagre 95.2 m.p.h. in 1930 and lasted a bare seven laps in the race. The fields degenerated for the most part into weird stock car specials or emasculated versions of the old racers of the 2 and $1\frac{1}{2}$ litre days. Race speeds, curiously enough, managed to rise from 100.448 m.p.h. in 1930 to 117.200 m.p.h. in 1937, although the one lap record stood at 124.018 m.p.h. from 1928 until 1937 when it was raised first to 125.139 and set at 130.492 m.p.h.

The only 1928 event run to the international formula was the European Grand Prix at Monza over 60 laps of the full circuit on the 9th September. Twenty-one cars were assembled, eleven 35B or C Bugattis (principally, Williams, Bouriat, Chiron, Foresti and Nuvolari), one P2 Alfa (Varzi/Campari), three 1927 Talbots bored out to 1750 c.c. (Arcangeli, Materassi and Brilli Peri), four 1.7-litre blown Maseratis (A. Maserati, Count Maggi and others), a 1925 Delage and two of the 1924/5 Talbot voiturettes. The race lasted 375 miles and initially lay between the Bugattis and Talbots, now showing something of their real potential, with Brilli Peri holding the lead after ten laps. Shortly after, a terrible disaster eliminated the Talbot team when Materassi got out

DISAPPOINTING EUROPEANS

365/6 DISAPPOINTING EUROPEANS: Louis Chiron (top) at Indy in 1929 with the doughty $1\frac{1}{2}$-litre Delage which could only finish 7th; (below) shorn of its superchargers the double-eight 4-litre Maserati only lasted seven laps there in 1930

367 *SUCCESSFUL REVIVAL: the advanced 1926/27 Talbots began to shew something of their potential in 1928/29*

THILLOIS

START

GUEUX

368 *The renowned Rheims circuit was first used for the Marne Grand Prix in 1928*

of control at 120 m.p.h. on the grandstand straight and the car flew into the crowd killing twenty spectators and injuring many others. This, at the time, was the worst accident in European racing since Paris-Madrid and caused a terrible outcry against Monza safety precautions, akin to that which followed a similar tragedy in 1961 when von Trips was killed. This, following Bordino's accident in Sicily, robbed Italy of two of her leading drivers: in 1927 it will be remembered that Materassi had won the Targa Florio and then by sheer daring had successfully fought Benoist until a few laps from the end of the Spanish Grand Prix. At the end of the day Ascari's 1924 lap record of 104.24 m.p.h. still stood against Arcangeli's fastest speed of 103.2 m.p.h., but Ascari's race record of 98.76 m.p.h. had at last fallen to Chiron's Type 35C Bugatti, which averaged 99.4 m.p.h. (3 hr. 45 min. 8⅕ secs.). Varzi and Campari shared the wheel of the second finisher in 3 hr. 45 min. 29 secs. followed by Nuvolari (Bugatti), Drouet (Bugatti), Maggi, Maserati (Maserati), Bouriat and Foresti on Bugattis being flagged off.

Several well known races were inaugurated in 1928, notably the Bordino Prize at Alessandria, the Montenero Prize and the Marne Grand Prix over the renowned Rheims circuit. The great Bordino himself had died practising on his Bugatti on the Targa Florio course in mid April and within days of his death the first of the series named in his memory

was run off over the tricky Alessandria circuit. Appropriately enough this gave Nuvolari his first victory in a race of consequence, with the dashing Materassi on his Talbot making fastest lap. Bordino and Campari were survivors of the pre-war days but Nuvolari, like Masetti, Ascari and Materassi, was of the new Italian school of drivers, although it was not until the early thirties that his famed mastery came to be enforced. Nuvolari made his first appearance in the Targa Florio a few weeks later in a large field which included Divo on Bordino's car, supported mainly by Chiron, Conelli, Minoia, Dreyfus, Foresti, Brilli Peri and Materassi, all on Bugattis. Other well known names were Ernesto Maserati, and Fagioli (Maserati) and Borzacchini, Campari and Marinoni (Alfa-Romeo). The only mention of Nuvolari in W. F. Bradley's account refers to his retirement with a caved-in piston head, the main source of comment being the legendary performance of the Czech Mme. Junek who finished in 5th place but managed to stay within sight of Divo for almost the whole race so that 'for 275 miles there was never more than a mile between the two cars and for threequarters of this distance one was right on the heels of the other . . . during the last round masculine endurance revealed itself . . . and from three seconds the lady dropped back until she was nine minutes behind the winner.'

At that time Divo was one of the toughest and most seasoned professional drivers in Europe and to have held him thus over the most arduous circuit in the world ranks as the finest effort of any woman racing driver in history. Divo's strength and experience earned him his victory for he had little practice or knowledge of the circuit, but he was eleven seconds outside Costantini's record of 1926. He was very closely followed home by Campari's $1\frac{1}{2}$ litre Alfa and Conelli's $1\frac{1}{2}$ litre Bugatti, both less than two minutes behind after nearly $7\frac{1}{2}$ hours racing. Campari's car was a blown $1\frac{1}{2}$ litre sports machine similar to the car on which he had just won the Mille Miglia but stripped to the extent of running with a bolster tank behind the driver and the oil tank and batteries in the mechanic's seat and, perhaps fatally, only one spare wheel. This could well have lost him the race as at one stage he had had to drive six miles on the rim to the nearest depot.

Bugatti's run of success continued at Alessandria where Nuvolari won the first Bordino Prize, although it was Materassi's Talbot which made the fastest lap. In 1927 the Rome Grand Prix had been a minor event which would have passed unnoticed but for being Nuvolari's first win in a motor race of any status; in 1928 he was less fortunate and victory went once more to Bugatti, this time Chiron's. For this race the organisers invited ten famous drivers, including Conelli, Campari, Brilli Peri, Minoia and the rising Nuvolari, to take part free of cost. In spite of this tribute to his rising fame the Flying Mantuan had to be content with his win at Alessandria, and he was not to win another race of Grand Prix status until his spectacular defeat of Varzi in the 1931 Targa Florio although he won both the R.A.C. T.T. and the Mille Miglia in 1930. During these lean years with opportunity seeming to knock at every door, he drove first Bugattis which were just not quick enough to beat the P2 Alfas and works cars from Molsheim, then, when he went on to the P2 Alfa, he found that this, too, had been superseded by the new Maseratis, with the deadly rival Varzi always one jump ahead.

On the 24th June 1928 the P2 Alfas returned to Cremona where, but four years before, they had made a triumphant debut. The circuit was of classic triangular shape and of an equally classic length of 39.1 miles, and, as in ancient times, the standing lap was the fastest when Campari set up a record of 108.6 m.p.h. to lead by a bare 50 yards from Nuvolari. These speeds under a torrid Italian sun wrought havoc with tyres and engines and only four of nineteen starters finished, Arcangeli's Talbot winning at 101.31 m.p.h. from Nuvolari (Bugatti) and Materassi also on Talbot. A fortnight later the equally classic if shorter circuit at Rheims saw Louis Chiron win the Marne Grand Prix for Bugatti at 82.5 m.p.h. with a fastest lap speed of 91.4 m.p.h. At Montenero a Talbot was again successful, this time with 'patron' Materassi himself driving to his last victory; Nuvolari, who was always peculiarly at home on this

twisting circuit, both before and after the race turned into the Coppa Ciano, made fastest lap which he contrived to do in all of the six races over this circuit between 1928 and 1935, besides winning three times. The great Benoist made a return to Grand Prix racing at San Sebastian, taking the wheel of a 2.3-litre Bugatti, along with Blancas and Lepori, against Chiron, the Algerian Marcel Lehoux, Williams and Divo on 2-litre models and Zehender and Torres on $1\frac{1}{2}$-litres—a Bugatti Grand Prix in fact if not in name. The race, over 434 miles of the same circuit used since 1923, produced some close work—Divo led for the first 120 miles but had by then lost all his brakes, and with no spare shoes his race was run! Chiron had lost time early in the race but was well and truly after Benoist who led after Divo's retirement. Poor Benoist had some harrowing memories of Spain, roasted in 1926, mercilessly pursued by the fiery Materassi in 1927 and now the same from Chiron in 1928. This time, however, he was not successful in holding off the pursuing Bugatti; at half distance he led by over $2\frac{1}{2}$ minutes but Chiron made this up with some record lappery and even managed to offset a further short pit stop in the closing stages to win by 1 min. 57 secs. at a speed of 80.52 m.p.h. slower by .06 m.p.h. than Benoist's winning average in 1927, although Chiron's new lap record of 88.25 m.p.h. was substantially faster than Benoist's 1927 speed of 85.41 m.p.h. The next day, in the same car, fitted with wings and a windscreen, Chiron won the Spanish Grand Prix for sports type cars: small wonder that the *Autocar* remarked that there were several features about the race which the average motorist had difficulty in understanding! One might well ask the old question, 'When is a sports car not a sports car?' and get the answer, 'When it's a sports car of course!'

Eight races went to make up the 1928 Grand Prix season and Grand Prix type cars ran in several others, such as the J.C.C. Brooklands '200' which was heavily criticized as an event for second-hand cars whose programme contained only one worth-while feature—the time-table of trains home! To such a level had the prestige of motor racing fallen in England in the space of twelve months. 'Casque' of the *Autocar* wrote of the season's calendar

'. . . it is becoming apparent that the movement is suffering from a surfeit of competitions which may have the same effect as the peaches and cyder had on that unpleasant person King John. What is needed and that very badly are good races but fewer of them. The competitor cannot possibly support the number of races at present appearing on the calendar and consequently some enter for one, some for another, the importance of the various races diminishes. . . .'

Well, whatever it may have seemed like in August 1928, the multi-race season had come to stay and increased in complexity until the coming of the German cars once more set

Formula racing far above the supporting events: ten major races will fall to be considered for 1929, eleven for 1930 and 1931, ten for 1932 and eleven again in 1933 and throughout the period speeds continued to rise as did the quality of cars, drivers and circuits and the racing itself. In England a long period of stagnation set in, no race of full international Grand Prix status taking place between the Grand Prix of 927 and the Donington Grand Prix in 1937 and no British driver winning a race of such status between Segrave's win at San Sebastian in 1924 and Dick Seaman in the German Grand Prix of 1938. As for a British car, it was not until the combination of Stirling Moss and Tony Brooks won the British Grand Prix in 1957 for Vanwall that those long lean 33 years came to an end.

Bugatti had won six out of the eight major races of 1928, leaving Talbot the other two. By 1929 the P2 Alfa-Romeos had been revived to such purpose that these doughty old warriors halved the ten races of the year with Bugatti. During 1928 Nuvolari had been racing in association with

his rival of the future, the Galliatese Achille Varzi; in 1929 Varzi went one better and acquired a P2 Alfa with which he won four races, including the Monza Grand Prix, then regarded as the supreme event for racing cars. It was rumoured that Count Brilli Peri would bring one of these cars over for the first B.R.D.C. 500-mile race at Brooklands, but this did not happen. The French and Spanish Grands Prix were run to the official formula and were pale shadows of their former selves, but in 1929 a new and exciting event made up for this—the Monaco Grand Prix, the first and greatest Round-the-Houses circuit. The race was won by Williams on a Bugatti with the amazing Caracciola on an SSKL Mercedes 2nd, having at one stage led the race. A 1927 Delage found its five speeds somewhat superfluous, its driver, de Rovin, never getting beyond 2nd and Williams claimed only to have achieved top gear in the closing laps when pressure had eased and Caracciola was over two minutes behind.

Count Florio's classic was held on the 5th May and this

369 FIRST ROUND-THE-HOUSES: The Monaco circuit which has always been the classic example of this type of course was first used in 1929

371 AMAZING: is the word to describe Caracciola's drive at Monaco with this type of large Mercedes

372 W. G. Williams

370 FIRST WINNER: of the Monaco Grand Prix was this Type 35 Bugatti driven by the enigmatic Englishman W. G. Williams, a staunch and successful Bugatti driver during these years

180

time the sports Alfas of Campari, Brilli Peri and Varzi were rather less of a match for the Bugattis. Brilli Peri did not quite equal Campari's time with a smaller car the year before, while Divo broke Costantini's 1926 record for the medium Madonie circuit by over five minutes, to win by 2 min. 2.8 secs. from Minoia also on Bugatti, with Campari 4th and Foresti 5th for Bugatti. For the closing event of the year Count Florio had adopted the traditional Monza Grand Prix formula of heats for different sizes of cars and a grand final, the classes on the 15th September being for 1½-litre, 3-litres and unlimited cars. The 1½-litre class was enlivened by the presence of the colourful American 'Leon Duray' with a violet Packard Cable Special, which was clearly the fastest in practice and was the car with which Duray held the Indianapolis track record of 124.018 m.p.h. from 1928 until 1937. Duray was not renowned for finishing at Indianapolis where he preferred to win a large number of the intermediate distance awards, and his performance at Monza was all of a piece. The races were over 62 miles or 22 laps of the fast inner circuit of 2.8 miles and in the first heat Duray was opposed by the Talbots of Arcangeli and Nuvolari and two Maseratis. His centrifugal blower gave him a slow getaway but by the fifth lap he had ousted Nuvolari from 2nd place and at half distance he had wrested the lead from the fiery Arcangeli. Two laps later and the Miller engine's lubrication system had had enough, leaving Arcangeli and Nuvolari an easy run through to the final. Duray brought his second Miller to the next class heat, claiming it was bored out to 1505 c.c. to the disbelief of sceptical Italians, who had threatened to lodge a protest before the race and require the Miller to be stripped for examination. Duray was marvellously unimpressed and countered by threatening to protest each and every one of their engines, knowing that some of them needed a couple of days to be stripped and re-assembled!

The second heat brought out the P2 Alfas of Brilli Peri and Varzi still wearing their original bull-noses and sporting the four-leaf-clover, together with four 2-litre Maseratis and three Bugattis. By the time the race settled down Brilli Peri had established a good lead, with Duray holding 3rd against severe pressure from Varzi. Before half distance and to the immense delight of the crowd Varzi had overtaken Duray and at half distance the second Miller had bitten the dust. The heat for the Heavy Brigade comprised the 4-litre 16-cylinder Maserati driven by Alfieri himself, two 38/250 sports Mercedes running stripped in the hands of Caflisch and the future Auto-Union driver Momberger and an old blown four-cylinder Mercedes which retired after three laps, leaving the other three to qualify. The final brought together the Talbots and Ruggieri's small Maserati, the Alfas and Borzacchini's middle-sized Maserati and the Mercedes and Maserati's big Maserati. A thrilling race raged hot and

furious in the opening rounds if Bradley's account is anything to go by:

'. . . the pack went by so closely bunched that in spite of my closest attention my only definite impression was that Maserati was in the lead . . . things happened with such rapidity that there was no time to make notes. Maserati, Varzi and Brilli Peri might have been covered with a handkerchief. . . .'

Eventually the handkerchief grew into a substantial horse blanket until Varzi, profiting by his rival's pit stops with tyre troubles, came through to win by nearly two minutes from Nuvolari, followed by Momberger, Brilli Peri and Caflisch. Varzi won at the high average of 116.83 m.p.h. with Maserati making fastest lap at 124.2 m.p.h., which compares interestingly with Duray's Indianapolis record of 1928.

Varzi and Brilli Peri cleaned up the remaining Italian races with their Alfas, Varzi winning at Alessandria, Rome and Montenero and Brilli Peri at Cremona where Varzi clocked 138.77 m.p.h. over the 10 kilometre timed stretch where Ascari had averaged 123 m.p.h. five years before when the cars were new. To Alfieri Maserati, however, went the fastest lap at 124.4 m.p.h., an unbelievable increase on Campari's 1928 speed of 108.6 m.p.h. Fittingly Bugatti ran up two victories on the 14th July—Chiron winning at the Nürburg Ring and another great French stalwart, Philippe Etancelin, winning the Marne Grand Prix at Rheims. On the whole the official Bugattis and P2 Alfas tended not to meet in 1929, although it is notable that in the three-hour Rome Grand Prix Varzi trounced the redoubtable Divo by over 10 minutes so, in spite of the score being level at five each for the season, I am inclined to give pride of place to the Alfas.

373 ANCIENT AND MODERN: mingle in this shot of Minoia (2nd in the 1929 Targa) refuelling his Type 35B Bugatti in the shade of a Roman viaduct

Chapter Twenty
1930 · The Ice is Broken

374 POLITICAL AGE: the new Italian cars of 1930/31 were its first harbingers. Here is Varzi talking to the Hereditary Prince of Piedmont who officiated at Monza where Varzi so narrowly won

In classical times Roman Heroes had trembled before Father Neptune the Earth Shaker, and before the new year was far advanced it was the turn of their descendants to bow before a new bearer of the old sea god's trident—Maserati of Bologna. In March 'Casque' remarked in his column in the *Autocar* that 'Maserati has set up *a sort of Thomson-Taylors* (a delightful piece of insular conceit that!) and is now making racing cars of all sorts and sizes to order. He is probably the man who is to build a batch of racing cars by order and under patronage of the Government to carry Italian colours in Grand Prix type races.'

Since the demise of the Gordon Bennett series the element of nationalism had been secondary in racing which remained essentially a battle between constructors and drivers with no political undertones. By the end of 1927 racing had ceased to be practical boardroom economics for the big manufacturers but, as time went by in the thirties, the attention of the Italian and German dictators became focused on it for political propaganda and in this way it received the economic shot-in-the-arm it so badly needed. Far away indeed were the days of 1902 when S. F. Edge reckoned the Napier Gordon Bennett victory had cost the firm a net £218! The new Italian cars of 1930/1 were the first emissaries of the Political Age of motor racing and they brought an end to the long reign of France as the traditional centre of the sport. Up till the end of 1927 racing was predominantly French. Its counsels, its constructors, its champions, indeed its very language were French in inspiration, origin and character. Even though the parent country had failed to win her own Grand Prix between 1913 and 1925, she had strengthened her position during the ensuing years through the victories of Bugatti and Delage who succeeded to the places of Peugeot and the same Delage in the years before 1914. At various times Germany, Italy, England and even America had made inroads into French supremacy, but it had always been a passing phase until France finally lost the habit of victory during the thirties. Even so the hard core of the sport continued to be French in spirit until the early post-1945 years and it is scarcely too fanciful to say that this great French inspiration has neatly spanned the combined careers of her two most long lived champions, Les Grands Louis-Wagner and Chiron.

However, long before the inspiration died, the driving force had withered with the retirement of Louis Delage and the subsequent eclipse of Bugatti, who with Peugeot were the triple pillars of French supremacy following the 1912 revival. Peugeot had never recovered from the loss first of Zuccarelli and then of Georges Boillot and were effectively dead from 1914. Delage and Bugatti found their feet in 1924 and spent that year and 1925 preparing for their ensuing years of triumph. Germany has always been a factor apart—Mercedes and Benz were, after all, both as old as motoring itself, but the American and Italian champions, Duesenberg, Fiat and Alfa-Romeo came and went, and as for the so-called 'English' Sunbeams, were they not French or Italian in all but name? So might the French well have argued in the early thirties but, given a plentiful supply of drivers of sufficient calibre a country will always rise to the top in the end and whilst France, England and Germany lagged or just rested on their laurels, a new generation of Italian drivers was springing up to succeed Cagno, Lancia, Minoia, Nazzaro and Bordino. During the twenties men of the stamp of Count Masetti, Antonio Ascari, Salamano, Count Brilli Peri, Giuseppe Campari, Emilio Materassi, Borzacchini, Fagioli, Nuvolari, Varzi and Arcangeli were perfecting their skill in the myriad minor races in Italy on car and motor cycle—as hard and prolific a school as the '500 c.c.' movement and its successors proved to be in England thirty years later after the second world war. Many of the great French drivers of the twenties and thirties were amateurs, but, like their latter day English counterparts, these Italians, were hard and seasoned professionals and it is small wonder that by the end of the twenties the seat of power had shifted decisively across the Alps to the classic Renaissance cities of Northern Italy—Bologna, Milan and Modena.

Not that Bugatti gave up easily—he countered each Italian advance steadfastly right through to 1935 but he had lost the initiative, and the French as a whole had lost their sense of L'Audace et L'Attaque, and, sadly for the sport they gave to the world, they have never regained it. Political support, even on a limited scale, came far too late in the thirties to make any impression on the Berlin-Rome Axis and since the war there has been no dominant French racing car and only two French drivers of significance—Jean Behra and Louis Rosier both long since dead. The others, Chiron, Sommer, Trintignant and Wimille were all well known during the thirties.

The increasing fixture list caused the 1930 season to open as early as the 23rd March with the relatively new Tripoli Grand Prix, a minor event which gave the four-litre Maserati, driven by Borzacchini, one of its rare victories from Arcangeli on a smaller Maserati and, another great Italian veteran to be, Clemente Biondetti on Bugatti. This Grand Prix was marred by the death in practice of Brilli Peri on one of the ill-fated Materassi Talbots. If not the Race of Millions it became later in the decade, the Tripoli Grand Prix was a very fast race even in 1930, Borzacchini's winning average being 91 m.p.h. Two weeks later the European season opened with the second Monaco Grand Prix which brought together the Bugatti team consisting of two litres of Chiron, Bouriat and Williams against the 2-litre Maseratis of Arcangeli and Borzacchini and a variety of independent drivers, including Arco on a Mercedes, Stuck on an Austro-Daimler, Biondetti now with a Talbot and the Bugattis of Dreyfus, Etancelin and Zehender. Two English entries had fallen by the wayside, Campbell having withdrawn his 1927 Delage and the 'super sports' Frazer Nash of Bowes having been excluded for lack of speed. The race was dominated by

375/6 LES GRANDS LOUIS: French inspiration has neatly spanned the combined careers of Louis Wagner (top) in the Darracq he drove at Le Mans in 1906 and (below) Louis Chiron, here in 1949 the year when he won his last French Grand Prix

377 Dreyfus made fastest lap and well deserved his win in the 1930 Monaco Grand Prix

378 NOR DEATH NOR HELL: ... 'flames licking round his neck were nothing to the ice cold Varzi ... on his way to join the Immortals' in winning the 1930 Targa Florio

the Bugattis, all the non-French entries dropping out in the first 12 laps and, like so many Grands Prix on this circuit, the event resolved itself into a question of who could beat Louis Chiron on his home ground. The challenge on this occasion came from the rising amateur René Dreyfus on a 2.3-litre Bugatti who succeeded in passing Chiron when he stopped for fuel after 80 of the 100 laps. After 90 laps Dreyfus had a lead of only two seconds but Chiron's car had seen better times by that stage and the gap opened to 22 secs. by the finish. Dreyfus had made fastest lap in 2 mins. 1 sec. (56.01 m.p.h.) and well deserved his win over the full weight of the works entry; the remaining finishers were the Bugattis of Bouriat, Zehender, Divo and Stuber and the winner's average was 53.64 m.p.h. which was faster than Williams' 1929 lap record.

With this resounding win under his belt Bugatti departed for the Targa Florio well prepared for a sixth successive victory. Whilst his team of Chiron, Divo, Williams and Conelli were on the island preparing under maestro Costantini, the Alfa-Romeo factory were putting the finishing touches to a revised version of the P2 car, which had at long last removed its characteristic bull nose front. Thus mounted Varzi won the third Bordino Prize at Alessandria, improving his best lap time from 68.6 to 70.7 m.p.h. and arrived in Sicily determined to drive this formidable machine over the Medium Madonie Circuit, which had been the graveyard of so many Grand Prix cars in the past, including the Alfa's great rival, the V-12 Delage. Even Campari opted to drive one of the new 1750 c.c. sports cars in preference to the P2. Nuvolari, also on the 1750, completed the Alfa team which was, if anything, even stronger than Bugattis. The three Maseratis from Bologna were driven by Ernesto Maserati, Borzacchini and Arcangeli, Borzacchini's being described as a 2½-litre model, which I feel unlikely as the car was never in the race. In spite of almost universal misgivings the race was a triumph for Varzi and the old Alfa. Varzi set up a new circuit record on his first lap and held the lead throughout the race apart from a short time at the beginning of the last lap and, though he won many great races in the thirties, this was perhaps the greatest tour de force of his astonishing career, as a sheer triumph of man over machine. In Bradley's eyes it classed him 'as the first driver Europe possesses at present' and Pomeroy has described it as 'a staggering feat of endurance and virtuosity'. In short it established Varzi as a driver of the first rank and re-inforced the fame of his wins in lesser races in the preceding years. It was also an appropriate manner for the great P2 Alfa-Romeo to score its last racing win although the game old cars fought doggedly on throughout the season in Italy.

After the first lap the three Alfas of Varzi, Nuvolari and Campari led the Bugattis of Chiron, Divo and Conelli, *all* having broken the record. Chiron then piled on the pace to overtake Nuvolari and Campari on elapsed time, but was still losing ground to Varzi after two of the five laps. During the third lap Varzi broke his spare wheel attachment and also lost the spare which made the rest of the race like a sword of Damocles especially as the spare had worn a small hole in the fuel tank. Thus after three laps Chiron had reduced the gap to less than two minutes and was still catching up. Varzi had started 12 minutes after Chiron and when he made a pit stop to change wheels after four laps it was calculated that he was actually about half a minute behind. Out on the circuit, however, Chiron was in trouble; first his young mechanic was suffering from Mal de Madonie and then, perhaps distracted by the lad's sufferings or inattentions, Chiron skidded on some loose stones on the descent from Polizzi and had to change two wheels. Twelve minutes behind Varzi was refuelling in the classic Targa manner whilst in full flight and the sword of Damocles soon turned into a flame thrower when fuel spilt on to the exhaust. Flames licking round his neck were nothing to the ice cold Varzi who drove fiercely on while the mechanic fought them with a seat cushion. On and on he flayed the veteran Grand Prix car till 'he roared through Campofelice and entered the five mile straightaway by the seashore—the only portion on which top gear could be used . . . the rev. counter crept up to the danger line of 6,000 to 6,200, to 6,300 and finally to 6,500. Something might go; it seemed that something MUST give way—but this was no time for caution' and anyway Varzi was on his way to join the Immortals of Motor Racing. He finally won in the record time of 6-55-16$\frac{4}{5}$ by 1 min. 48$\frac{2}{5}$ secs. from Chiron with Conelli 3rd, a mere 41 secs. ahead of Campari. Nuvolari was 5th some ten minutes later having been slowed with a broken front spring. Of the other Bugattis Divo had crashed in his 3rd lap and Williams had been in difficulty due to fatigue for much of the race, although he finished 7th with Divo's help. The Maseratis finished 8th and 11th and well away on time; however their hour was soon to come.

By 1930 the Sicilian bandits had been more or less disposed of but it is amusing to read of the Algerian Grand Prix a few weeks later which was distinguished by the presence of a 'wild and woolly collection of fighting native chiefs from the desert . . . (who) . . . being fully armed, were treated with the utmost respect, to the detriment of any pit work.' The ensuing Bugatti benefit was won by Etancelin, in spite of a cracked rib, from Lehoux and Dreyfus, and one wonders if a Touareg camel Grand Prix might not have produced more variety.

Three weeks after the Targa Florio Chiron and Bouriat on their Bugattis were doing battle at Rome with Nuvolari and Varzi on their P2 Alfas and Arcangeli with the new 2$\frac{1}{2}$-litre Maserati and this time it was the turn of a new car to win. In a sense Arcangeli had it easy because engine troubles over-

took Nuvolari, Varzi and Chiron but he had to fight off Chiron in a desperate finish on Bouriat's car to win by two fifths of a second with von Morgen, a German amateur, 3rd on Bugatti and Biondetti's Talbot 4th. To complete the Maserati triumph brother Alfredo won the 1100 c.c. event, though in the meanwhile Borzacchini and Ernesto were having a thoroughly frustrating time without their blowers at Indianapolis. Thus far the official Bugatti team and chiefly Louis Chiron himself had had an unhappy season of 2nd places which might so easily have all been 1sts with a little more luck and, now to cap it, le patron himself fell off his favourite horse and dislocated his shoulder and Jean Bugatti was hopping about on crutches after a spectacular accident involving an American car and a French tree. Then on Friday 13th June an accident of much deeper tragedy occurred on Lake Windermere when Sir Henry Segrave, holder of the World's Speed Records on land and water, died as a result of injuries when Miss England II capsized. Segrave had not taken part in a major race since the British Grand Prix of 1926 but he had exercised a tremendous influence on the English attitude to racing and in extolling his career Mr. H. Massac Buist put his finger on the essential features which raised Segrave above his great contemporaries in racing and record breaking when he wrote that it was he in particular 'who possessed the knack of making prestige secure' by his persistent success in whatever he set out to accomplish, and in general that :

'Until he made his mark there was a tendency abroad to believe that a British driver, though generally dependable and courageous, would certainly not be brilliant compared with the more mercurial champions of other lands.'

Perhaps W. F. Bradley was right not 'to rate him as an outstanding driver' but he was equally right to describe him as 'a gentleman in the very best sense of the word and an excellent ambassador for his country', yet he attained a measure of greatness not given to many when he dominated the opening laps at Lyons and won the Spanish Grand Prix in 1924. In the field of Grand Prix racing, 1924 represents his crowning achievement although his triumph was undoubtedly his win in the 1923 Grand Prix.

After the excitements at Rome Dreyfus continued his fine season with a win in the third Marne Grand Prix at the new record of 88.5 m.p.h. but with a fastest lap at 91 m.p.h. still slower than Chiron's 1928 record. The first formula event was the European Grand Prix at Spa but this was no more a Grand Prix than the Algerian affair and even had a staged finish with Bouriat letting Chiron through to win at 72.1 m.p.h. which was slower than Ascari's walk-over win in 1925 when he averaged 74.56 m.p.h. The Maseratis set the seal on their Rome debut during August with successive wins in the Coppas Ciano and Acerbo. Fagioli won the first of these,

379 The start of the 3-litre class at Monza shewing the new Maseratis (26 and 30) and the revised P2 Alfa (32)

with Nuvolari making fastest lap on the P2 Alfa and then for the Coppa Acerbo Varzi once again stole a march on Nuvolari by going over to Maserati and winning the first of the series on the magnificent Pescara circuit. Ernesto Maserati, back from America, was 2nd and Fagioli made fastest lap while poor Nuvolari had to be content with 5th place.

Once again September brought the Monza Grand Prix, this time on a slower 4.3 mile circuit with four qualifying heats, a repêchage for the unlucky and a final of 150 miles. As an indication of Fascist support, Mussolini's chief minister, Augusto Turati, started the first heat and the Hereditary Prince of Piedmont officiated for the final. The 2-litre heat was a narrow win for Etancelin over von Morgen and Minozzi, all on Bugattis at an average of 92.64 m.p.h. for the 62 miles but this was merely a prelude to the main heat for the 3-litre class which included the slightly bored out P2 Alfas, of Borzacchini, now changed from Maserati, Campari and Nuvolari. Their principal opponents, in the absence of an official Bugatti entry, were the new Maseratis of Varzi, Arcangeli and Fagioli. The Alfas were in constant tyre troubles and even Varzi burst a tyre when in the lead in the opening laps but the troubles of the Alfas were more serious and, although the newcomer Borzacchini managed to finish 2nd to Arcangeli, neither Nuvolari nor Campari

qualified for the final until the repêchage. Arcangeli's average was the fastest of the day—97.7 m.p.h. The Alfa team had been reluctant to start and only did so in response to the requirements of High Authority. The unlimited class provided a dull and slow race which Ernesto Maserati had no difficulty in winning at 90.8 m.p.h. from Caracciola (Mercedes), Stapp (Duesenberg) and Caflisch (Mercedes). As a result of the heats and repêchage all three Alfas qualified for the final, together with the four Maseratis, three Bugattis, two Mercedes and the Duesenberg and Scaron's 1100 c.c. Amilcar. The Alfa's tyre troubles were magnified under the intense pressure of the opening laps; although Arcangeli led it was Nuvolari who ousted Varzi from 2nd place and Campari who kept Fagioli out of 4th until the Alfa's tyres gave way. Then, with Nuvolari and Campari at the pits and Borzacchini's tyres shewing bald patches, the team wisely withdrew and left the Maseratis to fight it out. Varzi had a stop for plugs and it seemed that Arcangeli and Ernesto were safely booked for 1st and 2nd places: the spirit of the Targa Florio however descended upon Varzi who carved his way back into the race and finally pipped Arcangeli on the post to win by a nominal $1\frac{1}{5}$ second with Ernesto 3rd, then Minozzi's Bugatti surprisingly $1\frac{1}{5}$ second ahead of Fagioli on the fourth Maserati, followed by Etancelin, Caracciola, Stapp, Caflisch, and Scaron.

186

The closing races of the year were the Spanish and French Grands Prix. In the former Varzi continued his triumphal progress by winning after a fine battle with Lehoux, Etancelin and Dreyfus on Bugattis, during which Dreyfus overturned and the other two had mechanical ailments. Varzi went on serenely to win at a new record average of 86.82 m.p.h. with a record lap at 91.09 m.p.h. much the fastest speeds yet achieved on the Lasarte circuit. The French Grand Prix, run to the so-called formula, had taken place unusually late in the year on a fast 9.8 mile triangular circuit at Pau. Bugatti had hoped to enter two of his new twin camshaft 2.3-litre cars (Type 51) for Chiron and Divo but they were not ready either for this or the subsequent Spanish Grand Prix and the leading Bugatti drivers were Williams, Bouriat, Etancelin, Wimille (in his first French Grand Prix), Lehoux and Czaykowski. The only opposition was provided by Birkin's 4½-litre supercharged Le Mans Bentley running stripped and Seneschal once more on a 1½-litre Delage, which lost six minutes at the start. Etancelin led from the 8th to the 25th lap and won by 3½ minutes from Birkin's Bentley at 90.37 m.p.h. in a most pedestrian French Grand Prix, albeit an improvement on the farces of 1928/9. Due to the twisting nature of the circuit subsequently used for the Grand Prix de Pau series, the idea has grown up that Birkin's performance was achieved on a slow circuit terribly unsuitable for the Bentley, although this is far from the truth as the 1930 course was one of the fastest in France and of the classic triangular shape. It was an astonishing performance, none the less, particularly as the least slip or mechanical bother would have lost Etancelin the race, but it was only made possible by the low ebb reached in racing car design in the absence of the latest cars from Italy. Also run in September was the Masaryk Grand Prix over the long Brno circuit which was remarkable only because it was the last appearance in racing of the P2 Alfa-Romeo, Nuvolari finishing in 3rd place behind a pair of Bugattis, a sad but almost inevitable conclusion to the career of these much modified cars.

For the new season, however, a wind of change was beginning to blow. Bugatti was going over to twin camshafts and also experimenting with double-eight engines. Maserati was now a proven force with plenty more ideas up his sleeve and, finally, Alfa-Romeo were preparing a new straight-eight. As for drivers it had undoubtedly been Varzi's year par excellence with five victories on Alfa-Romeo and Maserati, Nuvolari, in spite of winning both the Mille Miglia and the Ulster T.T. for Alfa-Romeo had not won a racing car event since the 1928 Bordino Prize but was now at long long last about to start on his great period at the age of forty compared to Varzi's twenty seven. Campari, regarded as a veteran, was in fact only a few months older than Nuvolari, who, like Fangio, did not come to the full height of his genius till relatively late in life in what is generally regarded as a young man's sport.

380 The start of the 1930 French Grand Prix with Birkin's Bentley (18) towering over an assortment of Bugattis

381 The great French driver Jean-Pierre Wimille in his first French Grand Prix

382 The strain of Birkin's astonishing drive shews in every line of his face

Chapter Twenty One
1931/2 · Three Cornered Duel

383 MOST BEAUTIFUL: W. F. Bradley enthused over the new Type 51 with which Chiron (above) won the Monaco Grand Prix

Between 1931 and the coming of the P3 Alfa-Romeo in June 1932 the racing was closely fought between the various new types of Bugatti, Maserati and Alfa-Romeo with occasional intervention from Caracciola's super sports Mercedes. During 1929 and 1930 Maserati had had the edge over their rivals and in many ways continued thus but the new 2.3 Alfa-Romeos and the twin-camshaft 2.3 litre Bugatti (Type 51) made the racing very even. The year began sadly with the death of Montague Napier at Cannes at the early age of sixty. Although he had not been connected with motor racing for over twenty years he had been one of the pioneers of the six-cylinder engine and the detachable wire wheel besides producing engines that had won two Schneider Trophies for England. It is one of the sadnesses of British motor racing that he forsook racing cars for aeroplanes so soon.

At long last by 1931 the A.I.A.C.R. had learnt their lesson and eschewed their fancy regulations and formulae and acknowledged the *de facto formule libre*. Grand Prix races were to be of ten hours duration and no mechanics were to be carried. In addition a European championship for drivers with cash prizes was laid down on the basis of one point for a win, two for a second and so on, with eight points for a non-start, four points for retiring at half distance etc. so that the driver with least points became the winner. With racing starting at eight o'clock in the morning and lasting till six in the evening one was truly getting back to Edwardian standards of endurance. Prizes ranging from £1,220 for the winner to £303 for the fifth were to be awarded and whilst the sceptical Casque posed the question 'will there be any racing cars?' Monsieur Bugatti and Signor Maserati and Jano were busily providing a rousing answer. That Bugatti had been active to some purpose became apparent immediately Varzi let in the clutch of his new Type 51 car in the Tunis Grand Prix. Apart from mild tyre trouble during the middle of the race Varzi led throughout and won by nearly two minutes from Fagioli's Maserati. The new 2.3 Alfa-Romeos made their first racing appearance in the Mille Miglia, on the 12th April in the hands of Nuvolari and Arcangeli a few weeks later; Varzi was driving a 4.9 litre Bugatti but none of these quasi-racing cars were in luck, Caracciola scoring what was to rank as the only 'foreign' victory in this mighty series until Stirling Moss' brilliant drive, also for Mercedes, in 1955. Arcangeli, however, contrived only to lose eight minutes on Caracciola despite no less than nine tyre changes in the 375 miles between Brescia and Rome, while Nuvolari actually led at Rome. A week later at Monaco the new Bugattis of Bouriat, Chiron, Varzi and Divo met the Maseratis of Dreyfus and Fagioli but still no Alfa-Romeos.

W. F. Bradley enthused over the new Bugatti as 'one of the most beautiful and carefully prepared racing cars it has been my privilege to examine in a very long experience,' but as the cars raced up the hill after the start 'giving the impression, as seen from below, of a multi-coloured serpent wriggling with incredible swiftness,' it was Dreyfus' red Maserati that led, duelling with Williams' older Bugatti. The previous winners were ousted by Varzi after 10 laps and he held the lead from Chiron, Dreyfus and Fagioli for 19 laps. A burst tyre then lost Varzi four minutes and thereafter, drive as he might, he could not regain his lead. Chiron won at a new record speed of 54.09 by 3 min. 55 secs. from Fagioli, with Varzi only 9 secs. further behind. Dreyfus had fallen out with oiling problems, Caracciola's big and highly unsuitable Mercedes lost its clutch, but through it all our old friend André Boillot gamely plugged on with his old sleeve valve Peugeot (mounted in the ill-fated 5-valve car chassis going back to 1920) to finish 6th in what was his last big race.

Bugatti's run of luck was now sharply halted. First, *le patron* himself, had an accident in the original Royale and then Varzi lost an epic Targa Florio to Nuvolari on the new Alfa-Romeo. For one reason or another Bugatti decided to give the 1931 Targa a miss but Varzi, through his friendship with Costantini, obtained a Type 51 for the race against Nuvolari and Arcangeli on the new Alfas, Borzacchini and Campari on stripped 1750's and the Maseratis of Biondetti, Dreyfus and Fagioli. Varzi was the first starter and for three of the four laps he held a narrow lead of about two minutes from the Alfas, first of Borzacchini, then of Nuvolari. The weather worsened throughout the race and Varzi, lacking the front mudguards of the Alfas, like Napoleon was defeated by General Winter rather than his adversaries. He drove a race every bit as brilliant as when he had won the year before on the old P2 Alfa-Romeo, but this year it was Nuvolari's turn to score the big win that had so long escaped him. Varzi lost over 10 minutes on his last lap 'when mud and stones were flung up in such quantities that the bright red of the Bugatti disappeared . . . (and) Varzi threw away his useless goggles . . . (and) drove through seas of mud . . . sat in mud . . . swallowed mud . . . was blinded by it just when he most needed his sight, but he hung on grimly defiant'—and still, according to the historical film The Golden Age, with his characteristic cigarette clipped between his lips. In the end Varzi was beaten into 3rd place, narrowly ahead of Campari and behind Nuvolari and Borzacchini. The Maseratis had all met with disaster and Arcangeli limped home in 6th.

A fortnight later the first Grand Prix proper took place at Monza; the Bugatti team were opposed by Nuvolari and Arcangeli on 'Twin-Six' Alfas and Borzacchini and Campari on the 2.3's; Maserati, with two cars wrecked in the Targa Florio, could not make another team ready in the time. The 12-cylinder Alfas were ill starred; Arcangeli had a fatal accident in practice after which Alfas would have preferred to withdraw as they had after Sivocci's accident in 1923, but times had changed and all they got was a 'Start-and-Win' telegram from Mussolini. For the first two hours it seemed as if Varzi was going to cross Il Duce's wires, but no sooner had Chiron taken over than the car retired and left the race to the 2.3 Alfas of Campari-Nuvolari and Borzacchini-Minoia. Nuvolari had started with the 12-cylinder car but had retired after four hours and then shared Campari's 2.3. There is no film record of the dinner following the race, but one would dearly love to have heard Campari and Nuvolari singing the duet from Rossini's William Tell in which the hero, before firing the famous arrow, required his son to pray.

Four weeks later the French Grand Prix celebrated its 25th anniversary and the occasion was marked at Le Mans by a luncheon in the grandstands before the start of the 24 hour race. The winner, François Szisz and runner-up Felice

384 FIRST GRAND PRIX PROPER: the start of the Italian Grand Prix with Campari's Monza Alfa getting away from Lehoux (16) and Wimille (18), followed by Divo (14), Ivanowski (22), Senechal (Delage, 20) still setting his goggles, Varzi (12), Minoia (30), and directly behind him Nuvolari on the double-six Alfa

385 After the double-six car retired Nuvolari took Minozzi's place as Campari's relief driver on No. 26 Monza

Nazzaro had the places of honour beside such famous drivers as Cagno, Gabriel, Barriaux, Hemery, Rigal and the recently retired Louis Wagner, who had all driven in the original event, while representatives of Panhard, Brasier, Fiat, Mercedes, Darracq and Hotchkiss also attended. After all this excitement there had to be a French victory at Montlhéry, just as there had been an Italian one to mark the 25th anniversary of the Targa Florio earlier in the year. Maserati had entered a full team and, in the opening stages established a firm grip on the race with Fagioli leading from Chiron, followed by Dreyfus. The Alfas of Nuvolari, Campari and Minoia, by contrast, were clearly outclassed both on speed and at the pits, for this was the heyday of the Bugatti aluminium wheel which enabled the brake drum to be changed at the same time as the wheel; as if this were not enough, worn shoes were also replaceable in no more time

than was needed to effect a wheel change, so Bugatti had it all ways. The Montlhéry combined circuit was never renowned as an easy one on the drivers and the 10-hour marathon was a very exhausting experience. As a contemporary summed it up:

'The change from the concrete track to the macadam road brought a series of bumps which made it difficult for the drivers to remain in their seats. Despite their hold on the steering wheel they were frequently bumped right off their cushions and had to release pressure on the accelerator to hold the road. . . .'

'Men and machines were suffering from the ordeal; cars were skidding into and around the bends as if on ice. Even the most daring of the drivers hesitated to pass anywhere near the corners for cars were steering round in a terrifying manner. Eyston's hands were stripped of skin; Birkin's clothing was worn through. . . .'

but through it all the iron Varzi and the effervescent Chiron drove serenely on in the lead they had taken almost at the outset. Characteristically Varzi put in an extra lap at the end of the race and equalled his own best lap on his last of the day! But even his performance was overshadowed by René Seneschal who drove his little Delage single-handed into 5th place. Fagioli had retired with disintegrated brakes when lying 2nd and, although he had set up a new lap record at 85.6 m.p.h., he and Maserati had had a poor day. The Alfas had been in constant brake trouble and at one stage their mechanics had even prepared a spare axle with brakes ready adjusted to effect a complete change. Bugatti's unwonted attention to racing detail paid off handsomely; during the race his works cars led in the order Chiron, Divo, Williams about the half-way mark; though Williams fell out soon after the other two held their advantage till about half an hour from the end Divo had to retire out in the country

388 OUTCLASSED: the Alfa-Romeo of Campari

389 IRON TONIC: Varzi (nearest camera) with Chiron (facing camera) being congratulated by Campari after their long drive

386 Bugatti (in bowler) with Paul Panhard at Montlhéry

387 Fagioli is already out of this picture of the early morning start of the French Grand Prix. Others are: 18, Campari (2nd); 2, W. B. Scott (Delage); 32, Chiron (1st); 26, Ivanowski (Mercedes); and 12, Dunfee (Sunbeam)

390 EFFERVESCENCE: Chiron signalling victory to Varzi

191

391 *MIGHTY ATOM: René Senechal (here at Pau in 1930) who drove his Delage single-handed into 5th at Montlhéry*

392 *The Zehender-Minoia Alfa stops to change brake shoes at Montlhéry —Alfas even had a complete spare axle for quicker brake changes*

393 *Bugatti's greater speed at brake changing paid dividends, Here Chiron is having a vigorous discussion in the cockpit while Varzi calmly waits in the foreground*

394 *ANCIENT NAME: the Peugeot of Ferrant and Louis (not Victor) Rigal which finished 9th*

395 *Merz on the Mercedes he shared with Caracciola leads the Maseratis of Ghersi (20) and Biondetti (46)*

396 *Short measure for Borzacchini as he stands with Campari and the champagne after finishing 2nd*

allegedly because his engine had worked loose. In the end Chiron and Varzi won by some 27 miles from the Alfa-Romeo of Campari and Borzacchini, the official result being:

1. Chiron–Varzi	(Bugatti)	782·1 miles	
2. Campari–Borzacchini	(Alfa)	755 ,,	
3. Biondetti–Parenti	(Maserati)	737 ,,	
4. Birkin–Eyston	(Maserati)	736·7 ,,	
5. Seneschal	(Delage)	710 ,,	
6. Minoia–Zehender	(Alfa)	699·9 ,,	
7. Divo–Bouriat	(Bugatti)	699 ,,	(not running)
8. Dreyfus–Ghersi	(Maserati)	688 ,,	
9. Rigal–Ferrant	(Peugeot)	665 ,,	
10. Pesato–Felix	(Alfa)	656 ,,	
11. Nuvolari–Minozzi	(Alfa)	652 ,,	
12. Howe–Lewis	(Bugatti)	606·4 ,,	

Thus finished a French Grand Prix as long and gruelling as any since 1912 or 1906, a race of heroic if rather tedious proportions, which gave France her last win in her own classic until Louis Chiron himself did it again in 1947 and appropriately enough at Lyons. That there were truly heroes in Greece before Agamemnon is underlined by Stirling Moss himself who recently tried a Type 35 Bugatti and wrote

'It was a hard ride though. It proved one thing—that the drivers must have been very fit to have lasted in long distance races ... Its lack of comfort made me wonder if our G.P. drivers would match the speeds of their predecessors in cars of this era'.

The Spanish Grand Prix proving abortive, the final event in this exhausting series was the Belgian Grand Prix at Spa three weeks later. This time only 12 cars started as opposed to 23 at Montlhéry, the most significant absentee being Maserati who was holding himself in readiness for the German Grand Prix a week later. The opening 2½ hours produced a tremendous battle between Nuvolari and Varzi; before the race Ascari still held the lap record from the 1925 event at 81.5 m.p.h. but this was broken on the first and succeeding laps till eventually Chiron left it at 88 m.p.h. After 2½ hours drivers were changed and here the marvellous strength of the first Bugatti drivers began to tell: whilst Nuvolari and Varzi were well matched, Borzacchini was outdriven by Chiron to the extent of losing over two minutes in four laps (= about 36 miles). However after his record laps Chiron suddenly and dramatically appeared on foot, as if scorning to use the aid of a car against such opposition, requiring a magneto coupling. Sadly he got his Bugatti going again only to find deeper and more unspecified maladies 'which made it impossible for him to continue.' So the Nuvolari Alfa found itself with a slender lead over the Williams-Conelli Bugatti at half time, followed by Minoia (Alfa) and Divo (Bugatti).

Divo's run of misfortune continued in the afternoon when he dropped out with mechanical troubles and with only one

Bugatti left and a four-minute lead things must have seemed pretty safe to Nuvolari and Borzacchini. As they slowed down, Bugatti with admirable restraint brought in Conelli and changed drivers and brake shoes in 2 min. 2 secs.; Williams, driving at the top of his form, went after Borzacchini whom he caught during the ninth hour and not even the substitution of Nuvolari altered matters, the Bugatti winning by 6.8 miles, with Minoia's Alfa 3rd. Thus Minoia with a 2nd at Monza, 6th at Montlhéry and 3rd at Spa finished the series with the best performance for the European Championship, although one would have thought that Borzacchini who co-drove into 2nd in all three events had a better record! From an English point of view Birkin and Lewis did well to finish 4th on their Alfa 50 miles behind the winners.

The following week-end the circus were on the Nürburg Ring for the German Grand Prix, now considered of sufficient status to warrant the presence of W. F. Bradley who was much impressed:

'When the Nürburg Ring was planned,' he wrote, *'an intoxicated giant must have been sent out to trace the road. To drive around it is thrilling. To be whirled around by a Varzi, a Chiron or a Caracciola is a sensation never to be forgotten. The circuit starts with a straight stretch but immediately forgets itself and wriggles downhill; then it climbs up twisting and writhing as if in agony. From time to time the road rises to the skyline and whether beyond there is a left or a right hand turn can be learned only when the summit is reached. It impressed me as a pocket edition of the Targa Florio circuit—without the chasms.'*

NÜRBURGRING
(NORDSCHLEIFE)
LAP DISTANCE - 14·17 Miles

397 THRILLING DRIVE: by 1931 the Nürburg Ring racing was sufficiently important to warrant the presence of top correspondent W. F. Bradley

398 *INTOXICATED GIANT: a panoramic view of the Ring with Adenau Castle in the background*

399 *Very wet conditions on the Ring favoured Caracciola*

400 *The Shafer Special, here passing Birkin's Maserati, was remarkable only for being started by a portable starter*

The distance was the familiar 22 laps (311 miles) and heavy rain at the start favoured Regenmeister Caracciola and his big Mercedes. Pursued by Maseratis (Fagioli and Birkin), Bugattis (Chiron, Varzi, Bouriat and Williams) and Nuvolari's lone Alfa, Caracciola fought off the entire horde to win a brilliant race; the sun came out in the last six laps but this was too late although Chiron reduced the German's lead by 42 seconds in a desperate bid to win. Initially the Maseratis of Fagioli and Birkin were well placed but their abstention from Spa had done them little good and of the three only Birkin finished—in 10th.

Behind Caracciola, Fagioli, Nuvolari, Varzi and Chiron had waged great strife for 2nd place, the Bugattis eventually gaining 2nd and 3rd followed by Nuvolari. Caracciola raised the race record to 67.4 m.p.h. and Varzi the lap to 72.6 m.p.h. in spite of the rain. An American entry—'Red' Shafer on his Shafer Special—was remarkable only for being started on the grid by a portable electric starter. At the finish Caracciola was only concerned to find bath and bed, an idea not at all to the taste of Chiron and Varzi who 'discussed what they had done and what they ought to have done, then concluded "Let's have a drink." A cork popped.' After an airing in the hands of Campari at Montenero the misbegotten Double-Six Alfa-Romeos, which their Managing Director openly referred to as the outcome of a joke, were out at Monza for the September Grand Prix with Nuvolari and Campari driving. In the same vein Bugatti had entered two Type 54 4.9-litre cars for Chiron and Varzi, and Ernesto Maserati the 16-cylinder car which then held the 10-km. record at 152.9 m.p.h. These five Titans contested the unlimited heat over 14 laps of the 4.3 mile circuit in Homeric fashion. Varzi in fact led throughout, initially from Chiron before Nuvolari built up his challenge almost a foot at a time till he was at the tail of the Bugatti, when the inevitable tread went. The change took but 14 seconds and lost Nuvolari his chance of winning. Varzi slowed to win by 27 secs. from Chiron, Nuvolari and Campari, with Maserati nowhere.

The cars from Bologna had already made their mark with the brilliant debut of the 3-litre straight eight in the 3,000 c.c. heat which was utterly dominated by Fagioli and Dreyfus, who finished almost together and nearly 1½ minutes ahead of Champion Minoia. The final was contested by Nuvolari (double six Alfa), Chiron and Varzi (4.9 Bugattis), Fagioli and Dreyfus (Maserati), Minoia and Borzacchini (2.3 Alfas) and Lehoux's 2.3 Bugatti. Campari had trouble with one of his gearboxes and did not start and poor Nuvolari was disappointed again, breaking a piston after a mediocre start. However, nobody smelt Fagioli until Varzi forced the big Bugatti to the Maserati's tail after 12 laps. Thirteen—unlucky for some—certainly was for Varzi who lost a tread on that lap, while Chiron in 3rd, just ahead of Dreyfus, lost a lump of rubber which then cut through his brake cable. For a few seconds Monza seemed set for another of its disasters, but luck and skill were with Chiron, though he ceased to be in the race after the incident.

Nuvolari in person brought Minoia in and took over but to little avail, in all the excitement Fagioli too burst a tyre to show there was no ill will, letting Dreyfus into the lead. The slim Frenchman did not enjoy his position very long breaking a piston and Fagioli cantered in at an easy 96.6 m.p.h. to win by 1 min. 15 secs. from Eternal Second Borzacchini who had run quietly non-stop through the hail of bursting treads. Varzi was 3rd nearly another 3 mins. away, then Nuvolari on Minoia's car, Lehoux and Chiron sans brakes. Nuvolari and the Double-Six had the satisfaction of fastest lap at 101.23 m.p.h. in a meeting that had produced two new cars and an intriguing variety of technical interest.

Chiron, having had the first word at Monaco, appropriately had the last over the long Brno circuit for the Czech Grand Prix three weeks later. His luck held in the early stages when one of the most remarkable incidents in racing eliminated his chief rivals Fagioli, Varzi and Nuvolari when they were leading him. On the 2nd lap with a good lead Fagioli struck the pillar of a temporary bridge with his rear hub and brought the whole gimcrack erection down in front of his pursuers. Varzi took the main brunt clearing his way through by main force, miraculously without injury, but leaving some timbers which broke Nuvolari's back axle. Varzi then drove Nuvolari back to the pits and Fagioli retired the following lap, while accidents to Lehoux and Caracciola settled Chiron in an unassailable lead to win by nearly a lap from Stuck's Mercedes.

Since the end of 1927 the Grand Prix contenders had lacked the dominating influence of a great design from a major factory. Bugatti and Maserati were small and specialist outfits while Mercedes and Alfa-Romeo produced, by their standards, relatively pedestrian racing cars during this period. By the middle of 1932, however, all this was changed with the advent of the 2.6 litre monoposto Alfa-Romeo. Both Maserati and Bugatti fought hard and tenaciously against this new contender but the odds were always loaded against them, although both managed to give the new car some nasty surprises during 1932/33. Maserati received a serious blow with the death early in 1932 of Alfieri Maserati at a time when they were known to be carrying out experiments with front wheel drive for their new racing cars. At much the same time details were published of the more revolutionary four wheel drive Bugatti which never appeared in circuit racing. Varzi opened the score for Bugatti with a fairly easy win in the Tunisian Grand Prix, but the Alsatian équipe were badly mauled in the first major encounter at Monaco which as usual opened the European season. At first Chiron set a furious pace bent on repeating his 1931 victory, but soon Nuvolari carved through the field to settle on Chiron's heels until he overdid things while attempting to lap another car and pump up fuel pressure at the same time. The car hit the pavement rolled over and turned round in Nuvolari's path, who, characteristically, avoided an accident and went on to win the race. Varzi pressed him with another Bugatti but in 1932 it was Nuvolari's turn to win the Monaco Grand Prix, although diminishing fuel levels gave him some unpleasant moments

OSTROVAČICE

MASARYK
LAP DISTANCE - 18·2 Miles

ŽEBĚTÍN

KOHOUTOVICE

VESELKA

START

NOVÝ LISKOVEC

401 The long Brno circuit used occasionally in the thirties and after the war saw the last racing appearance of the P2 Alfa-Romeos

402 'BLACK AS A MINER'!—Marcel Lehoux, driver of Bugatti and later Alfa-Romeo

403 'WONDERFULLY PRECISE'—Albert Divo, former riding mechanic, was one of the most seasoned of professionals by the early thirties

404 ELEMENTAL FURY: 'Campari (nearest camera) brakes until his car shudders . . . and invariably skids . . .'

405 'FAST RUN FOR PLEASURE'—Caracciola, here with a monoposto Alfa at the French Grand Prix of 1932

406 'JOCKEY AND TIRED HORSE': a latter day but very characteristic view of Nuvolari flaying a weary car along

in the closing laps, when he was seen perhaps beseeching the Madonna that it might last to the end. It did, but his margin over Caracciola, driving his first race for Alfa Romeo was a very narrow one of 2$\frac{4}{5}$ secs.

Behind the winners Fagioli finished 3rd with his Maserati, never a lucky car at Monaco, then Earl Howe 4th on the first of the Bugattis having gone through non-stop. A few of W. F. Bradley's impressions of the drivers are worth repetition

'Lehoux is as black as a miner at the end of a day's work; (shades of the "Christie Minstrels" in the Amiens Grand Prix). Divo is wonderfully precise in the way he changes down, while Campari (who else!) brakes until his car shudders, changes down before going into the bend and invariably skids as he comes out. . . .'

'Nuvolari and Caracciola are less than three seconds apart and driving in entirely different manners. The former gives the impression of a jockey whipping a tired horse, and the latter of a man making a fast run for the pleasure of the thing. . . .'

Chiron's Bugatti had finished up within two feet of the harbour edge, narrowly escaping the immersion suffered by Ascari 23 years later. Chiron did have a sea trip across the harbour to the hospital but was up and about again in time to drive the Targa Florio three weeks later. Casque's comment on the incident is somewhat difficult to follow

'Frankly I think some of the crack Continental drivers are beginning to give their cars Hades just so long as they can manage to put up fast laps.'

With no Indianapolis-type lap prizes at stake, Chiron was presumably driving to win as best he knew and, in so doing, made a very understandable error of judgment when trying to do at least two too many things at once. Before the Targa Florio, in the Grand Prix de Rome Fagioli scored one of the rare wins of the 16-cylinder Maserati.

Nuvolari continued his winning way in the Targa with his 2.3 Alfa having for the first time what we now know as the Monza Alfa radiator shell. This was the last traditionally epic Targa and was fittingly dominated largely by Nuvolari with severe pressure from his old Bugatti rivals, Chiron and Varzi. Chiron drove a tremendously gallant race for four of the five laps but was physically not equal to the toughest race in the world after his recent accident. Varzi took over for the final lap but he could make little impression on either Nuvolari or Borzacchini. In the post-1945 years this event has regained much of its stature as a sports car race but it is to the years 1919-32 that one inevitably turns for the golden age of the Targa Florio; the years of Peugeot, Mercedes, Delage, Bugatti and Alfa-Romeo, of Boillot, Masetti, Divo, Costantini, Chiron, Varzi, Nuvolari, Antonio Ascari and Campari. The famous circuit that originally had out-Auvergned the Auvergne continued to tower like a Colossus over its lesser fellows, even the mighty Nürburg Ring, and fittingly after the war the event was restored to its classic setting where it remains the oldest extant series of races in history. There may have been dull Targas contested by poor fields, but the very nature of the event has always called for the stoutest that man can devise in heart and metal.

The last races before the new Alfa-Romeo appeared were held on successive week ends in Germany; at Avus the amateur Manfred von Brauchitsch with a specially stream-lined Mercedes won from a motley field of 'Big Bangers' ancient and modern, including the 4.9 Bugattis of Divo and Williams, Dreyfus' 16-cylinder Maserati and Campbell on a re-built 4-litre V-12 Sunbeam. The race itself was almost entirely between Caracciola and Brauchitsch, the Mercedes beating the Alfa by only 4 secs. at the fast speed of 120.7 m.p.h. Caracciola turned the tables on the Ring beating Dreyfus, now back on a Bugatti, by a short distance.

Quantitatively Alfa and Bugatti had shared the honours with Maserati a deserving 3rd and Mercedes an also-ran since the 1931 revival. Between June 1932 and June 1934 Bugatti and Maserati each won only three races of consequence and Alfa-Romeo all the rest (approximately eleven), which, in its way, was as big a reversal of fortune as that which followed the return of the German racing cars in 1934. It was not that Bugatti and Maserati were particularly outclassed by the Alfas; indeed there is evidence that the 3-litre Maserati was a faster car especially in the hands of Nuvolari. It seemed, however, that the others just could not consolidate the winning positions they frequently occupied, and in fact only one of their six wins was gained in competition with the new Alfas, this being in the Czech Grand Prix of 1932 when Chiron's 2.3-litre Bugatti won after the Alfas of Nuvolari and Borzacchini had both met with substantial mechanical troubles. It is one of those strange coincidences of history that the first driver to defeat the P3 Alfa in anything approximating to a fair fight was that same Ray-mond Sommer who accomplished the same feat over the equally unbeatable Type 158 in the post-war years. It is only fair to add that even Sommer's win (in the obscure Miramas Grand Prix of 1932) was gained due to a miscalculation of the lap position in the Alfa pits. On this dull and featureless circuit this would not be terribly surprising in almost any other équipe, but in one of Alfa's standing such an error must be counted quite inexcusable. There was nothing so fortuitous about Sommer's post-war win over the Alfas of Farina and Wimille in the Grand Prix of St. Cloud in 1946. This was the first race these cars had driven since winning the Tripoli Grand Prix in 1940 and both actually retired with transmission troubles prompting even so astute an observer as J. Eason Gibson to comment that it 'made one wonder what would come to them if we started having full length Grand Prix racing once again . . . at Tripoli in 1940 they had no opposition and one doesn't need a lot of gearbox on the Mellaha circuit'.

407 MIRACLE MAN: Sommer, who won the 1932 race at Marseilles from Nuvolari, after repeating the dose in 1946

With the wisdom of hindsight one could certainly query this statement and in a book not published till 1948 J. E.-G. ought really to have seen its error then. Still there is no gainsaying his conclusion that 'to assist in the breaking up of two works entries is pretty good for an independant'. It was, however, the last time that anyone attempted such lèse-majesté until J. F. Gonzalez and his Ferrari trounced the Alfas in their last season of racing at Silverstone in 1951[1]. Between St. Cloud and the 1951 French Grand Prix the Alfas only found themselves seriously out of the lead in the 1950 Belgian Grand Prix, when Sommer (who else?) contrived to hold the lead for no less than four laps after their first fuel stops had set them back between 20 and 30 seconds. Small wonder is it that Grande Vitesse wrote in The Motor —'once again Raymond Sommer, millionaire racer, who races for the hell of it stood out . . . like a giant among a crowd of very tall men'. Perhaps with memories of Miramas 18 years before where they said much the same thing, it was small wonder to find the Alfa team manager visiting the timekeepers 'more than once with the faintly puzzled expression of a man who does not believe Sommer really is on the same lap . . . and has indeed taken the lead'. Just occasionally history does repeat itself.

[1] I discount the Silverstone win of R. Parnell's Thinwall Special Ferrari in the rained off International Trophy earlier in 1951.

Chapter Twenty Two
1932/3 · Monoposto Supremo

408 MAESTRO: Nuvolari driving to victory in the 1932 French Grand Prix after his win in the Italian Grand Prix

The supremacy of the P3 Alfa takes us from June 5th 1932 when Nuvolari won the Italian Grand Prix at Monza on the car's first appearance in its original 2.6-litre form to the 1st July 1934 when Louis Chiron contrived its final and greatest victory in a race of full Grand Prix status by defeating the full panoply of the new German motor racing empire in one of the epic French Grands Prix at Montlhéry. For this race the car, although enlarged to 2.9 litres, was still in substantially original form, although it survived into 1935 by which time it had acquired first a 3.2 and ultimately a 3.8-litre engine, Dubonnet independent front suspension and reversed quarter elliptic springs at the back end. In this ultimate form Nuvolari won perhaps the most outstanding triumph of man over machine in motor racing history in the 1935 German Grand Prix, but by then the car had long passed out of its period of supremacy and, for that matter, out of its original form.

At Monza Nuvolari and Campari had the new Alfas, Fagioli the 16-cylinder Maserati, Chiron and Varzi 4.9 Bugattis and Borzacchini and Caracciola the older biposto 2.3 Alfas. Under international regulations the race was of five hours' duration and, with anything approaching decent pit work, the race would have been Fagioli's by the length of an autostrada. Thus Campari's first stop for a complete wheel change, fuel, oil and water occupied only 1 min. 29 secs. and Nuvolari's about the same time, while the wretched Fagioli took no less than 3 mins. 7 secs. for the same work. Nuvolari's second stop took 1 min. 50 secs.—a slightly longer time which perhaps accounted for the driver brushing a startled mechanic aside in the act of wiping the screen as he tore off in pursuit of Fagioli. Not that he need really have bothered because Fagioli's subsequent stop, which included a brief hand-over to Ernesto Maserati, took no less than 4¼ minutes and even then the car had to stop again a quarter of an hour later for Fagioli to take over. In the end Nuvolari won by 4.9 miles with Fagioli chasing him all the way, while the difference on basic pit stops of approximately four minutes more than accounted for this difference. Fagioli's lap record of 112.07 m.p.h. (3 min. 19⅗ secs.) was more than three seconds quicker than Nuvolari's best time and when both cars were racing together there was nothing even Nuvolari could do to counteract the Maserati's greater speed.

In the early stages Chiron's big Bugatti had led the race narrowly with Varzi in third position and both had led the race when the Italian cars were having their first pit stops. Varzi, however, dropped out with gear selection troubles after 26 laps and Chiron not long after with overheating caused by fuel blockages. Chiron later took over Divo's 2.3-litre car which he drove into 6th place, twelve miles behind the winner. This was not Caracciola's lucky day as his original car was delayed and, finally, put out by magneto troubles; like Chiron he later re-entered the race, finishing 3rd on Borzacchini's car after this driver had been injured by a flying stone. At all events, first blood well and truly to Alfa-Romeo whose entries finished 1st, 3rd and 4th.

Four weeks later they scored a resounding 1, 2, 3, win in the French Grand Prix run for the first time over the original Rheims circuit. On this occasion their drivers were Nuvolari, Caracciola and Borzacchini and the principal opposition lay in the 4.9 Bugattis of Varzi and Howe and the 2.3's of Williams, Chiron and Dreyfus. By the end of the first hour the sole interest lay in the eventual finishing order of the Alfas and who would be 4th. Although Chiron did get

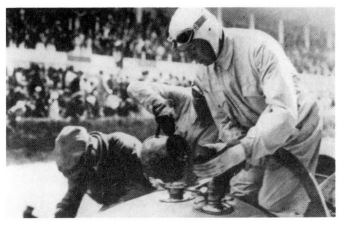

410 PRINCIPAL OPPOSITION: *Varzi refuels his Type 54 Bugatti at Rheims*

411 *Williams who was 6th*

409 SUPPORTING CAST: *Caracciola (18) and Borzacchini (30) with their monopostos at Rheims*

412 *Chiron's Type 51 gave the Alfas the best opposition but could only manage an indifferent 4th*

199

among the Alfas during the middle distance pit stop he was never a serious challenger and Nuvolari finished 1st about ½-mile ahead of Borzacchini with Caracciola roughly the same distance behind in 3rd. The German Grand Prix was not run under the 5-hour rule and at this stage it is interesting to compare the speeds and distances at Rheims and Monza. Rheims was basically the classic triangle with three hairpins joined by two straights and a slighter slower section, while Monza was the original full circuit with a very slight 'kink' or chicane. Thus:—

MONZA	(Miles)	m.p.h.	RHEIMS	(Miles)	m.p.h
1. Nuvolari (Alfa)	520·5	=104·1	Nuvolari	461·30	=92·26
2. Fagioli	515·6	=103·2	Borzacchini	460·06	=92·21
3. Borzacchini/ Caracciola	514·2	=102·8	Caracciola	460·53	=92·10
4. Campari	509·6	=101·92	Chiron	455·23	=91·05
5. Dreyfus (Bugatti)	509·5	=101·9	Dreyfus	451·17	=90·23
6. Divo/Chiron (B'g'ti)	508·2	=101·6	Williams	447·37	=89·47
7. Ghersi (Alfa)	494·7		Zehender (Alfa)	419·65	
8. Ruggieri (Maserati)	466		Felix (Alfa)	411·56	
9. Siena (Alfa)	406·8		Howe	387·15	
10. Premoli (Maserati)	360				

Fastest Lap: Fagioli at 112·07 m.p.h.   Nuvolari at 99·5 m.p.h.

These speeds were substantially faster than anything achieved on these circuits in previous years. The old race and lap records at Rheims stood to the credit of Lehoux's Type 51 Bugatti in 1931 at 89.49 and 92.48 m.p.h. respectively and Nuvolari's 1932 speeds were not beaten until the 1935 Marne Grand Prix by Dreyfus on the greatly improved 3.2 Dubonnet sprung Alfa-Romeo which averaged 98.03 m.p.h. over a shorter distance with a record lap at 102 m.p.h. The full Monza circuit had not been used for a race since 1928 when Chiron had set a race record of 99.4 with a blown 2-litre Bugatti, while the lap record still stood to the credit of Ascari's P2 Alfa at 104.24, dating back to 1924. In 1932, over a slightly slower course Nuvolari's average for five hours all but equalled the old lap record and, by a strange coincidence, was only fractionally slower than the new record set for Indianapolis that year at 104.114 m.p.h. over a comparable distance.

These vastly improved speeds were continued in the German Grand Prix over 354 miles of the Nürburg Ring two weeks later, where the same three Alfas met only one works Bugatti driven by Chiron. Varzi had an eye injury from Rheims and Chiron was only supported by Lehoux and Dreyfus as independants. Once again there was no strong Maserati opposition and, although Chiron got into 3rd on the second lap ahead of Borzacchini, he was soon out with ignition troubles, leaving the Alfas an even clearer run than at Rheims. The only excitement was really when Nuvolari 'forgot' it was Caracciola's race and began to pile on speed in the middle distance, but a suitably contrived pit stop of almost Maserati proportions redressed the balance and the German crowd rejoiced with the *Autocar's* correspondent

that 'the popular "Ruddy" (sic!) had won the Grosser Preis'. Dreyfus' Bugatti was way behind the last Alfa and nearly a quarter of an hour astern of the winner—

1. Caracciola	4–47–22.4/5	= 74·13 m.p.h.	3.	Borzacchini	4–54–33
2. Nuvolari	4–47–53.2/5		4.	Dreyfus	5– 1– 5

In the shorter Eifel Races earlier in the year Caracciola, on a 2.3 Alfa, had set new race and lap records of 70.7 and 72.8 m.p.h. respectively. Now over a much longer distance he had raised race average by nearly 4 m.p.h. and Nuvolari the lap speed by nearly 6 m.p.h. to 77.55 m.p.h.—and all this in a long race where the cars were never seriously challenged. In July and August Nuvolari, by this time almost by tradition, won the Coppas Ciano and Acerbo on the Montenero and Pescara circuits. At Pescara the superior speed of the P3 raised the respective race and lap speeds by 5 and 7 m.p.h. in round figures, but their winning ways were checked at the beginning and end of September, first by Chiron and mechanical mishaps at Brno and then by Sommer and dreaming pit managers at Miramas. Sandwiched between these débâcles, however, came another great battle with Fagioli's Maserati in the Monza Grand Prix, this time run over the full circuit. As was then usual this was the last big race of the season and everybody was hell bent on pulling out every available stop over the short distance involved with a whole winter to put the damage right! This time the heats were not according to engine size and were noteworthy for two incidents neither of which, happily, had serious consequences.

In the second heat Nuvolari and Fagioli were having one of their real battles in the middle of which Nuvolari left the track, jumped a low wall and returned to the course miraculously with only a buckled wheel and a bent axle, *still* contriving to finish 2nd ahead of Taruffi and Chiron. The heats were won at 111.6 m.p.h. (Caracciola), 106.3 m.p.h. (Fagioli) and 111.2 m.p.h. (Campari) for their 100 kilometres and in the repêchage the second disaster occurred when Earl Howe's 1927 Grand Prix Delage left the circuit and 'hit a tree which sliced the front axle . . . as cleanly as Crusader ever sliced infidel's head, then wrapped itself round a tree . . . so closely that the front axle and the differential were only six inches apart!' With no more than a slight tear in his overalls Earl Howe nonchalantly greeted those who rushed to the scene with 'I am afraid I have one car less', a truly classic gem of English understatement which one hopes did not fall solely on foreign ears.

The four P3's very nearly failed to start in the final following a protest against Fagioli's driving in the 2nd heat but good sense triumphed and, perhaps as well, so did the Alfas as Fagioli was slowed by plug bothers. Nuvolari also had his troubles with a punctured carburettor float and Campari actually failed to finish. After a great race with

413 ENGLISH UNDERSTATEMENT: 'I am afraid I have one car less!' Earl Howe on his 4.9 Bugatti

Nuvolari and Fagioli, Caracciola won in 1 hr. 7 mins. 15⅗ secs. at a new record average of 110.8 m.p.h. from

2.	Fagioli	1–8– 4.1/5	5. Varzi	1–10–5.4/5
3.	Nuvolari	1–9– 9.2/5	6. Chiron	1–10–18.2/5
4.	Borzacchini	1–9–23.4/5		

Nuvolari set a new lap record in his heat of 113.7 m.p.h. and the major European season concluded amidst yet more shattering of lap and race records.

All this had not passed unnoticed by the A.I.A.C.R. and whilst Mrs. Prideaux-Brune was calmly reading Herodotus amid all the clamour and chaos of the London Motor Show the governing body were laying down the formula that was to beget the most fabulous racing cars yet seen. For 1934/5/6 races were to last 500 kilometres and cars were to have a maximum weight of 750 kgs. without tyres, water, oil and fuel and a minimum width such that a rectangle measuring 850 × 250 mm. could be placed in the car on a level with the driver's seat. In the meantime the season of 1933 remained to be contested without rectangular seated drivers and, as it turned out, without the new Alfas. Presumably bored with a monopoly of success and virtually unchallenged, apart from Maserati at Monza, the firm decided to withdraw the cars and leave the Scuderia Ferrari to race a modified version of the 2.3 litre Monza in 1933. This was virtually unchanged apart from adopting an offset single-seater body and an engine bored out to 2.55 litres and was just about a match for the 2.3 Bugatti but none for the new 3-litre straight eight Maserati, whose success eventually brought the P3 out of its corner in the middle of the season.

Thus when the season opened Bugatti was the only works entrant in the Grand Prix field, the remaining contestants being independants, mostly organised into groups ranging from the Scuderia Ferrari which went racing in the grand manner to combinations such as that of Sommer and Zehender with new Maseratis or Caracciola and Chiron with

Alfas. Presided over by Count Trossi and organised by Enzo Ferrari, the Scuderia Ferrari had at their disposal six of the modified Monzas, five sports Alfas and two of the new Maseratis besides an assortment of 1750 Alfas and, though one can scarce credit the report, three M.G. Magnettes. For drivers they boasted Nuvolari, Borzacchini, Trossi himself, and a host of rising young Italians, Taruffi, Brivio, Siena, Comotti, and Tadini. Bugatti still had Varzi, Williams, Divo and Dreyfus besides Howe, Czaikowski and Lehoux and another young Algerian, Guy Moll, who later changed to Alfa. The erstwhile Bugatti drivers Etancelin and Wimille were also switching to Alfas and the sands of time were thus fast running out for Bugatti unless he could produce his rumoured new 2.8-litre car to replace the outclassed 2.3 and 4.9 racers. Apart from Earl Howe in England, Birkin was acquiring a new Maserati and Whitney Straight, then a Cambridge undergraduate, had one of the older Maseratis. Without the P3 Alfas speeds would probably be lower but each race was certain to be desperately fought with every man for himself and devil take the hindmost.

After two preliminary skirmishes in the snow at Pau (where incidentally Etancelin's Alfa was delayed by misfiring caused by snow melting on a plug lead) and blazing sun at Tunis the season began in earnest in April at Monaco. Practising was notable for Caracciola's dreadful accident which kept him out of racing for over a year and left him with a permanent limp. Both he and Chiron had equalled Varzi's record and then he overdid things and hit a wall sustaining severe injuries to his right leg. Nuvolari also came to grief on the same corner but only broke a rear axle. This race will always be remembered for producing the most classic of the many great duels between Nuvolari and Varzi which went on for 99 of the 100 laps and also, on a lesser plane, as the first race where starting positions were determined on practice times. From the inside berth Varzi shot into the lead and on the first lap headed Borzacchini, Lehoux and Nuvolari. During the second Nuvolari moved up behind Varzi and on the next lap he was in his wonted place—but only just, and so it continued for a further 96 laps. Of the hundred laps, Nuvolari led on 64 and Varzi on only 36, but on the vital last one. Nuvolari had the best of the race but Varzi won it and pace was such that the back-marker was lapped after only seven circuits. Behind the leaders an equally furious battle raged for 3rd place between Borzacchini's Alfa and 'Phi-Phi' Etancelin's smaller Monza Alfa, with the lead constantly chopping and changing. Then the fiery Phi-Phi had a skid at the 'chicane' and lost his 3rd place to the Italian. Nothing dismayed Etancelin drove with even greater fire, breaking Varzi's record on his 51st lap and catching Borzacchini again seven laps later. Another seven laps and Etancelin's race was run when his axle shaft broke—a sadly recurring Monza Alfa disaster. Just ahead the Nuvolari-

414 BATTLE ROYAL: The duel in the 1933 Monaco Grand Prix between Nuvolari and Varzi is one of the most famous in motor racing. Here Varzi leads on the first lap from Borzacchini in the dust

415/6 LESSER RIVALS: Behind Nuvolari and Varzi an intense battle raged between Etancelin's 2.3 Alfa which retired (top) and Borzacchini's improved Ferrari 2.6-litre Monza which finally finished 2nd

Varzi battle raged on unabated with the race average standing at 57 m.p.h. after 60 laps but still Nuvolari kept ahead. The enlarged Monza Alfa was slightly quicker than the Bugatti but the Bugatti was characteristically better on corners and it would only be possible for Varzi to get by with exceptional luck or daring or by risking mechanical disaster.

Somehow Varzi managed it on the 80th lap, but within four more laps Nuvolari was back again and with 98 laps gone the race looked signed, sealed and delivered to Nuvolari. However, no man won this great race twice in the pre-war era, even Nuvolari. Varzi got by again on the 99th lap only to be repassed yet again so that Nuvolari led till they reached the uphill Ave de Monte Carlo for the last time. Varzi now resolved on truly desperate measures, forcing the Bugatti up to 7500 r.p.m. on 3rd gear and past into the lead. Nuvolari's foot immediately went even further into the floor, but the Alfa baulked with a burst oil pipe. Hot oil caused a fire with Nuvolari coasting grimly on, as Varzi swept along his triumphal way to the chequered flag and vengeance for that mudswept Targa Florio defeat in 1931. Varzi also made a new record lap on his 99th circuit. Poor Nuvolari could not even rank as a finisher and Borzacchini, in 2nd, was unable to manage a tour d'honneur. Varzi's record average of 57.04 m.p.h. was not surpassed until 1935 when Fagioli fractionally improved it to 58.17 m.p.h. and raised the lap speed from Varzi's 59.77 to 60.08 m.p.h. It was not until 1937 when the titanic power outputs of the W125 Mercedes and C-Type Auto-Union were brought to bear on the circuit that there was any material increase on the 1933 speeds. During an equally stirring and uninhibited duel Brauchitsch raised the race average to 63.25 m.p.h. and Caracciola the lap record to 66.99 m.p.h. It is pleasing to recall that Nuvolari kept his ill used mount as his personal road car for a few years and that the car is still having an active competition life in South Africa.

The following Sunday saw Nuvolari walk away with the Bordino Grand Prix in the absence of Varzi who had won it the three previous years and then on the 7th May the grand adversaries were at it again with Varzi scoring yet another split second, if rather less meritorious, win, this time at Tripoli. In a field containing such great names as Nuvolari, Varzi, Borzacchini, Campari and Fagioli it was a rare privilege to find the Englishman Sir Henry Birkin leading on a Maserati for the first five laps and second to Nuvolari at half distance. Sadly, after this meteoric beginning Birkin was delayed by poor pit-work so that he could finish no higher than 3rd but it was a heart-warming performance at one of the lowest ebbs in British racing history. Tragically this was the dashing Birkin's last race: as is well known he sustained a small burn which set up blood poisoning from which he died on June 22nd. Apart from Birkin's performance the less said about this race the better, as it was the

TRIPOLI
LAP DISTANCE—8.14 Miles

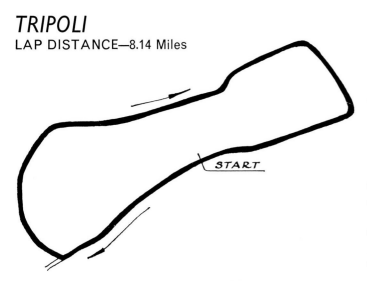

START

417 RACE OF MILLIONS: The famous Melaha circuit near Tripoli, unused since 1940, where lap speeds of over 140 mph were reached

historic one rigged by Nuvolari, Varzi, Campari and Borzacchini to enable Varzi to win and share with them an agreed percentage of the winning lottery ticket in concert with the man who had 'drawn' Varzi!

Two weeks later Varzi chalked up yet another and more genuine win for Bugatti with the big 4.9 Type 54 at Avus, with Czaikowski 2nd on a similar car ahead of Borzacchini and Nuvolari who tied for 3rd place. Practice was marred by a fatal accident to the veteran Mercedes driver Otto Merz who, unlike Archduke Franz Ferdinand, had escaped death on that hot sunny day in Serajevo nearly 19 years before, and was making a comeback after three years in retirement. The same day the well known Bugatti drivers Guy Bouriat, and Louis Trintignant, elder brother of Maurice, had fatal accidents in the Picardie Grand Prix, which was won by the popular and often unlucky Etancelin on a Monza Alfa. On 26th May Nuvolari won the annual Eifelrennen from Brauchitsch and Taruffi, then at the start of his long and versatile career. Two days later came the Targa Florio, which suffered from the clash with the German event; as a result only Borzacchini and Brivio of the better drivers were taking part in this great classic, which only shortly before had been regarded as second in importance and prestige to the French Grand Prix. After holding an easy lead in the early stages Borzacchini bent his Alfa considerably in an excursion off the road leaving Brivio with an easy win over an otherwise undistinguished field.

There have been few seasons quite like that of 1933 for sheer cut-and-thrust rivalry. The withdrawal of the monoposto Alfas had left Bugatti as the only constructor entering an official team, but somehow the epithet 'works sponsored' never seems to suit the erratic ways of Molsheim. As a result, with no dominating car and little in the way of team

'Management' a most glorious free-for-all ensued with Nuvolari, Caracciola, Chiron, Fagioli and Varzi all in their prime on cars of almost equal performance, challenged by seasoned men of the calibre of Borzacchini, Campari, Czaikowski, Dreyfus, and Stuck and a galaxy of rising talent—Etancelin, Taruffi, Sommer, Wimille, Lehoux and Moll—all at hand on very similar cars to take their places should any of the Big Five falter for even a split second.

So after a series of rousing preludes the scene was set for the 21st French Grand Prix—THE Grand Prix—to be held at Montlhéry. Sad absentees were the injured Caracciola and the mortally sick Tim Birkin, but everyone else was there, apart from Varzi, and in particular three past winners —Campari (1924), Chiron (1931) and Nuvolari (1932). In all its 27 years of sunlit history the Grand Prix had only been won once in successive years—by the legendary Boillot in 1912/13, though Lautenschlager (1908 and 1914), Nazarro (1907 and 1922) and Benoist (1925 and 1927) were all double winners and Campari had had a clear winning advantage in 1925 when the Alfas were withdrawn after Ascari's accident. Now here was the new Boillot—Tazio Nuvolari—the greatest virtuoso of the steering wheel since the Peugeot champion ready to set the seal on his triumphal years by a second successive victory in the classic motor race.

There had been hopes that the new 2.8-litre Bugattis would have been ready for the race but Ettore had never been a Boy Scout and to make matters worse the official Type 51's had not been overhauled since Monaco and were thus non-starters. This deprived the race of Nuvolari's greatest rival—Varzi—and with both Fagioli and Caracciola non-starters the race looked a good thing for the Mantuan. At the time the Montlhéry record stood at 136.778 k.p.h. set up by Fagioli's 16-cylinder Maserati. After three days concentrated effort in practice Chiron managed to lower this to 137.446 k.p.h. and on the final day Etancelin with another Monza Alfa achieved 137.330 with Sommer not far behind at 136.363, with the Maseratis of Zehender and Campari a little slower at 134.248 and 136.116 respectively. At this point the Scuderia Ferrari arrived and Nuvolari proceeded to put in a standing lap of 135.460 followed by successive laps at 139.578, 140.801, 140.889 and 141.242 k.p.h., which rather made nonsense of the fastest times till then. Perhaps inevitably Nuvolari had engine troubles after his five meteoric circuits causing him to take over Borzacchini's car for the race.

Rain threatened on the 11th June as the usual vast crowds poured in from all over France for the race which would lie principally between Nuvolari, Etancelin, Campari, Sommer and Chiron with Zehender (Maserati), Taruffi and Wimille (Alfas) and Lehoux and Czaikowski (Bugattis) competing for the left-overs. Earl Howe made a fast start but after the first of the 40 laps it was Nuvolari who led from Campari.

418 LAST LAP LOSER: Etancelin's face is a study in despair as he struggles to keep his Alfa ahead of Campari

419 IMPRESSIVE DEBUT: After his own car retired Nuvolari (above) took over Taruffi's car although Taruffi himself had been leading the French G.P. in his first season

420 LAST VICTORY: The great and beloved Campari being received by M. Chautemps after his second win in the French Grand Prix

Taruffi, Zehender, Chiron and Etancelin. Zehender fell back on the 2nd lap and on the 3rd Chiron and Etancelin both got through the less experienced Taruffi, though apparently not without much shaking of fists by the drivers supported by the Sydney Hill elements of the partisan crowd. After six laps Nuvolari stopped for over two minutes to change wheels and to balance things Chiron stopped with axle troubles. Two laps later the two champions were both out with the perennial complaint of the over-driven Alfa—transmission failure. This left Campari with a comfortable lead of 35 secs. over Taruffi with Etancelin 3rd, a second behind, followed by Zehender, Moll (Alfa) and Czaikowski. A series of routine pit-stops shook the order about during the next 100 kilometres: Campari especially was finding his car characteristically hard to handle and unstable, which made it proportionately more severe on tyres. Thus at 200 kms. the Maseratis were well and truly sandwiched by a bakery of Alfas:—

1. Taruffi	1–28– 9 = 136·131 k.p.h.		4. Zehender	1–29–42
2. Etancelin	1–28–10		5. Moll	1–29–59
3. Campari	1–28–40		6. Sommer	1–29–59

followed by Eyston and Zanelli also on Alfas.

Pit stops continued to govern the race order and seem to have been very lengthy—e.g. Moll took 2 mins. and Sommer 2 mins. 40 secs. for routine supplies and wheel changing. Campari was all the time gaining on Taruffi leading the French Grand Prix in his first season of Grand Prix racing. Came a great stir though when Nuvolari took over Taruffi's car and shot off in pursuit of the leaders—Campari, Etancelin and Moll. Soon after Moll had an even longer stop of 5 mins. 25 secs. losing 3rd to Nuvolari and 4th to Eyston. During all this Campari had been pressing on with all the weight his person and experience (to say nothing of his gargantuan snail dinners) could exert on the loud pedal against his remaining tyre stops. Even a 2-minute lead was not enough as he became 31 secs. down on Etancelin after his stop, which he had reduced slightly by 400 kms:

1. Etancelin	2–58– 8 = 134·730 k.p.h.		4. Sommer	3– 7–50
2. Campari	2–58–33		5. Moll	3–12– 9
3. Eyston	3– 5–30			

Etancelin's gearbox was causing him much anxiety and Moll's car was becoming increasingly troublesome so Montlhéry was living up to its name as a car breaker. On the 33rd lap Campari was 20 secs. behind Etancelin, then 11 on the 34th and 2 secs. on the 35th: then, like Moses within sight of the Promised Land, he had to make a final wheel change.

When he came to re-start the Maserati took a perverse fit and it needed the combined efforts of two mechanics and one of those by-standers, who always seem to crop up on these occasions, to urge the adamantine machine into life. The numbers employed constituted a technical breach of the regulations but luck was with the gallant Cavaliere not only in the Committee Rooms, where he was fined 1,000 francs after the race, but also on the circuit where Etancelin's car, still 60 secs. ahead, was fast becoming undriveable. On one corner he had to stop altogether to engage a gear so that his lead was inexorably whittled down from 56 secs. on lap 38 to 24 secs. on lap 39, Campari passing him on the last lap for his second victory in the Blue Riband of motor racing in 2 hrs. 48 mins. 45 secs. (131.143 k.p.h. = 81.49 m.p.h.) followed by

2. Etancelin	2–49–37		5. Moll	38 laps
3. Eyston	39 laps		6. Villars (Alfa)	34 laps
4. Sommer	39 laps			

From a British standpoint Eyston had driven an outstanding race on Bernard Rubin's Monza Alfa. Had the race been any longer he would certainly have caught Etancelin; also during the rain in the later stages his lap times were faster than any other drivers still racing, Campari included.

Thus the great and beloved Campari won his second Grand Prix and made up for the Montlhéry win that had eluded him in 1925. Nuvolari's run of ill luck continued at the revived Penya Rhin Grand Prix where he was delayed by engine trouble and could finish no higher than 5th in an indifferent field, while in the Marne Grand Prix at Rheims he was eliminated by back axle trouble. Here Etancelin made up in some measure for his misfortune at Montlhéry with a split second win over Wimille, with Sommer 3rd on Maserati and Whitney Straight 4th in his first continental appearance with his old 2½-litre Maserati which earned him considerable praise from experienced observers.

The works Bugattis had recovered from their hammering at Monaco by the 9th of July and appeared for the Belgian Grand Prix over the traditional and magnificent Spa circuit then considered by many to be the finest in Europe. The drivers were Varzi, Williams and Dreyfus and they were opposed by Nuvolari and Borzacchini (Ferrari Maseratis), Siena (Ferrari Alfa), Chiron, Sommer and Moll (Alfas), Lehoux (Bugatti) and Zehender (Maserati). In practice Nuvolari was not satisfied with the handling of his car and had the chassis strengthened at the Impéria works. The engine seemingly was man enough to stand up to over four hours of Nuvolari without similar fortification and the new combination was an instant success. Nuvolari won very comfortably although pressed by both Borzacchini and Chiron till they both retired. Varzi, this time, was well beaten into second place over three minutes behind, followed by Dreyfus, Lehoux and Siena. Nuvolari's average of 89.23 m.p.h. was faster than the 1931 lap record of 88 m.p.h. and he also set a new lap record of 92.33 m.p.h. At this point in the year Nuvolari left Ferrari and teamed up with Borzacchini to race the new Maseratis and the older 2.6 Alfas as independents, their places in the Scuderia being filled by

421 CONSOLATION PRIZE: Etancelin made up for his disappointment with a split-second win over Wimille (above) at Rheims

422 NAZZARO PROPELLED: the scene at Nice just after Felice Nazzaro started the race—Nuvolari on No. 2, the winner, lies 5th

Louis Chiron and Fagioli who had neither of them won a race all season.

Nuvolari descended on Nice for the Grand Prix on the 6th August and embarked on a tempestuous duel with Etancelin as soon as the great veteran Felice Nazzaro had started the race. The heat was as intense as the conflict and retirements were thick and fast but nothing seemed to stop the two leaders and Lehoux, until Nuvolari came brakeless to the pits for a 20 second adjustment, which left him 34 seconds behind Lehoux and 59 seconds behind Etancelin. This really put Nuvolari on his mettle and in remarkably short time he was past Lehoux, when he went wide on a corner and off after Etancelin. He, too, fell into error under Nuvolari's satanic pressure when he performed a complete *tête-à-queue* on a hairpin so that with 45 of the 95 laps gone Nuvolari was securely in the lead followed by Etancelin, Dreyfus, Wimille, Moll, Lewis and Lehoux, who lost more time first out on the circuit with another slide and then at the pits with tired brakes. The others had been driving steadily, realising that they had not quite the dash of the leaders, and now were beginning to reap their reward. Soon after, Etancelin lost a brake rod and gave up while Lehoux fell further back with more assorted troubles. The excitement was still not over for Wimille decided to catch Dreyfus and for ten laps there was barely daylight between the cars till his brakes gave out in the heat and finally Nuvolari won by a minute and a half from Dreyfus, followed by Moll, Fagioli, Lehoux and Lewis. Neither Chiron nor Fagioli had had a particular happy start to their Ferrari careers, but between them they won the remaining six races of the season, the explanation being the re-emergence of the 2.6 monoposto Alfa, which Ferrari had finally contrived to seduce from its jealous parents in Milan,

On the 13th August Fagioli opposed the field at Pescara

PESCARA
LAP DISTANCE—15.9 Miles

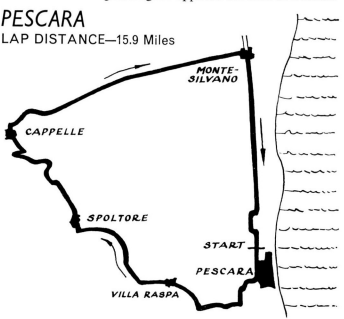

423 CLASSIC SURVIVAL: the magnificent Pescara road circuit was used for nearly thirty years of racing notably for the pre-war Coppa Acerbo series. It posed difficult carburation problems because of its variations of speed and height

but it was left to Campari and Nuvolari on their Maseratis to make the running till Campari crashed leaving Nuvolari well in the lead but, try as they might, nobody was to defeat the monopostos in 1933 and a pit stop delayed Nuvolari, who finished 2nd over two minutes behind Fagioli, with Taruffi (Maserati) and Varzi (Bugatti) 3rd and 4th. Nuvolari very slightly raised his 1932 lap record to 90.4 m.p.h. while Fagioli raised the winning speed from 86.89 to 88.03 m.p.h. A week later Fagioli scored a somewhat hollow victory in the Comminges Grand Prix at St. Gaudens in a race which lacked Campari, Nuvolari and Borzacchini. Nuvolari was in action at Miramas the following weekend where he dominated the 500 kilometre race till his Maserati broke its rear

axle with barely 100 kms. left and once again the monoposto scraped through, though even the disappointed Nuvolari must have been glad to see Chiron win his first race in a year. Oddly enough Zehender put in the fastest lap in the race which was about 1.4 secs. slower than Nuvolari's record in 1932.

And so the scene shifted a fortnight later to Monza for one of the most dramatic and tragic days in motor racing. Since 1927 the Italian Grand Prix and the heats and final for the Monza Grand Prix had taken place on separate days but this time they were to be run off on the same day with the big race in the morning. Competition promised to be unusually keen with the Italians all burning to win their great race and the independents equally keen to haul down the monoposto's colours as Sommer had done in 1932. Once more there were no works Bugattis, but Chiron, Fagioli and Taruffi had monopostos, Nuvolari and Zehender Maseratis and many others were mounted on Monza Alfas. The first ten laps produced a furious running battle betwen Nuvolari and the monopostos as first one, then the other attacked Nuvolari. Fagioli stopped at his pit after 10 laps leaving Taruffi to take up the challenge. This he did in no uncertain manner by actually leading Nuvolari and the race after 11 laps. Two laps later Nuvolari changed a wheel and lost three places and on the 18th Taruffi did likewise and never really got on terms with the race again.

At that point Chiron took up the running from Nuvolari, Fagioli and Zehender and a most interesting race ensued, governed in great measure by pit stops for fuel and wheel changes. At the 27th lap it was Nuvolari, Fagioli, Chiron; a few laps later Chiron and Nuvolari had changed round, then Fagioli stopped and after 35 of the 50 laps Chiron had a clear two minutes' lead over Nuvolari, then Fagioli, Lehoux gaining ground, and Zehender. At the 40 lap mark Chiron (plugs) and Nuvolari (wheels again) were at their pits and a lap later Chiron was out with a broken valve, all of which left Nuvolari with a slender but potentially winning lead of about half a minute for his 3rd successive Italian Grand Prix. Then with only two laps to go he coasted to his pit thumping a rear wheel and the race was over, Fagioli winning by 40 secs. with Zehender a very creditable 3rd, 3¼ minutes behind the winner in what was undoubtedly the most interesting race of the year.

After *Motor Sport's* correspondent had enjoyed 'a very third rate lunch during which . . . (he) . . . was charged 10 liras for a glass of water (about 3/6!)' the parade before the Monza Grand Prix began. This event was to be of three heats and a final and entries included Trossi (4½ litre Duesenberg—a Ferrari entry), Czaikowski (4.9 Bugatti), Borzacchini and Straight (Maserati), Moll and Lehoux (Alfa) and Campari (monoposto Ferrari Alfa with brakes on rear wheels only). In the first heat Czaikowski took the

Duesenberg in the early stages and won easily but not before the red American car had shed oil over the notorious South Curve. With rain already on the track the second heat was likely to be very dangerous and the parade was interrupted whilst a car went down bearing a large broom to clear the South Curve. In the meantime the burly Campari had received the tumultuous applause that invariably greeted him as the most popular driver in Italy and perhaps more than usual as he had announced this as his final appearance before retiring to the operatic stage.

Campari and Borzacchini led from the delayed start but that was the last spectators in the grandstands saw of these great drivers. On the opening lap the two cars hit the oil patch, inadequately cleared, and despite the great skill and experience of their drivers they crashed and were both killed almost instantly. In the meantime the spectators in the stands were astonished to see Balestrero on an outmoded Monza Alfa rumble past in the lead and the terrible news was soon all over the course.

Before the third heat could be started there was a drivers' meeting and more attempts to clear the South Curve causing a delay of about two hours while the crowd vented its displeasure with the customary succession of boos, cat-calls and whistles. The heat was eventually run off without disaster and the final then started. After the first lap Straight led though the race was clearly between Lehoux and Czaikowski and *Motor Sport's* correspondent recalled thinking with fatal prescience 'This will be a fine Bugatti finish . . . if Lehoux and Czaikowski . . . (do) . . . not race one another to death.' Sure enough on the 8th lap Lehoux appeared alone, Czaikowski having skidded on the fatal patch at well over 100 m.p.h. and left the road to have his petrol tank explode before help could be brought. . . .

The next week Chiron won his 3rd successive Czech Grand Prix on the leviathan Masaryk circuit at Brno with Fagioli 2nd, followed many minutes later by Wimille—a poor race over a rough circuit—and finally in October came the revived Spanish Grand Prix at San Sebastian. This was an interesting race in which the new 2.8-litre Bugattis made their long awaited appearance with their piano wire wheels and lower squatter lines, but still retaining a quasi-2-seater body. Driven by Varzi and Dreyfus they were beaten by Lehoux's Type 51 and were clearly no match for Nuvolari's Maserati or the two monoposto Alfas. Once again Nuvolari made the running storming past both Chiron and Fagioli by typically brilliant driving. This time, however, even he over-reached himself and finished the season against a tree but happily without very serious injuries. For the record it was Chiron's race again with Fagioli 2nd and Lehoux 3rd. The new Bugattis of Varzi and Dreyfus were 4th and 6th with Wimille's Alfa 5th.

For the intensity of its programme and rivalry the 1933

424/5 FATAL DAY: Borzacchini (above) and distinguished Bugatti driver and world hour record holder Czaikowski (below) who both perished in the miserable accidents on Monza's South Curve

season had been without precedent and whilst the latter months had been dominated by the Monoposto Alfas they had been devilishly hard pressed in most of their races by the genius of Nuvolari. Apart from him, however, their superiority was clear and the independents must have realised that the dog days in the sun which they had enjoyed between February and July were numbered. Still it had been magnificent while it lasted. Even more magnificent had been the long period of Italian leadership in racing car design and driving, which from its humble beginnings in the glorious defeat of the Fiats at Dieppe in 1912, had been such a dominant factor in racing between 1921 and 1933. Apart from the last flickerings of M. Henri's candle, the Lory Delages and Ettore Bugatti, who was Italian born anyway, every great racing car of the period had been Italian or, in the case of the S.T.D. cars, Italian designed. In addition Italy had supplied by far the greatest proportion of the leading drivers from Ascari, Nazarro and Bordino at the beginning to Nuvolari, Fagioli and Varzi at the end, with such great names as Masetti, Materassi, Borzacchini, Arcangeli and Brilli Peri in the middle of the period and, throughout the apparently eternal and indestructible Campari who in his career and outlook so aptly spanned the great gulf between the emergence of the Vintage era in 1912 and its glorious finale in 1933.

Following Minoia's retirement, Campari was the last survivor of the pre-war drivers, and the kind of man who elevates the everyday performance of his walk of life to the level of legend. A whole microcosm of these spring to mind—from the Great Lyons Sausage on his first Grand Prix win to his riding the wind perched in his Maserati like the incarnation of Mr. Bibendum in his last; Campari the gastronome cooking in convict pyjamas; Campari the opera singer and bon viveur : like Shakespeare's Fool a man for all waters cast in the rich mould of an 18th century eccentric—if you like, the Squire Western of motor racing, extracting every drop of zest there is in life and in many ways the character Georges Boillot might have become had he survived the old war. Somehow his death is symbolic because there would have been no place for Campari in the new motor racing firmament that came into being in 1934 even as in the end there was none for his great rival and contemporary Luigi Fagioli. In the new age there was room for only one truly independent spirit—the transcendental Nuvolari.

He too had become a living legend for the fire of his driving and the number of his victories, and may well have reached the full flowering of his genius in his battles with the monoposto Alfas during the latter part of 1933. Whatever Nuvolari did in that year was studded with his own special

brand of magic—the sort of thing George Monkhouse had in mind when he wrote

'The very sight of Nuvolari has for some reason which I cannot explain always sent "tingles down my spine," perhaps it was just his dynamic personality but I know that I was not alone in this feeling . . . To see Nuvolari in his heyday chin out sitting well back in the driving seat his outstretched hairy arms flashing in the sun as he made his blood-red Alfa perform seemingly impossible antics not once but corner after corner, lap after lap, the tyres screaming and the crowd yelling themselves hoarse was quite fantastic. There was something soul stirring about Tazio Nuvolari for, wherever he drove, thousands of spectators, whatever their nationality, "squeezed" for him, hoping against hope that he would achieve the impossible, nor did he often disappoint them.'

Like Stirling Moss in our own times so much of what Nuvolari achieved, particularly between August 1933 and September 1939, was done with inferior cars pitted against drivers of the very highest skill such as Chiron, Fagioli, Caracciola, Rosemeyer, Varzi and Lang. By contrast, during the early thirties when he generally had first call on the best Alfa Romeo could offer, he never seemed quite to stand so head-and-shoulders above the rest. Like Fangio or Moss, he was a driver for whom a slower or difficult car brought out his very finest driving ability and again like both Moss and Fangio he rarely, if ever, gave a bad performance, another rare quality in a top flight driver.

In almost every way the German revolution was a wonderful epoch-making step forward for racing save this one— that by re-establishing the Rule of the Factory it eliminated entirely from major Grand Prix racing the younger French drivers of the quality of Wimille, Sommer, Etancelin, Lehoux and to a lesser extent Dreyfus, all of whom had it in them to have been really first class drivers in the pre-war years. In many ways the French tradition in motor racing has never recovered from their rising generation being shunted into the sidelines at this stage in their careers. True Wimille got his chance in 1947/8 with Alfa-Romeo and Sommer too put up many sterling performances generally with outmoded cars, but with real motor cars on terms with the fastest what might all these fine drivers not have achieved? Of course politics made things difficult for French drivers in German or Italian teams after 1935 and Mercedes in particular like to retain German drivers for their leading places, but even so these Frenchmen must have felt even more frustrated than Nuvolari as they went on the rounds of minor Grand Prix and sports car events after they had touched, and on occasions even assumed, the mantle of the great in 1932/3.

426 REARGUARD ACTION: the latter part of 1933 was notable for the tremendous challenge by Nuvolari and the 3-litre Maserati to the supremacy of the monoposto Alfas

427 SPIRIT OF AN AGE: Campari perched in his Maserati rides the wind like Mr. Bibendum on the way to his last win

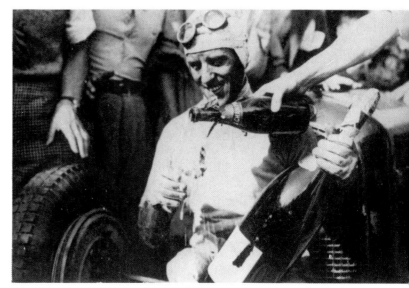

428 FOR ALL TIME: By the end of 1933 Nuvolari, like Boillot, had become a living legend for the fire of his driving and the number of his victories

PART FOUR
1934 to 1951 · The Early Moderns

The Spirit of the Time shall teach me Speed.
William Shakespeare: King John.

Chapter Twenty Three
1934 · The Old Order Changeth

435 THE OLD ORDER CHANGETH: as two Mercedes-Benz and the Auto-Union leave the two monoposto Alfas in the distance

'Great Deeds Need Great Preparations'—Heliodorus.

One of the great attractions of racing in the early thirties lay in the spectacle not only of man struggling against in machines of nearly equal performance but also in the often brutal struggle of man against machine. By the end of 1933 engine power had outstripped chassis design so much that Guidotti, Alfa Romeo's head tester, has said that with the monopostos 'the hardest job was not to get them around corners, but to keep them on the road where straights allowed the cars to approach their maximum speeds.' The

whole process underlying the German revolution against this design stalemate has been described with rare simplicity and clarity by L. T. C. Rolt in 'Horseless Carriage' and in describing its background I have drawn very heavily on this account.

Considered in terms of engine design it is doubtful if there had been any improvement since the Lory Delage of 1927 but apart from the introduction of front wheel brakes, chassis design had not really improved since 1914 so that the monoposto Alfa 'represented the ultimate that could be achieved within a convention that dated from the earliest days of motor racing. Yet such was the power developed that the road-holding ability of the chassis had become the decisive limiting factor on a road circuit.' As with the latter-day vintage sports car the villain of the piece was unsprung weight and by 1933 the point had been reached when the tail was almost literally wagging the dog or as Rolt puts it, 'the springs will no longer be capable of damping the forces generated by road shocks in the wheels and axles. The latter will therefore take charge and tend to destroy the stability and road-holding capacity of the vehicle. . . .'

Until 1934 designers adopted 'a crude though surprisingly

fusion of Mercedes and Benz in 1926 had given the engineers of Stuttgart an answer if they chose to look in their history books, which was precisely what Dr. Hans Nibel and Wagner, both from the old Benz Company proceeded to do. Benz influence predominated even more strongly in the more revolutionary Auto-Union which was partly designed by Adolf Rosenberger who had actually raced the rear engined Benz cars in the 'twenties. Thus it was that, with characteristic conservatism in basic principle of design, the German

436 . . . 'the hardest job was not to get them round corners . . .' Siena (Maserati) leads Lehoux's Alfa at Monaco in 1934

successful form of compromise . . . (by employing) . . . a flexible chassis frame . . . capable of withstanding stresses by absorbing them. In effect therefore the chassis itself became an additional damping device' and throughout the vintage period of racing car design 'a certain degree of flexibility was always maintained; indeed good road holding depended on this quality when spring movement was restricted.'

Now Morgan, Sizaire-Naudin and Lancia had all flirted with independent front suspension almost before the vintage era began and Alvis and Benz produced independently sprung cars in the 'twenties, 'yet it does not appear that even these few manufacturers who utilised independent suspension ever fully grasped its potential advantages.' In fact the

engineers once more contrived to take an immense stride forward, in part at least by looking carefully back.

The new formula was announced in October 1932 and was described by 'Casque' in the *Autocar* as a 'beautiful bombshell' and denounced roundly. 'How they arrived at it seems a mystery. The Italians are reported to say that the Germans wanted it and the Germans say the Italians were the authors, while it is suggested that Delage would only race if this limit was imposed. Now the weight limit strikes me as crazy . . . the proposed car would be about the weight of an M.G. Midget and have a speed of 120. Moreover any maximum weight limit seems to me ridiculous remembering that the engine size is unlimited. Of course it is not absolutely neces-

215

ly came to fruition.' By 1933 Adolf Hitler had seen to it that Rudi was to lack nothing in racing cars and what German publicity termed 'the Führer's overpowering energy' was to ensure that the formula was 'a measuring stick for German knowledge and German ability.' Also Sprach Adolf Hitler!

437 IN THE STEPS OF THE MASTER: Deputy Führer Hess with Dr. Ferdinand Porsche studying the new Auto-Union

438 WIELDER OF THE YARDSTICK

sary to run to these rules; England won't, America won't, I don't think Germany will and so it comes down to the French Grand Prix and Monza.'

In fact Germany stepped in and effectively saved the formula otherwise it might so easily have gone the way of all the other formulae since 1927 and Casque's prophecy was thus very nearly fulfilled because it was not until March 1933 that Mercedes-Benz decided to build cars to the Formula. At the time, however, it seemed a very curious idea as for years the cry had been for a fairly substantial minimum weight and Casque concluded that possibly 'one particular firm has a chassis that it thinks will comply with the rule.' The idea that Delage had pressed for the new formula was soon rejected by that manufacturer himself attacking the new rules along with the French press. Even then there were rumours of Mercedes participation as Casque dismissed the possibility of Caracciola driving a Mercedes again, depending 'on whether the plans to finance a Mercedes team actual-

The Italians, of course, had cars ready to hand which only needed very minor amendment to bring their narrow bodywork up to the required minimum width. Alfa-Romeo made the first of a series of bore increases bringing the cylinder dimensions up to 69 × 100 mm. and the swept volume to 2992 c.c. besides making slight amendments to the chassis detail. Secure behind a virtually unbeaten record and with a well tried car, Enzo Ferrari must have faced even the loss of Fagioli to Mercedes with equanimity and in any case he lost no time in securing the services of Varzi who was now leaving Bugatti. With Chiron, Trossi and the immensely promising Guy Moll the Italians made sure of the most powerful team of drivers. The terrible injuries sustained by Caracciola at Monaco had placed Mercedes in somewhat of a quandary which they had to resolve by importing Fagioli across the Alps. After his very successful three months with Ferrari, following years in the wilderness with Maserati, Fagioli must have felt that his hour had come with a vengeance and that as the fastest driver in his team he would have a clear right to win as he chose. Unhappily German nationalism and Alfred Neubauer had other ideas as the intrepid Italian was soon to discover in his first race on German soil.

A Mercedes team without Caracciola was unthinkable and the company spent a lot of time during the winter of 1933 persuading Rudi to resume his career. As if his injuries were not enough he had the sorrow to lose his first wife in a ski-ing accident that same winter and the future must have seemed bleak indeed to him as it was still touch-and-go whether he ever drove a racing car again. Instead of going foreign for their third driver Mercedes engaged the young Prussian aristocrat Manfred von Brauchitsch who, it will be remembered, had won the 1932 Avus Grand Prix in a specially streamlined Mercedes. Apart from a 4th place at Brno Brauchitsch had had little experience of Grand Prix racing in 1933 and virtually none of racing outside Germany. Other prospective drivers were the German motor cycling champion and record holder, Ernst Henne, who was of course even more of an unknown quantity than Brauchitsch.

The more revolutionary Auto-Union was no better equipped with drivers, having chosen the hill climb champion Hans Stuck as their leader and two other unknowns Prince Leiningen and Momberger as supports. Apart from his hill climbing prowess Stuck too was virtually unknown outside Germany and had little experience of European circuit racing and neither of his team-mates had even the experience of Brauchitsch. Germany might have the money and the cars but between them the teams could muster only one fit driver with active experience of the cut-and-thrust of modern Grand Prix racing. Bugatti, by contrast, had drivers in abundance but his other resources were limited and the new cars in a poor state of readiness. For works drivers he had Dreyfus, Wimille and Benoist, and in addition both Nuvolari and Taruffi were going to drive the cars as independents, so Bugatti had every chance of being in the money if he could only get his cars going properly *and* soon. Maserati had no regular works drivers but a few independents would be driving the 3-litre 1933 cars, notably Whitney Straight and his team, Earl Howe and Etancelin. Apart from their hydraulic braking systems, the cars were becoming sadly outmoded and played little part in the racing beyond a few spirited performances in 1934 by Nuvolari and Etancelin.

During the early months of 1934 both Mercedes and Auto-Union were busy with preliminary trials of both cars and drivers. During 1933 Count Czaykowski driving a 4.9 Bugatti in normal road racing trim had raised the world hour record at Avus to 132.87 m.p.h., which at that time consisted of two long straights joined by two relatively sharp

439 WELTPOLITIK: In the Third Reich motor sport had its own Korpsführer—Hühnlein a well-known figure at pre-war meetings

440 'Ferrari lost no time in securing the services of Varzi', here emerging from the tunnel at Monaco

141 ... 'the immensely promising Guy Moll ...'

442 At Monaco it was Dreyfus who led off from Chiron (16), Etancelin (14) and Trossi (22)

unbanked bends. In February 1934 George Eyston, with a slightly better streamlined special record breaking Panhard (and on the banked Montlhéry piste de vitesse), had raised this to 133.01 m.p.h. Back at Avus Stuck raised the record in March to 134.90 m.p.h., barely 2 m.p.h. faster than the Bugatti; whilst Stuck's was a good performance with a new car, it was not really notably faster and could well have been due to nothing more than better streamlining. Both Maserati and Alfa-Romeo were rumoured to be attacking Stuck's record, but perhaps significantly nothing came of it.

The early part of the season produced two wins for the relatively unknown Algerian driver Guy Moll and now driving for Ferrari, a defeat for Auto Union at Avus and a win for Mercedes in their first race on the Nürburg Ring. No German cars appeared at Monaco though Caracciola opened the course in a Mercedes and the race itself was very largely a case of The-Mixture-As-Before with Alfa, Bugatti and Maserati making the running. Trossi put in a desperately fast lap in practice and occupied pole position with Etancelin (Maserati) and Dreyfus (2.8-litre Bugatti) also in the front row. Etancelin repeated his fireworks of 1933 but could not really match Chiron who seemed comfortably set to be the first man to win twice at Monaco until, with 2 laps to go, he made an error of judgment (as he had done in 1931/2) hitting a sandbag and enabled Guy Moll to snatch a victory 'at the last permissible moment from one of the most famous drivers in the world on the course which he knew best of all.' Both the winning average and fastest lap were below 1933 speeds, even though there was considerable competition between improved models of the 1933 cars. Dreyfus finished 2nd a lap behind Moll without ever having seriously challenged the Alfas, followed by Lehoux (Alfa), Nuvolari (Bugatti) and Varzi (Alfa) with 98 laps covered. Three weeks later, driving a Maserati this time, Nuvolari came unstuck during a dice with Varzi on the tricky Alessandria circuit and finished up against a tree in a ditch. This was on the 22nd April and five weeks later the irrepressible Nuvolari was back at the wheel of the deodand Maserati with his injured leg in plaster for the Avus Grand Prix. It may be wondered whether, as the *Autocar* suggested, his recovery was 'greatly aided by the presentation from a local gymnastic club of a chunk of the tree against which the car crashed bearing the inscription

'To Tazio Nuvolari, intrepid ace of the wheel as a record of the providential obstacle which though preventing a sure victory saved a precious existence'.

Varzi might have had other ideas about that 'sure victory', but nobody could gainsay the iron courage of the maestro.

The Avus event was over 15 laps (183 miles) and, if there was disappointment over the withdrawal of the Mercedes team, the three Auto-Unions of Stuck, Leiningen and Momberger were on the line as the rain streamed down, opposed to Varzi, Chiron and Moll on Alfas with finned tails and faired wheels, Nuvolari, Siena and Howe on 3-litre Maseratis, Pietsch on an Alfa and Peter de Paolo on a four wheel drive Miller emphasising the formule libre under which the race was run.

Stuck literally steamed away from the field and was palpably unbeatable even though he would have to make a stop for new tyres. At first Chiron led the pack behind but Moll soon challenged and then passed the great Chiron showing that his win at Monaco was no idle flash in the pan. Even so he was about 85 secs. behind when Stuck stopped to change wheels with ten laps gone. At this early stage in their comeback the German team had not attained their fabulous speed in pitwork, and Moll was able to take the lead and win fairly comfortably at an average of 127.5 m.p.h. from Varzi, Momberger, Howe and Nuvolari. Stuck never got back into the race after his pit stop and retired soon after, as did Leiningen, Siena, de Paolo and Chiron at various stages—in brief, first blood to the Alfas and a nasty shock to Auto-Union.

Although the new cars were undoubtedly faster and more powerful than their 1933 counterparts, the first two races had been won at slower averages in spite of keen competition and it might have been thought that the A.I.A.C.R. really had achieved their age-old object of pegging speeds. The results of the next two races, in which the three leading teams were all engaged, soon swept away this 'optimism'. For the Eifelrennen on the Nürburg Ring Caracciola was still hors-de-combat, so there were two Mercedes for Fagioli and Brauchitsch against the Avus combinations of Alfa and Auto-Union. The new Mercedes took an instant lead shewing tremendous speed and their renowned supercharger wail; nothing that Stuck or, behind him, Chiron could do made any impression on the successors of Lautenschlager and Sailer. Fagioli finally succumbed to plug troubles but Brauchitsch won very easily from Stuck and Chiron over the substantial distance of 213 miles, at the record average of 76.12 m.p.h., the previous best being that of Caracciola at 74.13 in 1932. The lap record was raised by 1.45 m.p.h. from 77.55 to 79 m.p.h. This rise in speeds was continued at Montlhéry when the circus arrived to begin practice for the French Grand Prix, then still regarded as the great classic of the year. From the start of practice the old records were shattered and shattered again and with all five competing marques at full strength the chips were really down. Many great celebrities of the past were noted by the *Autocar's* representative—Chassagne, Rougier, Louis Wagner, René Thomas, 'that dark little man who drove a Mors (in Paris-Madrid) as one inspired all those years ago', and Jules Goux who had fought the Mercedes so desperately in their last appearance in the French Grand Prix twenty years before.

443 . . . 'Stuck raised the hour record in March to 134.90 mph'

444 . . . 'at Avus Stuck literally steamed away from the field . . .'

445 In the Eifelrennen . . . 'the new Mercedes took an instant lead shewing tremendous speed and their renowned supercharger wail . . .'

446 FIRST BLOOD: Brauchitsch won the Eifel race easily

447 GREATEST CELEBRITY: . . . 'that dark little man who drove a Mors as one inspired all those years ago . . .'

448 .. 'a second Maserati driven (when it went) by Zehender . . .'

449 DEVIL TAKE THE HINDMOST! . . . 'Chiron decided from his third row position that the race was going to be won from the front . . .'

At Lyons both Delage and Peugeot had borne the Tricouleur with every hope of winning but nobody could seriously think that the Bugattis of Dreyfus Benoist and Nuvolari were the equals of their ancestors. The two French champions, Etancelin and Chiron had gone over to Italian mounts and the French crowd looked to Chiron as their new Boillot to give them a 'French' victory to avenge the terrible defeat of 1914. The other Alfas were to be driven by Trossi and Varzi, two Auto-Unions by Stuck and Momberger, a second Maserati by Zehender and finally the Mercedes team of Fagioli, Brauchitsch and, at long last, Caracciola, who, like Nuvolari, was shewing the greatest courage in racing while still in considerable pain. All the greatest drivers and cars of the age were gathered together as at Lyons in 1914 and 1924 for one of those truly epic Grands Prix, even though many might have thought the result a sadly foregone conclusion.

Louis Chiron, however, had distinctly different ideas and decided from his 3rd row position that the race was going to be won from the front and the classic photograph of the start shows the pack still leaving the line with apparently no Chiron who had in fact succeeded in beating everybody including the camera (and incidentally the starter) as he tore away with Caracciola, Fagioli and Stuck in close pursuit. After two laps Stuck was hard on Chiron's heels and on the third he got past the Alfa but, try as they might, neither Fagioli nor Caracciola could quite catch Chiron. The ninth lap saw two serious inroads into the German Challenge when first Brauchitsch and then the leader Stuck slowed to their pits and after 10 laps, or quarter distance, Chiron led again. The next five laps were desperate indeed for Chiron, as Fagioli and Caracciola stalked him down even as Lautenschlager and Wagner had stalked Boillot, after Sailer's retirement had left him with a precarious lead. But this time a Frenchman and his car were equal to their task: Fagioli again broke the lap record in 5 mins. 6.3 secs., but Chiron, wonder of wonders, replied with 5 mins. 6 secs. (91.35 m.p.h.) and, that, as John said, was most emphatically THAT, as Fagioli then failed to appear at all following a brake failure, and Caracciola made a pit stop. This was for fuel, water and a change of rear wheels, and occupied the unbelievably long time of 80 secs. leaving Chiron with a substantial lead and Varzi in 2nd place. On the 16th lap Caracciola retired to the country, bringing Stuck's lame Auto-Union back to 3rd place followed by Benoist on the best of the Bugattis and Moll in Trossi's Alfa which had transmission troubles.

Around this time the other two Bugattis retired after a fitful and immaterial fluttering of their wings, the enlarged 3.3-litre engines being no improvement on the earlier 2.8-litre version. For the second year running Nuvolari had had a wretched French Grand Prix, but old veteran Benoist drove gamely on and even brought a touch of excitement to the last lap when everybody thought he had sent the lap record through the stratosphere till it was discovered he had simply taken a short cut home! After a succession of pit stops Stuck finally gave up after 32 of the 40 laps leaving the three Alfas the only official finishers and Benoist flagged off with 36 laps completed.

By his magnificent victory Chiron had at least in part avenged 1914 for France and driven the finest race of his long career. True he had not been hounded for anything like the full distance but those first hundred miles had been as testing a time as any driver could have wished for, when one mistake could well have cost Alfas the entire race. Fagioli in fact was the one who was tempted into error when he damaged a brake cable whilst mounting a bank in a vain endeavour to pass Chiron—probably the decisive factor in the race as his was the only German car that did not retire with self-induced mechanical failure.

The Germans scuttled back across the Rhine to prepare for their own Grand Prix in two weeks' time, while the Italian circus mopped up the Marne Grand Prix en route for the Nürburg Ring, where a 25-lap contest (356 miles) was to take place between the heroes of Montlhéry, Chiron, Varzi and Moll and their challengers, Caracciola, Fagioli and, a new man, Hans Geier for Mercedes and Stuck, Momberger and, another newcomer, Ernst Burggaller for Auto-Union, with Nuvolari, Zehender and H. C. Hamilton on Maseratis and a variety of independents, but no Bugattis. Once again the race lay between Stuck, Caracciola, Fagioli and Chiron, but this time the German cars set the pace and headed the procession once the race had settled down. Both Varzi and Chiron ran 3rd at various times and Chiron actually finished there but over eight minutes behind the winner Stuck, and six behind Fagioli. Stuck led for most of the race except when Caracciola briefly caught him around half distance,

450 RACE OF A LIFETIME: . . . 'a Frenchman and his car were equal to their task . . .'

451 SUCCESSION OF PIT STOPS: Stuck in frequent trouble

452 FULLEST FLIGHT: . . . 'Chiron had avenged 1914 for France and driven the finest race of his career . . .'

221

453 SHOT SHATTERED ARMADA or why the Germans gave the Marne a miss

454 Nuvolari had a new Maserati (six-cylinder 3½-litre) for the Italian Grand Prix

455 Right. The tricky and fast Bremgartern circuit used for the Swiss Grand Prix run between 1934 and 1955 was one of the greatest tests of driving skill in its day

but the effort was too much for Caracciola's engine and his car was not seen again. Varzi retired early on with stripped gears while Nuvolari reaped the reward of persistence with a well deserved 4th another nine minutes behind Chiron with Geier's Mercedes 5th.

Once again the Alfas had been decisively beaten on the Ring, and now the circus moved to Pescara with the score level at 2-all. The 19th August 1934, was the Black Day of the Scuderia Ferrari—Varzi, driving with all his traditional fury, burst two cars in his endeavours to hold the Germans; Chiron's car was destroyed by fire and, most tragic of all, the promising Moll wrecked his car in a fatal accident. Caracciola and Stuck made the pace from the start hotly pursued by Fagioli and Varzi, but soon Stuck and Varzi fell out; Varzi then took over Ghersi's Alfa and Caracciola was signalled to speed up in the face of the challenge from Varzi, Chiron and Moll. The result was one of Caracciola's very rare errors of judgment—it is a remarkable tribute to his skill that this was his last until the Italian Grand Prix of 1938.

Pit stops as usual affected the leading positions around half distance and by the time these had all been sorted out Fagioli had a lead of about 50 secs. over Moll and Varzi. Moll was driving at a terrific pace, and had already lost time through a slide before he attempted to pass Henne's Mercedes on the long straight at over 150 m.p.h. with fatal results in a most horrifying accident. Varzi's car failed at much the same time and Fagioli ran out an easy winner from his old rival Nuvolari (Maserati) and Brivio (Bugatti).

With his immensely full racing programme it must have been a fantastic effort for Ferrari to get three cars to the start of the first real Swiss Grand Prix and he had a limited reward in fielding the only team to finish, albeit in 4th, 5th and 7th. Mercedes had their full team back again but only Fagioli succeeded in finishing—in 6th—the race being an Auto-Union benefit with Stuck leading from the start and Momberger finishing 2nd. Salt was rubbed into Ferrari's wounds by Dreyfus, who brought his Bugatti into 3rd place, and, while it lasted, Nuvolari's Maserati, too, had been more than a match for the Alfas.

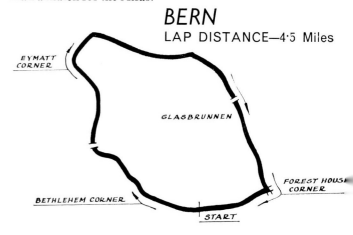

BERN
LAP DISTANCE—4·5 Miles

EYMATT CORNER

GLASBRUNNEN

FOREST HOUSE CORNER

BETHLEHEM CORNER

START

Nuvolari had a new 6-cylinder 3½-litre Maserati for the Italian Grand Prix over an improvised circuit at Monza which taxed brakes and drivers' patience and stamina to the extreme. Mercedes, Alfa and Auto-Union fielded three cars each, Comotti being promoted to the top flight for Ferrari. Mercedes had rather the best of the fight with Stuck this time, although they lost both Henne and Fagioli with miscellaneous troubles during the race. Caracciola shared the winning car with Fagioli to win his first race since the Monza Grand Prix in 1932. Stuck continued his successful season with a 2nd place shared with Leiningen; Trossi brought the first Alfa home in 3rd, four laps behind followed by an utterly brakeless Nuvolari, who might well have finished 2nd but for running the race with an empty hydraulic reservoir! This had been emptied before weighing-in to enable to the car to qualify and an anonymous somebody had neglected to refill it. This Monza circuit with 1600 corners in its 116 laps must have been peculiarly unpleasant to drive on and the winning average of 63.43 m.p.h. speaks for itself.

Bugatti had stirred himself into action for the Spanish and Czech Grands Prix at the end of September.

After a great deal of uncertainty due to the political situation the A.C. of Guipuzcoa put on the Spanish event over the picturesque Lasarte Circuit and produced a rattling good race between Mercedes and, surprise of surprises, Bugatti. Stuck seized a short-lived lead from the start but an oil pipe put him out soon after, leaving Caracciola ahead of Wimille. With one-third of the race past at ten laps Wimille still clung to 2nd, a mere 17 secs. behind, followed by Fagioli, Nuvolari and Dreyfus—a mere 61 secs. covering these five. Over the next five laps Fagioli piled on speed and caught up to within ten yards of Caracciola by half distance but was still pursued by the Bugatti team.

The two Mercedes continued at undiminished speed, Fagioli leading from the 10th lap, while misfortune struck two bad blows at Wimille: first his pit stop took over a minute longer and then he lost 5 minutes repairing a carburetter union after he had regained 3rd place. Dreyfus also had minor carburetter troubles which sent him down the field though Nuvolari drove with remarkable speed to finish a mere 24 secs. behind Caracciola, having been 1 min. 41 secs. behind him at 20 laps. Fagioli maintained a useful lead to the end, while Stuck, on Leiningen's car, did some Homeric motoring in the closing stages to bring his car into 4th place 16 secs. behind Nuvolari, having gained 1½ mins. on him over the last ten laps! Needless to say this included a new lap record, 4 secs. faster than the best Fagioli could do, and over 5 m.p.h. better than Nuvolari's 1933 record. The Alfas had a poor race and were noticeably slower than their three main competitors, Varzi, finishing 5th ahead of Wimille and Dreyfus more by good luck than anything else.

456 'IMPROVISED CIRCUIT'—the winning Mercedes-Benz leads Varzi and Nuvolari through a chicane at Monza

Bugatti continued his effort, if not his luck, in the Czech Grand Prix the following Sunday to the extent of fielding two cars for Benoist and Wimille to join the Monza contingent less Trossi. The inevitable quartet of Caracciola, Fagioli, Stuck and Nuvolari were soon hard at it in spite of the poor surface of the long circuit, a village with the delightfully obscure name of Ostrovacice bringing minor incidents to both Caracciola and Nuvolari, leaving Fagioli and Stuck out on their own. Without the benefits of independent suspension the Alfas were in trouble, Comotti breaking his fuel tank and Chiron an oil pipe on the rough surface, but nothing seemed to make any difference to the iron Nuvolari, who finished a rousing 3rd behind Fagioli, with Stuck the winner again. Practice was enlivened by a certain amount of car swapping, Nuvolari significantly driving an Auto-Union (as he had done at San Sebastian), and Stuck a Mercedes. Nuvolari's best lap of 14 mins. 15 secs. compares interestingly with Stuck's 14 mins. 5 secs. on Mercedes, Fagioli's race record of 13 mins. 16.2 secs. and Stuck's race best of 13 mins. 39 secs. on Auto-Union. There was also the extraordinary suicide of a Czech driver who turned up with a new 3½-litre Maserati purchased with borrowed money. The lender pressed her claim for its return, having been jilted rather tactlessly before the race, and the driver was arrested the day before practice. The Czech authorities evidently regarded imprisonment for debt as light-heartedly as 19th century England and the debtor was released for the first day's practice only to crash the car sensationally after a few laps raising a general presumption of suicide.

For forty years a year with a '4' in it had been magical in motor racing: 1894 had seen the first motor sporting event of all—the Paris-Rouen, ten years later had come the great Gordon Bennett race on the Taunus Circuit, then 1914 and Lyons, in 1924 the supercharger had come into its own and produced a new race of cars altogether and now 1934 had sent racing car design forward by another staggering leap and bound. Between 1914 and 1925 the Pomeroy speed index of the fastest car increased from 112 to 127.5; in 1932/3 it stood at 140—an increase of only 12.5 and in 1934 at 150—an increase of 7 per cent. in one season, quite the biggest jump until then. Independent suspension had obviously come to stay and no one realised this more clearly than Ferrari and Maserati. It was equally clear that larger engines were both feasible within the weight limits and essential to survival. Mercedes had started with a 3.3-litre engine of 78 × 88 mm. which they first bored out to 82 × 88 (3.7-litres) and then increased to 82 × 94.5 (3.99-litres) during 1934, the everyday b.h.p. going up from 302 to 348 and finally 430. Throughout 1934 Auto-Union had used their A Type V-16 model of 4.36-litres (68 × 75) developing about 295 b.h.p. In spite of its lower power output, greater difficulty to drive and lack of top line drivers, the Auto-Union was consistently faster and more successful than the Mercedes in 1934—a remarkable tribute to the skill and stamina of Stuck who had borne virtually the whole of the burden of the new car's effort on the circuit and on test.

The German cars started in ten races of which they won eight without being seriously challenged; Bugatti gave the Mercedes a good run in the Spanish Grand Prix and, over the latter part of the season, showed better results than Alfa-Romeo or Maserati. So long as they had the incomparable Nuvolari to drive them, the 3-litre and 3.5-litre Maseratis could make the German drivers hurry, but basically the Franco-Italian challenge faded utterly away after Chiron's

brilliant victory at Montlhéry. Stuck and Fagioli were the most successful drivers, each winning three races and two 2nds; Stuck shared 4th in the Spanish Grand Prix to Fagioli's 6th at Berne and put in three fastest laps to Fagioli's one to give him a fractionally better record over the season. Chiron had a win, two 3rds and three other places, Caracciola a win and two 2nds, Nuvolari two 2nds, one 3rd, two 4ths and a 5th, and Varzi two 2nds, two 4ths and a 5th. Of the rest Brauchitsch, after winning the Eifelrennen, was unlucky to crash in practice for the German Grand Prix, and, of course, Moll crashed fatally at Pescara after an immensely promising season. Nuvolari had driven for much of the season with a useless left leg, Taruffi, then a promising newcomer had crashed his 16-cylinder Maserati at Tripoli, leaving him out of the rest of the season. Poor Robert Benoist had had an uneventful comeback. Wimille had driven a very promising race at San Sebastian when, with a little more luck, he might well have finished 2nd and even challenged for the lead and had every chance of becoming a driver of great stature during 1935. Everything, however, would depend on who had the cars, and the speed with which the new Alfa-Romeos could be completed.

457 . . . 'poor Benoist had an uneventful comeback'

Chapter Twenty Four
1935 · German Consolidation

458 ... 'Auto-Union "went Italian" by engaging Varzi'

Realising the need for more top-flight drivers Auto-Union followed Mercedes' example and 'went Italian' by engaging Varzi to support Stuck after a great deal of intriguing had taken place. At the same time Nuvolari returned to Ferrari, it was said after political pressure from Il Duce himself. These moves caused some surprise because of Varzi's great record for Ferrari and also because, unlike Chiron, Nuvolari and Stuck, he had not been chopping and changing cars during practice in 1934. At all events the three principal constructors now had equal shares in the six ace drivers though, as usual, Ferrari had the strongest supporting chorus of Dreyfus, enticed from Bugatti, Trossi, Brivio and Comotti. Maserati now entrusted the management of their cars to the Scuderia Sub-Alpina and their driving to Etan-

celin and Zehender with a young Italian, Giuseppe Farina, as a reserve driver. Williams, Taruffi, Benoist and Wimille would form a sound team for Bugatti but his cars were, as always, an uncertain quantity.

Mercedes enlarged the W25 engine yet again for 1935 to its final size of 82 × 102 mm. (4.3 litres) in which state it developed 462 b.h.p. and also added the ZF self-locking differential. Auto-Union increased their engines to 4.9-litres and the output to 375 b.h.p., besides adopting the ZF differential. Bugatti, too, but with less cause, was content with detail alteration, merely increasing the engine of one of his cars to 3.8 litres.

By contrast Northern Italy was a ferment of activity. Maserati, as usual, worked on a bewildering variety of

459 . . . 'Mercedes were at full strength on the front row'

460 . . . 'Fagioli led virtually unchallenged throughout the race . . . .
Here he is with Soffietti's old Maserati

models, now with independent suspension of a fairly primitive nature, while Alfa-Romeo also pursued a variety of solutions to the problem posed by the new German cars. The basic solution was to be the new V-12 four-litre all independently sprung Type 12C-36, but this was a long time a-coming and in the meantime they gave the ageing monoposto a final face-lift by stepping up the engine first to 3.2 and then to 3.8 litres and by changes in the chassis. Here they applied reverse quarter elliptic springs to the back end and a form of i.f.s. devised by André Dubonnet to the front; at the same time hydraulic brake operation was adopted. The P3 Alfa was now in its final stage of development in which it was to gain its last and greatest victory. Finally for formule libre races two special cars were devised by Bazzi and Roselli to the requirements of Ferrari—the famous bimotore cars consisting of two coupled-up engines in an independently sprung chassis. Unlike the old double-six cars the two engines were not doubled up; one was fitted in front and one behind the driver who sat on top of the gearbox. One car had two 2.9 engines and the other two of the larger 3.2-litre engines, but neither achieved any spectacular results in racing, being dedevilled with tyre troubles. At Avus in 1935 Chiron finished 2nd to Fagioli's normal Mercedes and at Tripoli Nuvolari and Chiron finished 4th and 5th respectively; it is significant that in neither event did a bimotore Alfa put in fastest lap, although Nuvolari was reported as going all out for at least one lap at Tripoli when he passed Fagioli and Caracciola and got wheel to wheel with the leader Varzi.

The German teams increased their programme for the new season and one or both of them took part in 14 races as against ten in 1934. Auto-Union decided to give Monaco a miss once again but Mercedes were at full strength on the front row opposed to the Ferrari Alfas of Nuvolari, Chiron, Dreyfus and Brivio. Farina was making his debut in real Grand Prix racing with his team mates Zehender and the fiery Etancelin on Maserati. Fagioli led virtually unchallenged throughout the race to win from Dreyfus on a normally sprung 3.2 Alfa and Brivio on a 2.9 with Etancelin a lap behind. Etancelin had as usual driven a terrific race with his 3.7 Maserati actually passing Caracciola and causing him to burst his engine in his efforts to regain 2nd place. Not surprisingly Phi-Phi's tactics played havoc with the Maserati's oil pressure and brakes so he had to soft-pedal the rest of the race—hence his 4th place, but even this was quite an achievement. The new i.f.s. Italian cars did not seem very happy, Zehender's Maserati being very slow and Nuvolari's Dubonnet Alfa being notably difficult to handle although this was ascribed to the hydraulic brakes. Chiron, too, had an off-day and could only scrape home in 5th place, 3 laps behind the winner so in one way and another it had been a disappointing race, redeemed only by the impressive ease of Fagioli's win and the magnificent effort of Etancelin. It was also the first reported appearance of one Hermann Lang at the wheel of a Mercedes—in training sessions only however. His hour was yet to come.

Varzi drove a lone Auto-Union at Tunis against the Ferrari Alfas, the Subalpine Maseratis and Wimille's 3.3 Bugatti and had as little difficulty in winning as Wimille had in finishing 2nd and beating the Alfas. Unfortunately this did not hearten Bugatti sufficiently to start the following week at Tripoli where Auto-Union (Stuck and Varzi) had their first clash with Mercedes and the rest . . . as at Monaco, except that Nuvolari and Chiron had the two bimotores, described by Motor Sport as 'sombre' and 'almost evil looking' in comparison to the 'sleek white Mercs and squat elongated Auto-Unions.' Mercedes had been having valve troubles in practice on this fabulously fast circuit and Brauchitsch soon fell out thus in the race, which was determined largely by tyre changes. After Stuck's car had caught fire the race was fought out between Varzi, Fagioli and Caracciola with noises off—usually of exploding tyres—from Nuvolari's bimotore, victory ultimately going to Caracciola after Varzi had had two tyre stops in the last five laps, the first when he was well in the lead. The King of Tripoli thus had to be content with 2nd place, followed by Fagioli, then Nuvolari and Chiron, with the bimotores. In 1934 Varzi had won on a 2.9 Alfa at 115.67 m.p.h. and Chiron had made fastest lap at 124.48; Caracciola had now won at 123.03 with fastest lap at 136.81 m.p.h.

Three more races were held before the first great trial of strength in the French Grand Prix at Montlhéry—the Avus and Eifel races, and the Penya Rhin Grand Prix at Barcelona; on the Avus four Mercedes and Auto-Unions came out, the extra Merc. going to Geier and the Auto-Unions to Leiningen and another young man destined to achieve lasting greatness—Berndt Rosemeyer. The race was run in 2 heats of 5 laps each (c. 60 miles) and a final of twice this distance, the first four in each heat qualifying. Stuck won the first heat at 155 m.p.h., Caracciola the second at 148 m.p.h. and Fagioli the final at 148.83 with Stuck setting the lap record at 161.88 m.p.h. Fagioli was reported to have made one set of tyres last his heat and the final which must have given the bimotore drivers a touch of the green eye, to say nothing of Varzi who made three tyre changes in the final alone. By dint of carefully nursing the smaller bimotore Chiron finished 2nd ahead of Varzi, Stuck, Brauchitsch and Dreyfus on the last year's winning Alfa.

After these two orgies of speed the Eifelrennen must have seemed slow if not tame indeed; Mercedes again fielded four cars, this time giving the fourth to Hermann Lang, while Varzi and Stuck were now joined by Rosemeyer and Paul Pietsch. This, however, was not an Auto-Union day: Mercedes soon established a 1, 2, 3 position and with Varzi

461 'SLOW IF NOT TAME INDEED!'—Brauchitsch (7) leads the Eifelrennen from Rosemeyer, Varzi (2), Caracciola (5) and Fagioli (6)

reputedly unwell and Stuck's car off colour, it was all up to Rosemeyer. He, too, was not unvisited by mischiefs, losing in succession his windscreen, his goggles and helmet and then, for a time, two cylinders. However 14 seemed to do almost as well and the slowing of Fagioli and retirement of Brauchitsch brought him to Caracciola's tail. With remarkable coolness he then passed Rudi and had established a 9 secs. lead with two laps to go. Caracciola reduced this to 7 secs. as they set out on the last lap and by some superb driving he caught his young rival with barely a kilometre to go and won by less than 2 secs., with Chiron a minute and a half away in 3rd, Fagioli 4th and his protégé Lang, 5th.

Auto-Union were still having trouble with their new 5.6-litre engines so the Penya Rhin Grand Prix was largely a Mercedes (Caracciola and Fagioli) v. Alfa (Brivio and Nuvolari) affair. Nuvolari hounded the Mercedes brilliantly but neither he nor Brivio, who also drove exceedingly well, could make any real impression on Fagioli and Caracciola, who finished in that order.

Lang was not given a car at Montlhéry but Rosemeyer deservedly took his place with Stuck and Varzi; Ferrari fielded two cars of 3.5 litres for Nuvolari and Chiron, while the two Maseratis were driven by Zehender and Sommer. To everyone's sorrow Etancelin decided not to drive as the new 4-litre Maserati was still not ready. Lastly there was Benoist on the lone 3.8-litre Bugatti. Stuck and Varzi had new 5.6-litre engines in their cars, but all the Auto-Unions were ill at ease during practice and started with no great hopes of winning. Montlhéry followed the iniquitous practice of so many of the great circuits in France and Italy at this time by inserting chicanes largely to slow the German cars and give

462 CAUGHT SIR!: Benoist holds a fine one-hander when his bonnet flies off at Montlhéry

the native products a better chance. This the A.C.F. succeeded in doing and the first 14 of the 40 laps were enlivened by a mighty battle between Nuvolari and Caracciola: four litres of Mercedes versus three-and-a-half of Alfa-Romeo at the disposal of two of the greatest drivers of the day. Tazio was obviously at the height of his form, taking 'the chicanes every time quite 10 m.p.h. faster than anyone else with a half-turn right and left of the steering wheel' while the Germans slowed and then relied on their acceleration. Thus early Stuck and Varzi were falling behind while Rosemeyer never seriously got into the picture at all; Chiron, marvellously, was supporting Nuvolari in 3rd ahead of Fagioli and von Brauchitsch with the rest nowhere.

On the fifth lap as Benoist passed the stands the bonnet of his Bugatti flew off and 'fell like a blanket on the head of the unfortunate driver.' By a combination of luck and skill Benoist avoided a serious accident and continued at the tail end of the race for 34 trouble-studded laps, his car having been hastily and inadequately prepared. While Caracciola and Nuvolari battled wheel to wheel, Chiron drew to his pit, restarted slowly to the accompaniment of typical overstrained Alfa noises in the rear axle and retired after one more slow lap. This seemed only to inspire Nuvolari who increased his lead over Caracciola from 5 secs. at this point to 9 secs. five laps later (after 13 laps). On the 14th, however, Nuvolari slowed and Caracciola came round on his own followed by Fagioli and Brauchitsch. Nuvolari came in presently and retired with another dose of the familiar Alfa transmission sickness.

Whilst it had gone the Dubonnet-sprung Alfa had cornered and stopped superbly. Paul Frère has said that the earliest pictures of the modern four-wheel-drift are to be found of Nuvolari in the all-independent 8C-35 Alfa in the Italian Grand Prix later in 1935; this I doubt as a glance at a study of Nuvolari taking a right hander at Montlhéry shows —Motor Sport's caption observes—'Just look at those front wheels pointing at the grass'—as the great little man is pictured in what appears to be a classic drift with his left arm raised and stretched as far as the cramped driving positions of the day permitted. I have no doubt that it was this superlative technique that enabled Nuvolari to snatch so many chestnuts out of the German flames between 1934 and 1936 when the four wheel drift was in its infancy and that in fact Nuvolari came upon it much earlier as Ferrari seems to indicate in his memoirs.

The Mercedes were immediately flagged down by Neubauer and Caracciola eventually finished ½-second ahead of Brauchitsch, with Zehender 3rd two laps behind but a lap ahead of Fagioli's Mercedes. Rosemeyer brought Varzi's Auto-Union home 5th, five laps behind on the same lap as Sommer's Maserati—Montlhéry proving itself just as much a car breaker as ever in the last true French Grand to be held there[1].

Auto-Union were still out of action a fortnight later when Mercedes made that long delayed German début at Spa; Wimille, Benoist and Taruffi had 3.3 Bugattis, and Dreyfus and Chiron 3.5-litre Ferrari Alfas. Wimille made a good start and was only put out of 2nd by Brauchitsch at the end of the first lap, but that proved to be Bugatti's sole contribution to the race which he had won the year before. Bugatti was not the only one in trouble and Brauchitsch's Mercedes soon joined them in the graveyard leaving Caracciola seemingly in an unassailable lead in a race which, rumour had it, was to have been Fagioli's.

The bluff old Italian put on tremendous speed after his fuel stop and within 7 laps was at Caracciola's tail. They then embarked on an internal duel which Neubauer terminated by bringing Fagioli in for enforced relief by Brauchitsch, letting Dreyfus and Chiron into 3rd and 2nd places, while Fagioli and Neubauer exchanged compliments. After some fairly hectic driving Brauchitsch caught the Alfas again and even set up a new lap record but he could make no impression on Rudi who continued as if Fagioli was still behind him in spite of all Neubauer's signals to slow down for a Montlhéry-type 'finish'. Chiron finished 3rd in a state of complete collapse, while his team mate had had to be relieved by Marinoni. Dreyfus and Chiron ascribed their condition to the Mercedes fuel fumes and must have heartily wished that the Belgians had re-imposed that special duty on it which had caused the Germans to decline the 1934 event. Harold Nockolds, then Motor Sport's Continental Correspondent, thought little of this and remarked that the fuel smelt the same as at Montlhéry where Brauchitsch had followed Caracciola for 250 kilometres without any evil effects whereas Dreyfus only had the Mercedes in front of him for a few minutes!

[1] *I do not count the sports car events of 1936/7.*

463 UNLUCKY FIFTH: *Brauchitsch rising magnificently to the challenge on the Ring*

For the German Grand Prix Ferrari produced the final version of the monoposto Alfa, with Dubonnet front axle and a 3.8-litre engine for Nuvolari, Chiron and Brivio. Mercedes fielded their three chief drivers and Geier and Lang from the reserves, Auto-Union—Varzi, Stuck, Rosemeyer and Pietsch—Taruffi drove his semi-works Bugatti and Etancelin and Zehender Maseratis. The German Grand Prix was fast becoming the great race of the year thanks to the tremendous enthusiasm for motor sport in Germany which impelled spectators to converge on the Ring for two long nights and days before the race—Adrian Conan Doyle, sitting in the pinewoods by the Karussel as dawn was breaking on race day, wrote of a regiment of Nazis who had marched 350 miles to see the race and of the glimmer of camp fires lighting up sleeping forms round the trees. Perhaps some of this enthusiasm was engendered by a rumour the the Führer himself would attend and if so there must have been many disappointed spectators, though none so disappointed as would have been the Führer himself, had he actually been present!

In spite of a great deal of heated discussion, starting positions were still decided by ballot in deference to the drivers' alleged wishes—anyway it seemed to make little difference to Caracciola who made a start worthy of Chiron himself to lead before the field had left the pit area—from the fourth row! Initially Nuvolari held 2nd place until he was displaced by Rosemeyer who pulled back Caracciola's 12 second lead to only 4 secs. on the 4th lap. By the fifth lap both Chiron and Brivio were out with the usual transmission troubles and then Rosemeyer tried too hard and damaged his axle, slowing him to 5th where he stayed for much of the rest of the race. After his 2nd place on lap 1, Nuvolari sat it out for five laps, and then perhaps feeling time press, he took advantage of Rosemeyer's slowing to pass him and Brauchitsch into 3rd; then it was Fagioli's pit stop and Tazio was 2nd and on the 10th lap he passed Caracciola as well. On the 12th lap the four leaders all swept into the pits for fuel and wheels, taking a variety of times: Rosemeyer (4th)—75 secs.; Brauchitsch (3rd)—47 secs.; Caracciola (2nd)—67 secs. and, wait for it!, Nuvolari (1st)—2 mins. 14 secs. setting him back to 6th. As has ever been its wont, the Ferrari pit went mad and this time with some reason when the fuel pumping device broke and after those agonizing 134 seconds Nuvolari set off again for his Rendezvous With Glory.

229

464 ELEMENTAL GENIUS: Nuvolari's driving in the French and German Grands Prix with the fast dating Alfa-Romeo was something more than inspired

Stuck, Fagioli, Caracciola, Rosemeyer, all saw the Alfa's red tail disappearing in the distance at seemingly impossible angles during Nuvolari's epoch making 13th lap, but then Nuvolari had done just that at Montlhéry and his car had lasted barely 100 miles and there were still over 120 miles of the Ring to go. After 13 laps Nuvolari was 69 secs. behind but Brauchitsch, made aware of his danger, set a new record at 10 mins. 30 secs. and increased his lead at 14 laps to 86 secs.; another lap and he had gained another second but then Nuvolari started in earnest reducing the gap lap by lap—77 secs. (16), 63 secs. (17), 47 secs. (18), 43 secs. (19), 32 secs. (20); then with another desperate effort Brauchitsch increased it to 35 secs. as he went through for the last lap, making unhappy gestures at his near-side rear tyre. That tyre never lasted the 22 km. of the Ring and, instead of the winner's rostrum, Brauchitsch was lucky to grind home on the rim in 5th, the full order being

1. Nuvolari	4h. 8m. 39s.	4. Rosemeyer	4h. 12m. 51s.
2. Stuck	4h. 10m. 18s.	5. Brauchitsch	4h. 14m. 17s.
3. Caracciola	4h. 11m. 3s.	6. Fagioli	4h. 14m. 58s.

Poor Brauchitsch—he had really risen magnificently to the occasion and given of his very best but Nuvolari on that sort of form had an elemental genius that only one of his own stamp could have coped with. Brauchitsch's methods were altogether too crude and it was the very fire of his driving that wrought his own downfall. A contemporary had described his driving in the Belgian Grand Prix when pursuing the Ferrari Alfas in words that might well have been in Nuvolari's thoughts as he pressed after his adversary:

'Brauchitsch does not possess the genius of a Caracciola, a Fagioli or a Chiron, but he gets amazingly good results all the same. His approach to a corner is always rather ragged and involves a great deal of vigorous work with the steering wheel and some violent use of the brakes. . . .'

and, of course, severe wear on tyres. Much the same thing happened at Donington when he was under similar pressure from Rosemeyer in 1937 and after the 1938 German Grand Prix where he had another piece of shattering ill luck we find Giulio Ramponi writing to Dick Seaman who won:

'. . . the fact that you changed your tyres only once, he (Brauchitsch) twice proves that you were driving a better race. . . .'

In any event but for his misfortune at the pits, Nuvolari's stop would have taken at least a minute less which would have brought him back to the lead during the 10th lap.

It had been raining at the start and even though it dried out during the race the excess power of the German cars must have brought to mind Lord Acton's strictures on the corrupting influence of Absolute Power. The 300-odd b.h.p. of Nuvolari's Alfa probably represented the optimum power for limit driving on the Ring that day. As Peter Hull fairly concedes, Nuvolari was a little fortunate in finding the leading Mercedes and Auto-Union drivers hampered—Fagioli with troublesome shock-absorbers and Caracciola and Varzi by ill-health, and Rosemeyer by an assortment of troubles. This perhaps assisted him to make his spectacular climb back from 6th to 2nd so quickly. Hull also makes the

465 . . . 'Sure enough Stuck made one of his classic starts' as he leads Varzi (6), Rosemeyer (10), Fagioli (8) and Wimille (2) in the Spanish Grand Prix

excellent point that the Alfa's 'light weight, excellent cornering, *reliability* (sic!) and increased power output ... (made it) better suited to the Ring than the Auto-Unions' and that 'the chicanes in the French Grand Prix seemed to show that the Alfa-Romeo *in Nuvolari's hands* handled better on the slower corners than the Mercedes in its 1935 form. ...' Whilst doubting that the Alfa was then any more reliable than the German cars, I wholly agree with everything else he says, although the words 'in Nuvolari's hands' beg the entire question of whether it was man or machine that beat the Germans on their own ground—the one and only time a foreign car and driver achieved this on the Ring between 1934 and 1939. It was really as if Boillot had managed to win in 1914. *Verbum non amplius addam.*

After all their mid-season troubles it must have been a relief to Dr. Porsche to have all his cars finish on the Ring and he followed this up in the Coppa Acerbo where Varzi won at an average of over 6 m.p.h. faster than Fagioli's in 1934, in spite of the comparative emasculation of this great circuit by chicanes. No Mercedes were racing but Nuvolari was in his very best form until his car broke a valve when 2nd in the latter stages of the race. Rosemeyer who was timed at 172 m.p.h. over the kilometre finished 2nd.

Mercedes were back in the groove at Berne where their reserve driver Geier had one of the most spectacular accidents in history during practice when he miscalculated the highly tricky right hand bend by the pits. Lang took his place in the race and finished 6th behind Caracciola, Fagioli, Rosemeyer, Varzi and Nuvolari—no disgrace for any man. Chiron had the misfortune to crash and the Alfas were

generally no match for the German cars on this very fast circuit even in damp weather.

The sun of Italy again brought better luck to Auto-Union, this time at Monza when all four Mercedes fell out. On home ground Nuvolari and Varzi were in their finest form once more; Varzi set a cracking pace from the start and had established a ten second lead over Caracciola (3rd on the leading Mercedes) by 10 laps (43 miles). Fagioli had already quit with defective brakes and then the 13th lap brought a fiery end to Varzi's run when a piston collapsed. This left Stuck securely in a lead which he held for the rest of the race. Nuvolari had been biding his time in the new all independent 3.8-litre Alfa (the Type 8C-35) in 3rd place behind Caracciola but on the 27th lap he celebrated the explosion of Wimille's Bugatti by launching a spectacular attack on the leaders. A series of typically Tazio manoeuvres narrowed the gap by 5 seconds in 4 laps and he followed this up with a record lap 1⅕ secs. faster than Stuck's best time. Something had to go and this time it was the car which Nuvolari lost on one of the chicanes in a tête-à-queue, forfeiting all his hard-fought gain.

Stuck was winning the race at the pits as well as on the circuit, taking a mere 45 secs. to refuel and change rear wheels, compared to Caracciola's 1 min. 44 secs. and Nuvolari's 1 min. 17 secs. which included brake re-adjustment. All this coming and going left Stuck 58 secs. ahead of Nuvolari followed by Dreyfus and Caracciola after 41 of the 73 laps. During the next laps Caracciola and Brauchitsch fell out with transmission and brake failures, putting Rosemeyer in Pietsch's Auto-Union into 4th, followed by Lang,

Marinoni and Taruffi in the 3.8-litre Bugatti. The new Alfa did not handle so well with a full tank—or was it feeling the strain?—and before Nuvolari could get to grips with Stuck he was out with a collapsed piston. Lang evened the score when his engine gave up and then there were five. . . . In the closing stages Nuvolari took over Dreyfus' Alfa but only succeeded in breaking a valve finishing on 7 cylinders 1 min. 41 secs. behind Stuck and 3 laps ahead of Rosemeyer. Marinoni's Ferrari Alfa was 5 laps and Taruffi's Bugatti 14 laps behind the winner.

Chiron had been suffering from influenza and its after effects ever since the summer and was still sick from his Berne crash. Albeit he drove with all his panache and courage in the Spanish Grand Prix holding off Brauchitsch until he finally had to give up in 5th place after 28 of the 35 laps. Varzi had been much the fastest in practice and made the Auto-Unions greatly fancied for a second successive win. Sure enough Stuck made one of his classic starts and nobody could catch him—not even Fagioli and Caracciola driving with all their might—until his transmission failed around half distance. The other Auto-Union drivers had not been so lucky; Rosemeyer was slowed by pit stops and Varzi had been cut about the face on the 2nd lap by a stone. This and the slower relief driver (Pietsch) sent his car down to 9th before he could resume. His fastest practice lap had been 6 mins. 8 secs. and he now reduced this to 6 mins. 2 secs. and

then to 5 mins. 58 secs. Even so he never improved on his 9th place.

In 1934 Wimille had put up a magnificent challenge to the German cars and he used his experience of the circuit to hold 3rd behind Caracciola and Fagioli in the second half of the race. Mercedes were appreciably faster in 1935 and in the end Brauchitsch speeded up and passed him easily to give Mercedes their first 1-2-3 win in Grand Prix racing since 1914.

Mercedes decided to rest on their victories and leave the Czech Grand Prix four days later to Auto-Union where Varzi and Rosemeyer comfortably held off Nuvolari and Chiron until Varzi retired. This gave Rosemeyer his first Grand Prix win and a foretaste of what 1936 had in store. By contrast Chiron's return to form was anything but a pointer to the next season and turned out to be the last 'place' gained by him in a Grand Prix proper for many years.

Looking back on these years it is striking to note the extent to which drivers like Wimille, Dreyfus, Chiron and Nuvolari in particular were consistently able to press the leading German team drivers and clearly hold their own with any but the best on manifestly slower cars. Nuvolari continued to do this during 1936 but he was the last survivor and 1936 was the last season in which any non-German car had a dog's chance in a Grand Prix while the German cars lasted. The long Franco-Italian rearguard action went down in 1936 but with all its guns blazing.

466 DRIVER OF THE YEAR: Caracciola at full stretch in the Spanish Grand Prix

Chapter Twenty Five
1936 · The Rise of Rosemeyer

By the middle of 1935 a slimmer and sleeker Mercedes had begun to appear in practice for Grands Prix races; this car was powered by the M25E engine of 86 × 102 mm. (4.74 litres) developing 456 b.h.p. and had a shorter chassis than the original W25, the wheelbase being reduced by 11 ins. to eight feet. This was to meet the demand by drivers for a car that was easier to handle on the short or twisty circuits that were so much in vogue at the time. The odd thing about this car is that everyone seemed terribly happy about it at first—Chiron being quite ecstatic—'C'est une véritable bicyclette!'—when he tried it at Monza. Odder still was the fact that it won its first two races at Tunis and Monaco before everything went wrong.

Mercedes arrived for preliminary trials in December at Monza which were attended by their 1936 team drivers—Caracciola, Fagioli, Chiron and Lang, Brauchitsch being an absentee. Hitler himself approved Chiron's inclusion at a time when the position of a French driver in an Italian team was becoming difficult, after the League of Nations, with French support, had applied sanctions against Italy following the invasion of Abyssinia. As a result Dreyfus returned to France and dropped out of Grand Prix racing till 1938 while Chiron followed Fagioli to Stuttgart.

Maserati had at long last produced their V-8 for the Italian Grand Prix where Etancelin drove it for 14 laps when his throttle stuck open. Later in the year Farina failed to finish in the Donington Grand Prix and Varzi, reputedly unhappy with Auto-Union, had tested the car with evident satisfaction at Monza. Varzi did not return to his old love but stayed with Auto-Union along with Rosemeyer and Stuck, who was finding anti-Jewish feeling in Germany more than uncomfortable; he had been viciously victimised at the Feldburg Hill Climb in 1935 with vulgar posters about his being married to a Jewess. The 'overpowering energy' of the Führer was extending far beyond the formula as the yardstick by which the new Germany was to be judged.

Deprived of Chiron and Dreyfus, Ferrari promoted his junior drivers, Farina and Pintacuda to take their places by Nuvolari and Brivio while Trossi resigned his presidency of the Scuderia and went off to the Olympic Games at Garmisch in the Italian bob-sleigh team under the captaincy of Varzi with Cortese and the highly versatile Taruffi. Trossi was also experimenting with an intriguing radial 16-cylinder car for Grand Prix racing. Bugatti, faced with growing apathy in France, was diversifying himself in a thousand and one projects outside his Grand Prix cars and Wimille's drive at San Sebastian represented the effective swansong of Bugatti in Grand Prix racing. At the same time the A.C.F. announced that its Grand Prix would be for sports cars in 1936, a decision which the polished Wimille hailed as 'inelegant', even though he ultimately won the race! At the trials in February Taruffi caused some interest by trying an Auto-Union but it was not for another 19 years that he actually raced a German Grand Prix car. Then all of a sudden the intrigues were over and the cars were making for the blue Mediterranean at Monte Carlo.

To celebrate the best entry since the series began, the weather, for the first time, was atrocious; Chiron was making his first appearance on Mercedes and had made 2nd fastest practice time in his last pre-war Monaco Grand Prix, destined to be his shortest ever. On his first lap Tadini on a Ferrari Alfa scattered oil on the circuit and in the ensuing mêlée Chiron, Brauchitsch, Farina, Brivio and Trossi all ran into trouble and each other, in split seconds converting the 'chicane' bend into something out of Keystone Cops, gestures and all. When all the confusion had sorted itself out, Caracciola, ever the master in rain, was ahead of Nuvolari, Rosemeyer, Varzi and Stuck with special short chassis Auto-Unions. On the 10th lap Fagioli got into difficulty at the 'chicane' leaving Caracciola with the only Mercedes in the race. Nuvolari attacked at this critical point and established a ten-second lead over Caracciola by the 20th lap in an awe-inspiring battle between man, machine and the elements. Soon after, machine decided it had had enough and Nuvolari slowed gradually down losing 1st, 2nd and 3rd to Caracciola, Varzi and Stuck as the race progressed. Both these master drivers had given one of the clearest demonstrations of their superior skill over the first 30 laps; it was a pity the Alfa

was ultimately unequal to the task but Rudi's victory was well deserved in the highly tricky conditions. Faultless driving had brought him through one of the finest races of his career though Nuvolari was every whit his equal while his car had lasted. One tends sometimes to forget Nuvolari's absolute mastery in all conditions in praising the specialist expertise of individual drivers; while Caracciola might be Regenmeister and Rosemeyer Niebelmeister, there was and only ever has been one Maestro pure and simple.

Nuvolari appeared at Tripoli encased in plaster following a training spill at Monza but it was his erstwhile prime rival Varzi who carried off the day in a C-Type Auto-Union with a 6½-litre engine by 24 secs. from Stuck. Rosemeyer was 2nd till he caught fire after 18 of the 40 laps so the race was a real Auto-Union benefit, Varzi raising the race and lap record to 129.01 and 141.29 m.p.h. with only three wheel changes. Varzi had actually stolen a march on Stuck in the closing stages by driving flat out rather than in accordance with team orders and put up his record on the last lap, a flaming if flagrant finish to a magnificent Tripoli career which included three wins and a second (due to a last minute tyre burst) in four successive years. Fagioli (3rd) and Caracciola (4th) were the best for Mercedes.

Rosemeyer caught fire again at Tunis and Varzi had his only serious crash (before his fatal one 12 years later) when his Auto-Union did a series of end-to-end somersaults from 180 m.p.h. Varzi himself was thrown out, escaping injury miraculously. Chiron made the pace first and then dropped out leaving Caracciola the winner from Pintacuda's Alfa and the patient Wimille on Bugatti.

The German Afrika Korps then retired to the Fatherland with the remnants of the 300 tyres they had taken with them. However, not all their tyres or litres availed them at Barcelona where Nuvolari gave the full German teams a sound drubbing by leading for the whole of the 188 mile race in the face of the severest pressure from Caracciola who finished 2nd only seconds behind. Farina, recovered from an accident at Monza, rubbed more salt in the Herrenvolk's tail by bringing his 8C-35 into 3rd ahead of von Delius and Rosemeyer (Auto-Unions) and Chiron's Mercedes. On the mist-ridden Nürburg Ring a tremendous three cornered fight developed from the start between the first string drivers in each team; at first Caracciola led, then Nuvolari and finally, when the mist really fell, it was Rosemeyer who came through to win his first race on the Ring. Caracciola and Brauchitsch retired and Chiron's car was off colour while Lang was still then not equal to the task of coping with the likes of Nuvolari and his Ferrari colleagues, Brivio and Farina, who packed the places behind Rosemeyer.

The Mercedes débâcle continued at Budapest over a twisty short circuit; not one of them finished and Nuvolari managed to catch and beat Rosemeyer and Varzi. Tazio's

468 The start at Tripoli with Marshal Balbo, Governor of Tripoli, holding his flag over Man of the Year Rosemeyer (46), Chiron (10) and the field

469 Not even one of Marshal Balbo's famous smiles can have been much consolation to Stuck for the march Varzi had stolen on him

470 At first Caracciola led Nuvolari on the rain and mist ridden Nürburg Ring

next win at Milan was over Varzi only, but can have been no less satisfying and, with a record of a 2nd and three wins behind him, many wondered if the Maestro could cap it with another win in the German Grand Prix.

As it turned out he failed, but that was no disgrace in Rosemeyer's Great Year; he had the satisfaction of holding 2nd till he retired after 15 of the 22 laps. Stuck finished 2nd followed by Brivio on a 12C-36 Alfa. Fagioli-Caracciola drove the only Mercedes to finish—in 5th. Brauchitsch and Lang both retired, while Chiron brought his disappointing season to an end in a 140 m.p.h. crash when he left the road backwards and was nearly scalped. This was the last time he drove in a Grand Prix race until 1946, and one by one the pre-1934 leaves were beginning to fall off the tree of greatness.

There was, however, still plenty of fight left in those grizzled Italian warriors Varzi, Nuvolari and Fagioli. In the next three races they all played considerable parts. Nuvolari scored one of his all time tours-de-force on the Montenero circuit, one of his happy hunting grounds, where he opposed the formidable team of Rosemeyer, Stuck and Varzi and beat them after his 12C-36 had broken on the starting line and he had taken over Pintacuda's 8C-35! Such is true greatness, even though the Auto-Unions were almost brake-less not having been relined since the German Grand Prix. The Coppa Acerbo a week later was another Alfa-Auto-Union affair and for 150 of the 256 miles Nuvolari gave battle to Rosemeyer until his car gave way under the strain. Varzi was held up with plug troubles but still finished 3rd putting up fastest lap at 89.04 m.p.h. which was almost as fast as his 1935 record (90.9 m.p.h.) and achieved 183.64 m.p.h. over the timed kilometre. Delius' Auto-Union was 2nd and Brivio's Alfa 4th.

Stuck had grazed his elbow on one of the chicanes and spoilt the Auto-Union walk-over at Pescara but at Berne in the Swiss Grand Prix the next Sunday Auto-Union achieved the coveted 1-2-3, against the full teams of Mercedes and Alfa. Mercedes were making their first appearance since the German Grand Prix and were in even worse mechanical straits than Auto-Union had been in the middle of 1935. Things were also reported to be far from well in the Mercedes camp and rumours were rife that Caracciola was favoured, Fagioli was a known rebel, Brauchitsch wouldn't try and Chiron disliked the cars, leaving Lang as the only happy man. It was sadly reminiscent of what Dick Seaman wrote to George Monkhouse in 1939 after the Eifelrennen when 'Rudi did a terrific sulk ... (in which) ... he was assisted by Manfred who had shown childish behaviour all this year.' Motor Sport's Continental Correspondent suggested that a too rigid discipline had brought about smouldering resentments but the root of the trouble was really the cars. If the drivers had had regular drives in successful cars things would have been very different whatever their personal feelings.

At the start Caracciola led and Lang held 3rd and for a time it seemed as if the Stuttgart poltergeist had been laid. Nuvolari pressed and passed Lang but found the fast circuit too much for his car and fell back finally to retire as did all the other Ferrari cars. In the meantime Rosemeyer was going faster and faster and his 15th lap is now historic for being the only pre-war lap record on a Grand Prix circuit (used after the war) still to be standing—105.42 m.p.h. Wet conditions in 1937 and 1939 precluded the record being broken although Caracciola practised in 1937 at 107.14 m.p.h. and Lang in 1939 at 106.23 m.p.h. so that Rosemeyer's is not the fastest lap ever achieved there. As the nervous Swiss have not held their Grand Prix since the 1955 Le Mans disaster it is unlikely that this record will ever be broken now and its presence in the record book is an appropriate memorial to a meteoric driver. After Rosemeyer had passed Caracciola, Varzi began to press him for 2nd place and gradually the Mercedes challenge faded till only Lang's car was left in the race in 3rd place. Pained by a broken finger Lang handed over to Fagioli who had the bad luck to burst a tyre near the end which dropped him behind Stuck. This was bad luck but Stuck deserved the break for having driven with his injured arm swathed in bandages. The cruel Gods still made mock of Mercedes even after Fagioli's stop for just as he had caught Stuck again his engine started misfiring thus giving Auto-Union their 1-2-3 victory.

This race was also chosen by Bugatti for the launching of a new car which appeared brand new the day before the race. This was described as 'an experimental Type 59 fitted with the new T.50B engine and supercharged, the blower layout being similar to the Type 50 engine from which the modified

236

engine had stemmed.' It was also fitted with a bulbous radiator cowling and high-tailed streamlined body and was the first true single-seater Bugatti with central steering. At Berne it achieved little, retiring early on when the gear lever came adrift!

Like the Coppa Acerbo the Italian Grand Prix was another obstacle race and poor Stuck was in trouble again after a fine opening. Rosemeyer was still unbeatable in spite of everything Nuvolari tried and these two finished 1st and 2nd followed by Delius, Dreyfus, back with Ferrari, and Pintacuda.

Between 1934 and 1936 German cars had competed in 37 races with the following results (wins only): —

	1934	1935	1936		
Alfa-Romeo	3	1	4	=	8
Auto-Union	3	4	7	=	14
Mercedes-Benz	4	9	2	=	15

but over the next three years the balance of power shifted heavily to Mercedes as will be seen and after 1936 Alfa-Romeo never won another race in competition with German cars. Auto-Union held their own well in 1937 but after that they were generally always underdog however well Nuvolari might drive on occasions. The final three seasons before the war went:

	1937	1938	1939		
Auto-Union	5	2	2	=	9 (23)
Mercedes-Benz	7	5	5	=	17 (32)
Delahaye	–	1	–	=	1 (1)
Alfa-Romeo	–	–	–	=	0 (8)

1936 was thus the high-water mark for both Auto-Union and Alfa-Romeo. The new Mercedes had been a tragic failure leaving the field clear for Nuvolari's wizardry on tricky circuits where his magical skill still counted and where the Auto-Unions were additionally at a disadvantage, though the Alfas could not cope on fast circuits such as Tunis, Tripoli, Pescara and Berne. The year also saw the emergence of another driver of peculiar genius—Berndt Rosemeyer—and, as it turned out, the ending of three great careers—Chiron, Fagioli and Varzi, although all made successful comebacks in the post-war years.

At the end of the season it was still hoped that Chiron would go back to Mercedes to make up for two rather lean seasons and Ferrari was rumoured to be trying to achieve the impossible and weld Nuvolari, Varzi and Fagioli into an orderly team! In fact Auto-Union came very near to doing this putting up Fagioli and Nuvolari on two cars at Berne and Varzi in the Italian Grand Prix in 1937. In the end all three had passing flirtations with Auto-Union but only Nuvolari put in a full season's racing mostly on Alfa-Romeo. Chiron did not drive in Grand Prix races at all,

471 HIGH WATER MARK: 1936 was the last year even the wizardry of Nuvolari could make much impression on the German cars

Varzi only drove in the Italian Grand Prix and Fagioli drove an Auto-Union in three races without much luck. Fagioli was suffering from rheumatism at this time and faded from racing altogether after 1937, like Chiron, while Varzi continued to make unpredictable appearances, when the spirit moved him from his dolce vita.

Caracciola drove on, unmoved by the change and decay around him, with Rosemeyer his principal rival. Stuck had had a poor season in 1936 and he too faded from the scene without actually retiring. The place of the old champions was gradually being taken by the new generation of drivers who never fully measured up to their predecessors' stature with the possible exception of the fast maturing Lang and, in post-war years, Farina. France also vanished from Grand Prix racing in 1937 and Bugatti only started in one race after the 1936 Swiss Grand Prix—the 1938 French Grand Prix. Independent drivers had been on their way out in 1936, and 1937 killed them off almost entirely as it also did to works Maserati participation. This had been growing poorer and poorer throughout 1936, which is not surprising when one reads of Dick Seaman's experience in the German Grand Prix and Coppa Acerbo . . . 'in the course of three laps the filler cap sprung open, the mirror fell off, a front brake locked and the water temperature rose to 110°. It is the last time I shall ever drive a works Maserati.' However, the future had a brighter and more terrible fate in store for the promising young Englishman who was invited to join Mercedes at the end of 1936 in place of the great Fagioli, no easy place to fill for he had passed on his skill to all the Mercedes team, perhaps even in part to the great Caracciola himself, whose equal he always could have been, even in Rudi's triumphal 1935 season.

Chapter Twenty Six
1937 · Full Engagement

The 1937 season was the best of the 750 kg. formula and was contested by the largest cars since 1912. For many of us who saw the cars in their heyday it represents an all time high in racing and one summer's day in 1958 thousands at Oulton Park were privileged to have a peep into one of motor racing's most thrilling yesterdays when Peter Collins and Tony Brooks all too briefly demonstrated the mighty W125 Mercedes. The modern cars may go round corners faster and thus be able to put in laps at vastly increased speeds on the Nürburg Ring and at Monaco, which are the only comparable modern circuits, but is it really quite the same thing?

Feeling, like Ferrari in 1933, that their cars were as successful as they could be, Auto-Union made little basic change in their cars for 1937. Although there were rumours of new cars to come during the season, Alfa-Romeo did litttle during the winter beyond try a 4½-litre engine in the 12C-36 without much success. Mercedes, on the other hand, had abundant cause for heart-searching; the W25E was a design disaster and the 1934/5 cars were no longer fast enough so the Directors took the only decision they could in the middle of 1936 if they were to continue in Grand Prix racing at all. In fact the new car was conceived almost by accident; in February 1936 a new formula was decreed for 1937/9 based on a capacity limit of 3460 c.c. blown or 4½-litres unblown and a minimum weight (but including wheels and tyres) of 850 kg. In September the governing body had the happy inspiration to reduce the blown limit to the more orderly one of 3-litres, which must have endeared them to any constructor who had a blown 3460 c.c. engine ready by then! Mercedes were thus in the throes of designing a new chassis with a far longer wheelbase than the W25E and 3 ins. longer than the older W25B cars. It was thus possible to fit this with a much larger engine when the 750 kg. formula was extended.

If the conception of this classic car might be called fortuitous there was nothing fortuitous about its design or performance and it was a winner from the moment it first met the starter's flag. Once again the design was a typical Mercedes amalgam of tradition and modernity. Tradition was represented by the basic details of engine construction: two blocks of four cylinders made from steel forgings with welded up ports and welded water jackets gave the outline of the engine (apart from its two camshafts) in Pomeroy's words 'an almost startling resemblance to World War I Mercedes aviation engines.' Historical research produced a modified rear axle based upon a scheme originally devised by Trepardoux or Bouton for de Dion in the 19th century—the famous de Dion rear axle which became a *sine qua non* in racing car construction for almost twenty years until Mercedes themselves went back to swing axles in 1954/5. The engine itself measured 94 × 102 mm. (5660 c.c.) and in its most powerful tune developed 646 b.h.p. at 5800 r.p.m. compared with the C-Type Auto-Union which developed 520 b.h.p. at 5000 r.p.m. Mercedes had always had the edge over Auto-Union on the slower circuits: now they were ready to take them on successfully on the circuits where maximum speeds were more at premium. Small wonder then that the 1937 racing was so spectacular.

In one respect Mercedes broke with tradition: the new cars began the season with the familiar banshee-like shriek of their blowers as they cut in and out in the same way as had almost every blown Mercedes since the original 2-litre 4-cylinder car had run at Indianapolis in 1923. With a fitting sense of history Mercedes revised this lay-out and brought it into conformity with generally established practice in time for the 1937 Vanderbilt Cup Race in U.S.A. and the famous shriek was heard no more.

Ferrari, even without the fading Varzi and Fagioli, still had Nuvolari, Brivio and Farina plus a corrida of reserves including Trossi, Sommer, Pintacuda, Siena, Biondetti, Tadini and Severi. Mercedes conducted extensive tests on the Ring and at Monza during the autumn, winter and

473 THRONE OF POWER: *the cockpit of the most powerful racing car ever, the W 125 Mercedes-Benz*

spring, eventually announcing their team of Caracciola, Brauchitsch and Lang plus Dick Seaman, Zehender and Christan Kautz, a Swiss amateur who had done a small amount of fairly indifferent voiturette racing. In some respects the canons of Mercedes driver selection during 1934/9 and 1952/5 were obscure indeed, possessing all the exhaustive investigation one associates with the Germans, but on occasions utterly devoid of all common sense. Of the numerous unknown drivers they tried in races during the six pre-war years only Seaman and Lang made the grade—who really remembers Henne, Geier, Hans Hugo Hartmann, Brendel or Gaertner in motor racing except as names in old programmes? Then there were the disastrous trials in 1936/7 when 'under Neubauer's far-seeing (! !) supervision . . . 27 drivers underwent scrutiny.' In terms of driver selection Mercedes could have borne more closely in mind the old saying 'The fox is killed in the kennel' and been more far-seeing in their selection of trainees. They were in addition still notably wedded to the tradition of the works tester and nationally averse to the foreign star driver. This, coupled with the chronic lack of first class German drivers almost throughout history, was a trying handicap to them and undoubtedly enabled Auto-Union and Alfa-Romeo to pack places and even win races in 1934/6 when on strict performance they had no business so to do.

Auto-Union, though basically harder to drive, seemed to have more luck with their junior drivers: although they were never the equal of the Mercedes top liners, both Hasse and Müller each won a Grand Prix in 1937/9, but in general their

474 . . .'since 1935 the Avus circuit had been endowed with four steeply banked turns at either end . . .'—Fagioli's Auto-Union which made fastest lap at over 174 mph

475 The exciting 1st heat when Caracciola (35) beat Rosemeyer (31) by 2/5 sec.

driver situation was less satisfactory than Mercedes particularly following the retirement of Varzi, the gradual retirement of Stuck and, worst of all, the death of Rosemeyer in January 1938. If Dick Seaman's experience is any criterion their selection machinery was no better than Mercedes, as he became 'exasperated with Auto-Union's uncertainty and hesitation as to when their tests would be.' For 1937 the team would be led once again by Rosemeyer who, like Stuck in 1934, was going to carry the rest: Stuck himself would also drive along with Delius and Hasse, who had both driven soundly in 1936, and Hermann Müller who was a successful D.K.W. motor cyclist. Fagioli, Varzi and Nuvolari also all drove the cars during the year.

Tripoli did not seem itself without Varzi but it saw the crowning of a new king—Hermann Lang—who led almost throughout the race winning at the record speed of 134.42 m.p.h.—over 5 m.p.h. faster than Varzi's 1936 record. At one time Seaman and Caracciola were 2nd and 3rd but were slowed by sand getting into their superchargers and Lang was chased home by a cohort of Auto-Unions driven by Rosemeyer, Delius, Stuck and Fagioli. Stuck finally set the record for all time at 142.44 m.p.h. Nuvolari had required strong persuasion even to start and was soon out of the race and Brivio and Farina could only manage tenth and ninth places.

Since it had been last held in 1935 the Avus circuit had been endowed with one steeply banked turn at either end enabling lap speeds of nearly 180 m.p.h. to be attained. Being formule libre both Mercedes and Auto-Union produced some interesting 'one-off' cars: Mercedes had a V-12 engine of 5½ litres (82 × 88 mm.) giving 679 b.h.p. for record attempts and gave the streamlined record car to Brauchitsch, perhaps mindful of his win in 1932, Lang and Caracciola had streamlined 8-cylinder cars, Seaman an ordinary Grand Prix car and, most interesting of all, Goffredo Zehender with the Grand Prix chassis fitted with the V-12 engine. Poor Zehender! After sitting in the wings as relief driver throughout the 1936 German Grand Prix, whilst Lang, Fagioli or Caracciola did all the relieving he now proceeded to blow up the V-12 engine without really seeing what the car could do. For Auto-Union Rosemeyer drove a fully streamlined record car, Fagioli a car similar to Stuck's old record-breaker, and Delius and Hasse open racers.

The usual heats-and-final race produced an exciting 1st heat when Caracciola beat Rosemeyer by 2/5 sec. at 155.5 m.p.h. with record lap to Rosemeyer at 172.75—not quite as fast as Fagioli's best in practice at over 174 m.p.h. but near enough. Fagioli had gear selection troubles in the second heat which was won by Brauchitsch at 160.3 m.p.h. Tyres were obviously limiting performance and Mercedes decided that in the final Caracciola was to go flat out and risk a change of tyres, while Lang and Brauchitsch were to try and run non-stop, leaving Seaman with instructions to stay ahead of the open Auto-Unions. Both Caracciola and Brauchitsch were soon out with mechanical troubles and Rosemeyer slowed to check failing oil pressure leaving Lang to win a cleverly judged race by 2 secs. from Delius' open Auto-Union. Once again Seaman had been 2nd to Lang till burst tyres slowed him to 5th behind Rosemeyer and Hasse—first blood decidedly to Mercedes in the formule libre events.

Rosemeyer now pulled the score back to level pegging with two wins in succession. The first was in the Eifelrennen when he completed three successive victories on the Ring with a good win over Caracciola and Brauchitsch. Nuvolari finished 5th which involved beating Kautz, Müller and Delius on German cars—an achievement in itself in 1937. The Mercedes team had fuel pump troubles and it was after this race that they changed their supercharging arrangements in time for the Vanderbilt Cup on July 5th on the Roosevelt Speedway, Long Island. This ancient series had been revived in 1936 when Nuvolari's 12-cylinder Alfa had beaten Wimille's 4.7 Bugatti and now the German teams headed by Caracciola and Rosemeyer in person were going over along with Seaman and Delius. Nuvolari and Farina were both going again, and an Alfa, said by some to be the car Farina had driven in 1936, would be driven by the American Rex Mays. He had carried out some remarkable modifications to this car in the ensuing six months, and contrived 3rd fastest practice lap, being beaten only by Caracciola and Rosemeyer. Handicapped by an appallingly slow pit stop of 1 min. 18 secs. for fuel and tyres, Mays still managed to hold 2nd or 3rd place for most of the race. Nuvolari blew his own car up trying to pass Seaman in the early stages and relieved Farina at his fuel stop. He then set about first Delius (4th) and then the redoubtable Mays, whom he finally passed after tremendous efforts which over-stressed his engine, so after a hectic ten laps Tazio was back at the pits handing the dregs of an Alfa back to Farina.

Out in front Caracciola had led effectively for the first 22 of the 90 laps only to retire with a broken blower drive. Rosemeyer then went ahead followed by Seaman, who went through when Rosemeyer stopped for fuel, only to lose the lead when he in turn stopped. Seaman then caught up to within 9 secs. of Rosemeyer, but was running short of fuel and had to stop on his very last lap of all. Still, 2nd to Rosemeyer was warm work indeed and some consolation to Seaman for the possible 2nds he had missed both at Tripoli and Avus. Mays finished 3rd a lap behind with Delius 4th, Farina 5th and the American Thorne (Alfa) 6th. Writing after this race George Monkhouse expressed a hope that has still to be fully realised—

476 ANCIENT REVIVAL: Nuvolari takes an early lead in the 1936 revival of the Vanderbilt Cup

'It is to be hoped that now the Americans have had a taste of the thrills of Grand Prix racing by next year (!) they will have produced a genuine road-racing car. They have shown they have the drivers and everyone knows from past experience in other sports that once the Americans get down to a job of work they can "show the world", so why not in motor racing?'

Why not indeed? But in spite of Ford's forays at Le Mans and Indianapolis and the ill fated Scarabs we are still waiting. The way in which Mays' smaller Alfa was able to outpace the latest Ferrari cars, even when driven by Nuvolari, was the deepest of a long series of humiliations suffered by the Italians during 1937. His success was all the more surprising for being achieved on a medium pace circuit (winning average 82.56 m.p.h.) where the advantages of his centrifugal supercharger would have been less obvious than at Indianapolis or, for that matter, Tripoli—tempting thought. In the 1937 '500' the car had to be modified almost out of recognition to comply with the 'junk-formula' by removing the blower and fitting a two seater body and reducing the compression ratio to cope with ordinary pump fuel. By 1938 these rules had been changed to comply with the A.I.A.C.R. formula so the car appeared in racing trim but with an engine reduced to 3-litres and a live rear axle. All this improved its qualifying speed from 119.968 m.p.h. to 122.845 m.p.h. and enabled Mays to lead the 1938 race for 50 miles. However in the Vanderbilt Cup Mays became the only driver to finish a non-German car in the first 3 in a Grand Prix race in 1937.

While all these junketings were going on and the great trenchermen Neubauer and Uhlenhaut were devouring their

477 *Lang the fast starter leading the first lap of the German Grand Prix from Caracciola, Rosemeyer, Muller, Brauchitsch and Nuvolari*

478 *CHEMNITZ METEOR: The intensity of Rosemeyer's effort against the united might of Mercedes*

479 *DIFFICULT TASK: . . . 'Brauchitsch for once had driven with steadiness and cool judgment . . .'*

way through the best that the kitchens of the S.S. Bremen could offer them, the other half of the circus were converging on Spa for the Belgian Grand Prix. Some tremendous speeds were achieved, Hasse's winning average being faster than Brauchitsch's 1935 record when he was really hurrying. Lang raised the record lap to 108.8 m.p.h. and is credited with a speed of 193 m.p.h. over a kilometre against Stuck's 175 m.p.h. (slower than Varzi's speed at Pescara the year before). Stuck was in tremendous form, as, strangely for a hill climb champion, he so often was on a really fast circuit, but pit stops delayed the two fliers and it was left to Rudolf Hasse to win his first Grand Prix at the excellent speed of 104.07 m.p.h., with Stuck 2nd and Lang 3rd. Kautz survived several excursions off the circuit to finish 4th and Sommer's Ferrari Alfa was a poor 5th.

By the 25th July everybody was back in Europe to contest the German Grand Prix and a memorable race was promised. Auto-Union led 3-2 on outright wins in the season and had not been beaten on the Ring since the German Grand Prix two years before, while Mercedes had not won there since Brauchitsch won the Eifelrennen on the new car's first appearance in 1934. Although their reputation was not desperately at stake it was clearly a point of honour for the new cars from Stuttgart to recover their old supremacy dating back to the days when they had won the early German Grands Prix with those Wagnerian old S.S.K.'s. The battle started in practice but although he had five Mercedes, to say nothing of Nuvolari, to contend with, it was Rosemeyer who started in No. 1 position with a very clear advantage over his rivals. His speed of 9 mins. 46.2 secs. (87 m.p.h.) was then the fastest lap ever on the Ring and was 6 secs. faster than Brauchitsch and 8.9 secs. faster than Lang. Pomeroy refers to 'intense competition to make the fastest lap', while Monkhouse observes that 'most of the Mercedes drivers practised on the "training car" . . . which judging by some of their remarks, must have been a beast to drive. This was the car Brauchitsch had overturned at Spa.' In spite of their relative slowness in practice Monkhouse speaks of 'a great feeling of confidence at the Mercedes' table,' as well there might be with five superlative cars to oppose four slower Auto-Unions and Rosemeyer. It was Lang, ever the fast starter, who led on the first lap and then it seemed as if it was going to be Rosemeyer all the way after his record 2nd lap (9 mins. 53 secs. = 85.57 m.p.h.) gave him a 9 secs. lead. The next lap it was 11 secs., but by this time Caracciola was moving purposefully forward into 2nd as his juniors were palpably unable to cope with the Chemnitz Meteor.

If the 1913 French Grand Prix deserves to go down in history as the Tragedy of Guyot's Mechanic, then this race was to be the Sad Tale of Rosemeyer's Hub-Cap. In his anxiety to increase his lead Rosemeyer clouted a bank and lost the ears of a rear hub-cap besides damaging the wheel and came in at the end of his 4th lap, 28 seconds after

Brauchitsch on No. 3 Mercedes had passed. Another 2 mins. 28 secs. elapsed while the remnants of the hub-cap were knocked off with a cold chisel and hammer and Rosemeyer performed greater prodigies of acrobatics than even Nuvolari in his famous pit stop two years before. Alas for Rosemeyer the pace was too hot now to admit of another miracle victory and he did not even better his record 2nd lap during the ensuing 18 when he must have been trying all he knew: another excursion off the road on lap 8 made no difference to his place—tenth and last. In the meantime Mercedes were in a majestic position after 6 laps—1, 2, 3, 4 and 6. In 5th was Delius with the only Auto-Union anywhere and it is a little mystifying why he was not called in for Rosemeyer to take over, especially when one remembers that no less a figure than Nuvolari himself was called in thus later in the year in the Swiss Grand Prix.

However, Delius did not re-appear, having apparently lost control when challenging Seaman for 4th place. As a result both cars left the road and Delius died from his injuries—the first driver to be killed in one of the 'new' German cars during a 750-kg. formula race. This brought Kautz into 4th place on No. 5 Mercedes but his joy was shortlived for he left the road on the next lap and let the persistent Nuvolari into 4th. As always he was driving an inspired race on the Ring—5th fastest in practice in 10 mins. 8.3 secs. (83.9 m.p.h.) which he *improved* to 84.4 m.p.h. in the race: 'Rex Mays and centrifugal blowers indeed!' the great man might well have been saying as he blew out his cheeks and urged his time-expired car along. Way back in the field Rosemeyer was cutting through the tail-enders and by the 16th lap he had dispossessed Nuvolari from 4th. The next lap it was Lang's turn to run into bad luck when a tyre went flat and Rosemeyer was back on the leader board—a truly phenomenal effort. As if this was not enough he then set about catching Brauchitsch reducing his lead from 80 secs. on lap 19 to a mere 16 secs. at the end four laps later. Brauchitsch in turn was 46 secs. behind Caracciola who won at the record average of 82.7 m.p.h., nearly 1 m.p.h. faster than Rosemeyer's 1936 speed and over 2 m.p.h. faster than Brauchitsch's 1935 *lap* record.

The race had been notable for the brilliant driving of the Big Three: Rudi had driven a race of remarkable pace judgment even by his own standards finishing at an average only .18 m.p.h. slower than Rosemeyer's in the much shorter Eifelrennen and with a fastest lap of 85.4 m.p.h. He had piled on the pressure in the earlier stages just when it was needed and then driven on just fast enough to stay ahead in spite of a lightning stop for 23 secs. to change a rear wheel after 19 laps. Brauchitsch, for once, had driven with steadiness and cool judgment, no easy thing for one of his temperament, and this in many ways was precisely what Rosemeyer had not done—hence all his troubles. However, it is easy to be wise when harried by nothing more pressing

than time: Rosemeyer must have known the weight he carried that day and whilst his fight with the leaders may not have been as long as Boillot's it was as glorious and against odds no smaller. To take on five of the best cars Mercedes had produced since 1914 cannot have been any joke, though Rosemeyer always made light enough of it even to putting a lighted cigarette in the mouth of Rudi's Goddess of Speed Trophy during Korpsführer Hühnlein's speech at the prize-giving.

Seaman was still out of action a fortnight later at Monaco so his place was taken by the highly experienced Zehender who had presumably been forgiven his act of lèse majesté at Avus and now drove his first race for Mercedes. With the retirement from the Grand Prix field of Williams, Dreyfus, Chiron, Varzi and Fagioli and the death of Guy Moll, only Nuvolari and Caracciola were available to make the last pre-war bid to win twice at Monaco. At the last minute Nuvolari was unable to come as he was testing a new Alfa at Monza, so it was all up to Caracciola. Once again speeds were tremendously up on 1935 and Caracciola led off smartly as if he had every intention of tweaking that old superstition's nose. So it went on till 47 laps when he came in with misfiring which took over three minutes to cure and left Brauchitsch with a secure lead. After 69 laps Brauchitsch stopped and had trouble re-starting due to a brake locking (or was it, one wonders, one of Neubauer's delaying ruses?): choose how, it enabled Caracciola to draw up to Brauchitsch's tail and for 11 laps these two were hard at it.

480 . . . *'choose how it enabled Caracciola to draw up to Brauchitsch's tail . . .'*

243

481 HELLO STRANGER!: *The deplorable showing of the new Alfa sent Nuvolari off in disgust to Auto-Union at Berne*

482 At Berne 'Stuck redeemed Auto-Union fortunes slightly by one of his finest starts . . .'

483 . . . 'a crushing victory in damp conditions at 97.42 mph' for Caracciola at Berne

Brauchitsch, with the prospect of winning his first race since 1934, was damned if he would give way to Caracciola, Neubauer's flag or the devil himself and defied everything Caracciola (and Neubauer!) could do until, by a miracle of skill and courage, he nipped by on a bend during the 80th lap, but the old saw was not to be gainsaid and, like Chiron and Nuvolari in past years, it beat Caracciola as well. The very next lap his engine changed its note and its plugs and Brauchitsch had done it. The Auto-Unions had never been in the picture; both Rosemeyer and Hasse had crashed though Rosemeyer took over Stuck's car and did another of his spectacular drives through the field. This time he could not quite intercept the Mercedes 1-2-3, but he did block Zehender out of 4th place. Kautz redeemed a practice crash by finishing 3rd, which Zehender had occupied for much of the race.

After two rather ordinary years in 1935/6 the Monaco race had suddenly come to life with a vintage duel worthy of the old days of Nuvolari and Varzi, which produced a record lap by Caracciola at 66.99 m.p.h. (1 min. 46.5 secs.), which stood as a race record until 1955. A change of sky but not of weather took the Germans to Pescara where Fagioli was making one of his intermittent appearances on Auto-Union and Nuvolari was to produce the new Alfa-Romeo, now entered by the works but apparently not yet judged worthy to bear the Four Leafed Clover. The car was lower and sleeker than the 12C-36 and reputedly had a slightly bigger engine but failed badly in practice and dismally in the race, where it could barely keep up with Ruesch's old 3.8-litre, well known in Engand as the winner of the 1936 Donington Grand Prix and in Dennis Poore's hands after 1945.

Rosemeyer and Stuck were in rare form in practice and Caracciola did well to put in 2nd best lap to Rosemeyer, but in the race both Stuck and Rudi had mechanical bothers and Rosemeyer won easily at 87.61 m.p.h.—chicanes included—with a new record lap of 92 m.p.h.: a pity about those chicanes when you think that on the genuine road circuit in 1933 Nuvolari was record-lapping at 90.4 m.p.h. on the 3-litre Maserati. The deplorable showing of the new Alfa had the same effect on Nuvolari as the Ferrari Alfa troubles in the 1933 French Grand Prix and when they withdrew from the Swiss Grand Prix he appeared with Fagioli, Rosemeyer and Stuck on Auto-Union. In 1934/6 this would have been an utterly formidable line-up, but by 1937 it was somewhat jaded: in the race Fagioli was so exhausted that he had to be relieved by Nuvolari, who in turn had been flagged in for relief by Rosemeyer—a sad change for the great Italians. Under pressure for 3rd place on the 2nd lap poor Rosemeyer overdid it again and finally bogged down in a field trying to regain the circuit. Stuck redeemed Auto-Union fortunes slightly by one of his finest starts which enabled him to lead Caracciola during the opening laps. Caracciola, however,

244

was in his greatest form and simply unbeatable, drawing right away yet using fewer tyres than his more fiery rivals and capping his superb practice laps with a crushing victory in damp conditions at 97.42 m.p.h.

For once Lang was not dogged by misfortune and finished 2nd with Brauchitsch 3rd followed by Stuck and Rosemeyer, who had the consolation of fastest lap. During practice Caracciola had driven 'five laps, all in about 2 mins. 34 secs. the fastest being 2 mins. 32 secs. an average speed of no less than 107.14 m.p.h. Rudi's handling of the car during these five astonishing laps was one of the most impressive pieces of driving I have ever seen', wrote George Monkhouse and to this day no one has driven faster at Berne. In an age of ever falling records it is comforting to look at one achievement of a master which may well now stand not for an age but for all time.

Nuvolari was back with Alfa-Romeo at Montenero for the Italian Grand Prix and Varzi made his final pre-war appearance in Auto-Union distinguishing himself by being 2nd to Caracciola in practice. In the race, however, he had to give best to Nuvolari, although he did have the final satisfaction of finishing one place ahead of his oldest and greatest rival, who became bored and handed over to 'office-boy' Farina after half the race. Lang tried to 'do a Brauchitsch' but either Neubauer was not having it or Lang was too well disciplined and he finished 20 yards behind Caracciola with Rosemeyer 3rd, a recovered Seaman 4th, Müller 5th, then Varzi and Nuvolari-Farina.

In many ways the Masaryk Circuit was a mediaeval survival where even starting positions were still determined by lots. To start with Brauchitsch and Lang tried to make the running but it was soon clear that none but Caracciola could cope with Rosemeyer. Caracciola, however, seemed more than equal to the task and caught him with almost insolent ease. Rosemeyer bent a wheel on a corner, then, nothing daunted, proceeded to walk 1½-miles back to the pits, take over Müller's car *AND* catch Seaman to spoil yet another Mercedes 1-2-3. The last word was Caracciola's in that he raised the race average to 85.97 m.p.h. above Varzi's 1935 lap record of 85.21 and the lap speed to 94.59 m.p.h. where, needless to say, it still stands.

Mercedes had levelled the score at 3-3 after the German Grand Prix and had then shown much greater staying power than Auto-Union over the latter part of the season. The strain on Rosemeyer was clearly beginning to tell as his accident record of four minor crashes in these last six races shewed. By the end of the Masaryk race they had won seven races to Auto-Union's four and Caracciola had been declared European Champion for a second time. The twelfth and final race was held at Donington Park, which in those days was unique as being a country house circuit, barely over three miles in length—an immense contrast to Masaryk.

DONINGTON
LAP DISTANCE—3.125 Miles

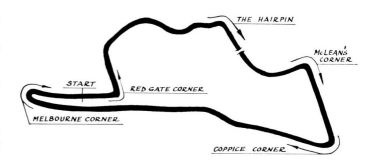

484 IMMENSE CONTRAST: the short country house circuit at Donington Park was quite different from any other used by the great teams

485 UP AND OVER!: Rosemeyer takes off in pursuit of an airborne Lang as they crest the rise from Melbourne Corner

486 GREATEST SINCE THE FLOOD!: Lang leads Caracciola, Seaman and Rosemeyer into Red Gate Corner

The impression created by the German racing juggernaut on the point-to-point atmosphere that was English motor racing in the thirties now seems as dated and stilted as the motor racing novels of Lord Cottenham, with the Donington bookmakers giving the same odds on Rosemeyer, Lang and Brauchitsch as Raymond Mays! The English driver Charles Martin was quoted by *Motor Sport* as calling it 'the greatest thing that happened since the Flood' and the race itself was as good as anything seen that whole year except that Caracciola, perhaps bored with success or just not enjoying the circuit, was not at his most deadly. Rosemeyer made up for it all, with his last and one of his greatest drives, in his race-long fight with Brauchitsch, who was possibly deprived of another win by an unlucky tyre loss. But he had been under great, perhaps for him, too great pressure from Rosemeyer and, as Monkhouse summed it up, 'no driver can drive as he had done . . . with the car snaking and sliding all over the road and sometimes off it—with smoke streaming off the tyres when accelerating out of the corners—without the possibility of such trouble.' At this distance in time it all sounds almost as far away as Bruce-Brown's Fiat at Dieppe in 1912, yet back within sight, sound and, most important, smell of the W125 in 1958, it might have been yesterday.

Seaman rounded off an unlucky season when Müller bumped him down from 5th place early on and Lang retired with shock absorber failure after being the first car over the crest of Melbourne Hill on the first shattering lap with all four wheels off the ground. The other five cars finished in the order Rosemeyer, Brauchitsch, Caracciola, Müller and Hasse.

In addition, during the year, German cars had taken part in two other races as far apart as Milan where Hasse had been 4th with a lone Auto-Union and Rio de Janeiro where Pintacuda had narrowly beaten Stuck, both races being very slow, won at 64.40 m.p.h. and 51.4 m.p.h. respectively. These races I have not included in the computation of races won but merely mention for the sake of completeness.

The 1937 cars combined all the speed of their ultra-modernity with all the surge and thunder of the old Dieppe days and would surely have rejoiced the heart of Gerald Rose had he then been following the sport. After a lean season in 1936, Caracciola had staged a shattering come-back particularly from mid-season when he was virtually invincible. The skill, the nicety and, most of all, the ease with which he dominated the untramelled power of the W125 even now makes one marvel particularly for its contrast with the methods of his rivals—Brauchitsch, Lang, Nuvolari and Rosemeyer. On 1937 form Caracciola was in a class of his own, although he did not have the problems of Rosemeyer and Nuvolari. Rosemeyer had a frustrating year: when things went well, he too was almost unbeatable but, unlike Caracciola, he tended to beat himself all too often. Of course it was asking too much of anyone, perhaps even Nuvolari himself, to take on the 1937 Mercedes cars and drivers single-handed. A more experienced and mature driver might have done better but it would have taken Nuvolari, Varzi, Fagioli, Fangio, Nazzaro, Boillot or Moss to have done it—and at their very best and most experienced. When one reflects that Rosemeyer had only $1\frac{1}{2}$ seasons motor racing experience before 1937 the sheer magnitude of his effort in actually winning as many races as Caracciola is brought home. Moreover with a little more luck and support from his team he could well have won the German Grand Prix, for there has never been a better driver on the Ring, and possibly the Swiss Grand Prix where he was also a master. In both races, however, he paid the penalty for minor errors almost certainly due to nervous tension in the opening laps when the full heat of the Mercedes attack was turned on. A little more calm in the opening laps of those two races and who knows?

Nuvolari's season had been almost a travesty: he had driven a superb race in the German Grand Prix but the rest of it had been the sort of outrage that a driver of his class should never have had to bear. Adversity and slower cars had frequently been his lot before, but even as an independent in 1934 he had been able to snatch the odd 'place' from under the Germans' noses. In 1937 there was a 4th on the Ring and the dubious consolation of beating one Auto-Union at Milan. For enduring all this and the disappointment of the new Alfa fiasco—to say nothing of being passed by Rex Mays' 'Bowes Seal Fast' Alfa—Nuvolari deserved almost as big a medal as Rosemeyer, beween whom there was such great personal regard, each respecting the plain guts and genius of the other. Better days were soon to come again for Nuvolari but, tragically, only as an indirect result of the death of Rosemeyer.

487 END OF SEASON BLUES: Caracciola was not at his most deadly

488/9 The race-long fight between Rosemeyer (1) and Brauchitsch (right) was a tremendous finish to a fabulous season's racing

PASSING OF THE TITANS

490/1 . . . 'the bright day is done, and we are for the dark'

Chapter Twenty Seven
1938 · The Litres Begin to Vanish

Having designed a chassis in 1936 with the 3/4½-litre formula in view, Mercedes had stolen a march on their competitors and, as if this were not enough, Auto-Union lost their only driver of consequence on January 28th 1938 when Rosemeyer crashed fatally in a record attempt. The folly of the Company in even allowing him to drive in the prevailing ice and cross-winds was almost criminal and, even allowing for Rosemeyer's tremendous courage and enthusiasm, one feels that Neubauer would never have allowed Caracciola out in such conditions and it is unlikely that Dr. Porsche would either. This proved an almost insuperable set-back to Auto-Union's 3-litre programme from which they never fully recovered in spite of the prodigious efforts of Nuvolari in 1939 and the latter part of 1938. By contrast Mercedes could afford to retain a driver of Seaman's class and race him but four times in the year where he was good enough to finish 1st, 2nd and 3rd in three races all of which he might easily have won. Auto-Union were perhaps paying heavily for vacillating with Seaman two years before. As it was, with Stuck in semi-retirement, Hasse and Müller, and Kautz, transferred from Mercedes, there was nobody capable of testing the new cars adequately and they must have blessed the fates for Nuvolari's accident with an Alfa in the early months of 1938.

Both German cars were V-12.s with one stage of supercharge and all round independent springing. Basically the Mercedes chassis was the same as that brought out for the W125 but 2½ ins. shorter, while the engine broke new ground in terms of high boost and r.p.m., the two Roots-type blowers achieving 18 p.s.i. and the 67 × 70 mm. engine peaking at 7800 r.p.m. when it originally developed 420 b.h.p. Ultimately in two-stage blown 1939 form this figure was increased to 483 at the same r.p.m. and the boost to 26.5 p.s.i. Twin o.h.c. and four valves per cylinder were retained besides the familiar welded steel water jackets To achieve a lower centre of gravity the engine was set across the chassis driving a propeller shaft to one side of the driver. Unlike the old Bugattis, however, the driver sat in the centre of the car which remained a true single-seater. The new car was on the drawing board in general outline in 1936 and on trial at Monza 12 months later—an achievement due as much to the immense technical skill and man-power available at Stuttgart as to the continuity of experience enjoyed by the design team of Engineers Wagner, Hess and Sailer.

The new Auto-Union was more truly a mid-engined car than its predecessors with engine dimensions of 65 × 75 mm. and developed 400 b.h.p. at 7000 r.p.m. Before the death of Rosemeyer they had also lost the originator of the car, Dr. Porsche, and for a time it was touch-and-go whether they raced at all, and there were even rumours that the new cars were to be front-engined straight eights! Like Mercedes they adopted 2-stage supercharging in 1939 achieving the very similar figures of 24 p.s.i. and 485 b.h.p. but still at 7000 r.p.m. Auto-Union have consistently used fewer r.p.m. than Mercedes. It is much to their credit (and not least that of Nuvolari in particular) that they were able to catch up with Mercedes performance so quickly: indeed the evidence is that by the end of 1939 they were better advanced than their rivals in the design of new 1½-litre engines for what was most generally anticipated as the post-1940 formula.

In 1938 the Alfa works, adopting the name Alfa Corse, took over the direction of Alfa-Romeos in racing, retaining Ferrari to run the team. Overall design was in the cultured hands of W. P. Ricart with Bazzi and one Gioachino Colombo under him. The famed remark of Pomeroy Senior to Coatalen after the 1913 Coupe de l'Auto—'I fancy I can see some of us ... looking up certain old drawings and pulling some old engines off the shelf'—might well have been the watchword at Portello in the winter of 1937/38. For a 3-litre formula their first call was on the time honoured 2·9-straight-eight, which they modified and put in an independent chassis, calling the car the 8C308. They obtained 295 b.h.p. at 6000 r.p.m. from the old warrior compared to the 1935 figure of 210 at 5400 r.p.m. but while this was a significant advance it was totally inadequate to deal with the German cars; during the year they also produced a V-12 (the 12C 312 of 66 × 73 mm.) and a V-16 (the 16C316 of 58 × 70). Recent information has shewn that this last was more truly a double-8 consisting of two of the new 1½-litre engines geared together which had been designed for Ferrari in 1937/8 and which ultimately powered the 158/9 Alfa-Romeo. Either of these V-designs ought to have been the ultimate answer, but their performance was disappointing: the best output of even the V-16 was 350 b.h.p. at 7000 r.p.m. and the V-12 was worse with only 320 at 6500 r.p.m.

Like Alfas with the 1½-litre straight eight, Maserati doubled up his 1½-litre 4CM engine to produce his 8CTF formula car in 1938. Bugatti was off on a similar tack by

492 LOWER CENTRE OF GRAVITY: *This side view of Lang at Rheims shews off the long low lines of the W 154 Mercedes-Benz*

493 CHANGING OF THE GUARD: *Dr. Porsche (left) departed from Auto-Union after 1937 and Dr. Feuereissen (centre) became responsible for race direction*

494 . . . *'The new Auto-Union was more truly a mid-engined car than its predecessors . . .' Nuvolari at Donington*

495 CRIMINAL FOLLY: *the folly of the Company in allowing Rose-meyer (shewn just before the crash) to drive in the prevailing ice and cross wind was almost criminal*

496 . . . *'Basically the Mercedes-Benz chassis was the same as that brought out for the W 125 . . .'*

497 CURTAIN UP: Caracciola leads the field at Pau with Dreyfus (2) the winner in 2nd

498 MADNESS IN MAY: Lang (46), Brauchitsch (44) and Caracciola (26) sweep to revenge at Tripoli with Trossi on the new Maserati challenging (10)

installing a new 3-litre engine of 78 × 78 mm. in his single-seater, and finally two French sports car manufacturers reversed the old adage by developing their 1937 sports models into 4½-litre unblown Grand Prix racers! Thus were born the long-lived Lago Talbots and the V-12 Delahaye which was to cause such a furore in the first race of the season.

In 1933 the Pau Grand Prix had been almost unique for being run off in a snowstorm and earlier on another circuit at Pau Sir Henry Birkin had caused a sensation by converting his 1929 sports car into a 1930 Grand Prix car and nearly carrying off the French Grand Prix itself. Now it was the turn of France's René Dreyfus to win the race of his life in what was essentially a stripped sports car against the latest thing in German Rennwagen. Pau was a typical French 'round-the-houses' circuit which did not favour the high powered German cars as they raced on their way a mere 60 miles away from the battlefields of the Spanish Civil War. When Nuvolari's 308 Alfa caught fire during practice one might have thought from the flames and fury that the war had covered those 60 miles, but it was only Nuvolari being borne ignominiously from his burning car, vowing never again to drive Alfa-Romeo or any other car for that matter. Sadly, he kept the first half, but relaxed the second oath soon after to follow his great compatriots Fagioli and Varzi across the Alps—to Auto-Union. In the race Wimille's Bugatti non-started, as well as Lang's Mercedes and the Alfas, but Dreyfus was there and Caracciola in the new W154 Mercedes and a white peaked cap! [1]

This piece of insouciance was matched and ultimately capped by Dreyfus coolly playing cat-and-mouse with his terrible adversary—as Dreyfus put it in a recent interview with the American Automobile Quarterly: 'I stayed close for a few laps . . . I wanted to see . . . if Rudi . . . had . . . some little surprise. It was not the case. I could hold him without trouble so . . .' then possibly with memories of Spa 1935, . . . 'I dropped back a bit. The exhaust fumes were very bad, very poisonous. . . . After a while . . I attacked Rudi again . . . and squeezed by . . . just to prove I could do it . . . Neubauer was out with his little red and black flag, making "faster" signs. He was not so happy. It made me laugh.' Well it was many a long day before anyone else laughed at a German car and it all rather calls to mind Georges Boillot's talk of 'ridiculing' those earlier Mercedes on the corners, but this time, in an obscure provincial motor race, a French driver in a French car had defeated the very latest thing in Mercedes racing cars, the first time such a thing had happened since the Sarthe Cup at Le Mans in 1913, and before that one had to go back to the early Grand Prix and Gordon Bennett days. As to the race itself, Caracciola had only a 6 secs. lead at half-distance (86 miles) when he refuelled and handed over to Lang which gave Dreyfus a lead of 1 min. 19

[1] Although this is not borne out by the photograph

secs. Lang drove furiously for the rest of the race but it was Dreyfus' day with a car more suited to the circuit and he won by 1 min. 51 secs. at 54.64 m.p.h. with fastest lap to Caracciola at 57.90 m.p.h. Comotti on a similar Delahaye was six laps (c. 10 miles) behind and the stragglers on ancient Maseratis were between fifteen and nineteen laps adrift.

The French Wisdom of Winter was made Madness in May when the circus descended on Tripoli for the last formula Grand Prix over that fastest of all road circuits. Lang, Brauchitsch and Caracciola appeared for Mercedes, with all three types of 3-litre Alfa in principal opposition. Biondetti, on the 16-cylinder was about 10 secs. slower than Lang (140 m.p.h.) in practice, but his challenge never materialized and it was left to Trossi in one of his intermittent and meteoric performances to put in a fast race lap (131.2 m.p.h.) and actually to lead the race on the 9th lap. The authors of The Racing Car were brutally right in describing this Maserati as 'simple and unpretentious and a complete outsider from the point of view of design trends, (and) a merely token effort on the part of the Maserati brothers to support Grand Prix racing' and its appearances during 1938 were all of this order—brilliant speed followed by mechanical disaster. Siena, a long standing Ferrari driver, had a fatal accident on a V-12 Alfa and the Hungarian independent Laszlo Hartmann, an indefatigable supporter of Grand Prix racing during this period, was also killed. Mercedes, however, triumphed 1-2-3, Lang leading Brauchitsch and Caracciola home and Sommer's 308 Alfa 13 mins. 35 secs. behind Lang in 4th: the next two places were filled by the 1½-litre Maseratis of Taruffi and Rocco ahead of Dreyfus' Delahaye which was no less than 25 mins. 49 secs. behind Lang: a fearful beating for the Italians and total eclipse for France.

The next race in the protracted 1938 season was the French Grand Prix, revived for Grand Prix cars after its two-year sports car interlude, and now transferred to the Rheims circuit last used for the race in 1932. France managed to produce four starters—two 4-litre Darracqs (or Lago Talbots if you will) of Etancelin and René Carrière, Wimille's Bugatti and the famed SEFAC, a motoring Rip van Winkle which had slumbered and non-started its way through the 750 kg. formula and was now about to complete its one lap in Grand Prix racing in the hands of Chaboud. Wimille had driven the Bugatti in a preliminary canter in April over a magnificent circuit the Irish had laid out at Cork which included a 6¼-mile straight and was described by The Motor as 'one of the finest in Europe'. True to Bugatti tradition, he managed only three laps in practice and seven cylinders in the race but even so averaged 147.25 m.p.h. over a timed section on the straight. No Delahayes appeared at Rheims, which was as well, and no Alfas either, which was a pity but perhaps understandable after Tripoli and both firms were rumoured to be improving their cars for later in the season.

499 RIP VAN WINKLE: the Sefac about to complete its one lap in Grand Prix racing

500 MOLSHEIM DISAPPOINTMENT: Wimille's Bugatti could only manage three laps in practice and seven cylinders in the race

501 CHEMNITZ CATASTROPHE: At Rheims Müller crashed in practice, while Kautz and Hasse (above) crashed on the 1st lap!

502 RARE EVENT: A delighted Brauchitsch at Reims after one of his infrequent victories

503 Brauchitsch's ill-luck returned on the Ring when his car caught fire

Mercedes, of course, were thoroughly ready and Auto-Union appeared with four new cars—including a stream-liner for Hasse and two others for Müller and Kautz: second string drivers and untried cars they may have been, but they still managed laps between 106 and 107 m.p.h. against the Mercedes bracket of 108/110 m.p.h. and Lang's race record of 105.90 m.p.h.

Müller crashed his Auto-Union in practice, Kautz and Hasse both crashed on the opening lap; Wimille finished a very slow first lap and the Sefac failed to complete its 2nd, leaving the remaining 300 miles to three Mercedes and two Darracqs. Caracciola nearly set his tyres alight on the line and made a very poor start into the bargain so the display of Grand Prix driving on that first lap was not particularly distinguished—perhaps for sheer lack of competitive practice, and Grande Vitesse may not have been so wide of the mark after all when he wrote in *The Motor* after Pau 'I have an idea that Caracciola is not used to the new car yet—I don't mean unused to the speed or the feel, but unused to seeing such high figures indicated on the r.p.m.' Odd though this comment may seem, the fact remains that, by his standards Rudi had a very poor season with a car that was streets ahead of its competitors and was quite unable to repeat his crushing wins of 1935 and 1937. For the record it was Brauchitsch who won the Grand Prix at 101.13 m.p.h. which was slightly slower than Dreyfus' 1935 lap record of 102 m.p.h. on the Ferrari Alfa of 3.2 or $3\frac{1}{2}$-litres. Caracciola was 2nd about 2 mins. behind with a slightly misfiring engine and Lang 3rd, a lap behind following delay in re-starting after a fuel stop. Carrière was 4th and last, 10 laps (c. 50 miles) behind. So, after 24 years, Mercedes had achieved another 1-2-3 in the Grand Prix, a feat only matched by Delage in 1927 in a similar runaway win and Alfa-Romeo in 1932 and 1934 when there had been rather better races. Pau was now a thing of the past and even though there were exciting rumours of Delahayes, newer and faster Talbots and Alfas and Maseratis, and further of Bugatti's challenge to the Germans, for the time being Mercedes were absolutely on their own and for them it had truly become a case of Not Victory But Annihilation.

For their own Grand Prix the Germans fielded their fullest teams—Seaman coming in with a fourth Mercedes and Auto-Union producing Nuvolari for the first time, and recalling Stuck to the colours in their latest cars; Hasse and Müller completed the team on the earlier normally bodied cars that had appeared at Rheims. Alfa sent Farina, Biondetti, Taruffi, Ghersi and Balestrero in a vain effort to make up in quantity what they clearly lacked in quality. Dreyfus and Comotti had Delahayes and the German Pietsch a $1\frac{1}{2}$-litre Maserati. Fast starter Lang set up a 13 second lead on the first lap, followed by Seaman, Caracciola and Brauchitsch then Hasse, Müller, Farina. On the 2nd lap Comotti retired and also Nuvolari after hitting a bank; then Lang fell back with plug troubles and Farina retired but still the three surviving Mercedes dominated the race, followed by the three Auto-Unions, then Lang and then Pietsch's voiturette Maserati ahead of the Alfas and Dreyfus! After seven laps the spectators saw something that had not happened since 1924[2]—an Englishman leading a major continental Grand Prix when Seaman passed Brauchitsch who was changing wheels. A lap later and they had changed places but the miracle had fleetingly happened. Further back Lang handed over to the Mercedes junior, Walter Baümer, former 750 c.c. Austin driver, and prepared to take over from Caracciola who was unwell. At half distance Müller brought his Auto-Union in for routine supplies and handed over to Nuvolari which pleased the crowd but made little other difference.

And so the race seemed set to run its course to another 1-2-3 for Mercedes and a second successive win for Brauchitsch, until his second stop after 16 laps when the refuelling pump overfilled and gushed the highly volatile fuel over the hot exhaust as a flame licked up on re-starting. Of a sudden all was frenzied but organised activity as Brauchitsch detached the steering wheel and leapt out while Neubauer directed the fire fighters, and in all the excitement nearly forgot to send Seaman on his historic way, now with a secure lead over Lang in Caracciola's car. Brauchitsch bravely started again when the fire had been put out but retired soon after and spoilt the completeness of Mercedes' win by letting Stuck into 3rd. Thus it was that after 14 years an Englishman, albeit on a foreign car, won a great continental Grand Prix from N.S.K.K. Chief Storm Leader Lang, also on a Mercedes. Stuck was 3rd nine minutes behind, followed by Nuvolari and Dreyfus who DID manage to beat Pietsch eventually.

During August the racing scene and Alfa Romeo had a much needed reviver when in three races Farina finished 2nd, 2nd and 5th. The first was the Coppa Ciano over the Leghorn circuit which was missed by Auto-Union and Seaman, but Trossi made a sensational appearance with the Maserati seizing the lead in the early stages until his engine burst after four of the 40 laps, leaving Mercedes well ahead again. Caracciola retired and then Brauchitsch stalled on sliding into some straw bales and lost his lead to Lang who seemed set for victory until three laps from the end he had to change a tyre and so lost to Brauchitsch by 39 secs. Subsequently the luckless Brauchitsch was disqualified for receiving outside assistance on restarting, leaving Lang the winner from the 16-cylinder Alfa of Farina, a 12-cylinder driven by Biondetti and Wimille (newly engaged by Alfa-Corse), an older model of Belmondo and Dreyfus' Delahaye no longer even a match for the Italians.

At Pescara Auto-Unions fielded three cars again but without much luck. Nuvolari blew up on the first lap,

504 A rather soulful Maestro samples the new Auto-Union in trials at Monza before his first drive on the Ring

505 In the interim Nuvolari had been trying the Welch Offenhauser at Indianapolis

506 Brauchitsch's ill-luck opened the way for Seaman to score a long overdue victory (centre) from Lang here shaking hands with Hühnlein

[2] This is not to denigrate W. G. Williams who won the first Monaco Grand Prix in 1929 and gave his life in the 2nd World War but this race was hardly of the status of the 1924 French and Spanish Grands Prix.

507 ITALIAN REVIVAL: *Trossi's Maserati chases the winning Mercedes of Lang at Leghorn followed by Farina's Alfa*

508 *The luckless Brauchitsch who was disqualified at Leghorn after passing the post first*

509 . . . 'at Pescara Auto-Union fielded three cars again but without much luck . . .'—Nuvolari leading Hasse

Brauchitsch fell out on the 2nd and then Lang caught fire leaving Caracciola leading Müller and Hasse. Luigi Villoresi, in his first Grand Prix drive, took over Trossi's Maserati and worked his way up to 2nd when Trossi took over only to burst the engine trying to catch Caracciola. When the Mercedes refuelled Müller took an Auto-Union into the lead for the first time in the year but promptly ran out of fuel leaving Caracciola to win from Farina again.

At the end of the month the Swiss Grand Prix attracted the full Mercedes and Auto-Union teams again and English hopes were mightily raised by Seaman's magnificent driving in practice when he achieved fastest lap at 103 m.p.h. The race was over 50 laps and, in spite of heavy rain, Seaman maintained a lead over the field for 11 laps although under tremendous pressure from Caracciola who was still the master in the wet and probably the greatest pre-war driver on the tricky Bremgarten circuit. Seaman drove his best race of the year and probably the best of his life to record fastest

510/11 *At Berne English hopes were raised by Seaman's form in practice (above) but in the race Caracciola's (below) skill in the wet remained undimmed and he took the lead from Seaman after 11 laps*

lap (95.9 m.p.h.) and to finish 2nd only 26 secs. behind Caracciola and a lap ahead of Brauchitsch. Stuck brought his Auto-Union into 4th and the patient Farina was 5th this time with the 16-cylinder Alfa.

The Alfa recovery continued in the Italian Grand Prix, now back at Monza, and Trossi even managed to get his Maserati home in 5th. Rain in the race following fine weather in practice is supposed to have played tricks on the Mercedes' carburetters; although the cars took an early lead, Caracciola of all people had a spin on the 2nd lap, Seaman and Lang retired after 16 and 20 laps leaving only Brauchitsch to struggle on in a shared drive with Caracciola on Rudi's damaged car. After taking the lead on the 8th lap Nuvolari drove faster and faster and won by a lap from Farina, with Brauchitsch/Caracciola 3rd, three laps behind, followed by Biondetti and Trossi. This was Nuvolari's 3rd and last win in his national Grand Prix and this, coupled with Italian cars in 2nd, 4th and 5th gave Italy a very useful record in the last four races.

512 *The Alfa recovery continued at Monza where Farina was 2nd to Nuvolari*

513 *Finally at Donington Nuvolari showed the crowd just why he was called 'Maestro!'*

514/5/6 *At Berne the patient Farina was 5th on Alfa-Romeo (top), Nuvolari (centre) had a bad day for Auto-Union and Jean-Pierre Wimille (bottom) made a welcome return to Grand Prix racing, for Alfa-Romeo*

517 FÜHRERPRINZIP!: . . . 'telling Mercedes they had won quite enough already . . .' here the famous Neubauer with his even more famous flag directs operations at Berne

518 . . . and 'brought a golden glow to the autumn of pre-war motor racing . . .'

Apart from Villoresi's Maserati which never achieved any startling position, the Italians ignored the Donington Grand Prix, as also did Caracciola who was stated not to like the circuit, but once again British spectators were rewarded with a fine race graced by H.R.H. the Duke of Kent and Korpsführer Huhnlein. In the race Nuvolari rolled back the years and the sleeves of his famed yellow sweater and showed the 60,000 crowd just why he was called 'Maestro'. Nuvolari and Müller, who had been improving steadily all the year, led quite easily for Auto-Union until Nuvolari had to stop for a plug change which left Müller just ahead of Seaman and Lang. At this point a back-marker dropped a sump full of oil on the descent to the so-called hairpin and pandemonium broke loose: needless to say the chief beneficiary was Nuvolari, who later 'smiled slightly on recollection and explained that he was taken right off the road well on to the grass, but did not fight the car unduly and so risk turning completely round. Instead he let the car more or less take its own course and continue on the grass back on to the road.' Brauchitsch and Baumer also got through, then Hasse crashed backwards off the road and Seaman stalled unluckily—which lost him his chance of the race. After all these pirouettings Müller still led but now Lang was breathing down his neck in place of Seaman (6th), followed by Nuvolari and Brauchitsch. Lang caught Müller and after all the routine stops were over, with 30 laps to go, he led Müller by 21 secs. and Nuvolari by 58 secs.

In the next ten laps Nuvolari put on the sort of performance Lang and Müller had probably never seen before, passing Müller and picking up 37 secs. on Lang. Aided by Lang's having broken his aero-screen Nuvolari went from strength to strength. He lapped Seaman on the 64th of 80 laps and caught Lang two laps later, it being noted that both Mercedes instantly let him by with a display of exemplary driving manners. Lang finished 2nd 1 min. 38 secs. behind, followed by Seaman, Müller and Brauchitsch all a lap behind. Nuvolari continued in brilliant form at the party after the race telling Mercedes they had won quite enough already and that they might have more luck if they made some new cars! This prophecy was well and truly fulfilled in 1939, but Dr. Feuereissen's was not so happy—'he could safely say all would be here again next year.' It was in fact to be 16 years before a German Grand Prix car raced on English soil again, but the memory of Nuvolari still lives on in his dashing attire of red helmet, yellow sweater and blue trousers as he sat 'grimly at the wheel of his Auto-Union . . . the most perfect subject for colour photography or for a painting,' bringing a golden glow to the autumn of pre-war motor racing.

256

Chapter Twenty Eight
1939 · High Boost

519 Lang who was almost unbeatable in 1939 winning the opening race at Pau

Mercedes had been complying with Nuvolari's 'directions' during the winter and the W163 was a considerable improvement on the 1938 W154 model. Auto-Union too had been busy but scratched from the Pau Grand Prix following Mussolini's ban on Italian drivers, including Nuvolari, racing there. Mercedes thus won an easy victory over an assortment of French machines, including the Sefac. Caracciola had troubles and fell back but Lang and Brauchitsch won much as they pleased. Lang improved the winning average to 56.09 m.p.h. although Caracciola's 1938 record was unbroken. Etancelin, driving with all his old vigour, was a popular and happy 3rd winning a race long battle after his own heart with his old rival Sommer on a 308 Alfa. Seaman had practised at Pau and had actually done fastest lap but did not get a car to drive in a race until the revived Eifelrennen in May. Once again Lang was in fire-cracking form winning at the record average of 84.14 m.p.h. and raising the

lap record to 86 m.p.h. (9 mins. 52.2 secs.); Nuvolari was little slower and finished 2nd only 11.2 secs. behind with Caracciola 3rd, 20 secs. further behind. The Mercedes, of course, stopped once while the Auto-Unions managed to run through non-stop. Seaman retired after a lap and Brauchitsch did little better, but the new Mercedes were obviously an immense improvement on the 1938 cars and Lang had become a driver of the very front rank as a race winner.

The Belgian Grand Prix was revived at Spa on the 26th June and this time full teams of Mercedes and Auto-Union met the Alfas of Farina and Biondetti. The race was run in almost impossible conditions, a heavy downpour reducing driving visibility almost to nil for much of the race. Although Farina jumped the start into an initial lead, he was soon swamped by the German pack led by Müller's Auto-Union, then Lang, then Caracciola, Seaman and Nuvolari. On the 9th lap even Caracciola found the conditions too

520 'Farina (leading still) jumped the start but was soon swamped by the German pack led by Müller's Auto-Union' as they storm up the hill after the start at Spa

521 Brighter skies greet Brauchitsch at Reims where (below)

522 Nuvolari seized an early lead

much for him when he left the road at La Source and was unable to restart his car. Seaman, continuing his magnificent Berne form, moved into 2nd place and then passed Müller keeping an average of 94.39 m.p.h. in those terrible conditions. At the same time Lang moved up to 2nd and Nuvolari came up to 3rd. With 20 out of 35 laps gone Seaman had a good lead over Lang; his average had fallen to 94.19 m.p.h. due to pit-stops but otherwise he had the race well in hand. Two laps later the La Source bend was his undoing; it is generally thought that he took the previous bend too quickly and found himself on the wrong line for La Source. At all events the car went off the road and hit a tree rendering Seaman unconscious while the newly filled tank burst into flames. No help could be given him for 20 or 30 seconds by which time Seaman had suffered burns that proved fatal; this was only the second fatal race accident to a German team driver since 1934 but 'to the world of English motor racing his loss was irreparable. As he himself once remarked when Rosemeyer was killed, it was the greatest blow since the death of Segrave,' and as his great friend George Monkhouse put it . . . 'of one thing I am convinced and that is that Dick died as he would have wished, doing what he like best and with victory in sight.'

Jim Burge, Seaman's former mechanic, attributed his success to 'his phenomenal patience and ability to remain unruffled by the many disappointments and hard luck which beset the best of racing motorists from time to time.' In this way he was perhaps a greater ambassador for England, at a very difficult time in her political history, than even Sir Henry Segrave whom he so much resembled and admired.

Nuvolari, too, had an accident four laps later leaving Lang secure in a lead which he cared so little about that he asked to give up during his second pit stop. He did re-start but dramatically not until his car had got to the very bottom of the hill past the pits with Hasse's Auto-Union right on his tail. Lang went on to win his 3rd Grand Prix of the season in succession—a performance equalled by Caracciola in 1937 and Rosemeyer in 1936, but very remarkable all the same. Caracciola had yet another incident in the French Grand Prix hitting a wall at the Virage de Gueux on the first lap when Nuvolari led the field through in a typical 45-degree slide with Lang hard on his tail. For seven laps these two staged an awe-inspiring battle for the lead which ended when Nuvolari drew to the pits with an engine covered in oil leaving Lang with a lead of 44 secs. over Müller at ten laps and an average of 110 m.p.h.

Soon after Brauchitsch dropped out but Lang was all the time literally soaring farther and farther out on his own sending the lap record up to 114.8 m.p.h. on his 20th lap. Why he had to continue at this tremendous speed is hard to understand and in the end he paid the price—or had Nuvolari forced this in those first seven laps?—falling out after 35 laps with a lead of nearly 2 mins. over Müller. Poor Lang was thus deprived of a fourth successive win but I doubt if he grudged it in the heat of his soul stirring battle with Nuvolari, which had brought the season to life for the first time.

Two weeks later Lang transferred his record breaking activities to the Ring with a practice lap of 9 mins. 43.2 secs. (87.5 m.p.h.) faster even than Rosemeyer's 9 mins. 46.2 secs. in practice for the 1937 Grand Prix. Brauchitsch had done 9 mins. 51 secs. and Caracciola 9 mins. 56 secs., while Müller had borne out his promise with 9 mins. 59.6 secs. As in 1937 Lang led on to the 2nd lap, but this time by no less than 27 secs! Behind him came Brauchitsch, Müller and Pietsch now on a 3-litre Maserati. On the next lap Lang slowed and Pietsch pushed the red of Italy into the lead for the first time in three years. His moment of glory was short lived with Nuvolari and Caracciola pressing strongly and after three laps Nuvolari led from Müller, with only Caracciola left as a serious Mercedes challenger—or so it seemed. The new Mercedes cadet driver was one Heinz Brendel who put in the fastest lap (81.10 m.p.h.) on his 4th lap to bring him up to 5th. He then passed Müller and was now sufficiently favourably placed to justify Neubauer's calling him in for relief by Lang whose 1939 talents were worthy of a more active seat than the pit counter. Brendel, however, overdid things after defiantly refusing to come in and Neubauer's face was a study, particularly when Brendel telephoned for a car to take him back to the pits!

By six laps Caracciola had passed Nuvolari halted briefly at the pits; then Nuvolari had a longer stop for plugs and after allowing for stops it was Hasse who led at half distance from Müller, Caracciola and Nuvolari. Hasse then ran off the road and Caracciola got past Müller for the last time to run out a fairly easy winner of his 6th German Grand Prix. Nuvolari retired after 18 laps leaving Pietsch a worthy 3rd for Maserati, their first Grand Prix 'place' since 1934.

This German Grand Prix was, with the 1938 Donington Grand Prix, the race with the longest spectator interest of the 3-litre formula and was a fascinating battle of tactics between Caracciola and the entire Auto-Union team for 18 of the 22 laps. Nuvolari's plug troubles made Rudi's task a little easier, but it was still a great victory in difficult racing conditions achieved in the classic Caracciola manner and with such ease that it is hard to accept that it was his last win in any motor race. Lang had had a frustrating Grosser Preis following a disappointing French Grand Prix, but he was back again in wonderful fettle for the Swiss Grand Prix on August 20th, the last race before the outbreak of war. During practice he was the fastest with 106.23 m.p.h. and started a firm favourite even against Caracciola who had already won the race in 1935, 1937 and 1938. The race was run in two qualifying heats and a final jointly with a 1½-litre voiturette event. This was the first time such events had been

523 *Then for 7 laps Nuvolari and Lang 'staged an awe-inspiring battle which brought the season to life for the first time . . .'*

524 *'Two weeks later Lang transferred his record breaking activities to the Ring with a practice lap at 87.5 mph . . .'*

259

525 *In the German Grand Prix Pietsch 'pushed the red of Italy into the lead for the first time in three years . . .'*

526 *In the end it was Caracciola who won 'with such ease that it is hard to accept this as his last win in any motor race . . .'*

527 *ALSO-RANS: In 1938/9 Alfa-Romeo, Delahaye and Talbot were generally faint and occasionally pursuing*

528 *LAST LINE-UP: Caracciola (nearest), Brauchitsch and Lang await the flag in the last pre-war race at Berne*

deliberately combined in a full Grande Epreuve since Dieppe in 1912 and, as in 1912, the fastest voiturettes nearly stole the Grand Prix cars' thunder.

Mercedes dominated the Grand Prix heat after an early challenge from Nuvolari had faded and Lang it was who won by 4.8 secs. from Caracciola, in spite of a fastest lap by Rudi at 104.32 m.p.h., with Brauchitsch 3rd. Practice for this race had been much enlivened by the tremendous speed of Farina in the 1½-litre 158 Alfa-Romeo and his best time of 2 mins. 45.2 secs. was faster than Dreyfus' new Maserati, but in the end was beaten by all the German cars. Farina won the voiturette heat as he liked and then absolutely electrified the spectators by holding 2nd place in the combined final for seven whole laps (c.40 miles) behind Lang until Caracciola finally devoured him and tore off in pursuit of Lang. The 30-lap final was too short a race for this great classic and reduced its stature very unnecessarily. It also deprived the spectators of the final round between Caracciola and Lang: old champion versus new champion. As it was, after his poor start Caracciola pulled Lang's lead down from 12 secs. after 20 laps to 3.1 at the finish 50 miles later. This rate of gain would have brought him up with Lang by about the 35th lap if the race had been run for its normal 50 laps and, on the damp tricky Bremgarten surface, there would have been a truly memorable battle as both cars were running well—or, who knows, neither might have lasted and Brauchitsch might have won instead of being 3rd for the 3rd successive year. At all events Rudi narrowly missed his hat-trick, having slightly misjudged his pace in the early stages. In 1934 and 1936 their cars performed poorly, but in the other four years Mercedes had gained every 'place' in the Swiss Grand Prix bar Rosemeyer's 3rd in 1935, while Caracciola had won three times and been 2nd the other time.

The shadows of war had been lowering over Europe even at the time of the Swiss Grand Prix and Hitler's invasion of Poland was two days old when the starter's flag fell at Belgrade for the final event in the 1939 calendar at 5 p.m. on the fateful 3rd September. The race lay between the Mercedes of Brauchitsch and Lang and the Auto-Unions of Nuvolari and Müller. Brauchitsch and Lang went ahead on the twisting hilly round-the-houses circuit, with Müller and Nuvolari biding their time, or just outpaced. With Nuvolari one could never be certain and Brauchitsch paid the price of uncertainty by pressing on that little too hard and spinning. This gave Müller the lead until he stopped for tyres and then it was Nuvolari all the way, even equalling Brauchitsch's lap record for good measure. Lang had a disappointing finale to his *annus mirabilis,* having to retire after being hit by a flying stone from Brauchitsch. Nuvolari's average for the 86-mile race (hardly worthy of a national Grand Prix) was 81.2 m.p.h., Brauchitsch was 2nd and Müller 3rd, and the magnificent six years furore of power and speed was at an end.

529 *The Polish war was two days old when Nuvolari (above in the German Grand Prix) won the Yugoslav Grand Prix*

530 *Right. GRAND FINALE: Brauchitsch 'opposite locks' towards the Cloud Capped Towers of the Grossglockner as the mists fall and the shadows of war lengthen*

During the eight pre-war seasons, 1932-9, motor racing had been almost continuously alive as never before as first the blue and red and then the silver cars thundered over European road and track circuits, raising dust and records, to say nothing of sieg-heiling German right arms and spectators' pulse beats everywhere they went. Now it was over and this time for seven years while 12 years were to pass before the W163.s raced again against a new generation of cars and drivers, and Auto-Union went to share the long eternal sleep of Fiat, Delage, Sunbeam, Peugeot and the other departed champions.

531 MOST SUCCESSFUL: If Caracciola was the most successful driver in winning three European Championships and more races . . .

534 . . . 'and Auto-Union went to share the long eternal sleep of Fiat, Delage, Sunbeam, Peugeot and other departed champions . .'

532 . . . Nuvolari was the greatest and probably the most versatile for the skill with which he had taken to the rear engined Auto-Unions . . .

535 . . . 'and the magnificent six year furore of power and speed was at an end . . .'

533 . . . while 12 years were to pass before the W 163's raced again against a new generation (Lang chases Gonzalez in the Argentine Temporada of 1951) . . .

Chapter Twenty Nine
Voiturette Interlude the Second

...'Young boys and girls
Are level now with men; the odds is gone
And there is nothing left remarkable'
          Wm. Shakespeare: Antony and Cleopatra

But for the 1914 war the Coupe de l'Auto would have been limited to 2½-litre cars, after being a 3-litre race in the four preceding years. After the war the Grand Prix first took over the old voiturette limit of 3-litres and then went by stages through 2-litres down to 1½, once again following a previous voiturette limit which had been popular in the period 1921/5. During the ensuing years 1100 c.c. or 1½-litres continued as the generally accepted limits for voiturette events which tended to precede the big races and to become specialised events of their own. Thus by 1937 there was a considerable voiturette calendar contested hotly by Bugatti, Maserati and E.R.A. Since 1935 E.R.A. had been having the best results overall though everyone had been well and truly worsted by Seaman's modernised 1927 Delage in 1936. Unhappily Prince Chula did not continue the good work of Seaman and Ramponi and this great car did not survive to challenge the new Italian cars which appeared in 1938. The

English E.R.A.s were becoming rather long in the tooth by this time and in any case, not being classic racing cars by the standards of the old Delage, they were unlikely to be able to cope with the new cars from Italy which were conceived along real Grand Prix lines.

The first was the 16-valve 4CL Maserati and the second the 158 Alfa-Romeo (or Alfette or Alfetta as they were often called before the war—a most detestable and undignified diminutive). With the decline of the Italian effort in Grand Prix racing after 1936, more and more attention was focused on these cars to the point when Ferrari commissioned Colombo in 1937 to create a 1½-litre Alfa, which in original form developed a modest 190 b.h.p. at 6500 r.p.m. compared to Seaman's reliable 195 b.h.p. with the Delage, but with their shorter stroke and simpler design they were obviously capable of very considerable development.

During 1938 they won the voiturette events before the Coppa Ciano and Italian Grand Prix but lost to Maserati, due to plug troubles, at Pescara and Modena. These victories decided the Italians to change all their 1939 races to 1½-litre affairs, significantly including the highly lucrative Tripoli Grand Prix. By this time, however, it was a reasonable certainty that the new formula due to begin in 1941 would at

536 *CLASSIC RACING CAR: 'Everyone had been worsted by Seaman's modernised 1926/7 Delage . . .'*

537 *'. . . A modest 190 bhp at 6,500 rpm . . .'—The Type 158 in original 1938 form*

least contain some opening for 1½-litre cars not only because there were plenty of them but also because, as the late Brian Twist wrote after Pietsch's performance in the 1938 German Grand Prix,

'*It seems, indeed, that greater equality would exist under the formula if the 4½-litre unblown cars were matched against the 1½-litre, instead of 3-litre supercharged machines. It is early yet, however, and no doubt the former type will be developed.*'

In the end the 4½-litre car was developed and, oddly enough by Enzo Ferrari himself in direct competition with his own original brain-child, the 158 Alfa, but it was to take nearly 13 years to bridge the gap. By the end of 1938 the 158 was the most potent voiturette in existence but was still very unreliable while the Maseratis, if not quite so unreliable, were less powerful and posed all the well known Maserati handling problems. However the Italians were not the only constructors who could read signs of the times and experiments with V-8 and V-12 1½-litre engines were also going on apace in Stuttgart and Chemnitz, which resulted in two V-8 Mercedes appearing at Tripoli in May 1939 driven by Lang and Caracciola. Against them were ranged no less than 25 Maseratis, including three works 4CL.s for Trossi, L. Villoresi and Cortese, and six Alfas in the capable hands of Farina, Biondetti, Pintacuda, Severi, E. Villoresi and Aldrighetti.

The W165 Mercedes was the greatest miracle of express racing car construction since Henry's 5-litre Indianapolis Ballot and, like almost every Mercedes, it went. The car itself in Pomeroy's expression 'was redolent of Untertürkheim practice' and was twin blown with a V-8 engine of 64 × 58 mm. producing 260 b.h.p. at 8500 r.p.m. Subsequently with two stages of supercharge, derived from development of the

538 *SURPRISE FOR IL DUCE!: The W 165 Mercedes-Benz embarks for Tripoli in 1939*

539 *LIKE ALL MERCEDES IT WENT: The cars of Lang (16) and Caracciola on the line with two Alfas facing Marshal Balbo's flag*

540 *KING OF TRIPOLI: Lang speeds to his 3rd successive win*

W163, the engine yielded 278 b.h.p. at 8250 r.p.m. By the time war broke out, Auto-Union had a V-12 1½-litre engine producing even more power (327 b.h.p. at 9000 r.p.m.) but this did not appear in racing form, although the 1½-litre Cisitalia gave a useful idea of what the Auto-Union would have been like in all matters bar actual performance. The authors of 'The Racing Car' have well described the production of the W165 as 'a technical exercise of extreme severity' and the Mercedes racing department was richly rewarded. By reason of their great speed and extreme similarity to the W163, which had already appeared at Pau, the Italians must have thought at first that they were up against the Grand Prix cars as Lang and Caracciola sailed right away with no apparent effort. Only Farina was able to offer any challenge, actually leading Caracciola to start with; however, the Alfa team wilted in the glaring heat until only Emilio Villoresi remained to limp home nearly eight minutes behind Lang and 4 mins. 10 secs. behind Caracciola. None of the works Maseratis even lasted out the first lap and the Italian defeat was total and humiliating. Lang's winning speed of 122.91 m.p.h. was fractionally slower than Caracciola's W25 in 1935 and quite a deal slower than the 1936/8 speeds. Oddly enough Lang's fastest lap was only 133.5 m.p.h. against Villoresi's streamlined Maserati which practised at 134 m.p.h. In spite of many exciting rumours in the early post-war years the W165 never raced again although they were at the Ring for the Eifelrennen when Seaman tried the car and described it in a letter to Monkhouse, 'It is very small and light to handle, but definitely goes, especially around slow corners. It is extremely easy to drive,' and then being a man of his times, 'However I must say I like the 3-litre better simply because it is more interesting.' Seaman's attempt to persuade Mercedes to enter the car for the Nuffield Trophy on June 10th at Donington sadly proved abortive.

Significantly Alfa-Romeo raced no more until the Coppa Ciano in August and by this time the cars had been considerably improved in detail besides being changed externally. As a result they won the Coppas Ciano and Acerbo and the Berne 1½-litre event with great ease in August 1939 and then swamped the decks in the last European motor race at Tripoli in 1940. This time Farina won at the greatly increased average of 128.22 m.p.h. compared to Varzi's 129.01 in 1936 and Lang's all time record in 1937 of 132.03 m.p.h.; Biondetti was 2nd and Trossi, back with Alfas after a long Maserati interlude, 3rd. Mercedes participation would have given the race an added interest but German motor power was then engaged in a more deadly battle in Northern France. At this stage the cars were probably in the form in which they appeared in 1946 when output had been increased to 254 b.h.p. at 7500 r.p.m., conversion to a roller bearing crankshaft having been made after the 1939 Tripoli débâcle.

541 UNFORTUNATE: The E-type E.R.A. of Arthur Dobson went well at Rheims and Albi (above) in 1939 but flopped sadly after the war

542 HISTORIC MOMENT: The start of the Bois de Boulogne race in 1945 with Etancelin leading with a Monza Alfa from Gérard, No. 4 Maserati and Sommer, No. 2 Talbot

543 'IT HAD TO LAST SOMMER A LONG TIME': Sommer leads Wimille (left) and Farina (right) at St. Cloud, with Nuvolari (4) in 5th place

544 'The Alfas also raced at Geneva where Farina (42) won from a sour-looking Wimille (18) . . .'

545 . . 'at Turin when Varzi finished one second ahead . . '

546 . . . 'and finally at Milan where it was Trossi's turn'

During 1947-51 Grand Prix racing was governed by the 4½-litres—unblown and 1½-litres blown limit that had long been anticipated and at first even the most advanced cars were modified versions of pre-war racers. There was also a strong element of 'Carried Forward' about most of the drivers, the leading Frenchmen being pre-war veterans like Sommer, Wimille, Chiron and Etancelin while the Italians fielded Varzi, Trossi, Taruffi and occasionally Nuvolari himself of the Old Guard plus Farina, Villoresi and Cortese of the more recent pre-war vintage. Alfa-Romeo also called on their head tester Consalvo Sanesi who was a newcomer. A large number of English independents ventured on to the continent with an assortment of E.R.A., Maserati, Alfa and Delage cars, including the unfortunate E-Type E.R.A. No national Grands Prix were run until 1947, although the first post-war race had taken place in the Bois de Boulogne on 9th September 1945. The 1946 races were many and varied but only those attended by the 158 Alfas could be said to have even remote Grand Prix stature. Their first appearance was on a short hilly circuit at St. Cloud on the outskirts of Paris on June 9th 1946. The front two rows contained Sommer (Maserati) and Wimille (Alfa), then Farina (Alfa) and Nuvolari (Maserati)—which about summed up the 1946 story. Sommer was at last coming into his own as a Grand Prix driver; Farina continued his long and successful career with Alfa; Wimille was setting himself up as the greatest driver of the 1945/9 period and Nuvolari was—just Nuvolari as long as his car or his health lasted.

The Alfas were reputed to have spent the later war years in a cheese factory and this disagreed with them rather more than actual burial had with the Bugatti voiturettes during the old war, for both Wimille and Farina retired with suspected transmission troubles leaving Sommer with the honour of being the last driver to win over the Alfas for five years. No one deserved this more but it had to last Sommer a long, long time. The Alfas also raced in the Grand Prix des Nations at Geneva, where Farina won, at Turin when Varzi finished one second ahead of Wimille and finally at Milan where it was Trossi's turn for one of his rare wins, achieved while coolly smoking his famous pipe. Behind these easily driven cars the battle usually raged fast and furious between the Maserati drivers, led by Sommer, Villoresi, Nuvolari and a Swiss pre-war voiturette driver, Baron de Graffenreid and occasionally Reg. Parnell who was beginning now to make a name for himself as Britain's most experienced driver in continental racing on his 1939 16-valve 4CL Maserati. When the Alfas were not racing the leading Maserati drivers had a good scrap among themselves with a mixture of French quasi-sports Delage, Delahaye and Talbot in vain pursuit. Also, as it was formule libre, Wimille kept his hand in with a 308 Alfa.

Although the 1946 season had been somewhat of shreds

and patches it was an immensely creditable beginning bearing in mind the havoc wrought by six years of total war on such obvious things as road, rail and sea transport, leave alone problems of supply, renewal of parts and general lack of expert knowledge particularly among the English fraternity. In spite of all this no less than nineteen races were run on the continent compared to but one in England and as John Eason Gibson put it:

'the intervening years seemed to fade like a bad dream ... straw bales lined the road, footbridges were going up and flags and streamers showed garishly against the white buildings ... right up to starting time there were few officials and certainly no spectators who knew precisely who would be driving what ...

then the most magical words
' "*Nuvolari is coming ... "*' and everybody knew that the sport had woken from its long war-laden slumber.

547 . . . '*Also as it was formule libre Wimille kept his hand in with a 308 Alfa . . .*'

548 MOST MAGICAL: '*the words—Nuvolari is coming—and everyone knew that the sport had woken . . .*' Here Nuvolari leads Sommer at Marseilles

Chapter Thirty
1947-8 · Quadrifoglio Supremo

Once Alfa Romeo had set their tackle in order after St. Cloud they won every race for which they entered until the British Grand Prix of 1951 and were not seriously challenged until the big unblown Ferrari appeared in the Italian Grand Prix of 1950. Five years of unchallenged supremacy with a car that was first designed in 1937 is a remarkable thought and an even more remarkable achievement which involved increases in b.h.p. of just over 50 per cent. and in r.p.m. of 40 per cent. over the original 1938 figures. Whilst it is unlikely that Alfas would have maintained such supremacy in the face of German competition, this does not detract from the excellence and skill of their development work over the years and the basic soundness of the design which permitted it.

Maserati too subjected their original 1939 car, the 4CL, to the same intensive development though their challenge had dwindled to nothing by 1950. This car had a 4-cylinder (78 × 78 mm.) 16-valve single-stage blown engine mounted in a box-section chassis frame with torsion bar i.f.s., good old ¼-elliptic rear springs and a live axle. The car was modified to the extent of a tubular frame in 1947 and designated the 4CLT and yet again in 1948 when it acquired two stages of supercharge and a longer and altogether sleeker body thanks to a lower tubular frame. In general form this car developed 260 b.h.p. at 7500 r.p.m. using a supercharger pressure of about 24 p.s.i. and had a road speed of about 160 m.p.h. and was known as the 4CLT/48 or San Remo model. Some cars were further developed to give another 20 b.h.p. or thereabouts but like the Psalmist's four-score years these cars were nothing but labour and sorrow to their owners.

The English E.R.A.s were 6-cylinder high-push-rod affairs developed from the 1933 Riley raced by Raymond Mays, and had high old fashioned chassis mostly employing short stiff semi-elliptic springs all round. Pomeroy quotes 190 b.h.p. at 7500 r.p.m. as the probable peak of performance of the A-B-C-D-type versions while the E-type was originally bench tested at 7000 r.p.m. when it developed 260 b.h.p. In 1939 this was a very satisfactory starting figure and would have stood comparison with the W165 itself. In practice for the 1½-litre event before the French Grand Prix the E-Type was reputed to have touched 170 m.p.h. down one of the straights but its post-war record belied such a thought and the car was still manifestly unready for serious racing long after sheer lack of performance had rendered it obsolete. Pomeroy sums this sorry car up succinctly.

'the skill exhibited in the detail design fell considerably short of the imagination shown in broad concept and despite considerable efforts made by the works under new organisation it was not possible to make the car raceworthy in its original form . . .'

or any other, as Peter Walker, Reg. Parnell, Peter Whitehead or Leslie Johnson would confirm.

The French Talbot was a development of the pre-war cars and like the E.R.A. was a push-rod six-cylinder with origins in the early or mid thirties. The 4½-litre engine (93 × 110 mm.) turned lazily over at 5000 r.p.m. producing 250 b.h.p. and a road speed of 155 m.p.h. Reliable almost to a fault this quasi-sports car had its odd day of glory when its faster brethren fell by the wayside but was never a serious challenger to the supercharged cars, as it could never get near enough to them to take advantage of its superior petrol and tyre consumption and on the one occasion when Sommer managed to do this, the engine rebelled.

During 1947-51 the voiturette class—or Formula 2 as it came to be known—was for 2-litre unblown cars and this class soon became dominated by a new car with a famous ancestry—the Ferrari. The formidable Commendatore had produced an 8-cylinder sports car which had been driven by a certain Alberto Ascari in the Mille Miglia of 1940 and after the war severed his connection with Alfa-Romeo along with Colombo and Bazzi, an old Scuderia man, to develop his own cars. These were based on a Colombo designed V-12 1½-litre sports car which was converted into a Grand Prix car in 1948 with the addition of a single-stage supercharger in time for the Italian Grand Prix at Turin. The engine originally had only a single overhead camshaft and was fitted in a very short chassis which made it hard to handle though, needless to say, Sommer tamed it to the extent of finishing 3rd to Wimille's Alfa and Villoresi's Maserati at Turin. By degrees during 1949 and 1950 it acquired both de Dion and swing rear axles, a longer chassis, two-stage supercharging and twin camshafts and romped away with the important races whilst Alfas had one of their Sabbatical years in 1949. Ferrari, however, like Bugatti, whom he so much resembled in rugged individualism, had a small

549 NEW CAR, FAMOUS ANCESTRY: Farina in the 1948 1½-litre single stage blown Ferrari at Turin

550/1 GREAT MIGHT-HAVE-BEEN: Two views of the Porsche designed Grand Prix Cisitalia

552 FAINT BUT PURSUING: the French Talbot which had its odd day of glory when its faster brethren fell by the wayside

553 The B.R.M. was a triumph of bold imaginative thinking—Raymond Mays demonstrates the original car in 1950

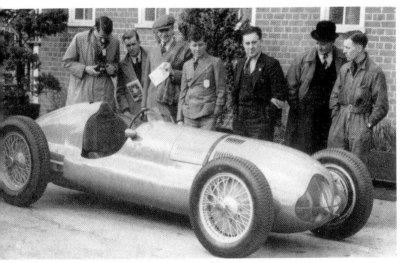

554 'In 1939 this was a very satisfactory starting figure'—the E-type E.R.A. in original form on test at Brooklands

555 . . . 'when it acquired a longer and sleeker body . . .'—the 4CLT/48 or San Remo Maserati

organisation which could not then cope with the expensive development and maintenance required by a highly stressed and complex blown car, so in 1949 his thoughts turned to the long abandoned Cinderella of the formula—the big unblown.

By this time he had an abundance of good chassis available and a new engineer, Aurelio Lampredi, to design and develop the engines. During 1950 first a 3.3-litre, then a 4.1-litre and finally the full $4\frac{1}{2}$-litre car appeared and gave the Alfas a very unwelcome fright in the Geneva and Italian Grands Prix. By 1951 the car was really ready to take on all comers and with Alfa-Romeo at the end of their development tether a series of races ensued which were as memorable as the titanic battles between Mercedes and Auto-Union.

Having tamed the original Grand Prix Ferarri Sommer went independent in 1949/50 with a Talbot in the interims of trying to coax some worthwhile performance out of the B.R.M., a British project conceived by the old E.R.A. combine of Mays and Berthon but this time on a national scale. This was not Sommer's first experience of such a project as he had been associated with the French C.T.A.-Arsenal in 1947. This was a V-8 engine of 60 × 65 mm. designed by M. Lory of vintage Delage fame which produced the very respectable test bed figures of over 270 b.h.p. employing 30 lbs. of boost from two stages of supercharge. Chassis and transmission were not M. Lory's work and were not good. It made two racing appearances—the first when the transmission broke at the start of the 1947 French Grand Prix and the second in practice for the 1948 event. The B.R.M. was a horse of a very different colour in that when it went it was one of the most thrilling racing cars of all time: the sadness was that it went too seldom and too late.

The car bristled with technical novelty at every point and posed problems of design, metallurgy, supply of materials and development work that would have taxed to the utmost the full pre-war resources of Stuttgart and Chemnitz combined. As it was, for a country house assembly shop to have attempted such a thing in post-war England was like asking Blériot to have flown the Atlantic in 1909. None the less it was the brilliant inspiration of this design, to say nothing of the continued irritation engendered by its failures, that played a very substantial part in bringing about the revival of British motor racing in the following years. In basic conception the car went on where the W163 Mercedes had left off—indeed the transmission and rear axle arrangements were very similar to the Mercedes of 1937/9. Air struts were used in the suspension, and ultimately disc brakes, but it was in the engine specification that the real magic of the car lay. This was a V-16 of 49.53 × 47.8 mm., with two valves per cylinder developing a conservative 430 b.h.p. at 11000 r.p.m. Fuel injection was the ultimate aim but, as raced, the mixture was drawn from two carburetters by a two-stage centrifugal supercharger devised by Rolls-Royce. In ultimate form the engine was developing 585 b.h.p. at maximum r.p.m. when the coil ignition was responsible for producing 85000 sparks per minute! During the years of the formula for which it was built the car started in three races, left the grid in two and finished in one, so those sparks were not so hard worked after all, but it was a triumph of bold imaginative thinking at a time when such virtues were rather at a premium in the depressed mood of post-war England.

At least the British engineers did better than the Italo/German Type 360 Cisitalia. This was designed to the order of Dusio by Dr. Porsche and was in many ways a 1½-litre Auto-Union, being developed by von Eberhorst who had been concerned with 1938/40 Auto-Union development. Writing in 1954/60 Pomeroy considered it 'the most interesting post-war racing car (and) one of the most ingenious design studies in the whole history of motor racing', and with the brains and experience available it was pity indeed that the funds to develop the car proved so lacking. The V-12 engine measured 56×51 mm., different from the experimental V-12 Auto-Union of 53×56 mm., but post-war emphasis was on bigger bore than stroke and the Cisitalia should have produced nearly 450 b.h.p. at 10500 r.p.m. Working on the Auto-Union figure of an actual 327 b.h.p. at 9000 r.p.m. in the early stages, Pomeroy's estimates are wholly acceptable even to an ultimate 550 b.h.p. assuming a reliable 12000 r.p.m. The real interest of the car, however, lay in its four-wheel drive and with the B.R.M. it must sadly go down as one of the greatest might-have-beens in the history of racing car design.

A bewildering series of races were held on the continent in 1947; only three of consequence were graced by the 158 Alfas—the Grands Prix of Switzerland, Belgium and Italy. At Berne there were heats and a final of 136 miles—rather an ersatz Grand Prix but a start to the post-war series of national Grandes Epreuves none the less. Even in this short distance Sommer's highly stressed Speluzzi-modified 2-stage 4CLT Maserati had to make a fuel stop while the Alfas were able to go through non-stop. Wimille led comfortably throughout to his appointed win followed by Varzi; behind them Sommer was thrusting really hard to make up for the double handicap of a slower car and a pit stop. Trossi and Sanesi on the other Alfas had some inferior fuel which slowed them, but nothing like Sommer's fuel stop which took the unbelievable time of 66 secs. Times had certainly changed since the earlier Swiss Grands Prix.

Sommer maintained his lead over Sanesi and so had the satisfaction of beating one Alfa at least, which was more than anyone else managed to do that year. In fact this was only achieved in equal fight by one other driver until the advent of the 4½-litre Ferrari—Villoresi who brought a

4CLT/48 Maserati into 3rd ahead of Sanesi at Berne in 1948; in addition Rosier (Talbot) finished 3rd ahead of Farina at Spa and 2nd ahead of Fagioli at Pescara in 1950, but in each of these cases the beaten Alfa had been slowed with mechanical troubles and had only limped in.

The Spa circuit had been speeded up by replacing the hairpin on the uphill climb after the start by a long curve, thus making pre-war comparisons misleading. Sommer did another of his Sanesi-teases blasting his way past him into 3rd on the 8th lap and holding on to it with might and main for five laps until the frame and a front cross member gave way! Wimille was seemingly not content to let Varzi have his turn on the winner's rostrum and they had a considerable duel in spite of all signals until Varzi stopped for over 11 minutes near the end for a replacement brake pipe characteristically 'looking incredibly angry and smoking everybody else's cigarettes.' Even so Varzi managed to finish 2nd, with Trossi 3rd after being delayed by a flying stone cutting his face—such a walk-over reminded Peter Hull of the 1925 Grand Prix of Europe at Spa 'when the Alfa Romeo drivers sat down to an impromptu meal in their pit so far ahead were their cars.' It is a strange and terrible thought how heavily the hand of tragedy lay over those two magnificently invincible teams of drivers in the European Grands Prix of 1925 and 1948—Ascari, Campari, Brilli Peri, Wimille and Varzi all died at the wheel and Trossi of serious illness.

556 Wimille, seemingly not content to let Varzi have his turn wins the revived Grand Prix de l'Europe at Spa in 1947

557 *GREMLINS ON THE WARPATH!*: New star Ascari looks disbelievingly at yet another Maserati tale of woe

558 *In the revived Italian Grand Prix at Milan Varzi leads a Maserati, Trossi who won and a modified sports Delage*

Another reminder of those great days came the following week when the name Ascari appeared in a French race programme for the first time in 22 years, but now on a 4CLT Maserati, entered by the Scuderia Ambrosiana. The fledgling Alberto drove a good fast race without ever leading, until his car retired with the inevitable Maserati thrombosis. At Nice a fortnight later, Ascari managed to finish 4th, after lying 3rd to Villoresi and Sommer for much of the race and 2nd after Sommer retired. After another retirement at Comminges in August he confirmed his immense promise in the Italian Grand Prix at Milan achieving 3rd fastest lap in the race and attracting the following tribute from John Eason Gibson, one of the shrewdest judges of a racing driver

'*Ascari (behind Trossi, Varzi and Sanesi) meanwhile was astonishing the crowd, and the experts ... and there were many excited spectators to be heard comparing him with his famous father and hailing him as a "nuovo astro del firmamento automobilistico Italiano."*'

After this his Maserati pulled out another gremlin from its capacious bag in the shape of disintegrating bodywork, necessitating a long pit stop which dropped him into 5th place behind the four Alfas of Trossi, Varzi, Sanesi and mechanic Gaboardi in the place of the disgraced Wimille.

Although they are strictly outside our terms of reference the two races at Modena and Turin at the end of season should just be mentioned as marking the first wins of two names that were shortly to become inextricably interwoven into the rich pattern of motor racing's highest honours—Ferrari and Ascari. In preparation for the prospective Formula 2, for blown 500 c.c. and unblown 2-litre cars, both races attracted the 6-cylinder 2-litre Maseratis of Ascari and Villoresi and a single V-12 2-litre Ferrari driven by Cortese at Modena and Sommer at Turin. Cortese made fastest lap and led till he had a series of pit stops; then a bad accident involving a Delage driven by Bracco led to the stopping of the race which was awarded to Ascari. Two weeks later at Turin over the Grand Prix circuit Sommer won the first Ferrari victory of all on a car that was clearly superior to anything e!se on the circuit—a rare experience for Sommer who really went motor racing in between his hilarious pit stops. His average for the 313 miles is variously given—Eason Gibson puts it at 67.5 *and* 2.88 m.p.h. faster than Varzi in the 158 Alfa which won in 1946, but R. King-Farlow's records shew that Varzi's average was 67.72 compared to 67.68 m.p.h. by Sommer! Thus quickly has Ferrari's first win become lost in the mists of legend.

Just before these minor events the French Grand Prix had been revived and at Lyons—not over the great circuits of 1914 and 1924 it is true, and without any Alfas, but it really brought European racing back to itself to have THE Grand

Prix starting again. Sommer was driving another new car—the C.T.A. Arsenal—which had ignition and almost permanent suspension troubles in practice and met with disaster on the starting line when the clutch jammed, then freed itself with such violence that it broke the back axle. Chiron had one of his great days here passing the fastest Maseratis in his single-seater Talbot and gammoning the unhappy Louveau in wonderful style in the closing stages. Apparently the Talbot was then suffering from a blown head gasket and 'although most of the time the engine was running on all six it made horrible noises when opened out. Thus to prevent Louveau's pit staff from learning the horrible truth and urging him to harry the Talbot, Chiron was forced to motor fairly gently when within earshot of the pits; and being Chiron of course, he smiled happily every time he came through, making lots of confident gestures—not only to his own pit but to friend Louveau's as well.' Motor races are not always won by the right foot alone and for sheer brass it is akin to the story of Walter Hagen, on the last green late in the day with one long putt for a one-stroke win, hauling his opponent out of the club-house to see him sink it. It would have needed all the talents of Stephen Potter himself to have judged a contest in Lifemanship between those two exponents. In the place where his father too had made his first appearance in the Grand Prix Ascari responded nobly to the calls of tradition by making fastest lap jointly with Villoresi and de Graffenried. Chiron's great contemporary Varzi was not racing at Lyons but had managed to win the unimportant Bari Grand Prix on a 158 Alfa in July from Sanesi and another pair of old timers—Balestrero and his 2.3 Monza Alfa-Romeo.

1947 had brought some long distance races and four national Grands Prix, Ferrari's racing début as competitor and winner, and a new driver of the first importance in Alberto Ascari. Alfa-Romeo were still quite unbeatable, and virtually uncatchable unless your name happened to be Sommer. The 4CLT Maserati was becoming distinctly time expired and the Talbot was not remotely quick enough and even after two full seasons pit work was described in scathing terms by Eason Gibson as being of 'lamentable standard. . . . Many drivers overshot their pits when coming in for fuel and when they did select the correct stall their staff seemed remarkably uninterested in getting the job done quickly and efficiently.' This and all the stops for fuel and plugs, plugs and yet more plugs: how long ago it all seems now!

During the year little had been heard of Nuvolari after his drive in the Mille Miglia, which will go down to history as one of his most epic. Driving an 1100 c.c. Cisitalia with exiguous open coachwork in the vilest of weather conditions the old sick maestro dominated the race in spirit and, for almost its full distance, in time and speed as well. His main rival was Biondetti on an unblown 2.9 Alfa saloon, who gained on the flat fast stretches, but on the tricky mountain sections there was still none to touch Nuvolari even at 56. At Rome after 444 miles he led by seven minutes; after an automobile autostrada section to Florence Biondetti had cut this to 4 mins.; between Florence and Bologna, as the news of his driving thrilled across Italy, Nuvolari had opened the gap to 9 mins. but in both controls he had had to stay in the car for fear of collapsing if he got out and as the weather worsened Biondetti closed for a kill he must have at least half wished not to make. Before Turin Nuvolari's engine had electrical troubles in the flooding rain and this lost time which he could never regain try as he might. In the end Biondetti beat him by the small margin of 15 mins. 4 secs., but Nuvolari's was the glory.

559 GAMESMAN EXTRAORDINARY: Louis Chiron winning the 1947 French Grand Prix

560 Right. THE TRUE GLORY: Nuvolari whose driving in the Mille Miglia of 1947/8 will go down to history shewn in the 1948 race

Alfa-Romeo made four appearances again in 1948 for the Swiss (European), French, Italian and Monza Grands Prix with their team of Wimille, Varzi, Trossi and Sanesi. After a very backwoods season in 1947· Farina came back in winning form to win the Grand Prix des Nations and the revived Monaco Grand Prix at the beginning of 1948 with an improved 4CLT Maserati. His fastest lap at Monaco of 62.32 m.p.h. compares interestingly with Caracciola's 1937 record of 66.99 m.p.h. and his average of 59.61 m.p.h. would have won the race in any year but 1937. For the 3rd time Chiron finished 2nd, this time in a Talbot and de Graffenried was a good 3rd. At one time the amazing Wimille had an 1100 c.c. Simca in 2nd and was lying 3rd when his engine gave up the unequal struggle after 60 of the traditional 100 laps. Nuvolari on a Cisitalia retired without playing much part in the race. Still on the Riviera a new Maserati—the 4CLT/48 or 'San Remo' model—appeared in the San Remo Grand Prix and won in the hands of Alberto Ascari who thus scored his first true Grand Prix win. Chiron had retired in this race as did another great veteran, making a come-back in his old love Maserati after nine years—the burly Luigi Fagioli.

561 For the 1948 Monaco Grand Prix Farina was back in winning form . . .

562 . . . while Wimille amazed everybody by the speed of his 1,100 cc Simca

By an odd twist of fate the third member of the great Italian triumvirate, Achille Varzi, now finished his last race (3rd) in the Nuvolari Cup at Mantua in a Cisitalia after the donor himself had led the field easily for eight of the 30 laps in a Ferrari. In practice for the Swiss Grand Prix Varzi took out a newly developed Alfa—the 158A or 158/47—in rain and mist and made one of his rare errors of judgment on the dangerous quarry section. The car overturned killing Varzi almost instantaneously; at least, there was nothing Louis Chiron could do to save his old team-mate and friend when he arrived on the scene of the tragedy a few seconds later. Apart from his sensational end-over-end crash at Tunis in 1936 this was Varzi's first serious accident in twenty years' racing and almost certainly his first serious error of judgment—a record even more remarkable than Caracciola's which only the more underlines the cruelty of his final luck. One of the happiest things, historically speaking, about the great Alfa years was the remarkably successful way in which they were able to resuscitate the great Italian maestri of the thirties—first Varzi in 1946/8, then Fagioli in 1950/1—and it has always been a sadness to me that Nuvolari himself was not given a run as well, but perhaps his oaths at Pau in 1938 had been too lasting! Tragedy stalked the wet Bernese woods that July week-end, for in the race the veteran Italian motor-cyclist and voiturette driver Tenni crashed fatally as did the Swiss driver Kautz when his Maserati hit a tree, involving de Graffenried and Fagioli also on Maseratis. There was also a multiple pile-up in the voiturette event won by Taruffi, with another old friend Hans Stuck 2nd, both on Cisitalias.

Wimille and Trossi had matters very much their own way, even though the new Maseratis of Villoresi, Ascari and Farina were an obvious improvement on the 4CLT's and Villoresi actually brought his into 3rd ahead of Sanesi's Alfa. Wimille had a quick stop for water and staged a grandstand finish into the slanting evening sun with Trossi, who won—his last win, too, as it turned out, before his sad death in 1949. Alfas came to the French Grand Prix a fortnight later for the first time since 1935; when last they had raced in The Grand Prix at Rheims they had been led to a triumphant 1-2-3 win by Nuvolari in the 2.6-litre monoposto in 1932. Now they were back again with three equally outstanding cars led by Jean-Pierre Wimille, who had himself striven vainly against the all conquering monopostos in that same race. With him were Sanesi and Ascari driving his one and only race for his famous father's firm. In practice Wimille, with the 158A made a tremendous effort to better Lang's pre-war records of 117.5 (practice) and 114.87 (race) but, in spite of a specially cleared circuit, could only manage 112.1 m.p.h., which even so was really remarkable on this high speed circuit with a car only half the size.

Whether there was anything really amiss with his car, or simply that he just wished to have some fun passing and repassing, Wimille made three extra pit stops, the last being to take on water due to a damaged radiator. This added a little interest to the race, this and Villoresi with the 4CLT/48 Maserati getting among the Alfas in the early laps, although with the Maserati's engine lacking the endurance of the Lord's mercy, Villoresi's fall was inevitable: Villoresi, who, in the later post-war years with his greying hair was to become the doyen of racing drivers, shared his 4CLT/48 with the Maestro himself. The great man had left his Ferrari at the frontier and claimed to have come on a busman's holiday! But then he had said he was at Berne in 1937 to drive his Contax not Auto-Unions. He told T. G. Moore he was going to drive till he died 'and I'm not dead yet' and that he looked forward to trying the new Ferrari in some small races before the Italian Grand Prix. In the race he drove a few characteristically very quick laps over the circuit where he had won Alfa's memorable victory in 1932 and had battled magnificently with Lang in 1939 and, with that, vanished quietly from the Grand Prix scene to die in his bed on 10th August 1953. One by one the great ones of the thirties were falling by the wayside though Chiron and Fagioli still seemed indestructible and had many great races before them. In the end Wimille won at 102.1 m.p.h. (record lap 108.14 m.p.h.) from Sanesi, with Ascari a cat's whisker behind. Villoresi finally struggled into 7th, five laps behind and astern of three Talbots. The British challenge had melted sadly away; two B-Type E.R.A.s were not even allowed to start and John Heath with the new Grand Prix Alta retired on the 7th lap.

Villoresi had some consolation in winning the Albi Grand Prix in August and then it was September and the Italian Grand Prix all over again at Turin. All three Italian constructors—how times have changed since!—had their fastest wares on parade: Wimille had the 158A, and Sanesi and Trossi 158 Alfas; three of the new Ferraris appeared in the formidable hands of Sommer, Farina and Bira plus a host of 4CLT/48's (Villoresi, Ascari, Taruffi, Cortese, de Graffenried and Parnell) and the usual Talbots. On the short Turin circuit the Ferraris were not the easiest cars to handle particularly in the wet and Farina retired after hitting a straw bale. Bira had transmission troubles but Sommer and Villoresi fought a race-long battle behind Wimille. Sanesi bent his front end after 41 laps and fared little better when he took over Trossi's which retired with blower troubles. Sommer finally finished 3rd behind Villoresi and Wimille, with the Maseratis of Ascari and Parnell 4th and 5th—not a bad day for Maserati and a promising start for Ferrari but Wimille and Alfa-Romeo were again the winners with no-one else effectively in sight.

Even though the Alfas could not twist the arms of the

563 LACKING ENDURANCE—and be it admitted, speed was the new Maserati at Rheims

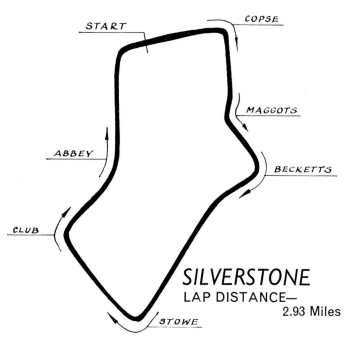

564 The perimeter circuit at Silverstone which was first used in 1949

565 HISTORIC RETURN: Ascari in the 1948 French Grand Prix drove his one and only race for his father's firm

566 NO LESS HEART-BREAKING: Count Trossi, who also died in 1949, smoking his famous pipe after winning the 1947 Italian Grand Prix

567 THINGS TO COME: the '500's on their opening lap with Stirling Moss on the inside

R.A.C. for adequate starting money, Villoresi and Ascari gave tired British eyes a taste of continental racing at Silverstone over a corkscrew course round runways and perimeter on a golden October day. The absence of the Alfas and the non-starting of the Ferraris of Sommer and Farina were disappointing as were the 4CLTs of Bira and Parnell: compensations, however, were the sight of maître Chiron, and Etancelin, still wearing what looked like the same cap as when last he had driven in England in 1938. As a revival of Grand Prix racing in England after 10 years this was an important occasion, but in retrospect it is important for an entirely different reason.

In July 1950 Kent Karslake published his readable and erudite history of the voiturette movement, which he ended after the 1925 season claiming that nothing really replaced the 1½-litre limit for voiturettes once this became the Grand Prix formula for 1926/7,[1] and using these words:—

'. . . by the coming of the second world war the (racing voiturette) seemed almost extinct.

'But when the war was over, a very remarkable thing happened; and curiously enough it took place not in France, which . . . had been the real home of the racing voiturette, but in England . . . (where) . . . after the war a group of enthusiasts . . . cast about for some means of . . . motor racing which should be financially less ruinous. They hit upon the happy idea of a class for cars with unsupercharged 500 c.c. engines and immediately the racing voiturette was born again. There was nothing very scientific about its new definition, but it had the inestimable virtue of being highly practical. And no one with the history of what had gone before in mind who watched these new voiturettes in their first long distance race at Silverstone in 1948 could fail to see the promise that a new epoch had begun.'

[1] I do not wholly agree with this view—for example what were all those 1½-litre cars racing in the thirties if they were not voiturettes? I know Karslake seeks to define a voiturette as 'a machine of relatively low power' but this really will not do for during the 1912/14 period two of the fastest cars in their years were the voiturette Sunbeam and Peugeot cars of 1912 and 1913. This however is perhaps pedantic carping in the light of the prophetic truth cited above.

And so it was that these puffing, panting little 500s which could barely finish those 50 miles in October 1948 have now turned into the present-day Grand Prix cars in which England has proved as supreme as ever were the Peugeots, Mercedes, Fiats, Sunbeams, Delages and Alfas of bygone days. For the record this was one of the few '500' events of those days that the young Stirling Moss did NOT win; and the 3rd man home was none other than Sir Francis Samuelson, that same 'Sampulson (sic!) who distinguished himself by taking a female mechanic[2] with him' to the French Cyclecar Grand Prix in 1913, and who still drives his 1914 T.T. Sunbeam with distinction in English V.S.C.C. events.

These excitements were at the time soon forgotten as the next big race loomed up. In October the Monza autodrome was re-opened by a Grand Prix preceded by a parade of old winners—Salamano, Chiron, Nuvolari, Fagioli, Caracciola and Stuck—and what wonderful memories they all brought back. In spite of his earlier statements Nuvolari did not drive but Chiron, game as ever, was racing with his Talbot even though he retired. Wimille, Trossi and Sanesi all had the 158A 'high boost' cars and Taruffi one of the less developed 158s. Wimille jumped ahead into his customary lead from the start but it was Sommer's Ferrari which pursued him hardest until the luckless driver had to retire with an attack of asthma. As the best Alfa lap was over 4 m.p.h. faster than the best Ferrari one, Sommer's was a truly doughty effort. Farina did not do so well but managed to lead Taruffi and the Maseratis till his transmission failed. Villoresi retired about the same time and Taruffi then regained 4th place behind Wimille, Trossi, Sanesi and Ascari. The Ferraris of Farina, Bira and Pola fared no better in the Penya Rhin Grand Prix a fortnight later when Villoresi won yet again, this time by a narrow margin from Parnell and a non-stop Chiron in 3rd.

The Alfas had now utterly dominated racing for three seasons after the St. Cloud nonsense in June 1946 and, at the end of 1948, the firm retired from Grand Prix racing for reputedly financial reasons although driver shortage may possibly have had something to do with the decision. Varzi had died in May and he was soon followed by his distinguished colleagues—Wimille and Trossi. Wimille's penchant for the small Simca-Gordini was well known and it turned out to be the death of him in the Argentine in January 1949. Neither Wimille nor anyone else seemed to know what really happened. Suffice it to say that he was 'apparently blinded by the rays of the rising sun combined with some dust kicked up by the horse of a policeman trying to force back spectators and crashed into a tree. He was universally considered 'not merely the greatest of the veterans racing today but also the greatest of all in the Grand Prix sphere . . . (who) . . . seemed in fact to drive better and better as the years passed.' As a token of the renown he had brought the nation he was posthumously awarded the Cross of the Legion of Honour and the President of the Republic went out of his way to quote some of his writings in a speech at Le Mans in 1949 on the occasion of the revival of the Grand Prix d'Endurance which had last been won by Wimille himself in 1939.

Count Trossi's end was no less heart breaking. For many years he had bravely fought against cancer, which must have accounted for his off days and halts for relief drivers over the years; in the interims he had shown himself a meteorically fast and polished and most gentlemanly driver who had given much to motor racing.

The deaths in such quick succession of their post-war invincibles made the 1948/9 close season a sad one indeed for Alfas but it opened the way for some very even, if slower, racing in 1949 between Ferrari, Talbot and Maserati.

569 GREATEST OF ALL: Wimille's penchant for the small Simca was well known—here he is the day before his untimely death at Buenos Aires in 1949

[2] Actually his wife on their honeymoon.

Chapter Thirty One
1949 · The Hound, the Trident and the Horse

570 Hound—*Etancelin:* Trident—*Fangio:* Horse—*Villoresi line up at Spa. Behind are Farina (12), Whitehead (6) Ascari (4), Rosier (24), and Campos*

If the title to this chapter sounds more appropriate to that of a fairy tale then it reflects the mood of drivers with Talbot, Maserati and Ferrari cars as they faced a season without Alfa-Romeo perpetually showing them the way home. In this respect 1949 was comparable to the 1933 season before the return of the monoposto Alfas, with Maserati as primitive and unreliable as ever but fast in the hands of the right driver, Talbot in the rôle of Bugatti winning occasional races when he could and Ferrari in his original rôle only as a manufacturer now, using the previous year's cars for most of the season and achieving a crushing victory with some newer ones in the Italian Grand Prix at the end. A few of the old actors were still in the field—notably Chiron, Etancelin,

Sommer and Taruffi. The outstanding car was the two-stage blown Ferrari which first appeared in the Italian Grand Prix in September, but the abiding memory of the season was undoubtedly the new Argentine meteor Juan Manuel Fangio. This was equally clear to contemporary observers for in a review of the year the *Autocar* wrote:

'*As to drivers it has been interesting to see the rise of Fangio ... who, while visiting Europe, showed his ability in no mean manner and is obviously in the first rank.*'

Fangio had driven in the Formula 2 event before the French Grand Prix in 1948 after racing against European drivers in the Argentine. Varzi and Villoresi had both taken cars to the

Argentine in 1947 where they had won and finished 2nd in alternate races and Fangio admitted to being surprised by the 'elegant simplicity' of the great Italians. At the time he was even more surprised and heartened by Wimille's reputed remark—'if one day he has a car that is right for his temperament, Fangio will perform miracles.' If this be an accurate report, then Jean-Pierre was as shrewd a judge of a driver as he was a great champion; whilst Fangio was almost devoid of temperament[1] as a driver in that he rarely, if ever, had an off day and had a skill that was almost miraculous in nursing a sick car home, there were certain

everyone but Farina and the two leading Ferrari drivers—and for two performances by Peter Whitehead in a 1949 single-stage Ferrari in winning the Masaryk Grand Prix, and all but winning the French Grand Prix itself from a full field. Finally in December the new B.R.M. was unveiled in readiness, one hoped, for some staggering performances to make up for its failure to race in 1949. In 1948 the Stationery Office published a work on the Development of German Grand Prix cars between 1934 and 1939 and early in 1949 its author, Cameron C. Earl, was guest-of-honour at a meeting in London where the chairman, George Monkhouse, gave a

571 MIXED BAG IN THE ARGENTINE: the start of the Rosario Grand Prix with a 308 Alfa, a 4½-litre of the type raced by Varzi in 1947 and a mixture of Ferraris and Maseratis

cars that did not suit his temperament. Thus even in machines like the big Ferraris or the 300 S.L.R. Mercedes, he was never such a pre-eminent sports car driver as some of his lesser contemporaries. Tragically Wimille did not live to be challenged by the first driver to emerge as a man of his own stature, but during the season it became clear that, apart from Fangio, another driver of classic stature had grown up in Alberto Ascari who was now becoming the leader of the Ferrari team and Villoresi his Fidus Achates.

No new nations or teams entered Grand Prix racing in 1949 but, from a British point of view, it was remarkable for a win at Jersey and a 2nd in the British Grand Prix by Bob Gerard driving an old pattern E.R.A. in fields that contained

solemn warning of new Mercedes, even then under construction for racing within two years and spoke of having seen pumps for direct fuel injection. Only a few weeks before the *Autocar* had interviewed Neubauer himself in a sparsely furnished office at Stuttgart and gathered that the chances of Germany coming back to Grand Prix racing in the prevailing economic conditions were next to impossible. At the time he was diligently recovering the lost racers of 1934-9 and earlier to reconstruct the Mercedes Museum and seemed resigned to the passing of the great days of German glory. Although they did not return to Grand Prix work until the middle of 1954, Monkhouse's prophecy was not so wide of the mark in that team of W 163s went to the Argentine

[1] *I know that this does not accord with, say, Ferrari's views but in this instance I discount these even as I discount much of what Fangio says about Ferrari, both views being grounded as much in an obvious mutual antipathy and ill-conceived prejudice as anything else.*

279

572 . . . 'remarkable for Bob Gerard driving an old pattern E.R.A. . . .'

573 Duncan Hamilton enjoying a moment of certain paternity!

574 TRIDENT SHAKER: Farina leaving a Ferrari at Spa

almost exactly two years after his speech. During the year Germany was re-admitted to the F.I.A. and in the ensuing winter Manfred von Brauchitsch journeyed to South America to drive a pre-war Maserati. In fact he did not start but thereby became the first German driver at least to enter a post-war Grand Prix.

On the 3rd April the 4CLT/48 Maseratis returned to San Remo; Fangio showed that his South American form was no flash in the pan and dominated the proceedings winning at an average of more than 4½ m.p.h. faster than Ascari's 4CLT/48 the year before. He carried a tremendous reputation before him to Pau on Easter Monday where his blue and yellow Maserati again showed absolute mastery: not even the famed Maserati reluctance to start deterred Fangio. When he stopped for oil towards the end of the race three mechanics in succession failed to start the car on the handle but all Fangio had to do was give one sharp pull and get back into the race before anyone could appreciate what had happened. He followed this with a win at Perpignan on May 8th but, to the disappointment of British enthusiasts, did not appear at either Jersey or Silverstone. Neither of these events attracted works Ferraris, but Villoresi, Parnell, Bira and de Graffenreid drove 4CLT/48's against Whitehead's single-stage Ferrari and a full complement of Talbots and E.R.A.'s. Surprisingly Gerard won at Jersey and was only 65.2 secs. behind de Graffenreid's winning Maserati at Silverstone, after the race had been led successively by Villoresi, Bira and Parnell. Whitehead's Ferrari was never a serious contender in either race; the car was a tricky one as both he and Raymond Mays, who drove another example at Silverstone, found. Jersey was run in heavy rain and Silverstone suffered from oil dropping to the amusement of Duncan Hamilton 'who had been expecting a happy domestic event, had some hair-raising turn-abouts and afterwards declared that even if his wife was not yet a mother he was sure that he was a father!' It was most notable that while the Maseratis had materially lost reliability since 1948, the 500s had clearly gained it in abundance and were now capable of surviving a 50-mile race in large numbers. By contrast the Talbots could barely even keep up with an aged, if meticulously prepared E.R.A.

Even before the war there had been rumours of a blown V-16 Talbot and in May 1949 the *Autocar* went so far as to publish an illustrated article on the project, without stating any measurements. The engine was a two-stage Roots blown narrow angle V-16 with one o.h. camshaft for each bank operating the exhaust valves direct through fingers interposed to take side thrust and the inlet valves on the inside of the V by very short push-rods. Classic roller bearings were used for the crankshaft and connecting rods but the real interest was centred on the 'fact that an aluminium bronze casting forms the combustion chamber, valve seats and the very small boss for the 10 mm. plug.' Into this lining the cylinder liners were screwed which gave a very large water space round each cylinder. A Wilson box and hydraulic brakes were all that was published on the remainder of the car and the rest of its performance, actual or potential, must remain even more of a cypher than those earlier mystery 1½-litre cars, the Itala and Fiat of 1926/7.

Farina put in one of his relatively rare 1949 appearances at the Belgian Grand Prix in June and made fastest lap in the race with his very potent Maserati at 101.64 m.p.h., within .30 m.p.h. of Wimille's 1947 best lap. Ferrari had redesigned the rear suspension on the team cars of Ascari and Villoresi, now driving their first race under the Prancing Horse of Baracca; Whitehead had resorted to the more homely expedient of adding a hundred-weight of ballast to the back end with marked improvement in handling. Belgium, 'all agog for its first sight of the fabulous Fangio, the Argentinian unstoppable force in Europe's 1949 Grands Prix' was sorely disappointed when a piston seizure stopped the Miracle Man in his first lap. Farina and Campos were left to uphold the Trident and mightily did Farina shake it under the Ferrari hooves until his very speed was his undoing on the 8th lap when he left the road. Ferrari pit-stops for tyres let Etancelin into the lead on his Talbot during laps 11, 12 and 13, the old Rouennais fire-brand burning as brightly as ever he had 15 and more years before and still with his famous cap, 'driving bright blue at every point of the course, cutting across verges, power-sliding the tighter turns and leaving a wake of black surface weals behind him at a dozen corners.'

By lap 14 Villoresi was back in the lead and Etancelin's gear-box was beginning to tire of being used as an electric mixer, but now it was Rosier who brought a hunting bay to the hound of Talbot as he pursued Villoresi. The Italian had to make two more pit stops and for all his speed it was the non-stop French tortoise that beat the halting Italian hare by 49 secs. in a race that had been fuller of interest and excitement than any previous post-war Grande Epreuve. Ascari and Whitehead packed their Ferraris home in 3rd and 4th ahead of Claes' Talbot which was one lap behind.

Once again Farina contrived fastest practice lap at Berne, sharing the first row with Bira's Maserati and Ascari. Sommer was back with a Talbot but the Argentine contingent were now running out of funds to keep their Maseratis properly overhauled and wisely, if sadly, missed the race. Ferrari had fitted Villoresi's car with long distance tanks to enable him to run non-stop and thus destroy the Talbot's advantage; Ascari, however, was going to stop so left the line like a shot from a gun and demonstrated in his driving a complete mastery of his difficult machine and superior technique to Villoresi as 'on fast open corners he set the four wheels drifting with a quick flick of the wheel and a light-

575 . . . 'the old Rouennais fire-brand burning as brightly as ever . . .'

ning correction.' Poor Villoresi! His tanks deceived him and he lost a clear-cut victory in a last minute stop, leaving Ascari to come through for his first Grand Prix win on but his second Formula 1 drive for Ferrari. Sommer (3rd), Etancelin, Bira and Rosier were the other finishers, the Talbots being by no means outclassed thanks to the fire of Etancelin and the 'usual flawless style' of Sommer, plus good m.p.g. of course.

Fangio was back for the Grand Prix at Rheims on the 17th July and had already whetted his appetite in the Formula II event on a Ferrari when he had led even Ascari on a similar car until his gear lever broke, while putting up eight new class lap records, compared with Ascari's two, and setting the record finally at 99.15 m.p.h. None of the three Cooper '1000's managed to survive the 126 miles. At 5 p.m. the Grand Prix cars were unleashed and to the surprise of many it was Campos who first challenged Villoresi on the pace making Ferrari, making a wonderful start from the 3rd row. Villoresi retired after only five laps and the Ferrari effort was now restricted to Whitehead as Ascari had nonstarted in common with the Maseratis of de Graffenreid and Fagioli. Campos and Fangio raced ahead and after 20 laps wonderman Fangio had a lead of 19 secs. over Campos and, what mattered more, of 1 min. 43 secs. over Chiron on the leading non-stop Talbot in 5th. Then he made his first fuel stop after 21 laps (1/3 distance) and dropped only two places. But Fangio's race and European season were nearly run: on the 25th lap he slowed and retired with a broken throttle linkage, a wretched ending to his boldly challenging entry on the European circuit. Campos, too, was soon in trouble and fell out with engine failure after 34 laps, leaving Bira leading Chiron by the slender margin of 34 secs. after 40 laps, with Whitehead only another 14 secs. away. Whitehead's car, newly rebuilt at the works, had not practised and

576 . . . 'none of the Cooper 1,000's managed to survive at Rheims'

577 To the surprise of many it was Campos who first challenged and then passed Villoresi's Ferrari

578 . . . 'Whitehead went from strength to strength taking the lead on the 54th lap . . .'

now started really motoring, closing on Chiron and, even after a fuel stop on lap 44 of 19 secs., was only 13 secs. behind Chiron after 50 laps. Bira had now fallen to 3rd a mere 3 secs. behind Whitehead and there the three of them were with 14 laps (70 miles) to go and all to play for. The last stops had been made and the chips were down.

Chiron was being at least warmed by a persistent oil leak, while Whitehead went from strength to strength taking the lead with the fastest lap of the race on his 54th (105.13 m.p.h.). By lap 58 he led by 6 secs., and then it happened, with victory almost there for an Englishman in The Grand Prix for the first time in 26 years. On that lap the Ferrari stuck in the 4th of its five gears and lost a vital 15 m.p.h. on the straights besides making the slow corners at their three ends almost impossible. Very creditably Whitehead struggled through those six heartbreaking laps watching the lead and then 2nd place vanish as first Chiron and then Bira went by. The crowd were naturally highly delighted at their national idol's 4th and last victory in the Grand Prix, although strictly the race was termed the Grand Prix de France and not the Grand Prix de l'A.C.F. in 1949![2]

The Zandvoort circuit in Holland staged its first big meeting in 1949, after the B.R.D.C. had christened it in 1948, in a race of two 65 mile heats and a final of 104 miles. Yet again Farina turned in the fastest practice lap with his Maserati, but finished his heat 2nd to Villoresi's Ferrari. In the 2nd heat Ascari and Parnell had a splendid fight which the British driver won while the Ferrari stopped immediately after the finish in the pit area for urgent mechanical attention. Whatever Ascari's troubles they cannot have been too serious as the Ferraris led the final as they pleased until Ascari lost a wheel and the lead five laps from the end leaving Villoresi to win easily from Farina, de Graffenried, Bira, Parnell, Etancelin and Gerard. In fact both Farina and Parnell were penalized for start jumping and were lowered to 4th and 6th in the results.

The first *Daily Express* Silverstone meeting was also a heats-and-final affair. By dint of some furious dicing Bira managed to beat Ascari by a split second in the first heat and Farina repeated the dose over Villoresi in the second. In this race Peter Walker made an E-Type E.R.A. perform reasonably well for the one and only time in its life actually holding 3rd place for some of the race ahead of de Graffenried. As at Zandvoort Ascari had troubles to sort out between heat and final: this time it was a seized blower that had to be replaced. Ascari, taking advantage of a ZF differential, led on the slippery course throughout the 90 mile final but was fiercely challenged by Farina in the second half. At first, however, it was Parnell who led the Maseratis continuing his fine form at Zandvoort where he had made fastest lap. After only 11 laps however he lost his oil pressure and Farina went by taking Villoresi at half distance and then setting about

[2] It was organised by the A.C. de Champagne and not the A.C.F.

282

579/80 . . . then when the Ferrari stuck in 4th gear Whitehead watched first Chiron (above) and then Bira (below) go by

Ascari too. For seven laps Ascari and Farina were wheel to wheel and then Farina, temporarily blinded by oil, glanced off the straw bales at Stowe Corner losing a vital 10 secs. He continued, however, at undiminished speed and finished less than 2 secs. behind Ascari and 36 secs. ahead of Villoresi. Peter Walker finally finished the E-Type in 5th behind de Graffenreid in considerable discomfort—'the steering kicked and wore great patches of soreness into his palms, the exhaust pipe burnt his foot badly, then the gear kept jumping out of third . . . and finally the radiator sprayed water back all over his face.' Whilst Walker had put up a truly courageous performance it was Farina whose driving was in a class of its own and drew this tribute from Pomeroy:

'*Farina's handling of an inherently slower car showed that something remains when engineering calculations are ended and beyond the scientifically correct line on a given radius bend . . . that blend of supreme skill with sheer courage which enables a man to force his car past another in a manner which takes him to the very edge of safety without crossing the border line which leads to disaster.*'

581/2/3: Whilst Ascari (top) won for Ferrari and Walker (centre) put up a truly courageous performance on the E-type E.R.A. it was Farina (bottom) whose driving was in a class of its own

584 THEN PRESTO—it was time for Italian Grand Prix in the Autumn glow of Monza's Royal Park with the new Ferraris leading already . . .

585 . . . and having matters very much their own way (Villoresi above)

586 . . . while the Milano Maseratis did not fare so well—Farina failing to finish after lying 3rd—

The death of the very fast and popular English driver St. John Horsfall cast a deep gloom over this otherwise sunlit meeting. Earlier in the year he had performed the remarkable feat of driving through the Belgian 24 hour race single-handed and was being strongly favoured for selection to drive the new B.R.M. when it finally appeared.

Shortly after, Farina got his own back at Lausanne where Ascari was plagued with oiling plugs, though Sommer's perhaps was the true glory with a faster average in the Formula II race (67.20 m.p.h. over 60 laps) than Farina's (65.81 m.p.h.) over the longer 90 laps Grand Prix. Then—Presto! It was time for the Italian Grand Prix again in the Autumn glow of Monza's Royal Park with the new twin o.h.c. 2-stage blown Ferraris appearing at long last and rumours of another Alfa-Romeo return—just as in 1933. In fact the Alfas non-started and the Ferraris had matters much their own way although they were, still substantially slower than the old 158A Alfas. In the race Ascari's fastest lap was 7 m.p.h. slower than Sanesi's 1948 record and his practice lap nearly 6 secs. slower than Wimille's; race average too was down by some 5 m.p.h. so the new Ferraris still had a very long way to go. Whitehead, Sommer and Bonetto all had single stage Ferraris geared up for reliability; Rosier and Etancelin led the Talbots and Farina and Taruffi had the Tipo Milano Maseratis with two of the largest blowers Grande Vitesse had ever seen boosting through 4 ins. diameter pipes and modified cylinder heads. Farina practised his in 2 mins. 7.8 secs. but in the race he failed to finish after lying 3rd early on, retiring, it was said, due to lack of power and thereby losing a certain 2nd place while Taruffi struggled grimly on to 'finish' 7th, 16 laps astern. Villoresi retired and Etancelin took another well deserved 2nd, followed by Bira, de Graffenried and Sommer, with Harrison's C-Type E.R.A. a good 6th only 58 secs. behind Sommer. As a race the Italian Grand Prix was a poor conclusion to what had otherwise been a closely fought season: retirements had been many ($62\frac{1}{2}$ per cent.) and the racing not especially close besides being well down on the previous year's speeds.

It is pleasant to record that Peter Whitehead had his consolation for losing the French Grand Prix when he won the revived Masaryk or Czech Grand Prix at Brno later in the month after a race long battle with Etancelin. The long circuit was still a source of dangerous accidents: several spectators were killed and at one corner Farina, Parnell and Bira all left the road at one time or another due to their vision being obscured by clouds of dust through which the race was run in the early stages. This was not the only reminder of the earlier years of motor racing during the year. Both in the Swiss and Italian Grands Prix there had appeared a car calling itself a Platé Special which was powered by one of the 1927 Talbot 8-cylinder engines

587 . . . in spite of two of the largest blowers ever seen boosting through 4-inch diameter pipes

589 Taruffi struggling grimly to 'finish' 7th, 16 laps behind—here leading Chaboud's Delahaye

588 WELL DESERVED was Etancelin's 2nd place on Talbot

590 GOOD SIXTH was T. C. Harrison's pre-war E.R.A.

mounted in a tubular chassis through which engine oil was passed in the optimistic hope of cooling it—one of Maserati's more mysterious practices—with rigid axles at either end. Rather more original was R. P. R. Habershon's 1927 Delage which competed at a V.S.C.C. meeting at Silverstone in July and then in the *Daily Express* meeting in August.

During the winter Alfa-Romeo improved the 158A still further, increasing r.p.m. to 8,500 and b.h.p. to 350 by detail changes but this served to limit the life of the engine to one race between overhauls. While this was probably a better reliability factor than the higher stressed Maseratis it did make the racing of blown cars highly expensive and for this and several other very good reasons Ferrari now instructed Lampredi to investigate the possibilities of big unblown engines. The 1949 racing had made it clear that over any distance a faster 4½-litre car than the Talbot would probably have won as it liked and also that even the newest Ferrari were nothing like fast enough to challenge the 1948 Alfas, let alone the improved cars that would be racing in 1950. Nor were the new Ferraris likely to be materially better than the Alfas in either m.p.g. or reliability to compensate for their lack of speed. Thus, unless Ferrari could pull something very startling out of the unblown hat, the outlook for him was poor indeed with his lesser resources in power, speed and hard cash.

591 *AMONG MY SOUVENIRS: The fiery and successful driving of Philippe Etancelin (talking to Nuvolari at Monza) was a feature of the season* . . .

592 *AY! EVERY INCH A KING: Nuvolari practising at Silverstone in 1950 in one of the new XK 120 Jaguars*

Chapter Thirty Two
1950 · 'Not Victory...'

The return of Alfa-Romeo in 1950 was an unbroken, indeed unchallenged run of triumph from April at San Remo to Silverstone at the end of August. During those five months the revived Alfas started in ten races and scored ten first, seven seconds, three thirds and a fourth. In one race they only ran one car; in another there was a multiple pile up which reduced them to one car and in a third Fagioli broke a spring when actually leading on the last lap, otherwise the score would certainly have been ten 2nds. By any standards this is an amazing record of success and reliability because many of their wins were achieved at far from touring speeds, even though they met with no serious opposition. Apart from anything else it showed how dull the 1949 season would have been with Alfa participation, so for this reason

and for the encouragement his wins in 1949 gave Ferrari the Alfa retirement was in many ways beneficial to the sport in the end. By tradition and ability Farina was their most obvious choice for a driver and Fangio on ability no less; there must have seemed a great deal less to be said for resurrecting Fagioli who had hardly driven a racing car since 1936. He turned out, however, to be a wholly reliable and most useful member of the team and managed to regain much of his old flair, speed and style, coupled with a consistency that none of his four great contemporaries were able to achieve in the post-war years. Varzi, Chiron and Nuvolari had some great moments during these years but not one of them was so successful as Fagioli in rolling back the years. In its own way it was the most remarkable thing about

Alfa's greatest year in racing, even if it was perhaps fortuitous for arising out of Sanesi's crash and Fagioli's own remarkable performance in the Mille Miglia where he finished 7th on an 1100 c.c. Osca.

Farina had had an accident in March and Alfa-Romeo therefore entrusted their single car at San Remo to Fangio who certainly did not disappoint his new employers on a circuit where even Ascari performed a tête-à-queue and finally crashed his 2-stage Ferrari. Fangio had already repeated his Pau victory on a Maserati so was in good form but, all the same, the responsibility was an anxious one especially in wet weather. However, he was more than equal to it and won with relative ease from Villoresi's 2-stage Ferrari. From the soaking Riviera to sunny England sounds like a nonsense novel but the sun shone out of a clear sky for Britain's first European Grand Prix to welcome not only His

late Majesty King George VI, but also the Alfa-Romeo team racing in England for the first time. In honour of the occasion they had invited Parnell to drive the fourth car and only a derangement of Fangio's valves, with 8 laps left, stopped a 1-2-3-4 win for the Alfas, which finished in the order Farina —Fagioli—Parnell.

As a matter of interest Fagioli was 2nd fastest in practice both at Silverstone and Monaco and was thus quickly finding his form. Chiron now on a 4CLT/48, Farina and Fagioli were all striving for a 2nd win at Monaco after respective intervals of 19, 2 and 15 years, but it was Fangio who led from the start and thus missed the massive pile-up on the first lap after Farina had skidded on a wet patch on the harbour front. This eliminated half the entry including two out of three Alfas and left Fangio a thoroughly uneventful drive till he finished with no other car within sight or

598 'None so successful as Fagioli in rolling back the years . . .' here he relaxes after the British Grand Prix

600 *LONE RESPONSIBILITY: Fangio with the only Alfa at San Remo and, in effect, at Monaco (above) won handsomely both times*

599 *In the early part of 1950 Ferrari fought a losing battle—here Villoresi's two-stage car leads Sommer's older pattern model at Monaco*

601 *Gerard still with his faithful E.R.A. leads a Talbot in vain pursuit of Fangio*

602 'They do sometimes let Fagioli lead . . .!'

603 Ascari in the final version of the 1½-litre blown Ferrari was most unsuccessful at the August Silverstone

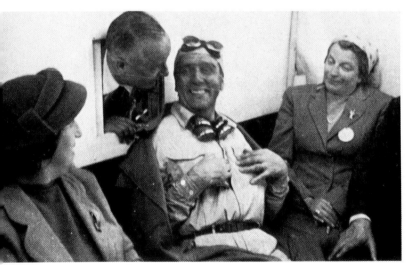

604 For all World Champion Farina's self-satisfaction to G. A. Vandervell (in hatch) after the British Grand Prix . .

sound. In practice Fangio had averaged 64.56 m.p.h. and managed 64.09 in the race besides winning at 61.33 m.p.h. so speeds were at last growing respectably near pre-war standards. The rest finished in the order Ascari, Chiron, Sommer, Bira, and Gerard still with his faithful E.R.A. Fagioli who was knocked into the mêlée arrived at the pits looking more savage than anyone 'Grande Vitesse' had ever seen, the famous rages of yore being still as undamped as his driving skill.

At Berne Villoresi's Ferrari had a de Dion rear axle but not even this could put him on the front row of the grid. Fangio circulated in 2 mins. 42.1 secs. (=100.48 m.p.h.) in practice which Farina improved to 2 mins. 41.6 secs. (=100.78 m.p.h.) in the race. Both Ferraris were out by the 9th lap and the race degenerated, if that be a fair word, into the usual high speed demonstration by Alfas till Fangio dropped a valve, this time with 9 laps to go, leaving Farina to "win" by .4 sec. from Fagioli. Rosier led the finishers, followed by Bira, then Bonetto with a Tipo Milano Maserati actually finishing a race. Speeds at Berne were still a long way below those of the Mercedes and Auto-Unions.

Sommer had driven a wonderfully fast race to win the FII event at Berne and now at Spa in a Talbot he was to drive the race of a lifetime. In practice he equalled Villoresi's 2-stage Ferrari time of 4 mins. 47 secs. and then in the race he passed Villoresi on the 5th lap and followed this by leading the Alfas after their first fuel stops. This really made them all hurry a little until Sommer's engine gave out after 20 of the 35 laps when he was lying 3rd still ahead of one Alfa! This time Fangio took the chequered flag after his disappointments at Berne and Silverstone, ahead of Fagioli, Rosier and Farina who had been delayed by loss of oil pressure. Both Ferraris finished: Ascari drove the experimental V-12 3.3-litre into 5th, followed by Villoresi on the 2-stage blown car. Poor Sommer had really done everything and more on a fast car's circuit and had shocked Guidotti to the extent that he tried to persuade himself and the organisers that Sommer had been a whole lap behind the Alfas before they had stopped! On occasions failure can be brilliant indeed.

In 1950 the French Grand Prix was the French Grand Prix again with no sports car nonsense and Fangio had an eye on Lang's 1939 record. In practice he managed to lower the race lap record of 114.87 with a speed of 116.2 m.p.h., but even this was not fast enough to deal with the practice record of 117.5 m.p.h. In the race Farina had fuel pump trouble and stopped 9 laps from the end but qualified as 7th finisher, Fangio winning at 104.83 m.p.h. with a fastest race lap of 112.35 m.p.h. Yet again Fagioli was 2nd—this was becoming so monotonous a placing that an *Autocar* photograph showing him leading Fangio at one stage was captioned 'They do sometimes let Fagioli lead'. What the irascible old gentleman might have said about such a thought fifteen years before beggars description. Alfas sent Farina and Fangio to Bari and Fangio and Fagioli to Pescara; both times they won but at Pescara Fagioli was deprived of 'HIS' victory by a broken spring on his last lap. Fangio was being pursued by Rosier and so had to press on to win rather than slow down and literally shunt Fagioli over the line. Another minor race by Alfa standards was the Daily Express Silverstone where Farina won from Fangio but before then they had met two unblown Ferraris of 3.3 and 4.1 litres in the Grand Prix des Nations at Geneva. Alfas fielded Farina, Fangio, Taruffi and de Graffenried on his native ground and were hard pressed by the Ferraris. Ascari with the bigger car tried grimly to hold Fangio and at least succeeded in keeping 2nd place for 62 of the 68 laps when he retired with water pouring from an exhaust pipe. Two laps earlier Villoresi, ahead of the Alfas of Farina, de Graffenried and Taruffi, had slid on some oil and had one of his very rare accidents. Farina also crashed trying to avoid him but de Graffenried and Taruffi brought their Alfas in 2nd and 3rd, 2 laps behind Fangio.

Ferrari had at last challenged the Alfas and had been ready poised to defeat at least three of them but for some damnable luck in the last 20 miles of the Geneva race. What was more he still had .4 of a litre in hand and as Grande Vitesse remarked 'this is, I think, the first time the usual Alfa column has been so long and so decisively disrupted.' Even then the shadows were beginning to lengthen over Portello and Alfas went forward to their last engagement at Monza, rather less lightheartedly than in previous years.

05/6/7 . . . both he (top) and Fangio (left above and right) found themselves having to work very hard for their money at Geneva against the new unblown Ferraris

291

Chapter Thirty Three
1950/1 · The Titans Walk Again

608 MASSIVE ENGAGEMENTS: The start of the French Grand Prix with Fangio and Ascari on either side of Farina whose tyres are nearly alight

The Italian Grand Prix in 1950 ushered in a series of massive engagements between the 158A and 159 Alfas and the 4½-litre unblown Ferrari. Of their nine meetings Alfas won six and Ferrari three, while Alfa put in 7 fastest laps to Ferrari's 2. Thus on balance Alfas had the better of the struggle but by the end of 1951 it was very clear that the 159 Alfa was a spent force while the Ferrari was even then not at the height of its development. The British B.R.M. was still barely raceworthy so that when Alfas withdrew after winning the 1951 championship, Ferrari had no worth while opponents and the 1½-litre formula died before it could run its appointed course to the end of 1953. Ascari's 4.1 Ferrari had shaken the Alfas at Geneva and at Monza, with the engine enlarged to the full 4½-litres (with only single o.h.c. to each bank), he frightened them through and through. Before the race the record laps in practice and the race stood to Wimille (1 min. 59.2 secs.) and Sanesi (2 mins. 0.8 secs. = 116.95 mp.h.) respectively. At the very start of practice Ascari set the target at 1 min. 59 secs. (118+ m.p.h.) the fastest speed ever on the new circuit. The Alfa drivers, notably Farina and Fangio with even higher boost cars giving 370 b.h.p., tried all they knew to beat this for the next two days only to have Ascari cut another .2 secs. off his record. Eventually Fangio managed to beat this with a time of 1 min. 58.6 secs. which could not have sent the Alfa équipe to a very easy sleep.

Alfas were going to have to make two stops for fuel to the Ferrari's one, but there were five Alfas—Sanesi and Taruffi coming in to swell the ranks—against the Ferraris of Ascari and Serafini in place of the injured Villoresi. Farina led from the start pursued by Ascari and then the remaining Alfas and Serafini. Sanesi was out by 12 laps—first blood to Ferrari and, as if to celebrate, Ascari passed Farina. Farina got by after two laps and Ascari, having made his point, sat on Farina's heels for six more laps and that was his race. Still there was no respite for Alfas: while Ascari walked in from the country Serafini was taking advantage of their first fuel stops to pull up to 3rd, 6 secs. behind Fagioli and about a minute behind Farina. Fangio had retired with gearbox failure about the same time as Ascari and the relentless game of Ten Little Nigger Boys went on. Neither Fangio nor Ascari was inactive for long: Fangio took over Taruffi's car at his fuel stop but lasted little longer with that one and then Ascari relieved Serafini. Actually he did little better than Serafini himself would probably have done in passing Fagioli at his second fuel stop. By this time Farina had the race sewn up in a bag and was slowing to orders though Ascari was near enough to be very troublesome if anything had gone wrong with the Alfa. Farina won by 1 min. 19 secs. from Ascari with Fagioli 3rd, 17 secs. further behind, then Etancelin about 20 miles adrift! At the end of it all Fangio, in the interims of blowing up two cars under him, had set a

new race record in 2 mins. flat (117.445 m.p.h.) while Farina had averaged 109.63 m.p.h. for the 313 miles, oddly enough, fractionally slower than Wimille's speed over the same distance in 1948.

At the time, the return match at Barcelona was eagerly anticipated but Alfa in the end thought better of it, obviously taking a more jaundiced view of the new challenger than Grande Vitesse's guarded comment after Monza

'Whether this race does indeed presage a swing-over to the hitherto somewhat despised unsupercharged 4500 c.c. type remains to be seen. It does look as if the existing highly supercharged 1500 c.c. engine is no longer necessarily unbeatable. Certainly there is new interest in the characteristics of the big unsupercharged engine if designed and developed with suitable resources, experience and data.'

If Ferrari read this measured prose he did not allow himself to be unduly deterred and appeared under the dusty skies of Barcelona with a full team of three cars, bringing in the old Trimmer Taruffi, against the two V-16 B.R.M.s of Parnell and Peter Walker, making their first appearance on the continent. In practice the Ferraris were 4 m.p.h. quicker and, although Parnell was timed at 186 m.p.h. over a kilometre on the 1.72 mile straight, hand timing over a corner section disclosed that the Ferrari averaged 96 m.p.h. to the B.R.M.'s 81 m.p.h.—a difference of about 2 secs. for only 500 yards. At the start Parnell's centrifugal blower made his car even slower than the Ferraris while Walker's car played a low trick on him spitting back through the blow-off valve and stalling dead. From 19th at the start Parnell pulled up to 4th after the first lap, 7 secs. behind Ascari. The next lap and Parnell was in with a sheared blower driver and the luckless Walker was dogged by sheer lack of power, of all things on that fantastic engine, till he finally retired after 33 of the 48 laps when 4th well behind a Simca and two Ferraris. He cannot have been helped by a stop for fuel alone which took the disgraceful time of 73 secs. Taruffi had a spin and lost a couple of laps which slightly spoilt the Ferrari walk-over but he was still 3rd behind Serafini and, of course, Ascari himself.

During these Spanish junketings Farina had been at the Paris Salon where he had been much struck by the possibility of the Bochory automatic transmission which he was going to fit to a 158 in the lively expectation of gaining several seconds per lap at Monza to say nothing of sundry lire from selling rights. More realistically the Portello works were busy squeezing the last drops of power from their magnificent old engine and also fitting up some of the cars with long distance fuel tanks in their sides. Experiments were also carried out with De Dion rear axles in place of the swing-axles in an effort to apply as much of their hard achieved

PRÈS NOUS LE DÉLUGE: The Alfa-Romeo team prep English weather at May Silverstone—(left to right) Sanesi, Farina, Bonetto, Fangio and manager Guidotti

610 The 4½-litre OSCA made a few unspectacular appearances in 1950/1

611 UNFORGETTABLE EXPERIENCE: . . .'only the English could race . . .' Parnell who was declared winner

power to the road. In Type 159 form the car gave 404 b.h.p. at 10,500 r.p.m. and consumed fuel at the rate of 1½ m.p.g. as it was necessary to use a very rich mixture to give better internal cooling. Even with full 65-gallon capacity two or more stops would be needed in a full distance Grand Prix but in the opening race they were likely to go through non-stop. This was the Daily Express event at Silverstone for which both Ferrari and Alfa-Romeo confirmed entries while the B.R.M.s remained inactive. Ferrari had been out at San Remo with a new 24-plug model giving an extra 500 r.p.m. and the first full engagement of the two marques at Silverstone was eagerly awaited. There was therefore great disappointment mixed with darker suspicions when Ferrari cancelled his entry saying he preferred long distance races to which Grande Vitesse added 'an unspoken parenthesis: "especially when up against the Type 160 Alfa Romeo."' Whether Ferrari did get cold feet or just could not be bothered matters not; his absence was a pity when one considers how well Parnell drove one of the earliest pattern 4.5 Ferraris entered by Tony Vandervell as The Thinwall Special and destined to become Britain's most famous formule libre car over the next few years. In the opening heat Parnell was up against Fangio and Felice Bonetto, another old-timer recruited in place of Fagioli; initially the Alfas led on acceleration and then after 5 of the 15 sprint laps Parnell was past and after Fangio. In practice Fangio had put in a new record of 1 min. 46 secs. (98.10 m.p.h.) while all he needed in his heat was 1 min. 48 secs. (96.29 m.p.h.) but Parnell had driven a fine race pulling out 42 secs. on Bonetto in 10 laps and keeping Fangio well up to the mark, so what might Ascari and the new car have done?

In the second heat Farina and Sanesi went rather faster; Farina opened in magnificent style, leaning well back in his classic manner with firm face and concentrated compressed mouth, with some four or five laps all around the 1 min. 47 secs. mark (97.19 m.p.h.) which was an improvement of over 3 m.p.h. on the 1950 race record. This was an altogether faster heat where Sanesi's time was in fact 5 secs. faster than Fangio's, and where Bira (4.5 Osca) Bob Gerard (1937 C-Type E.R.A.) and Trintignant (Simca) were faster than Bonetto in Heat 1. The final was eagerly awaited with the lively possibility of a great fight between Farina and Fangio and Parnell as the cars were wheeled out against a backing of sombre clouds. These burst with devastating suddenness, flooding the course with rain and hail and darkness lit up only by lightning so that no driver could see beyond his bonnet if that far. 'The hail lay on the track' wrote a contemporary 'so that on corners brakes merely locked the wheels and the cars went straight on and if there was another car or a marker tub in the way the driver could not even see it. Cars went off on to the grass, they spun round, they travelled forwards, backwards and sideways.' Bonetto led after lap 1, but then Parnell and Duncan Hamilton (Talbot) went ahead followed by Graham Whitehead (E.R.A.) and then, significantly, by lap 3—Fangio. Three laps later when the race was stopped Fangio had worked up into 3rd the placings being:

1. Parnell		16m. 48s. = 61·7 m.p.h.
2. Hamilton		17m. 9s.
3. Fangio		17m. 58s.
4. Whitehead	5 laps	14m. 40s.
5. Rosier	,,	15m. 7s.
6. Trintignant	,,	15m. 33s.
7. Rolt (ERA–Delage)		15m. 35s.
8. Claes (Talbot)		15m. 37s.
9. Farina		15m. 40s.
10. Bonetto		15m. 45s.

an unforgettable experience for anyone who took part in it in conditions which really only the English could race. With their elephant's trunk blower intakes the Alfa mechanics must have been as relieved as the drivers at the stoppage.

Things were not really much better in the Swiss Grand Prix at the end of the so-called Merry Month. Practice was, however, in wonderful weather and Fangio had a real 'go' at the pre-war records of Mercedes and Auto-Union, setting the 1½-litre record at 104.46 m.p.h. compared with 102.9 m.p.h. by Farina and 102.2 by Villoresi. Farina's 159 had long distance tanks and Sanesi's a de Dion axle; all three Ferraris had de Dion axles and single o.h.c., Taruffi being the third driver. Ascari was suffering from a burn so was not a really serious contender in the race. Fangio would have to make a fuel stop so went off as much like a rocket as he could in the downpour, followed by Farina, Sanesi, Villoresi, de Graffenried (Alfa), Ascari and Taruffi. After finding his feet in the opening laps Taruffi decided to go motor racing and between the 8th and 41st laps went through from 7th to 2nd rocketing the big car round this most testing circuit on its very limit . . . 'where others lifted a foot Taruffi pressed on regardless holding the car in a series of slides with a determination that was awe-inspiring to witness.'

Villoresi was less lucky losing his way on the 13th lap without injury and Ascari was off colour due to his burn so it was as well for Ferrari that Taruffi was in such form. After 23 of 42 laps Fangio led by over 40 secs. and stopped for 32 secs. for fuel, leaving just in time to tuck behind Farina's car. It took him 5 more laps to get by and he led for the rest of the race. Surprisingly Farina fell back and Taruffi gained till he was on the Alfa's tail with four laps to go. Farina then made a tremendous effort pulling out 2½ secs. on the 40th lap, but it was to no avail against the magnificent Taruffi, who got by on the 41st to finish 24 whole secs. ahead of Farina after only one more lap. Fangio was 55 secs. ahead of Taruffi and that after a pit stop, which shows what a magnificent race he had driven. Sanesi was 4th a lap behind, then came de Graffenried, Ascari, Chiron and Moss (H.W.M.) all on 40 laps. Chiron on de Graffenried's Maserati drove with much of his

612 *Things were not much better in the Swiss Grand Prix*

613 *It took Fangio five more laps to get by Farina*

614 *'Chiron . . . was lucky to catch Moss . . .'*

295

old skill but was lucky to catch Moss' Formula II car which ran short of fuel within sight of the finish.

By contrast brilliant sunshine greeted Farina and Parnell at Dundrod the following Saturday; Farina's car was not fitted with long distance tanks so at half distance (100 miles) he came in and went out again 3 secs. behind the Ferrari. It took the Italian another lap to get back in the lead and over the next 80-odd miles he built up a lead of 73 secs. Two other races in the same programme were won by Peter Collins (Cooper '500') and J. M. Hawthorn (2-litre Riley) of whom much more was soon to be heard.

Inspired by his trip to the Emerald Isle Farina descended on Spa for the Belgian Grand Prix where he seized the lead from Villoresi after the first lap and drove on at increasing speed, breaking all records (practice included), followed by the Ferraris of Villoresi and Ascari. Fangio had not driven a big-tank Alfa before, but quickly had the measure of it and, once he did, he was past the Ferraris and after Farina setting the record finally at 120.51 m.p.h. The Alfas stopped twice during the 316 miles: Farina lost a total of 1 min. 38 secs. at the pits against Ascari's single stop of 40 secs. only but the Ferraris still lacked the speed to deal with the Alfas on a really fast circuit. Thus Farina finished 1st, 2 mins. 51 secs. ahead of Ascari and nearer five ahead of Villoresi who had, however, spent over 2 mins. at the pits on three stops. Fangio had an unlucky day with his de Dion Alfa: when he stopped for wheels after 15 laps the left hand rear wheel jammed and could not be shifted so the whole hub had to be removed complete with wheel to which a new cover was then fitted in best Gordon Bennett style although in retrospect it is no quite clear why they could not have simply changed the tyre with the wheel in situ. All this took nearly a quarter of an hour and slowed Fangio over the rest of the race as he was unable to change the offending wheel again. In contrast to Varzi in 1947 Fangio was the soul of good humour, drinking and anointing himself with mineral water and sitting quietly while the minutes, the race and his championship hopes ebbed away. Eventually he finished 9th and last behind five Talbots; Sanesi and Taruffi on the third Alfa and Ferrari both retired. Farina's winning average of 114.26 m.p.h. was a substantial improvement on Fangio in 1950 and it was generally felt that the Alfas would have little difficulty in holding the Ferraris off at Rheims where speeds would be of much the same order.

However Ferrari had hunted up some more horses in the intervening ten days and the French Grand Prix of 1951 produced a soul-stirring series of opening laps with Ascari and Fangio playing the 1939 parts of Nuvolari and Lang. Both drivers made superb starts clearing the field comfortably by the end of the stands. In practice Fangio (119.99), Ascari (117.95) and Farina (118.63) had all beaten Lang's 1939 practice record, but it was Ascari who got ahead and

615 TEMPORA MUTANTUR: Fagioli, who was relieved by Fangio in the French Grand Prix, studying form with Farina

stayed there for nine laps. Then, like Nuvolari, he came to the pits in dire trouble: this time it was brakes and a rear axle that had 'given up the unequal struggle of braking as well as accelerating.' Fangio lasted but a lap longer before his car started misfiring and three laps later he was halted with magneto troubles which had tormented the Alfas throughout practice. Thus at 20 laps Farina was leading by 71 secs. from Villoresi, followed 12 secs. later by Fagioli, back with Alfas, then, at 3 secs. distance, Taruffi's replacement, the burly Argentinian José Froilan Gonzalez driving an inspired first race for Ferrari. In 5th nearly 3 further minutes behind was Parnell on the Thinwall. A lap later and Fagioli and Gonzalez were past Villoresi who spent the rest of the race sitting in a spray of oil but managed to keep going to finish 3rd.

After getting up to 2nd without any apparent effort Fagioli stopped for wheels and fuel with the normally tanked Alfa after 22 laps and was replaced by Fangio—Tempora Mutantur for poor old Fagioli who 'was obviously much overcome and on the verge of tears', as well he might be with the prospect of winning a really classic French Grand Prix, but, as Monkhouse goes on to say, 'it had to be because the Alfa pit realised that Ascari would almost certainly take over Gonzalez's Ferrari when he stopped for fuel.' This duly happened and after 40 laps when the first stops had all taken place Farina still held his lead now increased to 1 min. 17 secs. over the Fagioli-Fangio Alfa with Ascari, on Gonzalez' Ferrari, only 20 secs. behind. Lady Luck now took a hand sending Farina in to replace a thrown tread after 44 laps and as if this was not enough he overshot his pit and wasted 3¼ mins. Fangio stopped for fuel at the same time and Ascari now got back into the lead with his nearly brakeless Ferrari. These very brakes were now nearly Ascari's undoing and he was obliged to stop to tighten them after 50 laps, letting Fangio into the lead for the first time in nearly 200 miles.

After 60 laps, with about 85 miles to go, Fangio led by a minute from Ascari who in turn led Farina by over four minutes, with Villoresi 4th, 1½ minutes further away and the pattern of the race seemed virtually set. However the Gods had not finished their day's sport with Farina, who now felt the blight of the Alfa's ignition troubles as he fell first to Villoresi and then to Parnell to finish behind them in 5th after leading for over half of the race. Fangio won this 375 mile marathon at 110.97 m.p.h. and set a new lap record at 118.29 m.p.h. in a race that was undoubtedly the greatest French Grand Prix since 1934 and, up till that time anyway, one of the greatest in Fangio's career.

Thus far in the season the Alfas had shown themselves faster and as reliable as the Ferraris: the French Grand Prix, however, was the beginning of the end for Alfas and the end of the beginning for Ferrari. The Alfas might still be faster and their brakes better, but that extra fuel stop was the millstone they carried and on circuits where absolute speed counted that little less there was every possibility that they would not be able to gain sufficiently on the Ferraris to make up the necessary time. Once again the Silverstone crowds waited for those Ferraris that had disappointed them earlier in the year and in 1948 and, with no less critical anticipation, for those B.R.M.s that had been disappointing everybody everywhere for far too long. As it turned out nobody was disappointed and, while the B.R.M.s of Parnell and Walker did not set the Thames alight, they tried very hard to do this to their unfortunate drivers. To some extent their first and only proper race in the formula was overshadowed by the massive frame and efforts of Gonzalez: the iron grip of the Alfas had to be broken sometime and it was on the anvil of Silverstone that Gonzalez performed this historic feat in real blacksmith's style.

Ferrari has told how it was Sommer who first encouraged him to build the new unblown engines and great as I have always counted Gonzalez, it has always struck me how fitting it would have been had Sommer been spared to have repeated the doses of Miramas 1932, St. Cloud 1946 and Spa 1950, but by July 1951 this superb artist of the wheel had been dead nearly ten months. Sensation crowded into Silverstone from the first day's practice when Gonzalez caused banner headlines in the Daily Express with what was then believed to be the first 100 m.p.h. lap in 1 min. 43.4 secs.; Fangio was a whole second slower, then came Farina in 1 min. 45 secs., then Ascari, then Villoresi in 1 min. 45.8 sec all inside Fangio's May practice record of 1 min. 46 secs., clearly betokening a titanic struggle for the 14th July—Bastille Day with a vengeance with Gonzalez leading the

616/7/8 B.R.M. STORY: Mays and Sommer after the disaster of August 1950 (top), Parnell saves the marque at Goodwood in September (centre) and Walker in the 1951 British Grand Prix

297

619 . . 'the massive frame and efforts of Gonzalez . . .'

sans culottes or 'shirtless ones' as his own nation's President would more nicely have had it. That Saturday afternoon history visited Silverstone as all watching must have realised. First it was Bonetto in an early lead, from which he was quickly cut down by the mighty Gonzalez sweeping round the circuit in immense power slides, crouched over the wheel, glowering like a charging bull with his neck fitted with banderillas bearing four-leafed clovers. By 5 laps he held a lead of 5 secs. over Fangio himself with Bonetto 7 secs. further behind, then a group of Ascari, Farina and Villoresi, Sanesi and Whitehead (Thinwall 4.5 Ferrari); Parnell and Walker (B.R.M.) were already well outpaced after only 15 miles. Over the next 5 laps Fangio moved to tremendous purpose, pulling out that little extra that is the perquisite of genius, and increased the leading average from 93.48 to 96.29 m.p.h. (which was his fastest race lap in May!) to lead by a length from Gonzalez with Ascari, now 3rd, *26 secs.* behind, closely invested by compatriot Farina, then after a 5 secs. gap followed Villoresi and Bonetto similarly tied together.

And so the pattern of this great motor race unfolded itself—three pairs of Italian racing cars grappling desperately for 1st, 3rd and 5th places, a classic study of defence in depth. During the next 15 laps Fangio managed to build up a lead of 5.6 secs. over Gonzalez, aided as much by a record 13th lap (98.84 m.p.h.) as by Gonzalez' excursion into the country at Becketts. The gap between them and Farina, who now led Ascari by a couple of lengths, had now grown to 44.4 secs.; likewise Ascari had now got right away from Bonetto and he in turn from Villoresi, so, on balance, these 15 laps belonged to Alfa now in 1st, 3rd, 5th and 7th. This balance was all too precarious to overcome that extra fuel stop as Fangio and Farina well knew: during the next 20 laps both pulled out every trick in the book—Farina even broke the record again at 99.99 m.p.h. but all to no avail as Gonzalez was actually gaining on Fangio and passed him on the 39th lap. Farina by now was having rather the better of Ascari whom he led by 46 secs. after 45 laps (half distance); Farina was also 50 secs behind Fangio who was still right behind Gonzalez. Of course the Alfa stops changed the whole picture as the two leader boards at 45 and 50 laps show:—

45 LAPS (135 MILES)		50 LAPS (150 MILES)	
1. Gonzalez	+ 3 lengths on	Gonzalez	+ 1m. 13s. on
2. Fangio	+ 50·2 secs. on	Fangio	+ 36s. on
3. Farina	+ 46 secs. on	Ascari	+ 28s. on
4. Ascari	+ 1m. 26s. on	Farina	+ 1m. 3s. on
5. Villoresi	+ 17s. on	Villoresi	+ 27s. on
6. Sanesi		Bonetto	

All this time Gonzalez was slowly inching the average up till at 60 laps it reached the all time high of 96.8 m.p.h. when he had increased his lead over Fangio to 1 min. 29.8 secs.—16.8 secs. in ten laps. After 48 laps Fangio had stopped for fuel

620 'First it was Bonetto in an early lead . . .' followed by Gonzalez, Farina, Ascari and Fangio

621 DESPERATE STRAITS—DESPERATE MEASURES: Gonzalez achieves fastest practice lap with a push from Ascari

622/623 HISTORIC PATTERN: Fangio in pursuit of Gonzalez (left) and Ascari closely invested by Farina (right)

624 Too few gears and an unhappy face spell retirement for Ascari

625 Ascari bids Gonzalez carry on his great work at his pit stop

626 SENSATIONAL ENTRY: 'To Gonzalez and Ferrari was now the power . . .'

and wheels in 49 secs.; now after 61 laps it was Gonzalez' turn to take on fuel in 23 secs. only, yet after 70 laps he still led Fangio by 1 min. 19.2 secs., which shows his superior performance over this vital stage of the race when one would have expected Fangio to have pressed really strongly in response to his 'faster' signal which hung out fairly consistently.

A few laps before Gonzalez' stop Ascari had retired with too few gears and had been seen looking thoughtfully at Gonzalez' car at its pit stop. This time Gonzalez was suffered to continue even though he himself got out of the car with touching humility. He was hastily pushed back in again and bidden to carry on with his great work which he did calmly and efficiently, gradually relaxing, as well he might with a lead of 71 secs. at 75 laps. At this mark it was poor Farina's turn to meet trouble, taking to the grass at Abbey Curve with a burning car when in a very secure 3rd. Odd it was how Ascari and Farina, though well behind the leaders, had ended by bursting each other. And so the race ran to its appointed end with that calm that follows the storm, Gonzalez finishing with a lead of 51 secs. over Fangio, then Villoresi two whole laps behind in 3rd, then Bonetto—3 laps, then Parnell on the 1st B.R.M., 5 laps away but still ahead of Sanesi's Alfa, another lap behind, then Walker's B.R.M. 44 secs. behind, but only half a minute ahead of Brian Shawe-Taylor with the ex-Harrison 2-stage blown C-Type E.R.A.

To win Gonzalez had driven a real upstairs-downstairs-in-my-lady's-chamber race even lapping Sanesi on the wrong side of the marker tubs at one point, but desperate straits require desperate measures and it cannot have been as fierce as it looked out when his was the only Ferrari to finish in really good order. He had moreover out-driven Fangio fair and square, particularly when one remembers that Fangio had only stopped for 26 secs. longer, and it is perhaps the truest measure of this much under-rated driver's greatness that he had contrived this in his first complete European Grand Prix in a real car (with which he was not then over familiar) and on a circuit he had never seen before. I doubt if any driver, even Rosemeyer, has made a more sensational entry into top-flight motor-racing than Gonzalez in 1951 as the results will show. To Gonzalez and Ferrari was now the power and to Silverstone the glory of having staged one of the great and decisive motor races of the century. As 'King-Pin' wrote in *The Motor*—'To me it had everything . . . technically . . . as varied a menu as anyone could wish: fours, sixes, eights, twelves and sixteens, all on the line at once and a choice of unblown, single-stage and two-stage aspiration; dramatically it was a whole series of plays within a play—and the noise alone was the best thing we have heard in this country since the Germans came to Donington in 1938.' After the race *Motor Sport* found 'a host

of absorbing speculations—will Alfa field the 160 to meet the new ferocity of the Ferrari challenge, when will B.R.M. race again and how effectively, and has Fangio met his match in Gonzalez?' and ended with the decisive statement —'And HOW these Argentinians drive!' How indeed!

A fortnight later the Nürburg Ring helped to answer some of these queries. The German Grand Prix had been revived in 1950 as a formula-2 event when Ascari had won in a Ferrari. He showed his knowledge of the circuit by making fastest practice lap in 9 mins. 55.8 secs., then came the irrepressible Gonzalez underlining his quality with a lap in 9 mins. 57.5 secs., then Fangio in 9 min. 59 secs. and Farina with 10 min. 1 sec. Alfas had discarded Sanesi and at the last minute brought in Paul Pietsch giving the poor man only 3 laps practice in the last session. The *Autocar* seemed to think this mattered not too much, as he knew the course backwards which turned out to be an unfortunate choice of words as he finally left it in this manner during the race. It was, however, all of a piece with the general panic stations in the Alfa organisation where axle ratios were being changed and tyre sizes debated to the last moment in contrast to the slumbering peace in the Ferrari camp. Ferrari had brought in Taruffi on a fourth car and, after practice, was moving in for the kill as surely as the traditional tide of Ring-bound traffic was again converging on the circuit where, as usual, there was little peace in woods that reflected camp fires and rang with accordion music. The Ring was back in business but with only one survivor of the last Grand Prix in Pietsch who had actually led it at one stage in his 8CTF Maserati.

627 ALFA REARGUARD: Fangio who fought the Ferraris bitterly at Silverstone and the Ring to finish 2nd both times

628 QUESTION-MARK: 'When will B.R.M. race again and how effectively?' was the question as Peter Walker takes the flag

301

Bonetto's Alfa was early in trouble but Fangio was away this time and stayed there with Ascari and Gonzalez snapping at his tail then, in support, Farina and Pietsch followed by— and how they must have teased the *Autocar*'s unhappy reporter—'Nuvolari'! On the 2nd lap Pietsch was off the road for the first time and then on the 5th lap Ascari and Gonzalez passed Fangio who stopped for fuel. Two laps later Farina had trouble in his gearbox, which left four Ferraris (including Taruffi's which was off colour) against one Alfa even though it was driven by Fangio. After the Ferraris had stopped after 9 and 10 laps Ascari was ahead of Fangio, followed by Gonzalez, who had put in best lap to date; Fangio now put up the fastest of the day, equalling Ascari's practice time, and pulled the lead back from Ascari but still with all four Ferraris behind him. After 14 laps Fangio stopped again and restarted with an obviously deranged gearbox being reported to have only top speed left. If this be so his finishing 2nd only 30.5 secs. behind Ascari and over 4 mins. ahead of Gonzalez was a wonderful effort underlining his amazing ability to coax the utmost out of the most ailing of cars—a truly great drive to defeat by Fangio and a great victory for Ascari (his first since 1949) and Ferrari, who packed 3rd, 4th (Villoresi) and 5th (Taruffi) behind Fangio. No other Alfa finished at all—and July 1951 must rank as Alfa's darkest hour since August 1934 when they had met with such disasters at Pescara.

Perhaps significantly they ignored the Pescara Grand Prix (as the race was now called) which was a Ferrari benefit— but only just. Gonzalez was again in fine form taking the lead from Villoresi on the 3rd lap when he stopped to hand over to Ascari, who had retired on the first lap. Ascari fared little better with his second mount, which left Gonzalez with a commanding lead, which he increased steadily till he won by 7½ mins. from Rosier. Chiron lost a certain 3rd place to Etancelin almost in sight of the finish after hitting a straw bale due to a broken brake pipe. This was bad luck as he had achieved 3rd fastest practice lap incredibly keeping Gonzalez out of the front row. In the race, however, not even spectator Fangio's 'Slow-Down' signal to his compatriot could slow the new Argentine Flyer. On his going days, Gonzalez, like Sommer and Villoresi in the early post-war years, had what John Eason-Gibson describes as 'the continental driver's attitude to racing ... "Win or lose I get paid starting money and the people have paid to see ME. I'll show them just how good I am." '

Ferrari, by contrast, was riding the crest of the wave in both formulae and cannot have been too perturbed by the last minute entry of Fangio and Farina to oppose Ascari, Gonzalez, Villoresi and Taruffi at Bari on September 2nd, a fortnight before the Italian Grand Prix. Farina retired after 20 of the 65 laps but Fangio set off grimly determined to banish for ever the memory of his two second places in July.

For six laps (almost 20 miles) he was hounded by Ascari and then the Ferraris faded: Ascari gave up at the pits with a suspected seized engine and Villoresi and Gonzalez motored steadily some way behind Fangio. After 30 laps (c.100 miles) Fangio stopped for fuel and restarted 30 secs. later still in the lead and finally won by two laps (6.6 miles or a good 5½ minutes) from Gonzalez with Taruffi another two laps behind on a new 2½-litre unblown Ferrari which had first appeared at Pescara in readiness for the 1954 formula. Villoresi had retired after half distance, Taruffi had never been near the leaders and at the end of the race Gonzalez was quoted as saying, 'I am satisfied to run second. Fangio is a master.' Ascari had the consolation of fastest lap in a race where Fangio had very significantly put the clock back at least to June albeit only over 215 miles but with only top gear (again!) for the last third of the race.

No sooner had the cars revved their last at Bari than it seemed they were at Monza, particularly the Ferraris, who were set on avenging their defeat and notching up their third successive full Grand Prix win over the Alfas. Fangio, Farina and Bonetto had new 159's with de Dion axles and longer tails plus long distance tanks and an output conservatively estimated at 400 b.h.p. while de Graffenried, in place of the injured Sanesi, had an earlier 159. Ferrari, not to be outdone, fielded no less than five cars: the Brazilian Landi, on a car variously reported as a 1950 4½-litre or the new 2½-litre model, Taruffi on one of the earlier 1951 twin-plug cars and Ascari, Villoresi and Gonzalez on new models with a higher scuttle line, reshaped wind-screen and a higher faired tail. The remainder of the field comprised an assortment of French Talbots and Simca-Gordinis, Whitehead's older Ferrari, Rol on the 4½-litre Osca and two ill fated B.R.M.s for Parnell and chief mechanic Ken Richardson.

Parnell's engine had to be changed during practice after he had lapped in 2 mins. 2.2 secs. on a damp road without specially hurrying or intimate knowledge of the circuit, while Richardson did 2 mins. 5.6 secs., which was little worse than de Graffenried with the slowest of the Alfas in 2 mins. 5.2 secs. True that Richardson had little or no racing experience and that the B.R.M. équipe had been warned that his entry would not be sanctioned by the R.A.C., yet he had considerable experience of the car as chief tester and was obviously much more capable than, say, Gaboardi who had driven an Alfa at Milan in 1947. He was also faster than Stuck (2 mins. 7 secs.) when he practised with the car and, due possibly to Stuck's missing a gear, gearbox troubles developed on the morning of the race. While it is difficult to excuse the Bourne organisation for the deplorable impression created by all this, I have always felt the R.A.C. took the rôle of Maiden Aunt to extremes over Richardson's case. It all seems nigh incredible now when British cars have been dominating Grand Prix racing almost without interruption

629 MISERABLE ANSWER: A weary Raymond Mays surveys the dismal scene at Monza

630 The intensity of Alfa-Romeo's effort at Monza is written on every line of Fangio's face

631 WHO'S AFRAID OF—'Fangio over ¼ min up on Ascari at 12 laps lost a tread and 34 secs . . . and Ascari (above) was never again headed'

632 ALFA REARGUARD: Farina who made fastest laps at Silverstone and Monza where he shewed real greatness

since 1957 but at the time there was truth as well as disappointed vitriol in D.S.J's remark . . . 'the people behind the car . . . know little about real racing. . . .' In those days there were precious few people outside Northern Italy who did. The non-starting of both cars in such circumstances of public disgrace was a blow that was to have far-reaching consequences on the 1½-litre formula after 1951 and was the last appearance of the V-16 B.R.M. at a formula national Grand Prix, its end having come with a peculiarly miserable whimper.

The leading Italians had fought a tremendous battle during practice and Fangio's 1950 practice record would not even have placed him on the second row in 1951. Alfas had the edge with Fangio and Farina in pole positions with laps at 1 min. 53.2 secs. (124.53 m.p.h.) and 1 min. 53.9 secs. The best Ferrari times were 1 min. 55.1 secs and 1 min. 55.9 secs. by Ascari and Gonzalez, then Villoresi (1 min. 57.9 secs.), Taruffi (1 min. 58.2 secs.) and Bonetto (1 min. 58.3 secs.) in a well matched bunch. Nearly 2 secs. slower in practice, could the Ferraris live with the Alfas during the 312 mile race? Would their deficit of 1 to 2 secs. for each of the 80 laps be too much of a handicap? As it turned out the streak of unreliability which had first struck Alfas at Rheims and nigh paralysed them on the Nürburg Ring again played havoc with them at Monza. Thus Fangio, over ¼ minute up on Ascari at 12 laps, lost a tread and 34 more secs. in one loud explosion and Ascari was never again headed or even seriously challenged. De Graffenreid was out after one lap and Farina after seven—both with engine maladies and Fangio's car was not wholly happy finally retiring at half distance with a broken valve. So the honour of Portello rested solely on the square reclined shoulders of Dr. Farina after 28 laps, in Bonetto's car and 4th place behind Ascari, Gonzalez and Fangio. The retirement of Fangio let him into 3rd at half distance, 57 secs. behind Gonzalez and 2 mins. 26 secs. behind Ascari and followed by Villoresi (−21 secs.) and Taruffi in a high speed Ferrari double-decker sandwich.

This was a situation to put Farina really on his mettle and he started carving great chunks off Gonzalez's lead, getting within striking distance of the stout Argentinian before his next fuel stop at 55 laps. All this hard and hazardous work was reduced to nought by an appallingly slow stop of 1 min. 59 secs. and worsened by Gonzalez taking only 30 secs. two laps later. This left Farina with a net loss of 1½ mins. to make up and, game as ever, he did it only to have his prize dashed away a second time. This time it was a split fuel tank which had to be replenished with ten laps to go. Hell bent for Gonzalez Farina roared off again to finish the race 'with a fountain of fuel streaking along the road behind him—rather like driving a hand grenade with the pin out,' as *The Motor* graphically put it. A weary Ascari won by 45 secs. from a relieved Gonzalez with an even more relieved if disappointed Farina a lap away in 3rd, followed by Villoresi and Taruffi. Ferrari's was the sweeping victory but Farina's courage and record lap—1 min. 56.7 secs.=120.97 m.p.h.—are the things that stand out in one's memory. To have seen him, as Grande Vitesse did, driving as he had not done for years (if ever) 'adopting a high-speed crouch coming down the 1¼-mile straight past the stands ... really pressing on utterly regardless' was to have seen a great driver at his very best fighting the odds—and there can be no finer or more soul-stirring sight in motor racing.

A couple of weeks later English spectators were privileged to see Farina in an original 1950 Type 159 win three short races at Goodwood including a 5-lap handicap from scratch where again the memory will not fade of Farina like a Barracuda weaving through the minnows down the Lavant Straight and ultimately catching the last one—Stirling Moss' H.W.M.—on the last bend of the last lap.

The *Autocar* wrote well of this—'from the vantage point of the control tower (Farina) was quite something to see, a tiny object streaking down Lavant, round Woodcote in a long drift and accelerating tremendously out of the corner, damping out the snaking of the car as the full power came in and then whizzing past, a colourful snapshot, leaning back in the cockpit of his vermilion car, pale blue shirt sleeves flapping and an expression of great good humour and enjoyment on the big sunburnt face.'

Not surprisingly, no B.R.M.s went to Barcelona for the Spanish Grand Prix on October 28th preferring to stay at Monza for some much overdue high speed testing, during which Stirling Moss was reported as saying it stopped and went faster and developed more power than the Alfas but was not so good on corners. The eight Monza contestants were back again for the final round of Ferrari v. Alfa, with honours even in the Grandes Epreuves stakes—three each and all to race for: what more could anyone ask of the last race in the year? The race itself was of 275 miles (70 laps) and Ferrari planned to go through on one tankful of fuel while Alfas opted for two stops and smaller tanks to secure better handling. Alfas raced on 700 × 18 back tyres, but Ferrari made a fatal decision to use a larger section and smaller diameter tyre of 7.50 × 16. Combined with the weight of fuel carried, these smaller tyres were just not man enough for their task particularly with a 1¾-mile straight on the course and Ferrari had the agonizing experience of seeing the vital victory slip through the fingers of his mechanics as they coped with a succession of thrown treads —just like Fiat at Dieppe in 1912. In practice Ascari, with previous knowledge of the circuit, was much the fastest (2 mins. 10.59 secs.), then inevitably came Fangio (2 mins. 12.27 secs.), Gonzalez next (2 mins. 14.01 secs.) then Farina (2 mins. 14.94 secs.). So, when Ascari led round on the opening lap the race looked well set for Ferrari: if the cars could lead on speed with a full tank the poor old Alfas would

not have much of a chance with at least two pit stops before them. From the start Ascari had been supported by Gonzalez but after three laps Fangio made his bid, swallowing up Gonzalez and Farina in quick snaps and then really shaking Ascari by the ears. Backs-to-the-wall-and-bared-teeth motoring this by both drivers 'at terrific speeds taking their cars through the bends in enormous four wheel slides within a few inches of the pavement and within a few feet of the solid wall of spectators.'

All goods things have to come to an end and this time it was Ascari who was struck down on the 8th lap with the inevitable tyre troubles which had already assailed both Taruffi and Villoresi. From this point only Gonzalez exerted any influence on the race for Ferrari and even he was clearly outpaced by both Fangio and Farina. He finally got past Farina, on his second fuel stop, and at one stage was within 25 secs. of Fangio but on this occasion the Alfa position was secure and Fangio motored home to victory in the race and the driver's championship 54 secs. ahead of Gonzalez, with Farina 3rd nearly another minute behind, then Ascari and Bonetto two laps away and de Graffenried four laps down. Fangio's race average of 98.76 m.p.h. was faster than Ascari's 1950 race record lap (97.7 m.p.h.) and he had driven a beautifully judged race to win. It was a bad day for Ferrari, losing both Taruffi and Villoresi with a buckled wheel and oiling troubles respectively, and his tyre selection was nothing short of tragic, but at this distance in time it is hard to grudge Alfas the final win after their magnificent rear-guard action ever since the French Grand Prix in July when they had been so nearly beaten. Alfas had found some more reliability since Monza even though they were not under so much pressure from the Ferraris and it was this, plus Ferrari's tyre troubles, which just tilted the final result their way in the most exciting season's racing since the war and what was tactically the most interesting series of races in history.

What that most perspicacious of motoring writers King-Pin, or, give him his real name, D. B. Tubbs, wrote about the British Grand Prix was equally true of the whole series of seven Grandes Epreuves: they had everything—Sight, Sound, Dominion, Power and Planning. The races were won in the pits, and even sometimes on the veriest fringes of the circuit, on the designing board, and in their very planning while speeds were in some cases beginning to surpass those of the great German era. Could it be that this very lèse majesté would be too much for Stuttgart and who, with memories of the past, could have failed to miss a heart-beat at the reports of the Spitzenfahrer Caracciola himself, with Lang and Kling, being out on the Ring in the late Autumn with the old Mercedes Rennwagen again at the same time as England's own rising star Stirling Moss and others were trying to chase some of the nonsense out of the B.R.M. at Monza? Even then, however, Alfa participation in 1952 racing was uncertain and their ultimate withdrawal combined with the failure of B.R.M. to present their cars in raceworthy trim at the beginning of 1952 left Formula I such a one-sided affair for Ferrari that, one by one, the Grands Prix went over to Formula II. In this class there were at least some new cars from Maserati, H.W.M. and others to vary the supporting cast from the seared ranks of tired old Maseratis, time expired Talbots and the still-born B.R.M. Perhaps a little more patience would have produced some worthwhile formula I Grands Prix in 1952/3 but race promoters cannot exist on patience alone and the temper of Europe in the winter of 1951/2 was rather short of patience particularly with the fading prospect of the B.R.M. to challenge the Ferraris once Alfa-Romeo retired. Whatever else, it certainly resolved any lingering doubts Mercedes might have had about revamping their W165 after they had tried it again on the Ring that Autumn and set them busy designing the W196 that was to be the next really big step forward in racing car design.

Accordingly the extension of 'Formula I' in October 1951 for another two years fell on remarkably indifferent ears in design shops and promoters' offices alike. Moreover with the announcement of a $2\frac{1}{2}$-litre unblown and 750 c.c. blown formula from January 1954 common sense dictated an immediate change to Formula II as the logical proving ground for future $2\frac{1}{2}$-litre designs. It might have been different if the B.R.M. had made a race of it against the big Ferraris at Turin in April 1952 though I personally doubt it as most of the leading Grands Prix had already seceded to Formula II by then. A few races were run to the old formula in 1952/3—mostly in England between the B.R.M.s and a variety of 4.5 Ferraris, chiefly the Vandervell modified 'Thinwall Special'. In addition Ascari took one over to Indianapolis in 1952 where he impressed American observers by finding the groove so quickly. He retired when 8th (or 12th in some accounts) on the 40th lap after a wheel had collapsed, having discovered there was rather more to Indy than Bill Vukovitch's disarming understatement—'All you have to do to win is keep your foot on the throttle and turn left.' It was this very strain of continually turning left that caused the Ferrari's wheel failure. Although the B.R.M. performed better in these two years, the Thinwall had its measure in everything bar sheer speed and so, soul-stirring though the song of the 16-cylinders in full cry might be, it was but a sorrowing song even when propelled by Fangio and Gonzalez against the more reliable honest fustian of the Ferrari. At Albi in 1953, however, the British cars had an hour of glory when challenged by Ascari's works Ferrari and Farina on the Thinwall. From the start Fangio left Ascari, whose tyres nearly set the grid alight, and Farina. Unfortunately the B.R.M.'s tyres were unequal to the

633 LAST WORD: Fangio driving to his Championship and Alfa's needle victory at Barcelona

struggle and thrown treads caused Wharton on the third car to have an awe-inspiring accident at 130 m.p.h. and Fangio to retire leaving the steady Rosier to win by $\frac{1}{2}$ minute from Gonzalez on the third B.R.M. A weak and miserable record when compared to that of the pre-war Alfa-Romeo it was so confidently expected to supersede, the car that set 'a record of reliability and success without parallel in motor racing,' when between 1947-8-50-51 they 'raced a total of 18,153 miles an average of 6,800 racing miles per car for an overall reliability factor of 81 per cent.'

Fangio's win at Barcelona is the last time that a supercharged car has won a Grande Epreuve and for many 1951 represented the end of an age—in retrospect perhaps a primitive age, an age which relied on overt brute force more than concealed cunning in design, but an age which gave motor racing a surge and thunder worthy of the great pioneering days. Some, with more extremist views might go so far as to borrow the words with which the French writer Maurice Druon concludes his series of historical novels on the Valois Kings of mediaeval France

. . . 'the pen, as the old chroniclers say, falls from his hand and he has no desire to continue, at least for the present except to inform the reader of the destinies of some of the principal characters in this story.'

PART FIVE

Epilogues I and II

Appendices

'In my end is my beginning'
T. S. Eliot   East Coker

Epilogue I
Towering Shades and Great Contemporaries

'There is no merit where there is no trial; and, till experience stamps the mark of strength, cowards may pass for heroes.'
Aaron Hill.

Dr. Alessio of Alfa-Romeo denigrated the prospect of motor racing turning into a mere struggle between men, yet in the last analysis that is what the public pay to see and the prospect of ballistically controlled racing cars would be a poor substitute for the abiding interest of the human element. When all the chemical and metallurgical mysteries have departed it is on the Carlylean doctrine of the Great Man that the basic excitement and wonder of the sport rests. By these standards a Great Man must not only stand out head and shoulders from his lesser contemporaries in excellence, but also have the power on occasions to direct the channels of history even as Hercules diverted streams to cleanse the Augean stables. As Bernard Darwin wrote of W. G. Grace he is a man who, unlike other heroes,

'towers high over them ... his fame is of a different quality to theirs; many of them will live, if at all, only as figures in the W. G. legend; he was, as Tom Emmett said, "a non-such"'

and it is with the Non-Suches of motor racing that this chapter is concerned.

Yet even genius is fallible—it was written of W. G. when he made a celebrated 'pair':

Our Grace before dinner was very soon done
And Grace after dinner did not get a run,

nor does it eternally dwell on Olympian heights and again the story is told of W. G.'s remark to the young man who claimed never to have made a duck—'Then you go in last. You can't have played much cricket.'

In judging past and present one has to dodge between the twin pitfalls of being a mere *laudator temporis acti* on the one hand and refusing to credit that there were heroes outside one's own times on the other. Actual comparison is really impossible because of the immense changes in techniques dictated by developments in cars and circuits over the years, yet the basic skills and qualities remain the same in 1964 as they were in 1914—courage, resolution under pressure or in adversity, balance, judgment and a sense of speed. To some extent, therefore, one can relate the skills of drivers

through the different periods of history and even indulge the fancy overall but first one must consider the leading actors before trying to assess their relative merits.

The early Grand Prix age between 1906 and 1916 began with a substantial carry forward from the inter-town and Gordon Bennett days with Szisz, Nazzaro, Lancia, Wagner and Hemery the most successful. I am inclined to regard Lautenschlager as a lucky Grand Prix winner—lucky for many reasons in 1908 and for having the best car as well as Wagner's delays through an officious official in 1914. Of these drivers Hemery and Lancia were cast in the heroic mould but Szisz, Nazzaro and Wagner were all men of slight build belying the idea that great size and strength were essential perquisites for driving the great cars of the heroic age. In 1910/12 the American amateur David Bruce-Brown blazed like a meteor across the sky as the first great driver from the United States along with Ralph de Palma. Brown was a man of the highest promise and his early death at Milwaukee in 1912 a terrible tragedy. Unlike Brown, de Palma was an unlucky driver: in the Grand Prix he was disqualified in 1912, delayed by Vauxhall in 1914, and had troubles with Ballot in 1921 while his misfortunes at Indianapolis were legendary although he did contrive to win in 1915 with a Lyons Mercedes.

Of course Boillot was THE non-such of the age—le grand Georges who bestrode the Grand Prix field for three tragically brief years till he was enveloped in the holocaust of 1914. All this time Jules Goux was his faithful shadow basking in the reflection of the master apart from his great hour of glory at Indianapolis in 1913, with or without the champagne. Dario Resta was another slightly built man who started in the heroic age but had little success till he joined Sunbeam and nearly won the Coupe de l'Auto in 1912: his 5th in the 1914 Grand Prix was probably his finest drive even including his immensely successful American season in 1915 /16.

The Americans put their 1915/16 experience and the lesson of wartime aero engine practice to wonderfully good use in the early post-war years with a string of victories at Indianapolis and Jimmy Murphy's once-and-for-all All American intervention in the 1921 Grand Prix. Then it was all Fiat again and the rise of the second generation of Italian drivers—first Bordino and Salamano then Ascari, Campari and Count Masetti—with the veteran Frenchmen Goux, Thomas and Wagner still well in the running. England too was producing drivers—K. L. Guinness, who had been established before the war, and the new star, Segrave, who made history in 1923 when he won the Grand Prix. The new generation of French drivers also emerged in the mid-twenties—first Divo and Benoist, then Chiron, Etancelin, Lehoux and René Dreyfus. Italy replied with Costantini and the great trinity—Nuvolari, Fagioli and Varzi. During this time Germany had thrown up only one driver since the times of Sailer, Lautenschlager and Salzer: Rudolf Caracciola. Then came the new Frenchmen, Moll, Wimille and Sommer, the Italians Trossi, Brivio, Farina and Villoresi and the new Germans Stuck, Brauchitsch, Lang, Rosemeyer and Müller and Dick Seaman the lone Englishman.

Many of these drivers survived the second war and played leading parts in the 1945-8 period when yet another generation were still finding their feet, notably Alberto Ascari, son of Antonio, J. M. Fangio the Argentine meteor who first shook a staggered Europe in 1949, and his mighty compatriot J. F. Gonzalez whose appearance in 1951 was no less sensational. British drivers of this class were still very thin on the ground, Reg Parnell being probably the only real claimant. During the years 1945-51 the leading drivers were Ascari, Fangio, Farina, Gonzalez, Villoresi, Sommer and Wimille, with doughty veterans like Chiron, Fagioli, Varzi, Taruffi and Trossi playing remarkably strong supporting roles on occasions. Who was the greatest starting with these post-war years?

Personally I should plump for Fangio and Wimille. True Wimille did not have the competition in 1946/8 that Fangio and Farina had to cope with in 1951, but he was the first post-war driver to rival the pre-war German speeds with the 158 Alfa and his tremendous polish and experience showed him pre-eminently the greatest driver of the immediate post-war period. In many ways Wimille, like his great rival and contemporary Sommer, lived and died without realising his true potential. Relegated to sports cars and minor races after 1933 when he was a brilliant youngster, he was really beginning to show the world what they had missed in the pre-war years when he met his baffling and untimely death in 1949. Great as was Fangio in 1951, Jean-Pierre Wimille might so very easily have been that iota greater.

By contrast Fangio, like Caracciola, was able to realise the full majesty of his greatness in his Years of Victory from 1954 to 1957 but he was perhaps at his greatest in 1949 when he was making his name and in 1951 when he was battling against the rising might of Ferrari. Like Sommer, Moss and Nuvolari in particular, Fangio was a tremendous trier and this was never shown better than in his lean years with Maserati in 1952/3. Fangio was so much better in adversity than his greatest rival Ascari. Alberto was as great a driver as his father and, like him, he loved to get out in front at the start and lead at ever increasing speeds. If Ascari could do this and, in rowing parlance, take clear water he could be

634 Jean-Pierre Wimille pre-eminently the greatest driver of the immediate post-war period

635 Fangio, always a tremendous trier, was perhaps at his greatest in 1951

636 Alberto Ascari (winning the 1951 Italian Grand Prix) was as great a driver as his father and loved to lead at ever increasing speeds

309

637 . . . 'the very epitome of the polished long-arm style'—Farina in 1950, his Championship year

638 MR. MOTOR RACING: 'Villoresi simply *was* motor racing for *so much of the early post-war times* . . .'

639 *and here he is in a 4CLT/48 Maserati in 1949*

640 (Right.) Ascari, to whom Villoresi taught so much in his early days, with rising newcomer Stirling Moss in 1949

unbeatable, but did he once get behind, then he tended to drive with no less ferocity but often with a fatal disregard for his car's well being. But for this small flaw Ascari was generally the equal of Fangio.

Farina was a great driver who somehow just missed the very greatest heights: with him one always felt that it really *was* 99 per cent. perspiration and, with all respect to Thomas Edison, real genius should not need to work quite so hard. This was not readily apparent until 1951 and perhaps by then his brightest skills may have been behind him. In so many ways he was the very epitome if not the actual originator of the polished long arm style that has become almost universal nowadays: on his day, and particularly when he was a lone entrant, (as at Goodwood in 1951) or when everything rested on him (as at Monza in the same year) there could be no more formidable opponent and his stature can only be a matter of inches below that of his greatest contemporaries. Villoresi simply *was* motor racing for so much of the early post-war times that his retirement left an irreplaceable gap in peoples' hearts, although he had begun to fade from the greater heights as early as 1949 and had

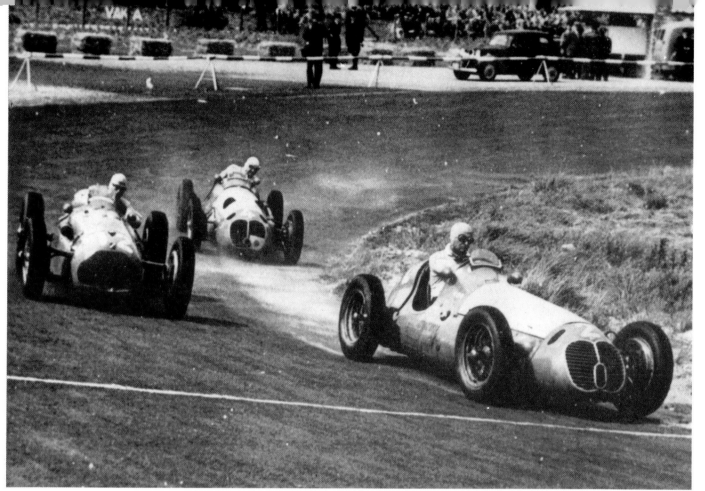

641 TIGERS THREE!: Fangio leads Gonzalez (4) and Sommer at Zandvoort in 1949

never really reached the greatest. Unlike any of the others in this group Villoresi was not a driver who ever managed to re-shape the destiny of a race against the odds, which must be the final touchstone of a great driver. The others—Fangio, Ascari, Wimille and Farina—all could and did—but none more successfully than Sommer and Gonzalez. Sommer never quite had the chance for one reason or another, but Gonzalez did in 1951 and seized it in his great hands with iron determination. I very much doubt if there has ever been a faster or more determined driver than Gonzalez, or one who learnt to go really fast as quickly as he did in 1951—and with such safety, whatever the appearances. In all his drives for Ferrari in 1951 Gonzalez never once crashed or retired, which is a record unequalled by Ascari, Fangio or Farina in that year. Had he driven for Ferrari in all the 1951 championship events he might very well have been the first Argentinian champion instead of Fangio. As it is his remains the glory of being the first driver to outdrive the full Alfa team in the supremacy of their power. Sommer had of course been the first to defeat them at St. Cloud and he shared with Fangio, Nuvolari and Moss that tremendous determination to win whilst going as fast as he could as long as he could which enabled him on occasion and against all odds to reverse the natural order of things.

So often brilliant failure is a more attractive facet than relatively uninteresting success and it was in those terms that Grande Vitesse wrote his moving epitaph in *The Motor* of Sommer: 'whether his list of successes is short or long

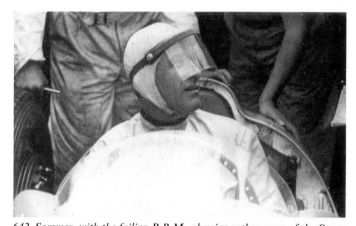

642 Sommer, with the failing B.R.M., shewing rather more of the Saxon than the Gaul

Sommer will be remembered for the quality of his make-up which seemed to combine so well the gaiety of the Gaul with the determination of the Saxon. In any case success is not necessarily a criterion and those who knew him will miss his bright example of how one should go really motor racing.' In so many ways Sommer's was a unique genius—a happy-go-lucky amateur united with a grim determined professional. Of course 'grim' is a relative term, like 'vintage' or anything else, and by Varzi's standards Sommer was a rustic clown. A very famous amateur footballer was once described by his contemporaries as 'that sombre athlete' and really this phrase might have been coined for the Sphinx of Galliate.

643 Seaman leading the Belgian Grand Prix of 1939 in appalling conditions with an ease worthy of Caracciola himself

Going back to the preceding period, the great drivers of the years 1928/39 were Chiron, Nuvolari, Varzi, Caracciola, Fagioli, Lang, Stuck and Rosemeyer: although they figured more or less during this period, Campari, Divo and Benoist really belonged to the pre-1928 years, while such drivers as Dreyfus, Moll, Lehoux, Müller, Trossi, Brivio, Hasse, Etancelin, Birkin, and possibly even Brauchitsch and Seaman, who all achieved great fame, never were absolutely in the class of the first eight. Of these Caracciola was the first to win a Grand Prix—the German in 1926—but Nuvolari was probably the first to start racing in about 1921 while Chiron was the last to give up, although Fagioli in the end was the one who kept his form best. For various reasons Varzi, Chiron and Fagioli retired from effective Grand Prix participation in 1935/6 and did not re-appear until after the war when they all raced with much more success than their more successful pre-war rivals Caracciola and Nuvolari, whose post-war appearances were curiously ill-starred. Caracciola drove an American machine at Indianapolis after wisely spending the war in Switzerland and had a terrible accident from which he had barely recovered in 1950, when he was back on the Ring testing the old pre-war cars for the Mercedes excursion to the Argentine in January 1951. Rudi thought little of this scheme but came back with joy to Mercedes in a 300 SL sports car for the 1952 Mille Miglia, in which he had not driven since 1932 when he led at Rome on Alfa-Romeo. In 1952 he finished 4th one place behind his great team-mate and rival Fagioli now on a touring Lancia and it was then planned that these two great veteran drivers were to share a Mercedes at Le Mans in June.

It is history that Lang made somewhat of a comeback to win a lucky race there but Fate hit tragically at the other two Mercedes veterans: Caracciola had a brake lock in the sports car race at Berne in May and never raced again after the third serious accident of his career, while Fagioli had been killed practising for the sports car race at Monaco in the same month. Lang went on to drive the W196 Mercedes at the Nurburg Ring in 1954 but was a mere shadow of his pre-war self and sang a disappointing swan-song. Lang showed promise in 1935, went under with the rest of the Mercedes team in 1936 and emerged as a driver capable of leading and winning major races in 1937. Although he won a second time at Tripoli in 1938 it was a dull season for him and gave no foretaste of his 1939 form when he was virtually unbeatable, winning every race in which he finished including the Grands Prix of Tripoli, Switzerland, Belgium, Pau and the Eifelrennen as well as dominating the French Grand Prix till his retirement and incidentally being German hill climb champion. As he also made a record or fastest lap in three out of his seven races, he stood out as by far the fastest and most successful driver of the year and probably of the whole 3-litre formula. The death of Seaman undoubtedly removed his most formidable rival in 1939, for on the evidence of his great form in 1938, which he continued in practice at the Ring and Pau in 1939, he was as fast as anyone in the Mercedes team. As proof of this, prior to his accident he was leading the 1939 Belgian Grand Prix in dreadful conditions with an ease worthy of the great regenmeister, Caracciola himself. Many reasons have been advanced for Seaman's fatal error of judgment but I have never heard one of the most probable suggested—sheer lack of racing practice: both Nuvolari and Caracciola also crashed in this race and Caracciola also did in the ensuing French Grand Prix. At that point Nuvolari had driven in the Eifelrennen only and Caracciola in that race and at Tripoli, while for Seaman it was his first race of the year. Just as in rowing so in motor racing is it often true that mileage makes champions and I have little doubt that Caracciola's indifferent form in 1938/9 was as much due to this, as the long gap in Lang's career after 1939 proved a stumbling block that he could not overcome. In this respect Lang, although poles apart temperamentally from Farina, shared his quality of being a 99 per cent. perspirationist. Caracciola had more of the flair of genius enjoyed by the great Italian and French drivers of his time and his falling off from his previous pedestal of almost invariably dependable genius was possibly as much due to lack of interest as anything else. Even at the end of 1939 he could still win a race with his head at the Ring and make the fastest lap on his beloved Bremgarten circuit.[1]

Rosemeyer, like Gonzalez, flashed like a star across the European firmament, achieving great fame almost in the twinkling of an eye and then departing as suddenly as he had arrived. No other driver ever succeeded in getting quite so much out of the unconventional Auto-Union as he did, although Stuck, Nuvolari and Varzi were all formidable performers with the car. Indeed the 1935/6 team which included Varzi, Stuck and Rosemeyer must rank as one of the strongest ever to line up in Grand Prix racing. After 1935 Stuck went through the same sort of reaction as Caracciola did in 1938/9, although his form tailed off more noticeably, but in the first two years of the 750 kg. formula he was a driver of the highest class and on a par in many respects and certainly for sheer speed with Fagioli, Caracciola, Nuvolari and Varzi. He also made a considerable comeback in Formula II racing after the war and in 1950 was reported as

645 TWINKLING STAR: . . . 'no other driver ever succeeded in getting so much out of the unconventional Auto-Union as Berndt Rosemeyer'

being in prospect of the odd drive in the 158/9 Alfas. I have always thought it a pity the Italians preferred Pietsch to Stuck for the 1951 German Grand Prix: at all events he could not have done worse and, in any case, was in a completely different class as a driver.

Now to turn the acid test on to the outstanding drivers of this period Chiron (in 1934), Fagioli (1934/5), Caracciola and Nuvolari (throughout) and Rosemeyer (1936/7) had that essential ability to reverse the natural order of things and turn a loser's race in their favour, the last three supremely, Chiron really only once (even though that once was enough for anyone else's lifetime) and Fagioli in 1934/5 when he was probably the fastest and most experienced driver in the German teams, second only in these qualities to the great Nuvolari. Varzi's career during 1934/6 was a sad one indeed: I am not alone in my belief that Varzi and Nuvolari, as different as the ice and fire of which their respective styles were compounded, were on a par in the years 1928-33, although Nuvolari's was the greater genius. Varzi, although Italian champion, had a frustrating season in the 1934 Grands Prix, and must have welcomed his translation to Auto-Union in 1935. Sadly, he was never able to make full use of his new car: by the time he had accustomed himself to it he had become enmeshed in the toils first of love and then of drugs, and turned, motor-racing-wise, into a Lost Weekend—Dolce Vita character. It is difficult to know whether the tragedy was greater for Varzi, motor sport, or Auto-Union. The tremendous speed of Varzi's reaction and the famed delicacy and accuracy of his driving could have made him the greatest of all Auto-Union drivers in the years 1935/9 and, of all the lost opportunities of motor racing history, I am inclined to place the illness of Varzi and Fagioli in 1936/9 highest. Both of these men dropped out of racing when they had years of top class driving in them and their post-war revivals add poignancy as well as distinction to their careers.

644 Stuck (in white cap) was a driver of very high class in 1934/5 (Nuvolari is by him in blue beret)

[1] The fact that Caracciola could drive at all after his injuries in 1933 is as remarkable a testament to his courage and skill as was the comeback of Ben Hogan after a similar accident, to the American golfing circuit in the late forties and early fifties.

'*Cruel but composed and bland*
'*Dumb, inscrutable and grand*

'*So Tiberius might have sat*
'*Had Tiberius been a cat*'

Between 1928 and 1933 the greatest 750 kg. drivers were learning and perfecting their art and the foundations of the modern technique of motor racing were being at least excavated, if not actually laid, by the Great Ones. It is, however, of Nuvolari and Varzi that one thinks chiefly, for their great rivalry on the circuit, for the near-perfection their vastly differing styles brought to racing technique, for the very contrast between the two men and, in retrospect, for their far reaching influence on the greatest of the post-war drivers. Both were ex-racing-motor cyclists but there the similarity ended. . . . 'Varzi had created his own driving style of which he was to remain the inimitable protagonist until the last . . . methodical, cold blooded, precise comparable to the best Swiss watch, whereas Nuvolari could be likened jokingly to a cuckoo clock liable to strike at the most unexpected moment and full of surprises.' Yet in their greatest duel, at Monaco in 1933, it was Varzi who cuckolded Nuvolari to win with a final lap two seconds inside the lap record while Nuvolari burst his engine. One almost blenches at the thought but, on this occasion, Varzi had played cat-and-mouse with the Maestro, the campionissimo himself. Varzi was the supreme example of the man who liked to come up from behind and scored many of his greatest victories in this style—Tripoli (1934 and 1936), Monaco and Avus (1933) and the thrilling Monza Grand Prix in 1930. This trait in his character is well described by Ferrari 'intelligent, calculating, grim when necessary, ferocious in exploiting the first weakness, mistake or mishap of his adversaries. He could well be described as pitiless,' but elsewhere Ferrari describes Varzi and Brivio as 'possessing the same gentlemanly chivalry at the wheel as Nazzaro and Minoia' and equally, Louis Chiron. Posthumus also speaks of his 'gentlemanly charm and sardonic sense of humour . . . calculated machine-like perfection, following his own wheel-tracks to the inch for lap after lap; when at bay he was magnificent, driving with grim ice-cold ferocity immensely fast but never making a mistake.'

Varzi inherited the precision as well as the immaculate turn-out and gentlemanly nature of the great Felice Nazzaro and engrafted on to it a grimness of purpose all of his own making and all this he passed on to Juan Manuel Fangio. Returning like a shade from the past at the age of 46, with his faithful mechanic Bignami to say nothing of his eternal cigarette Varzi was one of the earliest drivers to winter in the Argentine and there in 1948 he was introduced to Fangio then driving a Maserati for the first time. . . . 'he listened to my reactions and gave me some precious advice. . . The great Varzi spoke with simplicity. I hung on his every word. . . .' After that same race when Fangio calmed himself . . . 'studying the racing technique of the European champions whose style made our own look brutal and clumsy. . . .' Jean-Pierre Wimille singled him out as a future miracle man, but, tragically, neither Wimille nor Varzi lived to see their judgments fulfilled or, as they would have surely preferred, to drive in the same Alfa line-up against their Ferrari adversaries. Varzi's style as well as his name lived on in the Argentine and it was the most moving tribute to his great memory for the Argentine A.C. to name their 1949 Armada the Squadra Achille Varzi.

Fangio's most memorable victory in the 1957 German Grand Prix would have delighted Varzi—as would Brabham's in the 1964 International Trophy at Silverstone—and there is so much similarity between the manner and technique of Fangio's drive then and Varzi's pursuit of Arcangeli in the 1930 Monza Grand Prix when plug trouble cost him 1 min. 50 secs. Rejoining the race 'in an ice-cold fury (Varzi) made up the time in 60 tempestuous miles broke the course record on 11 consecutive laps and caught the astonished Arcangeli on the last corner of the last lap, to win a desperately exciting race by one-fifth of a second!' *Mutatis mutandis* it could just as well have been Fangio in that classic pursuit of Hawthorn and Collins.

In a sense it is easy to sing the praises of Varzi who never quite had as many as his skill warranted and nearly impossible to deal adequately with the greater genius of Nuvolari upon whom every conceivable superlative has already been lavished. Just as C. B. Fry and Hobbs did to cricket so did Varzi to motor racing in bringing an ice cold intellect to bear on the problems involved with results that are too well known to need further mention. By contrast Nuvolari was the 'W.G.' (or Bradman to a more recent age) whose genius enabled him simply to be styled the greatest who has ever lived. Of all the great drivers he was the most likely to confound expectation, the man who sent tingles down one's spine, who:

> Left a name at which the world grew pale
> To point a moral or adorn a tale.

Fagioli was the most consistently successful Mercedes driver in 1934/5 and continued to drive consistently well with the difficult W25E in 1936, but he was a sick and possibly disillusioned man by this time. True he had had two good years after leaving Ferrari but team orders were not to the taste of the independent spirit of the old Abruzzi Robber, as he was fondly known, when he felt himself 'as tall as any man in Illyria'. Shorn of team discipline his record with the W25A/B could have been as good as that of Caracciola whose equal he certainly was. Not so calculating as Varzi, not so phlegmatic as Caracciola, not so mercurial as Chiron nor as deeply gifted as Nuvolari, Fagioli was a clearing house of all his rivals' virtues: deeply experienced, rarely given to error, polished in his later years and very, very fast—he was a most formidable and tough adversary who brought his great knowledge to Germany and left a worthy disciple behind him in the rising Hermann Lang who

MAN OF FIRE

'*Of all the great drivers he was the most likely to confound expectation . . .*'

'*The Greatest Who Has Ever Lived . . .*'

650 '*A most formidable and tough adversary . . .*'—*Luigi Fagioli*

315

651 CLEARING HOUSE: *Fagioli in 1931*

652 SUCCESSFUL RETURN: *Fagioli in 1950: 'to shine for style in the company of Fangio and Farina is a remarkable tribute . . .'*

graduated in the traditional manner from mechanic to Grand Prix driver. He also contrived much the most successful comeback of his great comtemporaries in the post-war years: perhaps he no longer had the speed of the younger Alfa drivers, but the style and polish of his driving still stands in the memory: to shine for style in the company of Fangio and Farina is a remarkable enough tribute to any man, let alone one who had retired from racing due to ill health 13 years previously. In the cut-and-thrust of 1951 one would have thought Fagioli a 'natural' for the Alfa team, but instead they teetered about with Sanesi, de Graffenried, Pietsch and Bonetto, calling on the old master for only the French Grand Prix, which was his last great race and where he shared the winning car with Fangio—old and new champions. The old man distinguished himself by a remarkable detour into a ditch just short of Thillois hairpin where 'the car was over on the grass for 100 yards at 100 m.p.h. at an angle of 45 degrees, his head almost touching the tall grass, but he brought it back on to the road and took the corner without trouble.' This failure to deploy the fullest available driving strength is a characteristic not only of Alfa-Romeo at all times apart from 1950 (when oddly enough they least needed it) but in pre-war times, and for that matter in 1954/5, of Mercedes-Benz. The great experience, skill and toughness of Fagioli would undoubtedly have been a great support to Fangio and Farina in those desperately fought races in 1951 when Alfas were severely outgunned by Ferrari both technically and in terms of driver strength.

Between 1926 and 1939 Caracciola won six German Grands Prix and 16 other major races mainly for Mercedes but in 1932 for Alfa-Romeo. This in itself is a substantial achievement but success is not the only criterion of Greatness: when necessary Caracciola could 'tiger' as well as any man but it was such a softly spoken form of 'tigering', so much so that his rivals so often simply did not know what had hit them. This was especially true in rain where his extreme delicacy of touch made him able to tame the fiercest of cars and to drive at speeds that few other drivers could comprehend, let alone match. On occasions it was as if the natural laws of visibility and gravity were temporarily suspended by his genius. The old 2-litre 8-cylinder Mercedes of 1924/5 was never raced in France, but it did impress observers as being extremely difficult to drive and Raymond Mays who later drove it at Brooklands described it thus:

'. . . the thought came to me that it was only a matter of time before we killed ourselves on this machine.'

The 1926 German Grand Prix at Avus was, by the European standards of the time, a minor event except that it gave Rudi a chance to show what he could do with this killer in the rain. At the Ulster T.T. in 1929 nobody could touch him, again with a difficult car on an unfamiliar circuit, and it was the same years later at Berne in 1938 when Dick Seaman, at the top of his form, found Caracciola quite unbeatable in the wet. The fact that Seaman was able to challenge and even lead Rudi under such conditions adds immensely to his stature. The 1937 W125 Mercedes-Benz remains the most powerful Grand Prix car ever to have raced and the comments of Brooks and Collins who drove the cars in 1958 at only semi-racing speeds are revealing:

'... they were unanimous ... that those who had driven them in the past with the loud pedal down (e.g. Caracciola and Brauchitsch at Monaco or Caracciola at Berne—W.E.C.) must have been either extremely brave or completely lacking in imagination.'—Tempora Mutantur!

Only Caracciola really mastered these historic cars and his five laps during practice for the Swiss Grand Prix of 1937 *all* around 107 m.p.h. must represent the greatest testament to his skill. With Stirling Moss he is the only driver to have beaten the Italians on their own ground in the Mille Miglia; 21 years later (in 1952) Rudi astounded many by finishing 4th in this classic with the Mercedes comeback car, the 300SL. Before 1934 it was a considerable achievement for a non-Italian to win at Monza, which was what Caracciola had done with the original monoposto in the 1932 Grand Prix. Caracciola lacked the more obvious genius of the great Italians or the spectacle of Rosemeyer, and his skill was often only realised when the stop-watch was consulted. Yet Rudi at bay could be as memorable as Fangio or Nuvolari: then one saw him driving with heart and head— in 1939 he drove two classic races when people were beginning to rate him a back number after his accidents at Spa and Rheims. He out-drove and out-thought his team-mates and the Auto-Unions on the Nürburg Ring in poor weather conditions and drove a memorable race at Berne in his last Grand Prix for Mercedes. As the rain fell in the shortened final heat his pursuit of Lang, so nearly successful, was a wonderful example of a great driver grappling with his car, his rival, the weather, and most of all, himself. For all his 1939 supremacy Lang was lucky that that race was not 10 laps longer.

In many ways Louis Chiron, the last survivor of this great group, is the most difficult to assess. He assumed the mantle of Wagner and Benoist as the greatest French driver in 1928 and from then until 1935 he ranked with the greatest in Europe. Most memorable are Chiron's vivacious personality, the polished style of his driving and his masterful starting: who cares any longer if some of it was a bit on the 'quick' side? Chiron was Chiron and even starters had to turn a blind eye. The pinnacle of his pre-war career was his superb win in the 1934 French Grand Prix: after this he was dogged by much ill luck due to the declining powers of the Ferrari Alfas coupled with recurring illness in 1935. His selection for Mercedes in 1936 was amply justified but, of all

653 FORMIDABLE COMBINATION: the deep understanding between Caracciola and Neubauer was one of the foundations of Mercedes greatness 1934/9

654 REGENMESTER: 'in rain Caracciola was able to drive at speeds which few other drivers could comprehend . . .' here at Berne in 1938 when Seaman found him quite unbeatable

655 MEISTERSCHAFT: Caracciola setting up his all time practice record at Berne in 1937

656 *In 1928 Louis Chiron assumed the mantle of Wagner and Benoist*

657 *'Sheer Gascon Insouciance . . .'*

658 *Almost Italian Temperament*

the years to be forced into a new kind of racing car, 1936 on Mercedes was the worst and poor Chiron never had a chance with a car that defied even Fagioli and Caracciola. Had his translation to Mercedes occurred in 1935 much of subsequent racing history pre-war might well have had to be rewritten. From 1928 to 1933 he was on any account one of the fastest drivers in Europe; during 1934/5 he led the Ferrari counter-attack and conducted a magnificent rearguard action against the new German cars variously supported by Moll, Varzi, Trossi and Nuvolari. For sheer Gascon insouciance his refusal to bow to the superior German cars at Montlhéry in 1934 will go down to history as will his next French Grand Prix win in 1947 (I except the sports car event in 1937) when he 'gammoned' his rivals so successfully. Not D'Artagnan nor Henry of Navarre himself had a better touch of the Gasconade. Chiron's comeback after the war was tremendously successful and, needless to say, no less popular: motor racing had simply not been the same since his retirement in 1936. For all his almost-Italian temperament Chiron was a tremendous trier however hard the challenge, a quality which much endeared him to the pro-German crowds at the Ring in his years of adversity.

659 *PORTHOS: The melodious Campari dwarfs Nuvolari at Nice in 1933*

If Chiron was the dashing D'Artagnan, Caracciola the cool Aramis and Varzi the mercurial brooding Athos of their day, then their Porthos was surely the melodious Campari. Unlike his contemporaries we have so far considered, Campari never drove a 'modern' racing car but between 1924 and 1933 he showed himself a master of the post-1914 Grand Prix cars principally the P2 and P3 Alfas and sundry Maseratis. Campari may have been a greater character than he was a driver but in his day he was one of the toughest men to beat and one of the great drivers of his time. Campari was the last survivor of the original P2 team, Ferrari and Wagner having retired and Brilli Peri and Ascari being dead.

Going back now to 1912 we find a considerable 'carry-forward' from the Heroic Age and the early Coupe de l'Auto days. The great drivers of Dieppe were unquestionably Bruce-Brown and de Palma (Fiat) both Americans, Resta (Sunbeam) and Boillot and Goux (Peugeot). Sadly this was Brown's first and last European appearance: with de Palma he was and remains one of the three greatest American road racing drivers. It is not until the rise of Dan Gurney in recent years that America has produced a driver of similar quality: I am inclined to rank Phil Hill 6th in U.S.A. status below Tommy Milton and also Jimmy Murphy. Resta's placing is primarily on his brilliance in the States in 1915/16 although he drove a very fine race to finish 5th in the 1914 Grand Prix and was very unlucky not to win the Coupe de l'Auto (and 3rd place in the Grand Prix) in 1912. As for Boillot he was simply the *nonpareil* of his age and, of all the great drivers in 1914, it was passing cruel that he alone should have perished in the old war.

If Boillot had a fault it arose out of his intense pride and patriotic spirit. Like Farina in his later years he simply could not comprehend the possibility of defeat and it was this very pride that may have lost him his greatest win in 1914. Both he and Goux knew the Mercedes were better cars in terms of roadholding and, while the logical Goux was content to drive within the car's capabilities, Boillot drove his with an elemental fury that defied all logic, when only slightly more temperate tactics could well have saved both engine and tyres and kept him just ahead. For Boillot, however, this was not enough.

Whilst Goux was ultimately surpassed by Boillot and always lacked his daring and dash, he was a driver of great polish at a time when style was not always at a premium; he drove for many years with the greatest distinction and is the first European to have won at Indianapolis with a European car, a feat that has only been twice repeated and that as long ago as 1914 and 1916.[1] If for no other reason this is enough to put Goux in the Book of Immortality. Of René Thomas who won at Indianapolis in 1914 it is more difficult to write. He was at his best between 1914 and 1924, after which he gradually retired into racing management, displaying most marked reluctance to get into a racing Delage at San Sebastian in 1926. Thomas was a tough and experienced veteran but in my view lacking the greatest qualities of his contemporaries before or after the war, notwithstanding his winning Indianapolis in 1914 and achieving pole position there in 1919. In spite of the nihilistic brilliance of his win in the 1919 Targa Florio André Boillot never achieved either the glory or the cars of his elder brother: like Catiline he had plenty of eloquence but too little prudence and goes down to posterity as a One Speech Hamilton sort of driver. In the little known Aquila Italiana at Lyons in 1914 was one Bartolomeo Costantini who achieved fame as a Bugatti driver in the twenties in particular winning the Targa Florio

660 *Major Sedwick (left) with top American driver Johnnie Aitken (right), Goux (centre, left) and Boillot in 1914*

661 *André Boillot for all his brilliance never achieved the fame of his brother*

in 1925/6. W. F. Bradley has praised his delicate and accurate driving, characteristics in which he resembled his latter-day friend Varzi for whom he procured a Bugatti for the 1930 Targa. There was also a certain facial resemblance increased by Costantini's cigarette gripped between his lips and one wonders if Varzi did not absorb some of his style and methods from Costantini.

Since writing Jim Clark has, of course, made it three in 1965.

662 Felice Nazzaro was the greatest driver in the world at the age of 26 in 1907 and was able to stay at the top until he retired in 1924 by effortless and immaculate technique

663 Only Louis Wagner, also famed for his relaxed style, had a longer career at the top

664 Lautenschlager (right) was not the equal of his contemporaries

Nazzaro came back to racing in 1913 and his effortless and immaculate technique enabled him, like Fagioli, Goux and Wagner, to remain in the top flight long after almost all his contemporaries. Of these only Louis Wagner, who was also famed for his relaxed style, had a longer career at the top. I except the veteran Germans Lautenschlager and Salzer whom I do not consider ever to have been of the calibre of their French, Italian and English contemporaries. Bradley has put the difference so well in his account of the 1922 Targa Florio referred to at page 118. If Nazzaro was the veteran of Italian racing after 1914, then Bordino and Ascari were its new stars, the forerunners of Nuvolari, Varzi, Fagioli, Farina, Ascari II and Villoresi. Bordino was generally regarded as the fastest driver of the early and mid-twenties, with Ascari running him a close second. Both were fiery Latins whose only thought was to take the lead and drive as fast as possible from start to finish, and it was this very Garibaldino spirit that killed Ascari I—the fatal urge to go that little fatal bit faster than weather conditions warranted or the race position required. The decline of Fiat after the 1924 Grand Prix virtually finished Bordino's Grand Prix career which he only resumed in two short races with the 12-cylinder 1½-litre Fiat at Monza in 1927—with drivers like Ascari, Campari and Brilli-Peri, Alfas were perhaps rich enough not to need Bordino but it is a pity that room could not have been found for the most brilliant of Italian drivers in 1924/5 in either the Alfa-Romeo or Delage teams.

Apart from Wagner, the leading Frenchmen of the twenties were Benoist, Thomas, Divo and Goux, while the veterans Guyot and Hemery were still appearing from time to time. Both Benoist and Divo were effective only in the twenties: Divo was one of the last drivers before Lang to come up through the ranks, starting life as an S.T.D. riding mechanic and attaining great fame successively with S.T.D.,

665 FIERY LATINS: 'Bordino was generally regarded as the fastest driver of the mid-twenties . . .'

666 FIERY LATINS: . . . 'with Ascari running a close second'

667 Count Masetti in 1925, one of the best stylists of his time and Targa Florio expert

Delage and Bugatti. Benoist drove four seasons for Delage in 1924/7 culminating with his *Annus Mirabilis* in 1927. Impressive as this was, his pre-eminence was due as much to M. Lory as to Benoist himself: it would have been interesting to see how he and the Delage fared against Bordino's Fiat in 1927 and it should also be remarked that at San Sebastian, which was the only real 'drivers' circuit that year, Materassi was able to lead him for a time on a Bugatti that was decidedly inferior to the Delage. Benoist's status, like that of Divo and Thomas, remains somewhat of an enigma, though personally I should rank him higher than Divo, Segrave or Guinness and only slightly below the greatest Italians. On their showing at Lyons in 1924 both Segrave and Guinness were drivers capable of challenging Europe's best and Segrave won the Spanish Grand Prix on the difficult San Sebastian circuit later in the year. They had also both driven well in 1921/3 and, if Segrave's Spanish win had been achieved over the Alfa-Romeos as well, he would have a strong claim to the highest ranking as a driver of the twenties. As it is both he and Guinness rate slightly lower than Ascari, Benoist, Nazzaro and Bordino but higher than Divo, Thomas, Campari and Brilli Peri. The other great Italians of this period, who all died at the wheel, were Emilio Materassi, Count Masetti and Luigi Arcangeli; Masetti was one of the best stylists of the time and a great champion of the Targa Florio, who drove with distinction both for Mercedes and S.T.D. in various Grand Prix races until his untimely death in 1925. Like Bordino and Ascari I, Materassi and Arcangeli were both Garibaldinos—or speed merchants: it was only this that enabled Materassi to lead Benoist in the 1927 Spanish Grand Prix until he overdid things and let Benoist through to win. Arcangeli was a noted man of fire though never in the class of Nuvolari, Varzi and Fagioli.

668 Goux drove all through the twenties ending with an Indian Summer in 1926

669 Benoist drove four seasons for Delage culminating with his Nazzaro-like year in 1927

321

673/4 *Materassi (top) and Luigi Arcangeli (above) were both noted as Italians of fiery temperament*

670/1/2 *(Top left) Divo drove for S.T.D., Delage and Bugatti in the twenties and thirties (seated on wheel) often with Segrave (in car) and (left centre) K. Lee Guinness who were both capable of challenging Europe's best and (left) stout-hearted Jean Chassagne (holding steering wheel) ex-Clément-Bayard riding mechanic and Hispano-Suiza and Sunbeam driver*

For the years 1906-11 the outstanding drivers for speed were undoubtedly Duray, Lancia, Wagner, Nazzaro, Hemery and Bruce-Brown, with Szisz a very reliable man if not quite in the class of the others. Cagno also achieved considerable success during this time, Rigal drove a great race at Dieppe in 1908 as did Hautvast in the 1907 Kaiserpreis, but these and many other fine drivers of the period lacked the final touchstone of greatness in the six I have singled out. Perusal of the early chapters makes it clear that they were all in their differing ways and very different conditions men of outstanding calibre. For sheer all round enduring skill Nazzaro was undoubtedly the hardest man to beat, while Lancia on his day was the fastest driver in the world; Wagner, Duray and Hemery were all also capable of driving outstandingly fast. At this distance in time it is hard to assess their relative skills, but in the context of their times these men were the Fangio, Moss, Nuvolari, Caracciola, Bordino or Boillot of their age and Gerald Rose was right when he wrote

'The finest driver of 1949 cannot slide his corners any more skilfully than Jenatzy, Lancia or Hemery used to do. . . .'

Let us in conclusion honour and remember these the greatest of the original Grand Prix drivers as every whit the equals in the enduring skills of their profession of their successors.

675 By winning the four major events of 1904/5 Théry established himself as Europe's leading driver—here he is returning in triumph to Paris after the 1905 Gordon Bennett

677 A VERY RELIABLE MAN: François Szisz

678 the light-hearted Duray (centre) with Louis Delage (right) and designer Michelet around the 1914 Grand Prix car

676 (Left) Lancia, when going, was the fastest driver in the world and passed on his skills to riding mechanic Bordino

323

679 *Rigal who drove so well in 1908 with his Clément-Bayard at Dieppe*

682 *FASTEST FRENCHMEN: Louis Wagner*

680 *FASTEST FRENCHMEN: Victor Hemery*

683 *A Savannah 1908 group with (left to right) Wagner, de Palma, Nazzaro, Lancia (seated), Bordino and Fagnano*

684 *ANCIENT AND MODERN: Max Sailer, racing Director of Daimler-Benz and pace-maker of 1914, smokes a cigar with his 1938 team at Berne—(left to right) designer Uhlenhaut, Brauchitsch, Caracciola, Seaman and manager Neubauer*

681 *(Left) Bruce Brown (on wheel), Hemery (centre) and Haupt (front of bonnet)*

685 . . . 'Patience . . .'

686 . . . 'Judgment . . .'

687 . . . 'Concentration . . .'

688 . . . 'Sheer Hard Work . . .'

Passing from speculation into prejudice the greatest men of their periods can be stated as : —

1906-11 : Nazzaor, Lancia, Bruce Brown, Hemery, Wagner, Duray.

1912-33 : Boillot G., de Palma, Murphy, Bordino, Goux, Benoist, Varzi, Fagioli, Nuvolari, Caracciola, Chiron, Ascari,

1935-41 : Stuck, Rosemeyer, Seaman, Lang, Brauchitsch, Sommer, Villoresi L., Wimille, Fangio, Farina, Ascari, Gonzalez.

If one has to pick a winner in an imaginary race I should seek him out of Nazzaro, Varzi, Caracciola, Wimille and Fangio as the five most complete drivers in terms of technique, with, perhaps paradoxically, Nuvolari as the greatest for sheer driving genius and the most likely to reverse all the 'natural' laws and come through to win. But when all idle speculation is done and our dreams have melted into the air which distilled them, we are still left with the memories of more than half a century of the enduring human qualities of patience, concentration, judgement and sheer courage and hard work that still abound wherever drivers race and it is upon these very qualities that the past, present, and future of motor racing rest until the whole process is accomplished with push buttons or mirrors. Until then, with Flecker

> *We travel not for trafficking alone*
> *And surely they are brave who*
> *Tread the golden road to Samarkand.*[2]

689 . . . 'Courage . . .'

[2] These lines are reproduced by permission of Messrs. A. P. Watts & Sons as literary agents and executors and of Heinemanns as publishers of Hassan by James Elroy Flecker.

Epilogue II
The Revolutions of Time

*'To every thing there is a season, and a time
to every purpose under the heaven; a time to
be born and a time to die; a time to plant
and a time to pluck up that which is planted.'*
Ecclesiastes 3(i) and (ii)

The times, the seasons, births, deaths, sowings and castings out in racing history have been determined in greater part by financial considerations of one kind or another. In particular these have been responsible for: —

1. The slump of 1909/11 and 1928/30 and

2. The comings and goings of the great constructors, both of which have influenced the future design of the cars and the strength of the independent driver.

3. The demand for greater prize and starting money which brought about the selection of shorter open road circuits and then the construction of private roads and tracks resulting in greater income from charges to spectators. It also in turn increased the number of races and the degree of spectator interest to its present level.

4. The rise of commercial advertising and the bonus system which have deeply influenced the financial security and in turn the social position of drivers.

5. The trend towards standardisation of parts in more recent years.

Between 1912 and 1951 the distance of the French Grand Prix was reduced from nearly 1,000 to 375 miles and the circuit lap from $47\frac{3}{4}$ to 5 miles, although, fortuitously, the basic configuration of the circuits, remained similar, thanks largely to the influence of Roman and Napoleonic road builders. Just as distances have decreased, so have the numbers of races increased as well as the money needed to support them, until the present-day racing car calendar, often with a triple structure of Formula I. Grand Prix and Formula II and Formula III events, has emerged. In 1913 Jules Goux who drove in four races—Indianapolis, the Grand Prix, the Coupe de l'Auto and the Coupe de la Sarthe—was much the busiest driver. Now, half a century later, the drivers' championship events alone start in January and go on almost throughout the year in places as far apart as East London and Mexico City, and motor racing as a whole has spread itself beyond Cathay to the very Antipodes.

Motor racing is, and always has been, extremely expensive. Initially the enormous expansion of the motor industry coupled with low production costs put considerable profits into the constructors' pockets, out of which racing could be financed. While the first slump between 1909 and 1912 was due more to French pique than any trade recession and the situation in fact redressed itself by 1914, it was also caused by economic factors in the sense that supply of cars was at last beginning to outstrip demand. Again, once the war years had been forgotten, the twenties were a time of expansion until a combination of French supremacy and, more principally, economic depression struck a new blow at the sport in 1928. Up till then success in Grand Prix racing had been almost exclusively the privilege of the great manufacturer—Peugeot, Mercedes, Fiat, Sunbeam, Alfa-Romeo and Delage: smaller constructors like Duesenberg, Bugatti and Ballot and even the occasional independent such as Parry Thomas, Guyot and Halford had joined in from time to time, but Bugatti was the only one to do so with consistency and success in Europe. Between 1928 and 1933 this all changed in that Bugatti was joined by another small firm—Maserati, and the Scuderia Ferrari, a racing syndicate pure and simple, was formed in 1929.

In the years that followed, the independent, be he professional or amateur, came increasingly into his own, and by 1933 there was no major factory directly taking part in Grand Prix racing—a truly remarkable revolution. Since industrial profits had lessened, motor racing had been supported directly by a growing tally of prize funds and starting monies provided by organizers but this alone would never have sufficed had it not been that commercial and political interests discerned immense publicity potential in racing success. The Political Age of motor racing started with Mussolini in the early thirties and reached its zenith in the German Era between 1934 and 1939 when literally millions of pounds could be spent on a season's racing—a far cry indeed from the frugality of Edge's win for a net £218 in the 1902 Gordon Bennett!

As well as setting standards of expenditure which will probably never be exceeded, the re-entry of Germany in 1934 put an end to the independent entrant until the war was past and, after that, Alfa-Romeo perpetuated the Rule of the

Factory until 1951 with the smaller factories of Maserati and Ferrari their main rivals. Since 1951, however, another revolution has taken place in that racing has become increasingly the preserve of small specialist constructors like Maserati and Ferrari or even more specialised assembly and design establishments like Brabham, Lotus and Cooper all of whom actually use proprietary engines, or, again, great engineering combines like the Vanwall of G. A. Vandervell and the B.R.M. of Rubery Owen. Porsche have had a brief flirtation with Grand Prix racing and, of course, there was the fleeting and triumphant intervention of Mercedes in 1954/5, but, basically the years since 1939 have seen the gradual disappearance of the big car manufacturers from the Grand Prix scene. The only exception in recent years has been the interest shown by Ford in the Indianapolis '500' in 1963/5 and it may be that in the years of the new formula after 1965 this promising and interesting trend will be developed. However the independent driver and entrant are still at just as much of a disadvantage as ever: apart from anything else, no racing organisation is going to make available its latest engine, chassis or complete car and this, in itself, adds mountains of praise to the achievements of Rob Walker, Stirling Moss and Maurice Trintignant in 1958/61.

Almost inevitably with rising costs and lack of factory participation has come a significant move towards standardisation and the use of proprietary products—thus in 1964 all but one of the numerous British Grand Prix contestants were using the same engine, the V-8 Coventry Climax upon which so much recent British success has been based. Technical differences between the competing marques have, equally inevitably, become much more detailed although this is not to insult the varied brains of Colin Chapman, the Coopers and Jack Brabham by saying that the cars are all the same. It is, however, another sad instance of the inroads of the Dismal Science of Economics.

During the first period of our history from 1909 to 1916 the sport was recovering from the abandonment of the Grand Prix, which was ultimately redressed by the influence of a great series of U.S. Grand Prize and French Coupe de l'Auto races and the effect of Brooklands as a proving ground for the growing British motor industry. Thus by 1914 a new generation of European designers and drivers had grown up to dominate racing and influence design on both sides of the Atlantic. Also by 1914 the racing car had achieved a basic form which it retained till the end of 1933 with its cart sprung chassis, four wheel brakes and pointed-tail-semi-single-seater body. Engine design, however, was radically changed particularly in the light of war-time aero-engine development. This influence had been clear in the 1913/14 Mercedes racing engines and continued in the emergence of the multi-cylinder cars of the twenties. Although, in 1919, a four-cylinder Peugeot was able to defeat the European derived straight eights at Indianapolis, this was the last race of consequence to be won by such a car until the four-cylinder Maseratis became Grand Prix cars in the post-1945 period.

During the twenties promotion and construction economics brought a trend towards more Grand Prix races besides THE Grand Prix and over shorter road circuits and even specially constructed private road and track circuits, while the cars employed increasingly stressed, multi-cylinder supercharged engines. It was obvious at the same time that with shorter circuits and slowly improving road surfaces the days of the spare wheel and the riding mechanic were numbered and that it was only a matter of time before the conservatism of governing bodies and designers in Europe adopted the American trend towards single-seater bodies. Apart from improvements in detail of springing, brakes and chassis design, and with this a gradual lowering of the cars, this was the only change in the outline of the Grand Prix car between 1914 and 1933 so that a 1914 Grand Prix Fiat would have looked almost as at home in 1933 as a Monza Alfa at Lyons.

ACROSS THE GULF OF TIME

690/1 A 1914 Grand Prix Fiat (left) would have looked almost as at home in 1933 as a Monza Alfa (right) at Lyons

With the increasing speed and reliability of the cars, coupled with the decrease in lap distances, smart pit work became more important and effective pit signalling and direction more possible. Pomeroy has shown that Mercedes planned race directions and tactics as long ago as 1907, and the 1914 Grand Prix is often cited as another example of early race planning although I have not found any contemporary account which bears out that the Lyons Mercedes were significantly directed from their pits. I do not believe that effective direction was possible in races which consisted of relatively few laps over lengthy circuits, particularly when the races themselves were run on the basis of elapsed time and not from a scratch start. Directions could thus be as much as 2 laps out of date by the time they were signalled and I incline to the view that in almost every race until the 1922 Grand Prix it was very much a case of each man for himself and Devil take the hindmost. This is not to say that race tactics were not planned before 1922: there is plenty of evidence to the contrary and, in particular, I have no doubt whatever but that Sailer, starting only two minutes behind Boillot at Lyons, received instructions to join battle with the enemy and engage him on the circuit as smartly and closely as possible. To some extent this depended on the luck of the draw and it is possible that, without the early menace of Sailer, Boillot might not have stressed his engine so disastrously and thus have been able to last the race at a sufficient speed to have won it. The other Mercedes made relatively slow starts, in particular Wagner, and gradually speeded up and but for Boillot's mechanical troubles in the last five laps these initial delays might well have been fatal. Mercedes staked heavily on Boillot's character and consequently on Sailer tempting him beyond prudence in those opening laps.

Whatever the position in 1914, there was clear evidence of the most elaborate preparations by Fiat for the 1922 Grand Prix including a special refuelling device and different shaped signals to instruct the drivers. This was also the race when a fuel tank was changed in under a quarter of an hour. During the ensuing years speedy pit work assumed ever increasing importance—on one or two occasions in the early thirties it undoubtedly cost the Maseratis of Fagioli and Nuvolari a race and there is equally no doubt but that Bugatti's ability to change brake linings with wheels played a considerable part in enabling his cars to win so many of the long races run in the late twenties and early thirties. Due to their tremendous latter day efficiency the idea has gained credence that German pit work was always done with lightning speed and was also far in advance of anyone else's. In fact some of their work in the early years of the 750 kg. formula was decidedly inferior, which has already emerged from the race accounts. Of course from 1937 things became very different when Mercedes and Auto-Union were so closely matched that a race could well be won by split seconds at the pits as well as on the circuit. This became even more material when the highly stressed supercharged 3-litre and 1½-litre cars came into conflict with the more economical 4½-litre unsupercharged cars.

It took 12 years for the unblown challenge really to assume serious proportions although in their first formula race in 1938 Dreyfus had given a convincing demonstration of its possibilities. Yet designers seemed so mesmerized by the German school of thought that nobody really faced up to the challenge of designing an unblown 4½-litre as a racer *ab initio* until Ferrari in 1950. With Grand Prix distances then of between 250 and 375 miles it merely wanted a really quick '4½' to kill the blown cars stone dead and if the 1947/53 formula had run its full course it is very doubtful if even the B.R.M. could have won long distance races against the developed 4½-litre Ferrari. By the end of 1950 Ferrari was in a position to harry the Alfas mercilessly on the circuit and, once he was able to consolidate his cars' advantage at the pits by increasing their speed (as he did in 1951) the blown car was a spent force. Yet this was by no means apparent at the time and one must guard against the tendency to interpret the past with the wisdom of hindsight. In November 1950 Pomeroy posed the question in The Motor—'Has the B.R.M. failed?' and adduced powerful arguments in favour of the blown car whilst rejecting the B.R.M. adherence to the centrifugal lay-out. Having debated the pros and cons of the two designs Pomeroy writes this summary in bold type:

'On fundamental grounds it is correct to choose a 1½-litre supercharged engine against a 4½-litre unsupercharged type as the ideal instrument for winning Formula I Grand Prix races.'

Pomeroy then went through 'a formidable list of arguments in favour of choosing the unsupercharged engine' similar to those which I have rehearsed but pointed out that 'it suffers from one insuperable and perhaps fatal objection' which he again stated in bold type:

'However skilled the designer of an unsupercharged engine may be, and whatever resources are available in its development there is a ceiling of power which cannot be exceeded. The supercharged engine is not so limited and must be dominant if enough skill and money are lavished upon it.'

Of course that final 'if' could beg the whole question but it must be agreed that a reasonable amount of skill and money were lavished upon developing the Alfa even though, in fairness, it was then a 13 year old design. If the B.R.M. had been giving off something approaching its true potential by 1951 the blown engine might have been a practical answer; as it turned out it was still not a practical proposition in 1953 when, although the B.R.M. could easily outpace the 4.5 Ferraris at Albi, its tyres were unable to stand the strain.

While theory might favour the blown car, what Pomeroy termed 'hard practical facts telling in favour of the unblown type vitiated' the theory. At all events as soon as Practice was in a position to overcome Theory, King Blower was dethroned after his 28-year reign over Grand Prix design and Fangio's win at Barcelona in 1951 is still the last Grand Prix to be won by a supercharged car. This in itself is a development of great historical significance especially now that attention is again being paid to the supercharger in the light of the post-1965 Grand Prix formula.

Pit stops continued to matter at least down to 1957 when it will be remembered Fangio elected not to go through the German Grand Prix non-stop. Basically, however, once the blown engine ceased to be used after 1951, the pit stop gradually disappeared to the point nowadays that a leading driver, solely concerned to finish high up, might just as well withdraw after anything but the most lightning stop. The apotheosis of this process was reached in the 1964 Belgian Grand Prix when fuel calculation miscarried and nobody even had fuel available in the pits for topping up so that cars lay

As idle as a painted ship
Upon a painted ocean.

Lack of finance in the leading constructors had killed Grand Prix racing after 1927 until it was revived as an instrument of foreign policy by the dictators Mussolini and Hitler both of whom were considerable racing enthusiasts. Whether the subsequent decline of Italian fortunes after 1935 was the subject of one of those back-stairs discussions at the Brenner Pass is an idle speculation but the Italian decline is very hard to understand as their technicians and designers should have had the experience, money and skill (to say nothing of the drivers) to equal the Germans instead of failing all the way down the line as they did.

In the earliest times France had the pre-eminence in drivers with the Chevalier René de Knyff the equivalent of 'W.G.' in English cricket in all things apart from what our more restricted modern outlook might term W.G.'s questionable sporting standards, inherited as they were from an older and harder line of English sportsmen in the mould of H. O. Duncan's memorable ancestor Squire Osbaldeston. This continued right through to the late twenties when the initiative passed imperceptibly to Italy as producing two racing cars to France's one. During all this time Germany and, on occasions, Britain, America and Belgium occasionally contributed leading drivers but until 1934 the more celebrated drivers came from France and Italy. With the change to German leadership in racing car production German drivers came more into prominence in 1934/9 but after the war it was very much the mixture as before until the arrival of the Argentinians Campos, Fangio, Gonzalez and

692 KING-BREAKER: The 4½-litre Ferrari which dethroned the super-charged racing car

Marimon and the gradual rise of British drivers to the point when all the six leading drivers have British sounding names even though Gurney is American and Brabham and McLaren antipodeans. Since the war France has produced one driver of note in Jean Behra and Italy barely five including Alberto Ascari, Luigi Musso, Castellotti, Bandini and possibly Baghetti. America has done well with Gurney, Phil Hill and Ginther but Britain has excelled with Moss, Hawthorn, Collins, Brooks, Graham Hill, Clark, Lewis-Evans, Wharton and Surtees, as well as countless strong supporting drivers of a calibre previously provided almost exclusively by France and Italy.

The history under consideration is capable of fairly neat sub-division into 6 periods:

(1) 1906–1912   (4) 1928–1933
(2) 1913–1916   (5) 1934–1939
(3) 1919–1927   (6) 1940/1946–1951

and each of these periods in its turn had one particular year to be marked out with a white stone as excelling the others of its vintage, those seasons to which one inevitably looks back,

When the oldest cask is opened
And the largest lamp is lit.

For sheer drama and quality of entry the respective Grands Prix in 1908, 1914 and 1924 make these years stand out from the others in (1), (2) and (3) although the 1907 Grand Prix, the Savannah races of 1910 and 1911 and the '500' of 1915 were all desperately fought affairs; 1932 and 1933 were both good years in (4) but 1933 has my fancy because of its greater competitive interest. 1937, with its titanic rivalry between Auto-Union and Mercedes-Benz is the high point of (5) and, with Alfa-Romeo and Ferrari in similar pitched

693 INCREDIBLE SURVIVAL: Enzo Ferrari Semper Eadem with driver Gendebien (right)

battle, 1951 is the same for (6). Just as I have chosen 1933 out of its own period, I incline towards it as my own Golden Age in the face of the almost overpowering claims of the other four years, if only because in 1933 the element of Personal Competition was higher than in any of the other years, which were remarkable more for the struggle between marques rather than men. This is an intensely personal viewpoint, but what other year can summon up the presence of five such drivers as Caracciola (though hors-de-combat for almost all the year), Chiron, Nuvolari, Fagioli, and Varzi? In 1914 there was only one Boillot; great though the line-up at Lyons was ten years later, its greatest ones were not the equal of the men of 1933, while in 1937 there were only Rosemeyer and Caracciola and Nuvolari to share the mountain tops of the highest class and in 1951 only Fangio and Ascari, whatever the claims of Gonzalez and Farina.

For all its emotive drama I think the 1914 Grand Prix not so great a race as that of 1924 when the struggle between men and marques was keener: but for Boillot there would have been no race in 1914, while in 1924 any one out of Segrave, Guinness (Sunbeam), Bordino (Fiat), Campari and Ascari (Alfa-Romeo) or even Divo (Delage) might have won. If one excepts Nuvolari and Varzi at Monaco as a miracle all on its own, the Italian Grand Prix was the best race of 1933 but nowhere near the stature of the Lyons events. The German Grand Prix was the most interesting race in 1937 but again not on a par with the 1924 classic but, curiously enough, the British Grand Prix which is my own choice for 1951, must run it close for its extreme excitement, its varied field and, to the historian, the significance of its result which wrote FINIS to the reign of the supercharged Grand Prix engine. Lyons—1924 probably was the outstanding event as a race but for sheer drama its 1914 predecessor is my choice for the race I should choose from the time machine: again an entirely personal viewpoint.

Finally a word should be said about the changing constructors who have dominated the scene in the 43 years since 1906. In order of first appearance they have been Fiat and Mercedes (1906), Peugeot (1912), Delage (1913), Mercedes (1914), Sunbeam (1921), Bugatti (1922), Maserati (1929), Auto-Union (1934) and Ferrari (1948). Quantitatively, in terms of years of participation, Alfa-Romeo, Ferrari and Maserati share the honours if one extends the years of reckoning down to 1964, otherwise the order is Alfa, Bugatti, Sunbeam, Mercedes, Maserati, Fiat, Delage, Auto-Union, Peugeot and only then Ferrari. Of these only Ferrari is still racing. For all his youth as a Grand Prix constructor, his is an incredible survival: autocratic ruler of a small factory turning out hand built sports cars in minimal quantities, inevitably on a financial knife-edge, volatile, eccentric and even peevish to an extent that he is sometimes likened to Bugatti, Enzo Ferrari has been starting cars in European Grands Prix in every season since 1929. Moreover during most of these seasons whenever his cars have not been the out-and-out winners they have almost always been the car the winner himself has had to beat. His record since 1948 as

330

a Grand Prix constructor alone is without parallel and his whole career as an uninterrupted supporter of Grand Prix racing for 35 years makes him the great Semper Eadem of our, or probably any other time.

To keep up this amazing record he has generally been at least one move ahead of his competitors in a sport where there is no place for looking back—defying alike the revolutions of time and the rising generations to show him that 'period and end to all temporal things ... (that) ... end of names and whatever is terrene' so gloomily conjured up by Chief Justice Crewe. By continually moving with the times Ferrari has achieved the apparent miracle of making time stand still and avoid the fate of the other great constructors whose names are briefly mentioned and whose endeavours we have considered in the main historical narrative. As a result his products are winning races in 1966 just as surely as were his entries thirty and more years ago. For all that, however, Ferrari's has been a gentle rather than an absolute

dominion and for this reason he has, like the very years themselves, tended to slip by relatively unnoticed and even to be regarded as a very part of that Change which is the lifeblood of motor racing.

Without this change there would be no progress, only stagnation and, sad though the passing of 'our' champions, whoever they be, it has an inevitability, a dignity and even a majesty, can one, like Keats' Oceanus, but have the philosophy to accept it as part of the progress of evolution by which the Old Gods of Yesterday and To-day are eternally being surpassed:

'*And as we show beyond that Heaven and Earth*
In form and shape....
So on our heels a fresh perfection treads
A power more strong in beauty, born of us
And fated to excel us, as we pass
In glory that Old Darkness.'

Acknowledgments

The motoring movement is no longer quite short enough to be within the compass of a single man's memory but it is very nearly so and we are fortunate in still having with us Mr. W. F. Bradley whose wit and memory, I am delighted to say remains as sharp as ever. As long ago as August 1919 upon appointing him editorial representative on the continent The Autocar observed: —

'Mr. Bradley undoubtedly has acquired a more detailed knowledge of the motor movement and motor industry in France, Italy and Belgium than any other single individual. There is no person of note in the motor industry of these three countries to whom he is not known.'

Recently I have had the great pleasure of meeting Mr. Bradley and of discussing many topics with him personally and by letter and this, coupled with his writings over the years, has been of the greatest assistance in acquiring a sense of period authenticity.

Mr. Bradley's work still appears from time to time in Autocar and it is to this journal that I owe an enormous debt for permitting me the almost unfettered run of their photographic collection and for the endless trouble their staff have taken to hunt out ancient photographs from long forgotten files to meet my requirements. I am most particularly grateful to Ronald Barker, one of their Assistant Editors, for superintending this operation and for arranging various introductions for me, most notably Mr. Bradley himself and Peter Helck, and no less for the liberal use of his own photographic collection.

It would be impossible to contemplate any work of this kind without constant reference to periodicals, basically in my case, Autocar, Motor, Motor Sport, Automotor Journal, La Vie Automobile and l'Auto and my deepest thanks are due to those editors who have kindly permitted extracts to be used in my text. More specific acknowledgments for quotation are included as footnotes in the text and I am otherwise indebted to the following for leave to cite extracts:

Sir Robin Darwin, C.B.E., D.Litt.: Pack Clouds Away—Bernard Darwin

Herman Darewski Music Publishing Co.: Song—'I don't want to play in your yard'.

Rupert Hart-Davis Ltd. & M. Maurice Druon: The Lily and the Lion.

George Newnes Ltd.: Motor Racing with Mercedes-Benz—George Monkhouse. The Grand Prix Car—Laurence Pomeroy. From Veteran to Vintage—Laurence Pomeroy & Kent Karslake.

G. T. Foulis Ltd.: Bugatti—H. G. Conway: Dick Seaman Racing Motorist—H.R.H. Prince Chula of Siam. Targa Florio—W. F. Bradley. Split Seconds—Raymond Mays. Grand Prix Racing Facts and Figures—George Monkhouse & R. King-Farlow.

B. T. Batsford Ltd.: The British Competition Car—C. Posthumus. Sir Henry Segrave—C. Posthumus. The Vintage Motor Car—C. Clutton & J. E. Stanford. The Racing Car—C. Clutton, C. Posthumus & D. S. Jenkinson. The Motorists' Week-End Book, Motorist's Miscellany.

Cable Publishing Co. Ltd.: A Record of Motor Racing—Gerald Rose. Racing Voiturettes—Kent Karslake. The French Grand Prix 1906-1914—Kent Karslake. Motor Racing Memories—W. F. Bradley. Ettore Bugatti—W. F. Bradley. Motor Racing 1946—John Eason-Gibson. Motor Racing 1947—John Eason-Gibson.

Hamish Hamilton Ltd.: The Ferrari Memoirs—R. B. Hough.

The Hutchinson Publishing Group: The Lure of Speed—Sir Henry Segrave.

Constable & Co. Ltd.: Horseless Carriage—L. T. C. Rolt.

Frederick Muller Ltd.: 500 Miles to Go—Al Bloemker.

L'Automobile Club de l'Ouest: Les Vingt Quatre Heures du Mans—Roger Labric.

Cassell & Co. Ltd.: Three Pointed Star—D. Scott-Moncrieff and others. Nuvolari—Count G. Lurani. Alfa-Romeo—Peter Hull & Roy Slater.

Faber & Faber Ltd.: Collected Poems 1909-62—T. S. Eliot.

L. Scott-Bailey Esq.: Automobile Quarterly.

J. E. Stanford Esq.: Bulletin of the Vintage Sports Car Club Ltd.

The Statesman & Nation Publishing Co. Ltd.: The New Statesman.

Apart from references the biggest problem has been to find photographs to illustrate the cars, the drivers and changing racing conditions. Inevitably some of these have been seen before, although I hope that some will appear fresh to many readers. A variety of kind people have been to endless trouble to meet my wishes and have allowed me every possible facility to go through their collections. Of private individuals may I mention with especial gratitude Anthony Heal, Peter Helck, Rupert Instone, Ronald Barker, John Lloyd, Charles Lytle, Dr. J. K. Quattlebaum, Lt.-Col. Stubbs and the late Laurence Pomeroy. Many of the photographs I have used have come from their private collections: in these cases it has not been possible to identify the photographer and therefore no more specific acknowledgment of his skill can be given. Of factories I have had much help from S.A. Automobiles Peugeot in Paris and a wonderful portfolio of illustrations from Prince von Ürach and Herr Artur Keser of Daimler-Benz A.G.

However in the following cases my thanks are due to individual photographers for leave to reproduce their own work: —

Guy Griffiths Esq: Nos. 311, 572/3, 575, 580, 603, 609, 616, 618/9, 621, 623, 624, 627, 638, 642, 648/9, 687/8, 692.

Louis Klemantaski Esq: Nos. 309, 487, 490/1, 502/3, 510/11, 513/5, 523, 527, 535, 541, 557, 567, 581/3, 598, 604/7, 611, 620, 626, 628, 630/2, 139/40, 658.

George Monkhouse Esq.: Nos. 340, 352, 354, 470, 472/3, 479, 481, 507/8, 516, 525/6, 529, 531, 536/7, 552, 563, 615, 637, 645, 652, 655, 694.

Other photographs have come from the following journals or agencies: —

Autocar: Nos. 5, 9, 11, 13/15, 17, 20, 28/9, 37/43, 50, 53, 57, 62/3, 68, 72, 91, 95/8, 100, 102, 106, 114, 173, 180/2, 184, 212, 220/2, 225/8, 233/7, 239, 244/5, 247/56, 273/4, 279/85, 290, 308, 314, 316, 327/31, 334, 336/9, 346/8, 350, 355, 361/3, 387, 395/6, 398/400, 404, 422, 435, 448/9, 451/3, 499/501, 532, 534, 561/2, 565, 574, 576/7, 584/5, 588/91, 593, 599/602, 612/4, 617, 634, 662, 675, 691.

Associated Press: Nos. 322, 465/6, 476, 492, 497, 543, 549, 556, 570/1, 578, 633, 641, 643, 659, 685.

Indianapolis Motor Speedway Corporation: 118, 139, 161, 167, 190, 194, 215, 219, 262, 266, 301.

Keystone Press: 342/3, 533, 542, 558, 560, 566, 568, 569, 608, 629, 693,

Montagu Motor Museum: 317/8.

Motor Sport: 112, 364, 622, 625.

Planet News: 374, 468/9, 674.

Radio-Times Hulton Library: 55/6, 58, 103, 132/3, 136, 140, 145, 152, 154/5.

On a more personal basis I have already mentioned Peter Helck very briefly. He has been a mine of information on the American scene and has loaned me many treasured photographs for perusal, some of which appear in the text. Apart from the great help and pleasure of his correspondence he has also interrupted a highly busy professional schedule to fit in the four double page spreads which begin each part of the main historical text. Each of these has been specially drawn to typify our joint ideas of the spirit of each particular Age and it is a tremendous privilege for me to welcome the work of this great artist to these pages.

Whilst across the Atlantic both Dr. Quattlebaum and Mr. Bloemker have turned out their collections of Savannah and Indianapolis pictures and they, like Peter Helck and Charles Lytle, have entrusted many rare and irreplaceable photographs to the hazards of the post for my selection. Where one would be without the enthusiastic co-operation of such people I do not know. I have also found the collection of Anthony Heal particularly helpful in illustrating the very important American developments in the 1911-1925 period.

In a letter some time past Lytle made a slightly derogatory remark about the performance of Edwardian racing Vauxhalls and added charmingly:

'. . . this could be laid to prejudice as I shall have to admit that one of life's minor joys is to point out small errors in the works of the son of the constructor. . . .'

They were always very small ones indeed and, to my immense regret, it is a joy that I and so many others will have no longer. When 'Pom' heard by chance of this book he wrote immediately offering all the help he could give and I owe him a whole bookful of gratitude for so many things— the privilege of his Foreword, the supply of many rare photographs and information, the reading of my text and, perhaps most of all, the sheer pleasure of his table talk '. . . how often you and I
Have tired the sun with talking and sent him down the sky. . . .'
but alas no more.

In addition to 'Pom', the text has been read at various times by John Lloyd, Kent Karslake and Bunny Tubbs, who also volunteered to proof-read for me. They have all made highly valuable suggestions for its improvement and for these too I am immensely grateful. Guy Griffiths, Louis Klemantaski and George Monkhouse have given me the free run of their photographic collections and elsewhere I have had much generosity from M. le Grain-Eifel of the Commission Historique of the A.C.F. in Paris who allowed me to go through the Club's racing collection and to have my choice printed by Automobiles Peugeot through the good offices of their publicity chief in Paris, J. R. Broncard.

Other ageing prints have in many cases been skilfully copied and rejuvenated by my friend Barry Damon of Sky-fotos Ltd. (Lympne), to a point when they often far outshine the originals.

One other most important contribution to the illustration of this book has been made by my friend Dr. Lionel Stretton who has drawn maps of the thirty-one principal circuits and routes used during the years under consideration. These are the result of many painstaking hours snatched from a busy professional life and have involved him in most careful examination of the text and other sources. I am truly grateful to him for his work, his support and enthusiasm.

In conclusion there are the Publishers who have converted a mass of typescript and jumbled photographs into an artistic entity and here I should mention Mr. Gwyn Lewis who is responsible for the general lay-out of the pages and Messrs. Sadler and Timberlake who have generally supervised its production. As the Bard has it,

'For all, our thanks. . . .'

333

Appendices

'*There must be a beginning to any great matter but the continuing of the same unto the end until it be thoroughly finished yields the true glory.*'

Sir Francis Drake to Sir Francis Walsingham—17th May 1587 After Cadiz.

First I have set out in Appendix A the first, second and third finishers with a note of race distances and fastest laps in all material races considered in any detail in the text between 1894 and 1951. All results have been checked in the first instance against King-Farlow's tables in *Grand Prix Racing Facts and Figures*. Where these are silent—e.g. on fastest laps—I have double checked against the tables in *The Grand Prix Car*. Information as to events before 1909 has in all possible cases been checked against the tables in Rose's *Record* except for voiturette events with which he was not concerned. For these I have relied on Kent Karslake's *Racing Voiturettes*. It would be hard indeed to overestimate the debt owed to the writers of these four classic works by anybody interested in reading, let alone writing motor racing history.

Secondly I have extracted from this Appendix the contents of Appendices B and E which show the number of first second and third places won by drivers and marques in the years and periods under consideration. Their purpose is to shew at a glance which driver or car was the most successful in any given period, although one should again make the point that, in the case of drivers at least, sheer quantum of success is not necessarily the final criterion of the greatest quality.

I have not reproduced any of Rose's tables of individual lap times and positions, nor have I tried to furnish these for 'post-Rose' events, although some of these can be found in: —

1. *The Checkered Flag*—certain pre-1917 American events.
2. *The Great Savannah Races*—events run at Savannah between 1908 and 1911.
3. *Autocourse* magazine (1951 season).
4. *Grand Prix Racing 1906-1914*—the French Grands Prix during this time.

As to the rest, I should hope that someone with the industry, talents and archives of Mr. King-Farlow, if not he himself, will one day accept the challenge of this monumental research, even supposing such records still to exist for many of the races involved.

Thirdly I have quite unashamedly borrowed three sets of table almost in their entirety from Volume Two of the 1960 Edition of *The Grand Prix Car to form:*—

Appendix C: Specifications of Significant Cars.
Appendix D: Summary of Developments.
Appendix F: The 'Pomeroy' Speed Index.

These contents speak largely for themselves and whilst I could surely have compiled such tables for myself they would have owed so much to their originals that it seemed folly, to say nothing of impertinence, not to resort to the originals themselves. During the narrative I have referred to the 'Pomeroy' Speed Index almost as a term of art and it may therefore be convenient to the reader to have it available between these covers.

Appendix A · Table of Results 1894-1951

YEAR	EVENT	DISTANCE (MILES)	FIRST	SECOND	THIRD	AVERAGE FASTEST LAP (M.P.H.)	AVERAGE (M.P.H.)
1894	Paris–Rouen	78·75	Count de Dion (de Dion)	Lemaître (Peugeot)	Doriot (Peugeot)	11·6	
1895	Paris–Bordeaux–Paris	732	E. Levassor (Panhard)	Rigoulout (Peugeot)	Koechlin (Peugeot)	15	
1896	Paris–Marseilles–Paris	1062·5	Mayade (Panhard)	Merkel (Panhard)	Viet (de Dion)	14·5	
1898	Paris–Bordeaux	356·5	R. de Knyff (Panhard)	F. Charron (Panhard)	Breuil (Panhard)	22·1	
	Paris–Amsterdam–Paris	889·25	F. Charron (Panhard)	L. Girardot (Panhard)	Giraud (Bollée)	26·9	
1899	Paris–Bordeaux	351	F. Charron (Panhard)	R. de Knyff (Panhard)	L. Girardot (Panhard)	29·9	
	Tour de France	1350	R. de Knyff (Panhard)	L. Girardot (Panhard)	de Chasseloup-Laubat (Panhard)	30·2	
1900	Paris–Lyon =Gordon Bennett	353·75	F. Charron (Panhard)	L. Girardot (Panhard)		38·6	
	Paris–Toulouse–Paris	837·1	Levegh (Mors)	Pinson (Panhard)	Voight (Panhard)	40·2	

YEAR	EVENT	DISTANCE (MILES)	FIRST	SECOND	THIRD	AVERAGE (M.P.H.)	FASTEST LAP	AVERAGE (M.P.H.)
1901	Paris–Bordeaux incl.	327·6	H. Fournier (Mors)	M. Farman (Panhard)	Voight (Panhard)	53		
	Gordon Bennett		L. Girardot (Panhard)			37		
	Paris–Berlin	687	H. Fournier (Mors)	L. Girardot (Panhard)	R. de Knyff (Panhard)	44·1		
1902	Circuit du Nord	537·1	M. Farman (Panhard)	Marcellin (Darracq)	C. Jarrott (Panhard)	44·8		
	Paris–Vienna Paris–Innsbruck =Gordon Bennett	615·4	M. Renault (Renault)	H. Farman (Panhard)	Edmond (Darracq)	38·4		
			S. F. Edge (Napier)			36·1		
	Circuit des Ardennes	318·2	C. Jarrott (Panhard)	F. Gabriel (Mors)	W. K. Vanderbilt (Mors)	54	P. de Crawhez (Panhard)	57·1
1903	Paris–Bordeaux	342	F. Gabriel (Mors)	L. Renault (Renault)	Salleron (Mors)	65·3		
	Gordon Bennett	327·5	C. Jenatzy (Mercedes)	R. de Knyff (Panhard)	H. Farman (Panhard)	49·2	Foxhall Keene (Mercedes)	52·2(A)
							F. Gabriel (Mors)	51·7(B)
	Circuit des Ardennes	318·2	P. de Crawhez (Panhard)	L. Girardot (C.G.V.)	de Brou (de Dietrich)	54·3	P. de Crawhez	54·8
1904	Gordon Bennett Trials	331·05	L. Théry (Richard Brasier)	Salleron (Mors)	Rougier (Turcat-Méry)	62	H. Farman (Panhard)	68
	Gordon Bennett	317·86	L. Théry (Richard Brasier)	C. Jenatzy (Mercedes)	Rougier (Turcat-Méry)	54·5	L. Théry	55·3
	Circuit des Ardennes	367·4	Heath (Panhard)	Teste (Panhard)	A. Clément (Clément-Bayard)	56·4	lc Blon (Hotchkiss)	63·3
	Florio Cup	231·25	V. Lancia (F.I.A.T.)	Teste (Panhard)	V. Florio (Mercedes)	72		
	Vanderbilt Cup	284·4	Heath (Panhard)	A. Clément (Clément-Bayard)	Lyttle (Pope-Toledo)	52·2	Teste (Panhard)	70·8
1905	Gordon Bennett Trial	341·4	L. Théry (Richard Brasier)	G. Caillois (Richard Brasier)	A. Duray (de Dietrich)	44·9	L. Théry	50
	Gordon Bennett	341·4	L. Théry (Richard Brasier)	F. Nazzaro (F.I.A.T.)	A. Cagno (F.I.A.T.)	48·4	V. Lancia (F.I.A.T.)	52·6
	Circuit des Ardennes	367·4	V. Hémery (Darracq)	Tart (Panhard)	le Blon (Panhard)	61·6	Rougier (de Dietrich)	68·5
	Florio Cup	311·3	Raggio (Itala)	A. Duray (de Dietrich)	V. Lancia (F.I.A.T.)	65·1		
	Vanderbilt Cup	283	V. Hémery (Darracq)	Heath (Panhard)	Tracy (Locomobile)	61·5	V. Lancia (F.I.A.T.)	72·8
1906	Targa Florio	277·2	A. Cagno (Itala)	Graziani (Itala)	P. Bablot (Berliet)	29·1	A. Cagno (Itala)	32·6
	French G.P.	769·9	F. Szisz (Renault)	F. Nazzaro (F.I.A.T.)	A. Clément (Clément-Bayard)	63	P. Baras (Brasier)	73·3
	Circuit des Ardennes	371·2	A. Duray (de Dietrich)	Hanriot (Darracq)	Rougier (de Dietrich)	65·8	L. Wagner (Darracq)	70
	Vanderbilt Cup	297·1	L. Wagner (Darracq)	V. Lancia (F.I.A.T.)	A. Duray (de Dietrich)	61·4	Tracy (Locomobile)	67·6
	Coupe de l'Auto	145	Sizaire (Sizaire-Naudin)	Mennard-Lucas (Delage)	J. Goux (Lion-Peugeot)	36·2		
1907	Targa Florio	277·26	F. Nazzaro (F.I.A.T.)	V. Lancia (F.I.A.T.)	Fabry (Itala)	33·5	V. Lancia	34
	Kaiserpreis	292·6	F. Nazzaro (F.I.A.T.)	Hautvast (Pipe)	Jörns (Opel)	52·5	V. Lancia (F.I.A.T.)	53·5
	French G.P.	477·4	F. Nazzaro (F.I.A.T.)	F. Szisz (Renault)	P. Baras (Brasier)	70·5	A. Duray (de Dietrich)	75·4
	Circuit des Ardennes Kaiserpreis Class	371·2	J. C. T. Moore-Brabazon (Minerva)	Koolhoven (Minerva)	A. Lee Guinness (Minerva)	59·5	A. Lee Guinness	67
	G.P. Class		Baron de Caters (Mercedes)	A. Lee Guinness (Darracq)	C. Jenatzy (Mercedes)	57·3	C. Jenatzy	66·6
	Florio Cup	301·8	F. Minoia (Isotta-Fraschini)	V. Hémery (Benz)	Hanriot (Benz)	64·7	F. Minoia	66·5
	Coppa della Velocita		A. Cagno (Itala)	Demogeot (Darracq)	Rougier (de Dietrich)	65·2	A. Cagno	71·8
	Sicilian Cup	186	Naudin (Sizaire-Naudin)	V. Florio (de Dion)	Stabile (de Dion)	23·7		
	Coupe de l'Auto	189	Naudin (Sizaire-Naudin)	Sizaire (Sizaire-Naudin)	J. Goux (Lion-Peugeot)	40·7		
1908	French G.P.	477·4	C. Lautenschlager (Mercedes)	V. Hémery (Benz)	Hanriot (Benz)	69	O. Salzer (Mercedes)	78·5
	Florio Cup	328	F. Nazzaro (F.I.A.T.)	Trucco (de Dietrich)	A. Cagno (Itala)	74·1	V. Lancia (F.I.A.T.)	82·3
	U.S. Grand Prize	402·08	L. Wagner (F.I.A.T.)	V. Hémery (Benz)	F. Nazarro (F.I.A.T.)	65·2	R. de Palma (F.I.A.T.)	69·5

335

YEAR	EVENT	DISTANCE (MILES)	FIRST	SECOND	THIRD	AVERAGE (M.P.H.)	FASTEST LAP	AVERAGE (M.P.H.)
	Chari	107	Giuppone (Lion-Peugeot)	Cissac (Alcyon)		26·7		
	Sicilian Cup	186	Giuppone (Lion-Peugeot)	Camarata (de Dion)	Tasca (de Dion)	28·5		
	G.P. des Voiturettes	286	A. Guyot (Delage)	Naudin (Sizaire-Naudin)	J. Goux (Lion-Peugeot)	49·8		
	Coupe de l'Auto	250	Naudin (Sizaire-Naudin)	Sizaire (Sizaire-Naudin)	J. Goux (Lion-Peugeot)	47·8		
1909	Sicilian Cup	186	J. Goux (Lion-Peugeot)	Giuppone (Lion-Peugeot)		27·4		
	Catalan Cup	226	J. Goux (Lion-Peugeot)	Sizaire (Sizaire-Naudin)	Soyez (Werner)	35·9		
	Coupe de l'Auto	282	Giuppone (Lion-Peugeot)	J. Goux (Lion-Peugeot)	Thomas (le Gui)	47·5		
1910	U.S. Grand Prize	415	D. Bruce-Brown (Benz)	V. Hémery (Benz)	B. Burman (Marquette-Buick)	70·55		
	Sicilian Cup	186	G. Boillot (Lion-Peugeot)	Giuppone (Lion-Peugeot)	J. Goux (Lion-Peugeot)	34·9		
	Catalan Cup		J. Goux (Lion-Peugeot)	G. Boillot (Lion-Peugeot)	P. Zuccarelli (Hispano-Zuiza)			
	Coupe de l'Auto	282	P. Zuccarelli (Hispano-Suiza)	J. Goux (Lion-Peugeot)	J. Chassagne (Hispano-Suiza)	55·6		
1911	G.P. de France	403	V. Hémery (F.I.A.T.)	E. Friederich (Bugatti)	F. Gabriel (Rolland-Pilain)	56·71		
	U.S. Grand Prize	411	D. Bruce-Brown (F.I.A.T.)	E. Hearne (Benz)	R. de Palma (Mercedes)	74·75		
	Coupe de l'Auto	388	P. Bablot (Delage)	G. Boillot (Lion-Peugeot)	R. Thomas (Delage)	55·2		
1912	French G.P.	956	G. Boillot (Peugeot)	L. Wagner (F.I.A.T.)	V. Rigal (Sunbeam)	68·45	D. Bruce Brown (F.I.A.T.)	76·8
	Coupe de l'Auto	956	V. Rigal (Sunbeam)	D. Resta (Sunbeam)	E. Medinger (Sunbeam)	65·29		
	Coupe de la Sarthe	403	J. Goux (Peugeot)	Leduc (S.P.A.)	Crespelle (Crespelle)	73·01	G. Boillot (Peugeot)	80
1913	Indianapolis	500	J. Goux (Peugeot)	S. Wishart and R. de Palma (Mercer)	C. Merz and E. Cooper (Stutz)	75·93	P. Zuccarelli (Peugeot)	93·5
	French G.P.	566	G. Boillot (Peugeot)	J. Goux (Peugeot)	J. Chassagne (Sunbeam)	71·65	P. Bablot (Delage)	76·6
	G.P. de France	338	P. Bablot (Delage)	A. Guyot (Delage)	A. Pilette (Mercedes)	76·80	P. Bablot	82·5
1914	Indianapolis	500	R. Thomas (Delage)	A. Duray (Peugeot)	A. Guyot (Delage)	82·47	G. Boillot (Peugeot)	99·5
	French G.P.	467	C. Lautenschlager (Mercedes)	L. Wagner (Mercedes)	O. Salzer (Mercedes)	65·35	M. Sailer (Mercedes)	69·95
1915	Indianapolis	500	R. de Palma (Mercedes)	D. Resta (Peugeot)	G. Anderson (Stutz)	89·94	R. de Palma	98·6
	Chicago Derby	500	D. Resta (Peugeot)	Porporato (Sunbeam)	E. Rickenbacker (Maxwell)	97·60		
	Astor Cup	350	G. Anderson (Stutz)	Rooney (Stutz)	O'Donnell (Duesenberg)	102·6	D. Resta (Peugeot)	109·75
	Sheepshead Bay	100	D. Resta (Peugeot)	R. Burman (Peugeot)		107·93		
	U.S. Grand Prize	400	D. Resta (Peugeot)	H. Wilcox (Stutz)	H. Hughes (Ono)	56·13		
	Vanderbilt Cup	296	D. Resta (Peugeot)	H. Wilcox (Stutz)	E. Pullen (Mercer)	66·40		
1916	Indianapolis	300	D. Resta (Peugeot)	W. d'Alène (Duesenberg)	R. Mulford (Peugeot)	84		
	Chicago Derby	300	D. Resta (Peugeot)	R. de Palma (Mercedes)	J. Christiaens (Sunbeam)	98·61		
	Omaha	150	D. Resta (Peugeot)			99·02		
	Omaha	50	R. de Palma (Mercedes)			103·45		
	Astor Cup		J. Aitken (Peugeot)			104·8		
	Harkness Trophy		J. Aitken (Peugeot)			105·95		
	U.S. Grand Prize	403	H. Wilcox and J. Aitken (Peugeot)	E. Cooper (Stutz)	E. Patterson (Hudson)	85·59		
	Vanderbilt Cup	294	D. Resta (Peugeot)	E. Cooper (Stutz)	W. Wightman (Duesenberg)	86·98		
1919	Indianapolis	500	H. Wilcox (Peugeot)	E. Hearne (Durant/Stutz)	J. Goux (Peugeot)	87·95	R. Thomas (Ballot)	104·7
	Targa Florio	268	A. Boillot (Peugeot)	Moriondo (Itala)	D. Gamboni (Diatto)	34·19	A. Boillot	
1920	Indianapolis	500	G. Chevrolet (Monroe)	R. Thomas (Ballot)	T. Milton (Duesenberg)	88·16	R. de Palma (Ballot)	99·15

YEAR	EVENT	DISTANCE (MILES)	FIRST	SECOND	THIRD	AVERAGE (M.P.H.)	FASTEST LAP	AVERAGE (M.P.H.)
1921	Indianapolis	500	T. Milton (Frontenac)	R. Sarles (Duesenberg)	P. Ford and J. Ellingboc (Frontenac)	89·62	R. de Palma (Ballot)	100·75
	French G.P.	322	J. Murphy (Duesenberg)	R. de Palma (Ballot)	J. Goux (Ballot)	78·10	J. Murphy	84
	Brescia G.P.	322	J. Goux (Ballot)	J. Chassagne (Ballot)	L. Wagner (Fiat)	89·94	P. Bordino (Fiat)	96·31
1922	Indianapolis	500	J. Murphy (Duesenberg-Miller)	H. C. Hartz (Duesenberg)	E. Hearne (Ballot)	94·48	J. Murphy	100·5
	French G.P.	499	F. Nazzaro (Fiat)	P. de Vizcaya (Bugatti)	Marco (Bugatti)	79·20	P. Bordino (Fiat)	87·75
	Italian G.P.	497	P. Bordino (Fiat)	F. Nazzaro (Fiat)	P. de Vizcaya (Bugatti)	86·90	P. Bordino	91·3
	Targa Florio	268	G. Masetti (Mercedes)	J. Goux (Ballot)	G. Foresti (Ballot)	39·2	G. Masetti	41·3
1923	Indianapolis	500	T. Milton & H. Wilcox (H.C.S.-Miller)	H. C. Hartz (Durant-Miller)	J. Murphy (Durant-Miller)	90·95	T. Milton	108·17
	French G.P.	496	H. O. D. Segrave (Sunbeam)	A. Divo (Sunbeam)	E. Friederich (Bugatti)	75·31	P. Bordino (Fiat)	87·75
	European G.P. (Italy)	497	C. Salamano (Fiat)	F. Nazzaro (Fiat)	J. Murphy (Miller)	91·08	P. Bordino (Fiat)	99·8
1924	Indianapolis	500	L. Corum and J. Boyer (Duesenberg)	E. Cooper (Studebaker-Miller)	J. Murphy (Miller)	98·23		
	Targa Florio	268	C. Werner (Mercedes)	A. Ascari (Alfa-Romeo)	G. Masetti (Alfa-Romeo)	41·1	C. Werner	42·04
	European G.P. (France)	503	G. Campari (Alfa-Romeo)	A. Divo (Delage)	R. Benoist (Delage)	71	H. O. D. Segrave (Sunbeam)	76·7
	San Sebastian G.P.	386	H. O. D. Segrave (Sunbeam)	B. Costantini (Bugatti)	A. Morel (Delage)	64·12	B. Costantini	71·7
	Italian G.P.	497	A. Ascari (Alfa-Romeo)	L. Wagner (Alfa-Romeo)	G. Campari and E. Presenti (Alfa-Romeo)	98·76	A. Ascari	104·24
1925	European G.P. (Belgium)	503	A. Ascari (Alfa-Romeo)	G. Campari (Alfa-Romeo)		74·56	A. Ascari	81·5
	French G.P.	621	R. Benoist and A. Divo (Delage)	L. Wagner and Torchy (Delage)	G. Masetti (Sunbeam)	69·70	A. Divo	80·3
	Italian G.P.	497	G. Brilli Peri (Alfa-Romeo)	G. Campari and E. Minozzi (Alfa-Romeo)	B. Costantini (Bugatti)	94·76	P. Kreis (Duesenberg) / G. Brilli-Peri	103·21 / 104·03
	San Sebastian G.P.	450	A. Divo (Delage)	R. Benoist (Delage)	R. Thomas (Delage)	76·4	B. Costantini (Bugatti)	82·75
1926	French G.P.	316	J. Goux (Bugatti)			68·2	J. Goux	79·4
	European G.P. (Spain)	485	J. Goux (Bugatti)	E. Bourlier and R. Senechal (Delage)	B. Costantini (Bugatti)	70·4	J. Goux	81·5
	British G.P.	287	R. Sénéchal and L. Wagner (Delage)	M. Campbell (Bugatti)	R. Benoist and A. Dubonnet (Delage)	71·61	H. O. D. Segrave (Talbot)	85
	German G.P.		R. Caracciola (Mercedes)	C. Riecken (N.A.G.)	W. Cleer (Alfa-Romeo)			
	Italian G.P.	373	"Sabipa" (Bugatti)	B. Costantini (Bugatti)		85·87	B. Costantini	98·3
1927	French G.P.	373	R. Benoist (Delage)	E. Bourlier (Delage)	A. Morel (Delage)	77·24	R. Benoist	81·43
	Spanish G.P.	430	R. Benoist (Delage)	Count Conelli (Bugatti)	E. Bourlier (Delage)	80·52	R. Benoist	85·41
	European G.P. (Italy)	311	R. Benoist (Delage)	A. Morandi (O.M.)	P. Kreis and E. Cooper (Miller)	90·04	R. Benoist	94·31
	Milan G.P.	31	P. Bordino (Fiat)	G. Campari (Alfa-Romeo)	A. Maggi (Bugatti)	94·57	P. Bordino	96·59
	British G.P.	325	R. Benoist (Delage)	E. Bourlier (Delage)	A. Divo (Delage)	85·59		
1928	European G.P. (Italy)	373	L. Chiron (Bugatti)	A. Varzi and G. Campari (Alfa-Romeo)	T. Nuvolari (Bugatti)	99·4	L. Arcangeli (Talbot)	103·2
	Bordino Prize	159	T. Nuvolari (Bugatti)	A. Varzi (Bugatti)	F. Valpreda (Delage)	63·45	E. Materassi (Talbot)	64·3
	Targa Florio	335	A. Divo (Bugatti)	G. Campari (Alfa-Romeo)	Count Conelli (Bugatti)	45·65	L. Chiron (Bugatti)	46·2

YEAR	EVENT	DISTANCE (MILES)	FIRST	SECOND	THIRD	AVERAGE FASTEST LAP (M.P.H.)		AVERAGE (M.P.H.)
	Rome G.P.	243	L. Chiron (Bugatti)	G. Brilli Peri (Bugatti)	E. Materassi (Talbot)	78·55	L. Chiron	80·4
	Cremona Circuit	200	L. Arcangeli (Talbot)	T. Nuvolari (Bugatti)	E. Materassi (Talbot)	101·36	G. Campari (Alfa-Romeo)	108·6
	Marne G.P.	248	L. Chiron (Bugatti)	Gauthier (Bugatti)	Auber (Bugatti)	82·5	L. Chiron	91·4
	Montenero G.P.	139	E. Materassi (Talbot)	T. Nuvolari (Bugatti)	G. Campari (Alfa-Romeo)	52·77	T. Nuvolari	53·8
	San Sebastian G.P.	430	L. Chiron (Bugatti)	R. Benoist (Bugatti)	M. Lehoux (Bugatti)	80·58	L. Chiron	88·25
1929	Monaco G.P.	195	W. Williams (Bugatti)	E. Bouriano (Bugatti)	R. Caracciola (Mercedes)	50·23	W. Williams	52·7
	Targa Florio	335	A. Divo (Bugatti)	F. Minoia (Bugatti)	G. Brilli Peri (Alfa-Romeo)	46·21	F. Minoia	47·3
	Rome G.P.	243	A. Varzi (Alfa-Romeo)	G. Brilli Peri (Alfa-Romeo)	A. Divo (Bugatti)	80·2		
	Bordino Prize	159	A. Varzi (Alfa-Romeo)	B. Borzacchini (Maserati)	E. Maserati (Maserati)	68·24	A. Varzi	68·6
	Montenero G.P.	139	A. Varzi (Alfa-Romeo)	T. Nuvolari (Alfa-Romeo)	G. Campari (Alfa-Romeo)	54·17	T. Nuvolari	55·3
	Cremona Circuit	125	G. Brilli Peri (Alfa-Romeo)	A. Varzi (Alfa-Romeo)	E. Maserati (Maserati)	114·41	A. Maserati (Maserati)	124·4
	Marne G.P.	248	P. Etancelin (Bugatti)	J. Zanelli (Bugatti)	M. Lehoux (Bugatti)	85·5	P. Etancelin	88·6
	German G.P.	317	L. Chiron (Bugatti)	G. Philippe (Bugatti)	A. Momberger (Mercedes)	66·79	L. Chiron	69·97
	Monza G.P.	62	A. Varzi (Alfa-Romeo)	T. Nuvolari (Alfa-Romeo)	A. Momberger (Mercedes)	116·83	A. Maserati (Maserati)	124·2
1930	Monaco G.P.	195	R. Dreyfus (Bugatti)	L. Chiron (Bugatti)	G. Bouriat (Bugatti)	53·63	R. Dreyfus	56·01
	Targa Florio	335	A. Varzi (Alfa-Romeo)	L. Chiron (Bugatti)	Count Conelli (Bugatti)	48·48	A. Varzi	49·1
	Rome G.P.	162	L. Arcangeli (Maserati)	G. Bouriat (Bugatti)	H. von Morgen (Bugatti)	83·6	G. Bouriat	86·6
	Marne G.P.	248	R. Dreyfus (Bugatti)	M. Lehoux (Bugatti)	M. Doré (Bugatti)	88·50	R. Dreyfus	91
	European G.P. (Belgium)	373	L. Chiron (Bugatti)	G. Bouriat (Bugatti)	A. Divo (Bugatti)	72·1		
	Coppa Ciano	139	L. Fagioli (Maserati)	G. Campari (Alfa-Romeo)	A. Maggi (Bugatti)	54·47	T. Nuvolari (Alfa-Romeo)	57·2
	Coppa Acerbo	159	A. Varzi (Maserati)	E. Maserati (Maserati)	B. Borzacchini (Alfa-Romeo)	75·35	T. Nuvolari (Alfa-Romeo)	78·3
	Monza G.P.	149	A. Varzi (Maserati)	L. Arcangeli (Maserati)	E. Maserati (Maserati)	93·55	A. Varzi	100·6
	French G.P.	247	P. Etancelin (Bugatti)	Sir H. Birkin (Bentley)	J. Zanelli (Bugatti)	90·4		
	Spanish G.P.	323	A. Varzi (Maserati)	A. Maggi (Maserati)	H. Stoffel (Peugeot)	86·82	A. Varzi	91·09
1931	Monaco G.P.	195	L. Chiron (Bugatti)	L. Fagioli (Maserati)	A. Varzi (Bugatti)	54·09	L. Chiron	56·01
	Targa Florio	363	T. Nuvolari (Alfa-Romeo)	B. Borzacchini (Alfa-Romeo)	A. Varzi (Bugatti)	40·39	A. Varzi	43·8
	Italian G.P.	10 hours	G. Campari and T. Nuvolari (Alfa-Romeo)	F. Minoia and B. Borzacchini (Alfa-Romeo)	A. Divo and G. Bouriat (Bugatti)	96·17	T. Nuvolari	105
	French G.P.	10 hours	A. Varzi and L. Chiron (Bugatti)	G. Campari and B. Borzacchini (Alfa-Romeo)	C. Biondetti and Parenti (Maserati)	78·21	L. Fagioli (Maserati)	85·6
	Belgian G.P.	10 hours	W. Williams and Count Conelli (Bugatti)	T. Nuvolari and B. Borzacchini (Alfa-Romeo)	F. Minoia and E. Minozzi (Alfa-Romeo)	82·04	L. Chiron (Bugatti)	88
	German G.P.	255	R. Caracciola (Mercedes)	L. Chiron (Bugatti)	A. Varzi (Bugatti)	67·4	A. Varzi	72·6
	Monza G.P.	149	L. Fagioli (Maserati)	B. Borzacchini (Alfa-Romeo)	A. Varzi (Bugatti)	96·6	T. Nuvolari (Alfa-Romeo)	101·23
	Czech G.P.	308	L. Chiron (Bugatti)	H. Stuck (Mercedes)	H. von Morgen (Bugatti)	73·26	L. Chiron	75·36
1932	Monaco G.P.	195	T. Nuvolari (Alfa-Romeo)	R. Caracciola (Alfa-Romeo)	L. Fagioli (Maserati)	55·81	A. Varzi (Bugatti)	58·3
	Targa Florio	354	R. Nuvolari (Alfa-Romeo)	B. Borzacchini (Alfa-Romeo)	L. Chiron (Bugatti)	49·27	T. Nuvolari	50·7
	Avüsrennen	182	M. von Brauchitsch (Mercedes)	R. Caracciola (Alfa-Romeo)	H. Stuber (Bugatti)	120·07		
	Eifelrennen	198	R. Caracciola (Alfa-Romeo)	R. Dreyfus (Bugatti)	M. von Brauchitsch (Mercedes)	70·7	R. Caracciola	72·8

YEAR	EVENT	DISTANCE (MILES)	FIRST	SECOND	THIRD	AVERAGE (M.P.H.)	FASTEST LAP	AVERAGE (M.P.H.)
	Italian G.P.	5 hours	T. Nuvolari and G. Campari (Alfa-Romeo)	L. Fagioli and E. Maserati (Maserati)	B. Borzacchini and A. Marinoni and R. Caracciola (Alfa-Romeo)	104·13	L. Fagioli	112·22
	French G.P.	5 hours	T. Nuvolari (Alfa-Romeo)	B. Borzacchini (Alfa-Romeo)	R. Caracciola (Alfa-Romeo)	92·26	T. Nuvolari	99·5
	German G.P.	354	R. Caracciola (Alfa-Romeo)	T. Nuvolari (Alfa-Romeo)	B. Borzacchini (Alfa-Romeo)	74·13	T. Nuvolari	77·55
	Coppa Ciano	124	T. Nuvolari (Alfa-Romeo)	B. Borzacchini (Alfa-Romeo)	G. Campari (Alfa-Romeo)	53·91	T. Nuvolari	54·5
	Coppa Acerbo	190	T. Nuvolari (Alfa-Romeo)	R. Caracciola (Alfa-Romeo)	L. Chiron (Bugatti)	86·89	T. Nuvolari	90·3
	Marseilles G.P.	250	R. Sommer (Alfa-Romeo)	T. Nuvolari (Alfa-Romeo)	G. Moll (Bugatti)	109·14		
	Czech G.P.	308	L. Chiron (Bugatti)	L. Fagioli (Maserati)	T. Nuvolari (Alfa-Romeo)	67·67	L. Chiron	73·73
	Monza G.P.	124	R. Caracciola (Alfa-Romeo)	L. Fagioli (Maserati)	T. Nuvolari (Alfa-Romeo)	110·8	T. Nuvolari	113·7
1933	Monaco G.P.	195	A. Varzi (Bugatti)	B. Borzacchini (Alfa-Romeo)	R. Dreyfus (Bugatti)	57·04	A. Varzi	59·77
	Pau G.P.	132	M. Lehoux (Bugatti)	G. Moll (Bugatti)	P. Etancelin (Alfa-Romeo)	45·38		
	Tunis G.P.	292	T. Nuvolari (Alfa-Romeo)	B. Borzacchini (Alfa-Romeo)	G. Zehender (Maserati)	83·81		
	Tripoli G.P.	244	A. Varzi (Bugatti)	T. Nuvolari (Alfa-Romeo)	Sir H. Birkin (Maserati)	104·76		
	Avüsrennen	182	A. Varzi (Bugatti)	Count Czaykowski (Bugatti)	T. Nuvolari and B. Borzacchini (Alfa-Romeo)	128·48		
	Eifelrennen	213	T. Nuvolari (Alfa-Romeo)	M. von Brauchitsch (Mercedes)	P. Taruffi (Alfa-Romeo)	70·48		
	French G.P.	311	G. Campari (Maserati)	P. Etancelin (Alfa-Romeo)	G. E. T. Eyston (Alfa-Romeo)	81·52	G. Campari	86·6
	Marne G.P.	248	P. Etancelin (Alfa-Romeo)	J. P. Wimille (Alfa-Romeo)	R. Sommer (Alfa-Romeo)	90·59	G. Campari (Maserati)	96
	Belgian G.P.	370	T. Nuvolari (Maserati)	A. Varzi (Bugatti)	R. Dreyfus (Bugatti)	89·23	T. Nuvolari	92·33
	Nice G.P.	199	T. Nuvolari (Maserati)	R. Dreyfus (Bugatti)	G. Moll (Alfa-Romeo)	64·56		
	Coppa Ciano	149	T. Nuvolari (Maserati)	A. Brivio (Alfa-Romeo)	G. Campari (Alfa-Romeo)	54·18	T. Nuvolari	55·38
	Coppa Acerbo	190	L. Fagioli (Alfa-Romeo)	T. Nuvolari (Maserati)	P. Taruffi (Maserati)	88·03	T. Nuvolari	90·4
	Comminges G.P.	239	L. Fagioli (Alfa-Romeo)	J. P. Wimille (Alfa-Romeo)	G. Moll (Alfa-Romeo)	89·08		
	Marseilles G.P.	311	L. Chiron (Alfa-Romeo)	L. Fagioli (Alfa-Romeo)	G. Moll (Alfa-Romeo)	111·22		
	Italian G.P.	311	L. Fagioli (Alfa-Romeo)	T. Nuvolari (Maserati)	G. Zehender (Maserati)	108·58	L. Fagioli	115·82
	Monza G.P.	39	M. Lehoux (Bugatti)	G. Moll (Alfa-Romeo)	F. Bonetto (Alfa-Romeo)	108·99	Count Czaykowski (Bugatti)	116·81
	Czech G.P.	308	L. Chiron (Alfa-Romeo)	L. Fagioli (Alfa-Romeo)	J. P. Wimille (Alfa-Romeo)	63·57	L. Chiron	70·8
	Spanish G.P.	323	L. Chiron (Alfa-Romeo)	L. Fagioli (Alfa-Romeo)	M. Lehoux (Bugatti)	83·32	T. Nuvolari (Maserati)	96·59
1934	Monaco G.P.	195	G. Moll (Alfa-Romeo)	R. Dreyfus (Alfa-Romeo)	M. Lehoux (Alfa-Romeo)	55·86	Count Trossi (Alfa-Romeo)	59·7
	Avüsrennen	183	G. Moll (Alfa-Romeo)	A. Varzi (Alfa-Romeo)	A. Momberger (Auto-Union)	127·5	A. Momberger	140·33
	Eifelrennen	213	M. von Brauchitsch (Mercedes-Benz)	H. Stuck (Auto-Union)	L. Chiron (Alfa-Romeo)	76·12	M. von Brauchitsch	79
	French G.P.	311	L. Chiron (Alfa-Romeo)	A. Varzi (Alfa-Romeo)	C. F. Trossi and G. Moll (Alfa-Romeo)	85·55	L. Chiron	91·44
	German G.P.	356	H. Stuck (Auto-Union)	L. Fagioli (Mercedes-Benz)	L. Chiron (Alfa-Romeo)	76·39	H. Stuck	79·29
	Coppa Acerbo	321	L. Fagioli (Mercedes-Benz)	T. Nuvolari (Maserati)	A. Brivio (Bugatti)	80·26	G. Moll (Alfa-Romeo)	90·5
	Swiss G.P.	317	H. Stuck (Auto-Union)	A. Momberger (Auto-Union)	R. Dreyfus (Bugatti)	87·21	A. Momberger	94·42
	Italian G.P.	311	R. Caracciola and L. Fagioli (Mercedes-Benz)	H. Stuck and Prince zu Leiningen (Auto-Union)	Count Trossi and G. Comotti (Alfa-Romeo)	65·37	H. Stuck	72·59

339

YEAR	EVENT	DISTANCE (MILES)	FIRST	SECOND	THIRD	AVERAGE FASTEST LAP (M.P.H.)		AVERAGE (M.P.H.)
	Spanish G.P.	323	L. Fagioli (Mercedes-Benz)	R. Caracciola (Mercedes-Benz)	T. Nuvolari (Bugatti)	97·13	H. Stuck (Auto-Union)	101·96
	Czech G.P.	308	H. Stuck (Auto-Union)	L. Fagioli (Mercedes-Benz)	T. Nuvolari (Maserati)	79·21	L. Fagioli	81·23
1935	Monaco G.P.	195	L. Fagioli (Mercedes-Benz)	R. Dreyfus (Alfa-Romeo)	A. Brivio (Alfa-Romeo)	58·17	L. Fagioli	60·08
	Tunis G.P.	313	A. Varzi (Auto-Union)	J. P. Wimille (Bugatti)	P. Etancelin (Maserati)	101·2	A. Varzi	105·15
	Tripoli G.P.	326	R. Caracciola (Mercedes-Benz)	A. Varzi (Auto-Union)	L. Fagioli (Mercedes-Benz)	123·03	R. Caracciola	136·81
	Avüsrennen	122	L. Fagioli (Mercedes-Benz)	L. Chiron (Alfa-Romeo)	A. Varzi (Auto-Union)	148·83	H. Stuck (Auto-Union)	161·88
	Eifelrennen	156	R. Caracciola (Mercedes-Benz)	B. Rosemeyer (Auto-Union)	L. Chiron (Alfa-Romeo)	72·8	R. Caracciola	75·6
	Penya Rhin G.P.	165	L. Fagioli (Mercedes-Benz)	R. Caracciola (Mercedes-Benz)	T. Nuvolari (Alfa-Romeo)	66·99	R. Caracciola	68·94
	French G.P.	311	R. Caracciola (Mercedes-Benz)	M. von Brauchitsch (Mercedes-Benz)	G. Zehender (Maserati)	77·39	T. Nuvolari (Alfa-Romeo)	85
	Belgian G.P.	315	R. Caracciola (Mercedes-Benz)	M. von Brauchitsch and L. Fagioli (Mercedes-Benz)	L. Chiron (Alfa-Romeo)	97·8	M. von Brauchitsch	103·7
	German G.P.	312	T. Nuvolari (Alfa-Romeo)	H. Stuck (Auto-Union)	R. Caracciola (Mercedes-Benz)	75·43	M. von Brauchitsch (Mercedes-Benz)	80·73
	Coppa Acerbo	321	A. Varzi (Auto-Union)	B. Rosemeyer (Auto-Union)	A. Brivio (Alfa-Romeo)	86·6	A. Varzi	90·9
	Swiss G.P.	317	R. Caracciola (Mercedes-Benz)	L. Fagioli (Mercedes-Benz)	B. Rosemeyer (Auto-Union)	89·95	L. Fagioli	99·5
	Italian G.P.	313	H. Stuck (Auto-Union)	R. Dreyfus and T. Nuvolari (Alfa-Romeo)	P. Pietsch and B. Rosemeyer (Auto-Union)	85·17	T. Nuvolari	90·77
	Spanish G.P.		R. Caracciola (Mercedes-Benz)	L. Fagioli (Mercedes-Benz)	M. von Brauchitsch (Mercedes-Benz)	101·92	A. Varzi (Auto-Union)	108·11
	Czech G.P.		B. Rosemeyer (Auto-Union)	T. Nuvolari (Alfa-Romeo)	L. Chiron (Alfa-Romeo)	82·39	A. Varzi (Auto-Union)	85·21
1936	Monaco G.P.	195	R. Caracciola (Mercedes-Benz)	A. Varzi (Auto-Union)	H. Stuck (Auto-Union)	51·69	H. Stuck	56·01
	Tunis G.P.	237	R. Caracciola (Mercedes-Benz)	C. Pintacuda (Alfa-Romeo)	J. P. Wimille (Bugatti)	99·62	B. Rosemeyer (Auto-Union)	103·79
	Tripoli G.P.	326	A. Varzi (Auto-Union)	H. Stuck (Auto-Union)	L. Fagioli (Mercedes-Benz)	129·01	A. Varzi	141·29
	Penya Rhin G.P.	188	T. Nuvolari (Alfa-Romeo)	R. Caracciola (Mercedes-Benz)	G. Farina (Alfa-Romeo)	69·21	T. Nuvolari	71·85
	Eifelrennen	142	B. Rosemeyer (Auto-Union)	T. Nuvolari (Alfa-Romeo)	A. Brivio (Alfa-Romeo)	72·71	B. Rosemeyer	74·46
	Hungarian G.P.	155	T. Nuvolari (Alfa-Romeo)	B. Rosemeyer (Auto-Union)	A. Varzi (Auto-Union)	69·1	T. Nuvolari	71·84
	Milan Circuit	97	T. Nuvolari (Alfa-Romeo)	A. Varzi (Auto-Union)	G. Farina (Alfa-Romeo)	60·02	A. Varzi	62·26
	German G.P.	312	B. Rosemeyer (Auto-Union)	H. Stuck (Auto-Union)	A. Brivio (Alfa-Romeo)	81·8	B. Rosemeyer	85·52
	Coppa Ciano	130	T. Nuvolari (Alfa-Romeo)	A. Brivio (Alfa-Romeo)	R. Dreyfus (Alfa-Romeo)	74·8	T. Nuvolari	77·05
	Coppa Acerbo	257	B. Rosemeyer (Auto-Union)	E. von Delius (Auto-Union)	A. Varzi (Auto-Union)	86·48	A. Varzi	89·04
	Swiss G.P.	317	B. Rosemeyer (Auto-Union)	A. Varzi (Auto-Union)	H. Stuck (Auto-Union)	100·45	B. Rosemeyer	105·42
	Italian G.P.	313	B. Rosemeyer (Auto-Union)	T. Nuvolari (Alfa-Romeo)	E. von Delius (Auto-Union)	84·59	B. Rosemeyer	87·18
1937	Tripoli G.P.	320	H. Lang (Mercedes-Benz)	B. Rosemeyer (Auto-Union)	E. von Delius (Auto-Union)	134·25	H. Stuck (Auto-Union)	142·44
	Avüsrennen	96	H. Lang (Mercedes-Benz)	E. von Delius (Auto-Union)	R. Hasse (Auto-Union)	162·61	B. Rosemeyer (Auto-Union)	172·75
	Eifelrennen	142	B. Rosemeyer (Auto-Union)	R. Caracciola (Mercedes-Benz)	M. von Brauchitsch (Mercedes-Benz)	82·95	B. Rosemeyer	85·13
	Vanderbilt Cup	300	B. Rosemeyer (Auto-Union)	R. J. B. Seaman (Mercedes-Benz)	Rex Mays (Alfa-Romeo)	82·56	R. Caracciola (Mercedes-Benz)	84·5
	Belgian G.P.	315	R. Hasse (Auto-Union)	H. Stuck (Auto-Union)	H. Lang (Mercedes-Benz)	104·07	H. Lang	108·8
	German G.P.	312	R. Caracciola (Mercedes-Benz)	M. von Brauchitsch (Mercedes-Benz)	B. Rosemeyer (Auto-Union)	82·77	B. Rosemeyer	85·57
	Monaco G.P.	195	M. von Brauchitsch (Mercedes-Benz)	R. Caracciola (Mercedes-Benz)	C. Kautz (Mercedes-Benz)	62·35	R. Caracciola	66·99
	Coppa Acerbo	257	B. Rosemeyer (Auto-Union)	M. von Brauchitsch (Mercedes-Benz)	H. Muller (Auto-Union)	87·61	B. Rosemeyer	92

YEAR	EVENT	DISTANCE (MILES)	FIRST	SECOND	THIRD	AVERAGE (M.P.H.)	FASTEST LAP	AVERAGE (M.P.H.)
	Swiss G.P.	226	R. Caracciola (Mercedes-Benz)	H. Lang (Mercedes-Benz)	M. von Brauchitsch (Mercedes-Benz)	98·61	R. Caracciola	(P)107·14
	Italian G.P.	250	R. Caracciola (Mercedes-Benz)	H. Lang (Mercedes-Benz)	B. Rosemeyer (Auto-Union)	81·59	R. Caracciola	84·5
	Czech G.P.	271	R. Caracciola (Mercedes-Benz)	M. von Brauchitsch (Mercedes-Benz)	H. Muller and B. Rosemeyer (Auto-Union)	85·97	R. Caracciola	94·89
	Donington G.P.	250	B. Rosemeyer (Auto-Union)	M. von Brauchitsch (Mercedes-Benz)	R. Caracciola (Mercedes-Benz)	82·26	B. Rosemeyer and M. von Brauchitsch	85·52
1938	Pau G.P.	172	R. Dreyfus (Delahaye)	R. Caracciola and H. Lang (Mercedes-Benz)	G. Comotti (Delahaye)	54·64	R. Caracciola	57·86
	French G.P.	312	M. von Brauchitsch (Mercedes-Benz)	R. Caracciola (Mercedes-Benz)	H. Lang (Mercedes-Benz)	101·3	H. Lang	105·87
	German G.P.	312	R. J. B. Seaman (Mercedes-Benz)	H. Lang and R. Caracciola (Mercedes-Benz)	H. Stuck (Auto-Union)	80·75	R. J. B. Seaman	83·76
	Coppa Ciano	146	H. Lang (Mercedes-Benz)	G. Farina (Alfa-Romeo)	J. P. Wimille and C. Biondetti (Alfa-Romeo)	85·94	H. Lang and M. von Brauchitsch	89·17
	Coppa Acerbo	257	R. Caracciola (Mercedes-Benz)	G. Farina (Alfa-Romeo)	C. Belmondo (Alfa-Romeo)	83·69	L. Villoresi (Maserati)	87·79
	Swiss G.P.	226	R. Caracciola (Mercedes-Benz)	R. J. B. Seaman (Mercedes-Benz)	M. von Brauchitsch (Mercedes-Benz)	89·44	R. J. B. Seaman	(P)103
	Italian G.P.	261 / 261	T. Nuvolari (Auto-Union)	G. Farina (Alfa-Romeo)	R. Caracciola and M. von Brauchitsch (Mercedes-Benz)	96·7	H. Lang (Mercedes-Benz)	101·38
	Donington G.P.	250	T. Nuvolari (Auto-Union)	H. Lang (Mercedes-Benz)	R. J. B. Seaman (Mercedes-Benz)	80·49	T. Nuvolari	83·71
1939	Pau G.P.	160	H. Lang (Mercedes-Benz)	M. von Brauchitsch (Mercedes-Benz)	P. Etancelin (Darracq)	56·09	M. von Brauchitsch	57·83
	Eifelrennen	142	H. Lang (Mercedes-Benz)	T. Nuvolari (Auto-Union)	R. Caracciola (Mercedes-Benz)	84·14	H. Lang	86
	Belgian G.P.	315	H. Lang (Mercedes-Benz)	R. Hasse (Auto-Union)	M. von Brauchitsch (Mercedes-Benz)	94·39	H. Lang	109·12
	French G.P.	248	H. Muller (Auto-Union)	G. Meier (Auto-Union)	R. le Bègue (Darracq)	105·25	H. Lang (Mercedes-Benz)	114·87
	German G.P.	312	R. Caracciola (Mercedes-Benz)	H. Muller (Auto-Union)	P. Pietsch (Maserati)	75·12	R. Caracciola	81·66
	Swiss G.P.	150	H. Lang (Mercedes-Benz)	R. Caracciola (Mercedes-Benz)	M. von Brauchitsch (Mercedes-Benz)	96·02	R. Caracciola	104·32
	Yugoslav G.P.	86	T. Nuvolari (Auto-Union)	M. von Brauchitsch (Mercedes-Benz)	H. Muller (Auto-Union)	81·21	T. Nuvolari and M. von Brauchitsch	83·9
	Tripoli G.P.	244	H. Lang (Mercedes-Benz)	R. Caracciola (Mercedes-Benz)	E. Villoresi (Alfa-Romeo)	122·91	H. Lang	133·5
1940	Tripoli G.P.	244	G. Farina (Alfa-Romeo)	C. Biondetti (Alfa-Romeo)	Count Trossi (Alfa-Romeo)	128·22		
1946	St. Cloud G.P.	112	R. Sommer (Maserati)	L. Chiron (Talbot)	Ruggeri (Maserati)	67·99	L. Chiron	71·35
	G.P. des Nations	86	G. Farina (Alfa-Romeo)	Count Trossi (Alfa-Romeo)	J. P. Wimille (Alfa-Romeo)	64·10	J. P. Wimille	68·76
	Circuit of Turin	174	A. Varzi (Alfa-Romeo)	J. P. Wimille (Alfa-Romeo)	R. Sommer (Maserati)	64·62	J. P. Wimille	73·58
	Circuit of Milan	52	Count Trossi (Alfa-Romeo)	A. Varzi (Alfa-Romeo)	C. Sanesi (Alfa-Romeo)	55·59	A. Varzi and G. Farina (Alfa-Romeo)	56·7
1947	Swiss G.P.	136	J. P. Wimille (Alfa-Romeo)	A. Varzi (Alfa-Romeo)	Count Trossi (Alfa-Romeo)	95·42	R. Sommer (Maserati)	97·03
	Belgian G.P.	310	J. P. Wimille (Alfa-Romeo)	A. Varzi (Alfa-Romeo)	Count Trossi (Alfa-Romeo)	95·28	J. P. Wimille	101·94
	Bari G.P.	165·5	A. Varzi (Alfa-Romeo)	C. Sanesi (Alfa-Romeo)	N. Grieco (Maserati)	65·1	A. Varzi	70·68
	Italian G.P.	214	Count Trossi (Alfa-Romeo)	A. Varzi (Alfa-Romeo)	C. Sanesi (Alfa-Romeo)	70·29	Count Trossi	74·16
	French G.P.	314·2	L. Chiron (Talbot)	H. Louveau) (Maserati)	E. Chaboud	78·09	L. Villoresi, A. Ascari and E. de Graffenried (Maseratis)	82·4
1948	European G.P. (Switzerland)	181	Count Trossi (Alfa-Romeo)	J. P. Wimille (Alfa-Romeo)	L. Villoresi (Maserati)	90·81	J. P. Wimille	95·05
	French G.P.	310	J. P. Wimille (Alfa-Romeo)	C. Sanesi (Alfa-Romeo)	A. Ascari (Alfa-Romeo)	102·1	J. P. Wimille	108·14 (P)112·2

(P) *indicates a fastest lap achieved in practice.*

341

YEAR	EVENT	DISTANCE (MILES)	FIRST	SECOND	THIRD	AVERAGE FASTEST LAP (M.P.H.)		AVERAGE (M.P.H.)
	Italian G.P.	224	J. P. Wimille (Alfa-Romeo)	L. Villoresi (Maserati)	R. Sommer (Ferrari)	70·38	J. P. Wimille	(P)78·61
	Monza G.P.	313	J. P. Wimille (Alfa-Romeo)	Count Trossi (Alfa-Romeo)	C. Sanesi (Alfa-Romeo)	109·98	C. Sanesi	116·95
	Monaco G.P.	195	G. Farina (Maserati)	L. Chiron (Talbot)	E. de Graffenreid (Maserati)	59·61	G. Farina	62·32
	British G.P.	239	L. Villoresi (Maserati)	A. Ascari (Maserati)	F. R. Gerard (E.R.A.)	72·28	L. Villoresi	76·82
1949	San Remo G.P.	178	J. M. Fangio (Maserati)	B. Bira (Maserati)	E. de Graffenreid (Maserati)	62·87	B. Bira	64·66
	British G.P.	300	E. de Graffenreid (Maserati)	F. R. Gerard (E.R.A.)	L. Rosier (Talbot)	77·31	B. Bira (Maserati)	82·82
	Pau G.P.	87	J. M. Fangio (Maserati)	E. de Graffenreid (Maserati)	B. Campos (Maserati)	52·7	J. M. Fangio	56·85
	Belgian G.P.	315	L. Rosier (Talbot)	L. Villoresi (Ferrari)	A. Ascari (Ferrari)	96·95	G. Farina (Maserati)	101·64
	Swiss G.P.	181	A. Ascari (Ferrari)	L. Villoresi (Ferrari)	R. Sommer (Talbot)	90·76	G. Farina (Maserati)	95·1
	G.P. de France	310	L. Chiron (Talbot)	B. Bira (Maserati)	P. Whitehead (Ferrari)	99·98	P. Whitehead	105·1
	Zandvoort G.P.	104	L. Villoresi (Ferrari)	E. de Graffenreid (Maserati)	B. Bira (Maserati)	77·12	B. Bira	79·49
	International Trophy (Silverstone)	89	A. Ascari (Ferrari)	G. Farina (Maserati)	L. Villoresi (Ferrari)	89·58	A. Ascari	93·35
	European G.P. (Italy)	313	A. Ascari (Ferrari)	P. Etancelin (Talbot)	B. Bira (Maserati)	105·04	A. Ascari	(P)112·72
	Czech G.P.		P. Whitehead (Ferrari)					
1950	San Remo G.P.	178	J. M. Fangio (Alfa-Romeo)	L. Villoresi (Ferrari)	Pian (Maserati)	59·65	L. Villoresi	62·3
	European G.P. (Britain)	210	G. Farina (Alfa-Romeo)	L. Fagioli (Alfa-Romeo)	R. Parnell (Alfa-Romeo)	90·95	G. Farina	94·02
	Monaco G.P.	195	J. M. Fangio (Alfa-Romeo)	A. Ascari (Ferrari)	L. Chiron (Maserati)	61·33	J. M. Fangio	64·09
	Swiss G.P.	190	G. Farina (Alfa-Romeo)	L. Fagioli (Alfa-Romeo)	L. Rosier (Talbot)	92·76	G. Farina	100·78
	Belgian G.P.	315	J. M. Fangio (Alfa-Romeo)	L. Fagioli (Alfa-Romeo)	L. Rosier (Talbot)	110·05	G. Farina (Alfa-Romeo)	115·15
	French G.P.	310	J. M. Fangio (Alfa-Romeo)	L. Fagioli (Alfa-Romeo)	P. Whitehead (Ferrari)	104·83	J. M. Fangio	112·35 (P)116·2
	Bari G.P.	202	G. Farina (Alfa-Romeo)	J. M. Fangio (Alfa-Romeo)	S. Moss (H.W.M.)	77·31	G. Farina	81·28
	Pescara G.P.	257	J. M. Fangio (Alfa-Romeo)	L. Rosier (Talbot)	L. Fagioli (Alfa-Romeo)	83·95	J. M. Fangio	90·33
	G.P. des Nations	170	J. M. Fangio (Alfa-Romeo)	E. de Graffenreid (Alfa-Romeo)	P. Taruffii (Alfa-Romeo)	79·74	P. Taruffi	85·63
	International Trophy (Silverstone)	101	G. Farina (Alfa-Romeo)	J. M. Fangio (Alfa-Romeo)	P. Whitehead (Ferrari)	90·16	G. Farina	92·85
	Italian G.P.	313	G. Farina (Alfa-Romeo)	A. Ascari and D. Serafini (Ferrari)	L. Fagioli (Alfa-Romeo)	109·67	J. M. Fangio	117·44
	Penya Rhin G.P.	194	A. Ascari (Ferrari)	D. Serafini (Ferrari)	P. Taruffi (Ferrari)	93·8	A. Ascari	97·7
1951	Swiss G.P.	190	J. M. Fangio (Alfa-Romeo)	P. Taruffi (Ferrari)	G. Farina (Alfa-Romeo)	89·05	J. M. Fangio	(P)104·46
	Belgian G.P.	315	G. Farina (Alfa-Romeo)	A. Ascari (Ferrari)	L. Villoresi (Ferrari)	114·26	J. M. Fangio	120·51
	French G.P.	375	J. M. Fangio and L. Fagioli (Alfa-Romeo)	A. Ascari and J. F. Gonzalez (Ferrari)	L. Villoresi (Ferrari)	110·97	J. M. Fangio	118·29 (P)119·99
	British G.P.	260	J. F. Gonzalez (Ferrari)	J. M. Fangio (Alfa-Romeo)	L. Villoresi (Ferrari)	96·11	G. Farina	99·99
	German G.P.	283	A. Ascari (Ferrari)	J. M. Fangio (Alfa-Romeo)	J. F. Gonzalez (Ferrari)	83·76	J. M. Fangio	85·69
	Bari G.P.	215	J. M. Fangio (Alfa-Romeo)	J. F. Gonzalez (Ferrari)	P. Taruffi (Ferrari)	83·92	A. Ascari (Ferrari)	87·89
	Italian G.P.	312	A. Ascari (Ferrari)	J. F. Gonzalez (Ferrari)	F. Bonetto and G. Farina (Alfa-Romeo)	115·53	G. Farina	120·97
	Spanish G.P.	275	J. M. Fangio (Alfa-Romeo)	J. F. Gonzalez (Ferrari)	G. Farina (Alfa-Romeo)	98·76	J. M. Fangio	105·2

(P) *indicates a fastest lap achieved in practice.*

Appendix B · Table of Drivers' Successes,

PART ONE 1906–1911

DRIVER	FIRST	SECOND	THIRD	FASTEST LAP
Nazzaro	4	1	1	–
Cagno	2	–	1	2
Wagner	2	–	–	1
Bruce-Brown	2	–	–	–
Hémery	1	4	–	2
Duray	1	–	1	1
Szisz	1	1	–	–
Minoia	1	–	–	1
Lautenschlager	1	–	–	–
Lancia	–	2	–	3
Hanriot	–	1	2	–
Demogeot	–	1	–	–
Friederich	–	1	–	–
Graziani	–	1	–	–
Hautvast	–	1	–	–
Hearne	–	1	–	–
Trucco	–	1	–	–
Rougier	–	–	2	–
Baras	–	–	1	1
de Palma	–	–	1	1
Bablot	–	–	1	–
Burman	–	–	1	–
Clément	–	–	1	–
Fabry	–	–	1	–
Gabriel	–	–	1	–
Jörns	–	–	1	–
Salzer	–	–	–	1
Tracy	–	–	–	1

PART TWO 1912–1921

DRIVER	FIRST	SECOND	THIRD	FASTEST LAP
Resta	6	1	–	1
Aitken	3	1	2	–
Boillot G.	2	–	–	2
Murphy J.	2	–	–	2
Wilcox	2	1	–	–
de Palma	1	4	–	2
Thomas R.	1	1	–	1
Bablot	1	–	–	2
Boillot A.	1	–	–	1
Milton	1	–	1	–
Anderson	1	–	1	–
Lautenschlager	1	–	–	–
Chevrolet G.	1	–	–	–
Cooper E.	–	2	1	–
Wagner	–	2	1	–
Chassagne	–	1	1	–
Guyot	–	1	1	–
Hearne	–	1	1	–
Duray	–	1	–	–
Leduc	–	1	–	–
Wishart	–	1	–	–
Crespelle	–	–	1	–
Merz	–	–	1	–
Pilette	–	–	1	–
Rigal	–	–	1	–
Salzer	–	–	1	–
Bordino	–	–	–	1
Bruce-Brown	–	–	–	1
Sailer	–	–	–	1
Zuccarelli	–	–	–	1

PART THREE 1922–1933

DRIVER	FIRST	SECOND	THIRD	FASTEST LAP
Nuvolari	14	10	4	16
Chiron	13	3	2	10
Varzi	12	4	4	8
Fagioli	5	7	1	3
Benoist	5	2	2	3
Campari	4	7	5	3
Caracciola	4	3	3	1
Divo	4	3	3	1
Dreyfus	2	2	2	2
Etancelin	3	1	1	–
Brilli Peri	2	2	1	1
Ascari	2	1	–	2
Bordino	2	–	–	5
Goux	2	1	–	2
Lehoux	2	1	3	–
Arcangeli	2	1	–	1
Segrave	2	–	–	2
Williams	2	–	–	1
Nazzaro	1	2	–	–
Wagner	1	2	–	–
Conelli	1	1	2	–
Masetti G.	1	–	2	1
Materassi	1	–	2	1
Brauchitsch	1	1	1	–
Sénéchal	1	1	–	–
Sommer	1	–	1	–
Milton	1	–	–	1
Werner	1	–	–	1
Boyer	1	–	–	–
Corum	1	–	–	–
"Sabipa"	1	–	–	–
Salamano	1	–	–	–
Borzacchini	–	11	4	–
Bouriat	–	3	1	1
Bourlier	–	3	1	–
Costantini	–	2	2	3
Moll	–	2	4	–
Maserati E.	–	2	3	–
Minoia	–	2	1	1
Wimille	–	2	1	–
Maggi	–	1	2	–
Zanelli	–	1	1	1
Birkin	–	1	1	–
Cooper E.	–	1	1	–
Minozzi	–	1	1	–
de Vizcaya P.	–	1	1	–
Czaykowski	–	1	–	1
Bouriano	–	1	–	–
Brivio	–	1	–	–
Campbell	–	1	–	–
Hartz	–	1	–	–
Morandi	–	1	–	–
Philippe	–	1	–	–
Stuck	–	1	–	–
Murphy	–	–	3	–
Momberger	–	–	2	1
Morel	–	–	2	–
von Morgen	–	–	2	–
Taruffi	–	–	2	–
Zehender	–	–	2	–
Kreis	–	–	1	1
Biondetti	–	–	1	–
Bonetto	–	–	1	–
Dubonnet	–	–	1	–
Eyston	–	–	1	–
Foresti	–	–	1	–
Friederich	–	–	1	–
Marco	–	–	1	–
Marinoni	–	–	1	–
Thomas R.	–	–	1	–
Valpreda	–	–	1	–
Maserati A.	–	–	–	2

PART FOUR 1934–1951 I–1934/9

DRIVER	FIRST	SECOND	THIRD	FASTEST LAP
Caracciola	17	9	4	12
Rosemeyer	10	4	5	10
Nuvolari	8	6	4	7
Lang	7	5	2	7
Fagioli	6	5	2	3
Stuck	4	6	3	5
Brauchitsch	3	8	7	7
Varzi	3	6	3	7
Seaman	1	2	1	2
Chiron	1	1	5	–
Moll	2	–	1	1
Muller	1	1	3	–
Dreyfus	1	3	2	–
Farina	–	3	2	–
Delius	–	2	2	–
Brivio	–	1	5	–
Momberger	–	1	1	2
Trossi	–	–	2	1
Wimille	–	1	2	–
Leiningen	–	1	–	–
Mcicr	–	1	–	–
Pintacuda	–	1	–	–
Comotti	–	–	2	–
Pietsch	–	–	2	–
Villoresi L.	–	–	1	1
Biondetti	–	–	1	–
Belmondo	–	–	1	–
le Bègue	–	–	1	–
Kautz	–	–	1	–
Rex Mays	–	–	1	–
Lehoux	–	–	1	–
Zehender	–	–	1	–

PART FOUR 1934–1951 II–1939/40/46–51

DRIVER	FIRST	SECOND	THIRD	FASTEST LAP
Fangio	12	4	–	10
Farina	9	1	4	11
Ascari	6	5	2	5
Wimille	5	2	1	6
Trossi	3	2	3	1
Villoresi L.	2	4	5	3
Varzi	2	4	–	2
Chiron	2	2	1	1
Fagioli	1	4	2	–
Gonzalez	1	4	1	–
Sommer	1	–	3	1
Rosier	1	1	3	–
de Graffenried	1	3	2	1
Lang	1	–	–	1
Taruffi	–	1	3	1
Sanesi	–	2	3	1
Serafini	–	2	–	–
Bira	–	2	2	3
Gerard F. R.	–	1	1	–
Caracciola	–	1	–	–
Biondetti	–	1	–	–
Louveau	–	1	–	–
Etancelin	–	1	–	–
Whitehead	–	–	3	1
Villoresi E.	–	–	1	–
Ruggeri	–	–	1	–
Grieco	–	–	1	–
Chaboud	–	–	1	–
Campos	–	–	1	–
Parnell	–	–	1	–
Moss	–	–	1	–
Bonetto	–	–	1	–

DRIVER	FIRST	SECOND	THIRD	FASTEST LAP	DRIVER	FIRST	SECOND	THIRD	FASTEST LAP	DRIVER	FIRST	SECOND	THIRD	FASTEST LAP
Goux	3	2	5	–	Guyot	1	–	–	–	Mennard-Lucas	–	1	–	–
Giuppone	3	2	–	–	Moore-					Thomas R.	–	–	2	–
Naudin	3	1	–	–	. Brabazon	1	–	–	–	Chassagne	–	–	1	–
Sizaire	1	3	–	–	Guinness A. L.	–	1	1	–	Jenatzy	–	–	1	–
Boillot G.	1	2	–	–	Camarata	–	1	–	–	Soyez	–	–	1	–
Zuccarelli	1	–	1	–	Cissac	–	1	–	–	Stabile	–	–	1	–
Bablot	1	–	–	–	Florio	–	1	–	–	Tasca	–	–	1	–
de Caters	1	–	–	–	Koolhoven	–	1	–	–					

Appendix C · Specification of Successful Cars 1906-39

To achieve a more complete understanding of the specification of any car the following Notes showing the general type of construction followed should be read in conjunction with the specification tables appearing on the following pages.

ENGINE DETAILS

Crankcases—The only exception to the use of light alloy for crankcase construction was No. 123, which used a one-piece cast-iron cylinder block.

Cylinder Blocks—All engines had detachable cylinder blocks except Nos. 123 and 159 (bore cast with crankcase) and Nos. 151, 153, 156, 162 and 163, which had wet liners spigoted into the crankcase.
The detachable blocks were iron castings with the exceptions of Nos. 118, 124, 126, 128, 129, 130, 132, 137, 138, 150, 157, 158, 160 and 164, which used forged steel cylinder barrels with welded-up ports and water jackets. On Nos. 146, 154, 155, light alloy castings were used with dry liners.

Cylinder Heads—All cylinder heads were formed integral with the cylinder block except on Cars Nos. 123, 141, 142, 144, 147, 149, 151, 153, 156, 159, 162 and 163.

Sparking Plugs—All cars with high tension ignition had one 18 mm. sparking plug per cylinder except Nos. 110 and 112, which had two, and No. 118, which had three, 18 mm. plugs per cylinder.

Ignition—Cars Nos. 101, 102, 103, 104, 105, 106, 107, 108 and 109 had low tension magneto ignition; Cars Nos. 120, 122 and 123 had high tension coil ignition. All others had high tension magneto ignition.

Induction Systems—All cars running with a manifold pressure of over 1 ata. used continuously engaged Roots blowers except No. 129, which, in the 1923 French Grand Prix only, used the Wittig Vane type blower, and Nos. 130 and 140 which used Roots blowers engaged by a clutch coupled to the throttle linkage. In Nos. 129, 130, 131, 140, 150 and 157 pressure air was fed to the carburetters, in all other cases the carburetter was on the suction side of the blower. Two Roots blowers in series giving two-stage boost were used on Nos. 163 and 164.

Bearings—Ball (or roller) main bearings and white metal big-ends were used by Nos. 113, 114, 115, 115a, 116, 117, 119, 120 and 121. Lead-bronze main bearings and roller big-ends were used by Nos. 153 and 156. All roller (or ball bearings) were used by Nos. 126, 128, 129, 130, 131, 132, 133, 134, 135, 136, 136a, 137, 138, 139, 143, 148, 150, 155, 157, 158, 160, 162, 163 and 164. All others used plain bearings for the big-ends and main bearings.

Pistons—Cars Nos. 100, 101, 102, 103, 104, 105, 106, 107, 108, 109, 110, 111, 112 and 118, used cast-iron pistons. Cars Nos. 113, 114, 115, 115a, 116 and 117 used pressed or forged steel pistons. Car No. 120 and all higher numbers used light alloy pistons.

Camshafts—All o.h.v. engines used two overhead camshafts except 109 (push rods) and single o.h. camshafts on Nos. 110, 112, 117, 123, 133, 135, 139, 140, 151, 153 and 156.

1940-1951

ENGINE DETAILS

Crankcases—All the above cars used light alloy crankcases, Alfa-Romeo being split on the centre line of the crankshaft and Ferrari and B.R.M. beneath the centre line.

Cylinder Blocks—Alfa-Romeo used a detachable light-alloy cylinder block with inserted dry liners; Ferrari wet liners screwed into the combustion chambers and B.R.M. detachable flanged wet liners.

Cylinder Heads—B.R.M. used detachable cylinder heads; the Ferrari cylinder head was detached with liner and Alfa-Romeo integral with the block casting.

Sparking Plugs—All the cars used 14 mm. sparking plugs, number 169, having two plugs per cylinder.

Ignition—B.R.M. used coil ignition, all others magneto ignition.

Induction Systems—Alfa-Romeo had two-stage supercharging with Roots blowers in series, and B.R.M. two-stage supercharging with centrifugal compressors. Ferrari was unsupercharged, and had individual jet and choke assemblies for each cylinder.

Bearings—Alfa-Romeo used ball and roller bearings throughout; the other cars Vandervell three-layer plain bearings.

Camshaft Drive—Spur gears were used except on certain overhead camshaft models which used bevel gears and a vertical shaft, these being Nos. 112, 118, 123, 130, 133, 139, 140, 151, 153, 156, 162 and 163.

CHASSIS DETAILS

Brakes—All cars subsequent to No. 116 had mechanically operated four-wheel brakes with the following exceptions—No. 118 rear brakes only, No. 119 ran at Indianapolis with rear brakes only, and Nos. 123, 149, 150, 151, 153, 155, 156, 157, 158, 160, 161, 162, 163 and 164, which had hydraulic operation of four-wheel brakes. Mechanically driven servo assistance to the pedal effort was provided on Nos. 121, 124, 126, 128, 129, 132, 134, 136 and 136a. Cars Nos. 150 upwards (except 159) used two leading shoes, except Nos. 156, 162 and 163, which had four leading shoes.

Frames—All cars had riveted U-section frames except No. 150, with welded box construction; Nos. 151, 153, 156, 162 and 163 with welded circular section tubes; and Nos. 157, 158, 160 and 164 with welded oval section.

Suspension—Car No. 161 had quarter elliptic rear springs. Cars Nos. 133, 135, 139, 143, 148, 152 and 154 had reverse quarter elliptic rear springs, Cars Nos. 151, 155 and 159 had transverse semi-elliptic rear springs. Cars Nos. 150 and 157 had transverse quarter elliptic rear springs. Cars Nos, 153, 156, 158, 162, 163 and 164 had torsion bar rear springs. Cars Nos. 151, 153, 156, 161, 162 and 163 had torsion bar front springs. Cars Nos 150, 153, 154, 155, 157, 158, 160, 164 had coil front springs. Car No. 159 had a transverse semi-elliptic front spring. Cars Nos. 157, 160, 162, 163 and 164 had hydraulically damped springs. All other cars had semi-elliptic springs with friction damping.

Wheels—Cars Nos. 100–110 inclusive, and No. 112, used fixed wood wheels, all with Michelin detachable rims with the exceptions of Nos. 102 and 103. Cars Nos. 111, 113 and all higher numbers used Rudge-Whitworth detachable wire wheels, except Nos. 133, 139, 143 and 148, which had detachable wheels made from light alloy castings integral with the brake drums.

Rear Axles—Every car used bevel gears for the right-angle drive, but in Nos. 101, 102, 104, 105, 107, 108, 109, 110, 112, the final drive was by side chains, and in Nos. 157, 158, 160 and 164 by spur wheels. All used differential mechanisms with the exception of No. 100, but the Z.F. limited slip differential was fitted to Nos. 156, 157, 158, 160, 162 and 163.

Fuel Tanks—Rear-mounted fuel tanks were universally used except on Nos. 162 and 163, which had side tanks. Nos. 160 and 164 had a saddle-tank in addition to the rear tank.

Tyres—All cars up to No. 121 used beaded-edged tyres. All higher numbers had straight-sided tyres. Provision for carrying spare rims or wheels was made on Cars Nos. 100–121 inclusive, on Nos. 125, 133 and 139, and for Targa Florio race only, on No. 131. Cars Nos. 153–164 inclusive used a larger section tyre on the rear wheels than they did on the front wheels.

Pistons—Aluminium alloy.

Camshafts—Two overhead camshafts, except numbers 168 and 169 which had a single overhead camshaft with rockers.

Camshaft Drive—Spur gears, except for numbers 168 and 169 which had chain drive.

CHASSIS DETAILS

Brakes—B.R.M. used disc brakes with hydraulic servo assistance; all others hydraulically operated, two leading shoe, brakes.

Frames—Alfa-Romeo used oval tube frame; B.R.M. spaced round tubes; Ferrari tubes with triangulated reinforcement.

Suspension—B.R.M. had Lockheed air struts; Alfa-Romeo and Ferrari, transverse leaf springs fore and aft.

Wheels—All cars used detachable wire wheels.

Rear Axle—Alfa-Romeo and Ferrari had a central propeller shaft driving a gearbox mounted below the axle centre, final drive by spur wheels and a limited slip differential. B.R.M. a transversely mounted, five-speed, gearbox with offset propeller shaft driving the halfshafts through spur wheels.

Fuel Tanks—All cars had rear-mounted fuel tanks, numbers 167 and 170 having also scuttle or cockpit mounted tanks.

Tyres—All cars used larger section tyres on the back wheels than on the front wheels.

INDEX NUMBER	MAKE	YEAR BUILT	CYLINDERS NO., BORE AND STROKE	CAPACITY LITRES	PISTON AREA SQ. IN.	H.P.	R.P.M.	VALVES NO. AND ANGLE
100	Renault	1906	4/166/150	13	134	90	1,200	S
101	Richard Brasier	1906	4/165/140	12	134	105	1,400	S
102	De Dietrich	1906	4/190/160	18·1	175	130	1,400	S
103	Darracq	1906	4/170/140	12·7	140	120	1,500	S
104	Fiat	1907	4/180/160	16·2	158	130	1,600	60° inclined
105	De Dietrich	1907	4/180/170	17·3	158	120	1,250	S
106	Minerva	1907	4/145/120	7·9	102·5	90	2,200	E over 1
107	Mercedes	1907	4/175/150	14·4	149	120	1,200	Opposed
108	Mercedes	1908	4/155/170	12·8	117	135	1,400	Opposed
109	Fiat	1908	4/155/160	12	117	100	1,800	60°
110	Fiat	1911	4/130/190	10	83	120	1,650	4 vert.
111	Peugeot	1912	4/110/200	7·6	58·5	130	2,200	4 at 60°
112	Fiat	1912	4/150/200	14·1	110	140	1,700	4 vert.
113	Peugeot	1913	4/100/180	5·6	48·6	115	2,500	4 at 60°
114	Delage	1913	4/105/180	6·2	53·8	105	2,300	4 horizontal
115	Peugeot	1913	4/78/156	3	29·4	90	2,900	4 at 60°
116	Sunbeam	1914	4/81/160	3·3	31	92	2,800	Other con
117	Peugeot	1914	4/92/169	4·5	41·2	112	2,800	4 at 60°
118	Peugeot	1914	4/75/140	2·5	27·3	80	3,000	4 at 60°
119	Mercedes	1914	4/93/165	4·5	42	115	2,800	4 at 60°
120	Ballot	1919	8/74/140	4·9	53·2	140	3,000	4 at 60°
121	Monroe	1920	4/79/152	3	30·2	98	3,200	4 at 60°
122	Ballot	1920	8/66/112	3	41	107	3,800	4 at 60°
123	Frontenac	1921			Engine as Duesenberg (123)				
124	Duesenberg	1921	8/63·5/117	3	39·3	115	4,250	3 at 60°
125	Fiat	1921	8/65/112	3	41	120	4,400	2 at 90°
126	Sunbeam	1921	8/65/112	3	41	108	4,000	4 at 60°
127	Fiat	1922	6/65/100	2	30·8	92	5,200	2 at 96°
128	Miller	1923	8/58·8/89	2	33·6	120	5,000	2 at 90°
129	Sunbeam	1923	6/67/94	2	32·9	102	5,000	2 at 96°
130	Fiat	1923	8/60/87·5	2	35	118	5,600	2 at 96°
131	Mercedes	1924	4/70/129	2	24	120	4,500	4 at 60°
132	Alfa-Romeo	1924	8/61/85	2	36·2	165	5,500	2 at 100°
133	Sunbeam	1924	6/67/94	2	32·9	138	5,500	2 at 96°
134	Bugatti	1924	8/60/88	2	35	100	5,000	3 vert.
135	Delage	1925	12/51·3/80	2	38·7	190	7,000	2 at 100°
136	Bugatti	1926	8/52/88	1·5	26·3	110	5,500	3 vert.
137	Delage	1926			As 136A except exhaust on driver's side; twin blowers on left side and				
138	Delage	1927	8/55·8/76	1·5	30·5	142	6,500	2 at 100°
139	Talbot	1926	8/56/75·5	1·5	31	145	6,500	2 at 96°
140	Fiat	1927	12/50/63	1·5	36·5	160	6,500	2 at 100°
141	Bugatti	1926–30	8/60/100	2·3	35	135	5,300	3 vert.
142	Mercedes-Benz	1928	6/104/150	7·6	70	300	3,500	2 vert.
143	Maserati	1929	16/67/82	4	75	260	5,500	2 at 90°
144	Maserati	1929–31	8/64/98	2·5	41	175	6,000	2 at 90°
145	Bugatti	1931	8/60/100	2·3	35	160	5,500	2 at 90°
146	Alfa-Romeo	1931	8/65/88	2·3	41	160	5,400	2 at 100°
147	Alfa-Romeo	1931	12/65/88	3·5	61·5	200	5,000	2 at 100°
148	Alfa-Romeo	1932	8/65/100	2·65	41	190	5,400	2 at 100°
149	Alfa-Romeo	1934	8/69/100	2·9	46·5	210	5,400	2 at 100°
150	Maserati	1932	8/67/94	2·8	43·6		As No. 142	
151	Bugatti	1931	8/86/107	4·9	72	300	4,400	2 at 90°
152	Maserati	1933	8/69/100	2·9	46·5	205	5,500	2 at 90°
153	Mercedes-Benz	1934–5	8/82/94·5	4	65	430	5,800	4 at 60°
154	Auto Union	1934	16/68/75	4·4	90	295	4,500	2 at 90°
155	Bugatti	1934	8/73/100	3·3	52	240	5,400	2 at 90°
156	Auto Union	1935	16/72·5/75	4·95	102·5	375	4,800	2 at 90°
157	Alfa-Romeo	1935	8/72/100	3·2	50·2	265	5,400	2 at 100°
158	Alfa-Romeo	1935	8/77/100	3·8	51·5	305	5,400	2 at 100°
159	Auto Union	1936	16/75/85	6	109·5	520	5,000	2 at 90°
160	Mercedes-Benz	1936	8/86/102	4·74	72	494	5,800	4 at 60°
161	Mercedes-Benz	1937	8/94/102	5·66	86	646	5,800	4 at 60°
162	Delahaye	1938	12/75/85	4·5	82	220	5,500	2 at 90°
163	Mercedes-Benz	1938	12/67/70	3	65·5	468	7,800	4 at 60°
164	Maserati	1938	8/78/78	3	59·5	420	7,000	4 at 90°
165	Auto Union	1938	12/65/75	3	61·5	420	7,000	2 at 90°
166	Auto Union	1939	12/65/75	3	61·5	485	7,000	2 at 90°
167	Mercedes-Benz	1939	12/67/70	3	65·5	483	7,800	4 at 60°
168	Alfa-Romeo	1947	8/58/70	1·5	32·8	254	7,800	2 at 90°
169	Alfa-Romeo	1950	8/58/70	1·5	32·8	335	8,000	2 at 90°
170	Alfa-Romeo	1951	8/58/70	1·5	32·8	380	9,000	2 at 90°
171	Ferrari	1949	12/55/52·5	1·5	42·2	300	7,500	2 at 60°
172	Ferrari	1951	12/80/74·5	4·5	93·6	380	7,500	2 at 60°
173	B.R.M.	(1953)	16/49·5/48·3	1·5	47·8	525	10,500	2 at 90°

INDUCTION	GEARS	FRONT AXLE	REAR AXLE	SEATS	FRONTAL AREA SQ. FT.	LADEN WEIGHT CWT.	MAXIMUM SPEED
Ata	3	Beam	Torque Arms	2 Parallel	18	27–28	92 m.p.h.
,,	3	,,	Dead	,,	17	,,	94 m.p.h.
,,	4	,,	,,	,,	19	,,	98 m.p.h.
,,	3	,,	Torque Tube	,,	17	,,	94 m.p.h.
,,	4	,,	Dead	,,	18	,,	98 m.p.h.
,,	4	,,	,,	,,	18	,,	95 m.p.h.
,,	3	,,	Torque Arms	,,	18	,,	90 m.p.h.
,,	4	,,	Dead	,,	19	,,	95 m.p.h.
,,	4	,,	,,	,,	18	,,	104 m.p.h.
,,	4	,,	,,	,,	19	29	101 m.p.h.
,,	4	,,	,,	,,	18	33	100 m.p.h.
,,	4	,,	Hotchkiss	,,	16	28	100 m.p.h.
,,	4	,,	Dead	,,	18	31	102 m.p.h.
,,	4	,,	Hotchkiss	,,	16	27	108 m.p.h.
,,	5	,,	,,	,,	16	27	100 m.p.h.
,,	4	,,	,,	,,	14·5	21	95 m.p.h.
structural details as 1913 Peugeot							97 m.p.h.
Ata	4	Beam	Hotchkiss	2 Staggered	13	26	116 m.p.h.
,,	4	,,	,,	2 Parallel	—	21	92 m.p.h.
,,	4	,,	Torque Tube	,,	13	26½	116 m.p.h.
,,	4	,,	Hotchkiss	,,	15	28	118 m.p.h.
,,	3	,,	,,	2 Staggered	14	—	100 m.p.h.
,,	4	,,	,,	,,	12	23	112 m.p.h.
Chassis and body as 1920			Monroe (120)		14	—	105 m.p.h.
,,	3	Beam	Torque Tube	,,	12	23	114 m.p.h.
,,	4	,,	,,	,,	12	23	118 m.p.h.
,,	4	,,	Hotchkiss	2 Parallel	14	24	108 m.p.h.
,,	4	,,	Torque Tube	2 Staggered	12·2	18	105 m.p.h.
,,	3	,,	,,	1 Central	—	—	116 m.p.h.
,,	3	,,	Hotchkiss	2 Staggered	10·8	18·2	108 m.p.h.
1·3 Ata	4	,,	Torque Tube	,,	11	19·5	115 m.p.h
1·4 ,,	4	,,	,,	2 Parallel	12	23	115 m.p.h.
1·7 ,,	4	,,	,,	2 Staggered	11	20	135 m.p.h.
1·47 ,,	4	,,	,,	,,	10·8	20·7	125 m.p.h.
1·0 ,,	4	Beam	Torque Arm	2 Parallel	10·8	17·5	112 m.p.h.
1·5 ,,	4	,,	Hotchkiss	2 Staggered	11	21	134 m.p.h.
1·66 ,,	4	,,	Torque Arm	2 Parallel	10·8	18	110 m.p.h.
laden weight only 18·3 cwt.							
1·5 Ata	5	,,	Hotchkiss	1 offset	9·5	19·3	128 m.p.h.
1·95 ,,	4	,,	Torque Tube	,,	9·5	18	130 m.p.h.
1·7 ,,	4	,,	,,	,,	9·5	18	135 m.p.h.
1·66 ,,	4	,,	Torque Arm	2 Parallel	10·8	18·5	125 m.p.h.
1·5 ,,	4	,,	Torque Tube	,,	15	32	140 m.p.h.
1·5 ,,	4	,,	,,	1 offset	11·5	23	155 m.p.h.
1·6 ,,	4	,,	,,	,,	10·5	19	136 m.p.h.
1·66 ,,	4	,,	Torque Arm	2 Parallel	10·8	18·5	134 m.p.h.
1·66 ,,	4	,,	Torque Tube	1 offset	12	20	130 m.p.h.
1·6 ,,	4	,,	2 Torque Tubes and bevels	1 central	10·5	23	140 m.p.h.
1·6 ,,	4	,,	,, in Vee	,,	10·25	18·2	140 m.p.h.
1·6 ,,	4	,,	,, ,,	,,	11	18·7	145 m.p.h.
1·6 ,,	3	,,	Torque Arms	2 Parallel	13	22	145 m.p.h.
1·66 ,,	4	,,	Torque Tube	1 offset	10·5	19	145 m.p.h.
1·66 ,,	4	Wishbone	Swing Axle	1 central	11·8	20	175 m.p.h.
1·6 ,,	5	Trailing Arms	,,	,,	10·8	21·5	165 m.p.h.
1·6 ,,	4	Beam	Torque Arms	1 offset	11	19	150 m.p.h.
1·66 ,,	5	Trailing Arms	Swing Axle	1 central	10·8	21·5	180 m.p.h.
1·66 ,,	3	Dubonnet	2 Torque Tubes	,,	10·25	19	145 m.p.h.
1·66 ,,	3	Wishbones	Swing Axle	,,	11·5	20	150 m.p.h.
1·87 ,,	5	Trailing Arms	,,	,,	10·8	22·4	185 m.p.h.
1·9 ,,	4	Wishbones	,,	,,	12	20	180 m.p.h.
1·8 ,,	4	,,	de Dion	,,	12·5	21·8	195 m.p.h.
0·0 ,,	4	Leaf & Wishb'ne	,,	1 offset	14	23	140 m.p.h.
2·2 ,,	5	Wishbones	,,	1 central	12·5	23·5	180 m.p.h.
2 ,,	4	,,	Torque Tube	,,	12	22	170 m.p.h.
1·9 ,,	5	Trailing Arms	de Dion	,,	11·5	23·5	180 m.p.h.
2·6 ,,	5	,,	,,	,,	11·8	24	195 m.p.h.
2·65 ,,	5	Wishbones	,,	,,	12·5	24	195 m.p.h.
2·2 ,,	4	Trailing Arms	Swing Axle	,,	11·5	19½	160 m.p.h.
2·7 ,,	4	,,	,,	,,	11·5	20½	175 m.p.h.
3·0 ,,	4	,,	de Dion	,,	11·5	21½	195 m.p.h.
2·4 ,,	5	Wishbones	Swing Axle	,,	12·0	17	170 m.p.h.
1·0 ,,	4	,,	de Dion	,,	12·5	20½	185 m.p.h.
5·65 ,,	5	Trailing Arms	,,	,,	10·0	20	195 m.p.h.

347

Appendix D · Summary of Developments

DATE	CONDITIONS	TYPE OF CAR
1900–6	Pre-Grand Prix period of Gordon Bennett and other town-to-town races over distances up to 600 miles. 1904 and 1905 Gordon Bennett races run on closed circuits of 300 miles distance.	Cars changed from primitive types with 5-litre, 25 b.h.p. engines to 10–16-litre models developing 90–120 b.h.p. at 1,000–1,400 r.p.m. as used in the Gordon Bennett Races of 1903–5.
1906–7	First Grand Prix races organised by Automobile Club de France and run under weight limit of 2,240 lb., 1906; consumption limit 9·4 m.p.g., 1907, over 770 and 477 miles respectively. Road surface of water-bound macadam and tarred, with lap lengths of *circa* 50 miles duration and races 5–7 hours each day, with two-day racing in 1906. Competitors despatched singly, at intervals of 90 secs. in 1906, 60 secs. in 1907 on counter-clockwise courses. Pressure refuelling commonly used. First national racing colours in Grand Prix racing in 1907.	Similar to preceding Gordon Bennett models, using four-cylinder short-stroke engines of 12–18 litres capacity, developing between 100 and 120 b.h.p. Engine speed restricted to *circa* 1,200 r.p.m. with mainly short strokes and low tension magnetos. Fixed wooden wheels with limited use of detachable rims and equal division between propeller shaft and chain final drive. Steel channel frames straight in side elevation and plan with low-sided bodies consisting of two high-built seats with cylindrical fuel tank and spare wheels mounted behind them.
1908	Grand Prix formula restricted piston area to 117 sq. in., equivalent to 155 mm. bore diameter for four-cylinder engines; 127 mm. diameter for six cylinders. First use of "pits" in front of grand-stands.	Four cylinders, short-stroke push rod o.h.v. engines, developing 130–140 b.h.p. at 1,400–1,800 r.p.m. from 12 litres capacity. Frames, transmission systems and bodies on same general lines as 1906–7. Some cars used dropped frames and there was general use of relatively high scuttles and enclosed body sides.
1909–11	Grand Prix racing abandoned for four years. Old-established companies retired from competition work with the exception of Fiat in U.S.A. races and European hill-climbs. Voiturette racing enthusiastically supported by newly formed firms, such as Delage and Peugeot.	Nil.
1912	A.C.F. Grand Prix re-established with a two-day race over 955 miles, with no restrictions on weight or engine size. Circuit as employed in 1907–8, but tarred roads produced improved road surfaces.	Struggle between old and new forms, Fiat represented former in race with 14-litre, four-cylinder, short-stroke, o.h. camshaft engine with chain drive and fixed wooden wheels with detachable rims. Peugeot initiated new trend with smaller and lighter 7·6-litre long-stroke engine with propeller shaft drive (Hotchkiss system), and detachable wire wheels. The large cars developing 120–140 b.h.p. were challenged by 3-litre, four-cylinder, side-valve Sunbeams and Vauxhalls, developing 65–75 b.h.p. at 3,000 r.p.m. and weighing less than one ton. Sunbeam (third in Grand Prix) used tapering tails based on Brooklands experience.
1913	A.C.F. Grand Prix run under fuel consumption limited to 14 m.p.h. for cars weighing not less than 800 Kg. fitted with square backed bodies. Race run over 556 miles with lap distances reduced to 19·52 miles, resulting in cars being on different laps during end of race. Increasing interest in 3-litre car racing. Change to clockwise courses used for all subsequent Grand Prix events. First Saturday race, continued until 1925.	Grand Prix and 3-litre racing dominated by Peugeot, using four-cylinder long-stroke (2:1); twin camshaft engines developing 90 b.h.p. for the small size and approximately 130 b.h.p. in Grand Prix form. Taper tails on Grand Prix bodies excluded by regulation.
1914	4½-litre capacity limit for A.C.F. Grand Prix run over 20 laps of 23·3 mile circuit. Development of team tactics amongst entries received from 14 manufacturers.	General use of long-stroke, four-cylinder engines with four valves per cylinder operated by one or two overhead camshafts. Engine output *circa* 120 b.h.p. at 2,800 r.p.m. with cars weighing approx. 23 cwt. Seat height reduced by double drop frame side rails. Tapering-tail bodies employed by Peugeot.
1915–6–7–9	Racing confined to U.S.A. track events.	1914 Grand Prix cars uniformly successful with the post-war-built Ballot showing superior lap speed in 1919, although using traditional bolster tank body.
1920	Engines limited to 3 litres capacity by international formula, but racing restricted to U.S.A.	General use of long-tailed bodies under influence of high speeds attained at Indianapolis.
1921	International racing revived under 3-litre capacity limit. A.C.F. Grand Prix held over 10·6 mile circuit with very loose surface. Pits now abandoned in favour of road-level depots; pressure or gravity refuelling forbidden, and replaced by cans or churns.	Almost unanimous use of long-stroke, eight-cylinder engines with more than two valves per cylinder, developing 115–120 b.h.p. at 3,500–4,200 r.p.m. Wide use of long-tailed bodies with staggered seating and close under-cowling.

General form of the racing car established, together with initial appearance of many subsequent features such as I.F.S. (Bollée); inclined o.h.v. (Pipe); gate change, honeycomb radiator and overhead camshaft (Mercedes); friction shock absorbers (Mors); crash type gearbox (Panhard); girder type tubular frame and alcohol benzol fuel mixture (Gobron Brillie); propeller shaft drive with live axle (Renault), and de Dion type axle.	Richard Brasier, Darracq, Fiat, Mercedes, Mors, Napier, Panhard and Renault.
Fiat used inclined overhead valves operated by push-rods and Mercedes raced a six-cylinder overhead camshaft engine in 1907. Straight-eight engines were entered in the 1907 Grand Prix by Weigel, Porthos and Dufaux. First use of supercharging by Chadwick with centrifugal supercharger in Great Despair hill-climb (U.S.A.), 1907, and three-stage centrifugal supercharging in 1908.	Clément Bayard, Richard Brasier, De Dietrich, Fiat, Renault and Darracq.
Detachable wire wheels proposed for Napier Grand Prix cars, but banned by A.C.F. General use of detachable rims on fixed wooden wheels. Clément Bayard successfully used overhead camshaft engines and Motobloc initiate central flywheel.	Clément Bayard, Benz, Fiat, Mercedes, Richard Brasier and De Dietrich.
Independent front wheel suspension revived by Sizaire-Naudin in 1907 on Voiturette racing cars of restricted piston area. Use of stroke-bore ratios of up to 2·5:1 piston speeds of 3,000 ft./min. and multiple valves fostered by these regulations. First use of front brakes by Isotta Fraschini in Indianapolis 500 Mile Race of 1910 and Santa Monica (1911).	Nil.
Peugeot originated the twin overhead camshaft engine with four valves per cylinder and central plug location in a monobloc casting and carried forward their Voiturette experience to show the merits of the long stroke of 1.82:1 ratio) engine. Sunbeam and Vauxhall successes proved the possibility of engines with pressed steel pistons running at 2,800–3,000 r.p.m. in long-distance racing. All cars had high tension ignition.	Fiat, Feugeot, Sunbeam, Vauxhall.
Peugeot initiated two-piece bolted-up crankshaft (running in ball and roller bearings), inserted endwise through a barrel-type crankcase and dry sump lubrication, also used knock-off lock rings for detachable wire wheels. Increased employment of built-up pressed steel pistons. Last use of chain drive in racing of Grand Prix status by Mercedes in Sarthe Grand Prix. Mercedes pioneered use of separate forged steel cylinders with welded ports and jackets in same race. Delage used five-speeds and horizontal opposed valves. First appearance of sleeve valves (Mercedes at Indianapolis) and last appearance of side valve engines in Grand Prix racing.	Delage, Peugeot, Sunbeam; re-entry of Mercedes with privately sponsored team of experimental cars.
First use of four-wheel brakes in European racing by Delage, Peugeot, Fiat and Piccard Pictet. First use of combined engine and gearbox units by Fiat, and mica-insulated plugs (K.L.G.) fitted in Sunbeams. Delage tried positively closed valves and Vauxhall pioneered front springs passing through the front axle.	Delage, Mercedes, Peugeot, Sunbeam.
First successful use of eight cylinders in line by 4·9-litre Ballots and Duesenbergs (the latter having detachable cylinder heads) and of V.12 engine by Packard, all in 1919 Indianapolis race except Packard, which ran first in 1917 at Sheepshead Bay.	Ballot, Mercedes, Packard, Peugeot.
One out of four starters at Indianapolis had eight-cylinder in-line engines running at approximately 3,500 r.p.m. with an S/B ratio of 1·7:1. First use of light alloy pistons and multi-carburetters in Grand Prix racing.	Ballot, Duesenberg, Monroe.
First use in Grand Prix racing of hydraulically operated brakes, high-tension coil ignition, and three overhead valves per cylinder, and three-speed gearbox with central gear lever, all by Duesenberg. First use of mechanical servo brake operation (Ballot and Fiat), and of forged steel cylinders in group, and all-roller bearing crankshaft, both by Fiat in Brescia Grand Prix. First supercharged engine in European racing, the Mercedes using Roots blower in Coppa Florio. Experiments by Ricardo with alcohol blend fuel—RD1, RD2, etc.	Ballot, Duesenberg, Fiat.

DATE	CONDITIONS	TYPE OF CAR
1922	International 2-litre limit for Grand Prix racing. First national Grand Prix other than French (Italian); world's first artificial road circuit built in Monza Park; first massed start for A.C.F. (French) Grand Prix at Strasbourg.	Reduction in engine capacity leads to revival of four- and six-cylinder engines, developing 80–90 b.h.p. at 4,500–5,000 r.p.m. fitted into small cars weighing under 15 cwt. Fiat introduced wedge-shaped bodies, but bulk of cars continued with round sections using tapering tails. Last Grand Prix race in which spare wheels were carried on the car. Substantial improvement in road surfaces.
1923	As 1922.	Similar in general specification to 1922, but many makes reflected the superiority of Fiat in the previous year by producing cars of similar design and/or appearance.
1924	As 1923.	As 1923, with slight increases in stiffness and weight.
1925	As 1924; riding mechanic barred for first time, but mechanic's seat and driving mirror obligatory. A.C.F. (French) Grand Prix run on 7·6 mile lap on artificial road circuit (Montlhéry) for first time. Repair and replenishment of car continued to be restricted to driver and one mechanic alone as in all previous Grand Prix races. Belgian Grand Prix added to international calendar. First Sunday race (A.C.F.)	As 1924.
1926	Grand Prix cars limited to 1½-litres capacity with driver only, but mechanic's seat obligatory, and one mechanic only allowed to assist driver. General use of tracks for national Grands Prix.	Eight-cylinder in-line engines with roller bearings offset to left-hand side of car giving very low driving position and frontal area. Successful year by Bugatti, who continued 1925 chassis with modified engine to bring it within the capacity limit.
1927	As 1926, but mechanic's seat no longer obligatory.	As 1926, but Bugatti two-seater type outclassed.
1928–30	General disregard of internationally agreed formula with races run under *formule libre*. Feeble support for Grand Prix racing by manufacturers leading to entry lists made up of individuals competing as amateurs for sport or individuals for private advertisement or gain. Grand Prix of A.C.F. run as sports car race; first Sunday race on public road (1929).	Revived use of 2-litre models designed originally for 1922–5 formula. General use of two-seater bodies and chassis specification, making it possible to use cars for sports car events or general road use in addition to racing.
1930–3	No restriction on size of engine or car. Two mechanics in addition to driver(s) allowed to assist in repairs and replenishment. Re-introduction of works-sponsored teams and/or drivers. Contemporary with decline in importance of A.C.F. (French) Grand Prix, a great increase in races of Grand Prix status run by national or urban clubs, e.g., German and Czechoslovak Grands Prix and Rome and Monaco races. First starting line-up on practice times (Monaco Grand Prix, 1933). Revival of pressure refuelling.	Unsuccessful experiments with engines of between four and five litres capacity, developing *circa* 300 b.h.p. Decisively successful introduction of cars with single, central, seats placed above propeller shaft.
1934	Introduction of international formula limiting weight to 750 Kg. No restriction on size of engine. Four mechanics permitted to assist in repair and replenishment. Increase in number of Grand Prix status races became a permanent feature of the international calendar. Predominance of works' teams.	Initial successes secured by slightly modified 1933 cars; later events won by German cars developing 300–400 b.h.p., and many novel technical features. All Grand Prix cars except Bugatti used central single-seater bodies and all, with the exception of Auto Union straight-eight engines.
1935	As 1934. Portable electric starters first used by Auto Union at A.V.U.S. races. Elimination of successful amateur drivers by works-retained professionals.	As 1934, with larger engines and greater power output.
1936	As 1935.	As 1935, with engine capacity raised up to six litres and power available increased to over 500 b.h.p.
1937	Extension of 1934–6 750 Kg. formula for one year.	General use of engine sizes of between five and six litres with engine outputs of 520–640 b.h.p.

350

Design dominated by Fiat practice of welded cylinders with two valves per cylinder at 96 degree angle, roller-bearing crankshaft and big-ends, and torque tube drive. Revival of four- and six-cylinder engines. Vauxhall initiate one-piece connecting rods and detachable wet cylinder liners in R.A.C. T.T. car.	Fiat.
General acceptance of two-valve, two-camshaft engines with roller bearings throughout. First use (by Delage) of V.12 engine in road racing. First use by Bugatti and Voisin of aerodynamically formed bodies. First victory of supercharged engine in full Grand Prix racing secured by Fiat in European Grand Prix, which also saw first rear-engined racing car with independent rear suspension by swing axle, both featured by Benz cars.	Fiat, Sunbeam.
Light alloy wheel and brake drums fitted on Type 35 Bugatti. Designers tended to revert to eight-cylinder in-line engines. First use of superchargers aspirating mixture from the carburetter by Duesenberg at Indianapolis (with centrifugal blower) and Sunbeam in French Grand Prix with Roots blower. All Grand Prix status races won by supercharged cars using alcohol-benzol fuel.	Alfa-Romeo, Fiat, Sunbeam.
All Grand Prix cars supercharged except Bugatti, who in Targa Florio, scored last win in Grand Prix racing with an unsupercharged car. General increase in power and speed by detail development. Fiat fitted inter-cooler between blower and carburetter.	Alfa-Romeo and Delage.
All Grand Prix cars used supercharging. Predominance of offset single-seater, but first appearance in European road-racing of bodies with single central seats, these being used by Duesenberg and Miller in 1927 Italian Grand Prix, which marks last appearance of U.S.A. cars in European formula race.	Bugatti and Delage.
	Talbot and Delage.
Little development in engine design. Average speeds improved by detail development in suspension and braking systems. First use by European constructor of detachable cylinder head in Grand Prix racing on 2½-litre Maserati. Wide use on this car of magnesium alloy castings; cylinder head made of cast aluminium. Racing car design influenced by lack of works' teams and maintenance, and alternative entry in sports car racing. Roller bearings abandoned except by Bugatti.	Alfa-Romeo, Bugatti, Maserati.
Reintroduction of designs built purely for racing but designed under the influence of sports car requirements and making use of series production components. Engine size limited to 3 litres with a maximum of *circa* 5,500 r.p.m. and 200 b.h.p. Revival of hydraulic brakes by Maserati and of de Dion axle in racing by Miller at 1931 Indianapolis. Alfa-Romeo made first use of light alloy cylinder blocks with inserted dry liners and integral head with valves facing direct on light alloy seats and built twin-engined car with two propeller shafts followed by V shafts connecting to single engine. Last appearance of non-poppet valve engine (Peugeot in 1931 French Grand Prix).	Alfa-Romeo, Bugatti, Maserati.
First use of independent suspension for all four wheels on racing cars by Auto Union and Mercedes-Benz. Revival by Auto Unions of rear-engine mounting pioneered by 1923 Benz. First use of sixteen-cylinder V-type engine by Auto Union. Revival by Mercedes-Benz of welded steel cylinder construction with 60 degree four-valve heads and all-roller bearing crankshaft and of five forward speeds by Auto Union. Increases in engine size in German cars up to 3½–4½ litres. First use of torsion bar springs in Grand Prix racing by Auto Union for front suspension system, and of double reduction rear axle to give low propeller shaft height by Bugatti. First use of welded steel frames in the form of round tubes by Auto Union and rectangular box section by Mercedes-Benz. Revival of detachable wet cylinder liners by Auto Union.	Alfa-Romeo, Bugatti, Auto Union, Mercedes-Benz.
All successful Grand Prix cars used independent front suspension. Last Grand Prix victory by a car fitted with a live rear axle (Alfa-Romeo, German Grand Prix). Increase of engine size in German cars up to 5 litres and of engine output up to 400 b.h.p. All Grand Prix cars, except Bugatti, used hydraulic brakes. Torsion bar springs used for front and rear suspension units on Auto Unions. First use of larger diameter rims on rear wheels than on front wheels and Z.F. limited slip differential.	Alfa-Romeo, Auto Union, Mercedes-Benz.
Trend towards high alcohol content fuels (up to over 85 per cent), particularly by Mercedes-Benz. Introduction of two leading shoe brakes.	Auto Union, Alfa-Romeo, Mercedes-Benz.
Construction of Type 125 Mercedes-Benz which pioneered thin wall oval tube frame members, wishbone, i.f.s., with open coil springs, and road racing use of de Dion type rear axle. Car performance factors expressed in terms of b.h.p./ton and b.h.p./frontal area, reached an all-time high level. Outstanding reliability of German-built cars. Mercedes-Benz abandoned supply of pressure air from supercharger to carburetters (Vanderbilt Trophy). Development on German cars of Ethelyne-Glycol for cooling, and four leading shoe brakes by Auto Union. Hydraulic shock absorbers first used in Grand Prix racing (Mercedes-Benz).	Auto Union, Mercedes-Benz.

351

DATE	CONDITIONS	TYPE OF CAR
1938	Formula based on sliding scale of weight in relation to capacity: weight leading in effect to 3-litre cars weighing not less than 850 Kg.	Continued use of central single-seater bodies on chassis powered by engines developing 400–450 b.h.p. Marked reduction in height by Mercedes-Benz following upon transmission developments.
1939	As 1938.	As 1938, with engine power increased to 480–500 b.h.p.
1946	Extreme shortage of fuels, tyres and plugs, also general breakdown in international communications. Races run under *formule libre*.	Pre-World War II cars except ex-German teams. Alfa-Romeo the only entrant of works teams, with 1½-litre Type 158 models modified to two-stage boost for some entries.
1947–9	First three years of Formula I limiting engines to 1½-litre S. or 4½-litre U/S.	Competition between 4½-litre principle exemplified by six-cylinder Talbot with push-rod-operated valves, and 1½-litre S. types represented by four-cylinder Maserati with equal bore and eight-cylinder Alfa-Romeo with bore/stroke ratio 1·2:1. General use of tubular frames; transverse leaf springs; swing axle and drivers seated immediately above a central propeller shaft with single-stage reduction gears mounted ahead of bevel box.
1950–1	Revival of competition between works teams as sponsored by Alfa-Romeo and Ferrari.	Successful challenge to 1½-litre S. models by 4½-litre twelve-cylinder types with over 90 sq. in. piston area developing over 350 h.p. and weighing less than one ton.

Appendix E · Table of Successes by Marques

PART ONE 1906–1911

MARQUE	FIRST	SECOND	THIRD	FASTEST LAP
F.I.A.T.	7	3	1	2
Benz	1	5	2	–
Itala	2	1	2	2
Darracq	1	2	–	1
de Dietrich	1	1	3	1
Renault	1	1	–	–
Mercedes	1	–	1	1
Isotta-Fraschini	1	–	–	1
Pipe	–	1	–	–
Opel	–	–	1	–
Brasier	–	–	1	1
Clément-Bayard	–	–	1	–
Berliet	–	–	1	–
Marquette-Buick	–	–	1	–
Bugatti	–	1	–	–
Rolland-Pilain	–	–	1	–
Locomobile	–	–	–	1

PART TWO 1912–1921

MARQUE	FIRST	SECOND	THIRD	FASTEST LAP
Peugeot	17	4	2	5
Mercedes	3	2	2	2
Duesenberg	2	3	3	2
Delage	2	1	1	2
Ballot	1	3	2	2

1912–1921 Cont.

MARQUE	FIRST	SECOND	THIRD	FASTEST LAP
Stutz	1	6	2	–
Frontenac	1	–	1	–
Monroe	1	–	–	–
Sunbeam	–	1	3	–
Fiat	–	1	1	2
Mercer	–	1	1	–
Itala	–	1	–	–
S.P.A.	–	1	–	–
Crespelle	–	–	1	–
Diatto	–	–	1	–

PART THREE 1922–1933

MARQUE	FIRST	SECOND	THIRD	FASTEST LAP
Alfa-Romeo	31	35	23	19
Bugatti	27	27	31	26
Maserati	10	10	11	12
S.T.D. cars	4	2	3	4
Delage	7	7	7	5
Fiat	4	2	–	5
Mercedes	4	2	4	2
Duesenberg	1	–	–	1
Miller	1	2	4	1
Ballot	–	1	1	–
Bentley	–	1	–	–
O.M.	–	1	–	–
Peugeot	–	–	1	–

PART FOUR I–1934/9

MARQUE	FIRST	SECOND	THIRD	FASTEST LAP
Mercedes-Benz	32	26	16	28
Auto-Union	22	21	17	27
Alfa-Romeo	8	13	19	8
Delahaye	1	–	1	–
Bugatti	–	2	4	–
Maserati	–	1	4	1
Darracq	–	–	2	–

PART FOUR II–1939/40/46–51

MARQUE	FIRST	SECOND	THIRD	FASTEST LAP
Alfa-Romeo	28	20	16	29
Ferrari	8	13	10	5
Maserati	6	7	13	10
Talbot	2	4	6	1
Mercedes-Benz	1	1	–	1
E.R.A.	–	1	1	–
H.W.M.	–	–	1	–

Auto Union and Mercedes-Benz both reduced spring rates and used hydraulic shock absorbers. Independent rear suspension abandoned by both of these companies in favour of de Dion type rear axle coupled with torsion bar springs. Mercedes-Benz used propeller shaft inclined and offset in both planes which permitted very low mounting of central seat. Increased r.p.m. and supercharged pressures led to deterioration in specific fuel consumption and the need for much larger fuel tanks despite reduction in engine size and total horsepower. Auto Union pioneered side tank, and Mercedes-Benz scuttle tank filled from main rear tank. Revival of V.12 engine by Auto Union and Mercedes-Benz. Unsuccessful experiment by Auto Union of all-enveloping streamlined road-racing cars in A.C.F. Grand Prix at Rheims. Auto Union and Mercedes-Benz had five-speed gearboxes.

Auto Union, Mercedes-Benz.

Auto Union and Mercedes-Benz developed two-stage supercharging, using Roots blowers in series, and supercharge pressures of up to 2·65 Ata. Mercedes-Benz fitted turbo-finned brake drums and raised maximum possible engine speed to 10,000 r.p.m., with peak power developed at 8,000 r.p.m. Auto Union developed floatless carburetters.

Auto Union, Mercedes-Benz.

Most races run on short circuits at average speeds of under 70 m.p.h. over distances less than 100 miles.

Alfa-Romeo, Maserati.

Superiority of two-stage blown 1½-litre-engined cars over both the unblown type and twelve-cylinder 1½-litre models with single-stage blowing.

Alfa-Romeo, Ferrari, Maserati, Talbot.

Continued use of transverse leaf springs with general supersession of swing axle by de Dion axle at rear of car. Great attention given to brake developments characterised by improved friction lining and substantial increase in the width of the brake drum. Reduction of rim diameters to 17 or 16 in. in order to lower the unsprung weight. No marked change in other chassis design trends or bodywork. First appearance of sixteen-cylinder 1½-litre S. engine with two-stage centrifugal supercharging; and first appearance of suspension by airstruts in racing (B.R.M.).

Alfa-Romeo, Ferrari.

Appendix F · 'Pomeroy' Index of Speeds

YEAR	FASTEST CAR	MAX. SPEED M.P.H.	RELATIVE LAP SPEED
1906	Renault	92	100
1907	De Dietrich	98	102
1908	Mercedes	104	105·5
1912	Fiat	102	108
1913	Peugeot	108	109
1914	Mercedes	116	112
1919	Ballot	118	118·5
1920	Ballot	112	115
1921	Duesenberg	114	116
1922	Fiat	105	111
1923	Fiat	115	116
1924	Sunbeam	125	121
1925	Delage	134	127·5
1927	Delage	128	129
1928	Bugatti	130	127
1929	Alfa-Romeo	138	130
1931	Maserati	136	135·5
1932	Alfa-Romeo	140	140
1934	Auto Union	165	150
1935	Mercedes-Benz	175	153
1936	Auto Union	185	158
1937	Mercedes-Benz	195	163·4
1938	Mercedes-Benz	180	160
1939	Mercedes-Benz	195	165
1947	Type 158 Alfa-Romeo single-stage	160	150
1948	Type 158 Alfa-Romeo two-stage	170	155·7

YEAR	FASTEST CAR	MAX. SPEED M.P.H.	RELATIVE LAP SPEED
1949	1·5-litre Ferrari two-stage	165	154
1950	1·5-litre Alfa-Romeo two-stage Type 158/159	185	158·4
1951	Type 159/159A Alfa-Romeo	195	164·4
1951	4·5-litre U/S Ferrari	185	163·2

INDEX